D1614367

BICENTENNIAL EDITION

of

THE
EARLY PAPER MONEY
OF AMERICA

By

Eric P. Newman

An illustrated, historical, and descriptive compilation of data relating to American paper currency from its inception in 1686 to the year 1800

Encompassing issues of
THE ENGLISH COLONIES IN AMERICA (1690-1776)
THE UNITED COLONIES (1775-1777)
THE UNITED STATES OF AMERICA (1777-1787)
THE ORIGINAL AMERICAN STATES (1776-1788)
AMERICAN CITIES AND COUNTIES (1774-1796)
LA LOUISIANE (1718-1800)
BANKS OF ISSUE (1686-1800)
INDIVIDUALS, BUSINESSES, CHURCHES, AND
    OTHER ORGANIZATIONS (1729-1800)

Supplemented by
Current values of generally available bills under the direction of
RICHARD PICKER

1976

"Let us expel every Species of Luxury and Extravagance,—the Parents of Poverty and Ruin,—and banish the great cause of both—PAPER MONEY * * *"

Letter to the Editor
Boston Evening Post
January 8, 1750

"It is not more absurd to attempt to impel faith into the heart of an unbeliever by fire and faggot, or to whip love into your mistress by a cowskin, than to force value or credit into your money by penal laws."

Peletiah Webster
Political Essays (1791)

Library of Congress Catalog Card Number: 76-8365

Copyright © 1976 and 1967
WESTERN PUBLISHING COMPANY, INC.
Racine, Wisconsin
Printed in U.S.A. by Western Publishing Company, Inc.

9355   ISBN: 0-307-09355-7

To my charming wife
Evelyn
whose stream of
creative accomplishments
has continued to flow
during my years
of research

CONTENTS

(Issues and individual bills are listed under geographical categories)

PREFACE

It is a welcome opportunity to revise and expand a book written 10 years ago. Readers had been asked in the Preface of the first edition to suggest improvements, and fortunately there has been a steady and enthusiastic response. Not only were undescribed issues, notes, signatures, and varieties submitted, but discussion, correspondence, and research on controversial and previously unknown matters has led to extensive expansion, clarification, corroboration, and correction of the original book.

The paper money included in the first edition, published in 1967, was limited to bills issued up to the ratification of the U.S. Constitution in 1789. This Bicentennial Edition has extended the cut-off date to 1800, thereby permitting the inclusion of small change notes of the 1790-96 period, which group of fascinating issues has not been the basis of any prior publication. The date extension has also permitted a presentation from a numismatic point of view of the bank notes of the first Bank of the United States and other early banks incorporated under State laws.

New geographical sections have been added to include the French colonial regions now part of the United States and to cover the Northwest Territory.

Many new illustrations have been added to enlarge and improve the prior pictorial presentation.

Assistance and cooperation has come from many people and organizations. Richard Picker, beginning as soon as the first edition was published, has sent to me for study a steady stream of such early paper money as passed through his hands as a professional dealer. He has continually gathered and furnished information, raised inquiries, and demanded more satisfying answers on a myriad of matters in addition to developing the evaluation structure in this edition with the help of Ben M. Douglas. Joseph R. Lasser, beginning in recent years, has been a fountain of autographical and biographical information, particularly in the refinement of the signatures on Continental Currency. To Kenneth E. Bressett I am grateful for his patient and steady assistance in guiding the production of this book in the hope of satisfying the high standards which modern numismatic science demands. To these friends I am particularly grateful for their encouragement and devoted cooperation.

Others who were kind enough to furnish data for this edition include Douglas B. Ball, Ann Barrett, Christian Blom, Walter Breen, Mrs. Warren J. Broderick, David Cox, Jr., Maurice A. Crouse, Virgil H. Culler, James DuPont, Bernard Edison, C. John Ferreri, Leonard H. Finn, Thomas J. Fitzgerald, Dorothy Gershenson, Gordon Harris, William J. Harrison, Robert M. Hawes, Alfred D. Hoch, Julia Hoppe, Charles Johnson, Richard Jones, Don Kagin, W. Philip Keller, Sid Levinson, Bill Mason, Walt Mason, Rodney D. McCormack, Elvin Miller, Herbert Oechsner, Zola Packman, J. Roy Pennell, Elizabeth C. Reilly, George C. Rockefeller, S. Fred Rosenthal, Matt Rothert, Leonard Rothstein, Kenneth Scott, Austin H. Sheehan, Jr., Radford Stearns, Tracy G. Thurber, Robert A. Vlack, George W. Wait, Thomas P. Warfield, Frederick Weber, Edwin Wolf II, William W. Woodside and Charles M. Wormser.

Institutions whose facilities and staff were most helpful as to this revision include American Antiquarian Society, American Numismatic Society, American Philosophical Society, Chase Manhattan Bank, Connecticut Bank and Trust Company, Connecticut Historical Society, Historical Society of Delaware, Henry Ford Museum, Georgia Historical Society, Mercantile Library of St. Louis, Missouri Historical Society, Eric P. Newman Numismatic Education Society, Bank of New York, New York Historical Society, New York State Library, Rhode Island Historical Society, St. Louis University, Troy Public Library, Virginia State Library, Washington University, and Western Reserve Historical Society.

Last but not least, I wish to recognize as fundamental to this project the constant encouragement and enthusiasm of my wife, Evelyn E. Newman; the devoted proofreading acumen of my son, Andrew E. Newman; and the checking of some galley proofs by my 6 year old grandson, Daniel M. Newman, as a means of improving his reading skills.

Suggestions for further improvement are always welcome.

St. Louis, Missouri
April 1976

Eric P. Newman

PREFACE TO THE FIRST EDITION (1967)

The first comprehensive attempt to assemble historical and numismatic data on early American paper money was undertaken by Henry Phillips, Jr. who between 1862 and 1867 had completed sketches on Pennsylvania, New Jersey, Virginia, Vermont, Maryland, and Continental Currency. A Rhode Island study prepared by Elisha R. Potter in 1837 was republished by Phillips in 1866. A New York currency history by John H. Hickcox appeared in 1866 also. Phillips was unable to continue with North Carolina, South Carolina and Georgia as he planned. The history of Massachusetts currency published by Joseph B. Felt in 1839 and that of Connecticut prepared by Henry Bronson in 1865 were not sufficiently detailed to fit in with the Phillips project and material on New Hampshire and Delaware had not at that time been prepared by anyone.

In 1872 John W. Haseltine prepared a list of all of the issues and denominations he could assemble covering all of the colonies and the Continental Congress. This was followed in 1878 by the J. W. Scott priced and partially illustrated catalog of a much expanded list of issues and denominations which catalog was revised in 1879, 1889 and 1894. In 1927 D. C. Wismer published a check list based upon Scott's catalog. Wayte Raymond after acquiring Scott's numismatic division introduced in 1935 his *Standard Catalogue of United States Coins and Currency* which included Continental and Colonial paper money. Minor additions to those sections were made from year to year through the 1939 edition. In 1940 Raymond published the paper money separately as *The Standard Paper Money Catalogue,* the early American portion of which was confined to generally collectible issues and the rarer issues were included only as a list of dates of issue. Raymond's work contained much early American data assembled with the help of Fred C. C. Boyd, Harley L. Freeman, and D. C. Wismer. Prices for that catalog were revised in 1950 and 1955. In 1965, Ted N. Weissbuch and Richard T. Hoober patterned a revised and expanded price list on the Raymond catalog.

During the century of research and writing since Phillips, many specialized studies, auction catalogs, and other publications added extensively to the fund of knowledge relating to early American paper money. Nevertheless, there still seemed to be a need for a comprehensive and coordinated compilation of numismatic data as to early American paper money covering the full gamut of issues and denominations, whether extant or not, whether issued publicly or privately, describing varieties and unusual features, illustrating all available issues, giving historical background and statistics as to issues, authorization, signers, mottoes, engravers, printers, counterfeits, and other details, and including a categorized bibliography.

Toward such a goal the author has intermittently devoted more than a decade to the study of original and published records of all Colonies and States, to a review of the Archives of the Federal Government, to an examination of the major collections of early American paper money, to an analysis of the conclusions and data presented by others in their prior writings, and to many separate research projects in the field. This book is the result.

Many individuals and institutions have generously cooperated in the research necessary for this work. Harley L. Freeman, for over thirty years, had also compiled extensive information on the subject and graciously turned over his data to the author. For this kindness the author is particularly appreciative.

Other individuals who have given substantial assistance are Ann Barrett, Walter Breen, Kenneth E. Bressett, William H. Distin, Ben M. Douglas, John J. Ford, Jr., Richard T. Hoober, Marcus A. McCorison, Kneeland McNulty, Evelyn E. Newman, Richard Picker, Percy Rideout, Clifford K. Shipton, and Charles M. Wormser.

Of these, my friends Ben M. Douglas and Richard Picker, as professional numismatists, have prepared the present market values of generally collectible items.

Cooperation has also been received from many other individuals, including Charles J. Affleck, Richard Breadon, Edward R. Barnsley, James A. Brown, C. F. W. Coker, Sarah E. Freeman, George Fuld, Lee E. Hewitt, Alfred D. Hoch, Ivor Noel Hume, Charles E. Lee, Joan Martin, Andrew E. Newman, James Parrish, JoAnn Pinsky, J. Roy Pennell, Jr., Wayne S. Rich, Kenneth Scott, Abraham Slopak, Milton B. Smith, Howard E. Spain, L. Harold Spradley, Ivy N. Steele, Elvira Clain-Stefanelli, Vladimir Clain-Stefanelli, Don Taxay, Joseph Webber, Raymond H. Williamson, and Edwin Wolf II.

The facilities and help of many institutions have been made available, including American Antiquarian Society, American Numismatic Society, First National Bank of Boston, Boston Public Library, British Museum, British Public Records Office, Chase Manhattan Bank Money Museum, Library of Congress, Connecticut Historical Society, Connecticut State Library, Historical Society of Delaware, Essex Institute, Henry Ford Museum and Greenfield Village, Georgia Historical Society, University of Georgia, Harvard University, Johns Hopkins University, Maryland Historical Society, Archives Division of the Commonwealth of Massachusetts, Massachusetts Historical Society, Eric P. Newman Numismatic Education Society, New York Historical Society, New York Public Library, North Carolina Department of Archives and History, Historical Society of Pennsylvania, Philadelphia Art Museum, Library Company of Philadelphia, Smithsonian Institution, South Carolina Archives Department, Law Library Association of St. Louis, Mercantile Library of St. Louis, St. Louis Public Library, St. Louis University, Virginia Historical Society, Washington University, Colonial Williamsburg and Winterthur Museum.

The cooperation and assistance of all of the above are gratefully acknowledged.

In the early years of my research I was fortunate to have had the guidance and cooperation of Burdette G. Johnson and Fred C. C. Boyd, both of whom I wish had lived to see this project completed.

The use of the title, *The Early Paper Money of America,* for this undertaking is a further tribute to the research in depth, the mastery of organization, the accuracy of detail, and the clarity of expression demonstrated by Sylvester S. Crosby in his American numismatic classic, *The Early Coins of America* (Boston, 1875).

Suggestions for additions, revisions, and improved illustrations to what follows will be most welcome at any time and it is hoped that supplementary material based thereon will be published in the future.

St. Louis, Mo.
December, 1966

Eric P. Newman

INTRODUCTION

The Paper Money Experiment

The early paper money of America has the unique distinction of being the first authorized paper money issued by any government in the Western World. No country, state, or colony in Europe had previously issued publicly sponsored paper money.

In the fourteenth century Marco Polo had brought news that money printed on mulberry bark paper was circulated by the Emperors of China, but the Western World was little influenced by such practices. Economic theories as to the issuance of paper currency by governments and private groups finally entered the discussion stage by the seventeenth century. In 1661 the first paper money in Europe was issued by Stockholms Banco, a privately owned bank, to avoid the inconvenience of settling trade balances by physically transporting bulky Swedish copper plate money.

In Canada in 1685, when the French military payroll was delayed, *monnaie de carte* or *card money* was introduced as a temporary medium of exchange redeemable out of the first coin received from France. That paper money consisted of quarter sections of playing cards containing handwritten denominations and was duly signed and sealed by the intendant, Jacques Demuelles. This issue was declared legal tender, protected by counterfeiting punishments, and was redeemed within three months. The French Crown disapproved of the emission and construed the card money to be a personal promissory note of the intendant. New temporary Canadian issues followed in 1686, 1690, 1691, and 1692, each being officially disapproved in France. When redemption was deferred from year to year for lack of funds, card money was suppressed in 1701, only to rise again and again in an increasingly official status until its final elimination in 1757. In Acadia in 1703, the practice of issuing card money had also been undertaken. Whether the first emergency card money should be considered private promissory notes or quasi-public paper currency, it constitutes the first paper money of the Americas.

The Province of Massachusetts Bay had already begun the American venture in publicly authorized paper money before the Bank of England in 1694 and the Bank of Scotland in 1696 issued their paper currency. Both of these British banks were privately owned and operated. America was to become the proving ground

for paper money economics, and the entire world was to watch the test. Adam Smith was to study it as though it were done in his laboratory, and he included a discussion of it in his *Wealth of Nations* (1776). Economic philosophy was in a most immature state of development when American paper money appeared, as the "South Sea Bubble" in England and the "Mississippi Bubble" in France were clearly to demonstrate by 1720.

Early American paper money played a much more important role in numismatic history than did early American coins, because the issues of coins by or for the American Colonies were comparatively insignificant. After the issuance of Massachusetts and Maryland silver coinages in the seventeenth century, no other significant amount of American coins was put into circulation until 1783 when the Treaty of Paris officially closed the American Revolution. The tin Plantation farthings, the Rosa Americana coinage, and the Virginia halfpence had been rejected or withheld as circulating media, and the few token issues were economically inconsequential. The Nova Constellatio copper coinage of 1783, then the copper coinage of the American States beginning in 1785, and finally the establishment of the United States Mint in 1792 joined foreign coins in reestablishing coins instead of paper money as the principal circulating medium, but like the Phoenix, paper money continued to appear in various forms.

Payment for goods or settlement of balances in seventeenth century America was done primarily by bills of exchange drawn by or against British merchants, as specie was seldom available in America for that purpose. Because England had adopted a policy of withdrawing foreign coin which American colonists received in trade, there was a dire need for some available circulating medium in the American Colonies. Barter had become increasingly cumbersome and the only practical solution was a system of credit currency. The idea of a group of private persons to put assets in escrow to secure a limited amount of promissory notes was first considered in Massachusetts Bay, and such plans were referred to as "banks." One such bank had paper money prepared for issue in 1686 in convenient denominations, but the undertaking was abandoned.

Public paper money got its start in America when

Massachusetts Bay in 1690 paid for a military expedition to Canada during King William's War (1689-97) with Bills of Credit. To encourage general acceptance of such bills a 5% premium was promptly granted to those who might use them for tax payments. The second Colony to issue paper money was South Carolina, whose military expedition against the Spanish and Indians in Florida brought about an emission in 1703. Expenses of Colonial participation in Queen Anne's War (1702-13) resulted in paper money issues in 1709 by New Hampshire, Connecticut, New Jersey, and New York, followed by Rhode Island in 1710. North Carolina began its issues in 1712 to defend its frontiers against Indian raids.

These early emissions established the use of the term "Bill of Credit" as distinguished from the term "money." The justification for paper money was, in effect, a borrowing for a specific public expenditure rather than an issuance of a circulating medium. Since England never granted any Colony the right to issue coined money until 1773 (Virginia copper coinage), the expression "Bill of Credit" was retained to justify paper money issues mere- ly as a borrowing. Opinions on the justification or lack of justification for Bills of Credit were freely expressed, and prolific pamphleteering and other economic comment took place principally during the 1720 to 1749 period. The debtor class and the aggressive business interests often made a political issue out of the economics of Bills of Credit.

Each Colony found reasons to commence and continue its own emissions of paper money, because otherwise the bills of adjacent Colonies would have filled the vacuum. In Pennsylvania, New Jersey, and Delaware, the paper money of each Colony circulated generally in the other two because of their close economic ties. In the four Colonies in New England a similar situation existed, but from time to time restrictions would be adopted by one Colony to prevent the circulation of money of another. In 1705, however, a proclamation of Queen Anne required the Colony of New York (which then had no paper money) to circulate Massachusetts emissions, an order which the New York residents refused to obey.

Depreciation Before Paper Money

Before paper money was introduced into the American economy, depreciation through inflation had already worked its way into American monies of account. In 1642, Massachusetts Bay raised the value of the Spanish silver dollar from 4s6d to 5s, and Connecticut followed the next year. This created a differential between the sterling value of the Spanish dollar and its equivalent value in the money of account or nominal money of that Colony. Virginia in 1645 first rated the same coin at 6s, later at 5s, then back to 6s. A depreciation was solidified in Massachusetts Bay from 1652 to 1682, when that Colony minted silver coin with 22½% less silver per shilling than the standard English shilling. Maryland and New York set their standards by establishing a 6s rate for the Spanish dollar. The purpose of such deviations was to create a fixed premium for specie in a Colony's money of account in order to hold that specie in circulation within that Colony. English merchants and the Crown, in their pressure to have English and foreign silver and gold coin flow back to England, began a series of local Colonial regulations limiting the amount of American money of account which could be paid for such specie. This culminated in the Queen Anne Proclamation of 1704 which was reinforced by the Act of Parliament of 1707 (6 Anne, c.57), effective May 1, 1709, making 6s the maximum amount one Spanish dollar could pass for in the money of account of any American Colony and giving all other silver coin the same proportional maximum premium. This law was in effect until the American Revolution, and its standard was referred to as Proclamation Money. These established maximum evaluations were openly and continuously violated in the Colonies, in addition to being legally avoided by loophole transactions. The wording of the law failed to cover gold coins or uncoined silver and these unplanned omissions were taken advantage of to increase the premium of coin in relation to Colonial monies of account. American paper money therefore was born into an era in which artificial exchanges were customary, and the paper money of each Colony became a part of and at par with the money of account used by such Colony.

Development of Paper Money Uses

Receipts by Colonial Treasuries from the collection of duties, property taxes, and other fees were, at most, only enough to meet ordinary public administrative expenses. Long-term borrowing was not practical. Thus money for emergency payments and specific capital expenditures was unavailable unless Bills of Credit could be issued.

Military needs from time to time continued to justify

paper money issues. During King George's War (1741-48), expeditions from New England against Louisburg were financed in that manner. In the French and Indian War (1754-63), expeditions against Crown Point caused New York and the New England Colonies to issue paper money to cover the cost. Pennsylvania, New York, Delaware, Maryland, and Virginia used the same means to finance their operations against the French and Indians in the West.

In addition to military emergencies, issuance of Bills of Credit were authorized to repair or build jails, courthouses, harbors, lighthouses, buoys, forts, and other public works. The first issue in Maryland was used in 1733 to pay a nominal amount to those who were "taxed" by being forced to burn a portion of their tobacco in order to support the price of large tobacco inventories. In Pennsylvania in 1769 an issue was provided for the Relief of the Poor in Philadelphia. In Virginia in 1771, after public tobacco warehouses had been extensively damaged by floods, paper money was issued to meet the public obligation to holders of negotiable warehouse certificates. Other issues were to replace either worn out bills of prior issues or bills in issues which were extensively counterfeited.

However, the most effective method of issuing paper money for economic stimulation was through public loan banks. Commissioners to supervise a Loan Office were designated by an Assembly, and non-interest bearing paper money was emitted for loans in limited amounts to private individuals, with real estate mortgages or silver plate to be furnished as security. The interest from the loans would pay for the administration of the Loan Office and leave a balance for other public expenses. The period for repayment of the principal of the loans would correspond with the redemption dates of the paper money. South Carolina set up a Loan Office in 1712, Massachusetts in 1714, Rhode Island in 1715, New Hampshire in 1717, Pennsylvania and Delaware in 1723, New Jersey in 1724, North Carolina in 1729, Connecticut and Maryland in 1733, New York in 1737, and Georgia in 1755. The first paper money of Pennsylvania, Delaware, Maryland, and Georgia was for Loan Office purposes. Government loans of paper money stimulated business and supported land values, and the demand for more paper money for loans was constant. Rhode Island was able to pass legislation for nine suc-

cessive Loan Banks up to 1751, but other Colonies were more conservative or were held in check by their Assemblies or Governors. Due to English restrictions, some Loan Offices were liquidated prior to the Revolution, but Pennsylvania and New Jersey were trying to revive these lending institutions just before hostilities commenced. In 1786, after all issues of the Revolutionary War currency had collapsed, South Carolina and Rhode Island each reestablished their Loan Offices with new paper money emissions.

Circulating notes were also issued by private rather than public Loan Banks. One such bank was established in Connecticut in 1732, another in New Hampshire in 1734, and three in Massachusetts in the 1740-41 period, but the Colonial Assemblies or Governors promptly suppressed the banks in each case. In 1741 Parliament required the immediate redemption of all such private paper money regardless of its stipulated due date. The Virginia James River Bank came close to receiving official permission to organize, but instead its unissued notes were modified and used for public issues of the Colony of Virginia in both 1773 and 1775.

Georgia was originally administered from England by the Trustees for Establishing the Colony of Georgia in America. Georgia's first paper money was a series of convenient denominations of Bills of Exchange drawn in England on behalf of the Trustees and payable by the Trustees in England. These were called Sola Bills and were sent to the Colony to be used to pay expenses. They were designed to become bearer Bills of Exchange after their original endorsement in America and could then be presented for payment in England at any time.

Because Virginia's economy was based primarily on tobacco, the Colony in 1713 established public tobacco warehouses which issued certificates for tobacco deposited by private individuals. The tobacco was officially inspected and stored at public expense, and tobacco certificates were readily negotiable so that subsequent holders could withdraw the tobacco. Because of confidence in the reliability of this system, such certificates took the place of money for many years, and Virginia in 1755 was therefore the last of the American Colonies to adopt the paper money idea.

The basis for the many emissions of early American paper money is set out in the subsequent detailed portions of this catalog.

Depreciation Before the Revolution

America also has the dubious distinction of having had the first depreciation in value of publicly issued paper money. In 1713 the exchange of Massachusetts paper money had increased from the Proclamation Money

standard of 133 Massachusetts shillings for 100 shillings sterling to 150 Massachusetts shillings for 100 shillings sterling. The depreciation grew as shown in the following table:

Year	Massachusetts Exchange Rate to English Sterling Standard (Par 100)	Massachusetts Exchange Rate to Proclamation or Lawful Money Standard (Par 100)*
1702	133	100
1713	150	113
1717	225	169
1722	270	203
1728	340	255
1737	500	375
1741	550	413
1749	1100	825

*Minor differences from time to time between Queen Anne's Proclamation money standards and Massachusetts Lawful Money standards do not materially affect the exchange values.

The Massachusetts issue of Feb. 4, 1736(7) introduced a New Tenor issue, each denomination of which was equivalent in value to three times the same denomination of previously outstanding issues, the latter thereby becoming Old Tenor. Further depreciation occurred in both styles of currency so that when the issue of Jan. 15, 1741(2) was emitted, each of its denominations was set at a value of four times that of the same denomination in Old Tenor currency. The 1741(2) issue and its successors became known as New Tenor, and the issues between 1737 and 1740 were then designated Three Fold Tenor or Middle Tenor. Thus Massachusetts had Old Tenor, Middle Tenor (Three Fold Tenor), and New Tenor bills circulating at the same time, and all three issues continued depreciating until England, in 1749, sent sufficient English silver and copper coins to redeem 10 Old Tenor shillings with 1 shilling sterling (7½ Old Tenor shillings for 1 shilling of Proclamation or lawful money). New Tenor and Middle Tenor were both called in at 2½ shillings for 1 shilling sterling (1 shilling 10½ pence Middle Tenor for 1 shilling of Proclamation or lawful money). Special tables were printed for popular use in Massachusetts to aid in making calculations during the redemption which was completed in 1751, and to help convert Old Tenor prices into the new basis. From then until the Revolutionary War, Massachusetts had no new issues of paper money.

Rhode Island depreciation generally kept pace with Massachusetts until 1751, but then with the new issue of Mar. 18, 1750(1) and that of 1755, Rhode Island paper money dropped in value to 4 pounds Old Tenor for 6 shillings New Tenor, and finally by 1764 collapsed to 7 pounds Old Tenor for 6 shillings of New Tenor.

South Carolina, which had tied itself to sterling, had by 1746 reached a 700 to 100 depreciation, and this ratio continued until total collapse during the Revolutionary War.

North Carolina had its difficulties, but in 1748, on exchanging its money at 750 for 100 in Proclamation money, had no further significant depreciation until the American Revolution.

The Middle Colonies had minor fluctuations in their paper money but generally were able to control and redeem their issues with remarkable success throughout the entire Colonial period prior to the American Revolution.

In 1740 England became so concerned about the depreciation of American Colonial paper money that each Colony was required to prepare a detailed report on the status of its paper money. Although the figures submitted were not altogether accurate, and the excuses for the depreciated values somewhat unjustifiable, the reports were used as propaganda weapons to emphasize the need for further issuance of paper currency. Hearings in England continued intermittently until 1749, when the Crown finally recognized the right of New England Colonies to be reimbursed for military expenses in King George's War. After this was accomplished, most of the outstanding paper money of the New England Colonies was redeemed.

Another factor which harmed paper money value was the English requirement, beginning in 1710, that Americans pay postage in English sterling or the equivalent in silver plate at the rate of 4 pennyweights (96 grains) of silver plate for 1 shilling English sterling. England operated the inland and coastwise postal service in America as well as the transatlantic service and postage was payable by the recipient of a letter. Because these proceeds were remitted to England silver for postage was a constant drain on the supply of Colonial specie and thus deprived Colonial Treasuries of that much support for paper money issues.

A table of depreciation of paper currency of each Colony at critical periods is scheduled in Appendix C.

The difficulty in calculating constantly fluctuating values of Colonial currencies was increased by non-uniform methods of figuring value. Sometimes the value was expressed in terms of the various types of Spanish dollars; sometimes in terms of the value of silver plate; and sometimes in gold coin or other silver coin. Another common method in use was the most difficult to calculate, namely, the percentage advance of the Colonial currency over sterling. The most logical method was to calculate 100 times the ratio of Colonial currency to sterling, and this was the basis of the primary series of tables in J. Wright's 326-page *American Negotiator,* published in 1761 and thereafter to serve as the exchange calculator for American transactions. However, when customary prices are in an artificial money of account and there are many such monies of account each using the words "pounds," "shillings" and "pence," the complications and confusion must have been bewildering. When a negotiation or transaction in one Colony involved prices or payments in money of another Colony or Colonies, a long delay for calculations and an argument as to exchange rates must have been customary.

By studying the different periods and noting the conditions under which some issues collapsed and others retained their value, much was learned about paper money control. Because of Colonial responsibility and tightened English control, the last quarter century before the Revolution was comparatively free of further depreciation.

English Regulation of American Emissions

The general instructions of the Crown to English Governors of American Colonies were to deny approval of any legislation involving paper money issues except in a military emergency. The Crown also retained the right to veto any American law passed with a Governor's consent, but such action was of little practical value if the paper money had already been put into circulation by the time the matter was being reviewed in England. English merchants constantly pressured the Crown to stiffen control of paper money, and the colonists constantly urged that they should be permitted to handle their own monetary affairs.

During the eighteenth century the situation was complicated by an almost continuous military conflict in America between the English on the one side and the French, Spanish, or Indians on the other. The English needed military support from the American colonists, and this required prompt payment for expeditions, supplies, salaries, bounties, and fortifications. Since the money in Colonial Treasuries was barely sufficient to meet normal current expenses, a resort to paper money issues to meet military needs became a necessity. The Crown naturally preferred to permit Colonial issues of paper money redeemable by the Colonies out of future Colonial taxes rather than to undertake a direct outlay of funds by the Crown for military expenses.

In consequence of the 1740 review by the Crown of paper money conditions in the American Colonies, the English Parliament in 1741 (14 Geo. II, c.37) extended to America the South Sea Bubble Act originally passed in 1720 (6 Geo. I, c.18). The revision was intended to prevent sales of shares, to prevent investors from participating in business speculations, and to force all circulating notes of private American banks to become due immediately, regardless of their stated maturity. The Colonial Governors were also sent more stringent instructions regarding the control of paper money.

During the next decade in New England, when paper money went out of control, Parliament passed an Act effective Sept. 29, 1751 (24 Geo. II, c. 53) relating only to paper money of the New England Colonies. That Act provided: (1) No extension, reissue or deferment in the redemption dates or amounts of existing issues; (2) No change in the legal tender status of existing issues; (3) No extensions or relaxed enforcement of mortgage loans securing paper money issues; (4) No new legal tender issues of any kind; (5) No new issues of paper money for normal expenses unless redeemable from taxes within 2 years; and (6) No new issues of paper money for emergency expenses unless redeemable from taxes at face value plus legal interest within 5 years. This law had the effect of drastically limiting the amount of new paper money in New England and holding all new issues free of depreciation.

The paper money of Colonies other than the Carolinas had stayed reasonably stable. However, by the end of the French and Indian War, many new issues were outstanding, and certain English officialdom wanted the 1751 Act extended to all Colonies. Parliament refused to go that far but passed the Currency Act of 1764 (4 Geo. III, c.34), effective September 1, 1764, prohibiting extension of legal tender status beyond the retirement dates of outstanding issues and prohibiting any new legal tender issues. British merchants had been urging that the legal tender status of existing American Colonial paper money should not be applicable to them, but this preference was not seriously considered by the Crown.

By the number of new American Colonial paper money laws which were conditioned upon the Crown's approval, it is evident that England had effectively taken control of American paper money issues. The delays in obtaining approved legislation are illustrated by the May 10, 1768 New Jersey Act, which was disapproved by the Crown on March 26, 1769, reenacted with modifications on December 6, 1769, disapproved again by the Crown on June 6, 1770, reenacted with further modifications on March 11, 1774, and approved by the Crown with special conditions on February 20, 1775. Finally, because of the outbreak of hostilities, the conditions were disregarded and the currency was issued on March 25, 1776. New York had for many years arbitrarily emitted many of its paper money issues without waiting for the Crown's approval.

When a Colonial Governor would not consent to an Act authorizing the issuance of paper money, the Colonial Assemblies were not without means to obtain such consent. In New York the Governor's salary was not paid for over one year until he approved the 1737 paper money issue. In Massachusetts, Governor Shute's salary was reduced because of his unfriendly attitude toward paper money, and later, Governor Shirley, who was more tolerant, had his allowances increased because of it.

South Carolina refused to pass any laws of any kind for a period of four years until paper money legislation was included. In New Jersey, appropriations were held up for two years for the same reason. Because Colonial Governors and their administrations had to be paid by the Colony itself, Colonial Governors were often put in a position in which they could not freely exercise their discretion with respect to paper money authorizations.

The final English legislation affecting American paper money was an economic enactment brought about by public creditors who had not received payment of amounts due from Colonial Treasuries. In the hope of finding a remedy, Parliament passed an Act (13 Geo. III, c.57), effective September 1, 1773, giving the American Colonial legislatures the right to pass laws making any paper money voluntarily accepted by a public creditor from a Colonial Treasury a legal tender for taxes, debts, and duties payable by anyone to that Treasury. This had the effect of authorizing money to be shifted from one pocket to the other, and in so doing, breaking a log jam of unpaid debts and taxes.

The continuous efforts by the Crown to repress American paper money during the eighteenth century resulted in a steady habit of law violation by America's leading statesmen and merchants. Unnatural monetary restrictions not only were a major cause of the American Revolution but created a tactical training ground for fighting subjugation. The first two specific accusations set forth in *The Declaration of Independence* to justify the position of the United States were definitely applicable to the paper money legislation, namely:

"He has refused his Assent to Laws, the most wholesome and necessary for the public good.

"He has forbidden his Governors to pass laws of immediate and pressing Importance unless suspended in their Operation till his assent should be obtained; and when so suspended he has utterly neglected to attend to them."

Revolutionary War State Issues

From the commencement of the American Revolution, each State considered itself free of all English restraints on the issuance of paper money, even though the settlement of political differences with England seemed possible to some people prior to the Declaration of Independence. A profusion of emissions by each State to cover its own governmental and military expenditures kept engravers and printers busy. These emissions were entirely separate from those which the Continental Congress issued for use by disbursing agents of the Federal government.

Surprisingly enough, Pennsylvania, New Jersey, and Delaware dated their authorizations of Revolutionary War issues by a reference to the reign of George III in the text of the bills themselves. In Georgia a crown was used as the vignette on a five shilling certificate of 1776, but was soon eliminated in favor of a more patriotic seal. Some issues retained the English coat of arms for a short period, but new State Arms and mottoes soon made their debut in Massachusetts, Connecticut, Pennsylvania, New Jersey, Delaware, and Virginia.

The most propaganda-filled issue was that of the July 26, 1775 Maryland emission, which showed George III trampling on the Magna Charta while setting fire to an American city, and American Liberty trampling on slavery while backed by a large army. In several Massachusetts issues beginning with that of August 18, 1775, Paul Revere engraved on the back plate the motto ISSUED IN DEFENCE OF AMERICAN LIBERTY and showed a Minute Man holding a sword.

As a patriotic measure, New York and North Carolina in 1775 switched the denominations of their bills from English style money units to Spanish dollars, and in 1776 were joined by New Hampshire, Virginia, South Carolina, and Georgia. Maryland had already used Spanish dollars as the basis for its paper money denominations before the Revolution.

In South Carolina a group of patriotic citizens put out their joint personal promissory notes to support the Revolutionary cause pending the organization of the South Carolina Provisional Congress. In Virginia the Revolutionary government did not wish to lose the time necessary to engrave new money plates, so the Convention authorized a modification of two types of forms left over from the Colony's 1773 issue to be used until the new paper money was prepared.

The reason for each issue was usually not stated on the bills themselves, but some Georgia issues of 1777 indicated that they were for the "support of the Continental Troops" and a 1780 Virginia issue was "for the more effectual and speedy clothing the Army." With respect to redemption, the 1778 Georgia issue stated on its face that it was payable from the proceeds of properties confiscated from Tories.

The War caused the small amount of gold and silver coin to disappear from general circulation, and copper coins were also withdrawn for their intrinsic metal value or their use as metal. This left a severe scarcity of small change. Paper money was therefore printed in much lower denominations than had previously been authorized by Colonial Assemblies. In Massachusetts, Rhode Island, and Connecticut, bills as low as two pence were emitted; in New Hampshire, Delaware, and Pennsylvania, as low as three pence; in New York and North

Carolina $⅟₁₆; in Georgia $⅟₁₀; in Maryland $⅛; and in Virginia $⅙.

Prior to the Revolution, when an issue was to be redeemed in part on different dates, it was a Treasury responsibility to accomplish, but during the Revolution a new procedure was introduced by New Hampshire and Massachusetts. For such issues, a specific number of bills of each denomination were emitted bearing each due date on the face. Thus, in the course of printing, the engraved plates or the type had to be modified by changes in the due dates.

Because of the substantial movement of people during the Revolutionary War, the circulation of a mixed assortment of State currency, along with Continental Currency, was common. The credit of all paper money was initially dependent upon the outcome of the War, and difficulty in the calculation of values was aggravated as depreciation began in 1777.

Exchange rate problems during the American Revolution are well exemplified in General George Washington's Account Book (1775-1783). He starts out using Pennsylvania money and lawful money, changes to New York money and lawful money, then to dollars and lawful money; and after making an adjustment in accordance with the official scales of depreciation, his final calculation of recoverable expenditures was much less than the aggregate amount of actual disbursements for governmental purposes because he held the money before it was spent.

Some of the early Revolutionary War issues of New England Colonies and States were redeemed, but most War issues remained outstanding and became worthless. The pre-Revolutionary issues of New York, Pennsylvania, New Jersey, Delaware, and Maryland circulated along with the war issues of those States, until the final collapse. Thus the bulk of items available for collectors are those which were in circulation when this occurred.

A table showing the exchange rates during the Revolutionary War is included in Appendix D.

Continental Currency Issues

The $241,552,780 of Continental Currency issued by the Continental Congress during the American Revolution and its acceptance by the American People was a true test of loyalty to the ideal of independence. From the middle of 1775 Continental Currency circulated at par for one and one-half years. The Continental Congress used what specie it could obtain to purchase the essentials of war from foreign sources, and Continental and State paper money constituted virtually the only money in circulation within the country. The Continental Congress requested the States to levy taxes to redeem the Continental Currency, but most of each State's effort was directed toward military activity and taxes were neglected. The States were urged to support the value of the Continental Currency by giving it legal tender status and to control prices. Some States did not comply and others acted belatedly. Anyone who did not accept the paper money was declared a traitor, an enemy, or a Tory. Such measures had to be taken in desperation.

On 37 different dates specific amounts of Continental Currency were approved for emission by Resolutions of the Continental Congress, but for printing convenience the Continental Congress arranged for the text of the bills to include only 11 such Resolutions. The first issue carried the date of the commencement of the first Session of the Continental Congress, May 10, 1775, rather than the date of the currency Resolutions, but subsequent issues carried the specific date of a currency Resolution.

The English naturally refused to permit Continental Currency to circulate in areas they occupied and used every means to undermine public confidence in it elsewhere. A comic advertisement in the *New York Gazette* of October 28, 1776 read:

"Wanted, by a gentleman, fond of curiosities, who is shortly going to England, a parcel of Congress notes, with which he intends to paper some rooms. Those who wish to make something of their stock in that Commodity, shall, if they are clean and fit for the purpose, receive at the rate of one guinea per thousand for all they can bring before the expiration of the present month. Inquire of the printer. N. B. It is expected they will be much lower."

A pro-British item from the April 1, 1777 *Smythe's Journal* stated:

"The Pasteboard Dollars of Congress are now refused by the hottest among the rebels themselves. One, who was a member of a committee to punish those who might refuse them, was lately punished for refusing them himself; and, in short, every one is putting them off from himself, in exchange for almost anything that can be got for them. Yesterday, a Connecticut parson, with a parcel of the rag money in one of his moccasins, was taken at Kings Bridge and brought into New York. He was this morning obliged to chew up all the money, and declare, in the presence of a large assemblage of people, that he will not again pray for the Congress, or the doer of their dirty work, Mr. Washington."

The English participated in and encouraged the counterfeiting of Continental paper money, thus becoming the innovators of this type of economic warfare. The steady depreciation of the paper currency from the beginning of 1777 until its virtual demise in 1780 is set forth in a table in Appendix D. Debtors and speculators took advantage of the depreciation to pay off their debts. The rates of depreciation were subsequently codified in an attempt to establish fairness in such transactions. The loss to holders of currency, whether in the course of its collapse or at the conclusion of hostilities, was said by Benjamin Franklin and others to be justified as being a tax on the entire citizenry to pay for the War.

At the beginning of 1780, when the Continental Currency had depreciated to ⅟₄₀th of its face value, the Continental Congress desired to find a way to take it out of circulation. The only source of funds available was the States' payments of the tax quotas previously established, which were then substantially delinquent. The March 18, 1780 Resolution of Congress provided that the States could use $1 of a new issue of State money or $1 in specie to redeem $40 in Continental Currency, for which they would receive from the Federal Treasury a credit against their tax quotas. The amount of the new issue would be limited to one-twentieth of the amount of Continental Currency so turned in, but only six-tenths of it was to be for the State's use, the remaining four-tenths to be available for national use. Credit for the national four-tenths would also be given the States against their tax quotas. The bills constituting the new issue were to be due on December 31, 1786 plus 5% interest and were guaranteed by the United States.

The unwillingness of the public to accept revalued Continental Currency on any basis, the lack of confidence in the new issue, and the confusion due to the complexity of refinancing caused the plan to fail in a few months. However, an aggregate of $111,143,503 in Continental Currency was turned in. New guaranteed bills in the amount of $3,980,706 were issuable, of which the Federal government's share was $1,592,282. New Hampshire, Massachusetts, Rhode Island, New York, New Jersey, Pennsylvania, Maryland, and Virginia were the States which participated in the new issue, the others being either unwilling to do so or still occupied by British troops. The immediate depreciation of the new issue caused it to be emitted in limited amounts, and much of what was issued was soon paid back in tax payments to the Treasuries of the issuing States.

On November 18, 1776 the Continental Congress created The United States Lottery to generate profits to pay military expenses and to draw in Continental Currency as payment for the tickets. The scheme was designed to help prevent depreciation of the currency, but its six years of operation resulted in failure.

The worthlessness of Continental Currency is perpetuated in the colorful American colloquialism, "Not worth a Continental." Jonathan Carver in *Travels in America* (1778) comically stated, "The Congress paper dollars are now used for papering rooms, lighting pipes and other conveniences."

Finally, however, Continental Currency became exchangeable from 1790 to 1798 into U.S. Treasury bonds for 1% of its face value (See detail following the 1779 Continental Currency issue).

State Specie Paper Money Revival

In 1780 when the general collapse of all State paper money was obvious, some of the States independently undertook to emit new issues of paper money payable in specie. Pennsylvania began the practice with its April 29, 1780 issue, and Vermont, New York, New Jersey, Maryland, and North Carolina followed. These programs were entirely separate from the federally guaranteed State bills emitted under the March 18, 1780 Resolution passed by the Continental Congress to exchange for depreciated Continental Currency. By 1785 a State paper money mania had developed among the debtor classes, and further paper money issues payable in specie were made by Rhode Island, New York, Pennsylvania, New Jersey, North Carolina, South Carolina, and Georgia before the Federal government under the Constitution was established. Some issues at first suffered some depreciation, but in due course all were paid in full ex-

cept those of Rhode Island. In Massachusetts, in spite of the creation in 1784 of the Massachusetts Bank with the right of bank note issue, the refusal of the legislature to authorize State paper money caused Shay's Rebellion. Rhode Island's paper money of 1786 was created with legal tender status and resulted in the well-known case of Trevett vs. Weeden, in which the appeal from a summary judgment against a butcher for refusing to accept the paper money established the principle of trial by jury as part of the civil rights of citizens of the United States. Rhode Island's reluctance to ratify the Constitution of the United States until May 29, 1790 was based primarily upon the denial of the right of a State to issue its own paper money. The circulation of the 1783 and 1785 specie money of North Carolina until 1816 is detailed following those listings.

Provisions of the Constitution as to Paper Money

The collapse in value of the paper money of the Continental Congress and of the independent States was an experience which justified the Constitution of the United States specifically denying the States the right to issue paper money (Art. I, Sec. 10, Par. 1) and carefully omitting from the powers retained by the Federal government the same prerogative (Art. I, Sec. 8, Par. 5). Both the incorporation of banks and the packing of the United States Supreme Court for the Legal Tender decisions following the War between the States resulted in a circumvention of some of these restraints, but the Constitution still retains its original language as to paper money matters.

The Articles of Confederation adopted on June 26, 1778 had provided in Article XII that all Bills of Credit previously emitted under the authority of the Continental Congress were deemed a charge against the United States. Similarly, in 1787 the Constitution of the United States (Art. VI, Par. 1) assumed on behalf of the new government all of the obligations of the United States under the Articles of Confederation and thereby agreed to pay the Continental Currency issues as well as the State emissions guaranteed by the United States. No reference to a depreciated basis of payment was included. The exchange offer of U.S. Treasury bonds for 1% of the face value of Continental Currency specifically provided for the retention of full rights of those who did not wish to make the exchange. In spite of these provisions, there has been a continuing default by the United States in all such payments. Admittedly no citizen until the twentieth century had the right to sue the United States on these currency obligations, but now that such a right is available, no such claim has apparently been tested.

Paper Money from 1790 to 1800

The Bank of North America, incorporated by the Continental Congress in 1781, had successfully maintained its bank note circulation on a specie value basis since 1782 and was profitable. Other private interests soon organized to go into the banking business. The U.S. Constitution left the States the power to incorporate banks which could issue bank notes subject only to State regulation. Such issuing banks are described under the applicable geographical sections of this book.

The national government with other stockholders entered the banking business with the incorporation by Congress of the first Bank of the United States in 1791. The bank was intended to handle financial matters for both the U.S. Treasury and the public. Offices of Discount and Deposit were established in the largest American cities, and bank notes were issued from its principal office in Philadelphia as well as its other offices. This circulation is described under the applicable geographical sections of this book.

There was no regulation of private scrip under any laws in 1790. There was a desperate need for small change because of the collapse in value of copper coin issued by State franchised mints, private contractors, counterfeiters, and by the English. The national government desired to issue its own coin as a matter of practicality and was not yet prepared to set up its own mint. In 1787 it had had a costly and humiliating experience in contracting for the Fugio Cent coinage and seeing the contractor default after a minimal production.

Private issues, principally in New York and New Jersey, undertook to furnish small change notes for public use. Cities in those States joined in the note issuing spree.

Some churches in those States had received too many worthless copper coins in the collection boxes and baskets and undertook to issue "Church Money" which could be given back to them or redeemed by them. This scrip was small in size and circulated freely with private and city scrip in the trade of the areas in which it was issued. It remained in circulation until the U.S. Mint had provided a reasonable amount of copper coin to satisfy public needs and the confidence in the value of rejected coppers was restored.

A committee report to the New Jersey Assembly on June 7, 1790 described the problem of the small change notes and recommended the elimination of them as follows:

"from the depreciation of the Coppers, and the want of small change, a practice has almost universally prevailed throughout the state, of private persons issuing notes payable to the bearer for small sums; this practice the committee conceives to be improper, the same notes do not circulate throughout the state, and are therefore inconvenient to the holders; there is no security that they will be paid on demand, and indeed there are instances of persons issuing notes, and afterwards becoming insolvent, thereby defrauding the holders who are generally of the most ignorant class, and who ought therefore more particularly to be under the protection of the Legislature—Further, the notes increase the circulating paper medium, banish the small silver coins, and are a considerable profit to those who issue them, from the great number lost or destroyed in circulation, and which profit ought to be the emolument of the state and not of individuals.

"The committee therefore recommend, that a law should pass to prohibit all persons from issuing notes within this state, payable to the bearer for a less sum than   and which law would be similar to those which several European nations have found necessary to pass on the same subject."

Interest and Legal Tender

Although the concept of interest was natural to a Bill of Credit, the cost of interest to the Colony in addition to the face value was fully realized after the early experiences in redemption. Therefore interest on paper money was avoided by Colonial Assemblies wherever possible. Accrued interest on circulating money was impractical, as it would have to be recalculated each time a bill was passed. Sometimes the desire for interest from an issue caused people to retain paper money instead of using it for circulation. This was the problem when Virginia paper money of 1755 had its interest canceled prematurely because the bills were considered more advantageous to hold than to circulate.

Most issues, therefore, did not bear interest. The Crown, however, realized that without an interest obligation, some Colonies were perfectly satisfied to keep paper money in circulation indefinitely. Therefore, in New England, after 1751, England required any issue which was not to be redeemed within two years to bear interest. This was complied with until the American Revolution, although Massachusetts avoided paper money issues during that period. The Middle Colonies had become accustomed to interest-free paper money, and the Continental Currency followed that principle. By 1780, when the guaranteed issues were authorized, interest was reintroduced to help support their value.

To support the value of Bills of Credit, the Treasury of an issuing Colony accepted its own paper money in payment of taxes during the period prior to the final redemption date and would, if not limited by law, recirculate it. Because the redemption dates were often set well into the future, it was usually necessary to make the currency a legal tender in private as well as public transactions.

Acceptance of paper money in New York was required as early as 1711 at the risk of the debt being extinguished and penalties assessed. Other Colonies in due course passed similar legal tender laws. No problem with legal tender arose when paper money circulated at par, but only when it became depreciated. The British merchants complained about being forced to take depreciated paper money and agitated, without success, for an exemption with respect to themselves. In some situations merchants would enter into a contract requiring payment in specie or in commodities so as to be protected from the operation of the legal tender laws. In some Colonies, such as Rhode Island, the provisions of such a contract were illegal and the obligation could be satisfied by a paper money payment.

The interest and legal tender features of each issue are set forth under the descriptive sections.

Redemption, Cancellation, and Destruction

To provide funds to redeem paper money, it was customary to levy taxes, duties, and excises, and to allocate such proceeds for a number of years into the future. Since levies were lower if the redemption date was farther into the future, issues of postponed redemption were more popular with the colonists. The paper money was, in the course of its circulation, expected to find its way back to the Treasury in payment of the levies, and thus, by the time the redemption date or dates of the emission arrived, the Colonial Treasuries should have gathered the required amount of bills. Some paper money was made exchangeable at any time for specie then in the Treasury, but this was a theoretical right as specie was rarely available. If taxes sufficient to pay the amount to be redeemed were not collected, the due dates of the Bills of Credit were often extended and payment of taxes deferred. In South Carolina the Colonial government customarily issued circulating certificates to pay public

expenses before the annual Colony budget was approved, and only after approval was a tax levied to pay the outstanding certificates during the following year.

Many bills became invalid after their specific redemption date, but excuses for late presentation were usually honored. Ordinarily it was the Treasury which had to delay redemption when specie was required.

As bills were redeemed or paid into a Colonial Treasury, they were customarily counted at intervals by a committee appointed by the Assembly for that purpose and burned in the committee's presence. A certificate of burning was then signed and placed in the Treasurer's records. In this manner embezzlement, theft, and unauthorized reissue were controlled. Often these certificates made no distinction as to the issue or denomination destroyed, and thus the few remaining records of this type are usually difficult to interpret. Many issues circulated long beyond their due dates, and others were reissued by the Treasury without legislative authority.

When Revolutionary War paper money issues were redeemed, some of the bills were hole cancelled, slash cut, or X cut instead of or before being burned. As late as the twentieth century, Connecticut's State Archives still had many such bills on hand, and these eventually found their way into collections. Many cancelled guaranteed issues of New Hampshire and Massachusetts were similarly liberated. The March 18, 1780 Resolution of the Continental Congress provided that the Continental Currency to be redeemed was to be cancelled first with a one inch hole and subsequently burned when the Congress directed.

Printing and Engraving

Many techniques were used in producing the paper currency of early America. In North Carolina early bills were handwritten because there was no printer in the Colony. Printing from engraved plates was first adopted in New England and then selected by the southern Colonies. The plates were prepared by cutting the design and text into a sheet of copper by hand. To simplify the printing process several denominations were often engraved on one plate. The engraving artist was usually a silversmith, who sometimes was a printer too. To make a print the ink was applied onto the plate sinking into the intaglio portions. The flat surface was wiped clean, the paper laid on the plate, and covered with a pad over which a roller passed or on which a screw press squeezed. Two printings on a sheet in order to add the Crown's initials in a separate color were used in early New England issues, but other two-color printings from engraved plates were not usually undertaken because of the additional labor.

Printing from type, ornaments, and castings from cuts was accomplished by combining the elements in a printing chase and locking them together. A sheet of a group of denominations would be printed at one time. Cast lead type, usually acquired from England, consisted of letters, numbers, and ornaments which could be hand set. Type from many different fonts was often used on a single bill. Molds for some special ornaments were prepared in America and multiple lead castings made from them. Vignettes, insignia, borders, and frames were cut in wood, iron, or copper. A wood cut was usually prepared in such a manner that the high portions constituted the design to be printed, and wood in areas not to be printed was removed. The detail for iron and copper cuts was incised in metal, but the cuts themselves would not be used directly for printing. Lead would be poured over them to transfer the intaglio design to raised elements of a lead casting. Multiple castings could be made from the same iron or copper cuts so that bills printed on the same sheet could have identical ornamentation. These cast elements were mounted with nails on wood blocks for insertion into the printing chase. A similar process was used for the nature printing process invented by Benjamin Franklin, except that a refractory plaster cast of an actual leaf was used to make the lead casting instead of using a metal matrix as a mold. Cast cuts could be reused in later issues or renewed if broken at any time. The ink was applied to the raised surfaces with a roller or pad in the same manner as it was applied to printing in relief from type.

In the course of printing bills from type and castings, individual pieces of type or cast cuts occasionally became damaged, weak, or broken out. Sometimes replacement was undertaken if the defect was noticed. On rare occasions lines of type or a piece of type would shift in position. With respect to engraved plates, wear from wiping would sometimes make the printing of some parts weak, and reengraving took place when the results became poor. These printing difficulties are sometimes noticeable in comparing different specimens of a bill of the same denomination and issue.

The size of sheet to be printed and the number of bills for which there was space depended upon the press used. If a press was large enough, the faces as well as an equal number of backs could be set in one printing chase. In that way a sheet could be turned over vertically and rotated horizontally so that the faces and backs would be directly opposite. These were called double sheets. Registration of the face and back of the bill was accomplished by the use of two permanent upright nails flanking the middle of the printing bed so that the holes in the paper created by the first impression on a sheet could be reused when the sheet was set in on its opposite face. Two printings on one side of the same sheet were sometimes undertaken for uniface bills when the sheets of paper were twice as large as the printing chase. The second impression could also be made upon the opposite half of the other side. Two separate printings were also undertaken on one side of a sheet when two colors were desired. Franklin and Hall, however, printed in two colors on both sides of sheets for Pennsylvania beginning in 1759, and Hall and Sellers, their successors, printed the final issue of Continental Currency in this manner in 1779.

Sheet structure of some issues of bills is included in Appendix A.

After each impression the sheet was hung up on wires or laid out so that the ink would dry, as a sheet could not be printed on the other side or stacked when the ink was wet without risk of smearing or transfer.

The custody of the plates, cuts, and special insignia was often the responsibility of one or more specific committee members so that the printer would not have the risk of retaining them. Supervision of the press when notes were being printed was a duty assigned to appointed officials so that an excess of notes could not be clandestinely printed. When insignia or ornaments were to be reused at a later date, they were often separated and hidden by the committee.

Some issues of Connecticut and Massachusetts bills are printed from engraved plates on one side and printed from set type and raised ornamentation on the other. This required two entirely different printing techniques, and some of the issues engraved by Paul Revere appear to have been printed on the face by him and on the back by a printer who set the raised type.

The printer customarily printed extra sheets of bills to cover spoilage and sometimes for replacement of bills which would soon become worn. For example, Peter Timothy of South Carolina in printing 108,500 typeset bills for the March 6, 1776 issue made 3,044 extra bills. Franklin referred to his own extras as "Overplus" in a March 15, 1753 letter accompanying a delivery of Delaware bills which contained an excess of 1,180 bills in an order for 24,700 pieces.

Printing the authorized number of each denomination was sometimes a complex mathematical problem for the printer, who would not wish to use more sheets of paper than necessary. Extra labor was of less importance. The need of the public for more of certain denominations than others often resulted in different numbers of each denomination being authorized. The number of denominations in an issue was also subject to economic convenience. The presses then used for printing and the sheets of paper available for printing had specific dimensions, and the convenient size of the paper money adopted by a Colony would control the number of bills to be printed on a sheet. If all of the designated denominations would fit on and fill up one or two sheets and there was an equal number of each denomination to be printed on a sheet, the printer had a routine job to do. It was also simple for the printer to accommodate twice or three times the number of one denomination on a sheet by engraving or setting in type two or three of that denomination, provided that the total of all bills authorized could be produced from a specific number of full-sheet impressions. These were the practices for the cutting of and printing from engraved plates. Typeset printing, however, permitted a replacement of one denomination for another during the run by opening the chase and substituting one or more other or duplicate denominations or by modifying a denomination with a replacement of appropriate type and insignia. The puzzle was to determine how many impressions to make before changing the make-up of the chase and how many make-up changes were required for optimum efficiency.

The appropriate portions of a letter written by Franklin to accompany a shipment of unsigned sheets of the 1753 issue of £3,000 of Delaware bills is an example of the foregoing printing problem.

"Sir,   Philada. March 15. 1753

We send herewith all the Bills in a Trunk, containing as follows

	1s.	1s. 6d.	2s.	2s. 6d.	5s.	10s.
1st Sort 40 Quire, containing	4000	4000	4000	4000	—	—
2d Sort 11 Quire containing	1100	—	—	1100	1100	1100
3d Sort 9 Quire containing	900	900	—	900	900	—
4th Sort 4 Quire of half Sheets	—	200	—	200	400	—
	6000	5100	4000	6200	2400	1100

In the above, it is to be observed, that there are 100 of the 1s. 6d. Bills, more than there should be, which must be cut off, and put among the Overplus.

The Overplus is as follows

1st Sort   38 Sheets, which is one Short of our Memorandum
2d   Sort   13 Sheets which is one over
3d   Sort   13 Sheets which is three over
4th Sort   7 half Sheets, which is right.

So that I either made some small Mistake in our first Counting, or in this, I cannot tell which, for the Boat is just going, and we have not time to count again."

The issue was to replace worn out bills of the prior issue. Analyzing the contents of the letter, it appears that the requirements were 24,700 bills disregarding the sheets in the Overplus. He used 1,500 full sheets (25 sheets equal 1 quire) and 100 half sheets, the equal of 1,550 full sheets. The press made 3,200 impressions. His production of 4,000 bills of each denomination of the "1st Sort" was printed on 1,000 sheets, thus producing 4 bills of each of the 4 denominations on each such sheet or a total of 16 bills per sheet. Because these lower denomination bills had blank backs, it might be assumed that there were 4 faces of each denomination printed on one surface. The printing of the 2d, 3d, and 4th Sorts, however, included bills with printed backs (5s and 10s), and therefore the faces of 2 bills of each denomination must have been printed on each sheet surface to produce 4 of that denomination per sheet. This is based upon the customary economic practice of printing the faces and backs on each side of each sheet by turning over the sheet on its horizontal axis to produce proper registration. This reduces to 2 instead of 4 the number of faces

to be set up for each denomination. The half sheets contained 8 bills (4 of the 5s and 2 each of the others) and were also printed by being turned on their horizontal axis. Since two faces were typeset and used on full sheets for each denomination, the insertion of a plate letter enabled the two faces of the same denomination to be readily distinguished. Franklin's solution of his printing problem caused him to produce 100 too many bills of one denomination (1s6d). The mathematically inclined reader will find that Franklin needed only 1538 full sheets and 12 half sheets to complete the requirements without any further typesetting. This would use only 3100 pressings instead of 3200, but would have required 6 positional makeups for the chase rather than the 4 which Franklin used. Franklin would have therefore saved 100 pressings and 6 full sheets if he had shifted his makeup 2 more times. One hundred 1s6d saved would have pleased him and the printing labor would have been more than recovered by the makeup changes.

Printers and Engravers

Bills bearing the words "Printed by B. Franklin" or "Printed by B. Franklin and D. Hall" are found on some Pennsylvania, New Jersey, and Delaware issues. Bills engraved and printed by Paul Revere for Massachusetts and New Hampshire, however, do not bear his initials or name. Peter Zenger, a vigorous advocate of freedom of the press, printed some of the New York issues.

Famous silversmiths such as Jeremiah Dummer, Nathaniel Hurd, and John Coney engraved the plates for some New England bills. The artistry of Thomas Coram of Charleston, South Carolina, was demonstrated by elaborate mythological vignettes on the February 8, 1779 issue of his State. The Maryland issues of 1756 through 1774 show Jonas Green's initials on nature prints on the backs and on some border cuts on the face, but the border cuts were engraved by Thomas Sparrow, who worked his name into some of them.

James Smither of Philadelphia, who in 1778 was accused by Thomas Paine of counterfeiting Continental Currency for the British and by the Supreme Executive Council of Pennsylvania of being a traitor, identified himself as the engraver of some border cuts for 1772-76 Pennsylvania bills and was reliably said to have done similar work for the Continental Currency issues in 1775.

Elisha Gallaudet, whose identification appears as "E G FECIT" on one die variety of the coined 1776 Continental Dollar, began his paper money engraving by making the head, side border, and Arms cuts for the February 16, 1771 New York issue. This was followed by his engraving of the elaborate steam-operated water pump for the back and head cut for the face of the 1774-76 New York City issues. He then engraved the well known sundial MIND YOUR BUSINESS cut and the 13 links cut for the fractional denominations of the Continental Currency issue of February 17, 1776.

David Rittenhouse, who in 1792 became the first Director of the United States Mint, had previously used his artistic talents to engrave ornamental borders for the March 25, 1776 New Jersey issue, working his full last name into the £6 bill.

Henry Dawkins was employed as an engraver in 1780 by Treasury officials of the Continental Congress after he had served his sentence for counterfeiting 1775 Continental Currency, Connecticut, and Massachusetts paper money. He engraved the border cuts for the face as well as the panel surrounding the emblem on the back of the various denominations of the State issues guaranteed by the United States under the March 18, 1780 Resolution of the Continental Congress. For those issues he also skillfully modified some border cuts previously used on the faces of the January 14, 1779 Continental Currency issue so that they could be reused on the backs. The modfications consisted of eliminating or changing the denominational insignia on ten denominations of the 1779 issue which did not coincide with the denominations designated for the 1780 bills.

Amos Doolittle, John Draper, and William Harrison engraved plates for early bank notes and established well-known bank note engraving businesses.

Paper

The best available handmade rag paper was customarily used to print paper money. The rag content included both linen and cotton. In the early years of American paper currency, the Company of Stationers in England furnished the stock. As soon as paper making developed in America, local industry was favored. Lay wire markings from the laid paper process are quite evident on most early issues. After 1757 some woven paper was imported from England. Some Virginia money was printed on very thin rag paper, known as rice paper, but most issues were printed on thick coarse paper.

Watermarked paper for the Maryland issue of 1733 was sent over from England, but during the American Revolution New Jersey, Pennsylvania, and the Continental Congress issued some bills on watermarked American-made paper. Paul Revere's patriotism was evidenced by engraving the words AMERICAN PAPER on the copper plates for the Massachusetts Bay issue of May 25, 1775, but the paper contained a watermark of a Crown over GR.

On January 4, 1776, Stephan Crane of Milton, Massachusetts, sold to the Massachusetts Currency Committee thirteen reams of "Money Paper" which was paid for by Paul Revere in 1778. The principal source of the thick coarse paper for the Pennsylvania, Delaware, and Continental Currency issues was Ivy Mills (Thomas Wilcox, proprietor) of Glenn Mills, Pennsylvania, where the paper with blue fibres and mica was produced. New Jersey had its source of paper at Spotswood, New Jersey. There were other American paper mills making paper for legal, newspaper, and general commercial purposes, and some of that paper was used for paper currency as well.

The 1722 small change bills of Massachusetts were printed on parchment instead of paper in order to increase their durability. They also were the first non-metallic money to have a different shape for each denomination, having been made round, rectangular, and hexagonal.

Benjamin Franklin furnished two types of polychromed or marbled paper, a light weight one for the $20 Continental Currency bills of May 10, 1775 and a stronger one for the 1789 small change notes issued by the Bank of North America. This paper apparently was made in Merion, Pennsylvania.

Some New York Colonial issues and some City of New York issues were on laminated paper, a thin white layer comprising the face and a coarse dark brown layer on the back.

The rag content of the paper generally used for early American paper money was needed to enable it to withstand the dirt and wear to which it was subjected. Specimens in collections ordinarily show no greater deterioration than took place after their normal circulation.

Denominations

The different denominations used on paper money in Colonial and Revolutionary America are indicative of the myriad of changing economic conditions which confronted the people. The number of denominations officially adopted stagger the imagination, even within one Colony. Although each Colony used pounds, shillings, and pence as its denominational nomenclature for all or a portion of the period prior to Independence and some used that basis thereafter, these were monies of account which differed from Colony to Colony. A consolidation of these denominations follows.

Pence: 1, 2, 3, 4, 5, 6, 7, 8, 9, 10, 12, and 18.

Shillings: 1, 1s3d, 1s4d, 1s6d, 1s8d, 1s9d, 2, 2s3d, 2s4d, 2s6d, 2s8d, 3, 3s4d, 3s6d, 3s9d, 4, 4s4d, 4s6d, 5, 5s3d, 5s4d, 5s6d, 6, 6s3d, 6s8d, 7, 7s6d, 8, 9, 10, 11, 12, 12s6d, 14, 15, 16, 17, 17s6d, 18, 20, 22, 24, 25, 27, 28, 30, 36, 40, 42, 48, 50, 54, 60, 66, 72, and 100.

Pounds: 1, £1 10s, £1 12s, £1 15s, 2, £2 5s, £2 10s, 3, £3 4s, £3 10s, £3 12s, 4, 5, 6, £6 5s, 8, 10, 12, £12 10s, 15, 20, 25, 30, 50, and 100.

In the dollar denomination category, Rhode Island used $⅟₃₆, ⅟₂₄, ⅟₁₈, ⅟₁₆, ⅟₁₂, ⅑, ⅛, ⅙, ¼, ⅓, ½, 1, 2, 3, 4, 5, 6, 7, 8, 10, 20, and 30, which included the lowest dollar denomination of any jurisdiction. In dollar denominations Virginia used $⅙, ¼, ⅓, ⅔, 1, 2, 3, 3⅓, 4, 5, 6, 6⅔, 7, 8, 10, 13⅓, 15, 20, 25, 30, 35, 40, 45, 50, 55, 60, 70, 75, 80, 100, 150, 200, 250, 300, 400, 500, 750, 1,000, 1,200, 1,500, and 2,000, which included the highest denominations of any jurisdiction and several unique denominations. Maryland issued many unusual dollar denominations in its emissions which contained $⅟₁₅, ⅟₁₀, ⅑, ⅙, ⅕, ²⁄₉, ⅓, ½, ⅔, 1, 1⅓, 1⅔, 2, 2⅔, 3, 4, 5, 6, 7, 8, 16, and 20. North Carolina, among its twenty-six denominations in dollars, introduced $2.50, $7.50, $12.50, and $600. South Carolina provided a $90 denomination. The Georgia dollar denominations are aggregated under that section and contain such unusual denominations as $9, 11, 13, and 17. The Continental Congress was distinctive with its $65 denomination.

Specific weights of silver plate on certain foreign silver coin were sometimes used as the primary denominations of paper money issued by some of the American Colonies. In New Jersey from 1724 through 1776 the weight of silver plate was specified in ounces, pennyweights, and grains Troy measure as the denomination, and for convenience the exchange value in money of account was stated at 2 pennyweights 22 grains to the New Jersey shilling. In New York from November 1709 through July 1723 the denominations were in silver plate (the 1709 Silver Issue had an alternative in Lyon Dollars) and were stated to be equal to 2 pennyweights 12 grains to the New York shilling. Maryland issues from 1767 through 1780 used Spanish Dollars as the primary denominations and were stated to be convertible into English sterling exchange at the rate of 4s6d for each

Spanish Dollar. Early issues of the New England Colonies used denominations in their own individual pounds, shillings, and pence, making them equal to "Money" (meaning silver coin), but during the decade beginning in 1740 the equivalent in the weight of silver plate was in the text of the bill. New Hampshire in 1755 temporarily changed the equivalent for its money of account from silver plate to Spanish Dollars. Rhode Island from 1750(1) to 1755 changed its primary denominations to a specific weight of silver plate.

Indenture

To prevent counterfeits and altered bills from being redeemed and to audit the number issued, many series of bills were bound into pads or books with the denomination and part of the design intended to be retained on a stub. The same number was written on the stub and on the bill for identification purposes. The bills were cut off the stubs in an uneven manner with a knife or scissors so that on redemption they could be test fitted and verified. This procedure became impractical because of

the extra work involved in numbering and cutting and because the bills became tattered on the indented end as well as elsewhere. The expression "indented bill" was continued in use long after actual indenture was abandoned, as in the Pennsylvania issue of March 20, 1771. Unissued bills with a full stub are shown in the 1714 New York issue, the 1717 redated 1729 New Hampshire issue, and the 1733 Maryland issue.

Issued 1774 Maryland $2 bill showing insufficient removal of the stub, leaving the denomination, number, and full border design on the bill instead of being retained by the Treasurer.

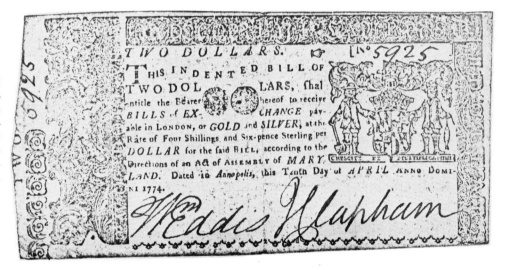

Signers

Manual signing of bills was done in ink as a protection against counterfeiting and as a control against printing or issuing more than were authorized. The number of signers depended on the authorizing legislation, and bills were signed by up to as many as six persons, as can be noted from the illustrations in the catalog. Sometimes lower denominations were signed by only one person, while higher denominations were signed by more, and where this occurs it is noted in the catalog. In some Virginia issues certain individuals were named to sign specific denominations for control and identification pur-

poses. Various colors of ink were sometimes used. The only exceptions to written signatures seem to be the 1722 small change issue of Massachusetts Bay, which had no signatures, and some small change notes issued between 1789 and 1796, which had printed signatures.

Some authorized signers listed in the catalog may not have signed any bills, because no bills with their autographs are known. Such persons may have been alternates or may not have been able or needed to perform the signing task. Conversely, many signatures found on bills are quite genuine, but according to available records these signers were not formally appointed. All known or authorized signers are therefore included. Signature combinations and signature frequency are not within the scope of this work since such data fall more properly in the autograph category. Some authorized signers must have permitted others to sign for them, since the same name is sometimes found in different handwriting.

A schedule of Continental Currency signers is set out in that section along with their authorization dates and the issues they signed.

The signers of Colony, State, and Continental Currency bills included many famous persons. Those connected with principal Revolutionary conventions and the establishment of the Federal government are hereafter listed, along with an identification of the issues which they signed.

Signers of the Declaration of Independence (1776):
Abraham Clark, NJ/02/20/76 (authorized but unknown).
George Clymer, PA/06/18/64.
William Ellery, RI/03/18/76.
Lyman Hall, GA/01/09/82.
John Hart, NJ/02/20/76, NJ/03/25/76.
Francis Hopkinson, PA/03/20/71.
Philip Livingston, NY/09/15/55.
Arthur Middleton, SC/00/00/50-69.
John Morton, PA/04/03/72.
George Walton, GA/00/00/75, GA/01/09/82.
James Wilson, CC/04/11/78, CC/01/14/79. (Sometimes by amanuensis and often confused with the signature of Joseph Wilson.)

Signers of the Articles of Confederation (1777):
Andrew Adams, CN/10/11/77.
Daniel Carroll, CC/02/17/76, CC/02/26/77.
William Ellery, RI/03/18/76.
Edward Langworthy, GA/06/08/77.
Henry Laurens, SC/00/00/60—Second Issue, SC/00/00/67.
John Mathews, SC/00/00/50-69, SC/03/06/76.

Daniel Roberdeau, PA/01/01/56, PA/06/15/67, PA/03/01/69, PA/03/20/71.
Jonathan Bayard Smith, CC/05/10/75, CC/11/29/75, CC/02/17/76, CC/05/09/76, CC/07/22/76.
Edward Telfair, GA/00/00/75, GA/00/00/76—shilling issue, GA/00/00/76 blue seal, GA/00/00/76 maroon seal.
George Walton, GA/00/00/75, GA/01/09/82.
John Williams, CC/02/17/76, CC/09/26/78, CC/01/14/79.

Delegates to the Stamp Act Congress (1765):
Joseph Borden, NJ/06/09/80.
Metcalfe Bowler, RI/03/01/66, RI/02/28/67, RI/05/03/75, RI/11/06/75, RI/06/00/80, RI/07/02/80.
George Bryan, PA/05/01/60.
John Cruger, NY/04/20/56.
Hendrik Fisher, NJ/02/20/76.
Christopher Gadsden, SC/04/10/74, SC/08/20/60.
Leonard Lispenard, NY/09/15/55.
Philip Livingston, NY/09/15/55.
Robert R. Livingston, NY/04/20/56.
Thomas Lynch, SC/00/00/67, SC/04/18/75.
John Morton, PA/04/03/72.
John Rutledge, SC/07/25/61, SC/00/00/67.
Henry Ward, RI/05/03/75, RI/11/06/75.

Signers of the United States Constitution (1787):
Gunning Bedford, Jr., CC/09/26/78.
John Blair, VA/04/07/62, VA/00/00/70, VA/07/11/71, VA/04/01/73, VA/09/00/73.
David Brearley, NJ/06/09/80, NJ/01/09/81.
Daniel Carroll, CC/02/17/76, CC/02/26/77.
George Clymer, PA/06/18/64.
William Few, GA/00/00/76—shilling issue, GA/05/04/78.
Thomas Mifflin, PA/03/20/71.
Charles Pinckney, Jr., SC/04/10/78 (different from Charles Pinckney, Sr.).
Charles Cotesworth Pinckney, SC/04/07/70.
John Rutledge, SC/07/25/61, SC/00/00/67.
James Wilson, CC/04/11/78, CC/01/14/79.

Numbering

Most issues of early American paper currency are consecutively hand numbered in ink. These numbers usually corroborate the statistics as to the number of each denomination of each issue actually emitted, as numbering for each denomination generally began with the number 1. Where there are different varieties or plate letters of the same denomination in the same issue, the numbering is usually continuous from variety to variety, as in the 1778 North Carolina issue or the Pennsylvania

issues. However, there are various exceptions in the numbering practices. Sometimes the numbering for the same denomination continues from issue to issue without beginning afresh, such as in some New York and Delaware emissions. Where substitution of new bills for worn bills was undertaken without special legislation, the numbering runs higher than the amount authorized, even though the amount outstanding was correct at any given time. Where a sheet contained several different denominations, the same number would sometimes be written on each bill on the sheet, as in the 1776 and 1777 Georgia issues. In other situations continuous numbering of all bills on such sheets took place, so that the same denomination bears numbering which skips uniformly, as occurs in the 1776 and 1777 Delaware issues.

There are situations where the number issued seems to have actually exceeded the number authorized. This might have taken place in emergencies or in situations where the bills were signed and numbered in anticipation of enabling legislation which was never passed because of economic changes or depreciation. It may also have occurred where the need for some denominations of an issue was greater than for others, and there was emitted more of one denomination than was authorized and less of another, so that the face value of the total issue was not exceeded.

Emblems and Mottoes

The paper money of early America contains many interesting and unusual emblems and mottoes in addition to the British, Colonial, and State Arms and Seals.

From *Come over & help us* on the 1690 Massachusetts issue to *Do as you would be done by* on a 1783 North Carolina bill, the charm of these moralistic insignia is inescapable. North Carolina is the most profuse in its quaint mottoes during the American Revolution with such examples as *Quaerenda Pecunia Primum est* (The search for money comes first), *Aut numquam tentes aut perfice* (Either finish or never begin), *Don't tread on me* above a rattlesnake, *Hit or miss* next to a hunter, etc. South Carolina in 1777 had a most prophetic motto, *Misera Omni Servatus* (Slavery of all kinds is wretched). One of Georgia's curious emblems was two floating jugs representing England and America with the motto *Si Colligimus Frangimur* (If we collide we break). Another Georgia motto *Libertas Carior Aura* (Freedom is more precious than gold) contradicts the first Latin North Carolina motto quoted above. In a New York 1776 issue there is a candelabrum of thirteen candles with the motto *Uno eodemque igni* (With one and the same fire).

These emblems and mottoes were principally selected or adapted from the many European emblem and motto books written by Camerarius, Weigels, Verrien, Saavedra, Alciatus, etc. The translation of all of the Latin mottoes is included in the listing of the bills on which they are found or with a convenient prior issue or description.

The most extensive use of emblems and mottoes was on the Continental Currency. Each integral denomination had an emblem and Latin motto which was retained through every issue. The public was naturally curious as to the meaning of the emblems and mottoes, and an explanation was published in the September 20, 1775 *Pennsylvania Gazette,* then in the December, 1775 *Pennsylvania Magazine,* and in contemporary almanacs. An interpretation of the meaning of the emblems and mottoes on Continental Currency is included under that section of this catalog.

Benjamin Franklin created the FUGIO MIND YOUR BUSINESS device.

Francis Hopkinson, who signed the 1771 Pennsylvania Bills of Credit and the Declaration of Independence, sought compensation in 1780 for designing "Seven Devices with Mottoes" used on the Continental Currency in the 1778 and 1779 issues. His claim was technically rejected because he had no voucher indicating any agreement for payment, but actually the denial was because his "fancy work" was deemed to be in the ordinary course of his service as a government employee.

Counterfeiting and Its Problems

Counterfeiting of early American paper money was a constant menace to the circulation of genuine bills. Some of these false pieces were of quality fine enough to cause entire genuine issues to be recalled and replaced. Capture of counterfeiters and passers was particularly difficult because (1) bills of one Colony or State were often passed in neighboring Colonies and States; (2) counterfeit bills or plates were often prepared in Europe; (3) genuine bills were often artistically crude and poorly printed, and (4) soiled, torn, patched and sewn bills made detection of counterfeits most difficult. Yet many arrests and prosecutions occurred because of the cooperation of the citizenry.

The death penalty for counterfeiting in many Colonies did not deter the counterfeiter, nor did branding, ear cropping, whipping, or the pillory. The bills in many Colonies, beginning with the New Jersey issue of July 2, 1746 and the New York issue of July 21, 1746, specified the death penalty on the bills themselves. TO COUNTERFEIT IS DEATH and many variations of the warning were prominently placed on many subsequent issues. The 1777 South Carolina issue has DEATH TO COUNTERFEIT printed twice on the back of each note. In a North Carolina issue of 1783, the warning reads COUNTER-

FEITERS BEWARE. **On an** April 10, 1759 New Jersey bill the warning is worked in with the denomination so as to read ONE POUND TEN SHILLINGS OR THIRTY SHILLINGS WHICH 'TIS DEATH TO COUNTERFEIT.

The most unusual counterfeit warning was:

TIEFRET.NUOCEDIVSIYGRELCFOTIFENEBTUOHTIWHTA EDTCAOT on the 1769 Georgia issue which, if read backwards, separated into words and rearranged, reads "To counterfeit is death without benefit of clergy vide Act," the last two words meaning "See the Act."

Some counterfeits are very important numismatically because without them the form of many issues would be entirely unknown. Counterfeits were often marked "counterfeit" in ink or defaced with a large X in ink. They were not subject to confiscation after discovery unless needed for prosecution. Innocent and embarrassed persons to whom counterfeits had been passed often discovered the fraud belatedly and could do nothing about it because they did not know who passed them. They retained the fakes, and for that reason counterfeits of early issues survive in far greater quantity than genuine bills. If the recipient had doubt about its genuineness, he required the payer to write his name on the back, and for that reason many genuine and counterfeit bills have an assortment of signatures on them.

Many means were employed to prevent counterfeiting. Engraving was done by the best craftsmen. Indenture designs and scrolls were placed on the back as well as the face. Printed bills had elaborate vignettes, ornaments, and many different type fonts. South Carolina in 1776 even used Hebrew and Greek letters and Zodiacal symbols. Franklin developed the nature printing process for leaf and cloth designs because manual copying could not produce nature's detail, lines of graduated thickness, or the graceful curves of stretched wet cloth. Paper of the best quality was used, some with colored threads, mica, watermarks, or polychromed (marbled) edges. Signatures were of little help as a preventative, but printing in two colors was a substantial deterrent.

So-called "secret marks" on bills were sometimes used as a means of detecting counterfeits rather than preventing counterfeits from being made. The problem of such a ruse was that most secret marks on genuine bills were usually just as obvious to the counterfeiter producing the false bills as to Treasury officials. If these marks were disguised as minutiae so that the counterfeiters might not notice them, then officials still could not announce the secret marks to the public without encouraging correction of the counterfeit plate or form. Engraving or setting type or designs slightly out of line could be copied just as odd sized, unusual, or deformed letters, numbers, or ornaments could be copied. Often movement of type or damage to type or ornaments in the course of printing would happen naturally and thus what appears to be a secret mark actually was not. Ink smears, dots, or blotches which often happened accidentally were the cleverest when used deliberately. The most obvious attempt to use secret marks to deter counterfeiting was in the Maryland issues of 1767, 1770, and 1774 in which errors and oddities in typesetting were combined with dots, blotches, accent marks, and rotated letters. Virtually all of these seem to be deliberate and not accidental and are described under those issues. The May 15, 1779 North Carolina issue contains secret marks in the text such as an accent circumflex, umlaut, carat, or dash, none of which are necessary to the text. They are described under that emission. In the Virginia issues of 1780 and 1781 Old English type is used on portions of the bills and there are many spelling errors in those issues. There could have been a shortage of Old English cast type at the Virginia printer or a typesetter with poor vision or knowledge, but the errors to anyone accustomed to reading Old English type would be so obvious that one wonders whether they were intended as secret marks or not.

Whether engraved bills or bills printed from type and cuts were better as a protection against counterfeiting was a topic of discussion throughout the eighteenth century.

The broad scope of counterfeiting is described in the extensive published material on the subject and is summed up in the 1768 *New York Journal or General Advertiser:* "It is said that they (the counterfeiters) have established a regular Chain of Communication throughout the whole Extent of the British Dominions in America and there are above an Hundred of them concerned in the different Provinces."

The most audacious advertisement relating to counterfeiting was inserted in the April 14, 1777 *New York Gazette* and the *Weekly Mercury* of the same date when New York City was still occupied by the British forces. In an effort to destroy the value of Continental Currency by the distribution of free counterfeits the notice read: "Persons going into other Colonies may be supplied with any Number of counterfeit Congress-Notes, for the Price of the Paper per Ream. They are so neatly and exactly executed that there is no Risque in getting them off, it being almost impossible to discover, that they are not genuine. This has been proved by Bills to a very large Amount, which have already been successfully circulated. Enquire for Q.E.D. at the Coffee-House, from 11 P.M. to 4 A.M. during the present month." George Washington commented as to this "unparalleled piece" that "no Artifices are left untried by the Enemy to injure us."

Bills of which counterfeits are known are marked with a Ⓒ in the listings in the catalog, and a description of counterfeits is in Appendix B. Illustrations of counterfeit bills are designated by a Ⓒ next to them. Many counterfeits have not been located and are known only through records and newspaper reports. There may therefore be some inaccuracies where an altered genuine bill was referred to as a counterfeit in such source material.

Counterfeit detector sheets of bills were printed and issued to Treasury personnel by Pennsylvania and by the Continental Congress for use in comparing suspected bills. These were printed along with the regular sheets, but customarily on blue paper. (Some May 10, 1775 Continental Currency detector sheets were on pink paper.) The double sheet of 16 bills was cut in half to make a single sheet of 8 bills for distribution to appropriate money handlers. They remained unsigned and unnumbered. Collectors have cut up some such detectors so that individual denominations are more often seen than those in sheet form.

Reproductions of bills made after the end of the circulating period of genuine bills are not identified as counterfeits because they usually contain printed signatures and printed numbering and are readily distinguishable as copies. However, where reproductions are reprints from original plates or forms after the end of the circulating period they are indicated by ® for reprint instead of being classed as counterfeit. A few such plates were located in the archives of New Hampshire, Massachusetts, Rhode Island, Virginia, North Carolina, and South Carolina, and used for reprinting. Some mutilated Massachusetts copper plates engraved by Paul Revere were located in 1854 and used for such reprinting. In some instances forged signatures and numbers are added to reprints to make them appear to be originals.

Alteration and Its Deterrents

The raising of the denomination of a genuine bill was a common form of rascality in early America. This practice could only be undertaken with one bill at a time and was therefore far less of a menace than counterfeiting. It was often done by erasing denominational portions of a bill and drawing in or pasting higher numbers over those areas. Cuttings from newspapers and advertisements were used. Penmanship with matching ink was often undertaken on both engraved and typeset bills.

Many methods were used to deter alteration. Some issues had a different vignette on each denomination so that a raised denomination would have the wrong vignette. Other bills had differently shaped borders around the text of each denomination. On occasion the back would be decorated on the higher denominations of an issue and be left blank or differently decorated on the lower. The denomination was often in many places on a bill and in different type fonts so as to make alteration difficult. Working the denomination into the border design or into the vignette was another deterrent. Different colors for each denomination were used in Connecticut for a short pe-

riod. In some Pennsylvania, Delaware, and New Jersey bills one or more crown symbols were keyed to a denomination as a 5 shilling equivalent. In some New York issues one or more pound weights or five pound weights were keyed to the pound denomination of the bills.

On many Pennsylvania issues from 1739 through 1776 the name of the province was spelled Pennsilvania, Pensylvania, Pensilvania, as well as Pennsylvania on various denominations as a means of preventing and detecting raised denominations, but finally this practice became so inconsistent that there was no coordination between the denominations and the particular variations in spelling. In another Pennsylvania issue the denomination in red Roman numerals was worked into the text.

On the margin of the New Jersey Act passed February 5, 1727(8) there are denominational insignia. These were used for denominational identification and to discourage alteration. Full moons and suns, with semicircles and quadrants of them, were selected for the nine basic denominations as illustrated below. These insignia were used for about 50 years on New Jersey bills.

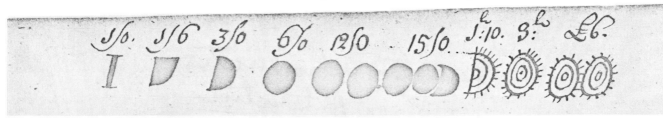

Alteration of dates took place occasionally when an issue was called for redemption, because some bills were not exchanged in time. This took place with respect to the May 20, 1777 and April 11, 1778 Continental Currency issues which were recalled for exchange because of British-sponsored counterfeiting. Fictitious dates therefore were inserted for continued circulation of a

bill and not for the numismatist.

Since bills which were altered could not be redeemed even for their original value, they were occasionally retained and are often the only known specimens of an issue.

Where illustrations used in the catalog had to be those of altered bills the symbol Ⓐ is placed adjacent to them.

Condition of Preservation

Much of the early American paper money is not found in choice condition. There are, however, uncirculated bills, principally from unissued remainders and from issues emitted toward the end of the Revolutionary War.

New money to exchange for damaged or worn bills was not usually available as it customarily required separate authorization. Thus some bills were permitted to circulate in tattered condition. They are often found torn at the folds and either pinned or sewn together or backed. The backing consisted of pieces of almanacs, letters, cloth, newspapers, or other available items pasted or sewn on for reinforcement purposes and often concealed the back design. Ragged edges and missing corners are often encountered on pieces which were extensively circulated or wherever the paper was not sufficiently strong for the heavy usage. Even many bills issued during the early part of the Revolutionary War were worn out before the end of hostilities, particularly those of low denominations.

Many bills have numbers written on their backs, as the bills were used for memoranda and calculations, in addition to the names of the persons from whom they were received.

Readable and complete bills of many scarce issues can be found in collections. However, the same condition standards used for a coin, which is a metallic product, should not be expected in an equally old paper product. Paper money had no intrinsic value and therefore no one saved paper money as one would accumulate gold or silver coin. Because paper money throughout the eighteenth century was subject to depreciation in value from time to time and during the American Revolution such depreciation was constant, it was deliberately kept in steady circulation, and as a result was subjected to as much wear as copper coinage and to much more wear than specie coinage.

Bills in crisp uncirculated condition or in untorn condition with natural folds can be graded in the same manner as other subsequently issued paper money. When fraying, holes, tears, stains, patches, and missing portions enter into grading, there can be many differences of opinion. For a collector to reject pieces with these defects as unacceptable for collection purposes is extensively limiting the scope and completeness of such holdings, but each collector must determine for himself the desirability of any defective bill.

Making Bits of Bills

The cutting by chisel of Spanish milled Dollars into bits for the purpose of making small change had its counterpart in early American paper money. The splitting of bills into half and quarter sections began innocently in the early part of the eighteenth century because of folding. The large size bills of the New England Colonies in particular were too large for a normal purse or pocket and were folded in two directions to be made small enough to fit. Almost each time a bill was spent or counted it was unfolded and then routinely refolded. Splitting began to take place along the folds and a partly torn bill would in due course separate into sections. There was no reserve supply for replacement of torn bills unless the Assembly authorized a specific issue for that purpose or an overrun by the printer was so used.

Customarily sections of most torn bills were sewn, pinned, pasted, or otherwise rejoined by the possessor. In some instances these sections became separated from the others or lost and the available sections became acceptable for such fraction of the original denomination as was equal to the portion presented.

The lowest denomination in bills of New Hampshire, Massachusetts Bay, and Rhode Island then was 1 shilling and of Connecticut 2 shillings. Small change was in short supply, particularly the lower denominations of Massachusetts Bay silver coinage. The English copper coinage was reluctantly accepted from time to time because it circulated at an overvalued rate. Thus the public was quick to realize the advantage of using sections of paper money as small change, and the practice of deliberately tearing bills into half and quarter sections to make change became acceptable. In 1722 the Massachusetts Bay Currency Committee was instructed to reckon with the problem. In 1726 the Connecticut Treasury was prohibited from accepting "broken money," but the practice continued unabated. After 1735 Connecticut faced the reality of the practice and marked each quadrant of some of its newly printed bills with the circulating value of a quarter section. As an example "Seven pence half-peny" was printed on the back of each quadrant of a 2 shilling 6 pence bill so that, if separated, each quadrant contained an accurate denominational value for further circulation. (See the illustrations under Connecticut.) No other Colony adopted this marking practice. Rhode Island in 1737 issued additional low-denomination bills for the purpose of withdrawing half and quarter sections of its bills from circulation.

Comparative Scarcity

The specific number of bills emitted in each denomination of an issue is designated in brackets thus, [ ], if the amount has been located in the records or can be conclusively calculated. Where the total face value of an issue is given but is not broken down into denominations, the number of each denomination can often be deduced from the sheet structure; but sometimes this may be erroneous if the issue was printed from part of an engraved plate or if some bills in a printing form were replaced with other denominations or eliminated in the course of the printing run.

In some issues the number of each denomination was left to the discretion of a committee; in others the number was left contingent upon reissues, redemptions, exchanges, or expenditures. As a result the emission statistics can only be partially complete. There can be deviations between the number authorized in the legislation, the number printed, and the number actually issued, but these are generally small differences unless an issue was not fully expended.

Small denominations wore out more quickly than larger ones and were exchanged sooner. This has affected available quantity, as in small denominations of early Delaware issues. Because of counterfeiting of some denominations of an issue, the genuine bills of such denominations were often withdrawn and different denominations reissued from circulated bills on hand in the Treasury or from an unissued supply. Thus certain genuine bills are scarce, while other denominations of the same issue are not.

Certain issues became invalid prior to or during the American Revolution, and therefore virtually the entire amount of such issues was redeemed, making examples rare. Other issues circulated without restriction or by extension until the final collapse of most paper money during the year 1780, and are therefore more plentiful. Emissions after 1781 were redeemed in specie, after suffering temporary depreciation. In New England, however, redemptions of the War period continued long after 1781.

Unissued remainders of a few issues, signed, partially signed, or unsigned, have from time to time been located and in that manner have become available to collectors in quantity.

The only true measure of scarcity is the availability of the bills themselves and the frequency with which they are included in collections, inventories, and sales. Although the prices for which they sell reflect some factors other than scarcity, comparative prices generally reflect how common or how scarce a particular bill may be.

Collectors

The collection of curiosities (known as The American Musaeum) which belonged to Pierre Eugene du Simitiére, a French artist who spent many years in America, was sold at auction in Philadelphia on March 10, 1785 and the description of lot #36 read: "American Money —A Collection of Parchment and Paper Money." He may have been the first collector in the field. The diary of William Bentley in 1787 and 1788 has references to interesting specimens of paper money he had gathered. The first extensive and scientific collection of early American paper money was gathered by Dr. Joshua I. Cohen of Baltimore, Maryland, beginning in 1828. His collection was purchased by the Henry Ford Museum in 1930.

Over one hundred years ago the research of Henry Phillips, Jr. on the subject of early American currency accelerated enthusiasm among many collectors. Dr. Thomas A. Emmet and Theodorus B. Myers made extensive collections which were donated to the New York Public Library. Simon Gratz and Frank Etting each formed large collections which were given to the Historical Society of Pennsylvania. In Philadelphia, John Haseltine, as a professional numismatist, gathered a fine collection which subsequently was acquired by another dealer, Henry Chapman. After adding much of the H. A. Chambers collection and other groups to his holdings, Chapman, at the time of his death in 1935, held the most extensive collection ever assembled. In the second quarter of the twentieth century, Charles J. Affleck, F. C. C. Boyd, Otto C. Budde, T. James Clark, Harley L. Freeman, Charles J. Hoadley, Eric P. Newman, Wayte Raymond, Jacob N. Spiro, and others assembled substantial collections. The Affleck and Budde collections were disbursed at auction sale after the deaths of the owners. The Clark, Raymond, and Chapman material was merged into the Boyd holdings, and subsequently John J. Ford, Jr., acquired the combined collection from the Boyd Family. The Hoadley collection was given to the Connecticut Historical Society. The Freeman collection was added to the Newman collection. Almost the entire Spiro collection was acquired by the American Antiquarian Society.

There are many collectors, museums, and historical societies who specialize in bills from their particular State and have developed important holdings. There are also many other more modern general collections which may not include as many varieties as the large collections, but which have many items which the larger collections lack. As is always the case, there are other fine collections with which the author is not familiar or concerning which the owners may prefer anonymity. Possibly because of the added interest in paper money generally and the enthusiasm generated by the American Revolutionary Bicentennial, there are many new collectors entering the field and many old holdings coming on the market.

It is a certainty that no collection can ever approach completion, because not only many denominations but many entire issues are without one surviving example. In addition there are many unique pieces and a large number of other major rarities. Each collector usually has a different motive for his interest in Early American paper money. The collecting appeal to some arises from the many differences between the various issues; to others it may be their historical significance, their autographs, their artistic elements, their economic complexities, their mottoes, their printing techniques, or otherwise. Whatever the reason, the bills have charm.

Old Style Years

In England and in the American Colonies prior to 1752, the year began on March 25 and ended on the following March 24. After 1752 the year was changed so as to begin on January 1 and to end on the following December 31 as it does now. Thus, dates falling in the period between January 1 and March 24 of any period prior to 1752 appear to be one year earlier than the year presently assigned to them. The system of year designation prior to 1752 is referred to as "Old Style" and the period thereafter referred to as "New Style."

In the dates on the paper money issues of the American Colonies, the Old Style year was used prior to 1752; thus, the Pennsylvania issue actually dated January 17, 1723 should be recognized under New Style dating as January 17, 1724. It is customary to refer to such a date as January 17, 1723(4) to show the year under both systems, and this procedure has been used in this catalog.

Confusion as to year designation existed in the American Colonies because some parts of Europe, including Scotland, had changed from the Old Style year to the New Style year long prior to 1752. Efforts were made to eliminate this confusion. For example, the Connecticut plates used for the May 8, 1740 issue were redated "Mar 14, 1744/5" for a new issue by including both the Old Style and the New Style years.

Method of Cataloging

All paper money, whether public or private, is listed in chronological order under the geographical area in which it was emitted, except New York small change notes. Issues of the national government are listed under Continental Currency.

The date of an issue is listed as the date which the bill or note actually carries on its face or back. Where the date of an Act, Resolution, or Ordinance is the only date printed on the face of the bill, that fact is incorporated into the heading of the issue. For example, the South Carolina issue with the December 23, 1776 Act on the face and 1777 on the back is listed as 1777 (December 23, 1776 Act).

The total face value of an issue is stated as the amount provided in the enabling legislation and is ordinarily in the money of account of the issuing Colony or State. This is followed by the equivalent in a related monetary exchange wherever both systems were used simultaneously, such as £225,000 ($600,000) in the New Jersey 1780 issue.

The date of enactment of legislation relating to an issue is given so that further desired detail may be readily located.

The reason for the issue, its legal tender status, its

due date, interest, indenture, engraver, printer, paper, watermark, signers, and other applicable items are given wherever possible.

Statistics as to reissue of bills and quantities destroyed are not given, as such data seem to be too incomplete to be included.

Wherever a denomination is printed on a bill in two or more separate exchanges, the official denomination is listed and is followed by the alternate denomination in parentheses, such as $½ (4s) in the New York August 13, 1776 issue.

Mottoes and emblems are noted and translated. Border varieties are described and plate letter varieties are included. Errors in printing and engraving are pointed out.

Wherever an example of a bill is known to be counterfeit ⓒ, unsigned ⓤ, unissued ⓤ, reprinted ⓡ, or a detector ⓓ, the listing is followed by the appropriate encircled symbol. This is in addition to the fact that a genuine bill was issued. In some cases only counterfeits or reprints are now known.

No attempt has been made to include the listing of bonds, notes, bills of exchange, or certificates of indebtedness which did not circulate from person to person as money, even though such items were dealt in by exchange brokers and merchants. Although interesting items of this sort, particularly those issued by Connecticut and Massachusetts, are often seen, they are not within the scope of this undertaking.

Illustrations

The illustrations used in this catalog have been obtained from many private and public collections throughout the United States with the cooperation of the owners. Only one denomination of each issue has been pictured unless there are different sizes or types of bills within the issue. It would be desirable to illustrate each available denomination, but this would require reduction in the size of illustrations and would not be practical for the benefits obtained. The face and back of bills illustrated are both shown except where the back is blank. With minor exceptions all illustrations are the exact size of the actual bills. Where no illustration is included with a listed issue, an example of that issue has not been located except in an instance or so where the piece was not made available for a copy to be made. Wherever

counterfeit, altered, or reprinted bills are used for illustration, no genuine issued unaltered bill has been located. Illustrations of counterfeit ⓒ, altered Ⓐ, unsigned ⓤ, unissued ⓤ, and reprinted ⓡ bills are marked accordingly with the appropriate symbol nearby. Ordinarily an illustration of a counterfeit bill is certain, but in cases where there is uncertainty as to its status no ⓒ marking is used next to the picture even though it is suspect.

In some instances bills are slightly overlapped for convenience of layout.

The source of each picture has not been given because changes in ownership occur from time to time; some owners for security reasons prefer the omission; and favoritism as to selection of pieces for illustration (the condition being equal) is eliminated.

Identification by Coding

A method for identifying a bill by code is sometimes desirable. No consecutive arbitrary numbering system is practical. It also seems better to codify a bill in a meaningful manner, instead of forcing someone to memorize or examine a listing for identification. The following code designations readily suggest themselves:

The first two letters represent the Colony, State, or area, viz: NH, VT, MS, RI, CN, NY, PA, NJ, DE, MD, VA, NC, SC, GA and FL, with CC for Continental Currency, LL for La Louisiane.

The next six numbers represent the date, the first two for the month, the next two for the day, and the next two for the year, applying the order customarily used in America. Since there is virtually no overlap the use of the final two numbers of the year can cause little confusion. Where the day of the month is not given 00 should be used in its stead; similarly, where no month

or day is given 00/00 may be used in their stead. Thus the issuer and date can be written CN/10/11/77, NH/04/29/80, NC/12/00/68, VA/00/00/70, etc. If a bill is redated the latest date should be used.

The abbreviated denomination would follow after a dash, thus: CC/11/29/75—$4, NY/02/16/71—£2, VT/02/00/81—1s3d, etc.

The plate letter, vignette, due date, motto, or any other variant within a denomination of an issue would then follow, thus: NJ/03/25/76—3s—A, MS/08/18/75—2s—1780, NC/04/02/76—$8—Rooster.

The ⓒ for counterfeit, ⓡ for reprinted, ⓤ for unsigned, ⓓ for detector, etc. could then be added. The condition would then complete the description.

It would not be essential to repeat the issuer or the date of issue in listing of several denominations of the same issue.

Abbreviations and Symbols

Ⓐ—Next to an illustration this symbol denotes that an altered bill is pictured.

*—Indicates a footnote.

Ⓒ—Denotes that counterfeits of the bill were made during its circulating period. Next to an illustration this symbol denotes that a counterfeit is pictured.

d—Pence (denarius) in the money of account of the Colony or State, but not English sterling unless specifically stated.

Ⓓ—Denotes that an unsigned counterfeit detector bill exists or existed.

$—Spanish milled Dollars, including Spanish Colonial mintages, even though the use of this symbol had not yet developed in early America.

dwt.—Pennyweight in Troy measure.

gr.—Grains in Troy measure.

£—Pound (libra) in the money of account of the Colony or State, but not English sterling unless specifically stated.

N.T.—New Tenor.

O.T.—Old Tenor.

Oz.—Ounces in Troy measure.

[ ]—Brackets are used only to contain the number of bills of a denomination which were issued, printed, or authorized.

Ⓡ—Denotes that reprints of a bill were made from the original plate or make-up many years after circulation had ceased. Next to an illustration this symbol denotes that a reprint is pictured.

s—Shillings in the money of account of the Colony or State, but not English sterling unless specifically stated.

Ⓤ—Denotes that unsigned, partially signed, or unissued bills or remainders from the original issue exist. Next to an illustration this symbol denotes that such a bill is pictured.

#—Used to denote the beginning of a new vertical row on a sheet of bills.

Collector Value of Bills

The value of a generally collectible item is separately set out after each denomination or variety in the various conditions in which the item is usually found. The values are indicated only for genuine pieces. No values are intended to be applicable to counterfeits, reprints, or detectors, even though such items are customarily collected, bought, and sold. Most collectors consider counterfeits which circulated along with genuine bills to have more or less equal value to genuine bills, sometimes because no genuine bills are available. Other counterfeits, such as English or Tory sponsored Continental Currency, have a special historical significance and sell for more than their genuine counterparts. Detector bills are much rarer than issued bills.

There are many bills and many entire issues which are not valued because there are not a sufficient number of reported sales to create a realistic market value. These range from scarce to exceedingly rare, and include unknown pieces. It should not be assumed that any such items which may be offered for sale should customarily have higher values than other items which are actually valued, although often that should occur on the basis of actual rarity. Where one or more denominations of a scarce or rare issue have had values established, such values are generally spread uniformly to all denominations of the issue, adjusted somewhat in proportion to the number issued.

The principal problem in valuation is that the number of existing pieces of other than the common issues is not sufficiently known. Description of pieces and condition of pieces in older catalogs has not been accurate enough. The limited number of collectors prior to the middle of the twentieth century did not bring about careful analysis of value. Many collections were sold in bulk rather than as individual pieces.

Values of bills are of temporary significance at best, while historical, informative and numismatic data are of permanent nature. Values depend upon supply and demand, which is affected by popularity, availability, promotion, economic conditions, timing, and the relationship with items in comparable collecting areas. There is always the effect of individual collector or investor competition for particular items or lack of such competition. There is sometimes the problem of artificial prices resulting from unannounced reserve bids at auction; the bidding up or repurchasing by owners of their own items; publication of auction prices of items which actually did not sell; and agreements by members of a group not to bid against each other.

Based upon his extensive experience in dealing with early American bills and upon study of auction sales up to the present, Richard Picker has directed the difficult task of setting values and the designation of items not to be evaluated.

Bibliography

In order to maximize the benefit to be derived from a study of prior publications, the bibliographical materials for this work have been divided into two categories: specialized works primarily relating to a specific geographical area, which are listed at the end of each specific section of this catalog; and general works, the listing of which follows in this section. The general works are subdivided into general historical works and general catalogs and listings.

Many of these references contain much important material in economic and political history. The compilation of data for this book, however, has been primarily devoted to the nature and use of the money itself, and thus many of such references should be referred to for expanded interests.

It will be noticed that in some instances statistics and statements in this book are not in accord with some material in prior publications. These differences should be expected because some past writers did not have the opportunity to check original sources and some relied on previously published information. Other writers speculated on interesting matters without having adequate facts available, the position of some turning out to be sound, and that of others proving to be incorrect. Some writing is little more than a restatement of material already published. These writings, nevertheless, filled an educational need and stimulated interest in the field and are included in the bibliography.

Because of the extent of detailed data in this undertaking, it was unfortunately impractical to include a separate citation to support each item that might deserve it. In addition some of the information was the result of study of the bills themselves.

GENERAL HISTORICAL WORKS

(See specific geographical areas for specialized references)

V. L. Bigsby, "Paper for Colonial Currency," *Whitman Numismatic Journal* (June 1964).

Leslie V. Brock, *The Currency of the American Colonies* (New York, 1975).

Charles J. Bullock, *Essays on the Monetary History of the United States* (New York, 1900).

Robert Chalmers, *A History of Currency in the British Colonies* (London, 1893).

Vladimir and Elvira Clain-Stefanelli, *Two Centuries of American Banking* (Washington, 1975).

Sylvester S. Crosby, *Early Coins of America* (Boston, 1875, 1878).

S. E. Dawson, "Old Colonial Currencies in America," *Coin Collector's Journal* (June 1879, July 1880).

William Douglass, *A Discourse Concerning the Currencies of the British Plantations in America* (Boston, 1740, 1751, 1760), reprinted. See also *The Numismatic Scrapbook Magazine* (June 1968, etc.).

Joseph E. Fields and Harley L. Freeman, "For the Love of Money," *Manuscripts* (White Plains, Spring 1959), reprinted in *The Numismatist* (March 1962, etc.).

John Fiske, *Critical Period of American History* (Cambridge, 1888).

Gilbert and Dean, *The Only Sure Guide to Bank Bills* (Boston, 1807, etc.).

Lynn Glaser, "The Beginnings of Colonial Currency," *The Numismatic Scrapbook Magazine* (December 1967).

William M. Gouge, *A Short History of Paper Money and Banking in the United States* (Philadelphia, 1833, and New York, 1835, 1840).

Jack P. Greene and Richard M. Jellison, "The Currency Act of 1764 in Imperial-Colonial Relations," *Wm. & Mary Quarterly* (October 1961).

Adolphus M. Hart, *History of the Issues of Paper Money in the American Colonies, Anterior to the Revolution* (St. Louis, 1851).

John Story Jenks, "A Talk about Paper Money," *Proceedings of the Numismatic and Antiquarian Society of Philadelphia,* Vol. 26, p. 231 (Philadelphia, 1913).

John J. Knox, *A History of Banking in the United States* (New York, 1900, 1903, and reprinted 1969).

Richard A. Lester, "Currency Issues to Overcome Depressions in Delaware, New Jersey, New York and Maryland 1715-37," *Journal of Political Economy* (Chicago, 1939), pp. 182-217.

M. Mazzei, *Recherches Historique et Politiques sur les Etats Unis de l'Amérique Septentrionale* (Paris, 1788).

John J. McCusker, "Colonial Paper Money," *Studies on Money in Early America* (New York, 1976).

Charles L. McKay, *Early American Currency* (New York, 1944).

C. C. Narbeth, "Notes of the American Colonies," *Seaby's Coin and Medal Bulletin* (July 1962).

Curtis P. Nettels, "Current Lawful Money of New England," *The American Historical Review* (October 1918).

————, *The Money Supply of the American Colonies before 1720* (Madison, 1934), reprinted.

Eric P. Newman, "Currency Used for Postage Payment," *The Posted Letter in Colonial and Revolutionary America* (State College, Pa., 1975).

————, "Franklin Making Money More Plentiful," *Pro-*

ceedings of the American Philosophical Society (Philadelphia, October 1971).

————, "Nature Printing on Colonial and Continental Currency," *The Numismatist* (February 1964, etc.), reprinted.

John M. Richardson, "Printers Whose Names Appear on Colonial Bills," *Coin Collector's Journal* (February 1936).

Elizabeth C. Reilly, *The Dictionary of Colonial American Printers' Ornaments and Illustrations* (American Antiquarian Society, Worcester, Mass., 1975).

Kenneth Scott, *Counterfeiting in Colonial America* (New York, 1957).

Thomas Snelling, *A View of the Coins Struck by the East India Company and in the West India Colonies* (London, 1769).

Jack M. Sosin, "Imperial Regulation of Colonial Paper Money, 1764-1773," *The Pennsylvania Magazine of History and Biography* (April 1964).

William G. Sumner, *A History of American Currency* (New York, 1874, 1876, 1878, 1884).

J. Wright, *The American Negotiator* (London, 1761, 1763, 1765, and Dublin, 1765).

Public laws and records in printed form, microfilm, microfiche, or manuscript.

GENERAL CATALOGS AND LISTINGS

Affleck-Ball Collection Sale Catalog, New Netherlands Coin Co., Inc., December 3, 1975.

Altman-Haffner Sale, Pine Tree Auction Company, Inc., April 28, 1975.

Bangs & Co. Sale Catalog, June 20, 1879.

William P. Bement Collection Sale Catalog, June 4, 1925

William W. Bradbeer Collection (Arnold Perl), Lester Merkin Sale Catalog, November 5, 1965.

Otto C. Budde Collection Sale Catalog, October 28, 1969.

Harmon A. Chambers Collection Sale Catalogue, June 19, 1908.

Joshua I. Cohen Collection Sale Catalogue, January 15, 1930.

Bulletin of the Connecticut Historical Society, October 1938 to April 1944.

John M. Connor Estate Collection, Samuel T. Freeman & Co. Auctioneers, November 17, 1970.

Grover C. Criswell, Jr., *North American Currency* (Iola, Wis., 1965; Citra, Fla., 1969).

Ben M. Douglas, *Colonial Currency, Continental Currency* (Washington, 1964).

John J. Ford and Walter Breen, *Numisma* (New Netherlands Coin Co., July-December 1955).

Harmer Rooke Numismatists, Ltd. Auction Sale, May 28, 1974.

Harmer Rooke Numismatists Ltd. Auction Sale, May 19, 1976.

John W. Haseltine, *Description of the Paper Money issued by the Continental Congress of the United States and the Several Colonies* (Philadelphia, 1872).

Stan V. Henkels Sale Catalog, October 17, 1895.

Edgar Allen Mason Collection, Stack's Auction Sale, May 4, 1956.

Elizabeth Morton Collection Sale, Pine Tree Auction Company, Inc., October 18, 1975.

New Netherlands Coin Co. 45th Sale Catalog, April 22, 1955.

Pine Tree Auction Galleries (John Carter Brown Library Sale, Part 2), May 22, 1976.

Pine Tree Rare Coin Auction Sale (The Promised Lands Coin Auction Sale), April 30, 1974.

Pine Tree Rare Coin Auction Sale (The G.E.N.A. '74 Sale), September 18, 1974.

Wayte Raymond, Scott's Special Coin List, No. 6 (April 1933).

————, *Standard Catalogue of United States Coins and Currency* (New York, 1935, 1936, 1937, 1938, 1939).

————, *The Standard Paper Money Catalogue* (New York, 1940, 1950, 1955).

————, *Coin Collector's Journal* (February 1940, etc.).

Oscar G. Schilke Collection, Federal Brand Enterprises Auction Sale, August 5, 1965.

J. W. Scott & Co., *Standard Catalogue No. 2, Paper Money* (New York, 1878, 1879, 1889, 1894).

Charles Steigerwalt Sale Catalog (Lancaster, n.d.).

Ted N. Weissbuch and Richard T. Hoober, *Price Catalogue of U.S. Colonial and Continental Currency* (Chicago, 1965).

D. C. Wismer, *Check List of Continental and Colonial Currency* (Hatfield, 1927).

CONTINENTAL CURRENCY

GENERAL EMISSIONS

May 10, 1775 Session
November 29, 1775 Resolution
February 17, 1776 Resolution
May 9, 1776 Resolution
July 22, 1776 Resolution
November 2, 1776 Resolution
February 26, 1777 Resolution
May 20, 1777 Resolution
April 11, 1778 Resolution
September 26, 1778 Resolution
January 14, 1779 Resolution
1782-1787 Indents

CONTINENTAL CURRENCY

May 10, 1775 Session

$3,000,000 ($2,000,000 and $1,000,000) in Continental Currency payable in Spanish milled Dollars was approved by the June 22-23 and July 25, 1775 Resolutions of the Continental Congress in Philadelphia, thus creating the first federally issued money. This emission, which was put into circulation in August 1775, was to pay the initial expenses of the American Revolution and was to be redeemed with taxes to be levied separately by each of the 13 United Colonies on a quota basis. Printed by Hall and Sellers of Philadelphia from a combination of cast border cuts, emblem cuts, nature prints and hand set type. Thick rag paper containing blue fibres and mica flakes was used on all except $20 bills and was made at the Ivy Mills, Chester County, Pennsylvania. This paper had previously been developed and used for Pennsylvania paper money. The $1 through $8 denominations of the Continental Currency were printed with 8 faces and 8 backs impressed on each side of a sheet, creating a double sheet of two sets of 8 bills each. The $30 bills were printed by inserting their face and back forms into one position after another on the double sheet form and removing one of the smaller denominations at a time. This minimized the number of impressions required to print the issue. The $20 bills were printed individually on thin and weak white paper furnished by Benjamin Franklin, the left side of which was polychromed by the marbling process. The $20 bills had no border cuts and were wider and shorter than the other denominations. The $20 and $30 bills had emblems on the back instead of nature prints. All nature prints used on the backs of the $1 through $8 denominations had previously been used or prepared for use on Pennsylvania paper money. These prints had been developed by a nature printing process invented by Benjamin Franklin. David Rittenhouse sent a bill to Congress for $48 for 36 border cuts, but the actual engraving was said by William Dunlap to have been done by James Smither who had cut and signed borders for Pennsylvania currency of similar style. Most of the emblem and motto cuts were copied from an emblem book by Dr. Joachim Camerarius in Franklin's library. To aid in counterfeit detection unsigned bills and sheets of bills printed at first on pink paper and subsequently on blue paper were distributed to officials for comparison purposes. Bills were numbered in dark red ink. Signers, emblems, mottoes, and nature prints are subsequently included in this section. Counterfeits of this and subsequent issues are described in Appendix B.

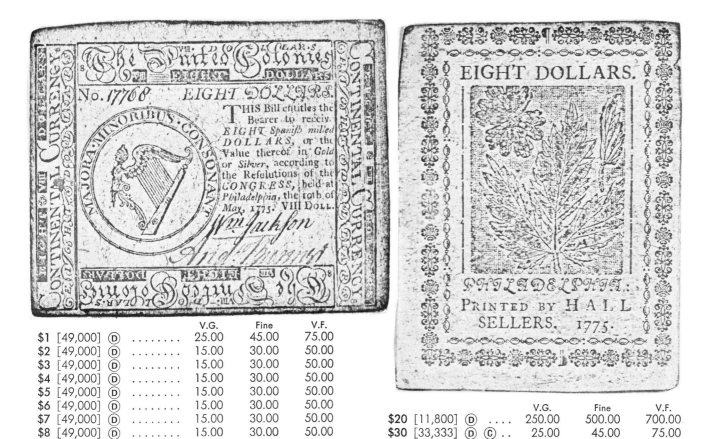

	V.G.	Fine	V.F.
$1 [49,000] Ⓓ	25.00	45.00	75.00
$2 [49,000] Ⓓ	15.00	30.00	50.00
$3 [49,000] Ⓓ	15.00	30.00	50.00
$4 [49,000] Ⓓ	15.00	30.00	50.00
$5 [49,000] Ⓓ	15.00	30.00	50.00
$6 [49,000] Ⓓ	15.00	30.00	50.00
$7 [49,000] Ⓓ	15.00	30.00	50.00
$8 [49,000] Ⓓ	15.00	30.00	50.00

	V.G.	Fine	V.F.
$20 [11,800] Ⓓ	250.00	500.00	700.00
$30 [33,333] Ⓓ Ⓒ ..	25.00	45.00	75.00

November 29, 1775 Resolution

$3,000,000 in Continental Currency payable in Spanish milled Dollars was authorized on Nov. 29, 1775. An additional $10,000 was approved on Jan. 6, 1776 to exchange for worn bills. The same style as the previous issue except that the denomination is placed under the emblem instead of at the end of the text. The Dec. 12, 1775 Resolution required the numbering to be different from the previous emission so all bills were numbered in bright red ink. Sheets for counterfeit detection were issued on blue paper. Signers, emblems, mottoes, and nature prints are subsequently included in this section.

CONTINENTAL CURRENCY

	V.G.	Fine	V.F.	Unc.		V.G.	Fine	V.F.	Unc.
$1 [83,611] ⑩	12.50	20.00	40.00	90.00	$5 [83,611] ⑩	12.50	20.00	40.00	90.00
$2 [83,611] ⑩	12.50	20.00	40.00	90.00	$6 [83,611] ⑩	12.50	20.00	40.00	90.00
$3 [83,611] ⑩	12.50	20.00	40.00	90.00	$7 [83,611] ⑩	12.50	20.00	40.00	90.00
$4 [83,611] ⑩	12.50	20.00	40.00	90.00	$8 [83,611] ⑩	12.50	20.00	40.00	90.00

February 17, 1776 Resolution

$4,000,000 in Continental Currency payable in Spanish milled Dollars was authorized on Feb. 17, 1776. Of this sum $1,000,000 was in fractional dollar denominations. The bills of $1 and over are in the same style as the previous issue. The fractional bills are smaller in size. Two sets of twelve fractional bills each were printed on a sheet, a set having three bills of each of the four denominations. Each fractional bill differs from the others of the same denomination by having different border cuts and by the use of plate letters. On the face of each fractional denomination directly under the top border and at the corners of the square enclosing the sundial device cut there are ornaments which are keyed to the denominations. Franklin's sundial rebus and the linked Colonies device were subsequently copied in designing the 1776 Continental Currency dollar coinage and the 1787 Fugio Cent coinage. Devices and borders of the fractional bills were cut by Elisha Gallaudet, then of Freehold, New Jersey. Counterfeit detection sheets of denominations of $1 and over are on blue paper. One signer for the fractional denominations and two for the integral denominations. Identification of signers, emblems, mottoes, and nature prints are subsequently included in this section. A double sheet of the fractional bills is illustrated in Appendix A.

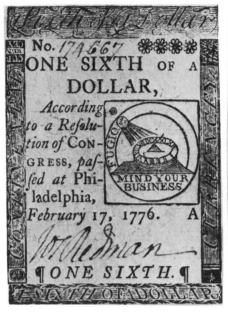

36

		V.G.	Fine	V.F.	Unc.
$1/6	Plates A, B, & C. CURRENCEY misspelled [600,000] ..	15.00	30.00	50.00	150.00
$1/3	Plates A, B, & C [600,000]	15.00	30.00	50.00	150.00
$1/2	Plates A, B, & C [600,000]	15.00	30.00	50.00	150.00
$2/3	Plates A, B ⓤ Ⓒ, & C [600,000]	15.00	30.00	50.00	150.00
$1	[130,436] Ⓓ	12.50	25.00	40.00	90.00
$2	[130,437] Ⓓ	12.50	25.00	40.00	90.00
$3	[130,436] Ⓓ	12.50	25.00	40.00	90.00
$4	[130,435] Ⓓ Ⓒ	12.50	25.00	40.00	90.00
$5	[65,217] Ⓓ	15.00	30.00	50.00	125.00
$6	[65,217] Ⓓ	15.00	30.00	50.00	125.00
$7	[65,217] Ⓓ	15.00	30.00	50.00	125.00
$8	[65,217] Ⓓ	15.00	30.00	50.00	125.00

May 9, 1776 Resolution

$5,000,000 in Continental Currency was authorized by the Resolutions of May 9, 1776 and May 27, 1776. The same style as the Nov. 29, 1775 issue, except that the bottom border of the face of the $4 denomination is not upside down as it is on all denominations of all other issues. Counterfeit detector sheets on blue paper. Signers, emblems, mottoes, and nature prints are subsequently included in this section.

		V.G.	Fine	V.F.	Unc.
$1	[138,889] Ⓓ	20.00	30.00	45.00	100.00
$2	[138,889] Ⓓ	20.00	30.00	45.00	100.00
$3	[138,889] Ⓓ	20.00	30.00	45.00	100.00
$4	Bottom border inverted [138,889] Ⓓ	20.00	30.00	45.00	100.00
$5	[138,889] Ⓓ	20.00	30.00	45.00	100.00
$6	[138,889] Ⓓ	20.00	30.00	45.00	100.00
$7	[138,889] Ⓓ	20.00	30.00	45.00	100.00
$8	[138,889] Ⓓ Ⓒ	20.00	30.00	45.00	100.00

July 22, 1776 Resolution

$5,000,000 in Continental Currency was authorized by the Resolutions of July 22, 1776 and Aug. 13, 1776. The same style as the Nov. 29, 1775 issue. The elimination of the $1 denomination was in contemplation of coinage of 1776 Continental Dollars in silver. A $30 denomination in the same style as the $30 of the May 10, 1775 issue was substituted in the printing form in lieu of the $1 bill. The B in the motto of the $5 denomination was originally engraved backwards and then corrected, causing it to appear as an H in this and the next two issues. Counterfeit detector sheets are on blue paper. Signers, emblems, mottoes, and nature prints are subsequently included in this section.

				V.G.	Fine	V.F.	Unc.
$2	[76,923]	Ⓓ	....	15.00	25.00	40.00	90.00
$3	[76,923]	Ⓓ	....	15.00	25.00	40.00	90.00
$4	[76,923]	Ⓓ	....	15.00	25.00	40.00	90.00
$5	B in motto appears as H						
	[76,923]	Ⓓ	....	15.00	25.00	40.00	90.00
$6	[76,923]	Ⓓ	....	15.00	25.00	40.00	90.00
$7	[76,923]	Ⓓ Ⓒ	....	15.00	25.00	40.00	90.00
$8	[76,923]	Ⓓ	....	15.00	25.00	40.00	90.00
$30	[76,923]	Ⓓ Ⓒ	....	15.00	25.00	40.00	90.00

November 2, 1776 Resolution

$5,000,000 in Continental Currency was authorized by the Resolutions of Nov. 2, 1776 and Dec. 28, 1776 in the same style as the previous issue. Counterfeit detector sheets are on blue paper. Signers, emblems, mottoes, and nature prints are subsequently included in this section. An additional issue of $500,000 in bills of $1/9, $1/6, $1/3, and $2/3 was also authorized by the Nov. 2, 1776 Resolution, but these fractional denominations were never printed pursuant to that authorization, because the fractional denominations of the Feb. 17, 1776 issue were still being signed and were in adequate supply through the fall of 1777.

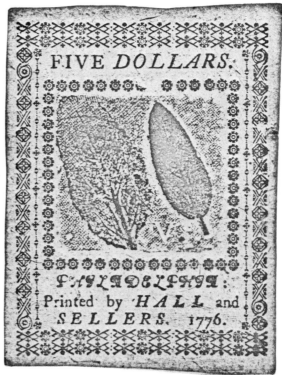

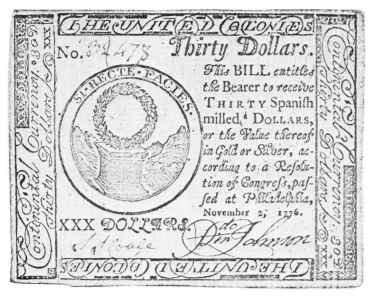

				V.G.	Fine	V.F.	Unc.
$2	[76,923] Ⓓ	....		15	25	45	100
$3	[76,923] Ⓓ	....		15	25	45	100
$4	[76,923] Ⓓ	....		15	25	45	100
$5	B in motto appears as H [76,923] Ⓓ.			15	25	45	100
$6	[76,923] Ⓓ	....		15	25	45	100
$7	[76,923] Ⓓ	....		15	25	45	100
$8	[76,923] Ⓓ	....		15	25	45	100
$30	[76,923] Ⓓ Ⓒ	.		15	25	45	100

February 26, 1777 Resolution

$5,000,000 in Continental Currency was authorized by the Resolution passed on Feb. 26, 1777 in Baltimore where the Continental Congress met from Dec. 20, 1776 to Feb. 27, 1777 because Philadelphia was occupied by British forces. Known as the Baltimore issue and in the same style as the previous issue except that Philadelphia was eliminated on the back as the place of printing. Yet the bills were probably printed in Philadelphia because the Continental Congress reconvened in that city on March 4, 1777. Speculation that the bills were printed in Ephrata, Pennsylvania is without foundation. Counterfeit detector sheets are on blue paper. Signers, emblems, mottoes, and nature prints are subsequently included in this section. Continental Currency began to circulate at a discount in January 1777.

			V.G.	Fine	V.F.	Unc.
$2	[76,923] Ⓓ	....	25.00	45.00	75.00	125.00
$3	[76,923] Ⓓ	....	25.00	45.00	75.00	125.00
$4	[76,923] Ⓓ	....	25.00	45.00	75.00	125.00
$5	B in motto appears as H [76,923] Ⓓ Ⓒ	....	25.00	45.00	75.00	125.00
$6	[76,923] Ⓓ	....	25.00	45.00	75.00	125.00
$7	[76,923] Ⓓ	....	25.00	45.00	75.00	125.00
$8	[76,923] Ⓓ	....	25.00	45.00	75.00	125.00
$30	[76,923] Ⓓ Ⓒ	....	25.00	45.00	75.00	125.00

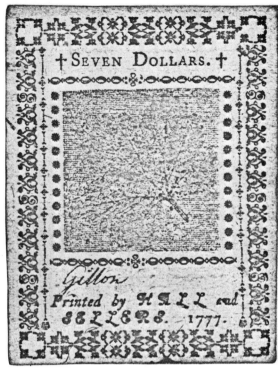

May 20, 1777 Resolution

$16,500,000 in Continental Currency was authorized by ten separate Resolutions passed between May 20, 1777 and April 18, 1778, the final $500,000 overlapping the approval of the Yorktown issue of April 11, 1778. The same style as the previous issue, except that the cuts for the top and bottom borders were modified to read UNITED STATES instead of UNITED COLONIES. A new emblem and motto cut for the $5 denomination erroneously contained an H in the motto instead of a B because the mistake in the prior issue was copied. The ornamentation and type fonts used on the back were changed. Due to extensive British-sponsored counterfeiting this entire issue was called for exchange prior to June 1, 1779 by the Jan. 2, 1779 Resolution, but the exchange date was extended to Jan. 1, 1781 by which time the bills were virtually worthless. When new bills were not available, receipts were issued by the Continental Loan Offices for exchanging bills of the May 20, 1777 issue for new bills by August 1780. Some exchanged bills are cancelled with two ¼-inch holes. Counterfeit detector sheets are on blue paper. Signers, emblems, mottoes, and nature prints are subsequently included in this section.

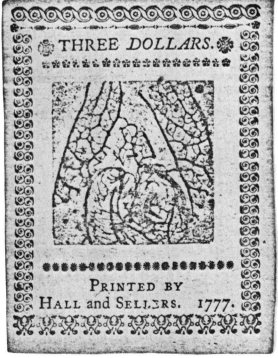

				V.G.	Fine	V.F.	Unc.
$2	[253,850] Ⓓ	....		35.00	60.00	90.00	150.00
$3	[253,839] Ⓓ	....		35.00	60.00	90.00	150.00
$4	[253,839] Ⓓ	....		35.00	60.00	90.00	150.00
$5	H in motto instead of B [253,840] Ⓓ	....		35.00	60.00	90.00	150.00
$6	[253,839] Ⓓ Ⓒ	....		35.00	60.00	90.00	150.00
$7	[253,840] Ⓓ	....		35.00	60.00	90.00	150.00
$8	[253,851] Ⓓ Ⓒ	....		35.00	60.00	90.00	150.00
$30	[253,850] Ⓓ Ⓒ	....		35.00	60.00	90.00	150.00

April 11, 1778 Resolution

$25,000,000 in Continental Currency was authorized by Resolutions passed at Yorktown (York, Pennsylvania) on April 11, May 22, and June 20, 1778 aggregating $15,000,000 and at Philadelphia on July 30 and Sept. 5, 1778 aggregating $10,000,000. Known as the Yorktown issue. Newly engraved border cuts are on the face. Newly prepared nature prints for the back of each denomination and decorative cuts were introduced to frame the nature prints. Type and typeset ornaments on the back were modified. Denominations below $4 were eliminated, the $20 reinstated, and a $40 denomination added because of inflation. The Continental Congress met at York from Sept. 30, 1777 to June 27, 1778 during which period Hall and Sellers conducted their printing business there. Due to extensive British sponsored counterfeiting the entire issue was called for exchange prior to June 1, 1779 by the Jan. 2, 1779 Resolution, but was extended to Jan. 1, 1781 by which time the bills were virtually worthless. Counterfeit detector sheets are on blue paper. Signers, emblems, mottoes, and nature prints are subsequently included in this section.

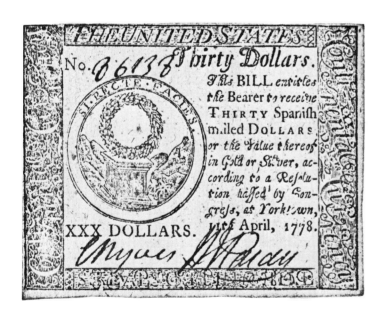

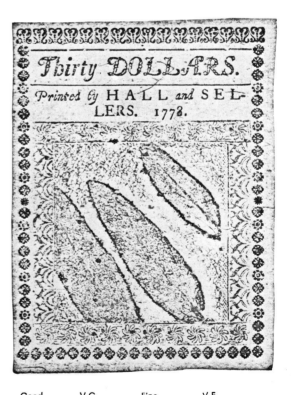

				Good	V.G.	Fine	V.F.
$4	[208,335] Ⓓ Ⓒ	....		85.00	150.00	250.00	400.00
$5	Undersized S in motto [208,330] Ⓓ Ⓒ	....		85.00	150.00	250.00	400.00
$6	[208,335] Ⓓ	....		85.00	150.00	250.00	400.00
$7	[208,330] Ⓓ Ⓒ	....		85.00	150.00	250.00	400.00
$8	[208,330] Ⓓ Ⓒ	....		85.00	150.00	250.00	400.00
$20	[208,330] Ⓓ Ⓒ	....		85.00	150.00	250.00	400.00
$30	[208,335] Ⓓ	....		85.00	150.00	250.00	400.00
$40	[208,335] Ⓓ Ⓒ	....		85.00	150.00	250.00	400.00

CONTINENTAL CURRENCY

September 26, 1778 Resolution

$75,001,080 in Continental Currency was authorized by nine separate Resolutions passed between Sept. 26, 1778 and July 17, 1779, a large portion being authorized and issued simultaneously with the Jan. 14, 1779 issue. The new $50 and $60 denominations have new emblems designed by Francis Hopkinson, new border cuts, and new back designs prepared by the nature printing process consisting of miniature archery items on a cloth background. Similar in style to the previous issue, but with different typeset ornaments on the back borders. These bills passed at about 22% of specie value when first issued. Counterfeit detector sheets are on blue paper. Signers, emblems, mottoes, and nature prints are subsequently included in this section.

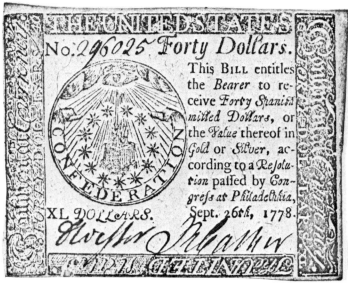

		Fine	V.F.	Unc.
$5	Undersized S in motto [340,914] Ⓓ	20.00	35.00	80.00
$7	[340,914] Ⓓ	20.00	35.00	80.00
$8	[340,914] Ⓓ	20.00	35.00	80.00
$20	[340,914] Ⓓ	20.00	35.00	80.00
$30	[340,914] Ⓓ	20.00	35.00	80.00

		Fine	V.F.	Unc.
$40	[340,914] Ⓓ Ⓒ	20.00	35.00	80.00
$50	[340,914] Ⓓ Ⓒ	20.00	35.00	80.00
$60	Lower part of p in passed soon was bent and then broke off [340,914] Ⓓ Ⓒ	20.00	35.00	80.00

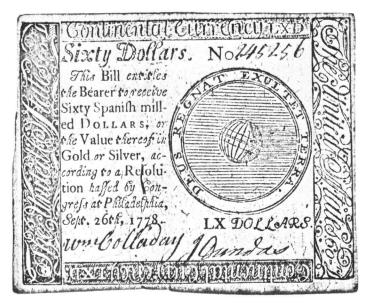

January 14, 1779 Resolution

$95,051,695 in Continental Currency was authorized by seven separate Resolutions passed between Jan. 14, 1779 and Nov. 29, 1779, the first portion being authorized and issued simultaneously with the Sept. 26, 1778 issue. The Jan. 14, 1779 Resolution provided for $50,000,400 to exchange for the May 20, 1777 and April 11, 1778 issues which were called for redemption because of extensive British-sponsored counterfeiting. Sixteen denominations of bills, including $7 and $8 denominations, were originally planned, but by the May 7, 1779 Resolution denominations of $70 and $80 were substituted for the $7 and $8 and the total number of bills to be issued was decreased accordingly. As a result the $70 and $80 denominations were printed on the same sheet as the six lowest denominations, which sheet was watermarked UNITED STATES in two lines. The $30 through $65 denominations were printed on sheets watermarked CONFEDERATION in two lines. New border cuts were engraved for the face and used the name of UNITED STATES OF NORTH AMERICA. New emblem and motto cuts of smaller size were similar to those used on corresponding denominations of prior issues. The emblem on the $3 bill has the birds' heads on the right side rather than on the left side as theretofore. Francis Hopkinson devel-

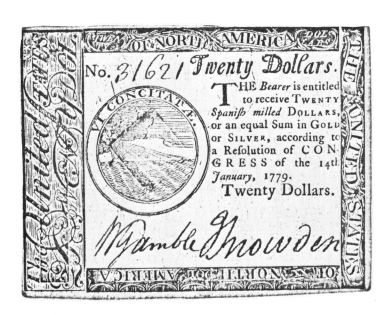

oped the new emblems and mottoes for the $35, $45, $70, and $80 denominations. On the backs are an entirely new set of leaf and cloth nature prints. On the face of all bills, portions of the emblem and the left border were printed in red, the balance of the bill being printed in black. Counterfeit detector sheets are on blue paper. By the time the final portions of this issue were issued the exchange had reached over $40 in bills for $1 in specie. Signers, emblems, mottoes, and nature prints are subsequently included in this section. The emblems and some border cuts on the face were subsequently used for the backs of the State issues guaranteed under the Mar. 18, 1780 Resolution of the Continental Congress.

				Fine	V.F.	Unc.
$1	[139,811]	Ⓓ	......	30.00	60.00	90.00
$2	[139,811]	Ⓓ	......	30.00	60.00	90.00
$3	[139,811]	Ⓓ	......	30.00	60.00	90.00
$4	[139,811]	Ⓓ	......	30.00	60.00	90.00
$5	[139,811]	Ⓓ	......	30.00	60.00	90.00
$20	[139,811]	Ⓓ	......	30.00	60.00	90.00
$30	[182,070]	Ⓓ	......	30.00	60.00	90.00
$35	[182,070]	Ⓓ	......	35.00	65.00	100.00

				Fine	V.F.	Unc.
$40	[182,070]	Ⓓ	.....	30.00	60.00	90.00
$45	[182,070]	Ⓓ	.....	35.00	65.00	100.00
$50	[182,070]	Ⓓ	.....	30.00	60.00	90.00
$55	[182,070]	Ⓓ	.....	35.00	65.00	100.00
$60	[182,071]	Ⓓ	.....	30.00	60.00	90.00
$65	[182,070]	Ⓓ Ⓒ	..	35.00	65.00	100.00
$70	[139,811]	Ⓓ	.....	40.00	75.00	125.00
$80	[139,811]	Ⓓ Ⓒ	..	50.00	90.00	150.00

Redemption of Continental Currency

All issues of Continental Currency continued to be a basis for speculation after their circulation ceased in April 1780. Although the Articles of Confederation had promised payment, it was not until the Constitution of the United States in 1787 gave validity to such obligations that some hope of partial payment revived. On October 9, 1787 Continental Currency was selling at $250 for $1 in specie. Finally by the Act of Aug. 4, 1790 Congress passed a provision for refinancing its debts and from Oct. 1, 1790 to Sept. 30, 1791 agreed to accept at the rate of $100 currency for $1 in bonds of indefinite maturity both the certificates for redemption of the May 20, 1777 and April 11, 1778 Continental Currency issues as well as all Continental Currency itself. Two thirds of the bonds were to be "Six Percent Stock of 1790" which bore 6% interest from Jan. 1, 1791 and one third of the bonds were to be "Deferred Six Percent Stock of 1790" which carried no interest until Jan. 1, 1800. Substantial amounts of Continental Currency were used for subscriptions, but many refrained because the law specifically provided that the rights of currency holders were not impaired if they did not make the exchange. The right to subscribe was extended to Mar. 1, 1793 by the Act of May 8, 1792; to June 30, 1794 by the Act of Mar. 2, 1793; to Dec. 31, 1794 by the Act of May 30, 1794; to Dec. 31, 1795 by the Act of Jan. 28, 1795; to Dec. 31, 1796 by the Act of Feb. 19, 1796; and to Dec. 31, 1797 by the Act of Mar. 3, 1797. Although $44,737,725 of bonds were issued the amount of Continental Currency so exchanged is not available. The bonds were paid by 1813 and those who did not subscribe for the bonds with Continental Currency received nothing. "Not worth a Continental" therefore did mean a 1% recovery for some holders.

1782-1787 Indents

After the end of hostilities the Continental Congress, although unable to redeem its paper money, was faced with the obligation of meeting the interest and principal obligations on its domestic and foreign bonds and paying the current expenses of the national government. Its source of revenue continued to be taxation by the States, each of which was to turn over such collections to the United States in an established proportion. Accordingly the Continental Congress anticipated such taxes by requisitioning the funds with issues of Indents in convenient denominations payable to bearer and receivable for taxes. In 1782 $1,200,000 was issued; in 1784 $667,744 $\frac{43}{90}$ths; in 1785 $2,805,071 $\frac{9}{90}$ths; in 1786 $1,606,560 $\frac{65}{90}$ths; and in 1787 $1,700,407. The use of the fractional sums in 90ths was for easy conversion into Pennsylvania, New Jersey, and Delaware money of account in which 90 pence was equal to one Spanish milled Dollar. By September 1787 Massachusetts, Connecticut, New York, Pennsylvania, Delaware and Virginia had paid in Indents aggregating $1,003,725 $\frac{57}{90}$ths leaving $4,672,815 $\frac{52}{90}$ths in circulation. No other States had turned in taxes for this account. The Indents depreciated about 20% for a short period but in due course were used for the payment of taxes and absorbed.

CONTINENTAL CURRENCY

The denomination in dollars is engraved into the border cut as well as being included in the typeset portions. Most of the few existing Indents are in integral amounts. Instead of serial numbers the Indents have a letter and number combination. The two known dates of issue are September 27, 1785 and October 11, 1787, but there must have been several other dates. The dates of issue are printed on the known examples. The paper is watermarked INTEREST surrounded by a rectangle. Signers are John Hardy and Michael Hillegas. There may have been additional denominations.

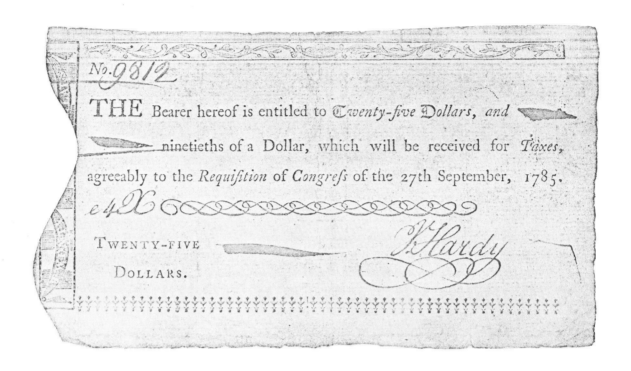

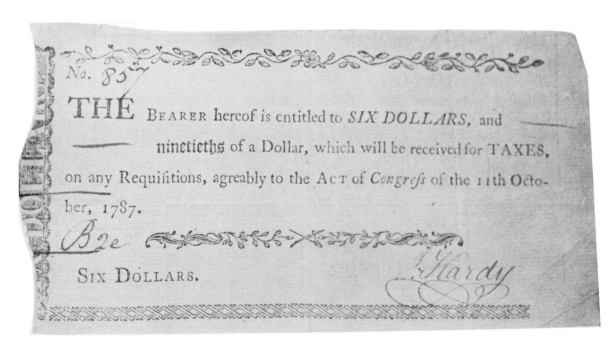

$1 $2 $4 $6 $8 $25

CONTINENTAL CURRENCY

The Emblems, Mottoes, and Nature Prints
on Continental Currency

(See catalog listings for illustrations)

EMBLEMS AND MOTTOES

$1/6, $1/3, $1/2, $2/3
The sun shining on a sundial. FUGIO. MIND YOUR BUSINESS. This is a device designed in the style of the moralisms of Benjamin Franklin's "Poor Richard." Interpreted literally it means, "I, the Sun, fly, therefore mind your business." Freely interpreted it means, "Time flies, so mind your business." The back shows a linked chain containing the names of the 13 colonies and AMERICAN CONGRESS WE ARE ONE. Both devices were created by Franklin.

$1
A weighted bowl on an acanthus plant. DEPRESSA RESURGIT (Though crushed it comes back).

$2
Grain being threshed by a flail. TRIBULATIO DITAT (Affliction enriches).

$3
An eagle and a heron fighting. EXITUS IN DUBIO EST (The outcome is in doubt).

$4
A wild boar charging into a spear. AUT MORS AUT VITA DECORA (Either death or an honorable life).

$5
A hand gathering food is bleeding because of pricks from thorns. SUSTINE VEL ABSTINE (Either survive or refrain).

$6
A beaver gnawing down a tree. PERSEVERANDO (By perseverance).

$7
A severe storm at sea. SERENABIT (It will be calm).

$8
A harp with 13 strings representing the 13 colonies. MAJORA MINORIBUS CONSONANT (The large colonies are in harmony with the small colonies).

All $20 Faces and 1775-77 $30 Backs
A strong wind blowing. VI CONCITATE (Driven by force).

Backs of 1775-77 $20 and $30
The sun shining on sailing ships in a calm sea. CESSANTE VENTO CONQUIESCEMUS (When the wind dies down we rest).

All $30 Faces
A wreath on a tomb. SI RECTE FACIES (If you perform righteously).

$35
A plough in a field. HINC OPES (Hence our wealth).

$40
The rays of an all-seeing eye shining on 13 stars surrounding a flame. CONFEDERATION.

$45
Beehives protected by a shed. SIC FLORET RESPUBLICA (Thus let the nation flourish).

$50
A stepped pyramid of 13 levels. PERENNIS (Everlasting).

$55
The sun coming out after a storm. POST NUBILA PHOEBUS (After dark clouds comes the sun).

$60
The earth. DEUS REGNAT EXULTET TERRA (God reigns, let the earth rejoice). The motto is from Psalm 97.

$65
A hand holding a balance scale. FIAT JUSTITIA (Let justice be done). The motto from which this is taken is FIAT JUSTITIA RUAT COELUM (Let justice be done though the heavens fall).

CONTINENTAL CURRENCY

$70

A healthy tree standing alone. VIM PROCELLARUM QUAD-RENNIUM SUSTINUIT (For four years it has withstood the force of storm).

$80

A large tree. ET IN SECULA SECULORUM FLORESCEBIT (And it will flourish for ages of ages).

The emblems and mottoes for the $1 through $7 and the face of $30 denominations were taken from the 1702 Mainz edition of *Symbolorum ac Emblematum Ethico-Politicorum* by Joachim Camerarius, which book was in Benjamin Franklin's library. The $8 emblem and motto is from *Idea Principis Christiano-Politici Symbolis* by Diego Saavedra, the 1660 edition of which was in an American library, probably Franklin's. The $55 emblem and motto is from *Emblematum Repositorium,* by J. C. Weigels and that of the $65 from insignia of courts of justice. The emblems and mottoes used on the $35, $40, $45, $50, $60, $70, and $80 denominations were developed by Francis Hopkinson who unsuccessfully sought compensation from the Continental Congress for this work.

NATURE PRINTS OF LEAVES ON BACKS

	1775-77 Issues	1778 Issues	1779 Issue
$1	Ragweed and Two Willows	—	Tansy
$2	Raspberry and Two Filberts*	—	Mulberry
$3	Skeletonized Elm and Maple Fruit*	—	Rose
$4	Skeletonized Maple Fruit*	Buttercup	Mulberry
$5	Betony and Sage*	Willow	Feverfew
$6	Buttercup	Sage	—
$7	Buttercup	Grape and Sage	—
$8	Henebit and Two Buttercups*	Three Sages	—
$20	(Emblem)	Buttercup	Grape
$30	(Two Emblems)	Three Willows	Climbing Fumitory
$35	—	—	Two Willows
$40	—	Carrot	Poterium
$45	—	—	Ground Ivy
$50	—	(Arrows)	Parsley
$55	—	—	Willow
$60	—	(Bow)	Willow and Poison Hemlock
$65	—	—	Parsley
$70	—	—	Maple
$80	—	—	Strawberry

*Identical nature print previously used on Pennsylvania issues.

CONTINENTAL CURRENCY

Signers of Continental Currency

Continental Currency bills of One Dollar and over were hand signed by two appointees, one signature in brown ink and one in red ink. Fractional denominations were signed by one person in ink of either color. Most appointees were private citizens nominated by Treasury officials and elected by ballot in the course of formal proceedings of the Continental Congress. Some of those nominated were not elected. There were at least 264 different authorized signers of Continental Currency, this being so large a number that signatures were rendered useless to the public as a means of counterfeit detection. At first appointees were designated for a specific issue, but subsequent authorizations were not limited as to issues to be signed. Signing took place over an extended period following the authorization of an issue. Signers were usually given 200 sheets of bills to sign at one time and after completion were given a receipt by a Continental Treasury official.

John Mease was named as a signer on four occasions. Joseph Watkins actually signed six issues, but most signers participated only in one or two issues. Signers were paid for their work either on a piece work or on an hourly basis. They were also required to number the bills in ink. Some signers seem to have permitted members of their family to sign as substitutes at times as there are obvious differences in signatures of the same name on genuine bills. A letter dated Oct. 22, 1779 from Joseph Nourse of the Continental Treasury Office in Philadelphia to Governor Caswell of North Carolina stated that "**it is found by experience that each signer so often varies his writing that the signature of one day differs materially from that of the next, and would afford very little assistance in detecting counterfeits**." On April 21, 1777, Michael Hillegas, Treasurer of the Congress, was delegated to appoint signers and to certify their names to Congress. No list of such appointments or of certification has been located and it is assumed herein that all of those who signed the issues of May 20, 1777, April 11, 1778, or September 26, 1778, without being directly named by the Congress were such Hillegas appointees. It is also probable that some signers of prior issues were Hillegas appointees because some portions of prior issues had not been fully signed by the date of his power to appoint signers.

The spelling of names of signers is complicated by the fact that the records of authorization sometimes differ as to spelling from one another and from the actual signatures on the bills. Where variations occur, the actual signature on the bills is listed as proper and any deviation noted in parenthesis. On counterfeit bills there are some fictitious signatures and some accidentally misspelled signatures, but most counterfeits have properly spelled forged signatures. The Official Broadside (See Appendix B) describing a few of the circulating counterfeits designates R. Davis and J. Duncan as fictitious signatures on the $40 counterfeits of April 11, 1778. There are some signatures which are difficult to decipher as well as other matters of uncertainty. It is hoped that readers will report any additional signature data to enable the listing to be further refined.

The research involved in revising and expanding the following alphabetical listing was most complex and required a review of many major collections, extensive biographical coordination, and careful analysis of uncertainties. This was graciously and enthusiastically undertaken by Joseph R. Lasser of Scarsdale, New York, to whom the author is most grateful.

Names of Signers	Appointment Dates	Issues Signed
Adcock, William	8/8/78	4/11/78, 9/26/78
Aisquith, William	12/27/76	11/2/76, 2/26/77, 5/20/77
Alexander, Charles	9/26/78	9/26/78
Alexander, Mark	1/8/77	11/2/76, 2/26/77
All, Isaac	8/14/78	9/26/78
Ash, James	3/9/76	2/17/76, 5/9/76, 7/22/76
Baird, Samuel	Hillegas Appointee	5/20/77, 4/11/78
Baker, Christopher (Charles)	7/23/79	9/26/78, 1/14/79
Barclay, Thomas	7/25/75, 12/11/75	5/10/75, 11/29/75, 1/14/79 Ⓒ
Barnes, Cornelius	12/11/75, 3/9/76	11/29/75, 2/17/76, 5/9/76, 7/22/76
Barney, Joshua (John)	2/12/77	2/17/76, 11/2/76, 2/26/77, 5/20/77
Barrell, Theodore	12/27/76	2/17/76, 11/2/76
Barton, Thomas, Jr.	7/25/75	5/10/75
Bayard, John*	7/25/75, 12/11/75	5/10/75, 11/29/75
Bedford, Gunning (Emmery), Jr.*	8/12/78	9/26/78
Billmeyer, J.	Hillegas Appointee	5/20/77, 4/11/78
Bond, George	2/23/79	9/26/78, 1/14/79
Bond, Phineas	12/11/75, 3/9/76	11/29/75, 2/17/76, 5/9/76
Boyd, John	12/27/76	7/22/76, 11/2/76
Brannan (Brannon), Benjamin	3/9/76, 1/4/77	2/17/76, 5/9/76, 7/22/76, 11/2/76
Bright, George	5/22/79	9/26/78, 1/14/79
Brooke (Brook), Clement	2/12/77	11/2/76
Brown, G.	Hillegas Appointee	4/11/78
Bryson, James	Hillegas Appointee	5/20/77, 4/11/78
(Bryson, S. Ⓒ)	—	5/20/77 Ⓒ, 4/11/78 Ⓒ, 9/26/78 Ⓒ
(Brisson, S. Ⓒ)	—	3/12/78 Ⓐ Ⓒ
Buchanan, R.	Hillegas Appointee	2/26/77
Budd, G.	Hillegas Appointee	5/20/77
Budd, Levi	5/22/79	9/26/78, 1/14/79
Bullock, Joseph	3/9/76, 8/8/78	2/17/76, 7/22/76
Bunner, Andrew	7/25/75, 12/11/75	5/10/75, 11/29/75
Caldwell, Samuel	12/11/75	11/29/75
Calhoun (Colhoun), James	12/27/76	11/2/76, 5/20/77
Campbell, George	12/11/75, 3/9/76	11/29/75, 2/17/76, 5/9/76, 7/22/76
Carleton, Joseph	2/23/79	9/26/78
Carroll, Daniel*	2/18/77	2/17/76, 11/2/76, 2/26/77
Cather (Caither), Robert	8/8/78, 2/23/79	4/11/78, 9/26/78, 1/14/79
(Cather, M. Ⓒ)	—	9/26/78 Ⓒ
(Carker, R. Ⓒ)	—	9/26/78 Ⓒ
Christ, H., Jr.	Hillegas Appointee	5/20/77
Cist, Charles	7/23/79	5/20/77, 4/11/78
Clarkson, John L.	8/6/79	—
Clarkson, Matthew*	12/11/75, 3/9/76	11/29/75, 2/17/76, 5/9/76
Claypoole, J.	Hillegas Appointee	5/20/77
Clymer, Daniel	7/25/75, 12/11/75, 3/9/76	5/10/75, 11/29/75, 2/17/76, 5/9/76, 7/22/76
Coale, Samuel Stringer	1/31/77	2/17/76, 11/2/76, 2/26/77, 5/20/77
Coale, W.	Hillegas Appointee	2/17/76, 2/26/77, 5/20/77
Coats, William	3/9/76, 5/22/79	2/17/76, 9/26/78, 1/14/79
Cockey (Cokey), John	12/27/76	11/2/76
Coit, Joseph (Joshua)	2/23/79	9/26/78, 1/14/79
Colladay, William	5/29/79	9/26/78, 1/14/79
Collins, Stephen	12/11/75, 8/11/78	11/29/75
Comegys, Cornelius	2/23/79, 5/13/79	9/26/78, 1/14/79

CONTINENTAL CURRENCY

Names of Signers	Appointment Dates	Issues Signed
Conner, G. . . . .—		4/11/78 ©
Coombe, Thomas 7/25/75, 12/11/75, 3/9/76		5/10/75, 11/29/75, 2/17/76, 5/9/76
Copperthwait, Joseph 8/8/78		—
Courtenay (Courtney), Hercules 12/27/76		2/17/76, 11/2/76
Cox, Paul .2/23/79		9/26/78, 1/14/79
Craig, William 7/25/75		5/10/75
Cranch, N. . . . . .Hillegas Appointee		4/11/78, 9/26/78
Creevey (Creery), Hans 2/12/77		11/2/76, 2/26/77, 5/20/77
Crispin, William 12/11/75		11/29/75
Cromwell, Richard 12/27/76		2/17/76, 11/2/76, 2/26/77, 5/20/77
Davis, R. . . . .—		4/11/78 ©
Donnell (Donald), Nathaniel 8/8/78, 2/23/79		4/11/78, 9/26/78, 1/14/79
Donnellan, Thomas 12/27/76		2/17/76, 7/22/76, 11/2/76, 2/26/77, 5/20/77
Dorsey, Caleb . . . . .Only Nominated 1/21/77		11/2/76
Dorsey, John 1/10/77		11/2/76
Dorsey, Robert 1/8/77		11/2/76
Douglass, George 3/9/76		2/17/76
Duncan, David 3/9/76		2/17/76
Duncan, J. . . . .—		4/11/78 ©
Dundas, James 2/23/79		9/26/78, 1/14/79
Edison, Thomas 2/23/79		9/26/78, 1/14/79
Eichelberger, George . . . . .Hillegas Appointee		5/20/77
Ellis, Joseph H. 8/8/78		—
Elms, S. . . . . .Hillegas Appointee		5/20/77, 9/26/78
Epplé, Henry 7/23/79		9/26/78, 1/14/79
Evans, Joel .12/11/75, 3/9/76		11/29/75, 2/17/76, 5/9/76
Evans, Robert 3/9/76		2/17/76, 5/9/76, 7/22/76
Ewing, T. . . . . .Hillegas Appointee		2/17/76, 5/20/77
Eyres, Henry . . . . .Hillegas Appointee		4/11/78
Eyres, Richard 9/26/78		9/26/78
Farmer, Lewis 8/8/78		4/11/78, 9/26/78
Ferrall, Patrick 8/6/79		9/26/78, 1/14/79
Foulke, Judah 7/25/75		5/10/75
Fox, Edward 8/8/78		4/11/78
Franklin, James 2/11/77		11/2/76
Fuller, Benjamin 12/11/75		11/29/75
Gaither (Gater), Edward 1/10/77		—
Gaither, Joseph 2/4/77		11/2/76
Gamble, William 2/23/79		9/26/78, 1/14/79
Gardner, Joseph* 2/26/79		9/26/78, 1/14/79
Garrigues, J. . . . . .Hillegas Appointee		4/11/78, 9/26/78
Garrison, Nicholas 12/11/75, 3/9/76		11/29/75, 2/17/76, 5/9/76, 7/22/76
Gibson, William 1/8/77, 2/11/77		11/2/76
Govett, William 12/27/76		11/2/76, 5/20/77
Graff, Jacob 7/23/79		1/14/79
Graff, John (Jr.) 5/29/79		9/26/78, 1/14/79
Gray, George, Jr. 3/9/76		2/17/76, 5/9/76, 7/22/76
Gray, Isaac .2/23/79		9/26/78, 1/14/79
Gray, William 8/8/78, 5/29/79		4/11/78, 9/26/78, 1/14/79
Grier, G. . . . . .Hillegas Appointee		2/17/76
Griffith, Dennis 2/8/77		2/17/76, 11/2/76, 2/26/77
Griffith (Griffiths), John 12/27/76		11/2/76, 2/26/77
Gutell, R. . . . .—		9/26/78 ©

CONTINENTAL CURRENCY

Names of Signers	Appointment Dates	Issues Signed
Hahn, M. ....Hillegas Appointee		5/20/77
Hammond, William 2/12/77		11/2/76
Hardy, William 8/8/78		5/20/77, 4/11/78, 9/26/78
Harvey, D. ....—		9/26/78 ©c
Hazlehurst (Hazelhurst), Isaac 7/25/75, 12/11/75		5/10/75, 11/29/75, 2/17/76
Hazlehurst, Robert 3/9/76		2/17/76, 5/9/76
Hazlewood, John 5/29/79		—
Helm, John 4/27/79		9/26/78, 1/14/79
Herandez, C. ....Hillegas Appointee		4/11/78, 9/26/78
Hewes, Josiah 3/9/76		2/17/76, 5/9/76, 7/22/76
Hiener, Casper ....Hillegas Appointee		5/20/77
Hiester, Joseph ....Hillegas Appointee		5/20/77
Hillegas, Samuel 3/9/76, 12/27/76		2/17/76, 5/9/76, 7/22/76, 11/2/76
Hopkinson, T. ....Hillegas Appointee		5/20/77
Houston, J. ....Hillegas Appointee		5/20/77
Howard, John 3/9/76		2/17/76, 5/9/76, 7/22/76, 4/11/78
Howell, Isaac 12/11/75, 3/9/76		11/29/75, 2/17/76, 5/9/76, 7/22/76
Hubley, Adam 3/9/76		2/17/76, 5/9/76
Hubley, Joseph 8/8/78		4/11/78
Humphreys, Richard 8/8/78		—
Irwin, Robert ....Hillegas Appointee		5/20/77
Jackson, William 7/25/75		5/10/75
Jacobs, Benjamin 3/9/76		2/17/76, 5/9/76, 7/22/76
Johns, Richard 1/8/77		11/2/76
Johnson, Horatio 2/13/77		2/17/76, 11/2/76, 2/26/77
Johnson, Rinaldo 1/31/77		2/17/76, 7/22/76, 11/2/76, 2/26/77, 5/20/77
Johnston (Johnson), James 3/9/76, 5/29/79		2/17/76, 5/9/76, 7/22/76, 5/20/77
Jones, Robert Strettell 7/25/75		5/10/75
Jones, T. (S.) ....—		4/11/78 ©c, 9/26/78 ©c
Kaighn, John 3/9/76		2/17/76
Kammerer, Henry 7/23/79		9/26/78
Kean, J. ....Hillegas Appointee		5/20/77
Kelso, James 12/27/76		2/17/76, 11/2/76, 2/26/77
Keppele, John 8/8/78		—
Ker (Kerr), Joseph 2/23/79		9/26/78, 1/14/79
Kimmell, Michael 7/23/79		1/14/79
King, John ....—		9/26/78 ©c
Kinsey, Philip 3/9/76		2/17/76, 5/9/76, 7/22/76
Kuhl, Frederick 7/25/75, 12/11/75, 3/9/76		5/10/75, 11/29/75, 2/17/76, 5/9/76
Kuhn, J. ....Hillegas Appointee		5/20/77
Kurtz, Peter ....Hillegas Appointee		2/17/76, 5/20/77, 4/11/78
Lardner, John 8/8/78		—
Lawrence, John 2/23/79		9/26/78, 1/14/79
Lawrence, Thomas 7/25/75		5/10/75
Leacock, John 2/23/79		9/26/78, 1/14/79
Leech, Thomas 3/9/76		2/17/76, 5/9/76, 7/22/76
Leiper, Thomas 8/8/78		—
Lemen, W. ....Hillegas Appointee		5/20/77 ©c, 4/11/78
Lester, G. L. ....Hillegas Appointee		5/20/77
Levy, Benjamin 12/27/76		2/17/76, 11/2/76, 2/26/77
Lewis, C. ....Hillegas Appointee		2/17/76, 2/26/77, 5/20/77
Lewis, Ellis 7/25/75		5/10/75, 11/29/75
Lewis, Francis, Jr. 8/14/78		—

CONTINENTAL CURRENCY

Names of Signers	Appointment Dates	Issues Signed
Lewis, Mordecai	7/25/75, 12/11/75, 3/9/76	5/10/75, 11/29/75, 2/17/76, 5/9/76
Little, James	8/14/78	4/11/78, 9/26/78
Loughead, James	8/8/78	—
Lux, Darby	2/18/77	11/2/76
Lux, William	Hillegas Appointee	2/17/76
Lyon, Samuel	9/26/78, 2/23/79	9/26/78, 1/14/79
Mackubin (Maccubin), Zachariah	2/7/77	2/17/76, 11/2/76, 2/26/77
Mahon, J.	Hillegas Appointee	5/20/77
Marshall, William	8/11/78, 8/14/78	9/26/78
Masoner, Jacob	5/29/79	9/26/78, 1/14/79
Massey, Samuel	3/9/76	2/17/76, 5/9/76, 7/22/76
Masters, William	3/9/76	2/17/76, 5/9/76, 7/22/76
McAlester, John	Hillegas Appointee	2/17/76
McCalister, A.	Hillegas Appointee	5/20/77
McHenry, John	Hillegas Appointee	2/26/77
Mease, John	7/25/75, 12/11/75, 3/9/76, 8/8/78	5/10/75, 11/29/75, 2/17/76
Meredith, Samuel*	7/25/75	5/10/75
Mifflin, George	7/25/75	5/10/75
Milligan, James	7/25/75, 3/9/76	5/10/75, 2/17/76
Mitchel, C.	Hillegas Appointee	4/11/78
Momegan, W.	Hillegas Appointee	4/11/78
Morris, Anthony, Jr.	7/25/75, 12/11/75, 3/9/76	5/10/75, 11/29/75, 2/17/76, 5/9/76, 7/22/76
Morris, Luke	7/25/75	5/10/75
Morris, Samuel	7/25/75, 12/11/75, 3/9/76	5/10/75, 11/29/75, 2/17/76, 5/9/76, 7/22/76
Morris, Samuel C.	12/11/75, 3/9/76	11/29/75, 2/17/76, 5/9/76, 7/22/76
Morris, Thomas	12/11/75, 3/9/76	11/29/75, 2/17/76, 5/9/76
Muir, F.	Hillegas Appointee	2/17/76, 5/20/77
Mullan (Mullen), Robert	2/23/79	9/26/78, 1/14/79
Nesbit, Alexander	8/8/78	—
Nesbitt (Nesbit), John Maxwell	7/25/75	5/10/75
Nevell (Nevill), Thomas	2/23/79	9/26/78, 1/14/79
Nicholas (Nichols), Samuel	8/8/78, 5/29/79	4/11/78, 9/26/78, 1/14/79
Nicholson, John	2/23/79	9/26/78, 1/14/79
Norris, Aquila	2/17/77	11/2/76, 2/26/77, 5/20/77
Nourse, Joseph	8/14/79	5/20/77, 9/26/78, 1/14/79
Ord, John	12/11/75, 3/9/76	11/29/75, 2/17/76, 5/9/76, 7/22/76
Paisley, I.	Hillegas Appointee	5/20/77
Parker, Joseph	12/11/75, 3/9/76	11/29/75, 2/17/76, 5/9/76, 7/22/76
Parr, C.	Hillegas Appointee	5/20/77
Patterson, George	1/14/77	11/2/76
Patton, Robert	8/8/78	—
Peale, St. George	2/1/77	11/2/76, 2/26/77, 5/20/77
Pearson, Isaac	3/9/76	2/17/76, 5/9/76, 7/22/76
Pennell (Pennel), Joseph	8/8/78	5/20/77
Peters, T.	Hillegas Appointee	5/20/77
Phile, Frederick	8/8/78	—
Philpot, John	1/8/77	11/2/76
Purviance, John	12/11/75, 3/9/76	5/10/75, 11/29/75, 2/17/76
Ramsey (Ramsay), William	8/6/79	1/14/79
Read (Reed), James	7/25/75, 12/11/75	5/10/75, 11/29/75
Read (Reed), John	5/22/79	9/26/78, 1/14/79

CONTINENTAL CURRENCY

Names of Signers	Appointment Dates	Issues Signed
Redman, Joseph	3/9/76	2/17/76, 5/9/76, 7/22/76
Reintzel, D.	Hillegas Appointee	4/11/78
Roberts, Robert, Jr.	7/25/75, 12/11/75, 8/11/78	5/10/75, 11/29/75, 9/26/78
Roberts, Robert A.	3/9/76, 8/12/78, 2/23/79	2/17/76, 5/9/76, 4/11/78, 9/26/78, 1/14/79
Ross, James	Hillegas Appointee	5/20/77, 4/11/78, 9/26/78
Rothrock, J.	Hillegas Appointee	2/17/76, 5/20/77, 4/11/78
Rownd (Round), Hampton	5/13/79	9/26/78
Rowan, James	8/14/78	4/11/78, 9/26/78
Royson, James	8/14/78	—
Rush, William	8/11/78, 8/12/78	4/11/78, 9/26/78
Russell (Russel), T.	Only Nominated 12/27/76	7/22/76
Ryves, E.	Hillegas Appointee	4/11/78, 9/26/78
Saltar (Salter), John	3/9/76	7/22/76
(Salter, Wm. ©)	—	1/14/79 ©
Schaffer (Shaffer), David, Jr.	7/23/79	—
Schreiner, Jacob	7/23/79	1/14/79
Scott, William	Hillegas Appointee	5/20/77
Sellers, John	3/9/76	2/17/76, 5/9/76, 7/22/76
Sellers, Nathan	3/9/76	2/17/76, 5/9/76, 7/22/76
Sellers, Samuel	3/9/76	2/17/76, 5/9/76, 7/22/76
Shaw, John, Jr.	3/9/76	2/17/76, 5/9/76
Sheaff (Sheaffe), William	8/8/78	4/11/78
Shee, John	7/25/75, 12/11/75, 8/14/78	5/10/75, 11/29/75, 7/22/76
Shee, Walter	3/9/76	2/17/76, 5/9/76, 7/22/76
Shoemaker, Charles	Hillegas Appointee	5/20/77
Short, J.	Hillegas Appointee	5/20/77
Shubart, Michael	7/23/79	9/26/78
Simmons, Ludson (Luson)	2/23/79	9/26/78, 1/14/79
Sims, Joseph, Jr.	7/25/75	5/10/75
Smith, Belcher Peartree	2/23/79	5/20/77
Smith, Jonathan Bayard*	12/11/75, 3/9/76	5/10/75, 11/29/75, 2/17/76, 5/9/76, 7/22/76
Smith, R.	Only Nominated 1/8/77	7/22/76, 2/26/77, 5/20/77, 9/26/78
Smith, Thomas	12/11/75, 3/9/76	11/29/75, 2/17/76, 5/9/76
Snowden, Jedediah	8/8/78, 2/23/79	5/20/77, 4/11/78, 1/14/79
Snowden, Joseph	8/8/78	4/11/78, 9/26/78
(W Colston)	—	9/26/78 ©
(U. Couden)	—	4/11/78 ©
Spear, William	Hillegas Appointee	2/17/76, 2/26/77, 5/20/77
Sprogell, Lodowick (Ludovic)	2/23/79	9/26/78, 1/14/79
Stewart (Stuart), D.	Only Nominated 12/27/76	7/22/76
Stretch, Peter	3/9/76, 8/8/78	2/17/76
Stretch, William	2/23/79	9/26/78, 1/14/79
Stringer, Richard	1/21/77	11/2/76
Strong, Matthew	5/29/79	—
Summers, D.	Hillegas Appointee	4/11/78
Swaine, Francis	7/23/79	9/26/78, 1/14/79
Sweny, T.	Hillegas Appointee	5/20/77
Taylor, John	2/13/77	2/17/76, 11/2/76, 2/26/77, 5/20/77
Thorne, William	8/8/78	4/11/78, 9/26/78
Tilghman, Tench	3/9/76	2/17/76
Tuckniss, Robert	7/25/75, 12/11/75, 3/9/76	5/10/75, 11/29/75, 2/17/76, 5/9/76
Tybout, Andrew	3/9/76	2/17/76, 5/9/76, 7/22/76

CONTINENTAL CURRENCY

Names of Signers	Appointment Dates	Issues Signed
Wade, F.	Hillegas Appointee	5/20/77
Walker, James	2/13/77	2/17/76, 11/2/76, 2/26/77
Walter, Joseph	8/8/78	9/26/78
(Welter, D. ©)	—	9/26/78 ©
Warren, Thomas	Hillegas Appointee	5/20/77
Watkins, Joseph	12/11/75, 3/9/76, 2/23/79	11/29/75, 2/17/76, 5/9/76,
		7/22/76, 9/26/78, 1/14/79
Watson, J.	Hillegas Appointee	5/20/77
Webb, William	12/11/75, 3/9/76	11/29/75, 2/17/76, 5/9/76, 7/22/76
Welch (Welsh), George	12/27/76	2/17/76, 11/2/76, 2/26/77, 5/20/77
Wetherill, Samuel	2/23/79	9/26/78, 1/14/79
Wharton, James	12/11/75	11/29/75
Whelen (Wheelen), Israel	3/9/76	2/17/76, 5/9/76, 7/22/76
Williams, John*	3/9/76, 5/22/79	2/17/76, 9/26/78, 1/14/79
Wilson, James*†	8/8/78, 7/23/79	4/11/78, 1/14/79
Wilson, Joseph	8/14/78	4/11/78, 9/26/78
Wister (Wistar), Daniel	5/29/79	9/26/78, 1/14/79
Wright, John	Hillegas Appointee	5/20/77, 4/11/78
Young, John, Jr.	8/8/78	4/11/78, 9/26/78
Young, Moses	Hillegas Appointee	
	and 2/23/79	5/20/77
(Young, G. ©)	—	5/20/77 ©
Young, William	1/14/77	11/2/76

*Member of the Continental Congress

†Signer of the Declaration of Independence. The genuine signature of James Wilson is written on the bills as "Jas Wilson" with a small s in the first name high above the preceding letter. An amanuensis substituted for James Wilson and also signed "Jas Wilson" with many differences, particularly the lack of a long sweep on the right side of W.

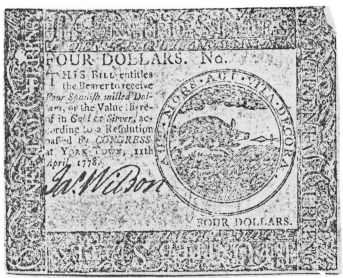

Genuine

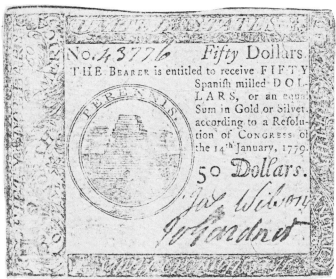

Amanuensis

CONTINENTAL CURRENCY

The signature of Joseph Wilson is always "J. Wilson" and can be readily distinguished by that abbreviation. It has several similarities to the signature of James Wilson.

Summary of Number of Signers

Appointment Dates	Number of Signers Appointed	Issues Signed by Appointees
7/25/75	28	5/10/75
12/11/75	36	11/29/75
3/9/76	60	2/17/76, 5/9/76, 7/22/76
12/27/76	14	2/17/76, 11/2/76, 2/26/77, 5/20/77
1/4/77 to 2/18/77	29	2/17/76, 11/2/76, 2/26/77, 5/20/77
Hillegas Appointees	55	2/17/76, 2/26/77, 5/20/77, 4/11/78, 9/26/78
Nominated but not elected. Probably also Hillegas Appointees	4	2/17/76, 7/22/76, 11/2/76, 2/26/77
8/8/78	30	5/20/77, 4/11/78, 9/26/78
8/11/78 to 9/26/78	13	4/11/78, 9/26/78
2/23/79	27	9/26/78, 1/14/79
2/25/79 to 5/22/79	9	9/26/78, 1/14/79
5/29/79	9	9/26/78, 1/14/79
7/23/79	11	9/26/78, 1/14/79
8/6/79 to 8/14/79	4	9/26/78, 1/14/79
Total Appointments	329	
Duplicated Appointments	65	
Persons Appointed	264	
Fictitious Signers on Counterfeits	16	
Total Names	280	

CONTINENTAL CURRENCY

CONTINENTAL CURRENCY REFERENCES

Samuel Breck, "Historical Sketch of Continental Paper Money," *Transactions of the American Philosophical Society* (Philadelphia, 1843), reprinted.

Charles J. Bullock, *The Finances of the United States from 1775 to 1789* (Madison, 1895).

"Continental Money," *Canadian Antiquarian and Numismatic Journal* (1879).

"Continental Paper Money," *The Numismatist* (April 1941).

"Devices on the Continental Bills of Credit," *American Journal of Numismatics* (October 1871).

Thomas L. Elder, "Vicissitudes of Continental Paper Money," *The Numismatist* (April 1925).

Benjamin Franklin, "Of the Paper Money of the United States of America," written in 1781.

Lynn Glaser, "Continental Currency," *Numismatic Scrapbook Magazine* (December 1963).

William M. Gouge, *A Short History of Paper Money and Banking in the United States* (Philadelphia, 1833 and New York, 1835, 1840, 1845).

Byron W. Holt, "Continental Currency," *Sound Currency* (New York, April 1898).

Richard T. Hoober, "Franklin's Influence on Colonial and Continental Paper Money," *The Numismatist* (December 1956).

Frank M. Katen, "Some Continental Currency Counterfeits," *Numismatic Scrapbook Magazine* (October 1951).

Charles E. Kirtley, "A Note on Colonial Counterfeiting," *Paper Money* (September 1975).

Joseph R. Lasser, "Continental Currency Signing Patterns," *The Numismatist* (May 1975).

Benson J. Lossing, "Continental Money," *Harper's Monthly Magazine* (March 1863).

Eric P. Newman, "The Successful British Counterfeiting of American Paper Money During the American Revolution," *The British Numismatic Journal* (1959).

——, "Historic Printing Plate Located," *Coin World* (December 8, 1961).

——, "Franklin and the Bank of North America," *The Numismatist* (December 1956).

——, "Counterfeit Continental Currency Goes to War," *The Numismatist* (January 1957, etc.), reprinted.

——, "Nature Printing on Colonial and Continental Currency," *The Numismatist* (February 1964, etc.), reprinted.

——, "Sources of Emblems and Mottoes for Continental Currency and the Fugio Cent," *The Numismatist* (December 1966).

Henry Phillips, Jr., *Continental Paper Money* (Roxbury, 1866).

——, "Continental Paper Money," *American Journal of Numismatics* (July 1871).

L. Miles Raisig, "The Continental Currency Makers," *Numismatic Scrapbook Magazine* (October 1960).

Lewis M. Reagan, "Continental Currency," *The Numismatist* (April 1942; March 1947).

Review of the Article on Continental Money in Harper's Magazine for March 1863 (1863).

Richard Rush, Old Continental Money, Document No. 107 of House of Representatives of 20th Congress, 1st Session (Washington, 1828).

Jacob N. Spiro, "Papers Relating to the Official Destruction of Continental Currency," *Numismatic Review* (July 1946).

J. W. Schuckers, *Finances and Paper Money of the Revolutionary War* (Philadelphia, 1874).

Peletiah Webster, *Political Essays* (Philadelphia, 1791).

Ted N. Weissbuch, "What Happened to the Continental Currency?" *Numismatic Scrapbook Magazine* (May 1966).

Lucius Wilmerding, Jr., "The United States Lottery," *The New York Historical Society Quarterly* (January 1963).

David C. Wismer, "Continental Money Plate Plowed Up," *The Numismatist* (March 1930).

Journals of the Continental Congress, papers of the Continental Congress, laws, archives of the United States, and newspapers.

See general references, catalogs, and listings following the Introduction.

CONNECTICUT

GENERAL EMISSIONS

July 12, 1709

July 12, 1709 Monogrammed AR

July 12, 1709 redated May 1713 (Scroll)

July 12, 1709 redated May 1713 (Flowers)

December 1, 1724

November 7, 1727

October 1728

May 1729

July 10, 1733

July 10, 1733 redated 1735

July 10, 1733 redated May 1740

May 8, 1740

July 10, 1733 redated July 8, 1740

May 8, 1740 redated May 10, 1744

May 8, 1740 redated October 11, 1744

May 8, 1740 redated March 14, 1744(5)

July 10, 1733 redated May 8, 1746

May 8, 1740 redated May 8, 1746

January 8, 1755

March 13, 1755

August 27, 1755

October 9, 1755

March 8, 1758

February 7, 1759

March 8, 1759

May 10, 1759

March 13, 1760

March 26, 1761

March 4, 1762

May 12, 1763

March 8, 1764

May 10, 1770

October 10, 1771

June 1, 1773

January 2, 1775

May 10, 1775

June 1, 1775

July 1, 1775

June 7, 1776

June 19, 1776

October 11, 1777

March 1, 1780

June 1, 1780

July 1, 1780

SPECIAL ISSUERS

New London Society for Trade and Commerce ★ August 1732

Union Bank in New London ★ 1792, etc. ★ August 6, 1792 ★ September 26, 1794

Hartford Bank ★ 1792, etc.

New Haven Bank ★ 1792, etc.

Chamber of Commerce in New Haven ★ December 3, 1794

Middletown Bank ★ 1795, etc.

Norwich Bank ★ 1796, etc. ★ September 12, 1796 ★ May 10, 1799

Hartford & New Haven Turnpike ★ 1799, etc.

CONNECTICUT

July 12, 1709

£24,000 (£8,000, £11,000, and £5,000) in indented Bills of Credit issued to pay for an abortive expedition against Canada pursuant to the May 1709, Oct. 1709 and Oct. 1710 Acts. Receivable for taxes at 5% advance, but not legal tender. Engraved on two copper plates by Jeremiah Dummer of Boston, the four highest denominations being on the "large" or "great plate" and the lowest four denominations being on the "small plate."

Colony Arms on the face plates contain the motto, SUSTINET QUI TRANSTULIT (He who transplants sustains himself). The Arms are surrounded by frames with a different shape for each denomination. The back contains an engraved scroll from the identical back plate used for contemporaneous Massachusetts Bay issues. Signers are John Chester, John Eliot, John Haynes, Caleb Stanly, and Joseph Tallcott.

2s	Diamond
2s6d	Six points and two convex sides resembling a pelt
3s	Rectangle with convexity on top and bottom
5s	Eight alternating arcs of two sizes
10s	Rectangular with one point on both top and bottom and with convexity on the sides ©
20s	
40s	Four leaflike points on both top and bottom plus irregular sides ©
£5	Large 270 degree arc at top, convex sides, and two winglike elements below

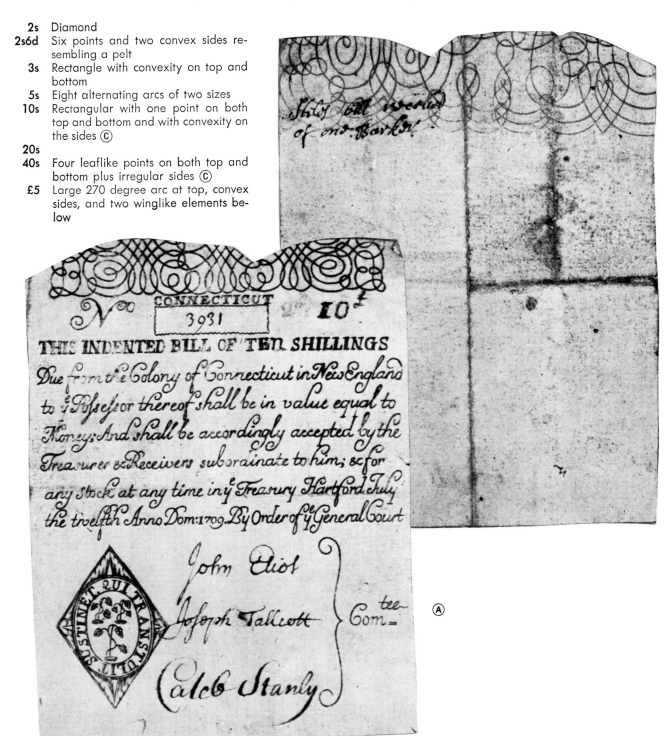

CONNECTICUT

July 12, 1709 Monogrammed, AR

£10,000 (£4,000 and £6,000) in indented Bills of Credit authorized by the May 1711 and June 1711 Acts. Identical to the first July 12, 1709 issue except that the paper obtained from the Company of Stationers in England was overprinted in red on the face with a large mirrored monogram AR (Anna Regina). The identical AR monogram is on contemporaneous Massachusetts and New Hampshire issues. On the faces SUSTINET QUI TRANSTULIT is on the oval Colony seal surrounded by frames with a different shape for each denomination as on prior issue. Easily and often altered. Signers are John Chester, John Eliot, John Haynes, Richard Lord, Caleb Stanly, Joseph Tallcott, and Hezekiah Wyllys.

2s	Diamond
2s6d	Six points and two convex sides resembling a pelt
3s	Rectangle with convexity on top and bottom
5s	Eight alternating arcs of two sizes
10s	Rectangular with one point on both top and bottom and with convexity on the sides
20s	
40s	Four leaflike points on both top and bottom plus irregular sides
£5	Large 270 degree arc at top, convex sides, and two winglike elements below

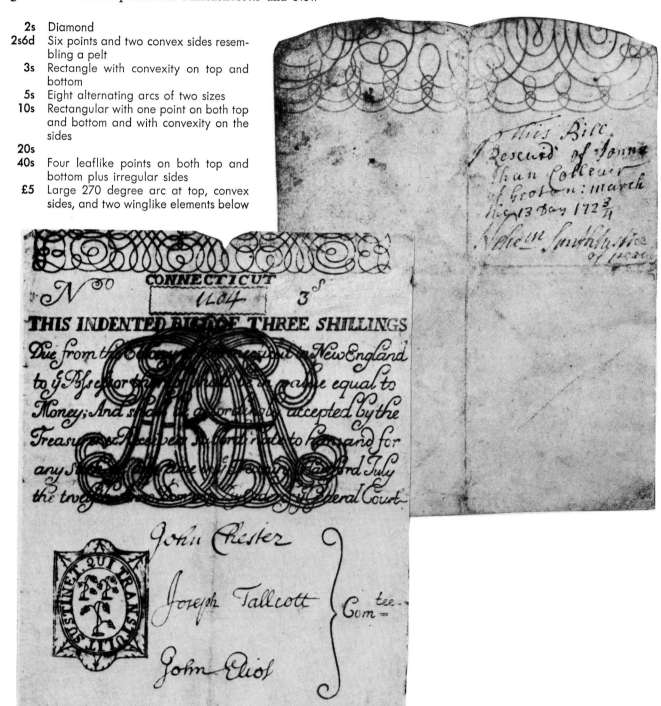

CONNECTICUT

July 12, 1709 redated May 1713 (Scroll on back)

£20,000 in indented Bills of Credit authorized by the May 1713 and June 1713 Acts to replace all prior issues because of the extensive practice of raising denominations by alteration. The July 12, 1709 plates were modified by adding "May 1713" below the original date, by engraving the denomination in script over the lower part of the face scroll, by placing a picture of a different animal on each denomination, and by writing the name of a different color on each denomination on the great plate. The AR monogram was used on bills from the great plate. The bills from the small plate were in black. The monogram, name of the color, animal and signatures were to be in the designated color on the bills from the great plate. All prior bills were to be replaced by November 1714 but this date was extended successively to June 1, 1721. Signers are John Eliot, John Haynes, Richard Lord, William Pitkin, Joseph Tallcott, William Whiting, and Hezekiah Wyllys.

2s	Dove
2s6d	Cock
3s	Squirrel
5s	Fox
10s	Lamb. Green
20s	Deer. Yellow
40s	Horse. Blue
£5	Lion. Red Ⓒ

61

CONNECTICUT

July 12, 1709 redated May 1713 (Flowers on back)

£10,000 (£4,000, £4,000 and £2,000) in indented Bills of Credit authorized by the May 1719, Oct. 1722 (to replace torn bills), and Oct. 1724 Acts. Identical to prior issue except that a flowered engraved plate was used to print the back instead of a scroll. In 1719 the face plates were reengraved in Boston. Printed by Timothy Green.

All bills issued by the Colony were made legal tender until 1727 by the Oct. 1718 Act, except where otherwise specified in the contract, and this status was extended until prohibited by the Crown in 1741. Same signers as prior issue. Signers of bills from great plate signed in red ink.

2s [7,853]	3s [7,853]	10s [599]	40s [599]
2s6d [7,853]	5s [7,853]	20s [599]	£5 [599]

December 1, 1724

£2,000 (half of £4,000) in indented legal tender Bills of Credit authorized by the Oct. 1724 and Nov. 1724 Acts primarily to exchange for torn bills. The face was identical to issue of July 12, 1709 redated May 1713. The backs of bills from the great plate have typeset text and a Dec. 1, 1724 date instead of flowers, the shape of the text differing on each denomination. Printed by Timothy Green. Same signers as the prior issue plus Matthew Allyn.

10s [236]	20s [236]	40s [236]	£5 [236]

November 7, 1727

£4,000 in indented legal tender Bills of Credit authorized by the Oct. 1727 and Nov. 1727 Acts to replace torn bills. The faces are identical to the issue of July 12, 1709 redated May 1713. The backs have typeset text in a different shape for each denomination and include the date. Printed by Timothy Green. Same signers as the prior issue.

2s	3s	10s	40s
2s6d	5s	20s	£5

October 1728

£4,000 in indented legal tender Bills of Credit authorized by the Oct. 1728 Acts to replace torn bills and for expenses. Identical to the prior issue except for the appropriate date in the text on the back. Same printer and signers as the prior issue.

10s	20s	40s	£5

May 1729

£6,000 in indented legal tender Bills of Credit authorized by the May 1729 Act to exchange for torn bills and for bills without printed backs. Bills without printed backs were to become unredeemable after May 1730. The faces were identical to the issue of July 12, 1709 redated May 1713. The date was in typeset text on the back. Printed by Timothy Green. Same signers as the prior issue.

2s	3s	10s	40s
2s6d	5s	20s	£5

August 1732

£10,000 (£30,000 authorized) in indented circulating notes loaned on twelve year mortgages by the "New London Society United for Trade and Commerce," a private organization founded in 1730 and incorporated in May 1732 by the Connecticut General Court. The notes were equal to all public Bills of Credit of the New England colonies and to silver at 16s per ounce. The engraved face and the typeset back were printed by Timothy Green. The seal consists of a ship with the motto AMOR PATRIAE VICIT (Love of country has conquered). Various shapes and designs on both face and back were used on each denomination to prevent alteration. This issue caused legislation in Feb. 1732(3) prohibiting private

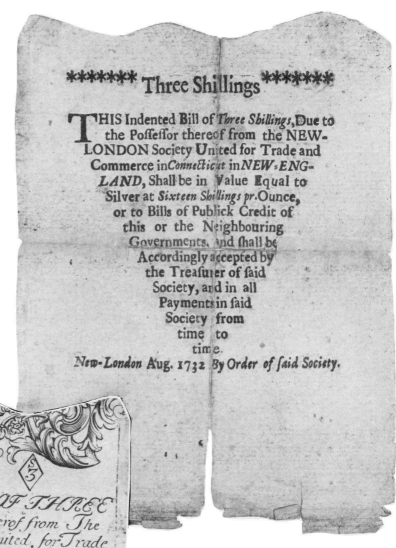

note issues and repealing the charter. The Colony authorized its own July 10, 1733 emission to be used in exchange for the New London Society notes. By the Acts of Oct. 1735, Oct. 1740, and May 1741 the issue was declared equivalent to counterfeit bills. Signers are Thomas Seymour, John Curtis, John Bissel, Solomon Coit, John Lee, Joseph Wright, and Thomas Traynor.

2s
2s6d
3s
5s
10s
20s
40s
£5

July 10, 1733

£30,000 in legal tender Bills of Credit issued pursuant to the Feb. 1732(3), May 1733, and Oct. 1733 Acts to exchange for "New London Society United for Trade and Commerce" circulating notes, to create new mortgage loans, and for public expenses. Redeemable by May 1, 1741. The faces were engraved on two copper plates (great and small) by Nathaniel Mors of Boston. The typeset backs contain the date. October was added to the face and back to distinguish the bills issued after the Oct. 1733 Act. Printed by Timothy Green. Signers are William Pitkin, Nathaniel Stanly, Joseph Tallcott, and Hezekiah Wyllys. Beginning at this time and continuing for over thirty years most paper money legislation was withheld from the public and not published in the printed Acts.

Since the 1709 emission the folding of bills had caused bills to tear and sections to separate. These sections circulated independently. By a Jan. 1719(20) Act of Massachusetts Bay Colony the redemption of sections of Connecticut bills in Boston was limited to half sections or more. In the May 1726 Act the Connecticut Treasury was prohibited from receiving any sections of bills after May 1, 1727. The practice of deliberately cutting up bills for change developed, making circulation of sections of counterfeit bills easier to pass. By the May 1736 Act sectioning of bills of 5s and over was prohibited and after May 20, 1737 sections were to be unredeemable. The practice continued, nevertheless, in spite of newspaper warnings, etc. "Broken money" given to Christianize Indians was exchangeable by the May 1737 Act. By the Oct. 1737, May 1738, and May 1741 Acts redemption of sections was extended.

2s	Dove	ⓒ
2s6d	Cock	
3s	Squirrel	
5s	Fox	
10s	Lamb	ⓒ
20s	Deer	
40s	Horse	ⓒ
£5	Lion	ⓒ

CONNECTICUT

July 10, 1733 redated 1735

£25,000 in legal tender Bills of Credit issued pursuant to the Oct. 9, 1735 Act to replace all prior emissions, particularly the July 10, 1733 issue because of extensive counterfeiting. The faces were identical to the July 10, 1733 issue with "1735" added. The face plates were to be cut deeper because they gave poor impressions. In each of the four quadrants of the typeset backs the text provided for circulation of sections of bills by including QUARTER OF THREE SHILLINGS or similar appropriate language for each denomination. This appears to be the first issue in America in which the exact circulating value of a quarter section was printed on the bill. Printed by Timothy Green. Signers are the same as the prior issue.

2s	Dove	10s	Lamb
2s6d	Cock	20s	Deer
3s	Squirrel	40s	Horse
5s	Fox ©	£5	Lion

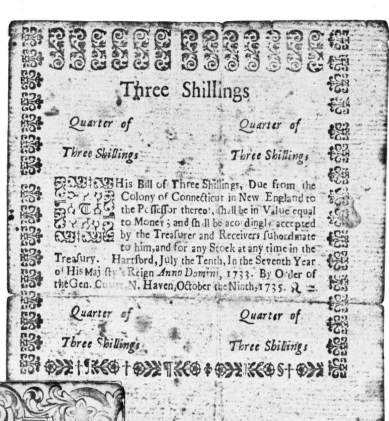

July 10, 1733 redated May 1740

£4,000 in Old Tenor legal tender Bills under the May 1740 Act for military bounties and the expense of an expedition against the Spanish West Indies. New Tenor bills under a contemporaneous act could not be prepared in time so the plates for the prior issue were modified by adding "May, 1740" and reused. Back typeset. Printer is Timothy Green. Same signers as prior issue except that George Wyllys is substituted for Hezekiah Wyllys.

10s	Lamb	[471]
20s	Deer	[471]
40s	Horse	[471]
£5	Lion	[471]

CONNECTICUT

May 8, 1740

£30,000 in legal tender New Tenor Bills of Credit issued pursuant to the May 1740 Act for mortgage loans, etc. New Tenor value was set at 3½ Old Tenor for 1 New Tenor and equivalent to silver at 8 shillings per ounce. The three lowest denominations are wide and the others are tall. The faces are engraved and the backs typeset. Printed by Timothy Green. The word "and" before the words "in the Treasury" was struck out on the face before signing because of the Crown's requirements, changing the redemption status. Same signers as the prior issue.

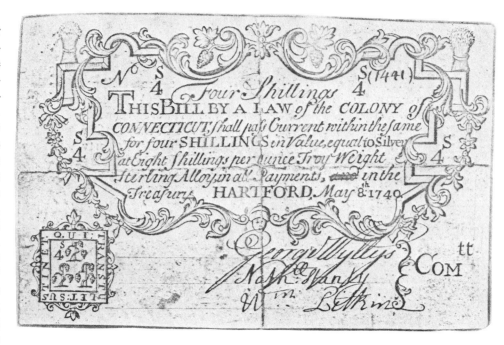

1s	12s
2s	20s Ⓒ
4s Ⓤ	40s
7s Seaven	£3

Ⓒ

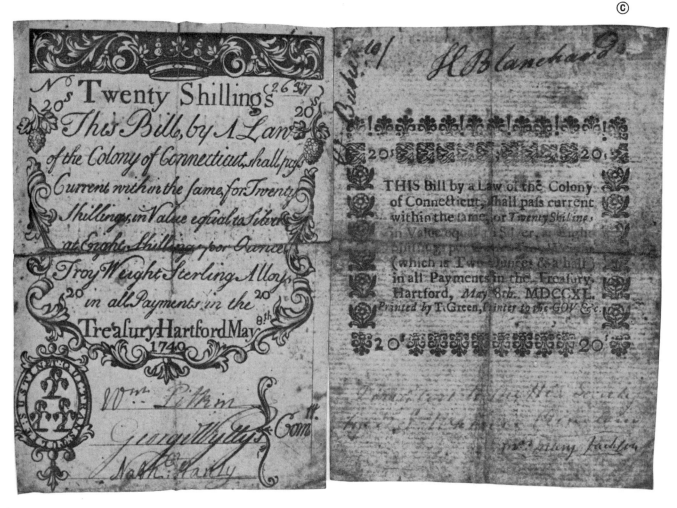

July 10, 1733 redated May 1740 on the face and July 8, 1740 on the back

£15,000 in Old Tenor legal tender Bills of Credit issued pursuant to the July 1740 Act because New Tenor bills were still delayed in preparation. £5,000 were to be exchanged for torn bills and £10,000 were for Colony expenses. The same face plate was used without further modification as in the prior issue and its wear is noticeable from its poor impressions. Typeset date is in the text on the back. The back text continued to anticipate the quartering of bills as theretofore. Printed by Timothy Green. Signers are William Pitkin, Nathaniel Stanly, Joseph Tallcott and George Wyllys. By the Nov. 1740 Act the legal tender status was voided pursuant to imminent legislation by the Crown prohibiting any legal tender.

10s	Lamb	[1,765]
20s	Deer	[1,765]
40s	Horse	[1,765]
£5	Lion	[1,765]

May 8, 1740 redated May 10, 1744

£4,000 in New Tenor Bills of Credit issued pursuant to the May 1744 Act for Colony expenses. Identical to the May 8, 1740 issue with "May 10, 1744" added on the face and the date changed in the typeset text on the back. Printed by Timothy

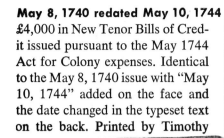

Green. Signers are Joseph Buckingham, John Chester, William Pitkin, Nathaniel Stanly, and George Wyllys.

1s		12s	
2s		20s	©
4s		40s	
7s	Seaven	£3	

May 8, 1740

redated October 11, 1744

£15,000 in New Tenor Bills of Credit issued pursuant to the Oct. 1744 Act to exchange for torn bills and for Colony obligations. The same face plates as the prior issue with Oct. 11, 1744 added without changing

the other dates. The latest date was also included in typeset text on the back. Printed by Timothy Green. Same signers as on prior issue.

1s		12s	©
2s		20s	
4s		40s	
7s	Seaven	£3	

©

May 8, 1740
redated March 14, 1744(5)

£40,000 (£20,000 and £20,000) in New Tenor Bills of Credit issued pursuant to the Mar. 1744(5) and July 1745 Acts for public obligations. Same face plates as prior issue with "Mar. 14, 1744/5" added without changing other dates. The latest date was included in the typeset text on the back.

Printed by Timothy Green. Because the great plate was unfit for use it was strengthened by recutting and additional insignia were added. Same signers as prior issue.

1s	7s Seaven	20s
2s	12s	40s
4s		£3

July 10, 1733 redated May 8, 1746

£3,000 in Old Tenor Bills of Credit issued pursuant to the May 1746 Act for use as small change. The same small face plate dated July 10, 1733 and redated Oct. 1735 had "May 8, 1746" added without changing the other dates. The latest date was included in typeset text on back. The backs also included provision for circulation of quarter sections of bills by including in each quadrant "Quarter of 2s & 6d. Seven-pence-half-peny" or similar appropriate language for each denomination. Printed by Timothy Green. Same signers as prior issue. By the Act of May 1747 no bills of other colonies were permitted to circulate in Connecticut. All Connecticut paper money issues were redeemed to a great

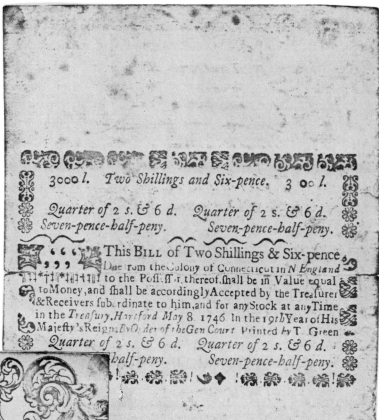

degree by copper and silver coin sent by the Crown in 1749 as repayment for expenses of the Cape Breton expedition. By the May 1753 Act the Connecticut Treasury was not to pay out any further paper currency.

2s	Dove	[4,800]
2s6d	Cock	[4,800]
3s	Squirrel	[4,800]
5s	Fox	[4,800]

CONNECTICUT

May 8, 1740 redated May 8, 1746

£20,000 and £37,000 in New Tenor Bills of Credit issued pursuant to the May 1746 and June 1746 Acts. The same face plates dated May 8, 1740 redated May 10, 1744, Oct. 11, 1744, and Mar. 14, 1744(5) had "May 8th, 1746" added without changing the other dates. Either May 8, 1746 or June 19, 1746 was included in the typeset text on the back along with initials of the Commissioners. The use of redated face plates for this and the prior issue resulted in the 2s denomination being issued in two completely different styles for the May 8, 1746 authorization. Printed by Timothy Green. Same signers as prior issue.

1s		
2s		
4s		
7s	Seaven	©
12s		
20s		©
40s		©
£3		©

January 8, 1755

£7,500 in Treasury Notes due May 8, 1758 with 5% interest issued for French and Indian War military expenses. Payable in lawful money equal to 9d sterling per shilling and prohibited from being legal tender by the 1751 Act of Parliament. Printed by Timothy Green from delicately detailed engraved cuts and set type on both the face and back. Hand near top of Colony Arms points to left on some denominations and to right on others. The former motto in the Colony Arms has been rearranged and abbreviated on a ribbon as QUI TRA SUS (He who transplants survives) and SIGILLUM : COLON : CONNECT-ICENSIS (Seal of the Colony of Connecticut) has been added. Signed and numbered in red ink. Signers are John Buckingham, John Chester, William Pitkin, and George Wyllys.

71

CONNECTICUT

January 8, 1755 (continued)

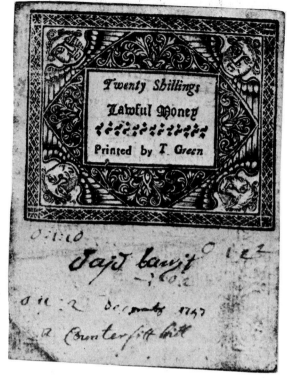

9d
1s
2s6d
5s
10s ©
20s ©
30s
40s

©

March 13, 1755

£12,500 in Treasury Notes due on May 8, 1759 with 5% interest. Similar to the prior issue and with the same signers. Old Tenor bills remaining in circulation were redeemable at 3½ for 1 in New Tenor interest bearing orders based upon coined silver at 58s8d Old Tenor per ounce or coined gold at 42 Old Tenor per ounce.

9d	1s	2s6d	5s	10s	20s	30s	40s

August 27, 1755

£30,000 in Treasury Notes due on Aug. 15, 1760 with 5% interest. Similar to the prior issue and with the same signers.

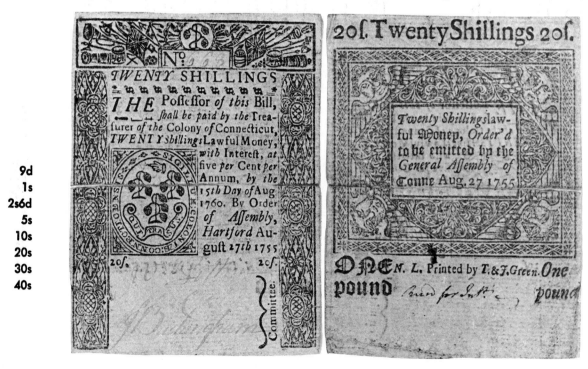

9d
1s
2s6d
5s
10s
20s
30s
40s

72

October 9, 1755

£12,000 in Treasury Notes due on April 1, 1760 with 5% interest. Similar to the prior issue and with the same signers.

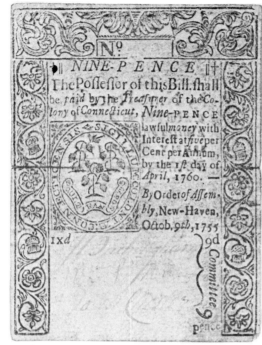

9d
1s
2s6d
5s
10s
20s
30s
40s

March 8, 1758

£30,000 in Treasury Notes due on May 1, 1762 with 5% interest. Same style, signers, and denominations.

February 7, 1759

£20,000 in Treasury Notes due on May 1, 1763 with 5% interest. Same style, signers, and denominations.

March 8, 1759

£40,000 in Treasury Notes due on Mar. 1, 1764 with 5% interest. Same style, signers, and denominations.

May 10, 1759

£10,000 in Treasury Notes due on May 1, 1763 with 5% interest. Same style, signers, and denominations.

March 13, 1760

£70,000 in Treasury Notes due on Mar. 1, 1765 with 5% interest. Same style, signers, and denominations.

March 26, 1761

£45,000 in Treasury Notes due on Mar. 26, 1766 with 5% interest. Similar to the prior issue. Signers are John Chester, Daniel Edwards, William Pitkin, and George Wyllys.

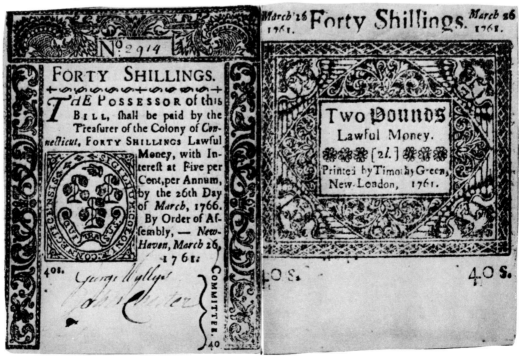

9d
1s
2s6d
5s
10s
20s
30s
40s ©

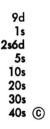

CONNECTICUT

March 4, 1762

£65,000 in Treasury Notes due on Mar. 4, 1767 with 5% interest. Similar to the prior issue and with the same signers. Abel Buel, engraver, type founder, diemaker and partner in the Connecticut copper coinage enterprise of 1785-89, was convicted of altering the 1s and 2s6d of this issue into 30s and as part of his punishment had his ear cropped and his forehead branded with a "C."

9d
1s
2s6d
5s
10s
20s
30s
40s ©

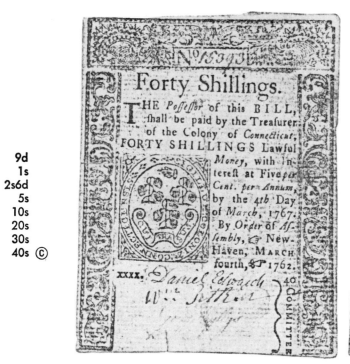
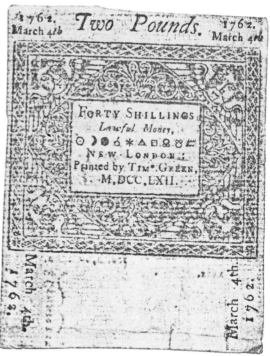

©

May 12, 1763

£10,000 in Treasury Notes due on May 1, 1765 with 5% interest. Similar to the prior issue and with the same signers.

5s
10s
20s
30s
40s

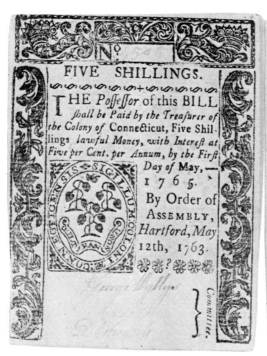
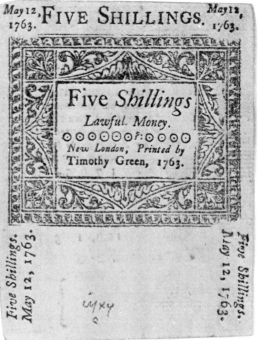

March 8, 1764
£7,000 in Treasury Notes due on Mar. 8, 1768 with 5% interest. Similar to the prior issue and with the same signers.

9d
1s
1s6d
2s6d
5s
10s
20s
30s ©
40s ©

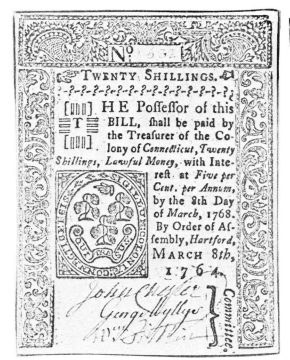

May 10, 1770
£10,000 in Treasury Notes due on May 10, 1772 with 2½% interest. Similar to the prior issue. Signers are John Chester, Benjamin Payne, William Pitkin, and George Wyllys. Slash or hole cancellation was usually used on redemption.

2s6d
5s
10s
20s
40s

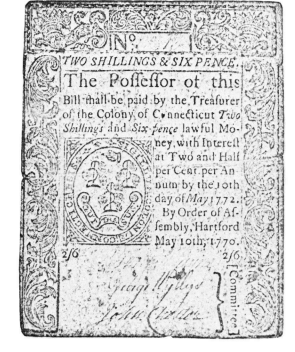

CONNECTICUT

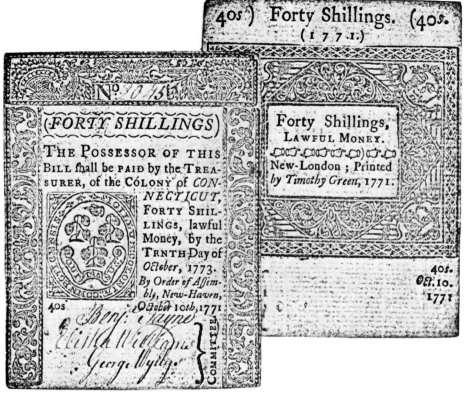

October 10, 1771

£12,000 in Treasury Notes due on Oct. 10, 1773, but without interest. Similar to the prior issue. Signers are Benjamin Payne, William Pitkin, Elisha Williams, and George Wyllys. Slash or hole cancellation was usually used on redemption. All paper money of other colonies was prohibited from circulation in Connecticut by the Oct. 1771 Act unless payable in specie with interest within 5 years, payable in specie without interest within 2 years, or unless issued by New York before Jan. 1, 1768. This prohibition was repealed in June 1776.

	Good	V.G.	Fine
2s6d	10.00	20.00	40.00
5s	10.00	20.00	40.00
10s	10.00	20.00	40.00
20s	10.00	20.00	40.00
40s	10.00	20.00	40.00

Values are for cancelled bills. One and one-half times the above value if uncancelled.

June 1, 1773

£12,000 in Treasury Notes due on June 1, 1775 without interest. Similar to the prior issue and with the same signers. Slash or hole cancellation usually occurred on redemption.

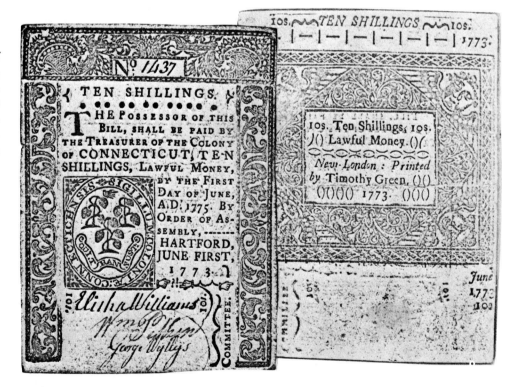

	Good	V.G.	Fine		Good	V.G.	Fine
2s6d	10.00	20.00	35.00	20s	10.00	20.00	35.00
5s	10.00	20.00	35.00	40s	10.00	20.00	35.00
10s	10.00	20.00	35.00				

Values are for cancelled bills. One and one-half times the above value if uncancelled.

CONNECTICUT

January 2, 1775

£12,000 in Treasury Notes due on Jan. 2, 1777 without interest. Similar to the prior issue. Signers are Benjamin Payne, William Pitkin, Thomas Seymour, Elisha Williams, and George Wyllys. Slash or hole cancellation usually occurred on redemption.

	Good	V.G.	Fine
2s6d	10.00	20.00	35.00
5s	10.00	20.00	35.00
10s	10.00	20.00	35.00
20s	10.00	20.00	35.00
40s	10.00	20.00	35.00

Values are for cancelled bills. One and one-half times the above value if uncancelled.

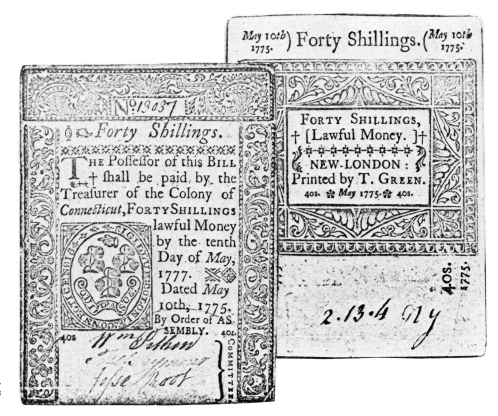

May 10, 1775

£50,000 in Treasury Notes due on May 10, 1777 without interest. Similar to the prior issue. Signers are Jabez Hamlin, Benjamin Payne, William Pitkin, Jesse Root, Thomas Seymour, Elisha Williams, and George Wyllys. Slash or hole cancellation usually occurred on redemption.

	V.G.	Fine	V.F.
2s6d	10.00	20.00	35.00
10s	10.00	20.00	35.00
20s	10.00	20.00	35.00
40s	10.00	20.00	35.00

Values are for cancelled bills. One and one-half times the above value if uncancelled.

June 1, 1775

£50,000 in Treasury Notes due on June 1, 1778 without interest. Similar to the prior issue and with the same signers. Slash or hole cancellation usually occurred on redemption.

	V.G.	Fine	V.F.
2s6d	10.00	20.00	35.00
6s	10.00	20.00	35.00
10s	10.00	20.00	35.00
20s	10.00	20.00	35.00
40s	10.00	20.00	35.00

Values are for cancelled bills. One and one-half times the above value if uncancelled.

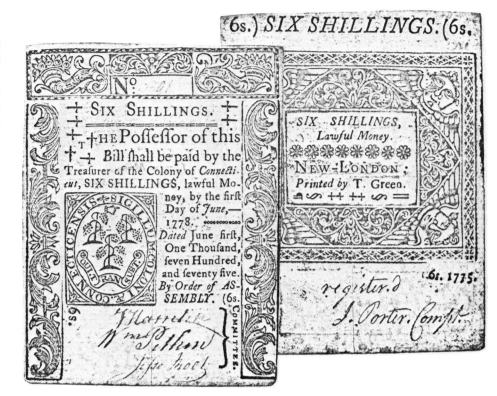

July 1, 1775

£50,000 in Treasury Notes due Dec. 31, 1779. Similar to the prior issue and with the same signers. Slash or hole cancellation usually occurred on redemption.

	V.G.	Fine	V.F.
2s	10.00	20.00	35.00
2s6d	10.00	20.00	35.00
6s	10.00	20.00	35.00
10s	10.00	20.00	35.00
20s	10.00	20.00	35.00
40s	10.00	20.00	35.00

Values are for cancelled bills. One and one-half times the above value if uncancelled.

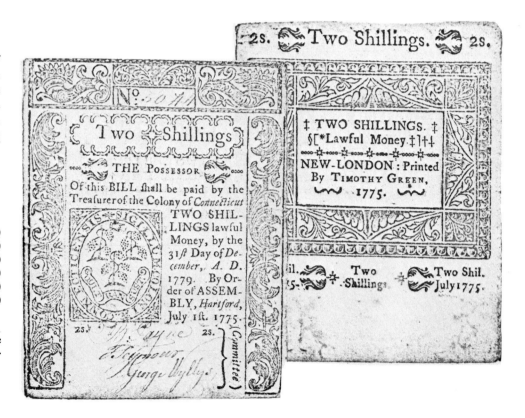

June 7, 1776

£60,000 in Treasury Notes due on Jan. 1, 1781. Similar to prior issue. £10,000 of the issue was 6s and below. Same signers as prior issue plus William Fisher. Some bills are slash or hole cancelled and others show redemption registration written in by the comptroller.

	Fine	V.F.	Unc.
1s ..	10.00	20.00	50.00
1s3d ..	10.00	20.00	50.00
2s ..	10.00	20.00	50.00
2s6d ..	10.00	20.00	50.00
3s ..	10.00	20.00	50.00
5s ..	10.00	20.00	50.00
6s ..	50.00		
10s ..	10.00	20.00	50.00
15s ..	10.00	20.00	50.00
£1			
£2 Back reads July 1, 1775			

Values are for cancelled bills. One and one-half times the above value if uncancelled.

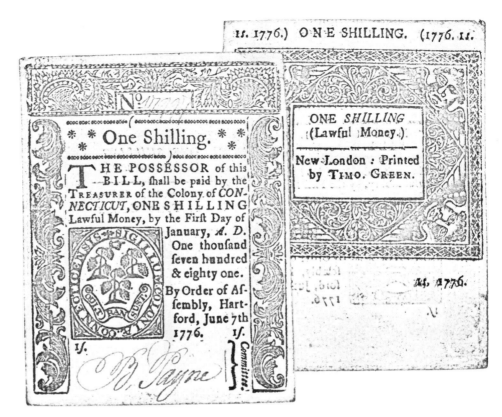

June 19, 1776

£50,000 in Treasury Notes due Jan. 1, 1782. Similar to prior issues. Same signers as July 1, 1775 issue. Connecticut and Continental issues made legal tender by Oct. 1776 Act. Some are slash or hole cancelled and others show registration by the comptroller in ink.

	Fine	V.F.	Unc.
6d ..	10.00	20.00	50.00
9d ..	10.00	20.00	50.00
1s ..	10.00	20.00	50.00
1s3d ..	10.00	20.00	50.00
1s6d ..	10.00	20.00	50.00
2s ..	10.00	20.00	50.00
2s6d ..	10.00	20.00	50.00
5s ..	10.00	20.00	50.00
40s ..	10.00	20.00	50.00

Values are for cancelled bills. One and one-half times the above value if uncancelled.

CONNECTICUT

October 11, 1777

£5,250 in Small Change Bills payable by Oct. 10, 1782. A small state seal with a hand near the top pointing to the left in all denominations. Blank backs. Usually signed and numbered in red ink. Some were printed on white paper but more commonly on coarse blue paper. The British captured 160 double sheets from Samuel Bishop in New Haven. Usually slash cancelled when redeemed. Some bills bear the clerk's registration in ink.

Signers are Andrew Adams, Samuel Bishop, Hezekiah Bissell, Ezra Bronson, John Brookes, John Chester, Pierrepont Edwards, Thomas Hayes, Abel Hine, Joseph Hopkins, Jabez Huntington, Isaac Lee, Lynde Lord, John Mackay, Thomas Mumford, Charles Phelps, Ebenezer Plummer, Jeremiah Ripley, Ephraim Root, Comfort Sage, Reuben Smith, Constant Southworth, Samuel Squier, Gad Stanley, John Treadwell, and Joseph Webb.

		Fine	V.F.	Unc.
2d	White paper	20.00	30.00	70.00
2d	Blue paper [60,000 combined]	10.00	20.00	40.00
3d	White paper	20.00	30.00	70.00
3d	Blue paper [60,000 combined]	10.00	20.00	40.00
4d	White paper	20.00	30.00	70.00
4d	Blue paper [60,000 combined]	10.00	20.00	40.00
5d	White paper	20.00	30.00	70.00
5d	Blue paper [60,000 combined]	10.00	20.00	40.00
7d	White paper	20.00	30.00	70.00
7d	Blue paper [60,000 combined]	10.00	20.00	40.00

Values are for cancelled bills. One and one-half times the above value if uncancelled.

March 1, 1780

£40,000 in Treasury Notes payable by Mar. 1, 1784 with 5% interest in Spanish milled dollars at 6s per dollar or the equivalent, pursuant to the Jan. 1780 Act. The same small State seal as was used on previous issue. Usually slash or hole cancelled on redemption. Signed and numbered in red ink. Signers are John Chester, Jabez Hamlin, Benjamin Payne, Elisha Williams, and George Wyllys.

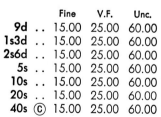

	Fine	V.F.	Unc.
9d ..	15.00	25.00	60.00
1s3d ..	15.00	25.00	60.00
2s6d ..	15.00	25.00	60.00
5s ..	15.00	25.00	60.00
10s ..	15.00	25.00	60.00
20s ..	15.00	25.00	60.00
40s ©	15.00	25.00	60.00

Values are for cancelled bills. Twice the above value if uncancelled.

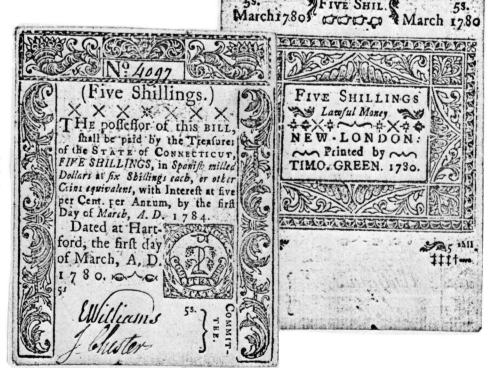

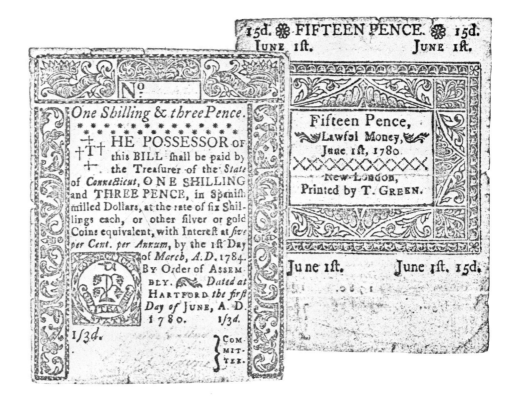

June 1, 1780

£50,000 in Treasury Notes payable by Mar. 1, 1784 with 5% interest pursuant to the May 1780 Act. This issue was in lieu of and exchangeable for the guaranteed issue authorized by Congress on Mar. 18, 1780 which guaranteed issue was apparently never printed. Similar to the prior issue and with the same signers plus William Pitkin. Slash or hole cancelled on redemption.

	Fine	V.F.	Unc.		Fine	V.F.	Unc.
9d	15.00	25.00	60.00	10s	15.00	25.00	60.00
1s3d	15.00	25.00	60.00	20s Ⓒ	15.00	25.00	60.00
2s6d	15.00	25.00	60.00	40s Ⓒ	15.00	25.00	60.00
5s	15.00	25.00	60.00				

Values are for cancelled bills. Twice the above value if uncancelled.

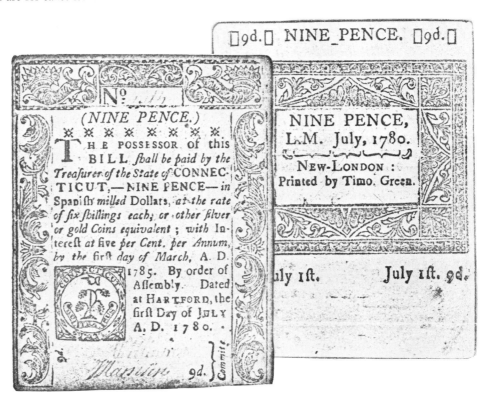

July 1, 1780

£100,000 in Treasury Notes payable by Mar. 1, 1785 with 5% interest pursuant to the May 1780 Act. Similar to the prior issue and with the same signers. Slash or hole cancelled on redemption.

	Fine	V.F.	Unc.
9d	15.00	25.00	60.00
1s	15.00	25.00	60.00
1s3d	15.00	25.00	60.00
2s6d	15.00	25.00	60.00
5s	15.00	25.00	60.00
10s	15.00	25.00	60.00
20s	15.00	25.00	60.00
40s	15.00	25.00	60.00

Values are for cancelled bills. Twice the above value if uncancelled.

Union Bank in New London ★ 1792, etc.

Organized on Mar. 5, 1792 as a partnership under the name, Bank of New London and Norwich, the Union Bank in New London was incorporated on May 30, 1792. Its capital was to be between $50,000 and $100,000 divided into shares of $100 each. Its debts including bank notes were not to exceed one and one-half times its capital plus its specie deposits. The $5 note of its original issue was counterfeited, causing an elimination of that denomination on June 30, 1795. Notes were signed by Jedediah Huntington, president, and John Hallam, cashier.

1792: $1 $5 © $10 $20   June 30, 1795: $2 $4 $6 $8

Union Bank in New London ★ August 6, 1792 and September 26, 1794

£575 "to furnish change which is much wanted in common dealings" was issued pursuant to the Aug. 6, 1792 authorization. Pursuant to the Sept. 16, 1794 authorization 4800 sheets of 32 notes each were circulated. Signed by Jedediah Huntington, its president, and John Hallam, its cashier. See further detail under prior issue.

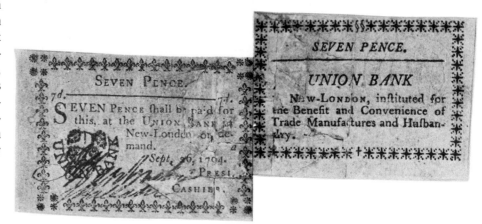

Aug. 6, 1792:   1d   2d   3d   Sept. 26, 1794:   1d   2d   4d   5d   6d   7d   8d   12d

Hartford Bank ★ 1792, etc.

The Hartford Bank was incorporated on May 29, 1792 with a capital of $100,000 divided into 400 shares of $250 each. The State was entitled to subscribe to an additional 40 shares. The debts of the bank including bank notes were not to exceed one and one-half times its capital plus its specie deposits. Its bank notes were signed by John Caldwell, president, and by Normand Knox, cashier.

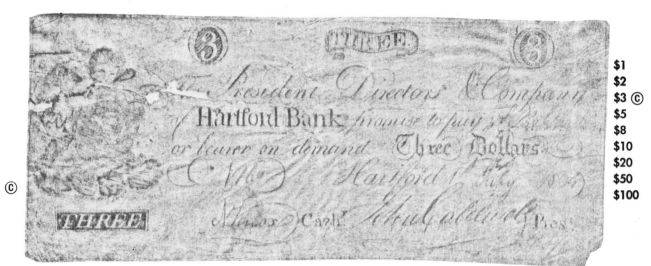

$1
$2
$3 ©
$5
$8
$10
$20
$50
$100

CONNECTICUT

New Haven Bank ★ 1792, etc.

The New Haven Bank was incorporated in October, 1792 with a capital of $100,000 which was changed in October 1795 to be between $50,000 and $400,000. Its shares were $200 each. Its debts including bank notes were limited to one and one-half times its capital plus its specie deposits. Its bank notes were signed by J. Beers, president, and W. Lyon, cashier.

$1 $2 $3 $5 $6 $7 $8 $10 $20 $50 $100

Chamber of Commerce in New Haven ★ December 3, 1794

Small change notes issued in New Haven, payable in silver, and signed by T. Daggett, treasurer. Wood cut on back with leaves representing the denomination. Other denominations probable.

1½d

Middletown Bank ★ 1795, etc.

The Middletown Bank was incorporated in October 1795 with a capital between $100,000 and $400,000 divided into shares of $100 each. Its debts including bank notes were limited to one and one-half times its capital plus its specie deposits. Its bank notes were signed by Elijah Hubbard, president, and Timothy Southmayd, cashier.

$1 $2 $5 $10 $20 $50

Norwich Bank ★ 1796, etc.

The Norwich Bank was incorporated in May 1796 with a capital to be between $75,000 and $200,000 divided into shares of $100 each. Its debts including bank notes were limited to one and one-half times its capital plus its specie deposits. Its bank notes were signed by Ebenezer Huntington, president, and Hezekiah Perkins, cashier.

50¢ $1 $2 $3 $5 $10 $20 $25 $50

Norwich Bank ★ September 12, 1796 and May 10, 1799

Small change notes issued at Norwich and signed by Ebenezer Huntington, its president, and Hezekiah Perkins, its cashier. Denominations are designated in both cents and pence on each note. Blank backs. Other denominations probable. See further detail under prior issue.

Sept. 12, 1796: 4¢ (3d), 8¢ (6d)

May 10, 1799: 3¢ (2d), 4¢ (3d), 7¢ (5d), 8¢ (6d), 11¢ (8d)

Hartford & New Haven Turnpike ★ 1799, etc.

The Hartford & New Haven Turnpike was authorized by the General Assembly in October 1798 and opened in the following year. Its scrip for passage tickets were engraved by Amos Doolittle of New Haven and printed on paper furnished by the Hudson and Goodwin Company. Signed by James Hillhouse, president. The unusual use of mills in a denomination was a result of the enthusiasm for the decimal system adopted by the United States and used in monetary conversion tables published after United States coinage commenced in 1793. The use of mills in a denomination was abandoned as impractical after half cents circulated freely.

5 mills	Sheep and pig	**6¢ 3 mills**	One horse sleigh
2¢	Horse, cow and donkey	**12¢ 5 mills**	Two two-wheeled vehicles
4¢	Horse and rider	**25¢**	Four-wheeled coach

CONNECTICUT

CONNECTICUT REFERENCES

Albert C. Bates, "Connecticut's Engraved Bills of Credit, 1709-1746," *Proceedings of the American Antiquarian Society* (Worcester, October 1936), reprinted.

William W. Bradbeer, *Connecticut Paper Money 1709-1793,* in Connecticut State Library (1923).

Henry Bronson, "A Historical Account of Connecticut Currency," *Papers of the New Haven Colony Historical Society* (New Haven, 1865).

Joseph Coffin, "Colonial Engravers and Printers," *The Numismatic Scrapbook Magazine* (November 1941).

"Connecticut Paper Money," *Historical Magazine* (March 1862).

Andrew McFarland Davis, "The Emissions of Neighboring Governments—Connecticut," *Currency and Banking in Massachusetts Bay* (New York, 1901).

———, "A Connecticut Land Bank of the Eighteenth Century," *The Quarterly Journal of Economics* (October 1898), reprinted.

Chester McArthur Destler, "The Union Bank of New London: Formative Years," *Connecticut Historical Society Bulletin* (Jan. 1959), Vol. 24, No. 1.

Gilbert and Dean, *The Only Sure Guide to Bank Bills* (Boston, 1806).

William F. Hasse, Jr., *A History of Money and Banking in Connecticut* (New Haven, 1957).

Richard D. Moore, "Connecticut's First Bills of Credit —1709," *Auctori Connec and Other Emissions* (Hartford, 1959).

Curtis P. Nettels, "The Beginnings of Money in Connecticut," *Transactions of the Wisconsin Academy of Sciences, Arts and Letters* (Madison, 1928).

Wayte Raymond, "Colonial Notes—Connecticut," *Coin Collector's Journal* (April 1934).

John M. Richardson, "Colonial Paper Currency of Connecticut," *The Numismatist* (June 1938); also in *The Numismatic Scrapbook Magazine* (June 1938).

———, "The Green Family, Printers of Colonial Bills in Connecticut and Maryland," *Coin Collector's Journal* (July 1935).

Kenneth Scott, *Counterfeiting in Colonial Connecticut* (New York, 1957).

Laws, archives, public records, and newspapers.

See general references, catalogs, and listings following the Introduction.

DELAWARE

GENERAL EMISSIONS

April 23, 1723 Act
November 2, 1723 Act
1729
March 1, 1734
December 1, 1739
February 28, 1746
January 1, 1753
May 1, 1756
March 1, 1758
May 1, 1758
June 1, 1759
May 31, 1760
January 1, 1776
May 1, 1777

SPECIAL ISSUERS

Caleb Sheward ★ January 8, 1777
William Buchanan ★ April 9, 1777
Bank of Delaware ★ 1795, etc.

DELAWARE

April 23, 1723 Act

£5,000 in Bills of Credit authorized by the April 23, 1723 Act and issued to make eight year 5% mortgage loans under a Loan Office system similar to that under which the April 2, 1723 Pennsylvania issue of bills was loaned out. Delaware then consisted of the three lower counties of the Province of Pennsylvania, namely New Castle, Kent, and Sussex.

November 2, 1723 Act

£6,000 in Bills of Credit issued pursuant to the Nov. 2, 1723 Act to make additional mortgage loans and corresponding to the Jan. 17, 1723(4) Pennsylvania issue of Bills of Credit. Delaware bills depreciated in value almost 25% because the people of Pennsylvania refused to accept them. However, in October 1726 the Pennsylvania Loan Office and a large group of Philadelphia merchants agreed to receive payments in Delaware bills on a par with Pennsylvania bills and the value of Delaware bills was restored. A reissue of both Delaware emissions of 1723 was authorized under a 1726 Act.

1729

£12,000 in Bills of Credit issued to make 16 year mortgage loans and corresponding to the Sept. 15, 1729 Pennsylvania issue. Probably printed by Andrew Bradford.

1s	2s	5s	15s ©
18d ©	2s6d	10s ©	20s ©

March 1, 1734

£12,000 in indented Bills of Credit. Elaborate floral and animal cuts engraved by Leech are on the top of the face for indenture. The English Arms are without background. The side and bottom borders as well as the text are typeset. The number of crowns is keyed to the denomination. The mottoes on the seal are DIEU ET MON DROIT (God and my right) and HONI SOIT QUI MAL Y PENSE (Evil to him who evil thinks). Blank backs. Printed by Benjamin Franklin. Signers are Jacob Kollock and Thomas Noxon.

1s
18d
2s
2s6d
5s
10s
15s
20s

DELAWARE

December 1, 1739

£6,000 in indented legal tender Bills of Credit issued to exchange for worn small denomination bills of the Mar. 1, 1734 issue. Similar to the Mar. 1, 1734 issue and with identical cuts. Blank backs. Plate letters were used to distinguish bills of the same denomination printed simultaneously. Printed by Benjamin Franklin. Signers are Jabez Maud Fisher, John Holliday, and Thomas Noxon.

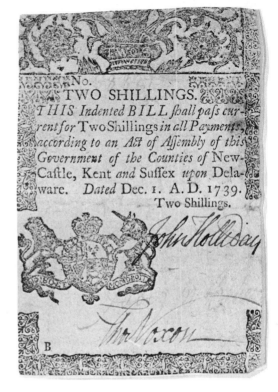

1s	Plate letters A & B	[12,000]
18d	Plate letters A & B	[10,000]
2s	Plate letters A & B	[8,000]
2s6d	Plate letters A & B	[12,400]
5s	Plate letters A & B	[4,800]
10s	Plate letters A & B	[2,200]

February 28, 1746

£20,000 in Bills of Credit issued pursuant to the Feb. 28, 1746 Act to exchange for prior issues and to continue Loan Office operations. In 1743 a similar authorization had been made but apparently no bills were issued as the Feb. 28, 1746 Act provided for the same action. The faces have English Arms in a rectangular background as well as top and bottom border cuts. The crowns are keyed to the denominations. On the back of the four highest denominations are nature prints below which are animal cuts. The backs of the four lowest denominations are blank. Printed by Benjamin Franklin. Signers are William Armstrong, Jno. Bunche, Thomas Clark, John Clowes, and Hugh Durborrow.

1s	Plate letters A & B
18d	Plate letters A & B
2s	Plate letters A & B
2s6d	Plate letters A & B
5s	Sea serpents
10s	Elephant, assorted leaves ©
15s	Horse, sage leaf
20s	Plate letters A & B. Lion, parsley

DELAWARE

January 1, 1753

£3,000 in Bills of Credit similar to the previous issue. The backs of the four lowest denominations are blank. The backs of the two highest denominations are the same as the corresponding backs on the previous issue. Printed by Benjamin Franklin and David Hall. Signers are William Armstrong, John Brinkley, and John Clowes. A letter dated Mar. 15, 1753 written by Franklin to Jehu Curtis is included and discussed in the Introduction and confirms many of Franklin's printing practices.

1s	Plate letters A & B	[6,000]
18d	Plate letters A & B	[5,000]
2s	Plate letters A & B	[4,000]
2s6d	Plate letters A & B	[6,200]
5s	Sea serpents, blackberry leaf	[2,400]
10s	Elephant, assorted leaves	[1,100]

May 1, 1756

£2,000 in Bills of Credit for military expenditures approved by a 1756 Act. Similar to the previous issue. The same backs as were used on the four highest denominations of the Feb. 28, 1746 issue were again used. Printed by Benjamin Franklin and David Hall. Signers are William Armstrong, Thomas Clark, and John Clowes.

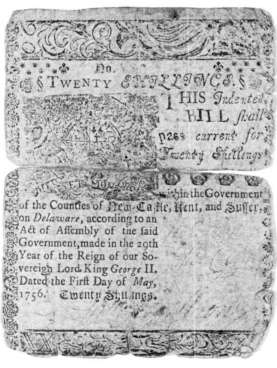

			Fair	Good	V.G.
1s					
18d					
2s					
2s6d					
	5s	Sea serpents, blackberry leaf	45.00	70.00	125.00
	10s	Elephant, assorted leaves	45.00	70.00	125.00
	15s	Horse, sage leaf	45.00	70.00	125.00
	20s	Lion, parsley	45.00	70.00	125.00

DELAWARE

March 1, 1758

£4,000 in Bills of Credit issued pursuant to 1757 Act to pay public expenses. Similar to the previous issue with some changes in nature prints but not in the engraved cuts. Printed by Benjamin Franklin and David Hall. Signers are William Armstrong, Thomas Clark, and David Hall.

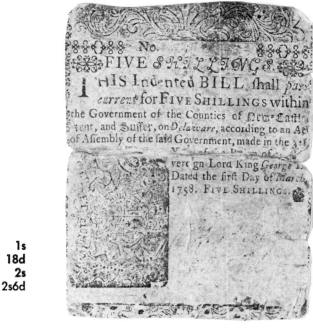

1s
18d
2s
2s6d

		Good	V.G.	Fine
5s	Sea serpents, blackberry leaf .	60	100	200
10s	Elephant, maple leaf	60	100	200

		Good	V.G.	Fine
15s	Horse, sage leaf	60	100	200
20s	Lion, assorted leaves	60	100	200

May 1, 1758

£8,000 in Bills of Credit issued to pay public expenses pursuant to a 1758 Act. Similar to the previous issue. **Printed by Benjamin Franklin and David Hall. Signers** are William Armstrong, Thomas Clark, John Clowes, and David Hall.

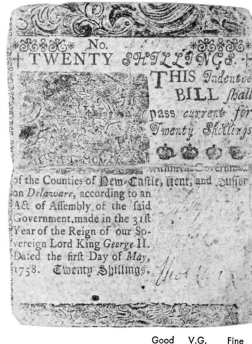

1s
1s6d
2s
2s6d

		Good	V.G.	Fine
5s	Sea serpents, blackberry leaf .	60	100	200
10s	Elephant, maple leaf	60	100	200

		Good	V.G.	Fine
15s	Horse, sage leaf	60	100	200
20s	Lion, assorted leaves	60	100	200

DELAWARE

June 1, 1759

£27,000 in legal tender Bills of Credit issued pursuant to the May 7, 1759 Act, £20,000 replacing the entire Feb. 28, 1746 issue and to be used by the Loan Office for new loans until June 1, 1773. The balance of £7,000 was for public expense and was redeemed in specie pursuant to the Nov. 2, 1762 Act. The English Arms are sideways on the six lowest denominations. The engraved animal cuts are from the Feb. 28, 1746 issue and are moved to the lower part of the back of the four highest denominations. On the upper part of the backs are a new set of nature prints. The backs of the four lowest denominations are blank. Printed by Benjamin Franklin and David Hall. Signers are William Armstrong, John Barns, and David Hall.

Plate letters to distinguish the two varieties of 20s bills are not used. There are many minor differences between these varieties, but the position of the period after "No" with respect to the Y below is used as the basis for differentiation.

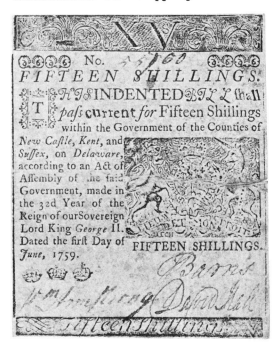

		Good	V.G.	Fine
1s	[5,000]	100.00		
1s6d	[8,000]	100.00		
2s	[5,000]	100.00		
2s6d	[5,000]	100.00		
5s	Sea serpents [8,000]	60.00	100.00	250.00
10s	Elephant [6,000]	60.00	100.00	250.00
15s	Horse [6,000]	60.00	100.00	250.00
20s	Lion, period over center of Y [7,750]	50.00	90.00	200.00
20s	Lion, period past right side of Y [7,750]	50.00	90.00	200.00

May 31, 1760

£4,000 in Bills of Credit issued pursuant to the April 28, 1760 Act. This issue was called for redemption in specie by the Oct. 31, 1761 Act. The English Arms are sideways in the three highest denominations. Another new set of small square nature prints are on the backs. Engraved cuts on the backs are eliminated. Printed in red and black on the face and in black on the back by Benjamin Franklin and David Hall. Signers are David Hall, Vincent Loockerman, and Evan Rice.

		Good	V.G.	Fine
20s	....	70.00	125.00	300.00
30s	I omitted in each THRTY	70.00	125.00	300.00
40s	Reversed D in borders	70.00	125.00	300.00
50s	....	70.00	125.00	300.00

May 31, 1760 (Continued)

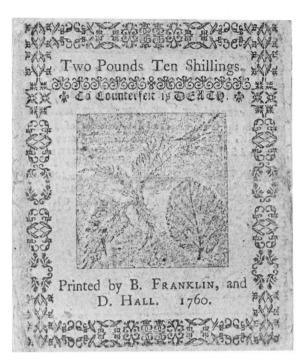

January 1, 1776

£30,000 in Bills of Credit issued pursuant to the Sept. 2, 1775 Act for 16 year mortgage loans, but to be redeemable on Jan. 1, 1788. Four different border cuts were on each denomination. English Arms are turned sideways on the six lowest denominations. Cuts of a sheaf of wheat are on the backs. Otherwise typeset. Not indented even though bills so state. Cuts engraved by James

Adams who also printed the bills. The thick paper containing blue thread and mica flakes is the same paper used for Continental Currency. The numbering of this issue is continuous on the sheets and disregards denominations. Signers are Thomas Collins, Boaz Manlove, John McKinly, and James Sykes.

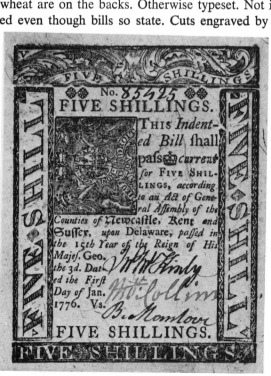

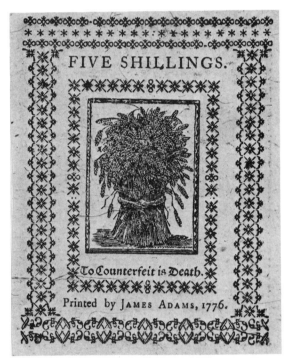

	Fine	V.F.	Unc.
1s [12,000]	20.00	40.00	90.00
18d [12,000]	20.00	40.00	90.00
2s6d [12,000]	20.00	40.00	90.00
4s [12,000]	20.00	40.00	90.00

	Fine	V.F.	Unc.
5s [12,000]	20.00	40.00	90.00
6s [12,000]	20.00	40.00	90.00
10s [12,000]	20.00	40.00	90.00
20s [12,000]	20.00	40.00	90.00

DELAWARE

Caleb Sheward ★ January 8, 1777

Private small change issued by a member of the Society of Friends of Wilmington. Date written in Quaker style. Blank backs. Border ornamentation also found on Georgia bills of 1776-7. Typeset. Other denominations are probable.

2d

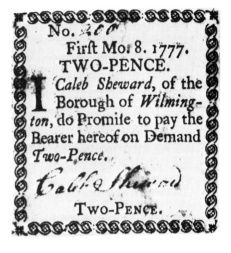

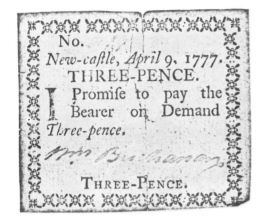

William Buchanan ★ April 9, 1777

Private small change issued by William Buchanan at Newcastle. Typeset. Blank back. Other denominations are probable.

3d

May 1, 1777

£25,000 in legal tender Bills of Credit pursuant to the Feb. 22, 1777 Act. £15,000 was for mortgage loans to be redeemed by Jan. 1, 1788 and £10,000 was for expenditure to be redeemed by May 1, 1782. New State Arms and borders were cut by James Adams for £24. Sheaf of wheat cuts were reused. Four lowest denominations are of small size. Printed by James Adams on thick paper containing blue fibre and mica flakes, the same paper then being used for Continental Currency. Legal tender discontinued on Nov. 4, 1780. Signers are John Clarke, Joshua Hill, John Jones, John Laws, Richard Lockwood, Alexander Porter, Abraham Robinson, John Thompson, and John Wiltbank.

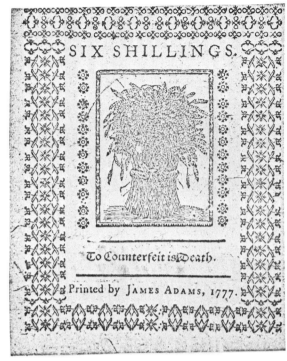

	V.G.	Fine	V.F.			V.G.	Fine	V.F.			V.G.	Fine	V.F.
3d [5,455] ..	15.00	30.00	50.00	1s [9,800] ..	10.00	20.00	35.00	5s [9,800] ..	10.00	20.00	35.00
4d [5,454] ..	15.00	30.00	50.00	1s6d [9,800] ..	10.00	20.00	35.00	6s [9,800] ..	10.00	20.00	35.00
6d [5,454] ..	15.00	30.00	50.00	2s6d [9,800] ..	10.00	20.00	35.00	10s [9,800] ..	10.00	20.00	35.00
9d [5,455] ..	15.00	30.00	50.00	4s [9,800] ..	10.00	20.00	35.00	20s [9,800] ..	10.00	20.00	35.00

Bank of Delaware ★ 1795, etc.

Beginning in business in 1795 before its incorporation on Feb. 9, 1796, the Bank of Delaware had a capital of $110,000. The State had the right to subscribe to 50 shares. Its engraved bank notes were signed by Joseph Tatnall, president, and John Hayes, cashier.

$5
$10
$20
$30
$50
$100

DELAWARE REFERENCES

Robert Aitken, *Waste Book,* Library Company of Philadelphia, ms.

Harrold E. Gillingham, "Counterfeiting in Colonial Days," *The Numismatist* (June 1929).

C. William Miller, *Benjamin Franklin's Philadelphia Printing* (Philadelphia, 1974).

Eric P. Newman, "Nature Printing on Colonial and Con-tinental Currency," *The Numismatist* (February 1964, etc.), reprinted.

Richard S. Rodney, *Colonial Finances of Delaware* (Wilmington, 1928).

Laws, archives and other public records.

See general references, catalogs, and listings following the Introduction.

FLORIDA

SPECIAL ISSUER

Unknown 177—

177—

Florida was under English rule from 1763 to 1783. Pensacola, the capital of West Florida, was captured by the Spanish in 1781. Nothing has been located concerning the illustrated issue, the engraved notes of which have differently designed borders and text layout. Each denomination apparently was printed in a different color as indicated by a salmon red color on one note and a greenish brown color on another. No evidence of the issuer or of the issued notes has been located, but Panton, Leslie & Co. who were the English fiscal agents and maintained one of their trading posts in Pensacola might have been connected with it.

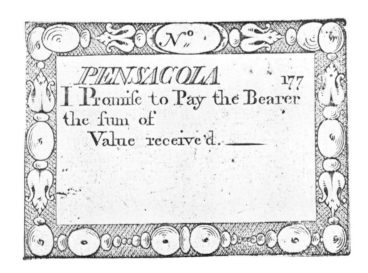

GEORGIA

GENERAL EMISSIONS

1735-50 Sola Bills
1735-45 Oglethorpe Bills
1755
May 1, 1760
1762
March 25, 1762
July 8, 1765
1766-7 Written Dates
1768-70 Tax Certificates
1769 Lighthouse Certificates
1773
(1774)
1775
1776 Sterling Denominations
1776 Light Blue Seal Dollar Denominations
1776 Maroon Seal
1776 Orange or Green Seal
1776 Fractional Dollar Denominations
1776 Blue-green Seal
1776 Black Vignette
(1776) Undated
1777 (No Resolution Date)
1777 (June 8, 1777 Resolution)
1777 (September 10, 1777 Resolution)
1778
January 9, 1782 Resolve
October 16, 1786

SPECIAL ISSUERS

Harris and Habersham ★ 1743-52
Unknown Savannah Issuer ★ 1775
Bank of the United States (Savannah Office) ★ 1793, etc.

1735-50 Sola Bills

£32,250 sterling in Sola Bills were provided by the issuance in England of bearer Bills of Exchange drawn by the accountant for the "Trustees for Establishing the Colony of Georgia in America" and countersigned by James Oglethorpe and others in America. The name, Sola Bill, was applied because, being intended for circulation, only one bill of exchange was drawn and was not followed by the second, third, and fourth bills of exchange which customarily followed the first. Sola Bills circulated in America until they were returned to England for payment. £4,000 were issued July 24, 1735, £3,150 on Aug. 4, 1736, £4,850 on Aug. 10, 1737, etc., until Mar. 27, 1750 by which time £32,250 had been issued. Sola Bills were indented and engraved. Marbled paper was used for the May 21, 1740 printing. On Mar. 8, 1742 Sola Bills were made payable "to order" instead of "to bearer" so that they could be made non-negotiable for their return to England by ship in case of seizure by a privateer. All Sola Bills were called for payment by Dec. 31, 1755, becoming unredeemable thereafter. Signers are J. Carman as accountant and Thomas Christie, James Habersham, Thomas Jones, James Oglethorpe, Henry Parker, William Spencer, and William Stephens as original payees.

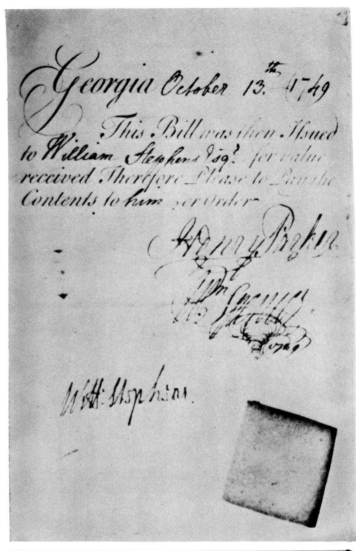

£1 Various forms [14,500]
£2 [500]
£5 Various forms [2,250]
£10 Various forms [450]
£20 [50]

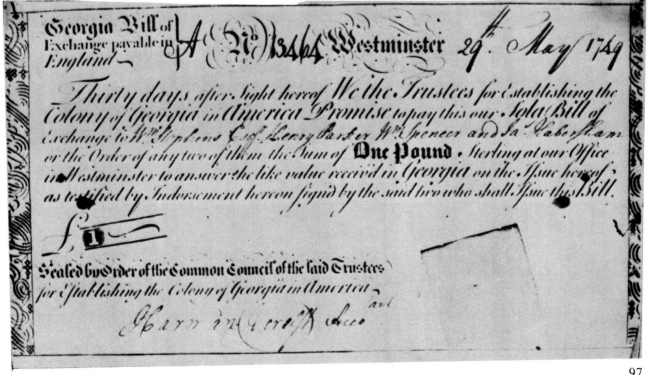

GEORGIA

1735-45 Oglethorpe Bills

Notes issued by James Oglethorpe on behalf of the Colony to supplement Sola Bills and to create a currency of small change. The number issued is based upon the highest serial number mentioned in available records.

1s [28,655]	4s [3,864]	5s [6,259]	£1 [5,520]

Harris and Habersham ★ 1743-52

Because of a deficiency of Sola Bills in circulation the partnership of Francis Harris and James Habersham, Savannah merchants, issued private scrip payable to bearer so that the people could pay their small obligations with money. Hand dated. Typeset. Other denominations are probable.

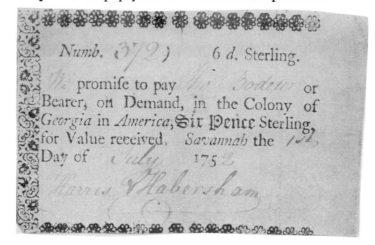

6d
18d
2s6d
4s
10s

1755

£7,000 sterling in legal tender Bills of Credit authorized by the Feb. 17, 1755 Act subject to the approval of the Crown and to be issued as the General Assembly directed. Commissioners of the General Loan were to lend out funds on security and provide for repayment of the issue by Dec. 1762. Typeset undated bills of 2s and below printed in Charleston, South Carolina. Indented bills of 2s6d and over engraved in Charleston with date on 5s and over. The sum of £2,785 was issued in 1755; £838 7s 1¼d on July 28, 1757 (£200 to replace worn bills); and £799 8s 11d on Mar. 27, 1759 for the public magazine, Tybee Island lighthouse and church improvements. Signers are Patrick Graham, Francis Harris, Clement Martin, James E. Powell, Edmund Tannatt, Alexander Wylly, and Henry Yonge.

2d	[3,600]
3d	[3,600]
4d	[3,600]
6d	[3,600]
9d	[3,600]
1s	[3,600]
1s3d	[3,600]
1s6d	[3,600]
2s	[3,600]
2s6d	Rose [3,600]
3s	[2,000]
3s6d	[2,000]
4s	[2,000]
5s	Bee [2,000]
10s	Bush and sickle [2,000]
20s	Woman operating thread winder [2,805]

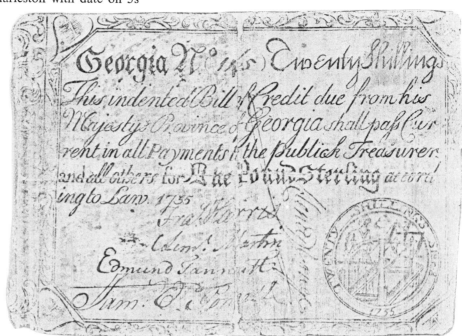

GEORGIA

May 1, 1760

£1,100 sterling in indented engraved certificates authorized by the April 24, 1760 Act for fortifications. One-fifth of the issue was redeemable on Oct. 1 of each year beginning in 1761. Signers are James Deveaux, John Graham, Noble Jones, William Knox, and William Russell.

£1   Blockhouses in the fortifications [1,200 emitted]

1762

£7,410 sterling in legal tender Bills of Credit authorized by the May 1, 1760 Act and approved by the Crown on July 2, 1761. The £4,400 of the 1755 issue remaining in circulation were called for exchange by Feb. 17, 1762. Worn bills were to be replaced at £200 per year. The life of the General Loan Authority was first renewed to 1769 and later to 1776 along with £6,500 of the currency. By the Sept. 16, 1777 Act the General Loan Authority was liquidated. Bills of 2s and under are

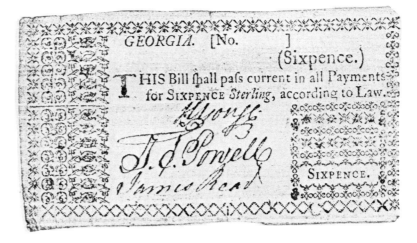

typeset, small in size and undated. Engraved plates for the 1755 issue were modified by changing the date in the text and in the vignette to 1762 and reused for large bills. Other bills dated 1762 are typeset with vignettes on the 5s and over. Signers are Francis Harris, Clement Martin, James E. Powell, James Read, Edmund Tannatt, Alexander Wylly, and Henry Yonge.

2d	
3d	
4d	
6d	
9d	
1s	
1s3d	
1s6d	
2s	
2s6d	
3s	
3s6d	
4s	
5s	Bee. Engraved
5s	Indian. Typeset
10s	Bush and sickle. Engraved
10s	Ship. Typeset
20s	Woman operating thread winder. Engraved
20s	Horse. Typeset. Printed in red and black

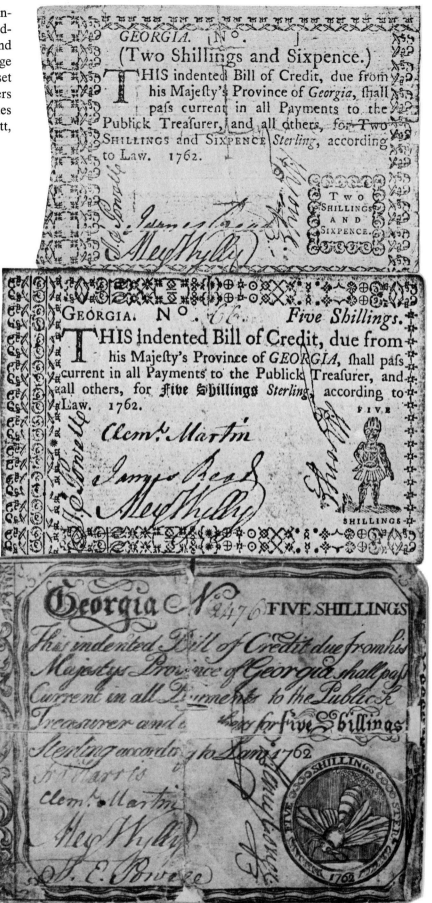

March 25, 1762

£540 sterling (£440 and £100) in indented engraved Certificates authorized by the Dec. 19, 1761 Act to fortify Cockspur Island and Midway River. Receivable for taxes until Mar. 30, 1767 and invalid thereafter. Signers are Grey Elliott, John Graham, Lewis Johnson, Noble Jones, and Alexander Wylly.

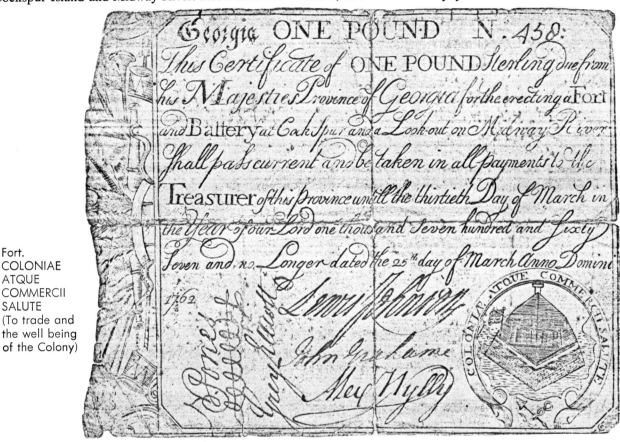

£1 Fort.
COLONIAE
ATQUE
COMMERCII
SALUTE
(To trade and
the well being
of the Colony)

July 8, 1765

£650 sterling in typeset red and black Certificates authorized by the Mar. 25, 1762 Act for fort, guard house and barracks construction. Receivable for taxes until Sept. 30, 1768 and invalid thereafter. Signers are William Ewen, Patrick Houstoun, Lewis Johnson, Noble Jones, and Alexander Wylly.

£1 House [1,120]

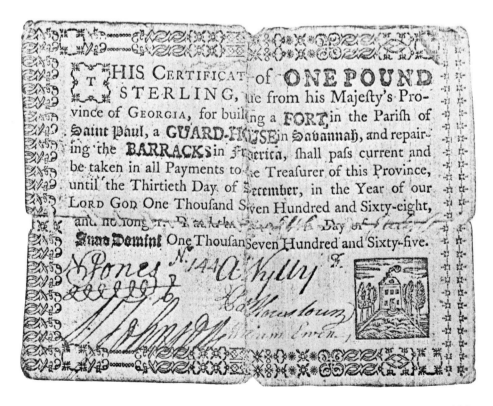

1766-7 Written Dates

£1,815 sterling in red and black typeset Certificates authorized by the Mar. 6, 1766 Act for encouraging settlers and rebuilding of the Savannah Court House. Receivable for taxes until Mar. 1, 1771 and invalid thereafter. Signers are Grey Elliott, William Ewen, Noble Jones, John Smith, and Alexander Wylly.

£1   SAVANNAH COURT-HOUSE
[2,523] Ⓤ

1768-70 Tax Certificates

Tax Anticipation Certificates authorized under the April 11, 1768 Act (£3,375 4s1d), the Dec. 24, 1768 Act (£3,046 16s8d), and the May 10, 1770 Act (£3,355 9s¼d). Receivable for taxes. Printed in red and black from set type. Handwritten dates. Signer is Noble Jones.

£5

1769 Lighthouse Certificates

£2,200 sterling in red and black typeset Certificates authorized by the Dec. 24, 1768 Act for rebuilding the lighthouse on Tybee Island. Receivable for taxes until May 1, 1772 and invalid thereafter. At base of note the comical counterfeiting warning is upside down, the words reading from right to left like Hebrew, the words are in both English and Latin, and the word order is scrambled. Reconstructed, the warning reads TO COUNTERFEIT IS DEATH WITHOUT BENEFIT OF CLERGY VIDE ACT (see Act). Signers are Grey Elliott, Noble Jones, Noble Wimberly Jones, John Milledge, and John Smith.

£1   Lighthouse. Written "9" in date
£1   Lighthouse. Printed "9" in date Ⓤ

1773

£4,299 sterling in Certificates authorized by the Sept. 29, 1773 Act to redeem all prior issues and to meet expenses. Receivable for taxes or exchangeable until Sept. 29, 1776 and invalid thereafter. This issue also must have been used to comply with another Sept. 29, 1773 Act for £520 to replace "decayed" bills issued by the Commissioners of the General Loan and £73 in bills destroyed by fire. Printed from type in red and black. Signers are Joseph Clay, Samuel Farley, Noble Jones, Noble Wimberly Jones, James E. Powell, Thomas Shruder, and William Young.

20s Ⓤ

(1774)

£800 sterling in typeset Certificates authorized by the Mar. 12, 1774 Act for military purposes. Receivable for taxes until Dec. 31, 1777 and invalid thereafter.

Signers are Nathaniel Hall, James Houstoun, John Jamieson, Noble Jones, Thomas Netherclift, and Thomas Shruder.

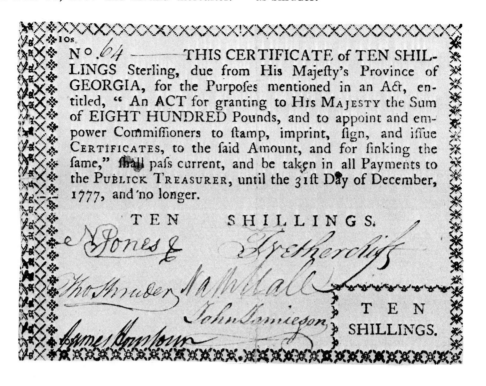

1s	[1,000]
2s	[500]
2s6d	[800]
5s	[1,200]
10s	[600] Ⓤ

Unknown Savannah Issuer ★ 1775

Private promissory note payable to bearer and issued in Savannah. Apparently printed by the same printer who printed Colony and State issues.

6d

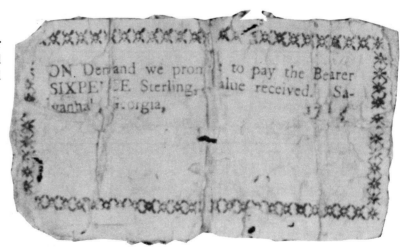

1775

£10,000 sterling in typeset Certificates authorized by the Provincial Congress of Georgia in a July 12, 1775 Resolve. Issuable as the Provincial Congress or Council of Safety required and to be redeemed three years after peace between Great Britain and America. Lower denominations are small and are printed in black. Higher denominations are large and are printed in red and black. Signers are Philip Box, Archibald Bulloch, Elisha Butler, Basil Cowpens, William Ewen, William Gibbons, John Houstoun, William LeConte, James Maxwell, William Maxwell, William O'Bryen, Edward Telfair, and George Walton.* Five signers were used on each Certificate.

*Signer of the Declaration of Independence.

1s6d	Sheaf of wheat
2s6d	
5s	One crown
10s	Two crowns
20s	
60s	
£5	Indian with bow and arrows

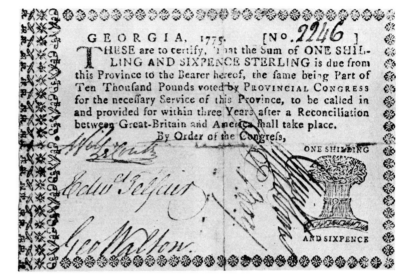

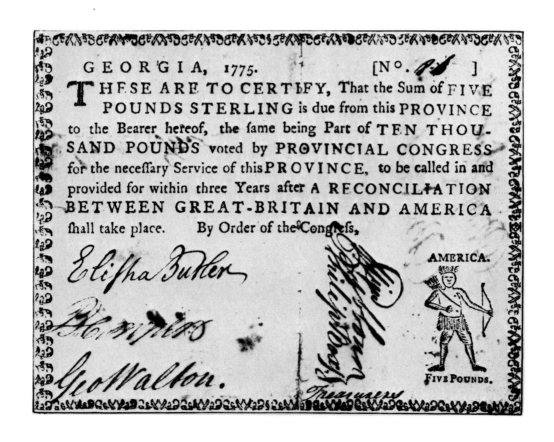

1776 Sterling Denominations

£12,572 19s in Certificates authorized by the Provincial Congress in 1775 to replace all outstanding issues. There are five sizes of certificates, the size increasing with the denomination. The two highest denominations are printed in red and black and the others are in black. Borders and text are typeset. The first 5s certificates had a crown as a vignette which, on being considered unpatriotic, was removed in favor of a light blue circular seal. Lower denominations are usually unnumbered. Signers are Peter Bard, William Ewen, William Few, William Gibbons, James Habersham, George Houstoun, Peter LaVien, Lachlan McGillivray, William O'Bryen, William Stephens, Samuel Stirk, Edward Telfair, Nehemiah Wade, Andrew E. Wells, and Richard Wylly.

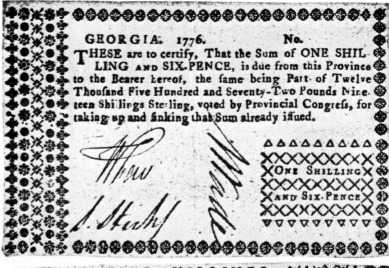

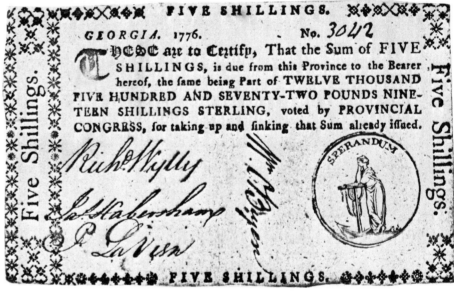

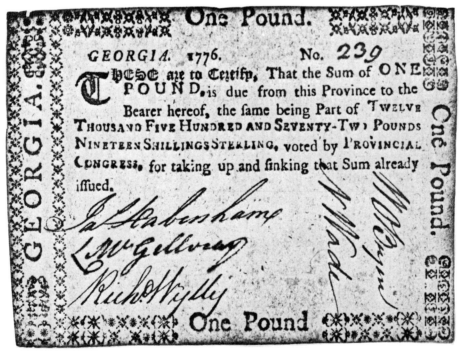

GEORGIA

		Good	V.G.	Fine
3d	Six border varieties	75.00	100.00	140.00

(a) Top, right and bottom borders each have different ornaments.
(b) Spiral type ornaments in top and bottom borders.
(c) Question mark in center of top and right borders.
(d) Odd ornament near right end of bottom border and 14 X ornaments to right of odd ornament in top border.
(e) Left border has almost one full line of symbols representing the earth and its equator.
(f) Odd ornament near right end of bottom border and 13 X ornaments to right of odd ornament in top border.

		Good	V.G.	Fine
6d	Seven border varieties	75.00	100.00	140.00

Same border varieties as (a), (c) and (d) of **3d**.
(g) Question marks in center of right and bottom borders.
(h) Diagonal colon in top border; exclamation point in right border; and period in bottom border.
(i) Colon near center of top and bottom borders; question mark in center of right border.
(j) Colon near center of top and bottom borders; in right border question mark is above middle.

		Good	V.G.	Fine
1s	Three border varieties	75.00	100.00	140.00

(k) The connection between the upper and lower portions of each of the two large border ornaments next to the inside line of the left border is on the right side.
(l) The connection between the upper and lower portions of each of the two large border ornaments next to the inside line of the left border is on the left side.
(m) The large ornament inside the juncture of the left and bottom borders is not part of either row.

		Good	V.G.	Fine
1s6d	Five border varieties	75.00	100.00	140.00

(n) Odd ornament near right end of top border; bottom ornament in middle line of left border has a period above it.
(o) Odd ornament near right end of top border; bottom ornament in middle line of left border is a small solid oval.
(p) Exclamation point in center of bottom border.
(q) Denomination box contains no X ornaments.
(r) Odd ornament near center of left side of top border.

		Good	V.G.	Fine
2s6d	Horse. Denomination along both right and left sides	90.00	125.00	175.00
2s6d	Horse. Ornaments instead of denomination along right side	90.00	125.00	175.00
5s	Crown. Two border varieties	125.00	175.00	250.00

(s) Seven ornaments between inside of left border and F in bottom border.
(t) Eight ornaments between inside of left border and F in bottom border.

		Good	V.G.	Fine
5s	Blue seal with SPERANDUM (One must hope). Border identical to variety (t) of **5s** with Crown	150.00	225.00	325.00
10s	Three border varieties	150.00	225.00	325.00

(u) No upright cross near each side of denomination in bottom border.
(v) Single crossbar on upright cross near each side of denomination in bottom border.
(w) Two crossbars on upright cross near each side of denomination in bottom border.

		Good	V.G.	Fine
£1	Same border as variety (u) of **10s**	150.00	225.00	325.00

GEORGIA

The 1776 and 1777 Georgia Dollar Emissions

The order of emission and the amounts of the Georgia dollar denomination issues of 1776 and 1777 are not determinable primarily because (1) the Council of Safety authorized expenditures from time to time without specifying any paper money detail; (2) many official records were burned during the British occupation of Savannah; (3) James Johnston who had been the official colony printer since 1763 remained loyal to England during the American Revolution and his shop, after confiscation, was operated by inexperienced personnel; and (4) the borders, text colors, seals, seal colors, dates, and denominations lack uniformity.

The 1776 and 1777 paper currency was printed in different sizes and on sheets containing either 4, 8, 9, 10 or 12 certificates. The certificates were generally composed of standard letters and printer's ornaments, each certificate on a sheet having a different arrangement of ornaments on its borders. Those denominations below $1 were always printed in black in one operation. Those of $1 and over usually had the border and some standard text printed in black in such a way that any desired denomination and some additional text could be added in red. Sometimes the portion printed in red was arranged so that several of the same denomination were printed on one sheet, resulting in the same denomination of an issue having many different borders. On other occasions, after a needed number of a denomination was completed, the denomination of some certificates was changed so that several different denominations would contain identical borders.

The first portion of the integral denominations of the June 8, 1777 issue had the word "in" printed in black in the sixth line while other words in the line were printed in red, but subsequently all of the sixth line was printed in red.

Sometimes minor border variations occur because one or more pieces of type broke or fell out in the course of printing and were replaced with ornamental type which differed from the original type.

On some sheets including the June 8, 1777 and September 10, 1777 issues the same serial number was written on all certificates. Where more than one of the same denomination was printed on such a sheet this resulted in more than one of the same denomination carrying the same serial number.

One of a group of seven circular emblematic seals was assigned to each denomination. These were applied by a separate overprinting of a sheet. A transposition of the seals for the $2 and $4 occurred when the 1776 light blue seal issue was prepared, but the error was noticed and corrected on the balance of the issue. In the 1777 issue the same seals impressed on the lower denominations were reused on the high denominations. Red, orange, green, blue-green, light blue, dark blue, and maroon colors were used in inking seals. When the orange ink supply was used up on one 1776 issue, green ink (or a color which faded to green) was used on the balance of the issue, so that otherwise identical bills are found with two seal colors. The June 8, 1777 and Sept. 10, 1777 authorizations have red seals for the four lower integral denominations and dark blue seals for the four higher ones. Some of the seals wore out from use and new seals with the same insignia were engraved. Differences between substituted seals can be readily noticed.

All 1776 issues have only the year as the date except for one issue which has no date at all. The denominations are quite "odd" and "numerous" in the 1776-1777 period and include $1/10, 1/5, 1/4, 1/3, 2/5, 1/2, 2/3, 3/4, 4/5, 1, 2, 3, 4, 5, 6, 7, 8, 9, 10, 11, 13, 15, 17 and 20, as well as eight denominations in pounds, shillings and pence.

Harley L. Freeman is entitled to particular recognition for his pioneering work over many years in the study of the Georgia border varieties and other Georgia numismatic data from which this listing was developed.

TRANSLATION OF MOTTOES ON SEALS

SUSTINE RECTUM   (Support what's right)

SI COLLIGIMUS FRANGIMUR   (If we collide we break)

LIBERTAS CARIOR AURO   (Freedom is more precious than gold)

OPRESSA SURGIT   (After being crushed it rises)

NEMO ME IMPUNE LACESSET   (No one will provoke me with impunity)

ET DEUS OMNIPOTINCE   (And Almighty God).

OMNIPOTENS is misspelled as OMNIPOTINCE.

ULTIMA RADIO   (The ultimate reckoning). RATIO is misspelled as RADIO.

GEORGIA

1776 Light Blue Seal
Dollar Denominations

Indented certificates printed in red and black on a sheet containing four subjects with different borders of ornamental type. Light blue circular seals. By error the seals for the $2 and $4 were transposed on part of the issue. Bills with borders (c) and (d) are also found in the 1776 maroon seal issue and the dateless issue. Signers are Peter Bard, William Ewen, William Gibbons, James Habersham, George Houstoun, Peter LaVien, Lachlan McGillivray, William O'Bryen, William Stephens, Edward Telfair, and Richard Wylly.

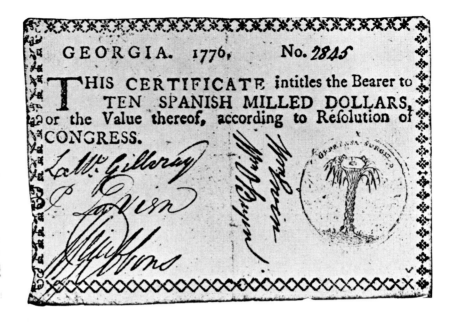

		Good	V.G.	Fine
$1	Justice. SUSTINE RECTUM. Two border varieties	75.00	100.00	140.00
	Same borders as $4 varieties (a) and (b) of this issue.			
$2	Floating jugs. SI COLLIGIMUS FRANGIMUR. Two border varieties	75.00	100.00	140.00
	Same borders as $4 varieties (c) and (d) of this issue.			
$2	Liberty Cap. LIBERTAS CARIOR AURO. (Erroneous seal)	100.00	125.00	175.00
	Same border as $4 variety (c) of this issue.			
$4	Liberty Cap. LIBERTAS CARIOR AURO. Four border varieties	75.00	100.00	140.00
	(a) All right border ornaments are identical.			
	(b) Odd ornament below middle in right border.			
	(c) Odd ornament above middle in right border.			
	(d) Exclamation point at center of inside line of left border.			
$4	Floating jugs. SI COLLIGIMUS FRANGIMUR. (Erroneous seal)	100.00	125.00	175.00
	Same border as $4 variety (d) of this issue.			
$10	Millstone on palm tree. OPPRESSA SURGIT. Two border varieties	100.00	125.00	175.00
	Same borders as $4 varieties (a) and (b) of this issue.			
$20	Rattlesnake. NEMO ME IMPUNE LACESSET	125.00	150.00	225.00

1776 Maroon Seal

Indented certificates printed in red and black on a sheet containing four subjects. The $10 and $20 have no other border than an engraved script GEORGIA on each side which cut was reused on the $40 of the 1778 certificates.

The $2 and $4 are from the same printing form used for the 1776 light blue seal issue. Same signers as the 1776 light blue seal issue.

		Good	V.G.	Fine
$2	Floating jugs. SI COLLIGIMUS FRANGIMUR	85.00	120.00	165.00
	Same border as light blue seal variety (c).			
$4	Liberty Cap. LIBERTAS CARIOR AURO	85.00	120.00	165.00
	Same border as light blue seal variety (d).			
$10	Millstone on palm tree. OPPRESSA SURGIT	90.00	125.00	175.00
$20	Rattlesnake. NEMO ME IMPUNE LACESSET	90.00	125.00	175.00

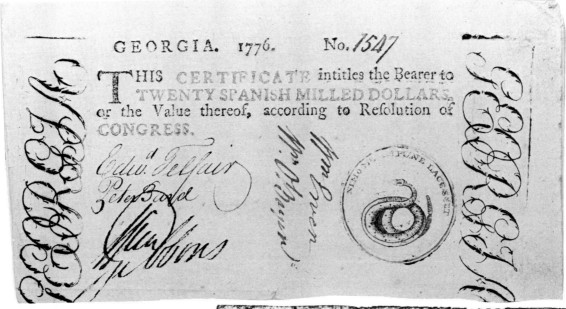

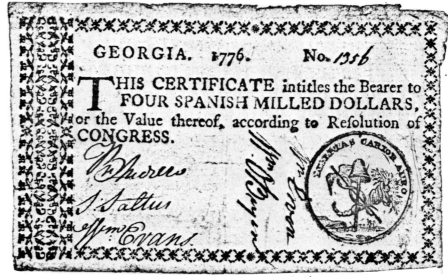

1776 Orange or Green Seal

Certificates printed in red and black on a sheet containing nine subjects with different borders of ornamental type. Orange ink was used for circular seals on all denominations until that ink supply was consumed. Greenish ink or ink which faded to that color was then used to stamp seals on the balance of the issue. Signers are Benjamin Andrew, William Evans, William Ewen, William O'Bryen, and Samuel Saltus.

		Good	V.G.	Fine
$1	Justice. SUSTINE RECTUM. Orange seal. Nine border varieties	80.00	110.00	150.00

(a) 13 ornaments to right of sunburst in top and bottom borders.
(b) Two different alternating ornaments in top, right and bottom borders.
(c) In top and bottom borders first ornament next to inside of left border differs from others.
(d) 13 ornaments to right of right vertical line in bottom border.
(e) 14 ornaments to right of right vertical line in bottom border.
(f) Two sunbursts in center of left border and 14 ornaments to right of sunburst in top and bottom borders.
(g) Four sunbursts in center of left border and 12 ornaments to right of sunburst in top border.
(h) Four sunbursts in center of left border and 14 ornaments to right of sunburst in top border.
(i) Some ornaments in three inside rows of left border match ornaments in other three borders. Also 14 ornaments to right of sunburst in top and bottom borders.

		Good	V.G.	Fine
$1	Justice. SUSTINE RECTUM. Green seal. Nine border varieties	90.00	125.00	175.00
	Same borders as $1 Orange seal varieties (a) through (i).			
$2	Floating jugs. SI COLLIGIMUS FRANGIMUR. Orange seal. At least four border varieties	80.00	110.00	150.00
	Same borders as $1 Orange seal varieties (f), (g), (h) and (i).			
$2	Floating jugs. SI COLLIGIMUS FRANGIMUR. Green seal. At least five border varieties	90.00	125.00	175.00
	Same borders as $1 Orange seal varieties (d), (f), (g), (h) and (i).			

		Good	V.G.	Fine
$4	Liberty Cap. LIBERTAS CARIOR AURO. Orange seal. Three border varieties	80.00	110.00	150.00
	Same borders as $1 Orange seal varieties (a), (b) and (c).			
$4	Liberty Cap. LIBERTAS CARIOR AURO. Green seal. Three border varieties	90.00	125.00	175.00
	Same borders as $1 Orange seal varieties (a), (b) and (c).			
$10	Millstone on palm tree. OPPRESSA SURGIT. Orange seal. Three border varieties ...	90.00	125.00	175.00
	Same borders as $1 Orange seal varieties (d), (e) and (f).			
$20	Rattlesnake. NEMO ME IMPUNE LACESSET. Orange seal. Three border varieties ...	100.00	135.00	185.00
	Same borders as $1 Orange seal varieties (g), (h) and (i).			

1776 Fractional Dollar Denominations

Typeset certificates printed in black on a sheet containing eight subjects with different borders of ornamental type. Signers are Benjamin Andrew, William Evans, William O'Bryen, Samuel Saltus, Thomas Stone, and Nehemiah Wade.

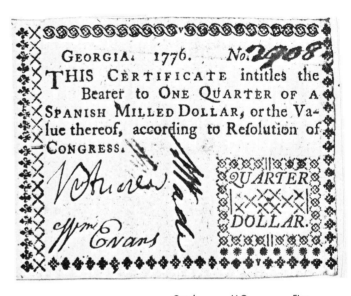

		Good	V.G.	Fine
$1/4	Eight border varieties	80.00	110.00	150.00
	(a) Two vertical lines separated by ornament on lowest line of denomination box.			
	(b) Nine ornaments in each line of left border and two adjacent vertical lines on lowest line of denomination box.			
	(c) Seven large and four small ornaments in each line of left border.			
	(d) Small v close to right end of bottom border.			
	(e) Two adjacent vertical lines in center of top border.			
	(f) Small v is seventh ornament from right end of bottom border.			
	(g) Only eleven ornaments to right of vertical line in bottom border.			
	(h) Line near center of right border.			
$1/2	Four border varieties	90.00	125.00	175.00
	Same borders as varieties (a), (b), (c) and (d) of this issue.			

1776 Blue-green Seal

Typeset certificates printed in red and black on a sheet containing eight subjects with different borders of ornamental type. Blue-green circular seals. The same borders are also found on the $2 and $3 of the 1777 issue. Same signers as on the 1776 Fractional Dollar Denomination issue.

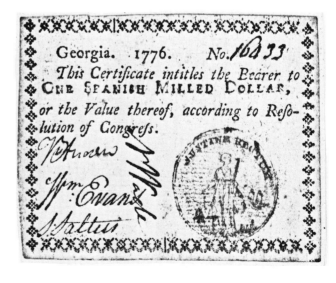

GEORGIA

		Good	V.G.	Fine
$1	Justice. SUSTINE RECTUM. Eight border varieties	90.00	125.00	175.00

(a) Spiral type ornaments on all four borders.

(b) Hourglass ornaments in center of top and bottom borders and ornaments resembling a large X superimposed on a small square in both side borders.

(c) 16 ornaments to right of vertical line in top border and 12 ornaments to right of vertical line in bottom border.

(d) Central ornament in top border has horizontal lines on its top and bottom.

(e) 12 ornaments to right of the vertical line in the top and bottom borders. Diamond ornaments on side borders.

(f) 12 ornaments to right of vertical line in top border and 11 ornaments to right of vertical line in bottom border. Diamond shaped ornaments on side borders.

(g) Hourglass type ornament in center of top and bottom borders and diamond shaped ornaments in side borders.

(h) Question mark in center of both top and bottom borders.

$4	Liberty cap. LIBERTAS CARIOR AURO. Two border varieties	150.00	200.00	250.00

Same borders as varieties (b) and (c) of this issue.

1776 Black Vignette

Indented typeset Certificate, being the only issue printed in red and black with the denomination only in black. Only issue payable in "Gold or Silver." Similar to (1776) Undated issue in style of black engraved vignette and in certificate size. Signers are Benjamin Andrew, William Ewen, Jonathan B. Girardeau, William Goodgion, William LeConte, John Martin, William O'Bryen, Quintin Pooler, Robert Rae, Samuel Saltus, and John Wereat.

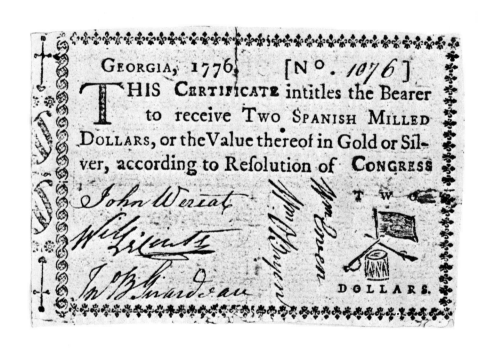

		Good	V.G.	Fine
$2	Flag, drum, sword and gun	125.00	200.00	325.00

(1776) Undated

Certificates printed in red and black in a sheet of eight subjects but lacking any date. The same style and size as the 1776 Black Vignette issue which may be a part of this issue. The tenure of the signers serving on the Council of Safety indicates issuance in late 1776 or early 1777. Each denomination has a distinctive engraved vignette in black. The border of a variety of $4 certificate is the same as both a variety of the $4 light blue seal issue and the $4 maroon seal issue. Signers are Benjamin Andrew, Adam F. Brisbane, Nathan Brownson, William Bryan, Richard Burkloe, Charles F. Chevalier, Jonathan Cochran, Job Colcock, John Elliott, William Ewen, Jonathan B. Girardeau, Joseph Gibbons, William Glascock, John Houstoun, William Jackson, William LeConte, William O'Bryen, Quintin Pooler, Daniel Roberts. John Screven, John Stark, John A. Treutlen, and John Wereat.

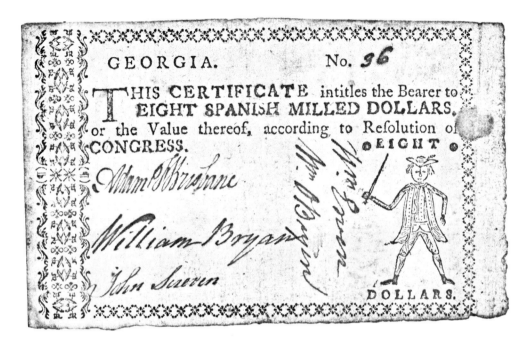

			Good	V.G.	Fine
$3	Crossed cannon		125.00	200.00	325.00
$4	Frontiersman. Two border varieties		125.00	200.00	325.00
	(a) Ornaments on inside line of left border are varied. Same border as variety (d) of light blue seal and maroon seal issues.				
	(b) Ornaments on inside line of left border are identical.				
$5	Barrel beehive. Two border varieties		125.00	200.00	325.00
	(c) Small cross in center of bottom border. Same border as variety (c) of light blue seal and maroon seal issues.				
	(d) Two exclamation points in top border and two inverted exclamation points in bottom border.				
$8	Man holding a cane. Two border varieties		125.00	200.00	325.00
	(e) Two horizontal lines in center of left border.				
	(f) Two parentheses at center of left border.				
$10	Cannon		125.00	200.00	325.00

1777 (No Resolution Date)

Typeset certificates printed in red and black. Circular blue-green seals except on $3 which has a black typeset denominational design. The $2 and $3 are small in size and were printed in sheets of eight certificates with the same border forms used for the 1776 blue-green seal issue. The higher denominations are larger in size and were printed in sheets of nine certificates with the same border forms used for the 1776 orange or green seal issue. Signers are Benjamin Andrew, William Evans, William Ewen, Jonathan B. Girardeau, William O'Bryen, Samuel Saltus, Thomas Stone, and Nehemiah Wade.

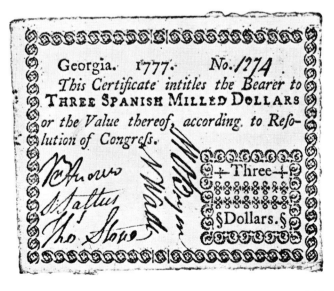

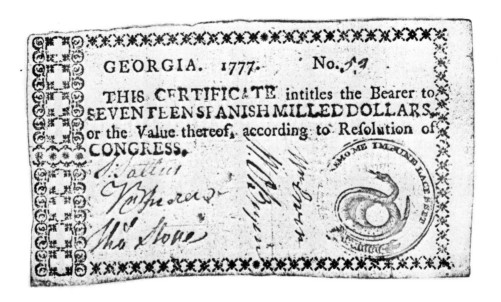

		Good	V.G.	Fine
$2	Floating jugs. SI COLLIGIMUS FRANGIMUR. Four border varieties	125.00	200.00	325.00
	Same borders as varieties (a), (b), (c) and (d) of the 1776 blue-green seal issue.			
$3	Typeset denomination design. Nine border varieties	90.00	125.00	175.00
	Same borders as varieties (a) through (h) of the 1776 blue-green seal issue. Border variety (b) has two variations in the interior denomination box ornamentation, sunbursts and hourglasses.			
$4	Liberty Cap. LIBERTAS CARIOR AURO. Same border as (c) of this issue	200.00	300.00	400.00
$5	Cannon. ET DEUS OMNIPOTINCE. Nine border varieties	110.00	140.00	200.00

(a) Ornaments do not reach intersection of right and bottom borders.

(b) Two sunbursts near center of bottom border.

(c) Question mark and exclamation point in bottom border. Same as border (e) of 1776 orange seal issue.

(d) 14 ornaments to right of sunbursts in top and bottom borders and no question mark in right border. Same as border (f) of 1776 orange seal issue.

(e) The two vertical lines separated by an ornament in the top border are directly over two similar lines in the bottom border.

(f) The two vertical lines separated by an ornament in the top border are slightly to the left of similar lines in the bottom border.

(g) 14 ornaments to right of sunburst in both top and bottom borders and question mark in right border.

(h) Sunburst flanked equally by ornaments in top border and unequally on bottom border.

(i) Sunburst to right of center of ornaments in top border and to left of center in bottom border.

$7	Hand. ULTIMA RADIO. Four border varieties	125.00	200.00	325.00
	Same borders as varieties (d), (e), (f) and (i) of this issue.			
$9	Justice. SUSTINE RECTUM. Four border varieties	125.00	200.00	325.00
	Same borders as varieties (a), (g), (h) and (i) of this issue.			
$11	Floating jugs. SI COLLIGIMUR FRANGIMUR. At least eight border varieties including border varieties (a), (b), (c), (d), (e), (g), (h) and (i) of this issue	200.00	300.00	400.00
$13	Liberty Cap. LIBERTAS CARIOR AURO. At least six border varieties including border varieties (c), (d), (e), (f), (h) and (i) of this issue	200.00	300.00	400.00
$15	Millstone on palm tree. OPPRESSA SURGIT. Nine border varieties. Same borders as varieties (a), (b), (c), (d), (e), (f), (g), (h) and (i) of this issue	125.00	200.00	325.00
$17	Rattlesnake. NEMO ME IMMUNE LACESSET. At least six border varieties including border varieties (b), (c), (d), (g), (h) and (i) of this issue	200.00	300.00	400.00

GEORGIA

1777 (June 8, 1777 Resolution)

Typeset Certificates payable in Continental Currency instead of Spanish dollars when Georgia exchange was 155.8 for 100 in specie. Issued pursuant to the June 8, 1777 Resolution to support troops, etc. Denominations of $⁴⁄₅ and under are printed in black and are slightly smaller than the higher denominations which are printed in red and black. Because of alignment difficulty in printing the red portion of the sixth line of the first group of certificates of $1 and over, the type was reset so that the sixth line would be only four words long and would be printed entirely in red. Red circular seals on $1 through $4 denominations and dark blue circular seals on $5 through $8. Signers are Edward Langworthy, William O'Bryen, Nehemiah Wade, Joseph Wood and Richard Wylly. Two or three signatures are on the fractional denominations and five signatures on the others.

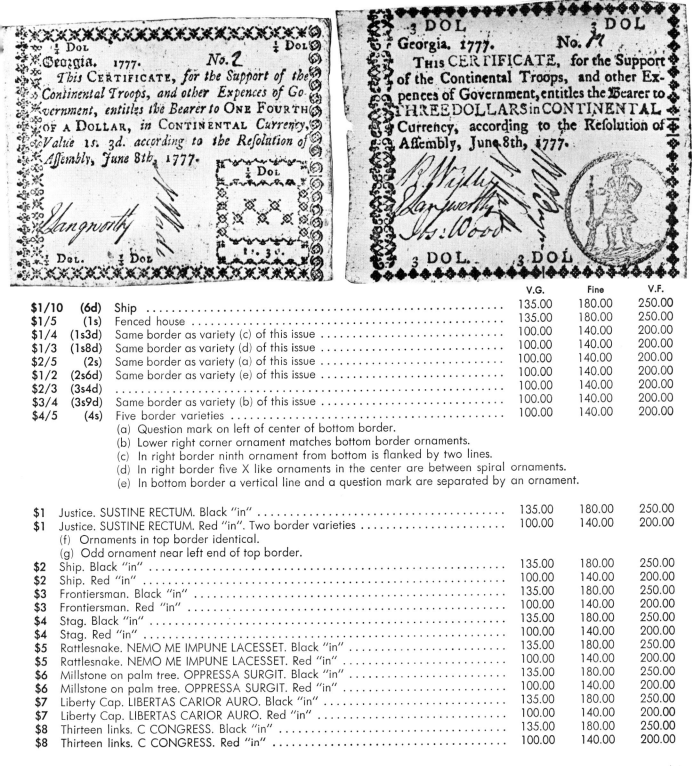

			V.G.	Fine	V.F.
$1/10	(6d)	Ship	135.00	180.00	250.00
$1/5	(1s)	Fenced house	135.00	180.00	250.00
$1/4	(1s3d)	Same border as variety (c) of this issue	100.00	140.00	200.00
$1/3	(1s8d)	Same border as variety (d) of this issue	100.00	140.00	200.00
$2/5	(2s)	Same border as variety (a) of this issue	100.00	140.00	200.00
$1/2	(2s6d)	Same border as variety (e) of this issue	100.00	140.00	200.00
$2/3	(3s4d)		100.00	140.00	200.00
$3/4	(3s9d)	Same border as variety (b) of this issue	100.00	140.00	200.00
$4/5	(4s)	Five border varieties	100.00	140.00	200.00

(a) Question mark on left of center of bottom border.
(b) Lower right corner ornament matches bottom border ornaments.
(c) In right border ninth ornament from bottom is flanked by two lines.
(d) In right border five X like ornaments in the center are between spiral ornaments.
(e) In bottom border a vertical line and a question mark are separated by an ornament.

		V.G.	Fine	V.F.
$1	Justice. SUSTINE RECTUM. Black "in"	135.00	180.00	250.00
$1	Justice. SUSTINE RECTUM. Red "in". Two border varieties	100.00	140.00	200.00

(f) Ornaments in top border identical.
(g) Odd ornament near left end of top border.

		V.G.	Fine	V.F.
$2	Ship. Black "in"	135.00	180.00	250.00
$2	Ship. Red "in"	100.00	140.00	200.00
$3	Frontiersman. Black "in"	135.00	180.00	250.00
$3	Frontiersman. Red "in"	100.00	140.00	200.00
$4	Stag. Black "in"	135.00	180.00	250.00
$4	Stag. Red "in"	100.00	140.00	200.00
$5	Rattlesnake. NEMO ME IMPUNE LACESSET. Black "in"	135.00	180.00	250.00
$5	Rattlesnake. NEMO ME IMPUNE LACESSET. Red "in"	100.00	140.00	200.00
$6	Millstone on palm tree. OPPRESSA SURGIT. Black "in"	135.00	180.00	250.00
$6	Millstone on palm tree. OPPRESSA SURGIT. Red "in"	100.00	140.00	200.00
$7	Liberty Cap. LIBERTAS CARIOR AURO. Black "in"	135.00	180.00	250.00
$7	Liberty Cap. LIBERTAS CARIOR AURO. Red "in"	100.00	140.00	200.00
$8	Thirteen links. C CONGRESS. Black "in"	135.00	180.00	250.00
$8	Thirteen links. C CONGRESS. Red "in"	100.00	140.00	200.00

GEORGIA

1777 (September 10, 1777 Resolution)

Typeset certificates issued pursuant to the Sept. 10, 1777 Resolution to support Continental troops, etc. Payable in Continental Currency at a time when Georgia exchange was 187.9 to 100 in specie. Denominations of $4/5 and under are printed in black and are smaller than the $1 and over which are printed in red and black. Red circular seals on the $1 through $4 denominations and dark blue circular seals on the $5 through $8. Signers are C. F. Chevalier, W. Hohendorf, William O'Bryen, Nehemiah Wade, and Richard Wylly. Two or three signatures are on fractional denominations and five signatures on the others.

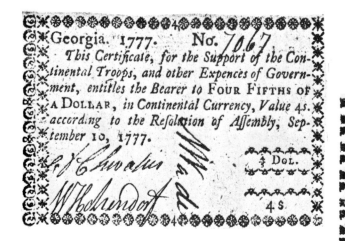

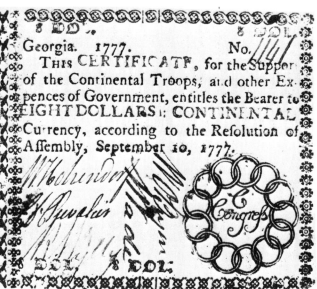

		V.G.	Fine	V.F.
$1/5	Four border varieties	125.00	175.00	225.00

Same borders as varieties (c), (h), (i) and (j) of this issue. In variety (c) the text contains Value 1s. In variety (h) the denomination in the box is inverted.

$1/2	Three border varieties	125.00	175.00	225.00

(h) Number 9 in center of top border.
(i) 11 ornaments to right of e in bottom border.
(j) 12 ornaments to right of e in bottom border.

$4/5	Seven border varieties	125.00	175.00	225.00

(a) Vertical line in center of top border.
(b) Oval shaped floral ornaments in top and bottom borders and no period after DOL or after 4s in denomination box.
(c) Oval shaped floral ornaments in top and bottom borders and period after DOL but not after 4s.
(d) Oval shaped floral ornaments in top and bottom borders and period after both DOL and 4s.
(e) Lower right corner ornament matches right border only and 4 is in top border.
(f) 12 ornaments to right of 4 in bottom border but no 4 in top border.
(g) 14 ornaments to right of 4 in bottom border but no 4 in top border.

$1	Justice. SUSTINE RECTUM	125.00	175.00	225.00
$2	Ship	125.00	175.00	225.00
$3	Frontiersman	125.00	175.00	225.00
$4	Stag	125.00	175.00	225.00
$5	Rattlesnake. NEMO ME IMMUNE LACESSET	125.00	175.00	225.00
$6	Millstone on palm tree. OPPRESSA SURGIT	125.00	175.00	225.00
$7	Liberty Cap. LIBERTAS CARIOR AURO	125.00	175.00	225.00
$8	Thirteen links. C CONGRESS	125.00	175.00	225.00

GEORGIA

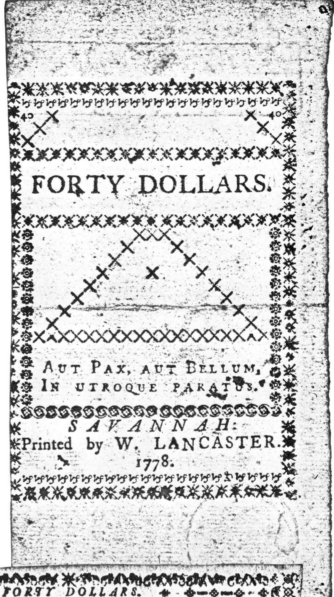

1778

£150,000 in Bills of Credit payable out of the proceeds of forfeited Tory estates pursuant to the May 4, 1778 Act when Georgia exchange was 531 for 100 in specie. Printed by W. Lancaster of Savannah in red and black on both face and back from typeset letters and ornaments previously used for other issues. Greenish blue circular seal keyed to each denomination. The engraved script GEORGIA, previously used on the $10 and $20 1776 Maroon Seal issue, was impressed in greenish blue on the $40 denomination. Printed in double sheets with four faces and four backs on each side. Signers are William Few, Charles Kent, William Maxwill, Thomas Netherclift, William O'Bryen, Nehemiah Wade, and Richard Wylly.

		V.G.	Fine	V.F.
$20	Rattlesnake. NEMO ME IMPUNE LACESSET (No one will provoke me with impunity). Four border varieties	135.00	180.00	250.00

    (a) Circular ornaments on outer row of left border of face and third ornament left of vertical bar in center of bottom border differs from adjacent ornaments.

    (b) Circular ornaments on outer row of left border of face and third ornament left of vertical bar in center of bottom border is the same as adjacent ornaments.

    (c) Floral ornaments on outer row of left border of face and 17 ornaments to right of vertical bar in bottom border.

    (d) Floral ornaments on outer row of left border of face and 20 ornaments to right of vertical bar in bottom row.

		V.G.	Fine	V.F.
$30	Wild boar. AUT MORS, AUT VICTORIA LAETA (Either death or victory is pleasing). Two border varieties	135.00	180.00	250.00

Same borders as varieties (a) and (b) of this issue.

		V.G.	Fine	V.F.
$40	Dove and Sword. AUT PAX, AUT BELLUM, IN UTROQUE PARATUS (Either peace or war, prepared for both). Two border varieties	135.00	180.00	250.00

Same borders as varieties (c) and (d) of this issue.

January 9, 1782 Resolve

£22,100 in indented typeset bearer certificates issued for military and public expense. Redeemable by Nov. 1, 1782 and receivable as specie in payment, for purchases of confiscated Tory estates. Denominations in pounds to be inserted by hand. Signers are Joseph Habersham, Lyman Hall*, Jared Irwin, and George Walton*. The signatures on the illustration are written by an amanuensis.

*Signer of the Declaration of Independence.

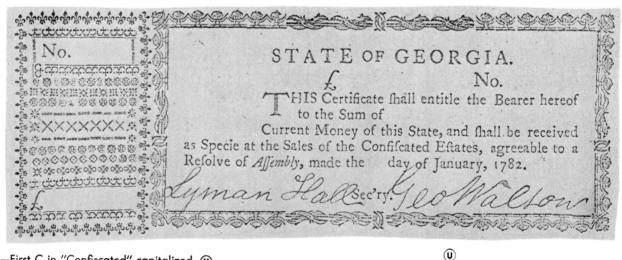

£—First C in "Confiscated" capitalized. Ⓤ
£—First c in "confiscated" in lower case. Ⓤ

Ⓤ

October 16, 1786

£50,000 in legal tender Bills of Credit authorized by the Aug. 14, 1786 Act to be loaned on real estate mortgage security. A value of 4s8d to the dollar was specified. The original redemption date of Aug. 14, 1790 was extended to Jan. 15, 1794 by the Feb. 1, 1789 Act, but legal tender status was revoked after August 14, 1790 by the Dec. 23, 1789 Act. By the Feb. 22, 1785 Ordinance all Georgia paper money issued during the Revolution was declared redeemable for taxes at $1000 for $1 in specie up to Aug. 22, 1785. This date was extended by Act of Feb. 13, 1786 to Nov. 13, 1786 after which date such issues were unredeemable. Printed by John E. Smith of Augusta on Dutch paper watermarked HONIG & ZOONEN. The vignette was engraved by Abernethie and featured the 1777 Georgia Constitution and PRO BONO PUBLICO (For the public good). A counterfeit warning was added for the first time since the 1769 Lighthouse issue. Signers are J. H. P. Carnes, William Daniell, W. Freeman, George Jones, J. Jackson, T. McCall, T. H. Napier, and W. Steele.

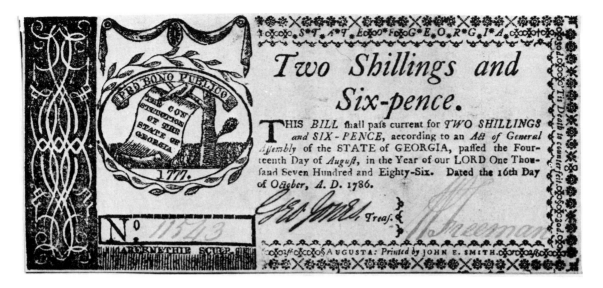

	V.G.	Fine	V.F.			V.G.	Fine	V.F.
6d [25,641]	125.00	175.00	250.00	5s [25,642]	125.00	175.00	250.00
1s [25,642]	125.00	175.00	250.00	10s [25,642]	125.00	175.00	250.00
2s6d [25,642]	125.00	175.00	250.00	20s [25,641]	125.00	175.00	250.00

Bank of the United States (Savannah Office) ★ 1793, etc.

The Office of Discount and Deposit in Savannah of the first Bank of the United States had issued $825,950 in bank notes by 1811. The bank notes were in the same form as other branch bank notes but were usually made payable to the order of and endorsed by the president of the Savannah branch. A description of the bank notes and other detail will be found under the parent bank in Philadelphia and other offices.

A flying eagle bearing the Arms of United States:	$5	$10	$20	$50	$100
A heraldic eagle with 13 stars surrounding its head:	$5	$10	$20	$50	$100
A heraldic eagle in an oval frame containing 15 stars:	$5	$10	$20	$50	$100

GEORGIA REFERENCES

Harley L. Freeman, "Bills of Credit of Georgia 1732-86," *The Numismatist* (July 1931).

William Estill Heath, "The Early Colonial Money System of Georgia," *The Georgia Historical Quarterly* (July 1935).

Milton B. Smith, "The Lighthouse on Tybee Island," *The Georgia Historical Quarterly* (September 1965).

"Paper Currency of the Province of Georgia," *Historical Magazine* (January 1858).

Laws, archives and other public records.

See general references, catalogs, and listings following the Introduction.

LA LOUISIANE

GENERAL EMISSIONS

Banque Royale ★ 1719-20
Treasury Notes ★ 1728
Billets de Cartes ★ 1735, etc.
Billets de Cartes ★ 1750
Bons ★ 1756, etc.
Spanish Certificates of Credit ★ 1775-89

SPECIAL ISSUES

Compagnie des Indies Storehouse Orders ★ 1721-2
Compagnie des Indies Billets de Cartes ★ 1722-3
Compagnie des Indies Billets de Caisse ★ 1726, etc.
Bons ★ 1785-1810

LA LOUISIANE

La Louisiane is used to refer to the French Colonial possession generally covering the Mississippi Valley, including areas drained by the Missouri, Ohio, and Mobile Rivers. In 1763 the eastern portion was ceded to England to become a part of its North American colonies which in 1776 became the United States. Also in 1763 the western portion was transferred to Spain which returned it to France in 1801. France in 1803 sold the western portion to the United States under which it became known as the Louisiana Territory. The northern part was referred to as Upper Louisiana.

Banque Royale ★ 1719-20

La Louisiane was the basis of a dream of limitless prosperity promoted by John Law. In 1717 he organized the Compagnie de la Louisiane ou d'Occident to exploit the wealth of that region. As part of Law's scheme La Banque Generale had been chartered on May 2, 1716 in France. The bank issued bearer notes for 10, 40, 100, 400, and 1,000 ecus in twelve series from June 16, 1716 to March 18, 1718. As the price of silver increased because of inflation circulating notes of 10, 50, 100, and 500 ecus were emitted in three series from June 18, 1718 to October 18, 1718. No examples of these issues have been located. By an Edict of December 4, 1718, the name of the bank was changed to Banque Royale which issued circulating notes to exchange for all the prior issues of its predecessor.

All emissions of the Banque Royale are on paper watermarked "Billet de Banque" and are impressed with the bank's seal. These bearer notes were guaranteed by the King and were issued from January 10, 1719 to September 2, 1720. Up to January 1, 1720, eighteen series of engraved notes aggregating 769,000,000 livres Tournois were emitted. Typeset notes beginning on January 1, 1720 were issued in three series aggregating the staggering total of 2,172,850,000 livres Tournois. The Bank Royale was interlocked with the Compagnie des Indies (successor in 1719 to Compagnie de la Louisiane ou d'Occident) in the speculative venture. The bursting of the "Mississippi Bubble" took place in May, 1720 when a 50% depreciation was ordered by the King of France, causing an economic catastrophe there.

On June 15, 1715 a special issue of French notes with denominations of 50 and 100 livres had been suggested for use in La Louisiane, but the plan was not carried out. On March 19, 1717, France had announced that new paper money would be sent to Nouvelle France, Martinique, and La Louisiane. The first delivery of Banque Royale paper money to the Compagnie de la Louisiane ou d'Occident was 25,000,000 livres in 1719. Although this money and later issues were to be spent on American development no proof as to whether or not these notes circulated in America has been located.

January 10, 1719 to January 1, 1720

Engraved issue with scroll work on the left end. Blank backs. Written signatures and dates.

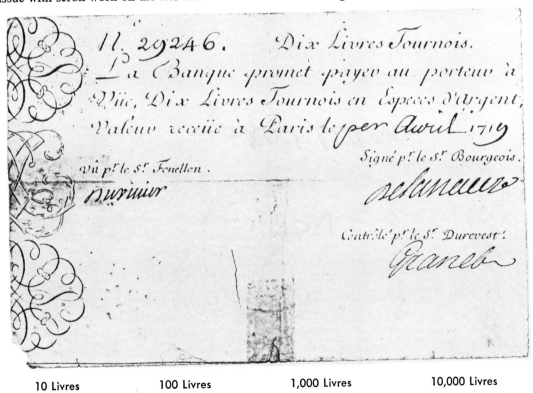

| 10 Livres | 100 Livres | 1,000 Livres | 10,000 Livres |

LA LOUISIANE

January 1, 1720

Typeset with BANQUE ROYALE along the left side of the sheet. Blank backs. Written signatures on the three highest denominations.

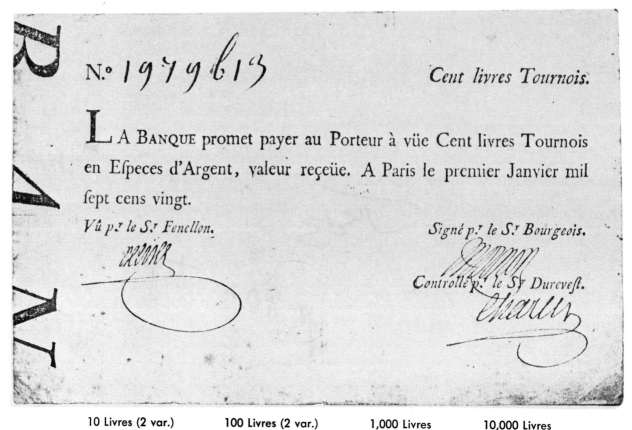

No. 1979613   *Cent livres Tournois.*

LA BANQUE promet payer au Porteur à vüe Cent livres Tournois en Efpeces d'Argent, valeur reçeüe. A Paris le premier Janvier mil fept cens vingt.

Vû p.r le S.r Fenellon.   *Signé p.r le S.r Bourgeois.*

                                               Controllé p.r le S.r Dureveft.

| 10 Livres (2 var.) | 100 Livres (2 var.) | 1,000 Livres | 10,000 Livres |

July 1, 1720

Notes issued to exchange for 1,000 and 10,000 livres notes of the prior issue. The word "Division" is above the body of the text.

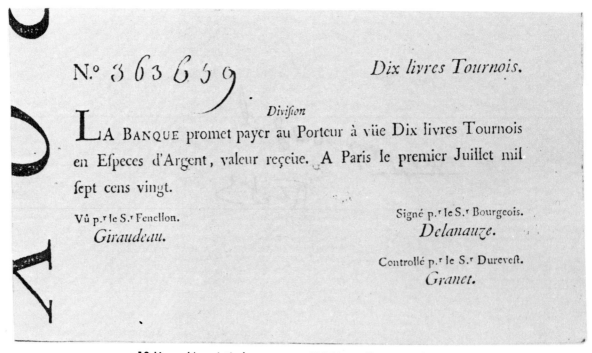

No. 363659   *Dix livres Tournois.*

                        Divifion

LA BANQUE promet payer au Porteur à vüe Dix livres Tournois en Efpeces d'Argent, valeur reçeüe. A Paris le premier Juillet mil fept cens vingt.

Vû p.r le S.r Fenellon.   Signé p.r le S.r Bourgeois.
Giraudeau.   *Delanauze.*

                                               Controllé p.r le S.r Dureveft.
                                               Granet.

| 10 Livres (4 varieties) | 100 Livres (2 varieties) |

122

September 2, 1720
Notes issued to exchange for prior issues. The edict of authorization is above the body of the text.

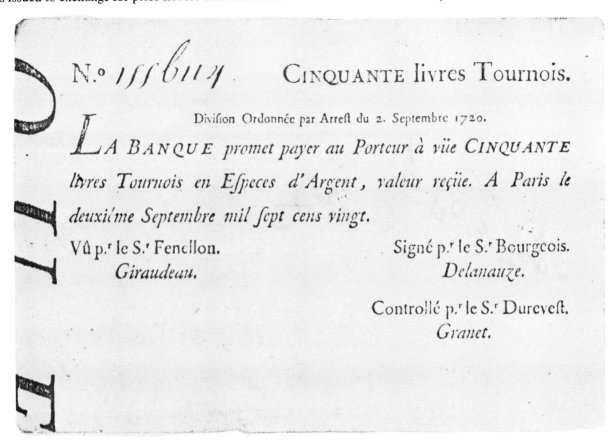

10 Livres   50 Livres

No examples of the next eight French and Spanish paper money issues have been located. These are known only through the research and writing of those who have examined the remaining original archives of the French and Spanish regimes. Much of the data is incomplete, unexplained, and confusing. Printing was not available in New Orleans until 1764 and thus whether prior issues were printed in France or elsewhere in whole or in part, or whether they were written by scribes is an open question. Similarly the size of the individual pieces is unknown and the means and extent of their circulation is unknown. Without examples of the paper money itself the comments which follow are subject to challenge. Nevertheless, an attempt is made to present this elusive subject rather than to omit it as its inclusion may stimulate further findings.

Storehouse Orders ★ 1721-22
The Compagnie des Indies in continuing the economic development of La Louisiane operated storehouses from which supplies could be withdrawn by those working on its behalf. The supplies were charged against the allotment of funds for each employee's services. Requests for such supplies had to be submitted to Compagnie officials for approval. After approval and before the specified items were withdrawn from the storehouses these orders circulated as a medium of exchange. By Ordinance of May 20, 1722 they were to be exchanged for card money by January 1, 1723, but those working far from New Orleans complained. On September 6, 1723 buying or selling Compagnie notes was declared illegal as they had depreciated in value. By 1725 all storehouse orders and cards were redeemed in New Orleans. The small change which consisted of 9 denier copper coins dated 1721 and 1722 was devalued to 6 deniers by 1724 when the coins were given legal tender status.

Billets de Cartes ★ 1722-3
Card money of the Compagnie des Indies was issued to redeem storehouse orders, following the practice in Canada. Its denominations ranged from 5 sous to 50 livres. The shape was tied into the denomination so that illiter-

ates could more readily use it. The cards bore two signatures.

Billets de Caisse ★ 1726, etc.

The Compagnie des Indies continued to issue paper currency to pay its debts and it was freely circulated. An ordinance of November 15, 1731 was passed because officials thought the issue interfered with the value of the King's coin and provided that the paper money would be worthless after 15 days unless exchanged for goods at French government storehouses in America. This was a factor in the elimination of the existence of the Compagnie des Indies and the transfer of development responsibilities to the King. The Compagnie paper money had depreciated to 35 livres to the piastre (Spanish dollar), but lingered in circulation until 1735.

Treasury Notes ★ 1728

50,000 livres in Treasury Notes were issued but were soon recalled because of counterfeiting.

Billets de Cartes ★ 1735, etc.

Although issued and signed in the manner often used in Canada, the King's La Louisiane card money became depreciated to the extent of 3 for 1, being similar to the experience with the paper currency of the Compagnie des Indies. On April 24, 1744 the Billets de Cartes were ordered to be redeemed on a 2½ for 1 depreciation basis and to be void after 2 months.

Billets de Cartes ★ 1750

By an Ordinance of February 1, 1750, a special issue of card money with denominations from 25 sols to 30 livres was emitted by the Colony to pay the King's obligations there. These notes were ordered withdrawn by the Crown officials in Europe on October 23, 1750 because the cards were issued only by Colonial authority. The money was extensively counterfeited by those who were described as "many important people." The genuine cards were exchanged for bills of exchange.

Bons ★ 1756, etc.

The practice of issuing promissory notes beginning with the words "Bon pour" (good for) drawn on the Colonial Treasury in New Orleans was undertaken at least by 1756 when notes of denominations from 10 sols to 100 livres were issued on the basis of conversion to bills of exchange on France in three months. These notes circulated until redeemed. In 1760 Governor Kerlerec proposed a 4,000,000 livres legal tender issue of numbered parchment bons, 6″ x 4″ in size, ranging in denomination from 6 sols to 5,000 livres and having the design of the King's Arms, but nothing was done. The practice of issuing bons must have continued because in 1766 when the Spanish took over the area west of the Mississippi River pursuant to the 1763 treaty ending the French and Indian War there was in circulation 7,000,000 livres in paper money issued by the French colonial authorities. The Spanish ordered that it be accepted for coin on the basis of 4 for 1 depreciation, creating substantial economic turbulence.

Spanish Certificates of Credit ★ 1775-1789

Under the Spanish regime certificates of credit and paper bills from one-half real upward circulated following the beginning of the American Revolution. After the 1788 fire in New Orleans a plan for Spain to redeem these obligations to rehabilitate the economy was proposed and accepted by the Royal Order of October, 1788. On January 16, 1789 redemption of all paper money in the Province began.

Private Bons ★ 1785-1810

Private bons were an element in the circulating medium, particularly in the Missouri River fur trade. Obligations were payable in peltry at established rates. Bons were given to suppliers by fur trappers and traders to be paid on the return from an expedition. Some were promissory notes and others were bearer obligations. An Illinois promissory note set forth hereafter illustrates the exchange value of various furs which were the official medium of exchange in Upper Louisiana. A translation follows it.

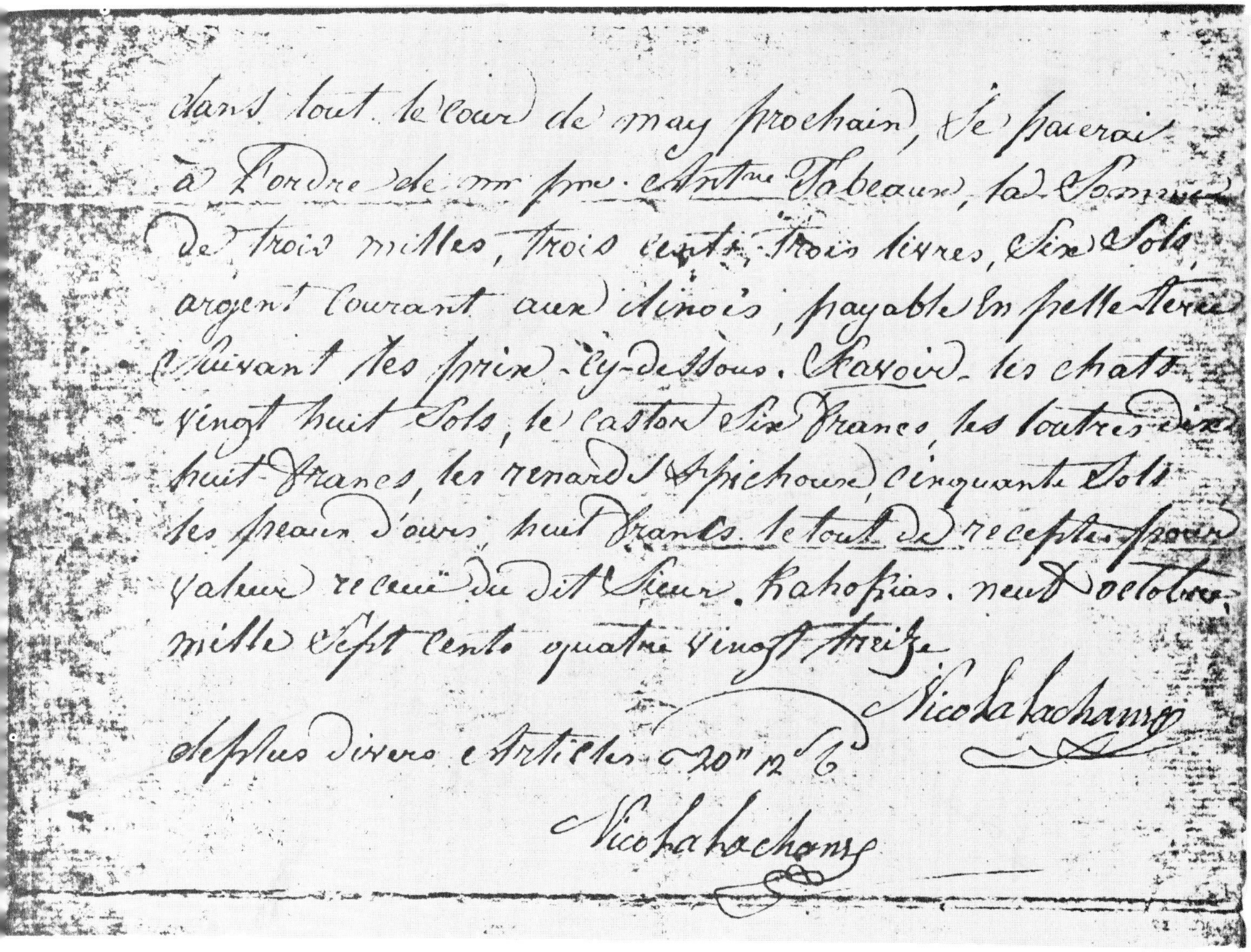

LA LOUISIANE

[handwritten document in French cursive]

dans tout le cour de may prochain, je payerai à l'ordre de mr pre. Antne Tabeau, la Somme de trois milles, trois cents trois livres, Six Sols, argent courant aux illinois; payable En Pelleterie suivant les prix Cy-dessous. Cavoir. les chats vingt huit Sols, le Castor Six Francs, les loutres huit Francs, les renards & pichoux Cinquante Sols les peaux d'ours, huit francs. le tout de recepte Valeur receuë du dit Sieur Kahokias. neuf octobre mille Sept Cents quatre vingt treize

Nicola Lachanse

desplus divers articles 20" 12 6

Nicola Lachanse

At the exchange rate of next May, I will pay to the order of Mr. Pierre Antoine Tabeau, the sum of three thousand three hundred three livres, six sols current money of Illinois, payable in peltry in accordance with the prices below, namely —raccoons 28 sols, beaver 6 francs, otter 18 francs, foxes lynx 50 sols, bear skin 8 francs, all on receipt for value received of said gentleman.

Kahokia 9 October 1793   Nicola Lachanse

In addition various articles

20 livres, 12 sols, 6 deniers

Nicola Lachanse

125

LA LOUISIANE

Missouri Circulating Bon Payable in Deerskin
Good for twelve Spanish silver dollars at the rate of two and one-half pounds of deerskin to the Spanish dollar—at St. Louis March 2, 1805.

On behalf of
    Francois Liberge
    Sam Solomon

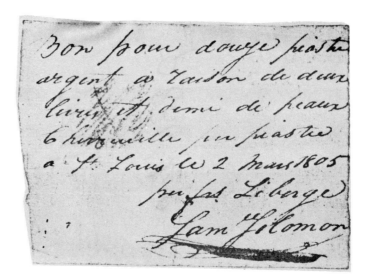

Missouri Circulating Bon
Good for three livres ten sols—current money, St. Louis
June 1, 1803
Reginald Loisel

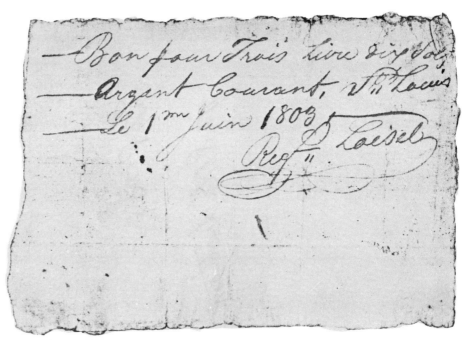

LA LOUISIANE REFERENCES

Caroline M. Burson, *The Stewardship of Don Esteban Miro* (New Orleans, 1940), pp. 275 and 277.

Charles Gayarré, *Louisiana: Its Colonial History and Romance* (New York, 1851), republished under various titles.

———, *Louisiana: Its History as a French Colony* (New York, 1852), republished under various titles.

Jean Lafourie, *Les Billets des Banque de Law* (Auxerre, France, 1952).

N. M. Miller Surrey, *The Commerce of Louisiana during the French Regime 1699-1763* (New York, 1916).

MARYLAND

GENERAL EMISSIONS

1733
June 2, 1740
October 1, 1748
April 6, 1751
July 14, 1756
January 1, 1767
March 1, 1770
April 10, 1774
July 26, 1775 Session
December 7, 1775 Session
August 14, 1776 Session
June 8, 1780 Act
June 28, 1780 Act
October 17, 1780 Act
May 10, 1781 Act
August 8, 1781

SPECIAL ISSUERS

Nathan West ★ 1761
Howe & Seyl ★ July 18, 1777
Bank of Maryland ★ 1791, etc.
Bank of the United States (Baltimore Office) ★ 1792, etc.
Bank of Baltimore ★ 1797, etc.
Bank of Columbia ★ 1800, etc.

1733

£90,000 in indented legal tender Bills authorized at session begun Mar. 13, 1732(3) primarily for the creation of a Loan Office which was to operate until Sept. 29, 1764. The Commissioners of the Loan Office were to purchase Bank of England stock out of a sinking fund arising from interest and principal payments. By Sept. 29, 1748 the sum of £30,000 in bills was to be retired from the sale of stock and the balance of bills was to be replaced with an emission marked "New Bill." To prevent poor tobacco from depressing the market, 30s in bills was to be paid to each taxable person for a required burning of 150 pounds of tobacco in both 1734 and 1735. The plates were engraved in England and the bills were printed on fine laid paper watermarked MARYLAND. Five bills of the same denomination were engraved on one sheet, the bills being distinguished by one to five stars placed after the denomination in the lower left corner. Issued at 25% discount under Sterling exchange. Handwritten dates. Signers are Richard Francis and Charles Hamond.

1s	[60,000]	Ⓤ	
1s6d	[60,000]	Ⓤ	
2s6d	[40,000]	Ⓤ	
5s	[40,000]	Ⓤ	
10s	[30,000]	Ⓤ	Ⓒ
15s	[30,000]	Ⓤ	
20s	[30,000]	Ⓤ	Ⓒ

Ⓤ

June 2, 1740

£5,000 in Bills ratified by the July 26, 1740 Act to support an expedition against the Spanish West Indies. This was one of many expenditures authorized by the Assembly from time to time to be paid out by the Loan Office and to be recovered with tax levies. Unused bill forms from the 1733 issue were dated and issued. Signers are John Bullen, Charles Hamond, and George Steuart.

1s
1s6d
2s6d
5s
10s
15s
20s

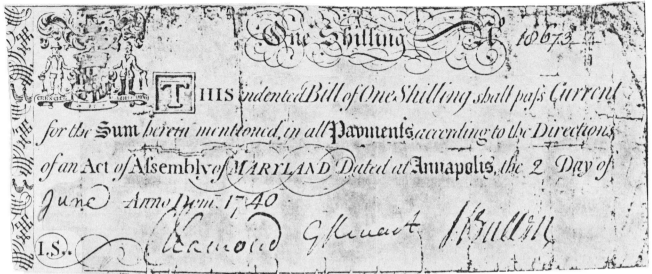

October 1, 1748

£60,000 in New Bills to replace two thirds of the 1733 issue pursuant to a requirement of the Mar. 13, 1732(3) Act. Unused bill forms remaining from the 1733 and 1740 emissions were dated and issued, but with the words "New Bill" handwritten on the face. **Signers** are J. Bullen, Richard Gordon, Charles Hamond, and George Steuart.

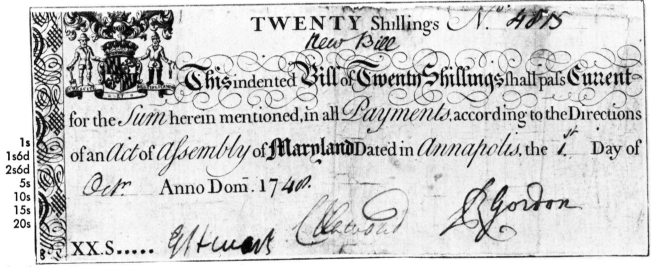

April 6, 1751

Identical to Oct. 1, 1748 issue except as to handwritten date.

July 14, 1756

£30,000 in legal tender Bills authorized by the May 15, 1756 Act which also permitted £10,000 in bills of prior issues to be put back into circulation. Three cast borders, two vignettes, and set type on the face. A different nature print on the back of each denomination, some showing the initials I.G. (Jonas Green) in large letters of punched dots within the print. Printed by Jonas Green of Annapolis who was required to turn over the "stamps and flowers" to the Loan Office Commissioners for safe keeping. The same cuts and nature prints were reused for the 1767, 1770 and 1774 issues. Signers are John Bullen, Charles Hamond, and George Steuart.

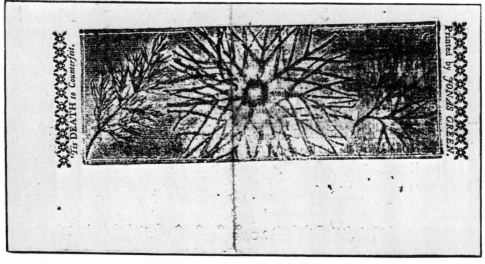

6d [10,000]	5s [12,000] ⓒ
1s [10,000]	10s [12,000]
1s6d [10,000]	15s [12,000]
2s [10,000]	20s [12,000]
2s6d [12,000]	

Nathan West ★ 1761

Small change promissory notes of Nathan West, redeemable in silver at his stores, his home, or at the places of business in Annapolis of Robert Couden or Nathan Hamond and to be withdrawn when the Colony or others issue small money. Other denominations were issued.

6d   2s6d

MARYLAND

January 1, 1767

$173,733 in indented Bills without legal tender status and authorized at the Nov. 1, 1766 Session. Payable at 4s6d sterling per dollar in bills of exchange between June 25, 1777 and Dec. 25, 1777. The Loan Office had been ordered closed at the Nov. 1, 1765 Session and all prior issues were made invalid after April 1, 1766. The Bank of England stock remaining after redemption of the prior issues was to secure this and following issues. By Act passed during the Nov. 8, 1779 Session, bills of this issue were to be deposited with the Treasurer of the Western Shore by June 1, 1780 or become invalid. Elaborate border cuts engraved by Thomas Sparrow containing either his initials or name as well as the initials or name of Jonas Green as printer. Nature prints from the July 14, 1756 issue were reused. Letters from many different type fonts were used to deter counterfeiting. Some words are improperly hyphenated and other words are divided by the Colony arms. In the $1 and $2 denominations tiny engravings of coined Spanish Dollars are the first use of coin illustrations on American paper money. For secret marks refer to the next issue. Thick weak paper. Signers are John Clapham and Robert Couden.

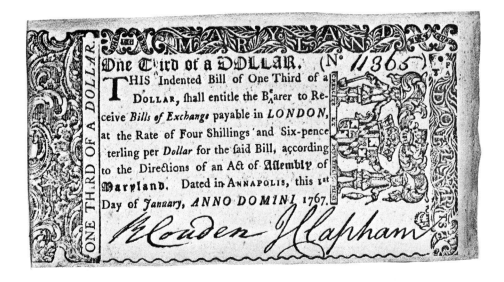

			Good	V.G.	Fine
$1/9	**(6d)**	[12,000]	12.50	20.00	30.00
$1/6	**(9d)**	Commas in Roman numerals [12,000]	12.50	20.00	30.00
$2/9	**(1s)**	Comma instead of period after Maryland [12,000]	12.50	20.00	30.00
$1/3	**(1s6d)**	Carets under small h in Third and small e in Bearer [11,999]	12.50	20.00	30.00
$1/2	**(2s3d)**	Small A between HALF and DOLLAR [12,000]	12.50	20.00	30.00
$2/3	**(3s)**	Caret under small h in Thirds [12,002]	12.50	20.00	30.00
$1	**(4s6d)**	Engraving of Spanish Dollar [12,000]	12.50	20.00	30.00
$2	**(9s)**	Engraving of two Spanish Dollars [12,000]	12.50	20.00	30.00
$4	**(18s)**	Caret under third the [6,318]	12.50	20.00	30.00
$6	**(27s)**	Three type sizes in MARYLAND [6,318]	12.50	20.00	30.00
$8	**(36s)**	Broken d in London [6,319] ©	12.50	20.00	30.00

MARYLAND

March 1, 1770

$318,000 in indented Bills without legal tender status and authorized at the Nov. 17, 1769 Session to be used for loans through the reestablished Loan Office. Payable between Oct. 10, 1781 and April 10, 1782 at 4s6d sterling per dollar. By Act passed during the Oct. 17, 1780 Session all outstanding issues prior to 1776 were to be exchanged at 40 (old) for 1 (new) or become invalid after Mar. 20, 1781. Similar in form to the Jan. 1, 1767 issue, but with payment in gold and silver added to the text. The nature prints from the July 14, 1756 issue were reused. Printed by Anne Catherine Green and William Green. Signers are John Clapham and Robert Couden.

"Secret marks" found on all except the lowest three denominations of the 1767, 1770, and 1774 issues seem to have been deliberately used for the detection of counterfeits and alterations. The listed marks continue from issue to issue without change.

$1/3—Cedilla under first c in according. Tiny J instead of a comma after Dollar in text.

$1/2—An accent mark is over a in Exchange.

$2/3—An accent mark is over the first i in Domini.

$1—Each N in INDENTED is rotated 180 degrees.

$2—A period is over a in Rate.

$4—Each N in LONDON is rotated 180 degrees.

$6—A dot follows ASSEMBLY.

$8—An accent mark instead of a comma is after DOLLARS in the text. The right bracket for the bill number is omitted.

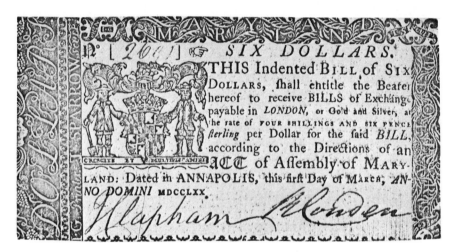

			Good	V.G.	Fine
$1/9	(6d)	A colon instead of a comma after ANNAPOLIS [18,000]	10.00	12.50	27.50
$1/6	(9d)	Commas in Roman numerals [18,000]	10.00	12.50	27.50
$2/9	(1s)	A comma instead of a period after Maryland [18,000]	10.00	12.50	27.50
$1/3	(1s6d)	Caret under small h in Third and small e in Bearer [21,000]	10.00	12.50	27.50
$1/2	(2s3d)	Small A between HALF and DOLLAR [18,000]	10.00	12.50	27.50
$2/3	(3s)	Caret under small h in Thirds [21,000]	10.00	12.50	27.50
$1	(4s6d)	Engraving of Spanish Dollar [21,000] ©	10.00	12.50	27.50
$2	(9s)	Engraving of two Spanish Dollars [21,000]	10.00	12.50	27.50
$4	(18s)	Caret under third the [12,000]	10.00	12.50	27.50
$6	(27s)	Three type sizes in MARYLAND [12,000] ©	10.00	12.50	27.50
$8	(36s)	Broken d in London [12,000] ©	10.00	12.50	27.50

MARYLAND

April 10, 1774

$480,000 in indented Bills without legal tender status authorized at the Nov. 16, 1773 Session. Payable between Oct. 10, 1785 and April 10, 1786 at 4s6d sterling per dollar. Of this issue $266,666⅔ were to be loaned through the Loan Office, $80,000 to be used for public expense and the balance to be exchanged for worn bills. By Act passed during the Oct. 17, 1780 Session all outstanding issues prior to 1776 were to be exchanged at 40 (old) for one (new) or become invalid after Mar. 20, 1781. Similar in form to the Mar. 1, 1770 issue, but on thinner paper containing mica flakes. The nature prints from the July 14, 1756 issue were reused. For an explanation of additional oddities in printing and secret marks refer to the 1767 and 1770 issues. Printed by Anne Catherine Green and Frederick Green. Signers are John Clapham and William Eddis.

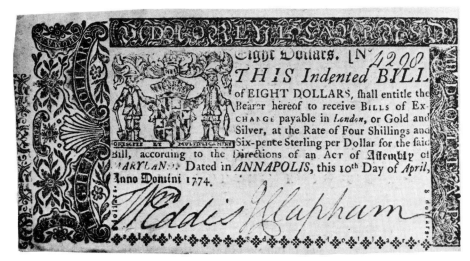

			V.G.	Fine	V.F.
$1/9	(6d)	A colon instead of a comma after ANNAPOLIS [27,000]	15.00	25.00	35.00
$1/6	(9d)	Commas in Roman numerals [27,000]	15.00	25.00	35.00
$2/9	(1s)	A comma instead of a period after Maryland [27,000]	15.00	25.00	35.00
$1/3	(1s6d)	Carets under small h in Third and small e in Bearer [31,000]	15.00	25.00	35.00
$1/2	(2s3d)	Small A between HALF and DOLLAR [27,000]	15.00	25.00	35.00
$2/3	(3s)	Caret under small h in Thirds [31,000]	15.00	25.00	35.00
$1	(4s6d)	Engraving of Spanish Dollar [34,500]	15.00	25.00	35.00
$2	(9s)	Engraving of two Spanish Dollars [31,500]	15.00	25.00	35.00
$4	(18s)	Caret under third the [18,000]	15.00	25.00	35.00
$6	(27s)	Three type sizes in MARYLAND [18,000]	15.00	25.00	35.00
$8	(36s)	Broken d in London [18,000] ©	15.00	25.00	35.00

July 26, 1775 Session

$266,666⅔ (£100,000 in Maryland exchange) in Bills issued pursuant to the Aug. 14, 1775 Resolve of the Maryland Convention to promote the manufacture of gunpowder. Payable in specie at Sterling rates by Jan. 1, 1786. On the face is a propaganda-filled woodcut by Thomas Sparrow, depicting Britannia receiving a petition of the Continental Congress, CONG PETI, from a female figure representing America; America trampling on a scroll marked SLAVERY and holding a Liberty Cap in front of American troops carrying the flag of liberty, LIB; and on the left George III trampling on the M (agna) CHARTA and applying a fire brand to an American city under attack by a British fleet. Side border cuts carry AN APPEAL TO HEAVEN and PRO ARIS ET FOCIS (For al-

tars and the hearth). On the back the figures of America and Britannia are shown achieving peace, PAX TRIUMPH-IS POTIOR (Peace is preferable to victory), LIBERTY, T. SPARROW, and FG (Frederick Green, the printer). The five highest denominations show a denomination in dollars, a denomination in Maryland money of account, and the exchange rate to convert the value into English sterling. Signers are Jeremiah Banning, James Brice, John Brice, Joseph Bruff, Joseph Davidson, John Duckett, Nathan Hammond, James Hindman, Thomas B. Hodgkin, Robert L. Nichols, William Perry, Samuel Sharpe, Peregrine Tilghman, Richard Tilghman, Jr., Richard Tootell, and Charles Wallace.

			Good	V.G.	Fine
$2/3		[10,512]	125.00	200.00	325.00
$1		[10,512]	125.00	200.00	325.00
$1 1/3		[10,512]	125.00	200.00	325.00
$1 2/3	(12s6d)	[10,512]	125.00	200.00	325.00

			Good	V.G.	Fine
$2 2/3	(20s)	[7,096]	125.00	200.00	325.00
$4	(30s)	[7,096]	125.00	200.00	325.00
$8	(£3)	[7,096]	125.00	200.00	325.00
$16	(£6)	[7,096]	125.00	200.00	325.00

MARYLAND

December 7, 1775 Session

$535,111⅑ in Bills ratified pursuant to the Jan. 13, 1776 Resolve to replace the July 26, 1775 issue and for military purposes. Redeemable in specie by Jan. 1, 1786 at Sterling rates. Borders on the face were engraved on copper in Philadelphia. Emblem on back with the motto SUB CLYPEO (under divine protection) and a shield. Printed by Frederick Green. Signers are the same as on the July 26, 1775 issue plus Henry Bannon, Thomas Gassaway, Jr., Frederick Green, Nicholas Harwood, Alexander Irvine, and Charles Irvine.

		Good	V.G.	Fine			Good	V.G.	Fine			Good	V.G.	Fine
$1/9	(6d)	7.50	12.50	20.00	$2/3	(3s)	7.50	12.50	20.00	$2 2/3	(12s)	7.50	12.50	20.00
$1/6	(9d)	7.50	12.50	20.00	$1	(4s6d)	7.50	12.50	20.00	$4	(18s)	7.50	12.50	20.00
$1/3	(18d)	7.50	12.50	20.00	$1 1/3	(6s)	7.50	12.50	20.00	$6	(27s)	7.50	12.50	20.00
$1/2	(2s3d)	7.50	12.50	20.00	$2	(9s)	7.50	12.50	20.00	$8	(36s)	7.50	12.50	20.00

August 14, 1776 Session

$535,111⅑ in Bills ratified pursuant to the Nov. 9, 1776 Resolve and redeemable Jan. 1, 1786. Due to the expenditure of a portion of the Dec. 7, 1775 issue intended to be used for the exchange of the July 26, 1775 issue, $120,000 of the Aug. 14, 1776 issue was set aside for such redemption. Same general form as the Dec. 7, 1775 issue. At the Feb. 5, 1777 Session both Maryland and Continental money were made legal tender. Signers are John Brice, Joseph Bruff, Thomas Dawson, John Duckett, Samuel Edmundson, Thomas Gassaway, Jr., Frederick Green, Nathan Hammond, Nicholas Harwood, Thomas B. Hodgkin, Alexander Irvine, Charles E. Irvine, Robert L. Nichols, St. George Peale, William Perry, Samuel Sharpe, Richard Tilghman, Jr., Richard Tootell, and William Wilkins.

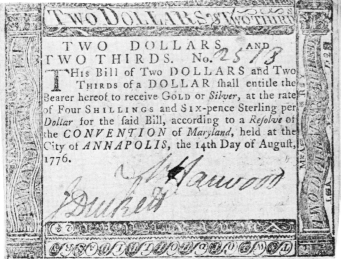 

			Good	V.G.	Fine
$1/9	(6d)	[40,000]	7.50	12.50	20.00
$1/6	(9d)	[40,000]	7.50	12.50	20.00
$1/3	(18d)	[40,000]	7.50	12.50	20.00
$1/2	(2s3d)	[40,000]	7.50	12.50	20.00
$2/3	(3s)	[32,000]	7.50	12.50	20.00
$1	(4s6d)	[32,000]	7.50	12.50	20.00

			Good	V.G.	Fine
$1 1/3	(6s)	[32,000]	7.50	12.50	20.00
$2	(9s)	[32,000]	7.50	12.50	20.00
$2 2/3	(12s)	[16,000]	7.50	12.50	20.00
$4	(18s)	[16,000]	7.50	12.50	20.00
$6	(27s)	[16,000]	7.50	12.50	20.00
$8	(36s)	[16,000]	7.50	12.50	20.00

Howe and Seyl ★ July 18, 1777

Private scrip for small change issued by Nicolaus Howe and John Seyl when coin was hoarded and unavailable. Ornaments and text are typeset. Other denominations are probable.

3d

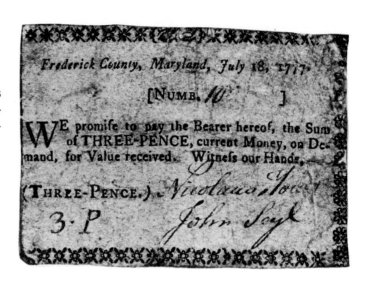

June 8, 1780 Act

£30,000 ($133,333⅓) in legal tender Bills known as Black Money and redeemable with 5% interest by May 1, 1786 pursuant to the June 8, 1780 Act. Same borders as two prior state issues, but their position was shifted. The back has State Arms. Printed by Frederick Green.

Issued by the Treasurer of the Western Shore and secured by assets in England and confiscated property. Signers are John Callahan, Joseph Cowman, Frederick Green, Nicholas Harwood, Thomas Johnson, Jr., and Isaac McHard.

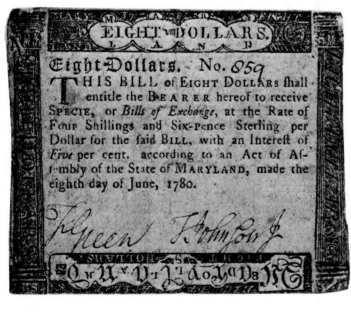

$1/9	$1/3	$2/3	$1 1/3	$2 2/3	$6
$1/6	$1/2	$1	$2	$4	$8

MARYLAND

June 28, 1780 Act

$346,000 in legal tender Bills payable in Spanish milled dollars with 5% interest by Dec. 31, 1786 was authorized by acts passed at the June 12, 1780 and Oct. 17, 1780 Sessions pursuant to a Continental Congress Resolution of Mar. 18, 1780, guaranteeing the payment of the bills and making the amount issuable dependent upon the amount of Continental Currency exchanged at $40 (old) for $1 (new). Face printed in black and back in red and black by Hall & Sellers in Philadelphia on mica-flaked paper watermarked UNITED STATES. Face border cuts and back cut surrounding emblem engraved by Henry Dawkins. Border cuts and emblem on back was from the Jan. 14, 1779 issue of Continental Currency. Signers are John Callahan, Henry Dickinson, Frederick Green, Nicholas Harwood, Thomas Johnson, Jr., Isaac McHard, Richard Tilghman, Philip Walker, and William Wilkins. The guaranty was signed by Benjamin Harwood and Thomas Harwood.

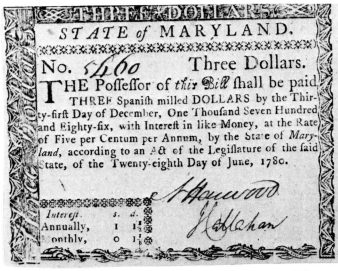

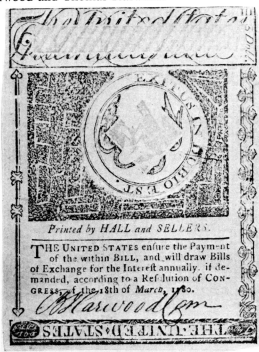

		V.G.	Fine	V.F.
$1	[6,922]	100.00	150.00	225.00
$2	[6,922]	100.00	150.00	225.00
$3	[6,922]	100.00	150.00	225.00
$4	[6,922]	100.00	150.00	225.00
$5	[6,922]	100.00	150.00	225.00
$7	[6,922]	100.00	150.00	225.00
$8	[6,922]	100.00	150.00	225.00
$20	[6,922]	100.00	150.00	225.00

October 17, 1780 Act

£5,400 sterling ($24,000) in small denomination bills to exchange for larger denominations of the June 8, 1780 issue pursuant to the Oct. 17, 1780 Act. Similar to the June 8, 1780 issue. Printed by Frederick Green. Signers are John Callahan and Thomas Johnson, Jr.

$1/15 (6d) [45,000] $1/10 (9d) [45,000] $1/6 (15d) [45,000] $1/5 (18d) [45,000]

MARYLAND

May 10, 1781 Act

£200,000 in Bills known as Red Money payable in specie at 7s6d per dollar between Dec. 25, 1784 and June 25, 1785 out of proceeds to be received from confiscation of Tory property. Printed by Frederick Green in red and black on face and back. Signers are John Callahan, Thomas Gassaway, Jr., Frederick Green, Nicholas Harwood, Thomas Johnson, Jr., and Isaac McHard.

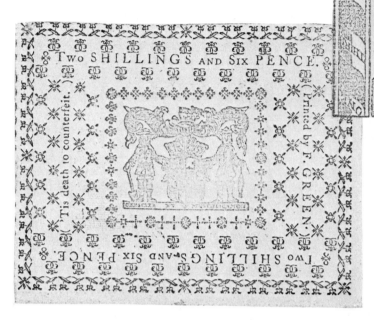

			V.G.	Fine
1s	Type borders [32,665] ...		125.00	200.00
1s6d	Type borders [32,665] ...		125.00	200.00
2s6d	($1/3) [32,665]		125.00	200.00
5s	($2/3) [32,665]		125.00	200.00
7s6d	($1) [32,652]		125.00	200.00
15s	($2) [32,652]		125.00	200.00
30s	($4) [32,652]		125.00	200.00
£3	($8) [32,652]		125.00	200.00

August 8, 1781

£5,500 in small change "tickets" issued in exchange for the bills issued under the May 10, 1781 Act. Printed in red by Frederick Green. Signer is Benjamin Harwood.

3d [60,000]
4d [60,000]
6d [60,000]
9d [60,000]

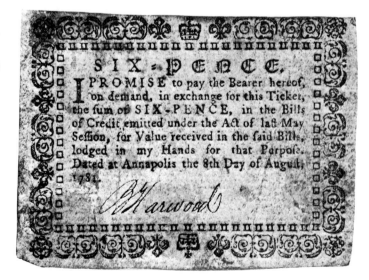

MARYLAND

Bank of Maryland ⋆ 1791, etc.

After attempting to organize in 1784 the Bank of Maryland was incorporated in 1790 with a capital of $3,000,000 and opened for business on July 1, 1791. Engraved notes contain plate numbers instead of plate letters. The 1 of the date is engraved. Blank backs. Signers of its first engraved notes are William Patterson, president, and Ebenezer Mackie, cashier.

Ⓤ

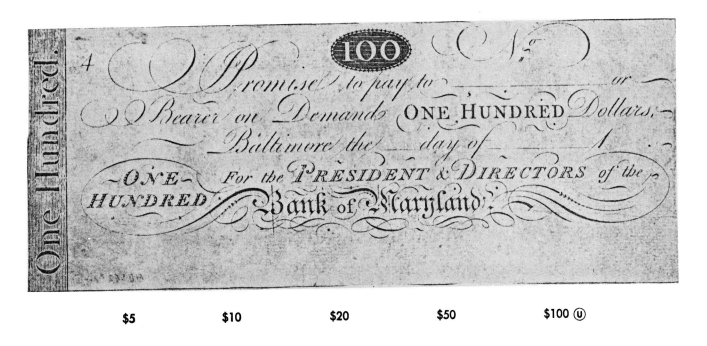

$5 $10 $20 $50 $100 Ⓤ

Post Note (Denomination written in). Blank backs.

Ⓒ

Bank of the United States ★ 1792, etc.

The Baltimore Office of Discount and Deposit of the Bank of the United States (first bank) operated from 1792 to 1811 and issued $371,865 in circulating bank notes. George Gale (1792-5), Archibald Campbell (1795-1800), and John Swan served as president and David Harris as cashier. A fuller description of branch bank notes and other branch bank data is included under Pennsylvania listings.

A flying eagle bearing the Arms of United States:	$5	$10	$20	$50	$100
A heraldic eagle with 13 stars around its head:	$5	$10	$20	$50	$100
A heraldic eagle in an oval frame containing 15 stars:	$5	$10	$20	$50 ©	$100

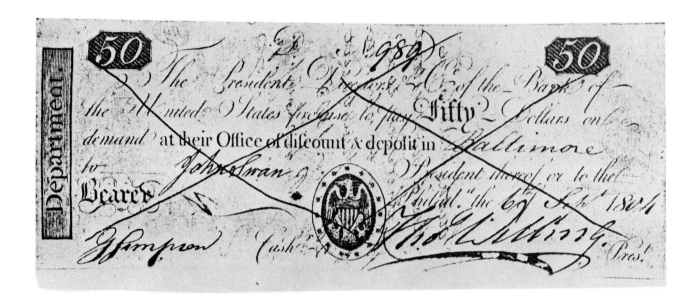

©

Bank of Baltimore ★ 1797, etc.

The Bank of Baltimore was incorporated on Dec. 24, 1795 with a capital of $1,200,000 and opened for business on Jan. 2, 1797. Its first engraved notes are signed by George Salmon, president, and James Cox, cashier.

$5	$10	$20	$50	$100

MARYLAND

Bank of Columbia ★ 1800, etc.

The Bank of Columbia was incorporated in Maryland on Dec. 23, 1793 with a capital of $1,000,000 in anticipation of the establishment of the United States Capital in the District of Columbia in 1800. The bank did **not** operate during the eighteenth century but later opened in Georgetown. Other denominations are probable.

$10

MARYLAND REFERENCES

Kathryn L. Behrens, *Paper Money in Maryland 1727-1789* (Baltimore, 1923).

Clarence P. Gould, *Money and Transportation in Maryland 1720-1765* (Baltimore, 1915).

Richard T. Hoober, "Financial History of Colonial Maryland," *The Numismatist* (August 1962, etc.), reprinted.

Eric P. Newman, "Nature Printing on Colonial and Continental Currency," *The Numismatist* (February 1964, etc.), reprinted.

"Paper Money Controversy in Maryland," *Canadian Antiquarian and Numismatic Journal* (1883).

Henry Phillips, Jr., "Some Observations on Early Currency of Maryland," *Proceedings of the Numismatic and Antiquarian Society of Philadelphia* (Philadelphia, 1867).

John M. Richardson, "The Green Family, Printers of Colonial Bills in Connecticut and Maryland," *Coin Collector's Journal* (July 1935).

Kenneth Scott, "Counterfeiting in Colonial Maryland," *Maryland Historical Magazine* (Baltimore, 1956).

Sebastian F. Streiter, "Sketch of Early Currency in Maryland and Virginia," *Banker's Magazine* (August 1851) and *Historical Magazine* (1857).

Laws, archives and other public records.

See general references, catalogs, and listings following the Introduction.

MASSACHUSETTS

GENERAL EMISSIONS

December 10, 1690
February 3, 1690(1)
November 21, 1702
November 21, 1708
May 31, 1710
May 31, 1710 redated 1711
October 14, 1713
May 26, 1714
October 14, 1713 redated 1714
October 14, 1713 redated 1716
October 14, 1713 redated 1716 ★
May 26, 1714 redated 1716
May 26, 1714 redated 1716 ★
October 14, 1713 redated 1718
May 26, 1714 redated 1718
October 14, 1713 redated 1719
October 14, 1713 redated 1721
May 26, 1714 redated 1721
October 14, 1713 redated 1722
May 26, 1714 redated 1722
October 14, 1713 redated 1723
May 26, 1714 redated 1723
October 14, 1713 redated 1724
May 26, 1714 redated 1724
October 14, 1713 redated 1725
October 14, 1713 redated 1725 †
May 26, 1714 redated 1725
May 26, 1714 redated 1725 †
October 14, 1713 redated 1727
May 26, 1714 redated 1727

October 14, 1713 redated 1728
October 14, 1713 redated 1731
October 14, 1713 redated 1733
May 26, 1714 redated 1733
October 14, 1713 redated 1735
May 26, 1714 redated 1735
October 14, 1713 redated 1736
May 26, 1714 redated 1736
October 14, 1713 redated 1740
May 26, 1714 redated 1740
June 1722
February 4, 1736(7)
February 4, 1736(7) redated 1737
1737
January 15, 1741(2)
January 15, 1741(2) redated 1742
June 20, 1744
1750
May 25, 1775
July 8, 1775
August 18, 1775
December 7, 1775
June 18, 1776
September 17, 1776
October 18, 1776
November 17, 1776
October 16, 1778
1779
May 5, 1780 Act
1781 Written Dates

SPECIAL ISSUERS

Private Bank ★ 1686
John Merrett ★ 1733
Merchants' Notes ★ November 30, 1733
Silver Bank (Specie Bank) ★ August 1, 1740
Manufactory Bills (Land Bank) ★ September 9, 1740
Bank Bills ★ May 1, 1741
Massachusetts Bank ★ July 5, 1784 ★ December 2, 1784 ★
    June 21, 1785 ★ September 21, 1789
Bank of the United States (Boston Office) ★ 1792, etc.
Union Bank ★ 1792, etc.
Nantucket Bank ★ 1795, etc.
Merrimack Bank ★ 1795, etc.
James Leach ★ July 1, 1796
Portland Bank (District of Maine) ★ 1799, etc.
Essex Bank ★ 1799, etc.

1686

A private bank intending to issue bank bills in connection with its loans on land was approved by the Council in 1686. A rolling press was bought and was used "for tryall of the plates and printing off some bills." The scheme was abandoned by 1688 and the bills were never issued. Denominations are unknown.

December 10, 1690

£7,000 in indented Colony or Old Charter Bills, being the first authorized public paper currency issued in the Western world (Europe and America). Approved by a Dec. 10, 1690 Order to pay military expenses for action against Canada. The faces are printed from an engraved copper plate containing four denominations. The Indian on the Colony seal is saying COME OVER & HELP US. The backs have engraved scrolls which are part of the indenture. Signers are Elisha Hutchinson, John Phillips, Timothy Thornton, Penn Townsend, and Adam Winthrop. See following issue for further data.

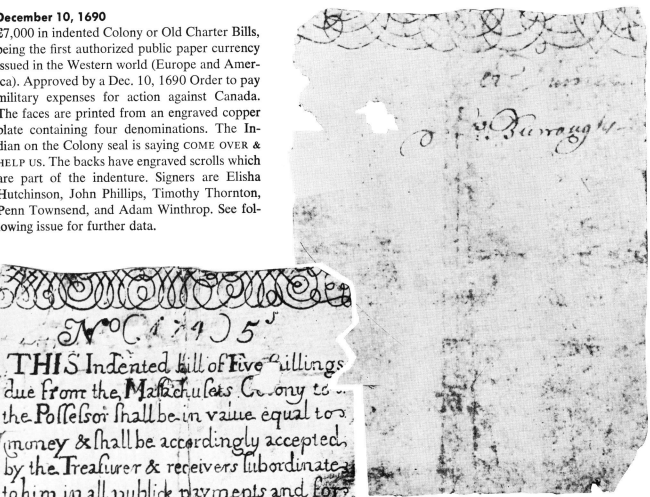

SIGILLVM: GVB: & SOC: DE MATTACHVSETS. BAY. IN: NOV. ANGL: (Seal of the Government and Society of Massachusetts Bay in New England).

5s [1,038]
10s [1,037]
20s [1,037]
£5 [1,037]

MASSACHUSETTS

February 3, 1690(1)

An aggregate of £40,000 for this and the previous issue of Colony or Old Charter Bills was authorized by the Feb. 3, 1690(1) and May 21, 1691 Orders. Receivable by Treasurer for taxes at 5% premium or payable at par with any specie on hand in the Treasury. Pursuant to a July 2, 1692 order all Colony bills were to be endorsed on the back by Jeremiah Dummer or Francis Burroughs for validation under the new status of Massachusetts Bay

as a Province. By Feb. 21, 1693(4) the bulk of Colony bills had been redeemed, but were reissued from time to time up to a total of £42,000 when on Nov. 21, 1702 further reissue was prohibited. Engraved on copper in the same manner as the Dec. 10, 1690 issue. The only known examples are fraudulently altered bills which have had their denominations raised from 2s6d to 20s. Signers are the same as on the Dec. 10, 1690 issue.

2s
2s6d
£3
£10

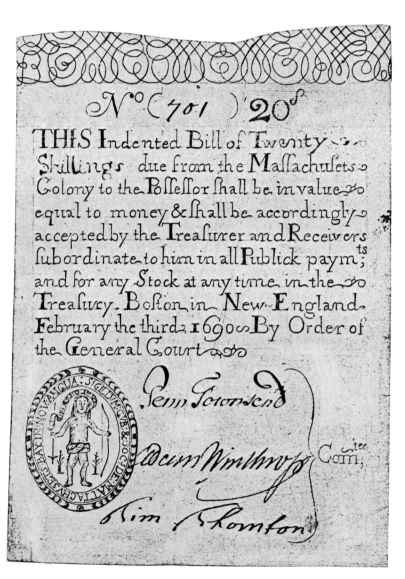

144

MASSACHUSETTS

November 21, 1702

£10,000 in indented Province Bills authorized by the Oct. 15, 1702 and Mar. 27, 1703 Acts. Engraved by John Coney on three new face plates known as the great plate, the middle plate and the lowest plate. A back plate containing a complex scroll was applied in red ink. The lower plate had two of each of the lower denominations. The great plate had two 20s and the middle plate one 20s. Each denomination had a differently shaped Arms.

The bills were printed by John Allen on a rolling press made by John Brewer. A specimen sheet from the middle plate (5s, 10s, 20s and 40s) exists with the back plate scroll overprinted vertically on the face. Bills were continuously printed, issued and reissued pursuant to sixteen separate Acts, the last of which was passed July 3, 1708. Signers are Nathaniel Byfield, Elisha Hutchinson, Samuel Legg, John Leverett, and James Russell.

2s	Two varieties
2s6d	Two varieties
5s	
10s	
20s	Three varieties Ⓒ
40s	
£3	
£5	

HONI SOIT QVI MAL Y PENSE (Evil to him who evil thinks).

MASSACHUSETTS

November 21, 1708

The same three face plates used for the issues dated Nov. 21, 1702 were altered by John Coney who cut an 8 over the 2 in the date. From the middle and lower plates £10,000 was authorized by the Oct. 29, 1708 Resolve. The face of the bills was overprinted with the mirrored monogram AR (Anna Regina) in red. The backs still retained the red scroll. Pursuant to the June 18, 1709

Resolve an aggregate of £30,000 more was to be printed from the three face plates, but pursuant to the Nov. 8, 1709 Resolve the extra 2s and 2s6d on the lower plate were altered to 3s and 3s6d respectively by John Coney before the last half of the issue was printed. Signers are Samuel Checkley, John Clark, Elisha Hutchinson, Ephraim Savage, Samuel Sewall, and Penn Townsend.

2s	Two varieties
2s6d	Two varieties
3s	
3s6d	©️
5s	
10s	©️
20s	Three varieties
40s	©️
£3	
£5	

©️

May 31, 1710

The same three face plates used for the Nov. 21, 1702 and Nov. 21, 1708 issues were further altered by John Coney by changing the 40s on the middle plate to 4s; by changing one 20s on the great plate to 40s and the other to 50s; and by changing the date on all bills to May 31, 1710. The face was overprinted in red with a mirrored monogram AR. A red scroll is on the backs of all except the four lowest denominations so as to deter alter- ation by raising denominations. £25,000 was autho- rized on June 29, 1710 and £15,000 on July 28, 1710. By the Nov. 4, 1710 Act all 20s bills dated Nov. 21, 1702 were called in because of extensive counterfeiting and £15,000 in new 20s bills were printed to replace the called denomination. Signers are Samuel Checkley, John Clark, Elisha Hutchinson, Samuel Sewall, and Penn Townsend.

2s
2s6d
3s ©
3s6d ©
4s
5s
10s ©
20s ©
40s ©
50s
£3
£5

©

May 31, 1710 redated 1711

£40,000 in indented Province Bills authorized on July 6, 1711 to finance a Canadian expedition. Issued for only two years at 40% advance with no right of reissuance. Made distinguishable from the May 31, 1710 issue by engraving the date "1711" on the right of the signature bracket. The face was overprinted in red with a mirrored monogram AR. Because of **counterfeiting**, this and all prior issues were declared invalid after Nov. 1, 1718 by the Act of Feb. 24, 1717(8). Signers are Samuel Checkley, John **Parker**, **Samuel Sewall, and Penn** Townsend.

4s
5s
10s
20s
40s
50s ©
£3 ©
£5 ©

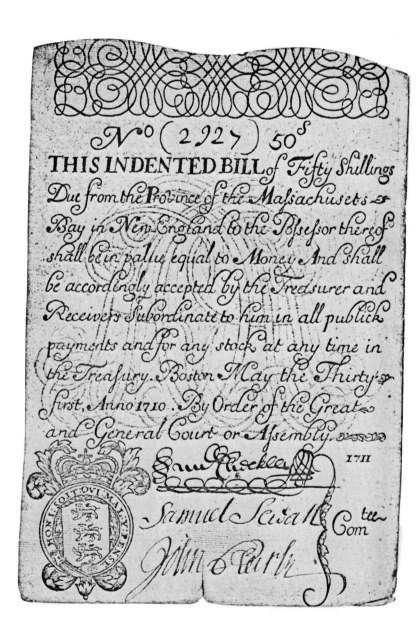

©

MASSACHUSETTS

October 14, 1713

£10,000 in indented Bills issued pursuant to the Nov. 10, 1713 Act to call in all prior issues of 3s6d and 10s bills because of counterfeits in circulation. Engraved on two new copper face plates with the denominations protected by the shape of the frame around the text. An engraved leaf design is on the back. No red overprint. In order to provide small money this issue included two denominations lower than theretofore issued. See subsequent redated issues for halving and quartering practices. Signers are Samuel Checkley, John Clark, Addington Davenport, Elisha Hutchinson, Samuel Sewall, and Penn Townsend.

1s	Trapezoid
1s6d	Octagon
2s	Semicircular scallops
2s6d	Irregular hexagon

3s	
5s	Arched vault
10s	Oval
20s	Mushroom top

May 26, 1714

£30,000 in indented Bills issued pursuant to the June 25, 1714 Act to exchange for old bills. Engraved on a new copper face plate in similar style to the plates for the Oct. 14, 1713 issue. An engraved leaf design is on the back. Same signers as the Oct. 14, 1713 issue.

30s	
40s	Pointed right end
60s	Heptagon
100s	Unframed text

In 1714 there was a plan projected by private individuals to establish a bank of credit for loans on property as had been done by other colonies. A £50,000 loan fund was therefore created by the Colony to stop the group from carrying out their plan. See May 26, 1714 redated issues for further detail on loans.

MASSACHUSETTS

October 14, 1713 Low Denomination Plate successively redated, 1714, 1718, 1719, 1721, 1722, 1723, 1725, 1727, 1731, 1733, 1735, 1736, and 1740

Commencing with the issue authorized by the Nov. 4, 1714 Act the low denomination plate was redated from time to time as Acts for new emissions were approved. The existing dates were left unchanged and each new date separately added. Due to a lack of small money in circulation the lower denominations printed from this plate were halved and quartered by the public prior to June 15, 1722 when a committee was ordered to investigate the practice. Signers are Samuel Checkley, John Clark, Elisha Cooke, Addington Davenport, William Dudley, Elisha Hutchinson, John Jeffries, William Payne, John Quincy, Samuel Sewall, Penn Townsend, John Wainwright, J. Willard, and A. Winthrop. See May 26, 1714 redated issues for further detail.

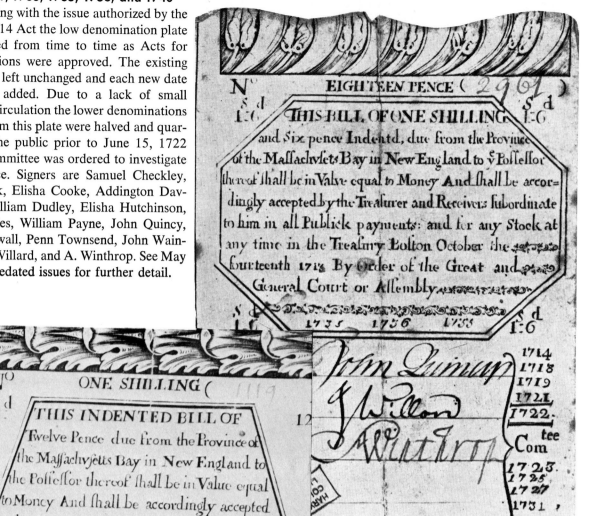

Above 18d bill is redated to 1736

12d (1s)
1s6d (18d)
24d (2s)
2s6d (Half Crown)

Adjacent 1s bill is redated to 1735

MASSACHUSETTS

October 14, 1713 Middle Denomination Plate successively redated 1714, 1716, 1716 ★, 1718, 1719, 1721, 1722, 1723, 1724, 1725, 1725 †, 1727, 1728, 1731, 1733, 1735, 1736, and 1740

Commencing with an issue of £10,000 under the June 25, 1714 Act the middle denomination plate was redated from time to time as new emissions were authorized. The existing dates were left unchanged. There were three more redatings on the middle plate than on either of the other plates. The insignia following the 1716 and 1725 dates were added to identify the second issue of each of those years. By the Feb. 21, 1727(8) Resolve a new marking was to be added to the 10s bills because of counterfeits. Same signers as the redated issues from lower plate. See May 26, 1714 redated issues for further detail.

Above 5s bill © is redated to 1740

3s (36d)
5s (Crown) ©
10s (Angel) ©
20s (Pound)

Adjacent £1 bill is redated to 1716 ★

May 26, 1714 High Denomination Plate successively redated 1716, 1716 ★, 1718, 1721, 1722, 1723, 1724, 1725, 1725 †, 1727, 1733, 1735, 1736, and 1740

Commencing with an issue of £80,000 under an Act passed during the May 30, 1716 Session the high denomination plate was redated from time to time as new emissions were authorized. The existing dates were left unchanged. Same signers as redated issues from the lower plate. The supporting legislation for issues from the high denomination plate and from the previously described middle and low denomination plates is as follows:

£50,000 to be loaned for 5 years at 5% interest and £40,000 to exchange for old bills was provided by the June 25, 1714 and Nov. 4, 1714 Acts; £5,000 by the June 23, 1716 Resolve of which £1,000 was to be from the middle plate and £4,000 from the high denomination plate; £100,000 to be printed from the two highest denomina-

Above £5 bill © is redated to 1727

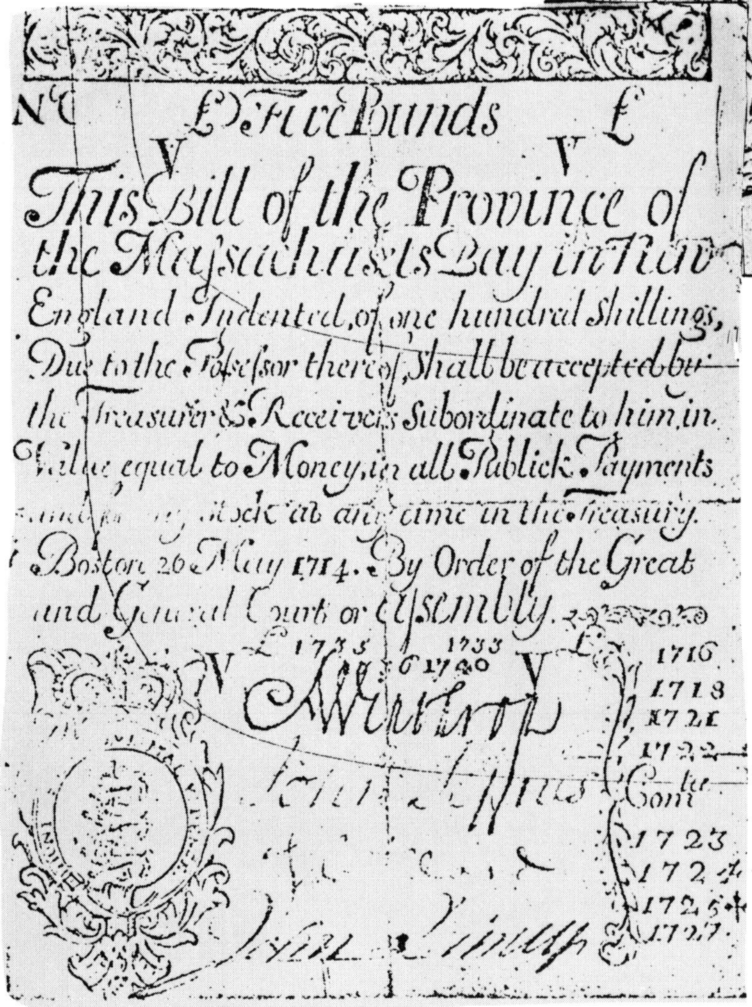

30s ©
40s
60s ©
100s ©

Adjacent £5 bill © is redated to 1740

tion plates was to be loaned for 10 years at 5% interest pursuant to the Act of Dec. 4, 1716; £6,000 by the July 3, 1718 Resolve and £5,000 by the Dec. 2, 1718 Resolve were specified as reemissions but apparently were new issues; £50,000 was approved for loans on Mar. 31, 1721(2) from all plates; £12,000, £13,000 and £20,000 were issued pursuant to Resolves of July 3, 1722, Jan. 14, 1722(3) and Jan. 18, 1722(3); £20,000 and £20,000 by the July 2, 1723 and Dec. 27, 1723 Resolves; £25,000 and £30,000 by the June 13, 1724 and Dec. 1, 1724 Resolves; £40,000 and £30,000 by the June 16, 1725 and Nov. 30, 1725 Resolves; £20,000 on June 16, 1726; £5,000 on Dec. 17, 1726; £16,000 on June 19, 1727; £12,000 on Jan. 13, 1727(8); £60,000 and £20,000 on Feb. 21, 1727(8); £10,000 from the middle plate on June 13, 1728; £20,000 on Sept. 24, 1729; £13,000 on Oct. 17, 1730; £1,000 and £6,000 on April 24, 1731; £5,400 on May 26, 1731; £3,800 on Feb. 3, 1731(2); £3,000 on April 28, 1733; £76,500 on Oct. 3, 1733; £3,000 on April 10, 1734; £29,570 on July 6, 1734; £3,000 in April 1735; £41,207 on May 28, 1735; £3,000 on Mar. 17, 1735(6); £3,000 on May 26, 1736; £18,000 on Feb. 9, 1736(7); and £80,000 on July 7, 1740 which was the last date of Old Tenor issues.

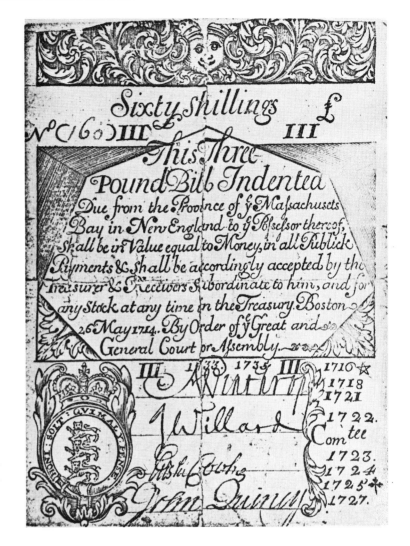

Above 60s bill Ⓒ is redated to 1735

June 1722

£500 in small change bills issued to prevent William Wood from introducing Rosa Americana base copper coinage into circulation in New England and to prevent halving and quartering of prior issues. Printed from set type on parchment pursuant to the May 30, 1722 Act.

Unnumbered and unsigned. The text and make up of the bills was used to print the official Act authorizing the issue. The shapes were used to simplify the determination of denominations. Some bills were torn in half to make smaller change.

1d   Round shape [40,001]
2d   Rectangular shape [20,000]
3d   Hexagonal shape [13,333]

John Merrett ★ 1733

Because of a scarcity of small Province bills and coppers John Merrett who operated Three Sugar Loaves & Canister on King Street in Boston issued bearer notes due on demand. They were designed so that they could be torn in half. Other denominations are probable.

2s   3s   5s

Merchants' Notes ★ November 30, 1733

£110,000 in Merchants' Notes issued by a private partnership of 102 participants in order to prevent an issue of Rhode Island bills of credit from flooding Massachusetts Bay. Repayable in silver at 19s per ounce, 30% by Dec. 30, 1736, 30% by Dec. 30, 1739, and 40% by Dec. 30, 1743. These promissory notes were payable to the order of Richard Clarke and endorsed by him on the back. The face and back were engraved on copper and contain the motto JUSTITIAE ERGO (For the sake of justice) and a hand holding balancing scales. Signers are James Bowdoin, Edward Bromfield, Jr., William

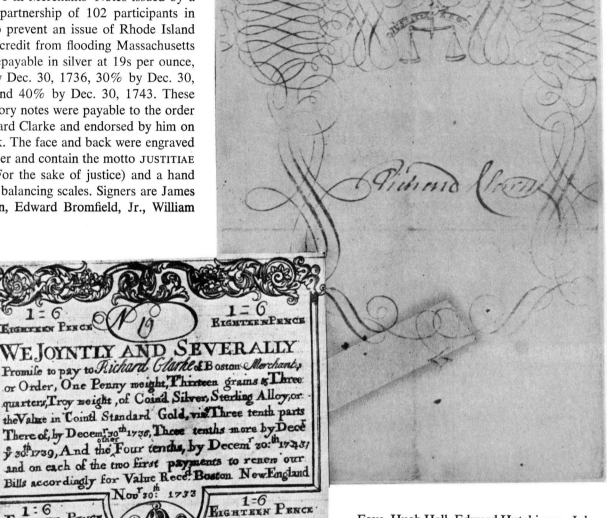

Foye, Hugh Hall, Edward Hutchinson, John Osborne, Samuel Sewall, Samuel Welles, Jacob Wendell, and Joshua Winslow.

1s6d	(1 dwt., 13¾ gr.)
2s6d	(2 dwt., 15¼ gr.)
6s	(6 dwt., 7½ gr.)
10s	(10 dwt., 12½ gr.)
20s	(1 oz., 1 dwt., 1¼ gr.)
£3	(3 oz., 3 dwt., 3¾ gr.)
£6	(6 oz., 6 dwt., 7½ gr.)
£10	(10 oz., 10 dwt., 12½ gr.)

MASSACHUSETTS

February 4, 1736(7)

£9,000 in indented New Tenor or Three Fold Tenor bills (3 Old Tenor for 1) issued pursuant to the Act published Feb. 9, 1736(7) and receivable at the Treasury at 6s8d per ounce of silver except for duties and lighthouse fees. Subsequently these bills became known as Middle Tenor. The faces were engraved with elaborate denomination designs and the Province Arms. The backs were printed from set type with elaborate cuts for indenture. Signers are William Dudley, John Jeffries, and John Wainwright.

	10d	1s8d	3s4d	6s8d	10s	20s	30s	40s

February 4, 1736(7) redated 1737

£27,000 (£1,000, £20,000 and £6,000) in indented New Tenor or Three Fold Tenor (later Middle Tenor) Bills issued pursuant to two June 30, 1737 Acts and a Jan. 9, 1737(8) Act. Printed from same plates as Feb. 4, 1736(7) issue with 1737 added without disturbing the existing date. Same signers as Feb. 4, 1736(7) issue.

10d
(2 dwt.,
12 gr.)

1s8d
(5 dwt.)

3s4d
(10 dwt.)

6s8d
(1 oz.)

10s
(1 oz.,
10 dwt.)

20s
(3 oz.)

30s
(4 oz.,
10 dwt.)

40s
(6 oz.)

MASSACHUSETTS

1737

£2,625 in New Tenor (later Middle Tenor) small change Bills authorized by the July 7, 1737 Act. John Bushell cut the ornamented wood block borders and put his initials or name on each denomination. Printed by John Draper who used the identical printing form to show the face of all of the bills in the official printing of the statutes. Backs are typeset. Signers are William Dudley, John Jeffries, and J. Willard.

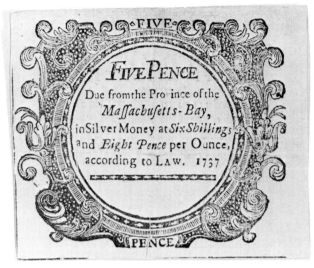
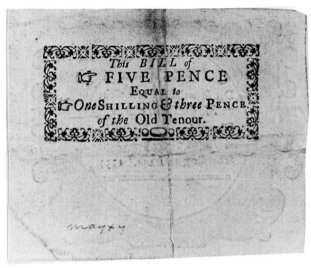

1d	Winged figures [30,000]	4d	Squirrel and turtle. JOHN BUSHELL SCULP [30,000]
2d	Angels with fruit [30,000]	5d	Circular frame [30,000]
3d	Lion [30,000]	6d	Tree and Indian [30,000]

Silver Bank ★ August 1, 1740

£120,000 in "Silver Bank," "Specie Bank" or "Merchants" Bills issued by a private partnership of 107 participants headed by Edward Hutchinson and organized in Boston to compete with the Manufactory Bank. Engraved bills issued to lend out with land as security. Payable by Dec. 31, 1755 to the order of Isaac Winslow in coined silver at 6s8d per ounce or the equivalent in gold. The bills contain vignettes and the motto FIAT JUSTITIA (Let there be justice). Signers are James Boutineau, James Bowdoin, Hugh Hall, Edward Hutchinson, Andrew Oliver, Thomas Oxnard, Edmund Quincy, Samuel Sewall, Samuel Welles, and Joshua Winslow. Other denominations are probable.

2s6d	(60 gr.) Wharf scene
5s	(5 dwt.) Skiff ©️
7s6d	(7 dwt., 12 gr.) Rowboat
15s	(15 dwt.) Ship
£10	(10 oz. in silver or 13 dwt., 13 gr. in gold) Two ships

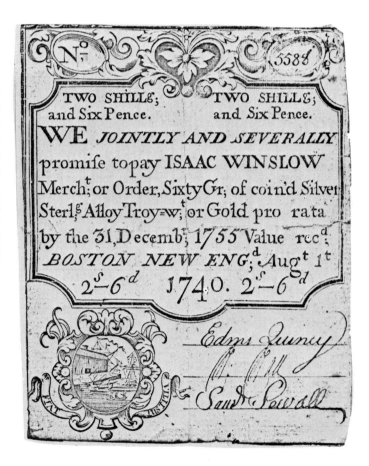

Manufactory Bills ★ September 9, 1740

£150,000 in Manufactory Bills or Land Bank Bills issued in Boston by a private partnership of 396 participants headed by John Colman. These engraved bills were issued with land as security; were to be current at 6s8d per ounce of coined silver; and were payable to the order of Joseph Marion in 20 years in Produce or Manufactures set out in the "scheme." Incorporation was refused and redemption of bills was forced by the Crown in 1741. The issue was the subject of spirited political and economic controversy. The bills contained the motto NEC PLURIBUS IMPAR (Not unequal to a greater number). Proofs of two incomplete trial printings exist. Signers are G. Chardon, Thomas Cheever, William Stoddard, Samuel Trusty, and Samuel Watts. Other denominations are probable.

3d	Incomplete engraving	Ⓤ
3d		
6d		
7s6d	Five misspellings in text	Ⓤ
7s6d		
20s		

Bank Bills ★ May 1, 1741

£50,000 in Bank Bills issued by a private partnership in Ipswich, Essex County, payable on demand to the order of James Eveleth in Produce or Manufactures or in whatever silver was in the partnership treasury at the rate of 6s8d per ounce. Engraved bills with the motto JUSTITIA REDIVIVA (Justice renewed). Signers are John Brown, Robert Choate, Edward Eveleth, Jonathan Hale, John Hadwen, Thomas Robinson, Eben Stevens, and Edwin Thurston, Jr. Other denominations are probable.

1d	Tree
3d	Tree
9d	Beehives
1s	Skiff
2s	Ship at wharf
5s	Ship on ways

January 15, 1741(2)

£30,000 in a legal tender issue of Second New Tenor bills equal to £120,000 of the Old Tenor bills and sometimes referred to as New Tenor bills. By the Jan. 15, 1741(2) Act three face plates were to be engraved, the four highest denominations on the "first plate," the next four highest on the "second plate" and the lowest six denominations on the "third plate." The backs of the lowest six denominations contain woodcut borders previously used on the face of the 1737 small change issue. All backs are typeset and include the date and the value in Old Tenor. Signers are J. Choate, Roland Cotton, Samuel Watts, and J. Willard.

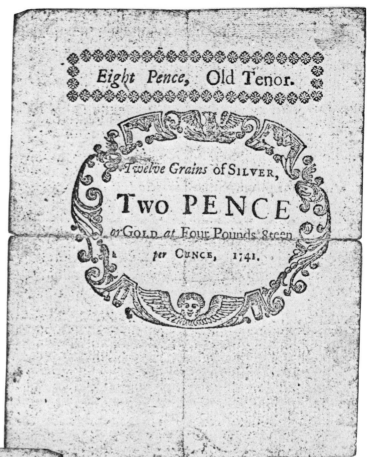

2d	(12 gr.) Circle
4d	(1 dwt.) Square
6d	(1 dwt., 12 gr.) Hexagon
8d	(2 dwt.) Octagon
1s	(3 dwt.) Oval
2s	(6 dwt.) Square with concave corners
3s	(9 dwt.)
4s	(12 dwt.)
5s	(15 dwt.)
10s	(1 oz., 10 dwt.)
15s	(2 oz., 5 dwt.)
20s	(3 oz.) Ⓤ
30s	(4 oz., 10 dwt.)
40s	(6 oz.)

January 15, 1741(2) (Continued)

This issue and the following two issues contain both the English Arms and the Massachusetts Arms.

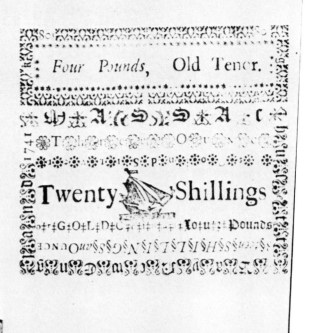

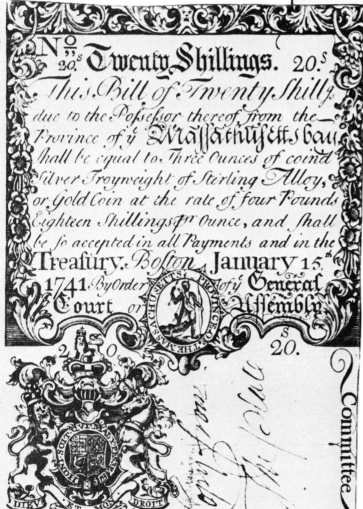

January 15, 1741(2) redated 1742

£39,000 in Second New Tenor Bills printed from same plates as the Jan. 15, 1741(2) issue but with 1742 added without disturbing the prior dating. The first £15,000 were authorized by the July 1, 1742 Act. Then £12,000 more were authorized by the Jan. 12, 1742(3) Act which issue, pursuant to the Jan. 14, 1742(3) Resolution, required denominational alterations to be made on the plates so as to change 4s to 2s6d; 3s to 15d; 2s to 9d; and 8d to 3d. £12,000 more were authorized by the Nov. 12, 1743 Act. Signers are Roland Cotton and J. Willard.

©

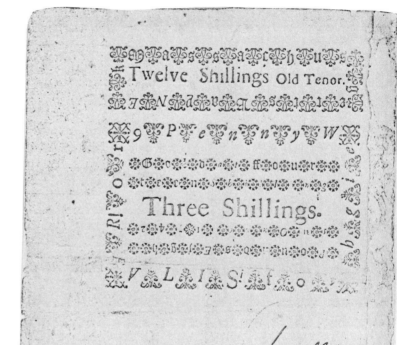

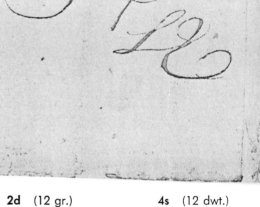

2d	(12 gr.)	4s	(12 dwt.)
4d	(1 dwt.)	5s	(15 dwt.)
6d	(1 dwt., 12 gr.)	10s	(1 oz., 10 dwt.)
8d	(2 dwt.)	15s	(2 oz., 5 dwt.)
1s	(3 dwt.)	20s	(3 oz.)
2s	(6 dwt.)	30s	(4 oz., 10 dwt.)
3s	(9 dwt.) ©	40s	(6 oz.)

Denominations from changed plates

3d	(18 gr.)	15d	(3 dwt., 18 gr.)
9d	(2 dwt., 6 gr.)	2s6d	(7 dwt., 12 gr.)

MASSACHUSETTS

June 20, 1744

Commencing with £26,037 10s authorized by the June 20, 1744 Act and continuing with eighteen more emissions through the Jan. 22, 1749(50) Act, Second New Tenor bills with a reduced silver equivalent were emitted and reemitted to a total of £666,837 10s. The Jan. 15, 1741(2) plates redated 1742 were substantially altered by substituting June 20, 1744 in place of Jan. 15, 1741 and by changing the silver equivalent in the engraved text. On the backs the date in the typeset text was changed to 1744 and the silver equivalent adjusted. Because most of these issues were for the military action

in the Cape Breton, Louisburg, and Canadian campaigns, the Crown repaid the colony in coin a total of £183,649 2s 7½d sterling which was used to redeem all outstanding bills of credit within one year after Mar. 31, 1750. Pursuant to the Jan. 26, 1748(9) Act one Spanish Dollar was exchanged for 45s in Old Tenor and for 11s3d in New Tenor (Middle Tenor) and Second New Tenor. Signers are Roland Cotton, R. Hale, J. Heath, J. Hutchinson, J. Jeffries, J. Quincy, Samuel Watts, Samuel Welles, and J. Willard.

2d	(11 gr.) Circle Ⓒ		2s6d	(6 dwt., 16 gr.)
3d	(16 gr.) Octagon Ⓒ		5s	(13 dwt., 8 gr.)
4d	(21 gr.) Square		10s	(1 oz., 6 dwt., 16 gr.) Ⓒ
6d	(1 dwt., 8 gr.) Hexagon		15s	(2 oz.)
9d	(2 dwt.) Square with concave corners		20s	(2 oz., 13 dwt., 8 gr.)
1s	(2 dwt., 16 gr.) Oval. 44 in date reversed		30s	(4 oz.) Ⓒ
15d	(3 dwt., 8 gr.)		40s	(5 oz., 6 dwt., 16 gr.) Ⓒ

1750

£3,000 ($10,000) in change bills secured by a deposit of Spanish Dollars and approved by Act of Jan. 27, 1749(50). Printed from decorative woodcut borders and set type. The vignettes consist of a pine tree, codfish and balancing scales with the motto REM RESTITUIT (He has restored the situation). Signers are A. Bordman, Roland Cotton, J. Hutchinson, J. Quincy, and Samuel Watts. New England paper money issues were restricted by the Crown after 1750.

$1/72 (1d)
$1/24 (3d)
$1/16 (4 1/2d)
$1/12 (6d)
$1/8 (9d)
$1/4 (18d)

May 25, 1775

£25,998 in indented Notes due on May 25, 1776 with 6% interest were authorized by the May 20, 1775 Resolve. An overrun of £254 was approved for issuance by the July 6, 1775 Resolve. Engraved by Paul Revere on three copper plates with three denominations on each. Below the vignette containing **M B C (M**assachusetts Bay Colony) for indenture are the words, AMERICAN **PAPER**. The same style of note was engraved by Revere for the New Hampshire issue dated June 20, 1775. Printed by Paul Revere on laid paper watermarked with a Crown over GR (Georgius Rex). Signers are Jedediah Foster, Abraham Fuller, Henry Gardner, Thomas Plympton, James Prescott, Ezra Richmond, and Lemuel Robinson. **By the Resolve** of June 28, 1775 clarifying a Resolve of May 1, 1775 bills of credit of all other colonies except Nova Scotia and Canada became legal tender.

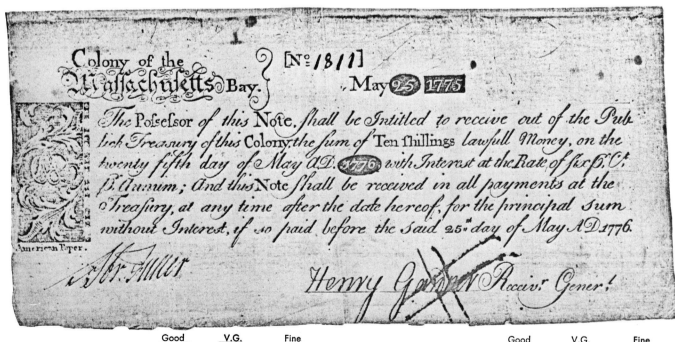

	Good	V.G.	Fine			Good	V.G.	Fine
6s [4,260]	300.00	500.00	900.00		15s [4,133]	300.00	500.00	900.00
9s [4,133]	300.00	500.00	900.00		16s [4,133]	300.00	500.00	900.00
10s [4,133]	300.00	500.00	900.00		18s [4,133]	300.00	500.00	900.00
12s [4,133]	300.00	500.00	900.00		20s [4,260]	300.00	500.00	900.00
14s [4,260]	300.00	500.00	900.00					

MASSACHUSETTS

July 8, 1775

£3,748 in indented Notes due on May 25, 1776 with 6% interest were authorized by the July 6, 1775 Resolve. The three copper plates for the May 25, 1775 issue were, after modification of the date by Paul Revere, reused by him for printing this issue. The plate for 20s, 14s, and 6s exists in slightly damaged condition and contains Revere's engraving of Harvard College on the other side. The plate for 10s, 18s, and 12s exists in defaced condition and contains Revere's engraving of the Boston Massacre on the other side. The plate for 16s, 15s, and 9s also exists and contains Revere's engraving of Rev. Samuel Willard on the other side. Signers are Abraham Fuller, Henry Gardner, Stephen Hall, and Lemuel Robinson.

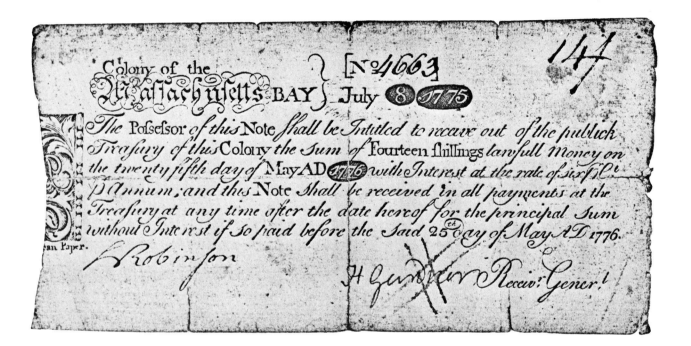

6s	[540]	®
9s	[667]	®
10s	[667]	®
12s	[667]	®
14s	[540]	®
15s	[667]	®
16s	[667]	®
18s	[667]	®
20s	[540]	®

August 18, 1775

£100,000 in "Sword in Hand" legal tender Bills engraved and printed by Paul Revere from two face plates and two back plates pursuant to the Resolve of July 6, 1775 and the Act of Aug. 23, 1775. The face has a small oval vignette of a ship, except on the 1s which has a pine tree in the oval. The back shows an American holding a sword in one hand and the MAGNA CHARTA in the other, surrounded by ISSUED IN DEFENCE OF AMERICAN LIBERTY and ENSE PETIT PLACIDAM, SUB LIBERTATE, QUIETEM (By arms he seeks tranquility under freedom). Because the issue was to be redeemed in the amount of £40,000 by Aug. 18, 1778, £30,000 by Aug. 18, 1779, and £30,000 by Aug. 18, 1780 each denomination was issued with three due dates, the plate being modified for each change. The 17s and 24s were originally printed with an erroneous 1777 due date which was in due course corrected to 1778 on the plate. There are some notes on which the 1777 due date is modified in ink before the plate was corrected. The July 6, 1775 Resolve included 13s, 19s, 60s, 80s, and 100s denominations which the Aug. 23, 1775 Act eliminated. Signers are Joseph Cushing, Daniel Hopkins, J. Palmer, Thomas Plympton, James Prescott, Ebenezer Sayer, and Joseph Wheeler. Red, blue and black ink was ordered to be used successively by each signer, but this was not always complied with.

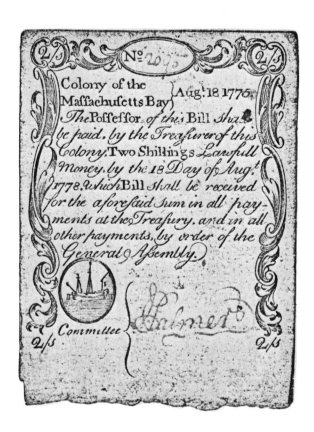

		Good	V.G.	Fine
1s	Three due dates [10,000] ...	500	800	1,500
2s	Three due dates [10,000] ...	500	800	1,500
2s6d	Three due dates [10,000] ...	500	800	1,500
4s	Three due dates [10,000] ...	500	800	1,500
5s	Three due dates [10,000] ...	500	800	1,500
6s	Three due dates [10,000] ...	500	800	1,500
7s6d	Three due dates [10,000] ...	500	800	1,500
8s	Three due dates [10,000] ...	500	800	1,500
10s	Three due dates [10,000]	500	800	1,500
11s	Three due dates [10,000]	500	800	1,500
12s	Three due dates [10,000]	500	800	1,500
17s	Three due dates [10,000]	500	800	1,500
20s	Three due dates [10,000]	500	800	1,500
24s	Three due dates [10,000]	500	800	1,500
30s	Three due dates [10,000]	500	800	1,500
40s	Three due dates [10,000]	500	800	1,500

December 7, 1775

£75,000 in "Sword in Hand" legal tender Bills printed by Paul Revere pursuant to the Dec. 22, 1775 Act. The two face plates and the two back plates of the Aug. 18, 1775 issue were altered to the extent necessary in the text and the denomination. All denominations except the 10s differ from the Aug. 18, 1775 issue. Through a printing error some bills had different denominations on the face and on the back. All bills are payable on Dec. 7, 1781 even though the Dec. 22, 1775 Act provided for £30,000 to be due Dec. 7, 1781, £22,500 to be due Dec. 7, 1782 and £22,500 to be due Dec. 7, 1783. The due date was apparently left unchanged because of the poor quality of due date changes on the plates for the Aug. 18, 1775 issue. The face plate for the lower eight denominations has been preserved. The plate for the counterfeit 42s was found in and still remains in Montrose, Scotland. Signers are Joseph Batchelder, Jr., Benjamin Ely, Daniel Hopkins, I. Morgan, William Pynchon, Thomas Rice, Dummer Sewall, and Joseph Wheeler.

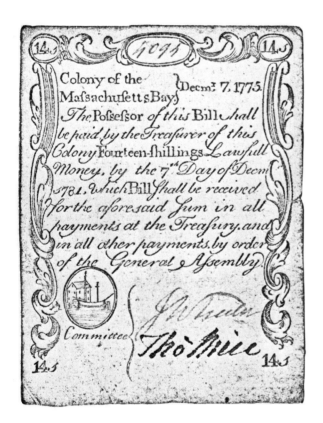

			Good	V.G.	Fine
8d	[6,250]	......	600.00	900.00	1,750.00
1s4d	[6,250]	......	600.00	900.00	1,750.00
1s6d	[6,250]	......	600.00	900.00	1,750.00
2s8d	[6,250]	......	600.00	900.00	1,750.00
3s Deemr.	[6,250]	.	600.00	900.00	1,750.00
3s4d	[6,250]	......	600.00	900.00	1,750.00
4s6d	[6,250]	......	600.00	900.00	1,750.00
7s	[6,250]	......	600.00	900.00	1,750.00
10s	[6,250]	......	600.00	900.00	1,750.00
14s	[6,250]	......	600.00	900.00	1,750.00
16s	[6,250]	......	600.00	900.00	1,750.00
22s	[6,250]	......	600.00	900.00	1,750.00
28s	[6,250]	......	600.00	900.00	1,750.00
36s	[6,250]	ⓒ ...	600.00	900.00	1,750.00
42s	[6,250]	ⓒ ...	600.00	900.00	1,750.00
48s	[6,250]	......	600.00	900.00	1,750.00

June 18, 1776

£100,000 in legal tender Bills authorized by the June 21, 1776 Act, one half of the bills of each denomination payable by June 18, 1778 and the other half by June 18, 1779. Bills of 5s4d and below are entirely typeset and are small in size. Bills of 6s and over have three border cuts and a cut of an American holding a sword and the Magna Charta. Bills of 6s and over have the denomination in dollars on the face and back. All bills are printed on coarse paper by Benjamin Edes. Bills of 6s and higher were called in for exchange for other bills by the Acts of Oct. 13, 1777 and Dec. 13, 1777. Bills of 5s4d and below of this and all prior issues were called in by Act of Oct. 13, 1778 for exchange for the Oct. 16, 1778 issue of bills. Signers are Jonathan Brown, S. Carlton, C. Davis, T. Dawes, Abner Ellis, A. Fuller, Daniel Green, Moses Gunn, S. Hall, Ter., Israel Hobart, Daniel Hopkins, D. Jeffries, John Lewis, Sam A. Otis, W. Palfrey, George Partridge, Samuel Thatcher, J. Wigglesworth, and George Williams.

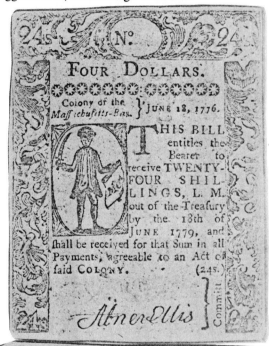

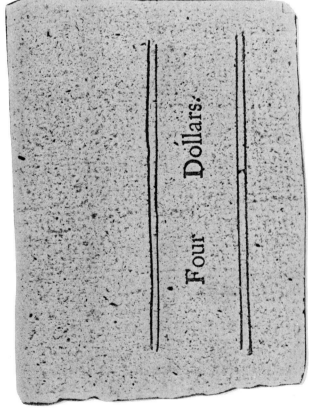

				Good	V.G.	Fine
3d	Two due dates	[8,000]		175	200	300
4d	Two due dates	[8,000]		175	200	300
5d	Two due dates	[8,000]		175	200	300
6d	Two due dates	[8,000]		175	200	300
9d	Two due dates	[8,000]		175	200	300
10d	Two due dates	[8,000]		175	200	300
1s	Two due dates	[8,000]	Ⓤ	175	200	300
1s3d	Two due dates	[8,000]		175	200	300
1s8d	Two due dates	[8,000]		175	200	300
2s4d	Two due dates	[8,000]		175	200	300
2s6d	Two due dates	[8,000]	Ⓒ	175	200	300
3s6d	Two due dates	[8,000]		175	200	300
4s	Two due dates	[8,000]		175	200	300
4s4d	Two due dates	[8,000]	Ⓒ	175	200	300
5s	Two due dates	[8,000]	Ⓒ	175	200	300
5s4d	Two due dates	[8,000]		175	200	300
6s ($1)	Two due dates	[8,000]		400	500	600
12s ($2)	Two due dates	[8,000]		400	500	600
18s ($3)	Two due dates	[8,000]		400	500	600
24s ($4)	Two due dates	[8,000]	Ⓒ	400	500	600
30s ($5)	Two due dates	[8,000]		400	500	600
36s ($6)	Two due dates	[8,000]		400	500	600
42s ($7)	Two due dates	[8,000]		400	500	600
48s ($8)	Two due dates	[8,000]		400	500	600

MASSACHUSETTS

September 17, 1776

£50,004 in legal tender Bills of Credit payable by Dec. 7, 1781 and authorized by the Sept. 16, 1776 Act. The two engraved copper plates for the face and back of the high denominations of the Dec. 7, 1775 issue were modified by Paul Revere for this emission by changing the date on both the face and the back and by changing COLONY to STATE in two places on the face. Signers are Jonathan Brown, Thomas Cook, C. Davis, Jonas Dix, Ichabod Goodwin, Henry J. Hill, John Lewis, and John Murray.

10s [4,630]		28s [4,630]	
14s [4,630]		36s [4,630]	
16s [4,630]		42s [4,630]	
22s [4,630]		48s [4,630]	

October 18, 1776

£75,000 in legal tender "Codfish" Bills due Oct. 18, 1784 and authorized by the Dec. 7, 1776 Act. The face plate for the twelve lowest denominations was engraved by Paul Revere and featured a codfish in the border design and the bills are small in size. The backs of the twelve lowest denominations are printed from set type and a cast cut of a pine tree. Nathaniel Hurd began to engrave both the face plates and the back cuts for the twelve highest denominations, but they were apparently completed by Revere. The backs of the twelve highest denominations include three border cuts, one central cut of a pine tree surrounded by OMNE TULIT PUNCTUM QUI MISCUIT UTILE DULCI (He won all the praise who mixed the useful with the sweet) and some set type. Revere apparently printed only the engraved faces and John Gill printed the backs of all bills. The twelve highest denominations were called in by the Act of Oct. 13, 1777 for exchange into notes by Jan. 1, 1778, but this was extended by the Act. of Dec. 13, 1777 to April 1, 1778. The twelve highest denominations contained dollar equivalents while the twelve lowest denominations did not. Signers are Nehemiah Abbot, Nathan Adams, Nathaniel Barber, D. C. Brown, David Cheever, William Drew, Jonathan Hastings, Thomas Ivers, Dummer Jewett, George Partridge, Ezra Sergeant, and Jonathan Wood.

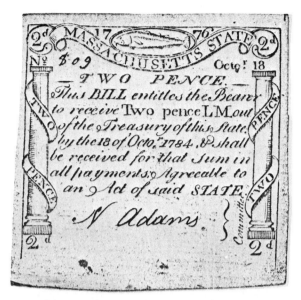

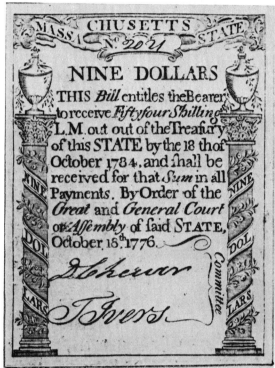

	Good	V.G.	Fine		
2d [5,143]	125.00	200.00	300.00	6s ($1)	[3,000]
3d [5,143]	125.00	200.00	300.00	12s ($2)	[3,000]
4d [5,143]	125.00	200.00	300.00	18s ($3)	[3,000]
6d [5,143]	125.00	200.00	300.00	24s ($4)	[3,000]
8d [5,143]	125.00	200.00	300.00	30s ($5)	[3,000]
9d [5,143]	125.00	200.00	300.00	36s ($6)	[3,000]
1s [5,143]	125.00	200.00	300.00	42s ($7)	[3,000]
1s6d [5,143]	125.00	200.00	300.00	48s ($8)	[3,000]
2s [5,143]	125.00	200.00	300.00	54s ($9)	[3,000]
3s [5,143]	125.00	200.00	300.00	60s ($10)	[3,000]
4s [5,143]	125.00	200.00	300.00	66s ($11)	[3,000]
4s6d [5,143]	125.00	200.00	300.00	72s ($12)	[3,000]

November 17, 1776

£70,038 (£50,004 and £20,034) in legal tender Bills of Credit due by Dec. 7, 1781 and authorized by the Oct. 29, 1776 and Dec. 6, 1776 Acts. The two engraved copper plates previously used for the Dec. 7, 1775 and Sept. 17, 1776 issues were further modified by Paul Revere for this emission by changing the date and by changing MAGNA CHARTA to INDEPENDANCE. The mutilated back plate exists and contains Revere's engraving of "A View of Part of the Town of Boston ***" on the other side. This emission and all bills of 6s and over

of prior issues were called for exchange by the Act of Oct. 13, 1777 and were to become unredeemable after Jan. 1, 1778. The redemption date was successively advanced to Dec. 1, 1778 by the Acts of Dec. 13, 1777, April 3, 1778, and June 4, 1778. Signers are Nehemiah Abbot, Nathan Adams, Nathaniel Barber, Jonathan Brown, David Cheever, Jonas Dix, William Drew, Ichabod Godwin, Jonathan Hastings, Jr., Israel Hobart, Thomas Ivers, Dummer Jewett, Joseph Noyes, Ezra Sergeant, and Jonathan Woods.

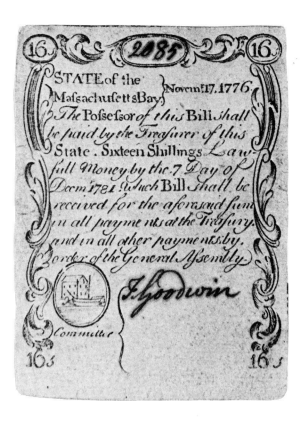

10s	[6,485]	Ⓡ	
14s	[6,485]	Ⓡ	
16s	[6,485]	Ⓡ	
22s	[6,485]	Ⓡ	
28s	[6,485]	Ⓡ	
36s	[6,485]	Ⓡ	
42s	[6,485]	Ⓡ	
48s	[6,485]	Ⓡ	Ⓒ

MASSACHUSETTS

October 16, 1778

£8,000 in legal tender Bills of Credit payable by Oct. 18, 1784 and issued to replace all bills of 5s4d and below dated on or before June 18, 1776. Originally £28,000 (30,000 bills of each denomination) was authorized by the Oct. 13, 1778 Act, but the delay and expense and the poor quality in printing such quantities were avoided by the Jan. 26, 1779 Act which provided for new plates and a higher range of denominations for £20,000 of the bills (see 1779 issue). The copper face plate for the twelve lowest denominations of the Oct. 18, 1776 issue was redated by Paul Revere and reused. The Pine Tree cast cuts on the back of the Oct. 18, 1776 issue were also reused. The type on the back of the Oct. 18, 1776 issue was reset. Revere apparently printed only the engraved faces and Thomas Fleet printed the backs. Signers are Nathan Adams, Jonathan Brown, Richard Cranch, Thomas Dawes, John Greenough, and George Partridge.

		Good	V.G.	Fine
2d	[8,571]	100.00	150.00	200.00
3d	[8,571]	100.00	150.00	200.00
4d	[8,571]	100.00	150.00	200.00
6d	[8,571]	100.00	150.00	200.00
8d	[8,571]	100.00	150.00	200.00
9d	[8,571]	100.00	150.00	200.00
12d	[8,571]	100.00	150.00	200.00
1s6d	[8,571]	100.00	150.00	200.00
2s	[8,571]	100.00	150.00	200.00
3s	[8,571]	100.00	150.00	200.00
4s	[8,571]	100.00	150.00	200.00
4s6d	[8,571]	100.00	150.00	200.00

1779

£20,000 in Substitute Denomination Bills emitted as part of the Oct. 16, 1778 issue, but payable by Dec. 1, 1782 pursuant to the Jan. 26, 1779 Act. Newly engraved face plate by Paul Revere with sun RISING. The backs contained set type and cast cuts of the pine tree previously used on Oct. 18, 1776 and Oct. 16, 1778 issues. The face plate is preserved. Revere apparently printed only the engraved faces and Thomas Fleet printed the backs. Signers are Jonathan Brown, Richard Cranch, Thomas Dawes, and George Partridge. Some bills are hole cancelled.

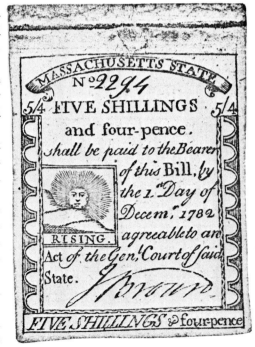

	Good	V.G.	Fine			Good	V.G.	Fine
1s [9,411] ⓡ	100.00	150.00	200.00	4s [9,411] ⓡ	100.00	150.00	200.00
1s6d [9,411] ⓡ	100.00	150.00	200.00	4s6d [9,411] ⓡ	100.00	150.00	200.00
2s [9,411] ⓡ	100.00	150.00	200.00	4s8d [9,411] ⓡ	100.00	150.00	200.00
2s6d [9,411] ⓡ	100.00	150.00	200.00	5s [9,411] ⓡ	100.00	150.00	200.00
3s [9,411] ⓡ	100.00	150.00	200.00	5s4d [9,411] ⓡ	100.00	150.00	200.00
3s6d [9,411] ⓡ	100.00	150.00	200.00	5s6d [9,411] ⓡ	100.00	150.00	200.00

May 5, 1780 Act

£394,000 (£460,000 less £66,000) equal to $1,313,333 in legal tender Bills of Credit payable in Spanish milled dollars by Dec. 31, 1786 with 5% interest was authorized by the May 5, 1780 and June 19, 1780 Acts pursuant to a Continental Congress Resolution of Mar. 18, 1780, guaranteeing the payment of the bills and making the amount issued dependent upon the amount of Continental Currency exchanged at $40 (old) for $1 (new). The face is in black and the back is in red and black. Printed by Hall & Sellers in Philadelphia on paper watermarked UNITED STATES. The face border cuts and the back cuts surrounding the emblems were engraved by Henry Dawkins. The border cuts and emblems on the back are from the Jan. 14, 1779 issue of Continental Currency. Sometimes surcharged in red INTEREST PAID ONE YEAR. Often hole cancelled on redemption. Signers are Loammi Baldwin, Richard Cranch, Thomas Dawes, Samuel Henshaw, Samuel Osgood, and Ebenezer Wales. Guaranty signed by Nathaniel Appleton, Peter Boyer, Joseph Henderson, and Thomas Walley.

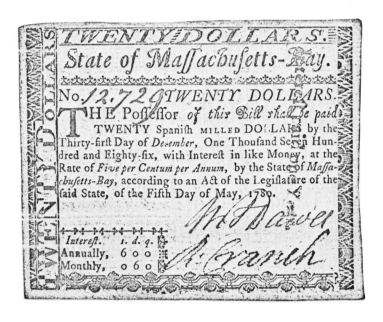
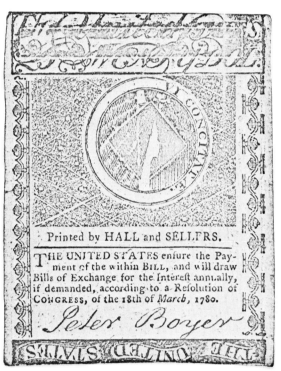

	Fine	V.F.	Unc.			Fine	V.F.	Unc.
$1 [26,267]	20.00	30.00	50.00	$5 [26,267]	20.00	30.00	50.00
$2 [26,267]	20.00	30.00	50.00	$7 [26,267] ⓒ	20.00	30.00	50.00
$3 [26,267]	20.00	30.00	50.00	$8 [26,267]	20.00	30.00	50.00
$4 [26,267]	20.00	30.00	50.00	$20 [26,267] ⓒ	20.00	30.00	50.00

Values are for cancelled bills. Value is doubled if bill is not cancelled.

1781 Written Dates

£51,000 ($170,000) in bearer Treasurer's Certificates with Spanish dollar denominations and receivable for taxes or payable in six months after date of issue at specie value. Top border cut reads COMMONWEALTH OF MASSACHUSETTS.

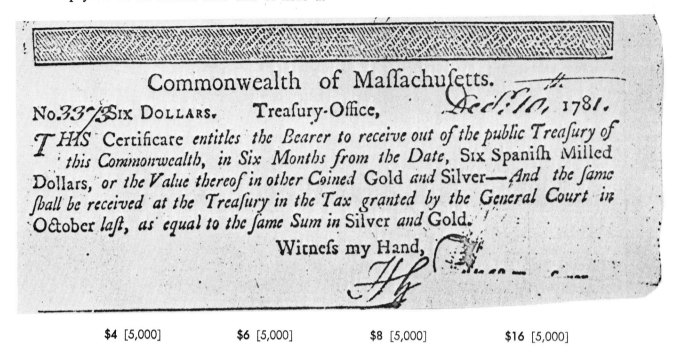

$4 [5,000] $6 [5,000] $8 [5,000] $16 [5,000]

Massachusetts Bank ★ July 5, 1784, etc.

$400,000 ($200,000 and $200,000) in Bank Notes of the Massachusetts Bank, incorporated as a private bank on Feb. 7, 1784 with a capital of $1,600,000. Engraved in Philadelphia and printed in Boston on laid paper, $100,000 being from the "large plate" and $100,000 from the "small plate." Another $200,000 was approved on Oct. 18, 1784. The bills bear written dates beginning on July 5, 1784. The notes were not to be recirculated after July 25, 1785 but this was subsequently countermanded. Signers are James Bowdoin, as president, and Samuel Osgood, as cashier. A special Act to protect the notes of the Bank against counterfeiting was passed Mar. 16, 1784.

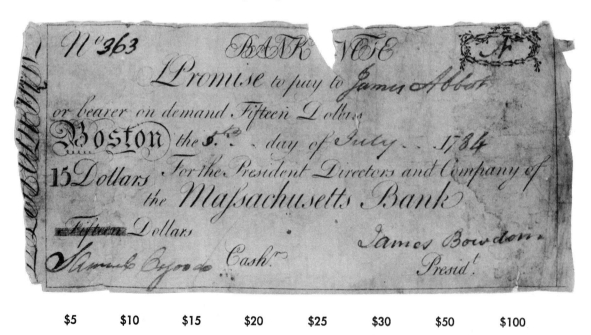

$5 $10 $15 $20 $25 $30 $50 $100

MASSACHUSETTS

Massachusetts Bank ★ December 2, 1784

$11,000 in engraved Bank Notes for smaller transactions. Originally the integral denominations had been approved on Nov. 22, 1784, but they were added to the Dec. 2, 1784 emission instead. All fractional denomination bank notes were withdrawn from circulation after Jan. 5, 1786. Same signers as the previous issue.

$1 [500] ⓤ	$2 [500] ⓤ	$3 [500] ⓤ	$4 [500] ⓤ
$1 1/2 [500] ⓤ	$2 1/2 [500] ⓤ	$3 1/2 [500] ⓤ	$4 1/2 [500] ⓤ

Massachusetts Bank ★ June 21, 1785

$255,000 in engraved Bank Notes which were limited in redemption to payment of debts due the Bank and to payment in specie only on the liquidation of the Bank. Approved on June 21, 1785, but withdrawn after Jan. 2, 1786 because of unacceptability. To prevent alteration the number of vertical lines on the left end corresponded with the number of letters in the written denomination. Signers were James Coffin Jones, as president, and Peter Roe Dalton, as cashier.

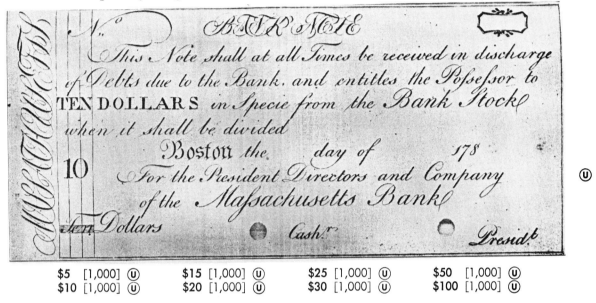

$5 [1,000] ⓤ	$15 [1,000] ⓤ	$25 [1,000] ⓤ	$50 [1,000] ⓤ
$10 [1,000] ⓤ	$20 [1,000] ⓤ	$30 [1,000] ⓤ	$100 [1,000] ⓤ

Massachusetts Bank ★ September 21, 1789

$1,080,000 in engraved Bank Notes printed by Joseph Callender on paper made in Philadelphia and watermarked with the denomination and the bank's name. By an Act passed March 9, 1792 the Massachusetts Bank was prohibited from circulating notes below $5.

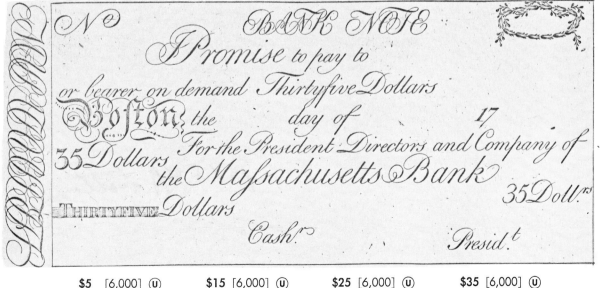

$5 [6,000] ⓤ	$15 [6,000] ⓤ	$25 [6,000] ⓤ	$35 [6,000] ⓤ
$10 [6,000] ⓤ	$20 [6,000] ⓤ	$30 [6,000] ⓤ	$40 [6,000] ⓤ

Bank of the United States ★ 1792, etc.

The Boston Office of Discount and Deposit of the Bank of the United States (first bank) operated from 1792 to 1811 and issued $435,680 in circulating bank notes. A fuller description of these branch bank notes and other branch bank data is included under Pennsylvania listings. George Cabot became the first president of the Boston branch bank.

A flying eagle bearing the Arms of the United States: $5 $10 $20 $50 $100
A heraldic eagle with 13 stars surrounding its head:

Ⓐ

$5 $10 $20 $50 $100

A heraldic eagle in an oval frame containing 15 stars:

Ⓒ

$5 Ⓒ $10 Ⓒ $20 Ⓒ $50 Ⓒ $100 Ⓒ

174

MASSACHUSETTS

Union Bank ★ 1792, etc.

The Union Bank was incorporated on June 22, 1792 for 10 years as the second bank in Massachusetts entitled to issue circulating notes. The capital was originally $400,000 to $800,000 with the State entitled to subscribe to an additional $400,000 which it did. The bank's debts including bank notes were limited to twice its capital plus its specie deposits. Notes below $5 were prohibited until 1805. A counterfeit engraved plate for the $10 note exists. Many issues after 1800 followed.

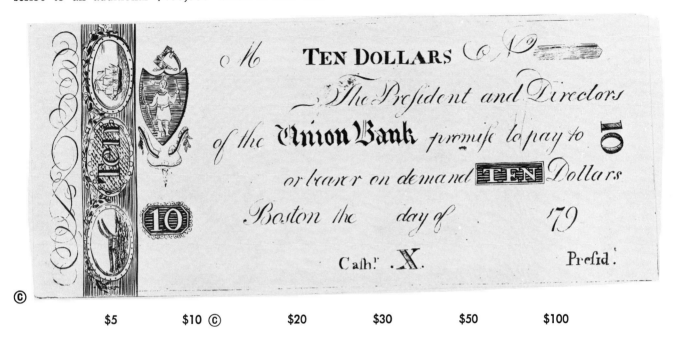

| $5 | $10 ©️ | $20 | $30 | $50 | $100 |

Nantucket Bank ★ 1795, etc.

The Nantucket Bank was incorporated on Feb. 27, 1795 for 10 years as the third bank in Massachusetts entitled to issue circulating notes. The capital was $40,000 to $100,000. Its debts including bank notes were limited to twice its capital plus its specie deposits. Notes below $2 were prohibited. It was entitled to become a branch bank of the Union Bank by May 1, 1795 if it so voted. Its notes were engraved. An early 19th century issue is shown below.

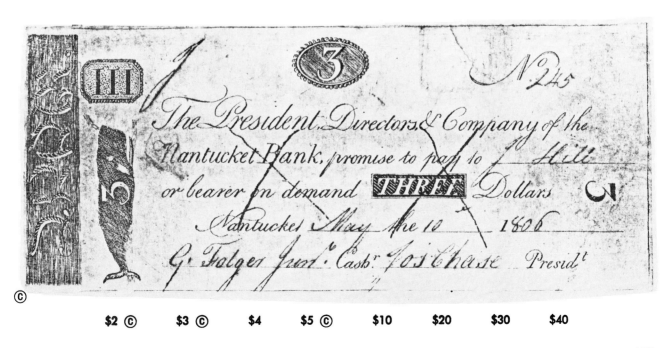

| $2 ©️ | $3 ©️ | $4 | $5 ©️ | $10 | $20 | $30 | $40 |

Merrimack Bank ★ 1795, etc.

The Merrimack Bank was incorporated on June 25, 1795 to operate at Newburyport with a capital of $75,000 to $150,000. Its debts including bank notes could not exceed twice its capital plus its specie deposits. Notes below $2 were prohibited originally but in 1799 the minimum denomination was raised to $5. The engraved notes bore the Continental Currency motto MIND YOUR BUSINESS. Signers are William Bartlett, as president, and Joseph Cutler, as cashier. Other denominations are probable.

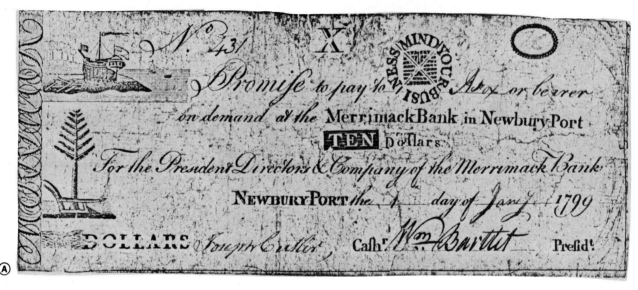

$2 $10

James Leach ★
July 1, 1796

Indented engraved promissory notes issued at Boston by a private banker. Plate letters.

$5   Envy's a Snake, the Growth of Ev'ry Clime.

Portland Bank ★ 1799, etc.

The Portland Bank was incorporated on June 15, 1799 for the District of Maine with $100,000 in capital. Its debts including bank notes could not exceed twice its capital plus its specie deposits. Notes below $5 were prohibited.

$5 $6 $7 © $8 $9 $10 $20 $30 $50

Essex Bank ★ 1799, etc.

The Essex Bank was incorporated on June 18, 1799 to operate in Salem with an authorized capital from $100,000 to $400,000. Its debts including bank notes could not exceed twice its capital plus its specie deposits. Notes below $5 were prohibited.

$5 $6 $7 $8 $9 $10 $20 $30 $40 $50 $100

MASSACHUSETTS

MASSACHUSETTS REFERENCES

Clarence S. Brigham, *Paul Revere's Engravings* (Worcester, 1954); Revised edition (New York, 1969).

Richard LeBaron Bowen, *Early Rehoboth* (Concord, 1945).

Sylvester S. Crosby, *The Early Coins of America* (Boston, 1875) p. 148-9.

Virgil Culler, "A Sense of Extreme Urgency," *Paper Money* (May 1975).

Andrew McFarland Davis, "Curious Features of Some of the Early Notes or Bills Used as a Circulating Medium in Massachusetts," *Publications of the Colonial Society of Massachusetts* (Cambridge, 1905), Vol. 10, p. 84.

————, *Tracts Relating to the Currency of the Massachusetts Bay 1682-1720* (Cambridge, 1902).

————, "The Massachusetts Bay Currency 1690-1750," *Proceedings of the American Antiquarian Society* (Worcester, 1898), reprinted.

————, "The Merchants Notes of 1733," *Proceedings of the Massachusetts Historical Society* (April 1903).

————, *Currency and Banking in the Province of Massachusetts-Bay,* 2 vols. (New York, 1900-1901).

————, *Colonial Currency Reprints 1682-1751,* 4 vols. (Boston, 1910), reprinted.

————, "Provincial Banks, Land and Silver," *Publications of the Colonial Society of Massachusetts* (January 1895).

E. H. Derby, *History of Paper Money in the Province of Massachusetts before the Revolution* (Boston, 1874).

Charles H. J. Douglas, "The Financial History of Massachusetts," *Columbia College Studies,* Vol. 1, No. 4 (New York, 1892).

"Early Massachusetts Paper Currency," *American Journal of Numismatics* (April 1871; July 1871; April 1873).

Joseph B. Felt, *An Historical Account of Massachusetts Currency* (Boston, 1839).

Tom Fitzgerald, "Authorization to Print First American Paper Money," *Paper Money* (September 1974), p. 218.

Lynn Glaser, "Paul Revere and the Massachusetts Currency," *Whitman Numismatic Journal* (February 1966).

N. S. B. Gras, *The Massachusetts First National Bank of Boston 1784-1934* (Cambridge, 1937).

Donald Kagin, "First Attempts at Banking in America," *The Numismatist* (May 1973).

————, "The First Attempts at Paper Currency in America," *The Numismatist* (April 1973).

Benjamin G. Lowenstam, "A Package of Colonial Notes," *The Numismatist* (July 1939).

Nathaniel Paine, *Remarks on the Early Paper Currency of Massachusetts* (Cambridge, 1866).

"Provincial Paper Issues," *American Journal of Numismatics* (October 1886).

John M. Sallay, "Depreciation and Redemption, Massachusetts and her Currency, 1750," *Numismatic Scrapbook Magazine* (January 1976).

E. W. Stoughton, "History of Massachusetts Currency," *Hunt's Merchants Magazine* (June 1840).

J. Hammond Trumbull, "First Essays at Banking and the First Paper Money in New England," *Proceedings of the American Antiquarian Society* (October 1884), p. 268.

Laws, archives, newspapers and other public records.

See general references, catalogs, and listings following the Introduction.

NEW HAMPSHIRE

GENERAL EMISSIONS

1709
May 20, 1717
May 20, 1717 redated 1714
May 20, 1717 redated 1717
May 20, 1717 redated 1722
May 20, 1717 redated 1724
May 20, 1717 redated 1725
May 20, 1717 redated 1726
May 20, 1717 redated 1727
May 20, 1717 redated 1729
April 1, 1737
April 1, 1737 redated August 7, 1740
April 3, 1742
April 3, 1742 redated 1743
April 3, 1742 redated February, 1744(5)
April 3, 1755
April 3, 1755 redated January 1, 1756

April 3, 1755 redated June 1, 1756
1759
March 1, 1760
January 1, 1761
May 1, 1761
January 1, 1762
(July 1) 1762
January 1, 1763
June 20, 1775
July 25, 1775
August 24, 1775
November 3, 1775
January 26, 1776
June 28, 1776
July 3, 1776
1777 with Handwritten Date
April 29, 1780 Act

SPECIAL ISSUERS

Merchants' Notes * December 25, 1734
New Hampshire Bank * 1792, etc.

1709

£8,000 (£5,000 to pay existing obligations and £3,000 additional) in indented Bills of Credit approved Dec. 5, 1709 and receivable for taxes at face value plus 5% interest. Known as "cypher'd bills" or "red figured bills" from the large red monogram AR (Anna Regina) appearing on the face in a normal and mirror image combination. The same monogram also appears on contemporaneous issues of Massachusetts and Connecticut. Engraved and printed by Jeremiah Dummer of Boston using two face plates of four denominations each. The paper was obtained from the Society of Stationers in England. Blank backs. An additional issue of £2,500 was approved on Dec. 2, 1710, £2,000 on Oct. 10, 1711, £500 on Oct. 15, 1712, and £1,200 on May 14, 1714. £1,000 in bills paid into the Treasury as taxes were

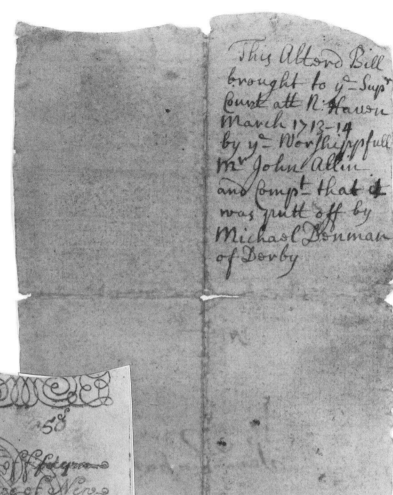

Ⓐ

reissued pursuant to the May 14, 1711 Act. Credit for 5% interest was cancelled by the Act of May 12, 1711. Signers are Theodore Atkinson, Mark Hunking, Samuel Penhallow, Charles Story, and William Vaughan. Six other denominations were issued.

The British Arms bear the motto HONI SOIT QUI MAL Y PENSE (Evil to him who evil thinks).

15s
50s

May 20, 1717

£15,000 in indented Bills of Credit authorized on May 18, 1717 for 11 year loans at 10% interest and secured by mortgages. Redeemable when money was in the Treasury. Engraved by Jeremiah Dummer of Boston on two copper face plates of four denominations each and two back plates. The three lowest denominations and the 25s were on one face plate while the three highest denominations and the 15s were on the other face plate. English Arms were on lower left within various ornamental frames keyed to the denominations and no vignettes in the signature area as found on later issues. Signers are John Gilman, George Jaffrey, and Joseph Smith.

| 1s | 1s6d | 4s6d | 15s ©| 25s | 30s | £3 10s | £4 |

May 20, 1717 redated 1714

£5,384 in indented Bills of Credit emitted to replace all bills printed prior to 1716 from the 1709 plates was authorized by the May 9, 1722 and Oct. 27, 1722 Resolutions. The monogram GR in both normal and mirror image was combined on the back. To distinguish this emission from the bills previously issued from the May 20, 1717 plates, the figure "1714" was engraved on the lower right margin of the four denominations on the small denomination plate. This was an unusual back-dating.

| 1s [3,368] | 1s6d [3,368] | 4s6d [3,368] | 25s [3,368] |

May 20, 1717 redated 1717

£500 in indented Bills of Credit with the date "1717" added below "1714" on the May 20, 1717 small plate were apparently printed in 1722 to anticipate the replacement of worn out bills of the May 20, 1717 issue. Authorization was not granted until the Jan. 7, 1725(6) Order which provided for replacement of bills printed after 1715. The first bills printed after 1715 were the original May 20, 1717 issue. The wording was intended to coordinate with the 1722 Resolutions for replacement of bills printed prior to 1716. The addition of 1717 was to distinguish the replacement issue from all other issues. Of this issue £200 was spent on Dec. 3, 1726 instead of being held for exchange purposes. Monogram GR on back. Signers are John Gilman, Thomas Lukor, and Joseph Smith.

1s [312]
1s6d [312]
4s6d [312]
25s [312]

Ⓐ

May 20, 1717 redated 1722

£2,800 in indented Bills of Credit authorized on May 9, 1722 and £2,000 on Oct. 27, 1722. The two May 20, 1717 face plates, the lower one of which was already redated 1714 and 1717, were redated 1722 without disturbing the prior dates. The monogram GR (Georgius Rex) in normal and mirror image form was on back of denominations printed from the lower plate and monogram CNH (Colony of New Hampshire) in normal and partly mirrored form was on the back of denominations printed from the upper plate. Signers are James Davis, Jonathan Frost, John Gillian, Mark Hunking, George Jaffrey, Joshua Peirce, John Plaisted, Peter Weare, and Richard Wibird.

(A)

(R)

1s
1s6d
4s6d
15s
25s
30s
£3 10s
£4

**May 20, 1717 successively redated
1724, 1725, 1726, and 1727**

As further issues were authorized the
two modified May 20, 1717 face plates
were redated by engraving a new date
on each denomination without disturbing the prior dates. Separate vignettes
for each denomination were added in
the 1724-27 period to discourage raising denominations by alteration. £2,000
was approved on Dec. 12, 1724; £2,000
on Dec. 31, 1725; £2,000 plus £500
for exchange on Jan. 8, 1726(7); and
£2,000 on May 20, 1727. Back plates
as in the previous issue. Signers are
Theodore Atkinson, Jonathan Frost,
Mark Hunking, George Jaffrey, Joshua
Peirce, and John Plaisted.

1s	Boar
1s6d	Bear
4s6d	Camel
15s	Cod
25s	Double headed eagle
30s	Stag
£3 10s	Pine Tree ©
£4	Indian

May 20, 1717 redated 1729

£1,700 in indented Bills of Credit which had already been "imprest" was approved by the Sept. 1, 1730 Act. Identical to prior issues but with 1729 added to face plates without disturbing prior dates. Face plates and CNH back plate are still in existence. £700 in bills in the Treasury had been reissued pursuant to the Dec. 19, 1729 Act. Signers are the same as the previous issue.

1s	Boar	®
1s6d	Bear	®
4s6d	Camel	®
15s	Cod	®
25s	Double headed eagle	© ®
30s	Stag	®
£3 10s	Pine Tree	®
£4	Indian	© ®

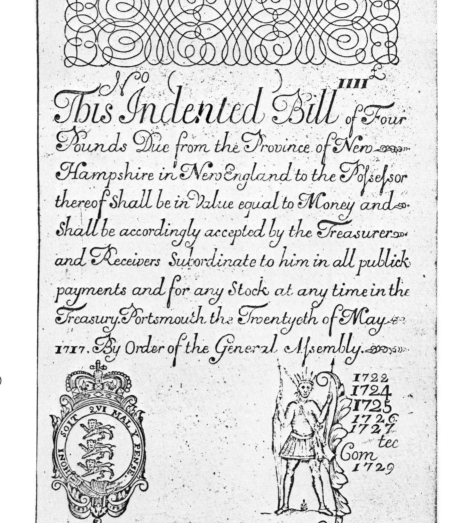

®

Merchants' Notes ★ December 25, 1734

Indented engraved private Promissory Notes sponsored by a group of private merchants because of the Crown's opposition to further paper money issues by the colony. Payable with 1% interest on Dec. 25, 1746 in bills of credit of any New England Colony. Endorsed on the back by Hunking Wentworth for circulation. The motto is BENEFICIO COMMERCI (For the benefit of trade). On Mar. 25, 1735 in Boston 198 merchants signed a pact not to accept the notes. By the April 18, 1735 Act Massachusetts Bay prohibited their circulation there but this Act was subsequently repealed by the Crown. Signers are Theodore Atkinson, John Downing, Jr., George Jaffrey,

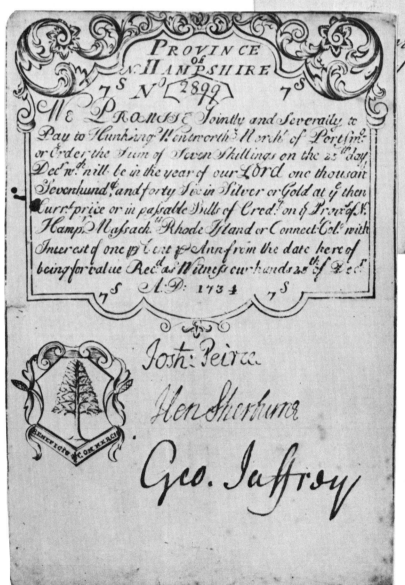

Joshua Peirce, John Rindge, Henry Sherburne, Samuel Smith, and Andrew Wiggin.

12d
 2s
 5s
 7s
10s N. Hamps inserted in margin

April 1, 1737

£10,000 (£6,500 plus £3,000 for exchange for worn bills plus a £500 reserve) authorized by the Mar. 23, 1736(7) Act and April 1, 1737 Order. Engraved on two copper plates of four bills each. Elaborate top border on the four lower denominations. Subsequently referred to as Cuba plates because of the reuse of the large denomination plate for financing the Cuban expedition in 1740. An additional £900 was authorized on Feb. 5, 1739(40). The plates for the four lowest denominations are still in existence.

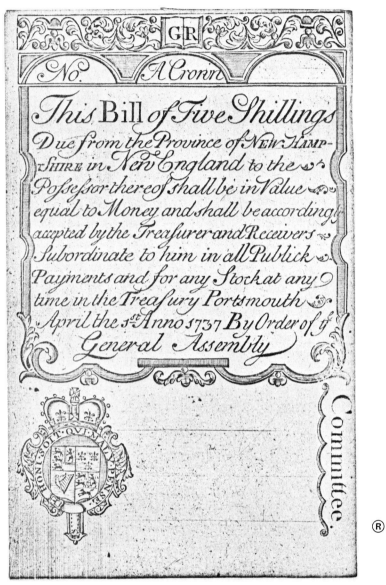

2s	[5,000]	®
3s	[5,000]	®
5s	Crown [5,000]	®
10s	Angel [5,000]	®
20s	(£1) [455]	
40s	(£2) [455]	
60s	(£3) [455]	
100s	(£5) [455]	

April 1, 1737 redated August 7, 1740

£2,700 in engraved Bills of Credit authorized by the Aug. 7, 1740 Act to be struck from the "large new plate" for bounties for Soldiers for the Cuban expedi-

tion. Identical to the previous issue, **but redated "Augst, 7th, 1740"** without disturbing the prior date. The plates still exist.

20s (£1) [246] ®
40s (£2) [245] ®
60s (£3) [245] ®
100s (£5) [246] ®

April 3, 1742

£4,720 in New Tenor legal tender Bills of Credit equal to four times the sum in Old Tenor bills. Elaborately engraved in Boston on two copper plates. The motto DIEU ET MON DROIT (God and my right) has been added to the Arms. Engraved backs were on the four highest denominations and contained the equivalents of four Old Tenor for one New Tenor. The backs of the four lower denominations were blank. Approved by the April

3, 1742 Act at 6s8d per ounce of silver. An additional £1,280 were simultaneously printed, held, and issued under the Sept. 28, 1743 Act. The back plate for the four highest denominations is still in existence. Signers are Theodore Atkinson, Charles Clarkson, John Downing, Ellis Huck, Jotham Odiorne, Jr., Joshua Peirce, George Walton, and Andrew Wiggin.

6d	(1 dwt., 12 gr.)	7s6d (1 oz., 2 dwt., 12 gr.) ®	
1s	(3 dwt.)	10s (1 oz., 10 dwt.) ®	
2s6d	(7 dwt., 12 gr.)	20s (3 oz.) ®	
6s	(18 dwt.)	40s (6 oz.) ®	

NEW HAMPSHIRE

April 3, 1742 redated 1743

£25,000 in New Tenor legal tender Bills authorized by the April 3, 1742 Act subject to the Crown's approval which came June 2, 1743. Used for mortgage loans. The date "1743" was added to the face plates of the previous issue and the silver equivalent remained unchanged. The backs of the four highest denominations are the same as on the previous issue and bear the Old Tenor equivalent. Inflation increased the price of silver from 6s8d to 8s per ounce late in 1743. Signers are Thomas Atkinson, John Downing, John Gage, Samuel Gilman, Clement Jackson, George Jaffrey, Jotham Odiorne, Jr., Thomas Parker, Joshua Peirce, Eleazer Russell, Joseph Sherburne, and Andrew Wiggin.

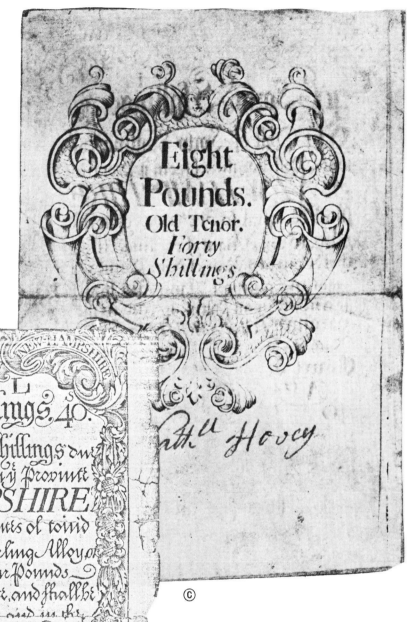

6d	(1 dwt., 12 gr.) [4,839]
1s	(3 dwt.) [4,839]
2s6d	(7 dwt., 12 gr.) [4,839]
6s	(18 dwt.) [4,839]
7s6d	(1 oz., 2 dwt., 12 gr.) (£1 10s O.T.) [12,500]
10s	(1 oz., 10 dwt.) (£2 O.T.) [12,500]
20s	(3 oz.) (£4 O.T.) [12,500]
40s	(6 oz.) (£8 O.T.) [12,500] ©

April 3, 1742 redated February 1744(5)

To finance the expedition against Louisburg £13,000 in bills were issued under the Act of Feb. 16, 1744(5) and each denomination on the two April 3, 1742 plates had the date added without changing the two prior dates. Without further redating, issues of £6,000 on July 6, 1745, £8,000 on Oct. 5, 1745, and £60,000 on July 12, 1746 were emitted, the latter to finance a Canadian expedition. In the £13,000 issue £2,000 consisted of the four lower denominations. In the £60,000 issue £5,000 consisted of the four bills on the low denomination plate. **Inflation** caused the price of silver to rise from 8s9d in 1745 to 15s New Tenor per ounce by the end of 1747. The paper money value strengthened to 14s per ounce in 1748. Signers are Theodore Atkinson, Thomas Davis, John Downing, John Gage, Peter Gilman, Samuel Gilman, George Jaffrey, Moses Leavit, Clement March, John Macmurphy, Jotham Odiorne, Jr., Samuel Palmer, Nathaniel Rogers, Eleazer Russell, John Sandburn, Joseph Sherburne, Sampson Sheafe, Samuel Smith, Samuel Solly, Ebenezer Stevens, Thomas Wallingford, Meshech Weare, L. Wibing, Richard Wibird, and Andrew Wiggin.

6d	(1 dwt., 12 gr.)	©
1s	(3 dwt.)	©
2s6d	(7 dwt., 12 gr.)	©
6s	(18 dwt.)	©
7s6d	(1 oz., 2 dwt., 12 gr.) (£1 10s O.T.)	
10s	(1 oz., 10 dwt.) (£2 O.T.)	
20s	(3 oz.) (£4 O.T.)	©
40s	(6 oz.) (£8 O.T.)	©

NEW HAMPSHIRE

April 3, 1755

£30,000 in New Tenor Bills of Credit authorized by the April 11, 1755 Act to use for the Crown Point expedition, the exchange being 15s N.T. for one Spanish Dollar or 333 N.T. to 100 in specie. Receivable with 1% interest for taxes. There were £23,000 in bills issued from the large denomination plate and £7,000 from the small denomination plate. The six bills on the "small"

plate are smaller in size than those on the "large" plate. PRO ARIS & FOCIS (For altars and the hearth) and CROWN POINT are on all bills. An additional £1,800 in bills was approved for issuance on April 1, 1756 and a remainder of £5,760 in bills was reapproved for issue. Signers are Theodore Atkinson, Peter Gilman, Jacob Hurd, Nathaniel Hurd, John Purnase, and Henry Sherburne.

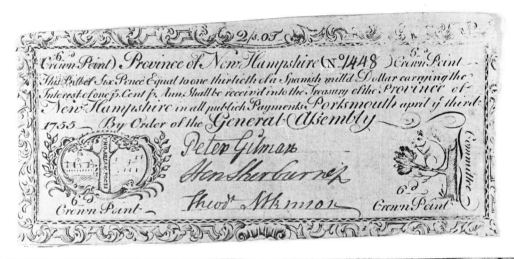

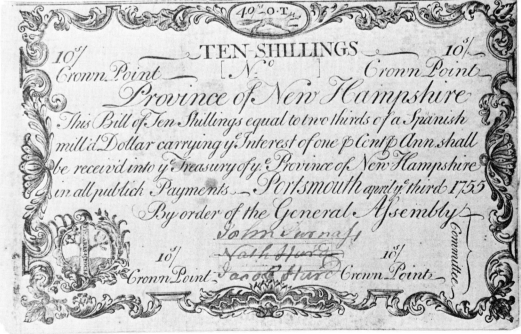

6d	(2s O.T., $1/30)	Squirrel in tree [6,748 plus]
1s	(4s O.T., $1/15)	Rabbit [6,748 plus]
3s	(12s O.T., $1/5)	Rooster [6,748 plus]
3s9d	(15s O.T., $1/4)	Bird flying [6,748 plus]
5s	(20s O.T., $1/3)	Bird on tree [6,748 plus]

7s6d	(30s O.T., $1/2)	Bird on ground [6,748 plus]
10s	(40s O.T., $2/3)	Fox [4,000 plus]
15s	(60s O.T., $1)	Squirrel [4,000 plus]
30s	(£6 O.T., $2)	Stag [4,000 plus]
£3	(£12 O.T., $4)	Wings [4,000 plus]

April 3, 1755 redated January 1, 1756

£15,000 in New Tenor Bills approved by the Sept. 5, 1755 Act. The large denomination plate of the April 3, 1755 issue was redated by adding "Jany 1, 1756" without disturbing the original dating.

10s (40s O.T., $2/3)	Fox	
15s (60s O.T., $1)	Squirrel	
30s (£6 O.T., $2)	Stag	
£3 (£12 O.T., $4)	Wings	

April 3, 1755 redated June 1, 1756

£30,000 in New Tenor Bills approved by the April 1, 1756 Act. The plates used for the two prior issues were redated by adding "June 1" to the large denomination plate and by adding "June 1, 1756" to the small denomination plate without disturbing prior dating. These plates still exist. £20,000 more were emitted under the Feb. 25, 1757 Act from the large denomination plate and £20,500 more under the Mar. 31, 1758 Act. Signers are Theodore Atkinson, Eleazer Russell, Henry Sherburne, Daniel Warner, John Wentworth, and Richard Wibird.

6d	Ⓡ
1s	Ⓡ
3s	Ⓡ
3s9d	Ⓡ
5s	Ⓡ
7s6d	Ⓡ
10s	Ⓡ
15s	Ⓡ Ⓒ
30s	Ⓡ
£3	Ⓡ

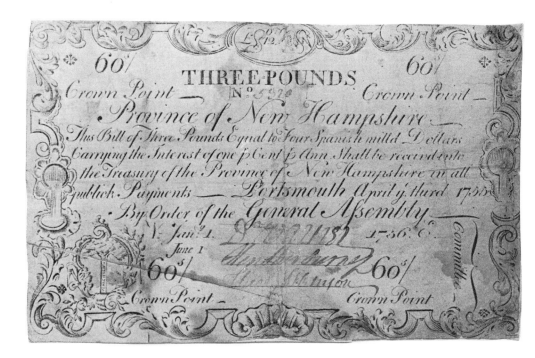

NEW HAMPSHIRE

1759

Bills of Credit bearing 2½% interest and payable in Sterling Bills of exchange were authorized because silver rose to 30s New Tenor per ounce against a nominal value of 17s3d per ounce. This created three separate standards of value for notes simultaneously in circulation, Old Tenor, New Tenor and Sterling. The Sterling Bills were hoarded and were valued at 6¼ N.T. for one or 25 O.T. for one. The first emission of Sterling Bills was £5,000 out of £15,000 authorized on May 23, 1759. The second emission of £8,000 was approved for printing on Nov. 1, 1759 and apparently issued. The balance were not issued. Printed from set type by Joseph Newmarch. Signers are Theodore Atkinson, C. Gilman, Clement March, Daniel Warner, and Richard Wibird.

6d   1s   2s6d   10s

March 1, 1760

£8,000 as the third emission of Sterling Bills issued out of £15,000 authorized on March 1, 1760 and due with 2½% interest on Dec. 25, 1764. Similar to the previous issue. The motto PAX BELLO POTIOR (Peace is preferable to war) is probably on all bills. The issue was extensively counterfeited. Signers are Theodore Atkinson, Eleazer Russell, Henry Sherburne, William Waldron, Daniel Warner, Theodore Westbrook, and Richard Wibird.

6d
1s
2s6d ⓤ
10s

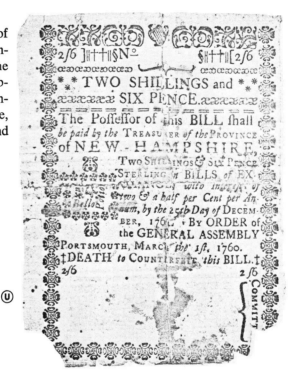

January 1, 1761

£7,000 as the fourth emission of Sterling Bills approved May 15, 1760 being the balance of £15,000 first authorized on March 1, 1760. Similar to the previous issue and with the same signers.

6d ⓤ
1s
2s6d
10s

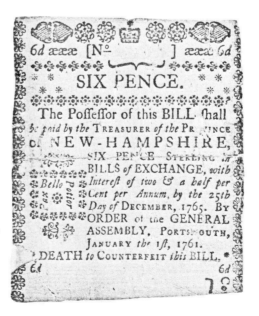

May 1, 1761

£20,000 as the fifth emission of Sterling Bills was authorized on April 20, 1761 to clothe and pay troops and due with 2½% interest on Dec. 25, 1765. Only £12,000 in bills were issued. Similar to the previous issue. Signers are Theodore Atkinson, C. Gilman, Clement March, Eleazer Russell, Henry Sherburne, Joseph Smith, Thomas Waldron, Daniel Warner, and Richard Wibird.

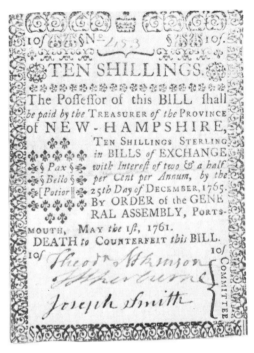

6d
1s
2s6d
10s   PAX BELLO POTIOR

January 1, 1762

The £8,000 balance of Sterling Bills out of the £20,000 authorized on April 20, 1761 was the sixth emission and was due on Dec. 25, 1766 with 2½% interest. Similar to the previous issue and with the same signers.

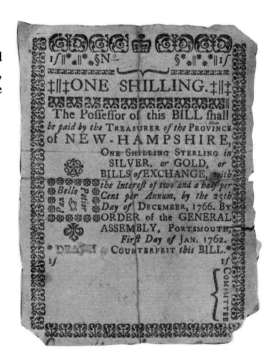

6d
1s   PAX BELLO POTIOR ⓤ
2s6d
10s

ⓤ

(July 1) 1762

£10,000 as the seventh emission of Sterling Bills to redeem Louisburg and Canadian expedition bills issued during the 1745-6 period. This was one-half of the £20,000 authorized by the June 25, 1762 Act and the balance was to await further authorization. Similar to the previous issue. The signers are the same as the previous issue except that Meshech Weare was added and Eleazer Russell was eliminated.

6d	1s	2s6d	10s

NEW HAMPSHIRE

January 1, 1763

£10,000 as the eighth emission of Sterling Bills, being the balance of the £20,000 authorized by the June 25, 1762 Act. Similar to the previous issue and with the same signers.

6d   2s6d

1s   10s

June 20, 1775

£10,050 in indented Treasury Notes authorized by the June 9, 1775 Resolve of the New Hampshire Provincial Congress and payable on Dec. 20, 1776, Dec. 20, 1777 or Dec. 20, 1778 with 6% interest. Engraved on copper and printed on laid paper by Paul Revere. Similar in style to the Massachusetts Bay issues of May 25, 1775 and July 8, 1775. The last numeral of the due date was written in ink in the body of the text. These notes are referred to as "Copperplate notes" in the Act of June 21, 1794. Signers are Nicholas Gilman and E. Thompson.

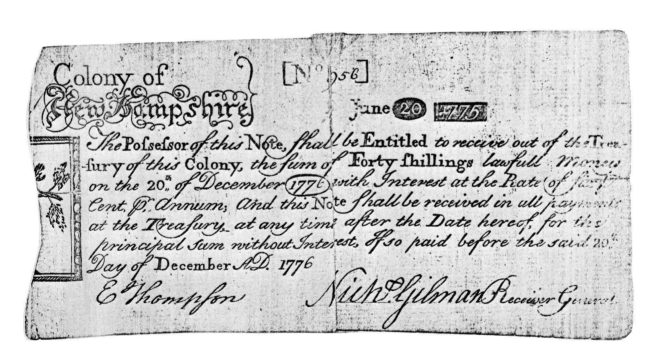

		Fair	Good	V.G.
1s	Three due date varieties. Large tree [3,000] Ⓡ	300.00	500.00	1,000.00
6s	Three due date varieties. Squirrel in tree [3,000] Ⓡ	300.00	500.00	1,000.00
20s	Three due date varieties. Two leaf designs [3,000] Ⓡ	300.00	500.00	1,000.00
40s	Three due date varieties. Tree with crossed trunks [3,000] Ⓡ	300.00	500.00	1,000.00

NEW HAMPSHIRE

July 25, 1775

£2,000 in indented Treasury Notes payable on Dec. 20, 1779 and authorized by the July 5, 1775 Resolve. Printed from typeset letters and ornaments on thin laid **paper**. Signers are Nicholas Gilman and E. Thompson.

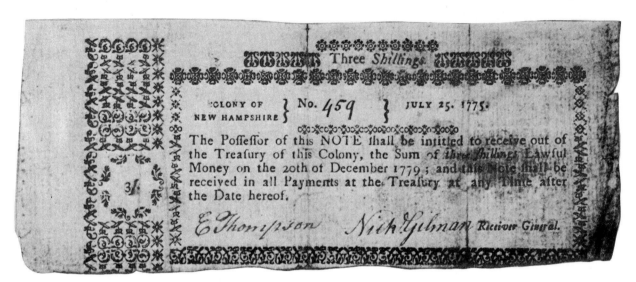

	Good	V.G.	Fine		Good	V.G.	Fine
6d [4,000]	100.00	175.00	300.00	1s9d [4,000]	100.00	175.00	300.00
9d [4,000]	100.00	175.00	300.00	2s6d [4,000]	100.00	175.00	300.00
1s6d [4,000]	100.00	175.00	300.00	3s [4,000]	100.00	175.00	300.00

August 24, 1775

£8,000 in indented Treasury Notes payable on Dec. 20, 1776, Dec. 20, 1777, or Dec. 20, 1778 with 6% interest and authorized by the July 5, 1775 Resolve **to coordinate with July 25, 1775 issue. Interest was** revoked by the Aug. 22, 1775 Resolve. Printed with typeset letters and ornaments on thin laid paper. **Signers** are Nicholas Gilman and E. Thompson.

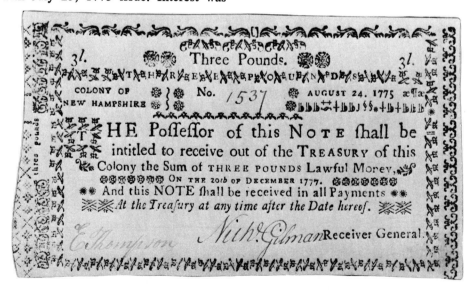

		Good	V.G.	Fine
5s	Three due date varieties [1,333]	150.00	225.00	350.00
10s	Three due date varieties [1,334]	150.00	225.00	350.00
15s	Three due date varieties [1,333]	150.00	225.00	350.00
30s	Three due date varieties [1,334]	150.00	225.00	350.00
£3	Three due date varieties [1,333]	150.00	225.00	350.00

NEW HAMPSHIRE

November 3, 1775

£20,000 in indented Treasury Notes payable in the amount of £4,000 on Dec. 20, 1779, £6,000 on Dec. 20, 1780, £4,000 on Dec. 20, 1781, and £6,000 on Dec. 20, 1782. Authorized by the Nov. 1, 1775 Resolve. The five highest denominations are larger than the others. Signers are John Calfe, Nicholas Gilman, and Sam Hobart. Daniel Fowle, the printer, and Robert Fowle, his nephew, severed their partnership in the printing business in 1774 over a difference of political opinion. Robert Fowle was a Tory and was later accused of making the counterfeits of this issue. He could have used type from his former enterprise. Apparently because of this counterfeiting, the House of Representatives on June 17, 1777 ordered all bills issued in 1775 to be called in and sunk.

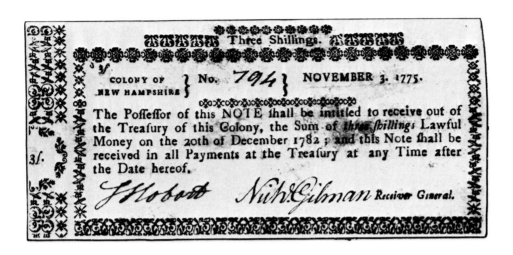

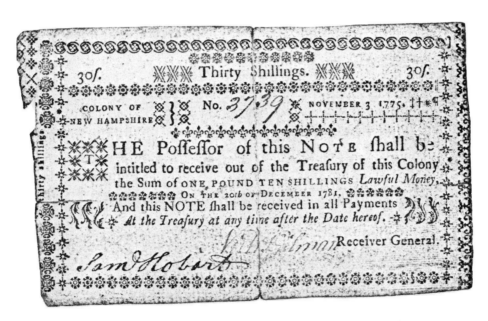

		Good	V.G.	Fine
6d	Four due date varieties [4,000]	150.00	225.00	400.00
9d	Four due date varieties [4,000]	150.00	225.00	400.00
1s6d	Four due date varieties [4,000]	150.00	225.00	400.00
1s9d	Four due date varieties [4,000]	150.00	225.00	400.00
2s6d	Four due date varieties [4,000]	150.00	225.00	400.00
3s	Four due date varieties [4,000]	150.00	225.00	400.00
5s	Four due date varieties [3,600]	100.00	175.00	300.00
10s	Four due date varieties [3,600]	100.00	175.00	300.00
15s	Four due date varieties [3,600]	100.00	175.00	300.00
30s	Four due date varieties [3,600] ©	100.00	175.00	300.00
40s	Four due date varieties [3,600] ©	100.00	175.00	300.00

January 26, 1776

£20,008 16s ($66,696) in Bills of Credit authorized on Jan. 26, 1776 and payable on Jan. 26, 1783, Jan. 26, 1784, Jan. 26, 1785, or Jan. 26, 1786 as specified. Type-set face and back printed by Daniel Fowle at Portsmouth. Signers are Joseph Gilman, Josiah Moulton, Joseph Smith, and Phillips White.

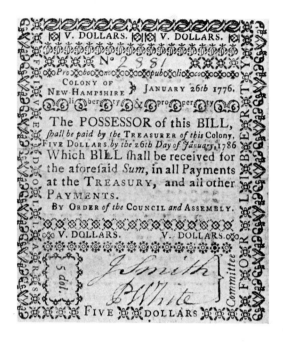
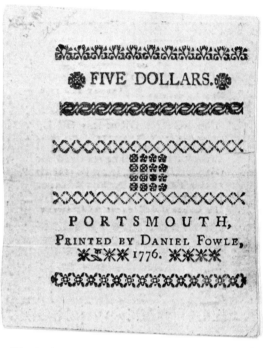

$1 Four due date varieties [3,176]
$2 Four due date varieties [3,176]
$3 SUB VERTUTE SPERAMUS (With morality we have hope). FOR LIBERTY. Four due date varieties [3,176]
$4 NIL DESPERANDUM (Nothing is to be despaired of). FOR LIBERTY. Four due date varieties [3,176]

$5 PRO BONO PUBLICO (For the public good). LIBERTY & PROPERTY. Four due date varieties [3,176]
$6 FOR DEFENCE OF AMERICAN LIBERTY. Names of committee members, MESHECH WEARE and LEVI DEARBORN, between ornaments. Four due date varieties [3,176]

June 28, 1776

£3,400 in legal tender Bills of Credit due either on Jan. 26, 1787 or Jan. 26, 1788 and authorized on June 17, 1776. Small typeset bills with blank backs. Signers are Benjamin Barker, Noah Emery, Peirce Long, Joseph Smith, E. Thompson, and **Phillips White.**

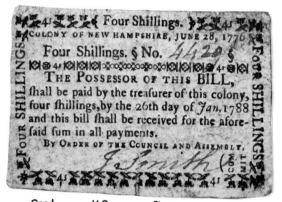

			Good	V.G.	Fine
3d	Two due date varieties	[6,000]	175.00	250.00	500.00
4d	Two due date varieties	[6,000]	175.00	250.00	500.00
5d	Two due date varieties	[6,000]	175.00	250.00	500.00
7d	Two due date varieties	[6,000]	175.00	250.00	500.00
8d	Two due date varieties	[6,000]	175.00	250.00	500.00
10d	Two due date varieties	[6,000]	175.00	250.00	500.00
1s	Two due date varieties	[6,000]	175.00	250.00	500.00
15d	Two due date varieties	[6,000]	175.00	250.00	500.00
2s	Two due date varieties	[6,000]	175.00	250.00	500.00
4s	Two due date varieties	[6,000]	175.00	250.00	500.00

NEW HAMPSHIRE

July 3, 1776

£20,160 ($67,200) in Bills of Credit payable on Jan. 26, 1789, Jan. 26, 1790, Jan. 26, 1791, or Jan. 26, 1792. Similar to the Jan. 26, 1776 issue. Typeset face and back **printed by Daniel Fowle at Portsmouth.** Signers are Benjamin Barker, Noah Emery, Peirce Long, Josiah Moulton, Samuel Philbrick, Joseph Smith, and **Phillips White.**

$1	Four due date varieties [3,200]
$2	Four due date varieties [3,200]
$3	SUB VERTUTE SPERAMUS. FOR LIBERTY. Four due date varieties [3,200]
$4	NIL DESPERANDUM. FOR LIBERTY. Four due date varieties [3,200]

$5	PRO BONO PUBLICO. LIBERTY & PROPERTY. Four due date varieties [3,200]
$6	FOR DEFENCE OF AMERICAN LIBERTY. Names of committee members, MESHECH WEARE and LEVI DEARBORN, between ornaments. Four due date varieties [3,200]

1777 with Handwritten Date

£30,000 in four year 6% interest indented bearer Notes authorized on Jan. 14, 1777 and April 1, 1777 to pay bounties to Continental troops. Typeset with UNION worked into the ornamental borders. The month and day of issuance is handwritten. The denomination is both printed and handwritten. Signers are Noah Emery, Nicholas Gilman, and Joseph Smith. These did not circulate as currency.

£5 UNION [3,000]
£10 [1,500]

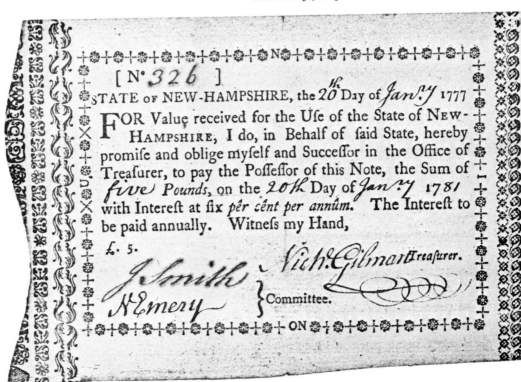

197

April 29, 1780 Act

$145,000 in legal tender Bills of Credit payable in Spanish milled dollars by Dec. 31, 1786 with 5% interest pursuant to the Act of April 29, 1780 and in accordance with a Continental Congress Resolution of March 18, 1780, guaranteeing the payment of the Bills and making the amount issued dependent upon the amount of Continental Currency exchanged at $40 (old) for $1 (new). Face in black and back in red and black. Face border cuts and back cut surrounding the emblem were engraved by Henry Dawkins. Border cuts and emblem on the backs are from the Jan. 14, 1779 issue of Continental Currency. Printed by Hall & Sellers in Philadelphia on paper watermarked CONFEDERATION in two lines. Usually punch cancelled. Signers are James McClure, Joseph Pearson, and E. Robinson. Guaranty is signed by John Taylor Gilman or Nicholas Gilman.

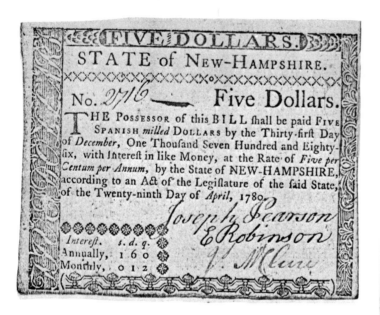

		V.G.	Fine	V.F.
$1	[2,900]	45.00	60.00	90.00
$2	[2,900]	45.00	60.00	90.00
$4	[2,900]	45.00	60.00	90.00
$5	[2,900]	45.00	60.00	90.00
$7	[2,900]	45.00	60.00	90.00
$8	[2,900]	45.00	60.00	90.00
$20	[2,900]	45.00	60.00	90.00

Values are for cancelled bills. Value is double the amount shown if uncancelled.

New Hampshire Bank ★ 1792, etc.

The New Hampshire Bank was incorporated in 1792 for 50 years with a capital of $160,000. It operated at Portsmouth. Its bank notes were signed by Oliver Peabody, president, and Daniel R. Rogers, cashier, and payable at the Bank of the United States in Philadelphia.

$1 $2 $3 $4 $5 ⓒ $10 ⓒ $15 $20 ⓒ $30

NEW HAMPSHIRE

NEW HAMPSHIRE REFERENCES

Charles J. Bullock, "The Paper Currency of New Hampshire," *Essays on the Monetary History of the United States* (New York, 1900).

Forest W. Daniel, "A Colonial Counterfeit," *Paper Money,* Vol. 7, No. 2 (1968).

Andrew McFarland Davis, "New Hampshire Notes 1735," *New England Historical and Genealogical Register* (October 1903), reprinted.

————, "The Emissions of the Neighboring Governments," *History of Currency and Banking in Massachusetts Bay* (New York, 1901).

Richard T. Hoober, "Financial History of Colonial New Hampshire," *The Numismatist* (August 1964).

Wayne S. Rich, "New Hampshire Numismatics," *The Nonagon* (1963-4).

Kenneth Scott, "New Hampshire Tory Counterfeiters Operating from New York City," *The New York Historical Society Quarterly* (January 1950).

————, "Counterfeiting in Colonial New Hampshire," *Historical New Hampshire* (1957).

Laws, archives and other public records.

See general references, catalogs, and listings following the Introduction.

NEW JERSEY

GENERAL EMISSIONS

July 1, 1709
July 14, 1711
January 24, 1716(7)
March 25, 1724
March 25, 1728
March 25, 1733
March 25, 1737
July 2, 1746
May 15, 1755
September 8, 1755
January 26, 1756
June 22, 1756
April 12, 1757
June 14, 1757
November 20, 1757

May 1, 1758
October 20, 1758
April 10, 1759
April 12, 1760
April 23, 1761
April 8, 1762
December 31, 1763
April 16, 1764
February 20, 1776
March 25, 1776
June 9, 1780 Act
1781 (January 9, 1781 Act)
1784 (December 20, 1783 Act)
1786

SPECIAL ISSUERS

Hibernia Furnace ★ May 1, 1774
James Craft ★ August 6, 1776
James Craft ★ October 11, 1776
Moore Furman ★ November 1, 1776
Isaac Craig ★ April 21, 1777
Azariah Hunt ★ July 26, 1786
Burlington Nail Company ★ August 29, 1786
Seeley & Merseilles ★ January 19, 1787
Colhoun & Brush ★ November 7, 1787
Isaac L. Milnor ★ December 1, 1787
Borough of Elizabeth ★ March 25, 1790
Reuben Chadwick ★ May 3, 179(?)
First Presbyterian Church at Newark ★ December 16, 1790
City of New Brunswick ★ January 7, 1791
City of Perth Amboy ★ February 10, 1792
Society for Establishing Useful Manufactures ★ January 1, 1794
W. & R. Colfax ★ July 4, 1794
City of New Brunswick ★ March 10, 1796

July 1, 1709

£3,000 in legal tender Bills of Credit were approved by the June 30, 1709 Act for a proposed Canadian Expedition. By mistake a design on the stub for indentation was omitted and English Arms (3 lions) were used instead of British Arms (shield). Originally valid until Sept. 1, 1711, but extended by the Mar. 13, 1713(4) Act. Authorized signers were Thomas Farmer, Elisha Parker, Thomas Pike, and John Royce, three of whom were to sign each bill, but Adam Hude signed without authority in lieu of John Royce who died. These violations caused lack of confidence in the issue so that by the Act of Feb. 10, 1710(1) the bills were revalidated. By the Act of July 16, 1711 the erroneous form was specifically approved.

5s [2,000]		40s [200]	
10s [1,000]		£5 [200] ©	
20s [600]			

July 14, 1711

£5,000 (12,500 ounces of silver plate) in legal tender Bills of Credit for the proposed Canadian military operations were issued pursuant to the July 16, 1711 Act and were to be valid until April 1, 1717. Signers are Joseph Billup, John Burrow, Thomas Farmer, and Adam Hude, three of whom were to sign each bill.

2s6d	(6 dwt., 6 gr.) [4,000]	20s	(2 oz., 10 dwt.) [1,000]
5s	(12 dwt., 12 gr.) [2,000]	40s	(5 oz.) [500]
10s	(1 oz., 5 dwt.) [1,000]	£5	(12 oz., 10 dwt.) [300]

January 24, 1716(7)

£4,670 (11,675 ounces of silver plate) in legal tender Bills of Credit were approved by the Jan. 25, 1716(7) Act and were to be valid until Dec. 1, 1718. Printed by William Bradford. Signers are John Harrison, John Kay, John Kinsey, and David Lyall, three of whom were to sign each bill.

2s	(5 dwt.) [1,000]	16s	(2 oz.) [500]
4s	(10 dwt.) [1,000]	20s	(2 oz., 10 dwt.) [1,170]
5s	(12 dwt., 12 gr.) [1,000]	30s	(3 oz., 15 dwt.) [500]
8s	(1 oz.) [500]	40s	(5 oz.) [550]
10s	(1 oz., 5 dwt.) [1,000]		

March 25, 1724

£40,000 in Proclamation money (116,666 oz., 13 dwt., 8 gr. of plate) authorized by the Act of Nov. 13, 1723 for Loan Office purposes. Legal tender until Mar. 25, 1736 and invalid after June 25, 1736. Loaned on security of real estate or specie at 5% interest with 12 year amortization and known as the "First Bank." An equivalent circulating value in money of account was also stated based upon the then current rate of silver at 8s per ounce. Because of many Irish-made counterfeits circulated through New York the issue was ordered in 1727 to cease circulation "between man and man" by Nov. 1, 1728 and to be invalid after Nov. 1, 1729. Large indented bills printed by William Bradford from cast cuts, wood blocks and set type. Signers are Peter Bard, Robert Lettis Hooper, John Parker, and James Trent. Substitute signers were Jacob Daughty and Enoch Vreeland.

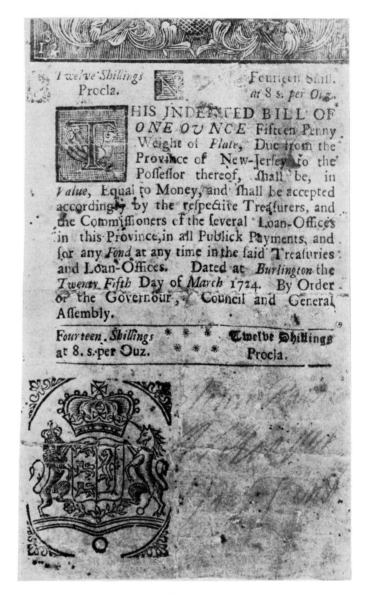

1s	(2 dwt., 22 gr.)	[14,000]
1s6d	(4 dwt., 9 gr.)	[12,000] Ⓒ
3s	(8 dwt., 18 gr.)	[8,000] Ⓒ
6s	(17 dwt., 12 gr.)	[8,000] Ⓒ
12s	(1 oz., 15 dwt.)	[8,000] Ⓒ
15s	(2 oz., 3 dwt., 18 gr.)	[8,000]
30s	(4 oz., 7 dwt., 12 gr.)	[8,000]
£3	(8 oz., 15 dwt.)	[4,000] Ⓒ

March 25, 1728

£24,760 (72,216 oz., 13 dwt., 8 gr. of plate) in Proclamation money (£28,886 13s 4d circulating value) authorized by the Act of Feb. 10, 1727(8) to replace the Mar. 25, 1724 issue which had been extensively counterfeited. Legal tender "between man and man" until Mar. 25, 1736 and invalid after Nov. 1, 1736. Printed under contract with Samuel Keimer of Philadelphia whose employee, Benjamin Franklin, cut and cast the ornaments, built the press and printed the issue. No examples of this issue are known, but a drawing of the layout of a bill was included in the authorizing legislation. Signers are Isaac Decow and John Stevens.

1s	(2 dwt., 22 gr.)	[12,200]
1s6d	(4 dwt., 9 gr.)	[8,000] Ⓒ
3s	(8 dwt., 18 gr.)	[7,000]
6s	(17 dwt., 12 gr.)	[6,000 but 5,000 specified]
12s	(1 oz., 15 dwt.)	[5,000]
15s	(2 oz., 3 dwt., 18 gr.)	[4,000]
30s	(4 oz., 7 dwt., 12 gr.)	[4,000] Ⓒ
£3	(8 oz., 15 dwt.)	[1,000] Ⓒ
£6	(17 oz., 10 dwt.)	[1,000]

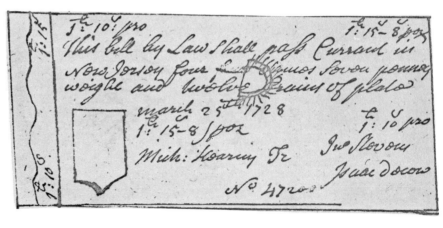

March 25, 1733

£25,000 (£20,000 plus £5,000 to exchange for worn bills) in Proclamation money (£29,166 13s 4d circulating value) authorized by the Act of July 8, 1730 subject to Royal approval which was granted on May 4, 1732. Legal tender "between man and man" until Mar. 25, 1749 and invalid after Sept. 25, 1749. Issued for mortgage loans and known as the "Second Bank." Arms bear the mottoes DIEU ET MON DROIT (God and my right) and HONI SOIT QUI MAL Y PENSE (Evil to him who evil thinks). Printed by Andrew Bradford. Blank backs. Signers are Andrew Johnston, Michael Kearny, Caleb Raper, and Richard Smith. Alternates were Samuel Bickley and John Stevens.

1s	(2 dwt., 22 gr.)	[16,250]
1s6d	(4 dwt., 9 gr.)	[12,500]
3s	(8 dwt., 18 gr.)	[10,000]
6s	(17 dwt., 12 gr.)	[7,500]
12s	(1 oz., 15 dwt.)	[7,500] ⓒ
15s	(2 oz., 3 dwt., 18 gr.)	[5,000] ⓒ
30s	(4 oz., 17 dwt., 12 gr.)	[2,500]
£3	(8 oz., 15 dwt.)	[1,250]
£6	(17 oz., 10 dwt.)	[625]

March 25, 1737

£50,000 (£40,000 plus £10,000 to exchange for worn bills) in Proclamation money authorized by the Act of Aug. 13, 1733 subject to Royal approval which was finally granted on May 4, 1735. Although news of approval came promptly after authorization the formal document was deliberately withheld by an obstinate American official until he was ordered on June 28, 1736 and again on August 24, 1736 to deliver it. The issue was secured by mortgage loans and known as the "Third Bank." Legal tender "between man and man" until Mar. 25, 1753 and invalid after Sept. 25, 1753. The equivalent in silver is the same as was provided for prior issues. Printed by Benjamin Franklin whose Pennsylvania Gazette on July 22, 1736 said that he was "at Burlington with the Press, laboring for the publick Good to make Money more plentiful." In this issue Franklin invented and introduced the art of nature printing from leaf casts by transferring a sage leaf image to the back of the bills. No examples of this issue are known but in 1772 on the death of Robert Hude 2,724 bills of this issue including all eight denominations were found partially and fully signed in his effects and were ordered burned by the Provincial Council. Signers are John Allen, Isaac Decow, Robert Hude, and John Stevens. Alternate signers are William Cox and Robert Smith.

1s [32,500] ⓒ	**6s** [15,000]	**30s** [5,000]
1s6d [25,000]	**12s** [15,000]	**£3** [2,500]
3s [20,000]	**15s** [10,000]	**£6** [1,250]

July 2, 1746

£16,000 (£10,000 for military expense plus £6,000 to exchange for worn bills) authorized by the Act of June 28, 1746. Legal tender as "Money of America" until Mar. 25, 1753 and invalid after Sept. 25, 1753. The equivalent in silver is the same as was provided for prior issues. Printed by Benjamin Franklin. The face of the two highest denominations was printed in red and black. The back contains a nature printed sage leaf. Signers are John Allen, William Burnett, Isaac Decow, Samuel Nevill, Samuel Smith, and Stephen Williams.

1s	Plate letters A & B [10,400]	15s	Plate letter A [3,200] Ⓒ
1s6d	Plate letter A [8,000]	30s	Plate letter A [1,600]
3s	Plate letter A [6,400]	£3	[800]
6s	Plate letter A [4,800] Ⓒ	£6	[400]
12s	Plate letter A [4,800]		

May 15, 1755

£15,000 as the First War Issue of Bills of Credit. Authorized on April 22, 1755 to pay for military action against the French. Legal tender to May 15, 1760 and invalid after Nov. 15, 1760. The equivalent in silver is the same as was provided for prior issues. Printed by James Parker with a nature print of a sage leaf on the back. Signers are Thomas Bartow, Daniel Smith, Jr., Abraham Hewlings, and John Smyth.

1s	Plate letters A, B, & C [9,720]	15s	Plate letters A, B, & C [3,000]
1s6d	Plate letters A, B, & C [7,520]	30s	Plate letters A, B, & C [1,500]
3s	Plate letters A, B, & C [6,000]	£3	Plate letters A & B [750]
6s	Plate letters A, B, & C [4,500]	£6	No plate letter [375]
12s	Plate letters A, B, & C [4,500]		

September 8, 1755

£15,000 as the Second War Issue of Bills of Credit. Authorized on Aug. 20, 1755 to be legal tender until Sept. 8, 1760 and invalid after Mar. 8, 1761. The equivalent in silver is the same as was provided for prior issues. The face of the higher denominations is in red and black and the lower denominations in black. Sage leaf backs. Printed by James Parker at Woodbridge. Signers are Jacob Dehart, Joseph Hollinshead, A. Johnston, Samuel Nevill, Henry Paxson, and Daniel Smith, Jr.

1s	Plate letters A, B, & C	[9,720]
1s6d	Plate letters A, B, & C	[7,520]
3s	Plate letters A, B, & C	[6,000]
6s	Plate letters A, B, & C	[4,500]
12s	Plate letters A, B, & C	[4,500]
15s	Plate letters A, B, & C	[3,000]
30s	Plate letters A, B, & C	[1,500]
£3	Plate letters A & B	[750]
£6		[375]

January 26, 1756

£10,000 as the Third War Issue of Bills of Credit. Authorized on Dec. 24, 1755 to be legal tender until Jan. 26, 1761 and invalid after Jan. 26, 1762. The equivalent in silver is the same as was provided for prior issues. The faces of the 15s and under are in black; of the £6 are in red and black; and of the others are in red. Sage leaf backs in black. Printed by James Parker. Signers are Hugh Hartshorne, Joseph Hollinshead, A. Johnston, Samuel Nevill, John Smyth, and Joseph Yard.

1s	Plate letters A, B, & C	[6,500]
18d	Plate letters A, B, & C	[5,000]
3s	Plate letters A, B, & C	[4,000]
6s	Plate letters A, B, & C	[3,000]
12s	Plate letters A, B, & C	[3,000]
15s	Plate letters A, B, & C	[2,000]
30s	Plate letters A, B, & C	[1,000]
£3	Plate letters A & B	[500]
£6		[250]

NEW JERSEY

June 22, 1756

£17,500 as the Fourth War Issue of Bills of Credit and £3,500 to replace worn bills. Authorized on June 2, 1756, to be legal tender until June 22, 1761 and to be invalid after Dec. 22, 1761. The equivalent in silver is the same as was provided for prior issues. The faces of the 15s and under are in black and of the others are in red and black. Sage leaf backs in black except the £6 which is in green. Printed by James Parker. Signers are William Burnett, Hugh Hartshorne, Joseph Hollinshead, A. Johnston, Joseph Smith, and John Smyth.

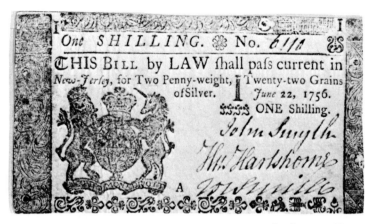

		Good	Fine	Unc.
1s	Plate letters A, B, & C [9,750]	25.00	75.00	200.00
18d	Plate letters A & B [7,500]	25.00	75.00	200.00
3s	Plate letters A & B [6,000]	25.00	75.00	200.00
6s	Plate letters A & B [5,000]	25.00	75.00	200.00
12s	Plate letters A, B, & C [5,500] Ⓒ	25.00	75.00	200.00
15s	Plate letters A & B [5,000]	25.00	75.00	200.00
30s	Plate letters A, B, C, & D [2,000]	35.00	90.00	250.00
£3	Plate letters A & B [1,250]	50.00	125.00	
£6	[625]	85.00	175.00	

April 12, 1757

£10,000 as the Fifth War Issue of Bills of Credit. Authorized by the Mar. 21, 1757 Act to be legal tender until April 12, 1762 and to be invalid after Oct. 12, 1762. The equivalent in silver is the same as was provided for prior issues. Faces of the £6 are in red and black and of the others in red. Sage leaf backs are printed in black except the £6 which is in green. Printed by James Parker. Signers are Hugh Hartshorne, Joseph Hollinshead, A. Johnston, Samuel Nevill, Samuel Smith, and John Smyth.

		Good	V.G.	Fine
15s	Plate letters A & B [1,334]	50.00	75.00	100.00
30s	Plate letters A, B, C, & D [2,000]	50.00	75.00	100.00
£3	Plate letters A & B [1,000]	100.00	150.00	225.00
£6	[500]	125.00	175.00	275.00

June 14, 1757

£5,000 as the Sixth War Issue of Bills of Credit. Authorized by the June 3, 1757 Act to be legal tender until June 14, 1762 and invalid after Nov. 14, 1762. The equivalent in silver is the same as was provided for prior issues. The faces of the £6 are printed in red and black and of the others in black. Sage leaf backs are in black. Printed by James Parker. Signers are Hugh Hartshorne, Joseph Hollinshead, A. Johnston, Samuel Nevill, Samuel Smith, and John Smyth.

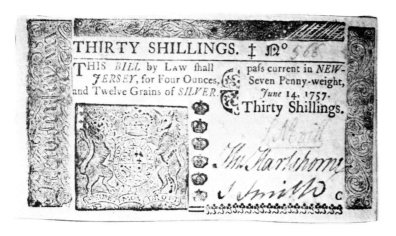

		Fair	Good
15s	Plate letters A & B [677]	70.00	100.00
30s	Plate letters A, B, C, & D [1,000]	60.00	85.00
£3	Plate letters A & B [500]	85.00	125.00
£6	[250]	125.00	200.00

November 20, 1757

£30,000 as the Seventh War Issue of Bills of Credit. Authorized by the Act of Oct. 12, 1757 to be legal tender until Nov. 1, 1773 and invalid after May 1, 1774. The equivalent in silver is the same as was provided for prior issues. The faces are printed in red and black. Sage leaf backs are in black. Printed by James Parker. Signers are Hugh Hartshorne, Joseph Hollinshead, A. Johntson, Samuel Nevill, Samuel Smith, and John Smyth.

		Fair	Good	V.G.
6s	Plate letter A [3,000]	30.00	60.00	90.00
15s	Plate letters A & B [4,000]	25.00	50.00	75.00
30s	Plate letters a, b, & C [6,000]	20.00	40.00	50.00
£3	Plate letters A & B [3,500]	25.00	50.00	75.00
£6	[1,100]	45.00	125.00	200.00

May 1, 1758

£50,000 as the Eighth War Issue of Bills of Credit. Authorized by the Act of April 4, 1758 to be legal tender until Nov. 1, 1778 and invalid after May 1, 1779. The equivalent in silver is the same as was provided for prior issues. The faces are printed in red and black. Sage leaf backs are in black. Printed by James Parker. Signers are the same as the previous issue.

		Fair	Good	V.G.
6s	Plate letter A [5,487]	15.00	25.00	50.00
15s	Plate letters A & B [7,000]	15.00	25.00	45.00
30s	Plate letters A & B [10,000]	10.00	15.00	30.00
£3	Plate letters A & B [5,700]	15.00	30.00	55.00
£6	[1,834]	30.00	50.00	90.00

October 20, 1758

£10,000 as the Ninth War Issue of Bills of Credit. Authorized by the Act of Aug. 12, 1758 to be legal tender until Oct. 10, 1763 and invalid after Oct. 20, 1764. The equivalent in silver is the same as was provided for prior issues. The faces of the 30s and £3 are in red and black; of the £6 in red and brown; and of the others in black. The back of the £6 is in brown and the other sage leaf backs are in black. Printed by James Parker. Signers are Joseph Hollinshead, James Hude, A. Johnston, Samuel Smith, John Smyth, and Joseph Yard.

		Fair	Good	Fine
1s	Plate letters A & B [6,500]	35.00	45.00	95.00
18d	Plate letters A & B [5,000]	45.00	60.00	125.00
3s	Plate letters A & B [4,000]	50.00	60.00	125.00
6s	Plate letters A & B [3,000]	55.00	70.00	145.00
12s	Plate letters A & B [3,000]	55.00	70.00	145.00
15s	Plate letters A, B, C, & D [2,000]	65.00	80.00	165.00
30s	Plate letters A, B, C, & D [1,000]	75.00	90.00	185.00
£3	Plate letters A & B [500]	85.00	110.00	210.00
£6	[250]	125.00	150.00	275.00

NEW JERSEY

April 10, 1759

£50,000 as the Tenth War Issue of Bills of Credit. Authorized by the Mar. 17, 1759 Act to be legal tender until Nov. 1, 1767 and invalid after May 1, 1768. The equivalent in silver is the same as provided for prior issues. The faces are printed in red and black. Sage leaf backs are in black. Printed by James Parker. Signers are Joseph Hollinshead, A. Johnston, Samuel Nevill, Daniel Smith, Jr., Samuel Smith, and John Smyth.

		Fair	Good	V.G.
6s	Plate letters A & B [5,487]	15.00	25.00	35.00
15s	Plate letters A & B [7,000]	12.00	20.00	25.00
30s	Which 'tis Death to counterfeit. Plate letters A & B [10,000]	15.00	22.00	30.00
£3	Plate letter A. O in Ounces is sometimes broken so as to resemble C [2,850]	15.00	25.00	35.00
£3	Plate letter B [2,850]	15.00	25.00	35.00
£6	[1,834]	25.00	40.00	60.00

April 12, 1760

£45,000 as the Eleventh War Issue of Bills of Credit. Authorized by the March 25, 1760 Act to be legal tender until Nov. 1, 1773 and invalid after May 1, 1774. The equivalent in silver is the same as was provided for prior issues. The faces of 30s and above are in red and black. The faces of the other denominations and all backs are in black. Printed by James Parker. Signers are Hugh Hartshorne, A. Johnston, Samuel Nevill, Daniel Smith, Jr., Samuel Smith, and John Smyth.

		Fair	Good	V.G.
1s	Plate letters A & B [9,720]	15.00	25.00	40.00
18d	Plate letters A & B [7,500]	15.00	25.00	40.00
3s	Plate letters A & B [6,000]	15.00	25.00	40.00
6s	Plate letters A & B [4,500]	15.00	25.00	40.00
12s	Plate letters A & B [13,500] ©	15.00	25.00	40.00
15s	Plate letters A & B [9,000]	15.00	25.00	40.00
30s	Plate letters A, B, C, & D [4,883]	15.00	25.00	40.00
£3	Plate letters A & B [2,759]	20.00	35.00	60.00
£6	[1,875]	25.00	45.00	75.00

April 23, 1761

£25,000 as the Twelfth War Issue of Bills of Credit. Authorized by the Act of April 7, 1761 to be legal tender until Nov. 1, 1778 and invalid after May 1, 1779. The equivalent in silver is the same as was provided for prior issues. The faces are in red and black and the backs are in black. Printed by James Parker. Signers are Joseph Hollinshead, A. Johnston, Samuel Nevill, Thomas Rodman, and Samuel Smith.

		Fair	Good	V.G.
12s	Plate letters a & b [1,372]	30.00	50.00	100.00
15s	Plate letters A & B [3,500]	25.00	45.00	90.00
30s	Plate letters A, B, C, & D [5,000]	15.00	25.00	50.00
£3	Plate letters A & B [2,850] Ⓒ	20.00	30.00	60.00
£6	[917]	30.00	50.00	100.00

April 8, 1762

£30,000 as the Thirteenth War Issue of Bills of Credit. Authorized at the session ended Mar. 10, 1762 to be legal tender until Nov. 1, 1780 and invalid after May 1, 1781. The equivalent in silver is the same as was provided for prior issues. The face of the £6 is in red and blue and the other faces are in red and black. Backs are in black. Printed by James Parker. Signers are A. Johnston, Samuel Nevill, Thomas Rodman, S. Skinner, and Samuel Smith.

		Fair	Good	V.G.
12s	Plate letters A & B [1,600]	25.00	40.00	80.00
15s	Plate letters A & B [4,084]	20.00	35.00	70.00
30s	Plate letters A, B, C, & D [5,850] Ⓒ ..	10.00	25.00	50.00
£3	Plate letters A & B [3,330] Ⓒ	15.00	30.00	60.00
£6	[1,219]	25.00	40.00	80.00

December 31, 1763

£20,000 (£10,000 plus £10,000 to exchange for worn bills) in Bills of Credit authorized at the session begun Nov. 15, 1763. Legal tender until Dec. 31, 1781 and to be invalid after Dec. 31, 1782. The equivalent in silver is the same as was provided for prior issues. The face of the £6 is in red and blue. The faces of the 30s and £3 are in red and black. The faces of the others are in black. Backs are in black. Printed by James Parker. Signers are Jonathan Johnston, S. Skinner, Joseph Smith, Richard Smith, and Samuel Smith.

		V.G.	Fine	Unc.
1s	Plate letters A, B, C, & D [13,000]	15.00	30.00	100.00
18d	Plate letters A & C [5,000]	15.00	30.00	100.00
18d	Plate letter B. Italic instead of upright "t" in "Penny-weight" [2,500]	15.00	30.00	100.00
18d	Plate letter D. PLATE misspelled PTATE [2,500]	45.00	90.00	125.00
3s	Plate letters A & B [8,000]	15.00	30.00	100.00
6s	Plate letters A & B [6,000] ©	15.00	30.00	100.00
12s	Plate letters A & B [6,000] ©	15.00	30.00	100.00
15s	Plate letters A & B [4,000] ©	20.00	40.00	125.00
30s	Plate letters A, B, C, & D [2,000]	50.00	100.00	
£3	Plate letters A & B [1,000] ©	75.00	150.00	
£6	[500]	100.00	200.00	

April 16, 1764

£25,000 in Bills of Credit authorized at the session ended Feb. 23, 1764. Legal tender until Dec. 31, 1782 and to be invalid after Dec. 31, 1783. The equivalent in silver is the same as was provided for prior issues. The face of the £6 is in red and blue. The faces of the others are in red and black. Backs are in black. Printed by James Parker. Signers are Jonathan Johnston, S. Skinner, Richard Smith, and Samuel Smith.

		Good	V.G.
12s	[1,372]	35.00	70.00
15s	Plate letters A, B, D, and without plate letter [3,500] ©	20.00	40.00
30s	Plate letters A, B, C, D, F, & G [5,000] ©. (Counterfeits of Plate letters B & G only, the former containing the misspelling SHILLIGNS on the back)	25.00	50.00
£3	Plate letters A, B, & D [2,850 for all £3] ©	25.00	50.00
£3	No plate letter. Solid sun	25.00	50.00
£3	No plate letter. Split sun	25.00	50.00
£6	[917]	100.00	200.00

Hibernia Furnace ★ May 1, 1774

Bills issued in "light money" (paper money) and receivable at the store of the Hibernia Furnace, near Rockaway, Morris County. This smelter was known as the Adventure Furnace and was built in 1765 by Samuel Ford, who became a notorious paper money counterfeiter. Signed by Lord Stirling who purchased the furnace in 1771.

1s	Plate letters A, B, C, D, E, & F
3s	Plate letter E
5s	Plate letters B, C, & D
10s	Plate letter A

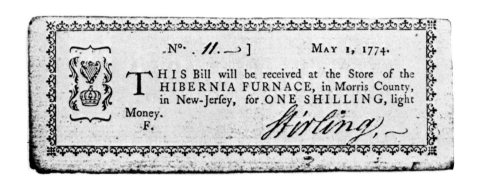

February 20, 1776

£30,000 in Proclamation Money authorized by Ordinance of the Provincial Congress on Oct. 28, 1775 and redeemable by Dec. 21, 1786. The issue was not printed by Feb. 28, 1776 when the amount was increased to £50,000 5s and the redemption date extended to Dec. 21, 1791. Invalid after June 21, 1792. Made legal tender on Sept. 20, 1776. The faces are in red and black. The back contains an engraved cut of a leaf rather than a nature print. Printed by Isaac Collins at Burlington on mica flaked paper watermarked NEW JERSEY. Some notes signed by Hart and How were plundered in a military raid, circulated before the third signature was added, and were therefore invalid. Signers are Caleb Camp, Alexander Chambers, Abraham Clark*, John Cowenhoven, John Dennis, Azariah Dunham, Joseph Ellis, Hendrick Fisher, John Hart*, Samuel How, Abraham Hunt, Samuel Tucker, and William Tucker.

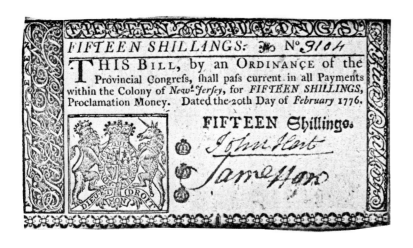

		Good	Fine	V.F.
6s	[5,000]	50.00	75.00	100.00
15s	[6,667]	40.00	60.00	80.00
30s	Plate letters A & B [10,000] ..	30.00	45.00	60.00
£3	Plate letters A & B [9,500] ...	30.00	45.00	60.00

*Value doubles with signature of John Hart, signer of the Declaration of Independence. Bills with signature of Abraham Clark have not been located.

March 25, 1776

On May 10, 1768 £100,000 in legal tender Bills of Credit were authorized subject to the Crown's consent. The Act was rejected by the Crown for legal tender reasons on Mar. 26, 1769. A renewed authorization on Dec. 6, 1769 provided for £100,000 in Loan Office bills of credit and £25,000 to replace worn bills, but was rejected by the Crown allegedly because the issue lacked legal tender provisions. On Mar. 11, 1774 the 1769 legislation was reenacted and after extensive delays was approved by the Crown on Feb. 20, 1775 with conditions. When the American Revolution began the conditions were deemed void and the bills were issued. The portion for replacement of worn bills was expended pursuant to an Act passed Dec. 11, 1777 and bills arising from Loan Office earnings were made available for legislative appropriations by the Act of April 17, 1778. The notes were made legal tender by Act of Sept. 20, 1776 and called in by Jan. 1, 1780 pursuant to the Act of June 8, 1779. David Rittenhouse who in 1792 became the first Director of the United States Mint engraved at least the decorative border for the £6 on which he cut his name. The faces of the £3 and £6 are in red and blue. The faces of the other denominations are in red and black. Nature printed backs printed in black by Isaac Collins on mica flaked paper watermarked NEW JERSEY. Signers are Jonathan Deare, John Hart*, Jonathan Johnston, Joseph Smith, Robert Smith, John Smyth, and John Stevens, Jr.

		Fine	V.F.	Unc.
1s	Plate letters A, B, & C [81,250]	25.00	40.00	100.00
18d	Plate letters A, B, & C [62,500]	25.00	40.00	100.00
3s	Plate letters A & B [50,000]	25.00	40.00	100.00
6s	Plate A. Small coat of arms [18,750] .	25.00	40.00	100.00
6s	Plate B. Large coat of arms [18,750] .	25.00	40.00	100.00
12s	Plate letters A & B [37,500]	25.00	40.00	100.00
15s	[25,000]	25.00	40.00	100.00
30s	[12,500]	30.00	50.00	125.00
£3	Bees on back. Umlaut instead of of dot over i in Reïgn [6,250]	50.00	90.00	175.00
£6	RITTENHOUSE in tiny letters in center ornament of left border of face [3,125]	75.00	125.00	250.00

*Value doubles with signature of John Hart, signer of the Declaration of Independence.

James Craft ★ August 6, 1776

Private small change circulating notes issued at Burlington. Blank backs. Other denominations are probable.

4d NIL DESPERANDUM (Never lose hope). A & H
6d NIL DESPERANDUM

James Craft ★ October 11, 1776

Private small change circulating notes issued at Burlington. Many border mottoes. Blank backs. Other denominations are probable.

2d   HONI SOIT QUI MAL Y PENSE (Evil to him who evil thinks); SERENABIT (It will be calm); a very early use of the abbreviation U.S.A.; PRO BONO PUBLICO (For the public good); and NIL DESPERANDUM (Never despair).

3d

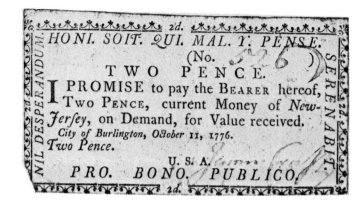

Moore Furman ★ November 1, 1776

Private small change circulating notes issued at Pitts-Town. In Trenton, Moore Furman had been in partnership with Azariah Hunt, who personally issued circulating notes in 1786. Moore Furman also signed the New Jersey State issue of 1786. Blank backs. Other denominations are probable.

3d
6d

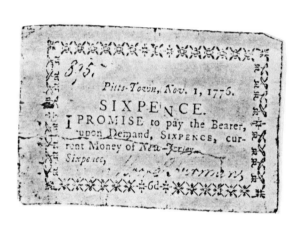

Isaac Craig ★ April 21, 1777

Private small change circulating notes issued at Freehold. Blank backs. Other denominations are probable.

3d

June 9, 1780 Act

£225,000 ($600,000) in legal tender Bills of Credit payable in Spanish milled dollars by Dec. 31, 1786 with 5% interest was authorized by the June 9, 1780 Act. Guaranteed by the United States pursuant to the March 18, 1780 Resolution of the Continental Congress making the N.J. issue dependent upon the amount of Continental Currency exchanged at $40 (old) for $1 (new). Legal tender terminated as of May 1, 1782 by the Act of June 13, 1781. Paid out at depreciated current exchange rates pursuant to the Dec. 29, 1781 Resolution. By the Dec. 21, 1784 Act bills were revalued at $3 in

bills for $1 in specie. The faces are in black and the backs in red and black. Printed by Hall & Sellers in Philadelphia on paper watermarked UNITED STATES. Face border cuts and back cut surrounding device were engraved by Henry Dawkins. Border cuts and the device on the back are from the Jan. 14, 1779 issue of Continental Currency. Sometimes surcharged in red "Int. Pd. 1 Yr." or variants. Signers are David Brearley, Philemon Dickinson, Moore Furman, John Imlay, Robert Neil, and Benjamin Smith. Guaranty signed by Joseph Borden and Joseph Kirkbride.

	V.G.	Fine	V.F.
$1 [12,000]	45.00	55.00	65.00
$2 [12,000]	45.00	55.00	65.00
$3 [12,000]	45.00	55.00	65.00
$4 [12,000]	45.00	55.00	65.00

	V.G.	Fine	V.F.
$5 [12,000] ©	45.00	55.00	65.00
$7 [12,000]	45.00	55.00	65.00
$8 [12,000]	45.00	55.00	65.00
$20 [12,000]	45.00	55.00	65.00

1781 (January 9, 1781 Act)

£30,000 in legal tender Bills of Credit redeemable by Dec. 31, 1787. Legal tender terminated as of May 1, 1782 pursuant to the June 13, 1781 Act. Paid out on a depreciated basis at current exchange rates pursuant to the Dec. 29, 1781 Resolution. By the Dec. 21, 1784 Act bills were revalued at $3 in bills for $1 in specie. The

faces contain the N.J. State seal. The nature print of the sage leaf on the back has its stem opposite the left side of the face of the Bill, thus differing from all prior issues. Printed in black by Isaac Collins at Trenton on paper watermarked NEW JERSEY. Signers are David Brearley, Philemon Dickinson, Robert Neil, and Benjamin Smith.

	V.G.	Fine	V.F.
6d [20,000]	100.00	150.00	200.00
9d [20,000]	100.00	150.00	200.00
1s [20,000]	100.00	150.00	200.00
1s6d [20,000]	100.00	150.00	200.00
2s6d [20,000]	100.00	150.00	200.00

	V.G.	Fine	V.F.
3s6d [20,000]	100.00	150.00	200.00
3s9d [20,000]	100.00	150.00	200.00
4s [20,000]	100.00	150.00	200.00
5s [20,000]	100.00	150.00	200.00
7s6d ($1.00) [20,000]	100.00	150.00	200.00

1784 (December 20, 1783 Act)

£31,259 5s in Tax Notes approved by the Dec. 20, 1783 Act. The State seal is on the face. The date and a nature print of a sage leaf are on the back. The stem is opposite the left side of the face as in the previous issue. Recalled within one year. Printed by Isaac Collins on paper water-marked NEW JERSEY. Signers are James Ewing and James Mott.

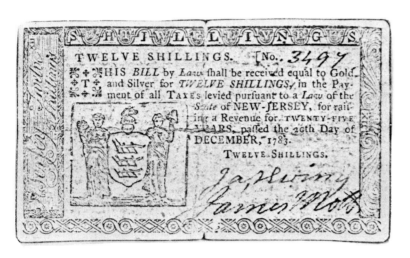

2s6d		[3,976]
3s9d	($1/2)	[3,976]
5s		[3,976]
7s6d	($1)	Bees on the back [3,976]
12s		[3,976]
15s		[3,975]
30s		[3,977]
£3		[3,000]
£6		[1,200]

1786

£100,000 in Loan Office Bills of Credit authorized on May 17, 1786. Legal tender until Dec. 5, 1798 and invalid after June 5, 1799. Legal tender was reaffirmed by the Nov. 3, 1786 Act. Printed by Isaac Collins with the faces in red and black and the backs in black. The stem of the sage leaf nature print is opposite the right side of the face and contains SIC which apparently is an abbreviation of "Sculpsit Isaac Collins." The paper is watermarked NEW JERSEY. Signers are Maskell Ewing, Moore Furman, Benjamin Smith, and Benjamin Van Cleve.

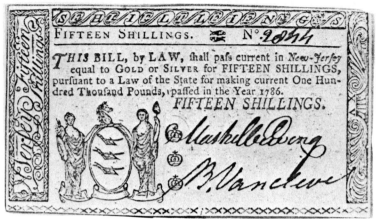

		Good	V.G.	Fine
1s	Plate letters A, B, & C [50,000]	150.00	200.00	275.00
3s	Plate letters A, B, C, & D [40,000] ...	150.00	200.00	275.00
6s	Plate letter A. Bees [17,500]	150.00	200.00	275.00
6s	Without plate letter. Bees [17,500] ...	150.00	200.00	275.00
12s	Plate letters A & B [35,000]	150.00	200.00	275.00
15s	[20,000]	175.00	225.00	300.00
30s	[10,000]	175.00	225.00	300.00
£3	Bees on back [5,000]	200.00	250.00	325.00
£6	[2,500]	225.00	275.00	350.00

Azariah Hunt ★ July 26, 1786

Private small change notes issued by Azariah Hunt at Trenton where he previously had been a partner of Moore Furman, who issued circulating notes in 1776. Printed in red. Other denominations are probable.

3d

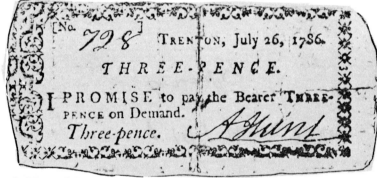

Burlington Nail Company ★ August 29, 1786

Small change notes issued by John Little and Joseph Bloomfield at Burlington with the motto: "He that despiseth Three Pence will never be worth a Groat." Printed by Matthew Carey of Philadelphia. Other denominations are probable.

3d

Seeley & Merseilles ★ January 19, 1787

Private small change circulating notes issued at Bridgetown. Blank backs. Other denominations are probable.

6d

Colhoun & Brush ★ November 7, 1787
Private small change notes issued at New Market. Blank backs. Other denominations are probable.

3d

Isaac L. Milnor ★ December 1, 1787
Private small change circulating notes issued by Isaac L. Milnor, a merchant of Philadelphia. Blank backs. Other denominations are probable.

6d Black ink   9d Green ink

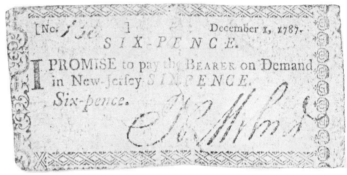

Borough of Elizabeth ★ March 25, 1790
Small change notes issued by the Corporation of Elizabeth. Printed by S. Kollock of Elizabeth Town.

1d   3d   4d
      6d   9d

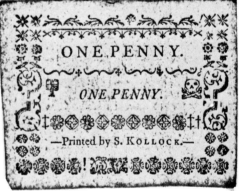

Reuben Chadwick ★ May 3, 179(?)
Small change note without place of issue. Blank backs. Other denominations are probable.

2d

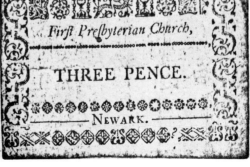

First Presbyterian Church at Newark ★ December 16, 1790
Church Money issued by the First Presbyterian Church at Newark and signed by Elias Boudinot, its president. He later became the third Director of the United States Mint. Printed by S. Kollock of Elizabeth Town.

1d (undated)   2d (undated)
3d   4d   6d   9d

City of New Brunswick ★ January 7, 1791

Small change notes approved by the Common Council of the City of New Brunswick with a due date of Jan. 1, 1796. Signed by John Plum as commissioner. Printed by A. Blauvelt.

1d   2d   3d

City of Perth Amboy ★ February 10, 1792

Small change notes of the Corporation of Perth Amboy to be good for four years. Printed by A. Blauvelt. Other denominations are probable.

2d   3d   6d

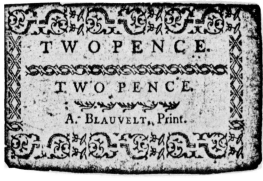

Society for Establishing Useful Manufactures ★ January 1, 1794

Small change notes issued at Patterson and signed by Peter Colt, secretary. Denomination in cents rather than pence. Other denominations are probable.

1¢   10¢

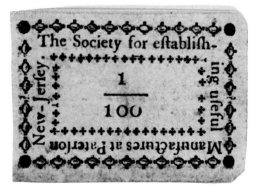

W. & R. Colfax ★ July 4, 1794

Small change notes issued at Pompton. Typeset. Other denominations are probable.

2d

NEW JERSEY

City of New Brunswick ★ March 10, 1796
Small change notes issued to replace the Jan. 7, 1791 issue which was due on Jan. 1, 1796. Printed by A. Blauvelt.

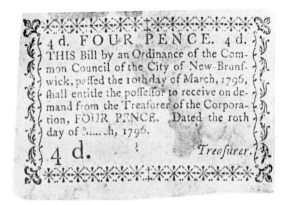 

1d Ⓤ   2d Ⓤ   3d Ⓤ   4d Ⓤ

NEW JERSEY REFERENCES

William Benedict, "James Parker, The Printer of Wood-bridge," *Proceedings of the New Jersey Historical Society* (1923).

William W. Bradbeer, "New Jersey Paper Currency 1709-1786," *Proceedings of the New Jersey Historical Society* (1923).

Joseph Coffin, "An Early American Printer," *The Numismatic Scrapbook Magazine* (February 1942).

Herbert Eccleston, "John Hart—Signer of the Declaration of Independence and Colonial Notes," *Paper Money,* Vol. 12, No. 3, p. 118 (1973).

Richard F. Hixson, *Isaac Collins, A Quaker Printer in 18th Century America* (New Brunswick, 1968).

Richard T. Hoober, "Colonial Paper Currencies of Pennsylvania and New Jersey," *The Numismatist* (December 1944).

———, "Finances of Colonial New Jersey," *The Numismatist* (February 1950, etc.), reprinted.

Francis B. Lee, "Paper Money and Counterfeiting in the Colony of New Jersey," *Proceedings of the American Numismatic and Archeological Society* (New York, 1896), and in *New Jersey as a Colony and as a State* (New York, 1902).

C. William Miller, *Benjamin Franklin's Philadelphia Printing* (Philadelphia, 1974).

Eric P. Newman, "Franklin Making Money More Plentiful," *Proceedings of the American Philosophical Society* (Philadelphia, Oct. 1971).

———, "Nature Printing on Colonial and Continental Currency," *The Numismatist* (February 1964, etc.), reprinted.

Henry Phillips, Jr., *A Catalogue of the New Jersey Bills of Credit* (Philadelphia, 1863), reprinted in *Historical Sketches of the Paper Currencies of the American Colonies* (Roxbury, 1865).

"Relic of Benjamin Franklin's Printing Office," *The Numismatist* (August 1921).

Kenneth Scott, "Earliest Counterfeiting in New Jersey," *Proceedings of the New Jersey Historical Society* (January 1957, etc.).

Jacob N. Spiro, "Furman & Hunt," *Coin Collector's Journal* (November 1941).

———, "Isaac Collins, Printer," *Coin Collector's Journal* (January 1943).

———, "Tis Death to Counterfeit," *The Numismatic Review* (June 1943).

Laws, archives, newspapers and other public records.

See general references, catalogs, and listings following the Introduction.

NEW YORK

GENERAL EMISSIONS

May 31, 1709
November 1, 1709 (Shilling)
November 1, 1709 (Silver)
July 20, 1711
July 1, 1714
July 5, 1715
November 28, 1717
November 10, 1720
July 2, 1723
July 10, 1724
July 22, 1724
November 16, 1726

October 20, 1730
November 15, 1734
December 10, 1737
October 20, 1739
May 10, 1746
July 21, 1746
November 25, 1747
March 25, 1755
May 12, 1755
September 15, 1755
February 16, 1756
April 20, 1756

April 15, 1758
April 2, 1759
April 21, 1760
February 16, 1771
September 2, 1775
March 5, 1776
August 13, 1776
June 15, 1780 Act
March 27, 1781 Act
April 18, 1786
February 8, 1788

SPECIAL ISSUERS
NOTES OTHER THAN SMALL CHANGE NOTES

New York City ★ August 25, 1774 ★ August 2, 1775 ★ January 6, 1776 ★ March 5, 1776
City and County of Albany ★ June 22, 1775 ★ February 17, 1776
Unknown Issuer ★ June 6, 1776
Scrip Payable in Army Bills ★ Undated
Bank of New York ★ 1784, etc.
Bank of the United States (New York Office) ★ 1792, etc.
Bank of Albany ★ 1792, etc.
Bank of Columbia ★ 1793, etc.
Manhattan Company ★ 1799, etc.

SMALL CHANGE NOTE ISSUERS (1789-1799)

William Adams
City of Albany
N. Aldridge
J. H. & W. Baker
E. Bicknell & J. Becker
Egbert Bogardus
W. Y. Burrough
Cayuga Bridge Company
John Clark
Constitutional Society
William Cooper
M. Croswill & Co.
Edward Dale
Daniel Davis
Davis & Clark
R. Davis & J. Schoonhoven
Stephen Day & Son
Samuel DeRiemer
Genesee Company

German Reformed Church
    of Schohary
George & Thomas Hale
City of Hudson
J. & A. Hunt
Janes & Dole
Corporation of Kingston
Lansingburgh Museum
Lutheran Church in Schoharie
Benijah Morris
City of New York
New York Manufacturing Society
Ananias Platt
John Portens
J. Porter
City of Poughkeepsie
Presbyterian Congregation of Ballston
Presbyterian Congregation in Troy
John Prince

William Radclift & Co.
Reformed Dutch Church
    of Canajohary
Reformed Dutch Church
    at Schenectady
Reformed Dutch Church
    at Stone Arabia
Reformed German Church
    in Herkemertown
James Rogers
Isaac Schultz
Shepard & Allen
Society of Mechanics at Hudson
Solomon Tryon
Union Society
Walsh & Loudon
Walsh & McAuley

May 31, 1709

£5,000 in indented Bills of Credit approved by the June 8, 1709 Act and receivable for taxes without interest. Printed by William Bradford from set type and with a scroll wood cut on the top for indenture. Blank backs.

Four notes were printed side by side on one sheet. Signers are Johannes DePeyster, Robert Lurting, Lawrence Reade, and Robert Walter.

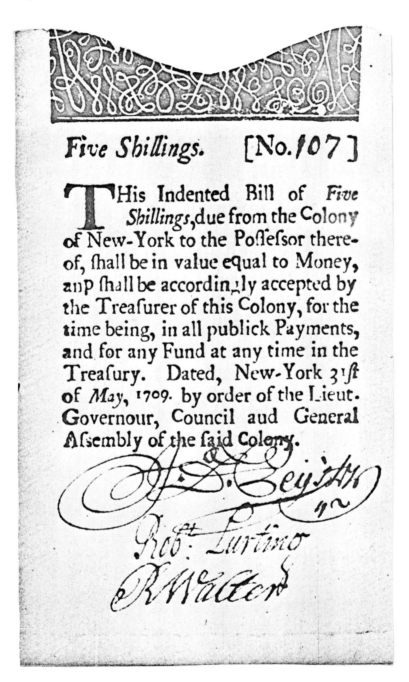

5s	"&" in fourth line of text [1,400]
5s	"d" in first "and" is inverted [1,400]
10s	Governor [500]
10s	Governour [500]
20s	[600]
40s	[600]
£5	[400]

November 1, 1709 Shilling Issue

£4,000 (14,545 "Lyon Dollars") in indented Bills of Credit approved by the Nov. 1, 1709 Act and receivable for taxes with 2½% interest. Interest was subsequently revoked. Silver ducatoons of Holland were referred to in New York as "Lyon Dollars" because of their rampant lion insignia. Same general form as the May 31, 1709 issue. Printed by William Bradford. Signers are Johannes DePeyster, Johannes Jansen, Robert Lurting, and Robert Walter.

Fifty Shillings, (No. 1552
at half a farthing per diem Int.

THis Indented Bill of *Fifty Shillings*, due from the Colony of New-York, to the Poſseſsor thereof ſhall be in value equal to Money, & ſhall be accordingly accepted by the Treaſurer of this Colony, for the time being, in all publick Payments, and for any Fund at any time in the Treaſury. Dated, *New-York*, the 1*ſt* of *November*, 1709. by order of the Lieut. Governor, council & General Aſsembly of the ſaid Colony.

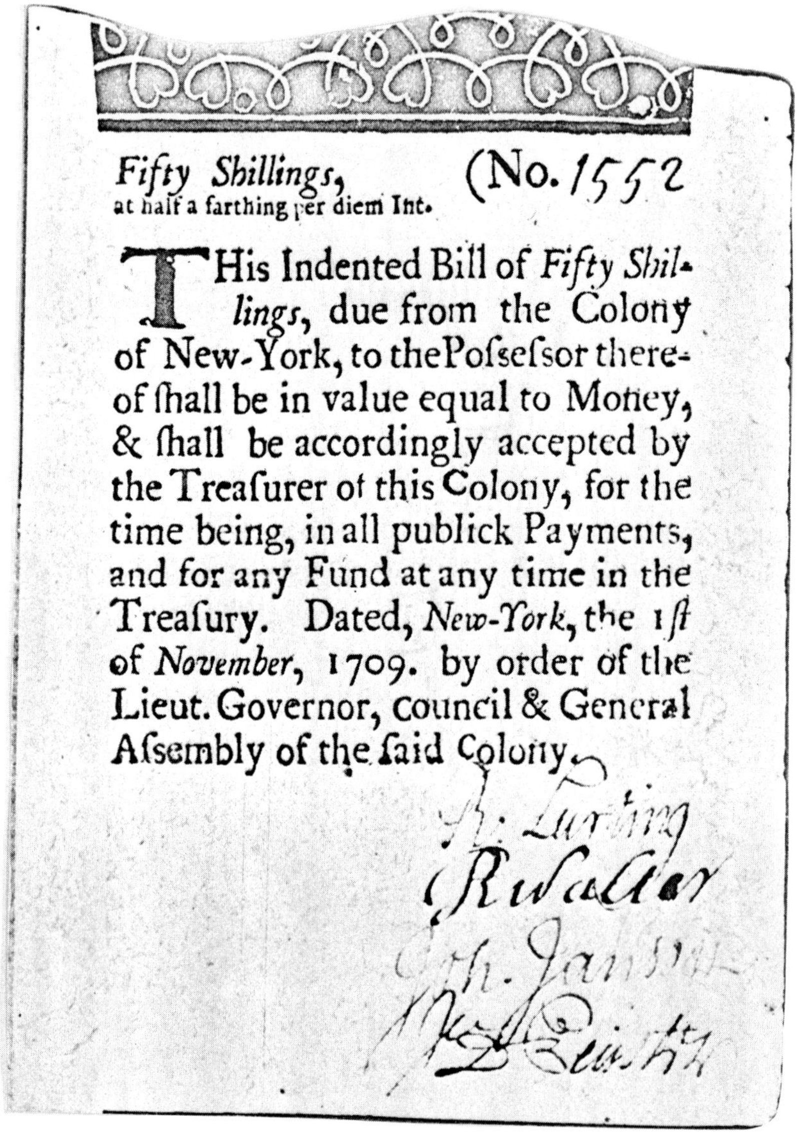

25s [800]
50s [400]
£5 [400]

November 1, 1709 Silver Issue

£4,000 (14,545 "Lyon Dollars" or 10,000 ounces of Silver Plate) in indented Bills of Credit approved on Nov. 12, 1709 and receivable for taxes with 2½% interest. Interest was subsequently revoked. One "Lyon Dollar" equalled 5s6d New York money of account or 13 pennyweights, 18 grains of Silver Plate. Same general form as the previous issues. Printed by William Bradford. Same signers as the Nov. 1, 1709 Shilling Issue.

2 Ounces, 15 Pennyweights (4 Lyon dollars). GOVERNOR [169]
2 Ounces, 15 Pennyweights (4 Lyon dollars). GOVERNOUR [168]
5 Ounces, 10 Pennyweights (8 Lyon dollars) [300]
11 Ounces (16 Lyon dollars) [300]
13 Ounces, 15 Pennyweights (20 Lyon dollars) [300]

July 20, 1711

£10,000 (25,000 ounces of Silver Plate) in indented Bills of Credit approved by the July 26, 1711 Act. Same general form as previous issues. Arms of the City of New York were not included as ordered. The spelling of Fund has been changed to Fond. Printed by William Bradford. Signers are Johannes DePeyster, Robert Lurting, and Robert Walter.

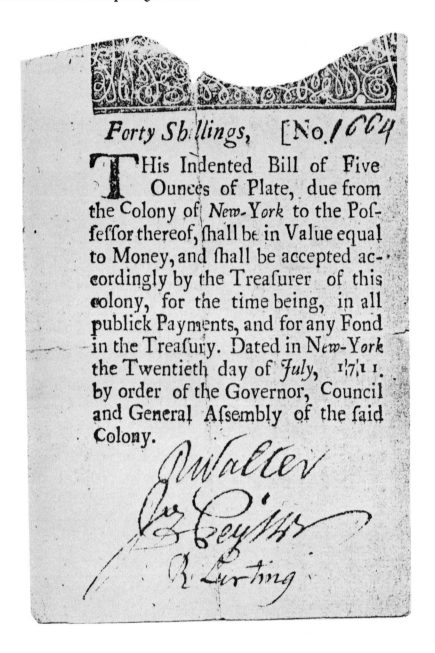

¼ ounce	(2s)	[1,000]
½ ounce	(4s)	[1,000]
1 ounce	(8s)	[1,000]
2 ounces	(16s)	[1,000]
2½ ounces	(20s)	[500]
5 ounces	(40s)	[1,000]
10 ounces	(£4)	[500]
20 ounces	(£8)	Each C in the three uses of COLONY is different in size. [250]
20 ounces	(£8)	Each C in the first and last uses of COLONY is the same size. [250]

July 1, 1714

£27,680 (69,200 ounces of Silver Plate) in legal tender indented Bills of Credit approved by the Sept. 4, 1714 Act and by the Crown on June 17, 1715. Bills were to circulate until Dec. 31, 1739 and thus acquired the name of "First Long Bills." The denomination in both Plate and New York Money of Account is included in the text in the alternative whereas in prior issues either one or the other basis was specified in the text. The Arms of the City of New York were again omitted contrary to order. The spelling of Fond is retained. Bills are narrower than prior issues. The stub which was ordinarily cut off and retained by the Treasurer in the course of indenture is shown on the accompanying illustration of an unissued unsigned bill. Printed by William Bradford. Signers are John Cruger, Robert Lurting, David Provoost, and Robert Walter.

7 dwt., 12 gr.	(3s)	[4,000]
15 dwt.	(6s)	[2,000] Ⓤ
1 oz., 10 dwt.	(12s)	[1,500]
1 oz., 17 dwt., 12 gr.	(15s)	[1,200] Ⓒ
3 oz., 2 dwt., 12 gr.	(£1 5s)	[1,000]
3 oz., 15 dwt.	(£1 10s)	[800] Ⓒ
6 oz., 5 dwt.	(£2 10s)	[800]
7 oz., 10 dwt.	(£3)	[1,000] Ⓒ
12 oz., 10 dwt.	(£5)	[720]
15 oz.	(£6)	[700] Ⓒ
18 oz., 15 dwt.	(£7 10s)	[500]
25 oz.	(£10)	[568]

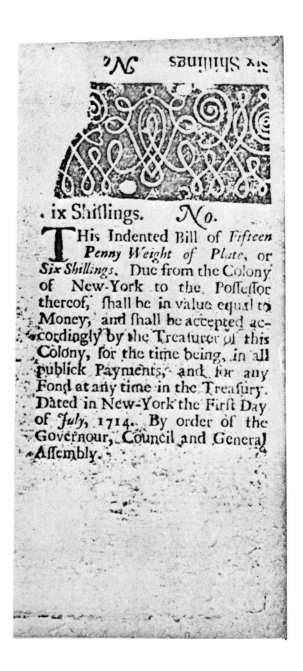

July 5, 1715

£6,000 (15,000 ounces of Silver Plate) in indented Bills of Credit approved by the July 5, 1715 Act and to be good for five years. Only £1,200 were emitted before the Crown vetoed the Act. Some of those issued were continued in circulation through 1724 by the Acts of Nov. 10, 1720, Dec. 1722, and Nov. 1724. Printed by William Bradford. Signers are John Cruger, David Provoost, John Read, and Robert Walter.

12 dwt., 12 gr.	(5s)	[1,200]	
1 oz., 5 dwt.	(10s)	[1,000]	Ⓒ
2 oz., 10 dwt.	(20s)	[1,000]	Ⓒ
5 oz.	(40s)	[200]	

10 oz.	(£4)	[200]
12 oz., 10 dwt.	(£5)	[200]
25 oz.	(£10)	[200]

November 28, 1717

£16,607 (41,517½ ounces of Silver Plate equal to "Sevil, Pillar or Mexico" plate) in indented Bills of Credit approved Dec. 23, 1717 and known as "Second Long Bills" from their maturity in 1740. Sevil (Spanish), Pillar (Peruvian), and Mexico Plate refers to coined silver acceptable on an equal weight basis. Arms of the City of New York were inserted within the text and reading SIGILL. CIVITAT NOV. EBORAC (Seal of the City of New York). Otherwise the issue is similar to the previous issues with the spelling of Fond retained. Printed by William Bradford. Signers are John Cruger, Johannes Jansen, David Provoost, and Robert Walter. In the example illustrated a ficticious denomination of £6 is created by altering Shillings to Pounds and by altering Pennyweights to Ounces.

5 dwt.	(2s)	[5,630]
10 dwt.	(4s)	[4,000]
15 dwt.	(6s)	[3,000]
1 oz.	(8s)	[2,200]
1 oz., 5 dwt.	(10s)	[1,000]
1 oz., 10 dwt.	(12s)	[1,000]
2 oz.	(16s)	[1,000]
2 oz., 10 dwt.	(20s)	[1,000]
5 oz.	(40s)	[1,000]
7 oz., 10 dwt.	(£3)	[1,000]
10 oz.	(£4)	[1,391]

November 10, 1720

£2,000 (5,000 ounces of Silver Plate) in indented Bills of Credit approved on Nov. 19, 1720. Originally good for 5 years, but extended to Sept. 1, 1733 by the Acts of Nov. 10, 1725, June 17, 1726, Aug. 31, 1728, July 12, 1729, Oct. 17, 1730, and Oct. 14, 1732. Same form as previous issue. Printed by William Bradford. Signers are Gerardus Beekman, Johannes Jansen, Jacobus Kip, and David Provoost.

2 dwt., 12 gr.	(1s)	[6,001]
3 dwt., 18 gr.	(1s6d)	[4,000]
6 dwt., 6 gr.	(2s6d)	[4,000]
7 dwt., 12 gr.	(3s)	[4,000]
8 dwt., 18 gr.	(3s6d)	[1,714]

July 2, 1723

£2,140 (5,350 ounces of Silver Plate) in indented Bills of Credit approved on July 6, 1723 and good until July 1, 1726. Same form as the previous two issues. Printed by William Bradford. Signers are Gerardus Beekman, John Cruger, Johannes Jansen, Jacobus Kip, and David Provoost.

8 oz., 15 dwt.	(£3 10s)	[299]
11 oz., 5 dwt.	(£4 10s)	[243]

July 10, 1724

£6,630 in indented legal tender Bills of Credit approved on July 24, 1724 and good until July 1, 1729. Money of account replaced silver as the basis for this and future emissions. The denomination is cut into the top border design and also placed within the Arms of the City of New York. Printed by William Bradford. Same signers as the previous issue.

1s3d	(15d)	[5,000]
3s9d		[4,000]
7s6d		[3,000] ©
14s		[1,495]
£1 12s		[800]
£3 4s		[380]
£3 12s		[250] ©

July 22, 1724

£3,000 in indented legal tender Bills of Credit approved by the July 24, 1724 Act to replace worn bills and good until July 1, 1729. Same form as previous issue. Printed by William Bradford. Same signers as the July 2, 1723 issue.

1s [4,000]	2s [2,000]	3s [2,000]	4s [2,000]	8s [800]
1s6d [3,000]	2s6d [1,800]	3s6d [2,000]	6s [1,000]	12s [800]

November 16, 1726

£3,000 in indented legal tender Bills of Credit approved on Nov. 11, 1726 to replace worn bills. Smaller in size than the prior issues, but with the same Arms cut. Signers are Stephen DeLancey, Robert Livingston, Jr., Frederick Philipse, and Anthony Rutgers.

1s [2,000]
1s3d [1,600]
1s6d [3,000]
2s [2,000]
2s6d [1,800]
3s [2,000]
3s6d [2,000]
4s [2,000]
6s [1,000]
8s [800]
12s [800]

Ⓐ

October 20, 1730

£3,000 in indented legal tender Bills of Credit approved on Oct. 17, 1730 to replace worn bills. Same general form as the previous issue. Printed by William Bradford. Signers are Henry Beekman, Philip Van Cortlandt, John Cruger, and Frederick Philipse.

2s6d [4,000]	5s [2,000]	10s [2,000] Ⓒ	20s [1,000]

NEW YORK

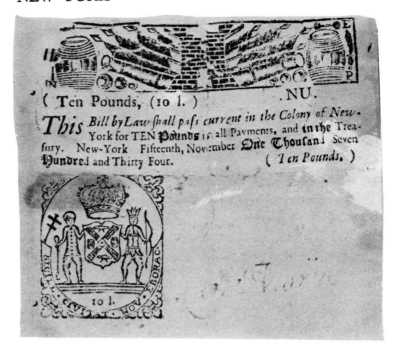

November 15, 1734

£12,000 in legal tender Bills of Credit approved on Nov. 28, 1734 for fortifications and good until Mar. 25, 1746. Allegorical symbols in top border cuts. Small cut of the Arms of the City of New York under the typeset text, both cuts having been engraved by Charles Le Roux. Number is abbreviated NU. Printed by William Bradford. Signers are Stephen Bayard, John Cruger, Frederick Philipse, and Cornelius Van Horne.

5s	[2,000]	©
10s	[1,000]	©
20s	[1,000]	
£2	[800]	
£3	[800]	
£5	[600]	
£10	[300]	

December 10, 1737

£48,350 in legal tender Bills of Credit approved on Dec. 16, 1737 and originally good for 12 years. Mortgage loans were to be made with £40,000 of the issue at 5% interest. The redemption date was extended to April 3, 1768. Border cuts on the top and left sides of the Bills were engraved by Charles Le Roux. The cut of the Arms of the City of New York was reused from the prior issue. Pound weights were keyed to the higher denominations to deter alteration. The denomination was removed from within the Arms to a position below them. A line through the center of the border of the two highest denominations was used to discourage alteration. The abbreviation of number was changed back to No. Printed by John Peter Zenger with blank backs. Signers are James Alexander, G. Beekman, A. DePeyster, B. Hinchman, Peter Jay, Simon Johnson, P. Lefferts, James Roosevelt, S. Rowe, Peter Schuyler, James Stringham, and Stephen Wood.

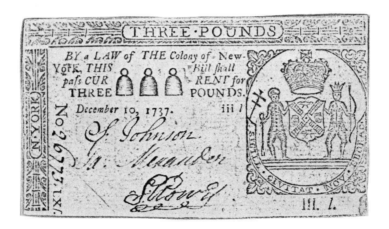

5s	[10,000]	©
10s	[7,700]	
20s	[5,000]	©
£2	[4,000]	©
£3	[3,000]	©
£5	[2,000]	
£10	[1,000]	©

231

October 20, 1739

£10,000 in legal tender Bills of Credit approved on Oct. 25, 1739 to exchange for worn bills and to be redeemed by Nov. 1, 1767. Similar to the previous issue with a line in the borders of the two highest denominations to discourage alteration. Printed by William Bradford. Signers are David Clarkson, A. DePeyster, Peter Jay, John Moore, and William Roome.

5s	[4,000]	£3	[500]
10s	[3,000]	£5	[400] ©
20s	[1,000]	£10	[200]
£2	[500]		

May 10, 1746

£13,000 in legal tender Bills of Credit approved on May 13, 1746 for defense and to be redeemed in January, 1748. Similar to the previous issue but with borders on the top and the right sides and with Arms on the left. The denomination has been moved back inside the Arms. The issue was recalled on Oct. 27, 1755 because of counterfeits. Printed by James Parker. Signers are Henry Cruger, Robert Livingston, Jr., Paul Richard, and Cornelius Van Horne.

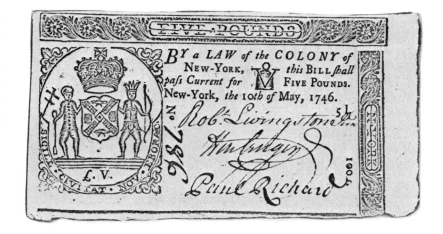

£2	[650]	£5	[650]
£3	[650] ©	£10	[650]

July 21, 1746

£40,000 in legal tender Bills of Credit approved on July 15, 1746 for military expense and to be redeemed by Jan. 1756. New border cuts are at the top and serpent column cuts are on both sides. Arms are on the right side. Warning to counterfeiters was added, but the punctuation was omitted from Its. Pound weights were continued to be keyed to denominations. Printed by James Parker. Signers are Isaac DePeyster, Abraham Lynsen, Paul Richard, and Cornelius Van Horne.

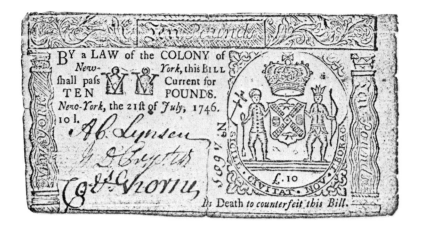

10s	[1,860]	£3	[1,860] ©
20s	[1,860]	£5	[1,860]
£2	[1,860]	£10	[1,861]

November 25, 1747

£28,000 in legal tender Bills of Credit approved on Nov. 25, 1747 for military purposes and redeemable by Nov. 25, 1756. Arms on the left and numbering is changed to read upward. Otherwise similar to the previous issue. Printed by James Parker. Same signers as the previous issue.

20s [3,500]	£5 [1,250]
£2 [1,250]	£10 [1,250]
£3 [1,250]	

March 25, 1755

£45,000 in legal tender Bills of Credit approved on Feb. 19, 1755 to finance the first expedition to Crown Point and to be redeemed by Nov. 1761. Arms are on the right. The top borders of the Dec. 10, 1737 issue were reused without alteration protection lines. The location of the vertical numbering was moved and reads downward. The abbreviation of number is changed to NUMB. Printed by James Parker on white paper with blank dark coarse paper backs. Signers are Oliver DeLancey, Isaac DePeyster, Nicholas Gouverneur, and John Livingston.

10s [2,092]	£3 [2,092]
20s [2,092]	£5 [2,092]
£2 [2,093]	£10 [2,094]

May 12, 1755

£10,000 in legal tender Bills of Credit approved on May 3, 1755 and to be redeemed by Nov. 1762. Similar to the prior issues but with the Arms on the left, no left border, and with the position and abbreviation for the number changed. Printed by James Parker. Blank dark coarse paper backs. Signers are David Clarkson, James DePeyster, Gabriel Ludlow, and Abraham Lynsen.

5s [2,000]	£3 [300]
10s [2,000]	£4 [250]
20s [1,100]	£5 [200]
£2 [1,250]	£10 [200]

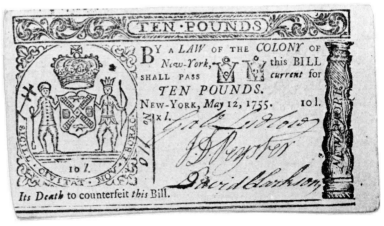

September 15, 1755

£8,000 in legal tender Bills of Credit approved on Sept. 11, 1755 and to be redeemed by Nov. 1761. Similar to the Dec. 10, 1737 issue. An apostrophe is inserted in It's. Printed by James Parker. Blank dark coarse paper backs. Signers are Leonard Lispenard, Philip Livingston*, Frederick Philipse, and Beverly Robinson.

5s	[1,200]	£3	[300]
10s	[1,000]	£4	[300]
20s	Plate A & B [1,000]	£5	[300]
£2	[300]	£10	[200]

*Signer of Declaration of Independence.

February 16, 1756

£10,000 in legal tender Bills of Credit approved on April 1, 1756 and to be redeemed by Nov. 1761. The Arms are on the right side. A rectangular border is on the left side and a serpentine column on the right side, both being from prior issues. Number is again abbreviated as Numb. The apostrophe in Its is again eliminated. Otherwise in same form as Dec. 10, 1737 issue. Printed by James Parker. Blank dark coarse paper backs. Signers are Henry Cruger, Paul Richard, William Walton, and John Watts.

£10 [1,000]

April 20, 1756

£52,000 in legal tender Bills of Credit approved on April 1, 1756 and to be redeemed by Nov. 1766. Similar to the previous issue, but with punctuation restored in It's. Printed by James Parker. Blank dark coarse paper backs. Signers are John Cruger, Robert R. Livingston, William P. Smith, and John Van der Spiegel.

20s	[2,000]	£5	[4,000]
£2	[1,000]	£10	[2,200]
£3	[2,000]		

April 15, 1758

£100,000 in legal tender Bills of Credit approved on Mar. 24, 1758 to finance the second expedition to Crown Point and redeemable by November 1768. Similar to the prior issue but with the side rectangular border and the serpentine column interchanged. Printed by James Parker. Blank dark coarse paper backs. Signers are David Clarkson, Henry Cuyler, Jr., Peter Livingston, and David Van Horne.

		Good	V.G.	Fine
£5	[4,000]	40.00	60.00	150.00
£10	[8,000]	30.00	40.00	100.00

April 2, 1759

£100,000 in legal tender Bills of Credit approved on Mar. 7, 1759. The first word of the counterfeit warning is changed to 'Tis. Similar to the previous issue but the dark coarse paper backs were eliminated. The numbering has been placed horizontally. Printed by William Weyman on thin paper. Signers are Andrew Barclay, Nathaniel Marston, Lawrence Reade, and John Morin Scott.

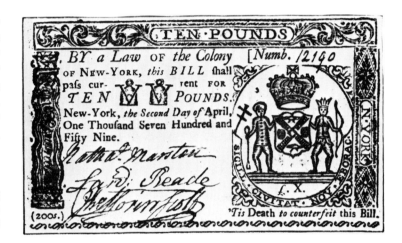

		Good	V.G.	Fine
£2	[10,000] ...	40.00	60.00	100.00
£5	[6,000] ...	40.00	60.00	100.00
£10	[5,000] ...	40.00	60.00	100.00

April 21, 1760

£60,000 in legal tender Bills of Credit approved on Mar. 22, 1760. Similar to the prior issue except that the side borders conform to the two 1756 issues. Printed by William Weyman on thin paper. Signers are John Bogert, Jr., Elias Des Brosses, Robert G. Livingston, and John Van Horne.

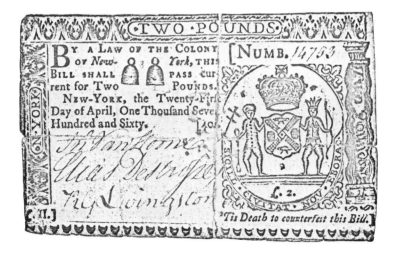

			Good	V.G.	Fine
£2	[10,000]	©.	40.00	60.00	100.00
£5	[3,000]	...	40.00	60.00	100.00
£10	[2,500]	...	40.00	60.00	100.00

February 16, 1771

£120,000 in Bills of Credit receivable for taxes pursuant to an Act originally passed in 1769, reenacted on Jan. 5, 1770, revoked by the Crown on Feb. 14, 1770 and reenacted Feb. 16, 1771. Decorative top border, left border, and Arms of New York City cut and cast by Elisha Gallaudet who also made the cuts for the New York City Water Works notes and the dies for the 1776 Continental Currency coinage. Printed by Hugh Gaine on thin laid paper. Due to extensive counterfeiting followed by a suggestion in a newspaper, sep-

arate backs showing three counterfeiters on the gallows were authorized in March 1773 to be pasted on all genuine bills in circulation, but this was never done. Signers are Theophylact Bache, Walter Franklin, Henry Holland, A. Lott, and Samuel Verplanck.

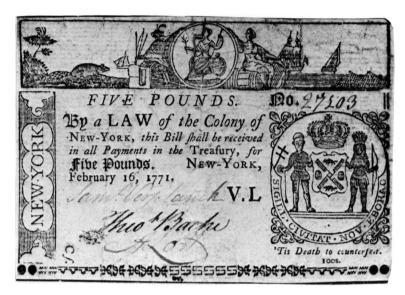

			V.G.	Fine	V.F.
5s	[8,000]	©	30	50	100
10s	[8,000]	©	30	50	100
£1	[6,000]	©	30	50	100
£2	Four variations [5,000] .		30	50	100

    (a) Comma after February. Stars on bottom border have 12 points.
    (b) No comma after February. Stars on bottom border have 12 points.
    (c) Stars on bottom border have 12 points except 7th from right.
    (d) Stars on bottom border have 8 points.

			V.G.	Fine	V.F.
£3	[6,000]	©	30	50	100
£5	[6,000]	©	30	50	100
£10	[6,000]	©	30	50	100

New York City ★ August 25, 1774

£2,400 (originally £2,500) in Promissory Notes of the City of New York known as New York Water Works notes and constituting the first paper money issued by an American City. The 4s was issued but by error not authorized and 4,000 of the 6d were authorized but not printed. On the back is an illustration of the proposed steam operated water pump of Christopher Colles. The face has a top border cut but the other borders are typeset. The cuts were engraved by Elisha Gallaudet. Printed by Hugh Gaine in red and black on the face and in black on the back. Signers are John H. Cruger, Whitehead Hicks, Jacob Lefferts, and J. Watts, Jr.

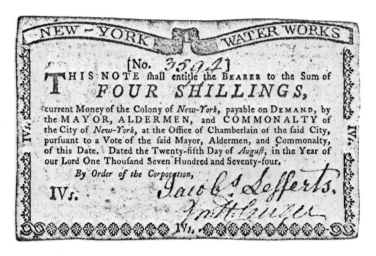

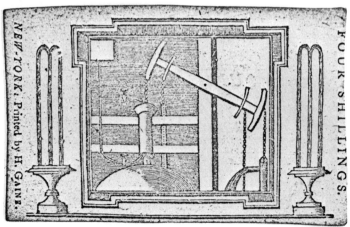

		Fine	V.F.	Unc.
1s	[4,000]	25.00	45.00	100.00
2s	[4,000]	25.00	45.00	100.00
4s	[4,000]	25.00	45.00	100.00
8s	[2,500]	25.00	45.00	100.00

Four minor varieties of each denomination.

NEW YORK

Albany ★ June 22, 1775

Promissory Notes of the City and County of Albany payable in New York currency by Sept. 1, 1775. Typeset with a cast left border cut. Signers are Jacob Lansing Jr., Jacob C. Ten Eyck, Samuel Stringer, and Abraham Yates, Jr.

2s
5s
10s
20s
40s

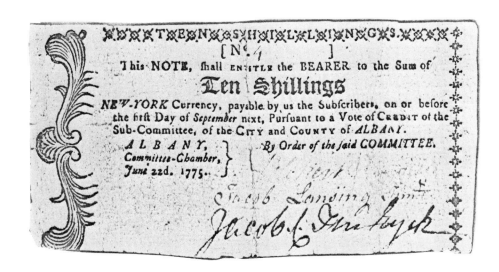

New York City ★ August 2, 1775

£2,500 (originally £2,600) in Promissory Notes of the City of New York known as the second Water Works issue. In the same form as the Aug. 25, 1774 issue, but the back of the 8s is dark coarse paper and some of the other denominations have darker backs than faces. The 1s was not issued (one unsigned trial piece is known) although 2,000 were authorized. Signers are George Brewerton, John H. Cruger, Whitehead Hicks, William Waddell, and J. Watts, Jr.

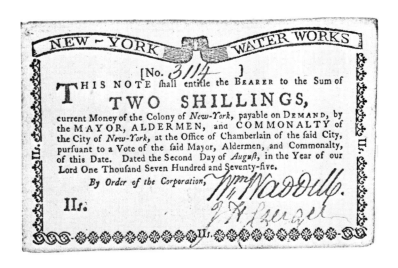

	Fine	V.F.	Unc.
1s Ⓤ			
2s [5,000]	25.00	45.00	100.00
4s [4,000]	25.00	45.00	100.00
8s [3,000]	25.00	45.00	100.00

Four minor varieties of each issued denomination.

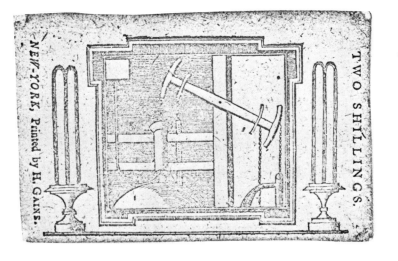

September 2, 1775

$112,500 (£45,000) in legal tender Bills of Credit payable in Spanish milled dollars, one-half on Mar. 1, 1776 and the balance on Mar. 1, 1777 pursuant to the Sept. 2, 1775 Resolution. The due dates were subsequently extended for one year. Newly engraved border, Arms, and emblem cuts on the face and back. The emblems and mottoes were copied from an emblem book by J. C. Weigels. The warning to counterfeiters was discontinued. Printed on thick paper by John Holt. Signers are Garrit Abeel, Evert Bancker, Anthony L. Bleecker, Abraham Brinckerhoff, John Broome, Jeremiah Brower, William Denning, Abraham Livingston, A. Mesier, Eleazer Miller, Jr., Robert Ray, John Reade, John Sebring, Thomas Tucker, and Theodore Van Wyck. Originally three signers were required but this was reduced to two signers by the Dec. 16, 1775 Resolution.

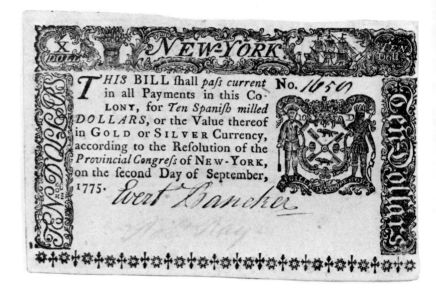

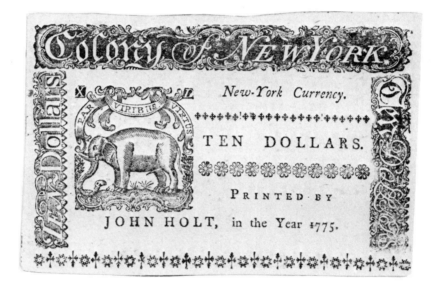

		V.G.	Fine	V.F.
$1/2	Planting a tree. POSTERITATE [5,000]	40.00	60.00	100.00
$1	Sheaf of wheat. ACERVUS E PARVIS GRANDIS [10,000]	40.00	60.00	100.00
$2	Pair of storks. SALUTARIS SIBI PARENTIBUSQUE [5,000]	40.00	60.00	100.00
$3	Ten Commandments. LEX REGIT ARMA TUENTUR [5,000]	40.00	60.00	100.00
$5	Candelabrum. UNO EODEMQUE IGNI [5,000]	40.00	60.00	100.00
$10	Elephant. PAR VIRIBUS VIRTUS [5,000]	40.00	60.00	100.00

(Mottoes are translated under the March 5, 1776 issue.)

NEW YORK

New York City ★ January 6, 1776

£2,750 in Promissory Notes of the City of New York, known as the third Water Works issue, was approved by Act of Council on Jan. 5, 1776. The small 3 above T indicates the third issue. Same cuts and set type as in prior issues. Dark coarse paper backs on all denominations. Printed by Hugh Gaine in red and black on the face and in black on the back. Signers are N. Bayard, George Brewerton, John H. Cruger, Andrew Gautier, and J. Watts, Jr.

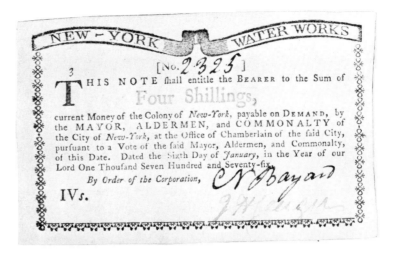

	Fine	V.F.	Unc.
2s [2,500]	30.00	55.00	125.00
4s [2,500]	30.00	55.00	125.00
8s [5,000]	30.00	55.00	125.00

Four minor varieties of each denomination.

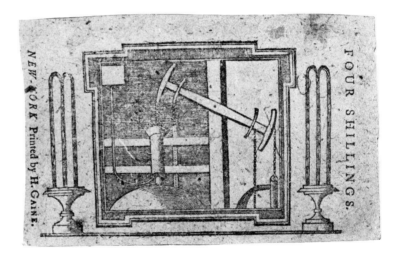

Albany ★ February 17, 1776

Promissory Notes of the City and County of Albany payable in Continental Currency. Printed from set type and a decorative top border cut. Signers are John T. Beeckman, Jacob Cuyler, Samuel Stringer, and John Van Rensselaer.

		Good	V.G.
$1/8	(1s)	100.00	175.00
$1/6	(1s6d)	100.00	175.00
$1/4	(2s)	100.00	175.00
$1/2	(4s)	100.00	175.00
$5/8	(5s)	100.00	175.00

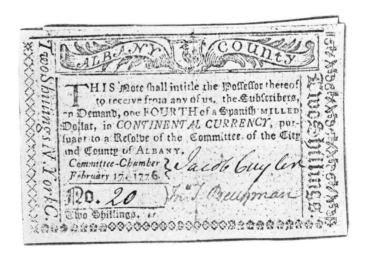

March 5, 1776

£55,000 ($137,500) in legal tender Bills of Credit with one-third payable respectively on Mar. 1, 1779, Mar. 1, 1780 and Mar. 1, 1781. Approved by the Mar. 5, 1776 Resolution but 6,000 additional $1/8 bills were ratified by the Aug. 13, 1776 Resolution raising the total to $138,250. Similar in form to the Sept. 2, 1775 issue, but on the new fractional denominations the emblems and mottoes are very small and are also copied from an emblem book by J. C. Weigels. Printed on thick paper by Samuel Loudon. Signers are Jacob Abramse, Thos. Arden, Jr., Frank Bassett, Luke Bassett, John Bathram, Peter Byvanck, G. Cornell, A. W. DePeyster, Daniel Dunscomb, Jr., Jacob K. Duryee, C. Duyckinck, Jr., Nicholas Fish, George Hazard, William Heyer, James Jarvis, Henry H. Kip, John H. Kip, P. Kitellas, Jr., Abraham C. Lott, Phillip Lott, Jonathan Marchalk, J. Osthout, Cornelius Ray, Samuel Ray, W. Remsen, John I. Roosevelt, N. Roosevelt, P. Schermerhorn, Robert Smith, Andrew Stockholm, Jonathan Thompson, Abraham Van Alstyne, A. Van Tuyl, Peter Van Zandt, William Willcocks, Josh. Winter, and J. Woodward.

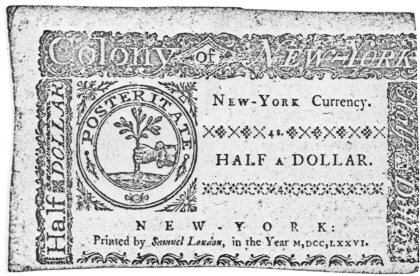

				V.G.	Fine	V.F.
$1/8	(1s)		Fire. NON DIU (Not for long) [30,000]	25.00	50.00	75.00
$1/6	(1s4d)		Stork. NE IMPROVISO (Not unexpectedly) [30,000]	25.00	50.00	75.00
$1/4	(2s)		Book and candle. CLARET AB ICTU (It shines from use) [30,000]	25.00	50.00	75.00
$1/3	(2s8d)		Three wreaths. HIS ORNARI AUT MORI (To be decorated with these or to die) [30,000]	25.00	50.00	75.00
$1/2			Planting a tree. POSTERITATE (For posterity) [30,000]	25.00	50.00	75.00
$2/3	(5s4d)		Eagle. FORTIS A FORTE (Strength comes from strength) [30,000]	25.00	50.00	75.00
$1			Sheaf of wheat. ACERVUS E PARVIS GRANDIS (Great accumulation from small things) [30,000]	25.00	50.00	75.00
$2			Pair of storks. SALUTARIS SIBI PARENTIBUSQUE (Fortunate for itself and its parents) [2,350]	45.00	80.00	120.00
$3			Ten Commandments. LEX REGIT ARMA TUENTUR (Law rules, arms guard) [2,350]	45.00	80.00	120.00
$5			Candelabrum. UNO EODEMQUE IGNI (With one and the same flame) [2,350]	45.00	80.00	120.00
$10			Elephant. PAR VIRIBUS VIRTUS (Virtue is equal to strength) [2,350]	45.00	80.00	120.00

New York City ★ March 5, 1776

£2,000 in Promissory Notes of the City of New York known as the fourth Water Works issue. Small 4 over T indicates the fourth issue. Same form as the prior New York City issues. Printed by Hugh Gaine in red and black on the face and in black on the back. White paper on the face and dark coarse paper on the back. Signers are Benjamin Bragge, Abraham Brasher, John H. Cruger, Andrew Gautier, and D. Mathews.

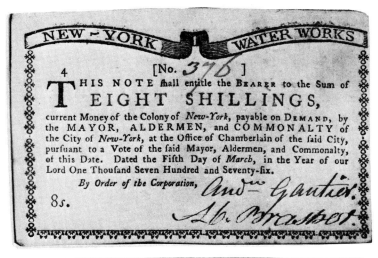

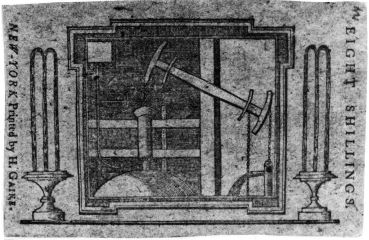

		Fine	V.F.	Unc.
4s	[5,000]	25.00	50.00	135.00
8s	[2,500]	25.00	50.00	135.00

Four minor varieties of each denomination.

Unknown Issuer ★ June 6, 1776

Private scrip issued at Manchester, Dutchess County. Other denominations are probable.

$3/4 (6s)

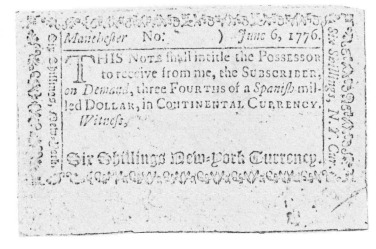

NEW YORK

Scrip Payable in Army Bills

Scrip payable in New York Currency with Army Bills. Nothing has been learned about this issue. If Woodhouse is a place name it has not been located. Typeset and printed on laid paper.

1s

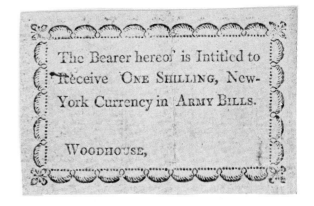

August 13, 1776

$500,000 (£200,000) in legal tender Bills of Credit issued pursuant to the Aug. 13, 1776 Resolution. Same form and emblems as the Mar. 5, 1776 issue but the warning to counterfeiters is reinstated. As in contemporaneous Continental Currency issues the $1 denomination was omitted in anticipation of coined Continental silver dollars. Printed by Samuel Loudon on thick paper. Signers are Matthew Adgate, Abraham B. Bancker, Evert Bancker, Abraham K. Beekman, William Beekman, Jr., C. Crygier, Archibald Currie, David Currie, William I. Elsworth, Jonathan Goodwin, D. Hoper, Robert King, Jonathan Lawrence, A. Mesier, Benjamin Newkerk, B. Sebring, Jr., Isaac Sebring, J. J. Sebring, Johannes Sleght, L. Thiersted, Benjamin Verplanck, J. V. Voorhis, Jr., Alexander Webster, and Josh. Winter.

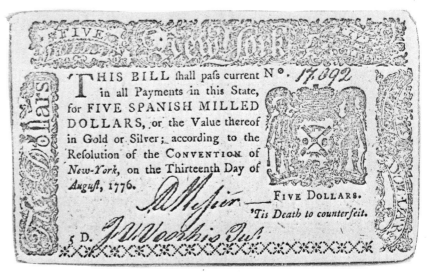

			Good	V.G.	Fine
$1/16	(6d)	[105,868]	20.00	35.00	60.00
$1/8	(1s)	Fire. NON DIU [105,867]	20.00	35.00	60.00
$1/4	(2s)	Book and candle. CLARET AB ICTU [105,867]	20.00	35.00	60.00
$1/2	(4s)	Planting a tree. POSTERITATE [105,866]	20.00	35.00	60.00
$2		Pair of storks. SALUTARIS SIBI PARENTIBUSQUE [20,000]	25.00	40.00	75.00
$3		Ten Commandments. LEX REGIT ARMA TUENTUR [20,000]	25.00	40.00	75.00
$5		Candelabrum. UNO EODEMQUE IGNI [20,000]	25.00	40.00	75.00
$10		Elephant. PAR VIRIBUS VIRTUS [20,000]	25.00	40.00	75.00

(Mottoes are translated under the March 5, 1776 issue)

NEW YORK

June 15, 1780 Act

$487,500 (£195,000) in legal tender Bills of Credit payable in Spanish milled dollars with 5% interest on Dec. 31, 1786 pursuant to the June 15, June 30, Oct. 7, 1780 and Mar. 27, 1781 Acts. Guaranteed by the United States according to the Resolution of Congress of Mar. 18, 1780. The amount of the issue was only $70,625 and was based upon $2,825,000 in Continental Currency exchanged at $40 (old) for $1 (new). Abraham Yates, Jr., claimed that he counted, punched and packed this sum for which he charged the prescribed commission of ⅛% or $3,531 in specie dollars. The Continental Congress reduced his claim on Oct. 9, 1787 to $111 in specie

dollars by valuing the Continental Currency at its depreciated value when he received it. The face is in black and the back is in red and black. Printed by Hall & Sellers in Philadelphia on mica flaked paper watermarked CONFEDERATION in two lines. The face border cuts and the back cut surrounding the emblem were engraved by Henry Dawkins. The border cuts and the emblems on the back are from the Jan. 14, 1779 issue of Continental Currency. See the Mar. 27, 1781 issue for the balance of the emission. Signers are Evert Bancker, Reynard Mynderse, and Henry Rutgers. The guaranty is **signed** by Abraham Yates, Jr.

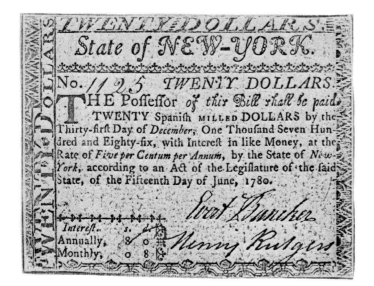

		Good	Fine	V.F.
$1	[1,413]	200.00	250.00	350.00
$2	[1,413]	200.00	250.00	350.00
$3	[1,413]	200.00	250.00	350.00
$4	[1,413]	200.00	250.00	350.00
$5	[1,413]	200.00	250.00	350.00
$7	[1,413]	200.00	250.00	350.00
$8	[1,413]	200.00	250.00	350.00
$20	[1,413] ©	200.00	250.00	350.00

NEW YORK

March 27, 1781 Act

Because all of the June 15, 1780 issue could not be put into circulation at the legal tender value required by the Continental Congress, a Mar. 27, 1781 Act provided for the unissued balance of $416,875 of the June 15, 1780 authorization to be reprinted in a different form of note and circulated at its current value. The United States guaranty was eliminated and the 5% interest made payable annually. Printed by John Holt in black with a typeset face and an allegorical cut on the back. Some bills bear a printed endorsement in red, "Int. pd. one Year." Signers are A. Laurence and G. Livingston.

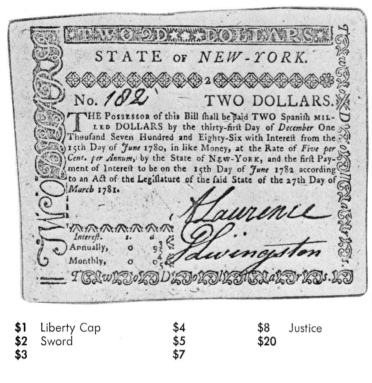

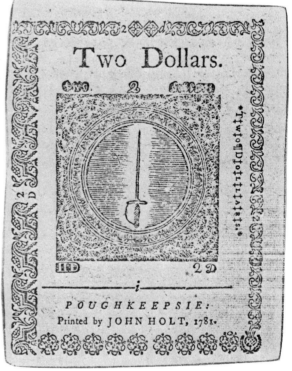

$1	Liberty Cap	$4		$8	Justice
$2	Sword	$5		$20	
$3		$7			

April 18, 1786

£200,000 in Bills of Credit receivable for taxes pursuant to the April 18, 1786 Act and redeemable by June 1800. The borders on the sides and the top of the face and the New York State Arms were cut by Peter Maverick. Printed by Samuel Loudon. Blank backs. Due to extensive counterfeiting this issue was to be exchanged by June 1789 for the Feb. 8, 1788 emission pursuant to the Feb. 8, 1788 Act, but was extended to Jan. 1, 1791 by the Act of Mar. 8, 1790. Signers are Evert Bancker, John DePeyster, Jonathan Lawrence, William Heyer, and Henry Remsen.

5s	EXCELSIOR (Higher) in white	[24,000]
5s	EXCELSIOR in black	[24,000]
10s		[20,000]
£1		[24,000] ©
£2		[10,000]
£3		[10,000]
£4		[6,000] ©
£5		[4,000]
£10		[6,000] ©

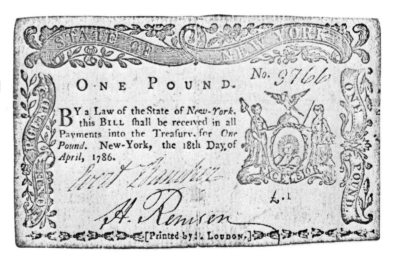

February 8, 1788

£200,000 in Bills of Credit receivable for taxes and legal tender until Dec. 31, 1800. Issued pursuant to the Feb. 8, 1788 Act to replace the heavily counterfeited April 18, 1786 emission. Four face borders, the State Arms, and allegorical back vignettes were engraved by Peter R. Maverick (1755-1811). A warning to counterfeiters was reinstated. Printed on thick paper by Hugh Gaine in red and black on the face and in black on the back. Signers are Hendrick Wyckoff, Daniel McCormick, John DePeyster, and Nicholas Hoffman.

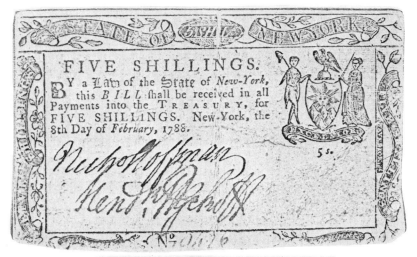

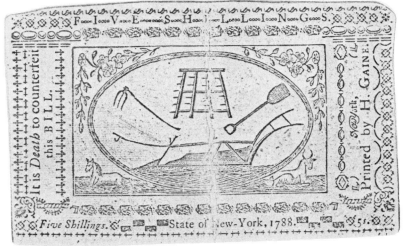

5s
10s
£1
£2
£3
£4
£5
£10

CIRCULATING NOTES OF BANKING INSTITUTIONS

Bank of New York ★ 1784, etc.   ©

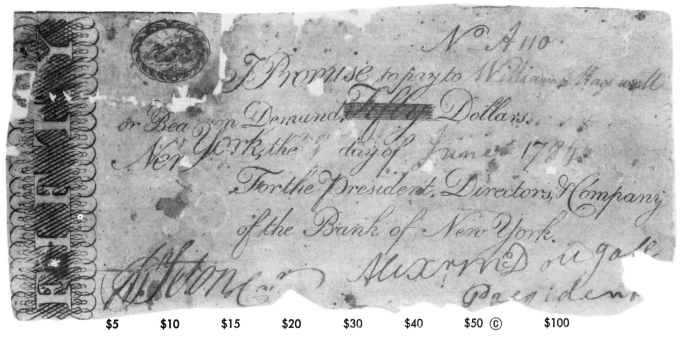

$5 $10 $15 $20 $30 $40 $50 © $100

245

Bank of New York (Continued)

The Bank of New York began to operate in New York City on June 9, 1784 as a modest unincorporated private banking operation. An application for a charter from the New York legislature in 1785 was unsuccessful but on March 21, 1791 it was incorporated. This bank is still in operation. Its early presidents were Alexander McDougall (1784-5), Jeremiah Wadsworth (1785-6), Isaac Roosevelt (1786-91), Gulian Verplanck (1791-9), and Nicholas Gouverneur (1799-1802). Its early cashiers were William Seton (1784-94) and Charles Wilkes (1794-1825). All of these officers signed its early bank notes except Jeremiah Wadsworth. The first type of **bank notes issued beginning in June 1784** was payable in specie (Spanish) dollars and aggregated $234,520. The denomination in capital letters was in the left side border panel.

When the State of New York issued paper money pursuant to the Act of April 18, 1786, the Bank of New York issued undated bank notes payable in that State currency. These were termed "paper notes" and were a combination of an engraved top border, an engraved left side denomination shield, and a typeset text. The engraving was probably done by William Rollinson, as they are quite similar in design to post notes engraved for the bank's use by him.

| £1 | £2 | £4 ©️ | £10 |

Small denomination bank notes payable in specie were issued between 1786 and 1791.

| $1 | $2 | $3 | $4 |

After incorporation in 1791 three new fully engraved currency plates were used containing two counters at the top and a spelled out fanciful denomination in the left panel.

Low denomination plate:	$5 ©️	$10	$15	$20
High denomination plate:	$30	$40 ©️	$50	$100
Highest denomination plate:	$300	$400	$500	$1,000

Bank of New York (Continued)

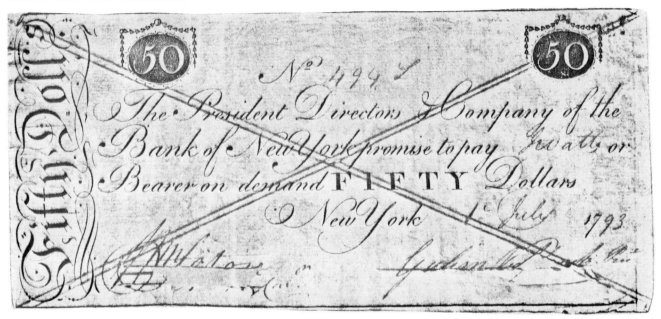

In 1795 a new four subject plate of $5 and $10 notes was engraved by William Harrison, Sr. Of this and the prior issue almost $3,500,000 were emitted by the Bank of New York during the eighteenth century and further styles of notes continued to be issued until all bank notes were taxed out of existence in 1864.

Bank of the United States ★ 1792, etc.

The New York City office of Discount and Deposit of the Bank of the United States (first bank) operated from 1792 to 1811 and issued $1,254,530 in circulating bank notes. A fuller description of these branch bank notes and other branch bank data is included under the Pennsylvania listings.

A flying eagle bearing the Arms of the United States:

| $5 | $10 | $20 | $50 | $100 |

A heraldic eagle with 13 stars surrounding its head:

| $5 | $10 | $20 | $50 | $100 |

A heraldic eagle in an oval frame containing 15 stars:

| $5 | $10 | $20 © | $50 | $100 |

Bank of Albany * 1792, etc.

The Bank of Albany was incorporated on April 10, 1792 until May 1811 with a maximum capital of $240,000 divided into 600 shares of $400 each. The State had the right to subscribe for 50 shares additional. The bank notes were to be signed by the president and the cashier.

The debts including bank notes were limited to three times the capital plus the amount of specie deposits. No 18th century issues have been located and an early 19th century issue is shown below.

Bank of Columbia * 1793, etc.

The Bank of Columbia in Hudson was incorporated on March 6, 1793 until May 1811 with a capital of $160,000 divided into 400 shares of $400 each. The State had the right to subscribe for 50 shares additional. Debts including bank notes were limited to three times the capital plus the amount of specie deposits. Thomas Jenkins was the first president and signed the bank notes with the cashier. No 18th century issues have been located and an early 19th century issue is shown below.

$2 © $4 © $5 $10 ©

Manhattan Company ★ 1799, etc.

The Manhattan Company was incorporated on April 2, 1799 to supply water to New York City with the right to use its surplus for money transactions not in violation of law. Aaron Burr was the principal organizer. Its capital was a maximum of $2,000,000 divided into shares of $50 each. Because there were no laws regulating banking it immediately became a banking competitor to the Bank of New York, deliberately bypassing the water supply enterprise. An illustration of one of the many early 19th century issues is set out below.

Ⓒ

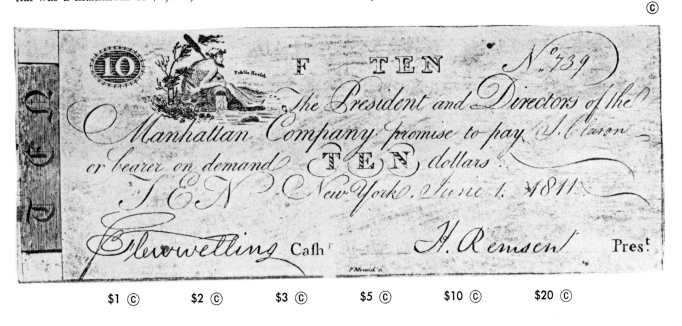

$1 Ⓒ $2 Ⓒ $3 Ⓒ $5 Ⓒ $10 Ⓒ $20 Ⓒ

SMALL CHANGE NOTES (1789-1799)

New York small change notes including Church Money were a substitute for coppers during the small change panic which began in July, 1789. On March 3, 1787, the New York Assembly had received a committee report which emphasized the fraud on the public resulting from the circulation of genuine and counterfeit British halfpence and copper coinage of adjoining States at far above their intrinsic value. Thereupon the Assembly lowered the value of all coppers from 14 to 20 to the New York shilling effective August 1, 1787. The situation continued to deteriorate because of continued coining and imports of copper coinage and by 1789 some merchants advertised that they would accept in trade 60 coppers for one New York shilling. At that time the New York City Council was recommending 48 coppers to be equal to one N.Y. shilling. The result was a general refusal to take coppers at any price. The people of the State of New York were particularly affected by the problem of making change. An acceptable medium consisting of paper notes of small denominations was the result. Some churches did not want unacceptable coppers placed in their contribution boxes and were, therefore, among the leaders in issuing "Church Money" change so as to receive donations which were redeemable or had general acceptance. Although the Presbyterian Church of Albany issued copper one penny tokens, other churches throughout the State had extensive issues of small change paper money printed. Cities, merchants and other organizations also became paper money issuers. The insufficient production of copper coinage by the United States Mint from 1793 to 1802 delayed the restoration of copper coinage in lieu of small change paper notes in many areas and thus the paper notes are usually found substantially worn. Although most small change paper notes were issued in New York, some were used in the neighboring states of Connecticut, Rhode Island, Pennsylvania and New Jersey (see listings under those States).

The extensive numismatic collection formerly in the New York State Library included many small change notes issued in New York. These were listed in a catalog published in 1856. The collection was destroyed in the fire of 1911 along with books, manuscripts and other Library holdings.

The listings which follow are in alphabetical order rather than chronological order because many are undated and others have no issuer or no place of issue. Some pieces which are not now sufficiently identifiable are illustrated at the end of this group. The spelling of names sometimes differs from printed census or other records and the spelling used on the paper money itself is relied upon. Where county locations are given they are as of the date of the issuance of the note rather than the county as it may thereafter have been changed.

Selling prices are not included because of an insufficiency of sales data at present.

William Adams ⋆ Undated

Small change notes issued at New Windsor, Ulster County. Blank backs.

1d

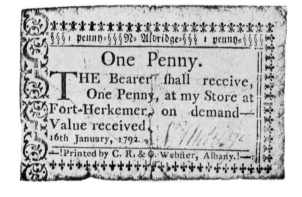

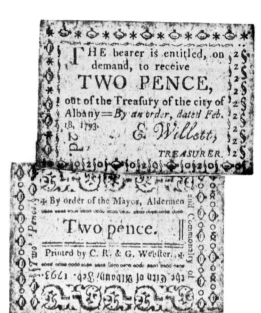

City of Albany ⋆ July 3, 1790 to February 18, 1793

The Common Council of the City of Albany approved small change notes on six occasions, the date of authorization becoming the date of the notes except the Feb. 13, 1792 resolution for the Jan. 13, 1792 notes. Printed signature of E. Willett, Treasurer. Various small sizes. The faces of the August 28, 1790 issue are printed in red.

July 3, 1790:	1d [2,400]	2d [2,400]	3d [2,400]		
Aug. 28, 1790:	1d [5,600]	2d [5,600]	3d [5,600]		
Mar. 26, 1791:	1d [6,000]	2d [6,000]	3d [6,000]		
Jan. 13, 1792:	1d [8,000]	2d [8,000]	3d [8,000]		
Sept. 5, 1792:	1d [12,000]	2d [12,000]	3d [12,000]		
Feb. 18, 1793:	1d [7,200]	2d [7,200]	3d [7,200]		
	4d [7,200]				

N. Aldridge ⋆ January 16, 1792

Small change notes issued at Fort Herkemer, Montgomery County. Blank backs.

1d
2d
3d

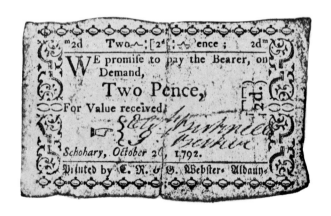

Jonathan H. & William Baker ⋆ March 9, 1791

Small change notes issued at Schohary, Albany County. Blank backs.

1d
2d
3d

Edward Bicknell & J. Becker ⋆ October 26, 1792

Small change notes issued at Schohary, Albany County. Blank backs. Other denominations probable.

2d

Egbert Bogardus ★
May 17, 1793
Small change notes issued at Fish-Kill Landing, Dutchess County. Signatures printed on face and written on back.

1d
2d
3d

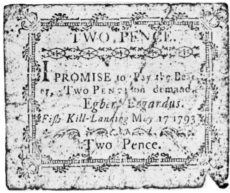

W. Y. Burrough ★ **November 2, 1789**
Small change notes issued at Hudson, Columbia County. Hand numbered. Blank backs. Other denominations probable.

2d

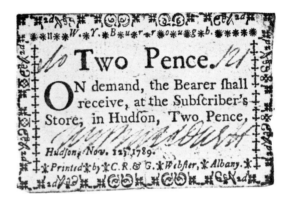

Cayuga Bridge Company ★
September 12, 1799
Toll bridge scrip issued at Cayuga and drawn on Manhattan Bank, New York City. Engraved by Peter Maverick of New York City. Signed by Thomas Wentworth and James Smith. Handwritten date. Blank backs. Other denominations probable.

6¼ cents

John Clark ★ **Undated**
Small change notes issued at North Troy. Plate letters. Other denominations probable.

2d

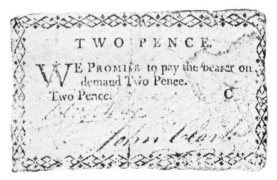

NEW YORK

Constitutional Society ★ January 11, 1791

Small change notes issued in Dutchess County with printed signature of Edmund Per Lee, Treasurer. Printed by Nicholas Power at Poughkeepsie. Hand numbered. Blank backs.

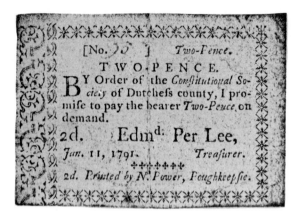

1d
2d
3d
6d

William Cooper ★ January 25, 1790

Small change notes issued at Cooper's Town, Otsego County, by its founder, William Cooper, who was the father of the novelist, James Fenimore Cooper. Hand numbered. Issuer's name printed and written. Quaker style date. Blank backs. Other denominations probable.

3d
4d
6d
9d

M. Croswill & Co. ★ Undated

Small change notes issued at Catskill-Landing, Albany County. Blank backs. Other denominations probable.

4d

Edward Dale ★ Undated

Small change notes without place of issue or date.

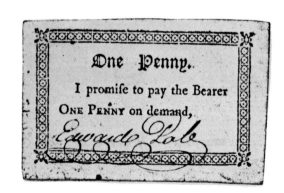

1d

Daniel Davis ★ January 20, 1791

Small change notes issued by a storekeeper on Quaker Hill, Dutchess County. Hand numbered. Blank backs. Other denominations probable.

4d

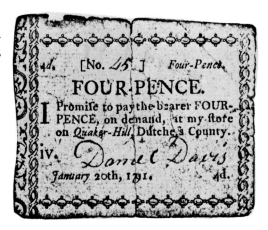

Davis & Clark ★ December 22, 1790

Small change notes issued by a storekeeper in Ballston (Ballstown), Albany County. Printed by R. Barber & Co. of Albany. Blank backs. Other denominations probable.

1d
6d

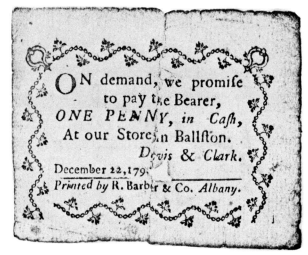

Richard Davis, Jr. and Jacoburt Schoonhoven ★ September 10, 1789

Small change notes issued at Waterford, Albany County. Wood block border. Hand numbered. Blank backs. Other denominations probable.

3d

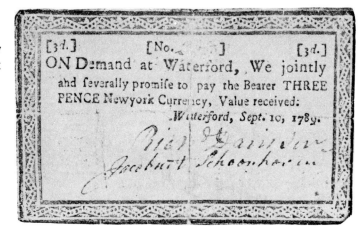

Stephen Day & Son ★ February 15, 1792

Small change notes issued at Catts-Kill, Albany County. Other denominations probable.

5d

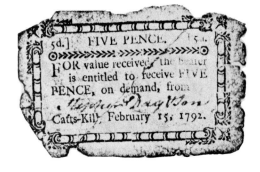

Samuel DeRiemer ⋆ September 1, 1790
Small change notes issued by stores of Samuel De-
Riemer (DeReimer) in Montgomery County and
advertising Babington's Patent. Blank backs. Other
denominations probable.

5d

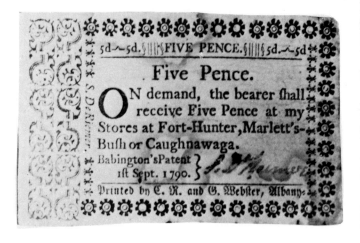

**Genesee Company ⋆
September 10, 1790**
Small change notes
issued by Genesee
Company of Dutchess
County with printed
signature of I. Knick-
erbacor & Co. (John
Knickerbacker). Print-
ed by A. Stoddard of
Hudson. Other de-
nominations probable.

4d

German Reformed Church of Schohary ⋆ Undated
Church Money of the Consistory of the German Reformed
Church of Schohary (Schoharie) signed by George Recht-
myer and Peter Snyder. Printed by C. R. & G. Webster of
Albany. CHURCH MONEY on back.

1d

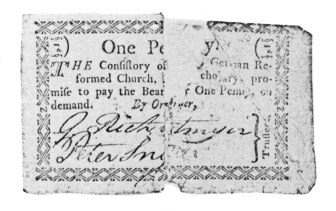

**George and Thomas Hale ⋆
February 6, 1792**
Small change notes issued at
Catts-Kill, Albany County.
Printed by A. Stoddard of Hud-
son.

1d

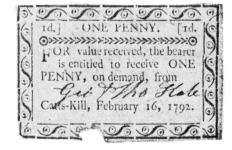

City of Hudson ★ October 26, 1790 and November 5, 1792

Small change notes issued by the Corporation of the City of Hudson, Columbia County. Printed by A. Stoddard of Hudson. The signature of the treasurer, Stephen Paddock, was hand-signed on the 1790 issue and printed on the 1792 issue. Other denominations probable.

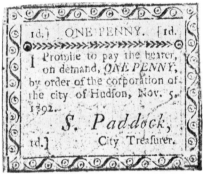
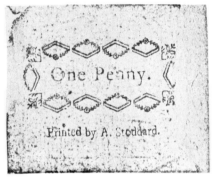

Oct. 26, 1790:

1d	2d	3d
4d	7d	8d

Nov. 5, 1792:

1d	2d	3d

J. & A. Hunt ★ January 1, 1791

Small change issue of J. & A. Hunt of Troy, Rensselaer County. Other denominations probable.

3d

Janes & Dole ★ December 31, 1790

Small change notes issued by Elijah Janes and James Dole in Lansingburgh, Rensselaer County. Printed by C. R. & G. Webster of Albany. Blank backs.

1d

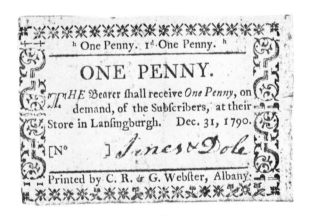

Corporation of Kingston ★ September 8, 1790

A total issue of £75 in small change notes by the Corporation of Kingston, Ulster County. Printed by Mandeville & Co., and by its successor, Mandeville & Westcott. Blank backs.

1d
2d
3d

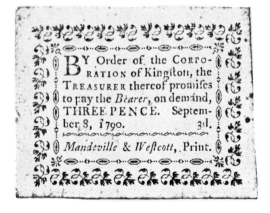

Lansingburgh Museum ★ October 20, 1792

The Lansingburgh Museum was formed in 1775 as a library and educational organization. Small change notes were issued in Lansingburgh with 27 merchants of Rensselaer County pledged to accept them. James Dole was treasurer.

1d
2d
3d
4d

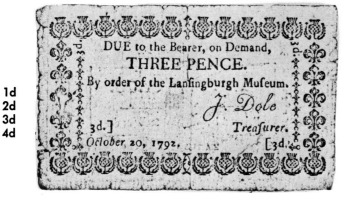
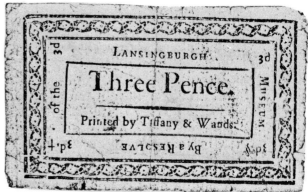

Lutheran Church in Schoharie ★ March 17, 1797

Church Money of the Consistory of the Lutheran Church of Schoharie formed in 1743. Signed by David Sternbergh and Henricus Schaefer whose given names are printed. Other denominations probable.

2d

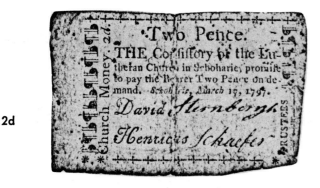

Benijah Morris ★ August 15, 1792

Small change notes issued at Whitestown, Oneida County. Printed by C. R. & G. Webster of Albany. Other denominations probable.

3d

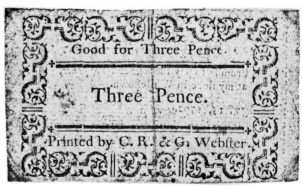

NEW YORK

City of New York ★ February 20, 1790

The Common Council of the Corporation of the City of New York approved an aggregate of £9,660 in notes to satisfy "the want of small change" and to prevent the great losses "to the poorer classes of citizens from the circulation of base coppers." The original authorization of Feb. 26, 1790 was for £1,000 but only £902/2 was printed by Hugh Gaine of New York with 12 notes to the sheet at a cost of £25. Further authorizations were £1,097/18 on May 14, 1790; £1,000 each on Mar. 11, 1791, Oct. 4, 1791, Sept. 23, 1793 and May 26, 1794; then £2,000 on Jan. 12, 1795; £600 on Nov. 11, 1795; and £1,000 on Aug. 29, 1796. Destruction of redeemed notes by burning was recorded from Feb. 17, 1792 intermittently through May 28, 1798. A rumor that the notes were called for redemption was reported on Jan. 21, 1799 and denied. By April 22, 1799 the appearance of London-made counterfeits brought about a call for redemption of the entire issue by June 1, 1799. Printed signature of Daniel Phoenix.

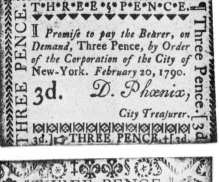

1d [367,333]
2d [367,333] ©
3d [367,333]

New York Manufacturing Society ★ June 22, 1790

Small change notes with printed signature of A. Robertson, Treasurer, and others with Henry Ten Brook, Treasurer. Printed by Hugh Gaine of New York City. MIND YOUR BUSINESS on back of all notes.

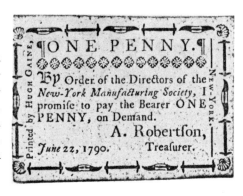

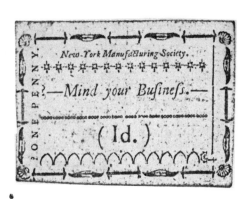

Robertson:
| 1d | 2d | 3d | 4d |

Ten Brook:
| 1d © | 2d | 3d © | 4d |

Ananias Platt ★ December 31, 1790

Small change notes issued at Lansingburgh, Rensselaer County. Printed by C. R. & G. Webster of Albany. Blank backs.

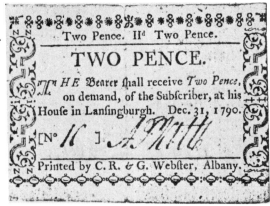

1d
2d
3d

NEW YORK

John Portens ★ Undated
Small change notes issued at Little-Falls, Herkimer (Herkemer) County. Printed by C. R. & G. Webster of Albany. Written signature. Blank backs. Other denominations probable.

1d
2d
4d

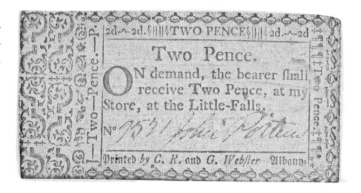

J. Porter ★ Undated
Small change notes issued at Millton, Saratoga County. Numbered by hand. Printed by C. R. & G. Webster of Albany. Blank backs. Other denominations probable.

1d
4d

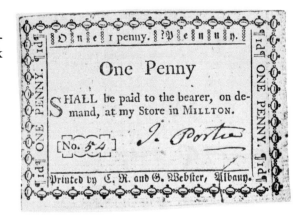

City of Poughkeepsie ★ March 19, 1791
Small change notes of the City of Poughkeepsie, Dutchess County, signed by Peter Tappan, Treasurer. Printed by Nicholas Power of Poughkeepsie. Blank Backs. Other denominations probable.

1d
2d

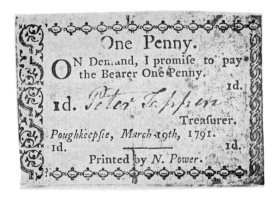

Presbyterian Congregation of Ballstown ★ Undated
Church Money of the Trustees of the Presbyterian Congregation of Ballstown, Albany County, signed by H. Baldwin. Printed by Barber and Southwick of Albany. Other denominations probable.

1d   2d   4d   6d

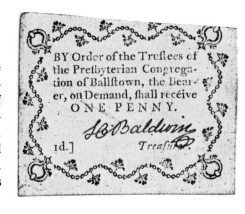 

258

NEW YORK

Presbyterian Congregation in Troy ★ August 28, 1792
Church Money of the Trustees of the Presbyterian Congregation in Troy, Rensselaer County, signed by Ephraim Morgan, Treasurer. Printed by C. R. & G. Webster of Albany.

1d
2d
3d
4d

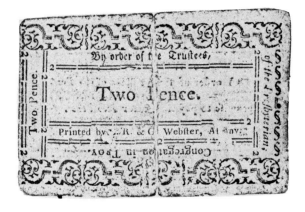
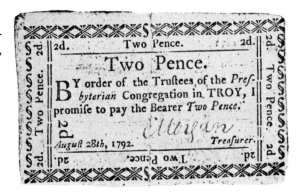

John Prince ★ January, 1791
Small change notes issued at Schenectady, Albany County. Printed by C. R. & G. Webster of Albany. Blank backs.

1d

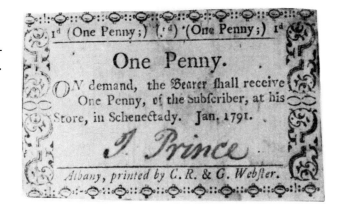

William Radclift & Company ★ May 2, 1791
Small change notes issued in Rhinebeck, Dutchess County. Numbered by hand. Printed by Nicholas Power of Poughkeepsie. Blank backs. Other denominations probable.

1d
3d
4d

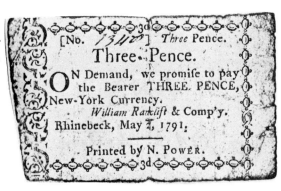

Reformed Dutch Church of Canajohary ★ **February 4, 1793**

Church Money issued by the Trustees of the Reformed Dutch Church of the upper part of Canajohary, Montgomery County, signed by Jacob Maskell, Treasurer. Printed by C. R. & G. Webster of Albany.

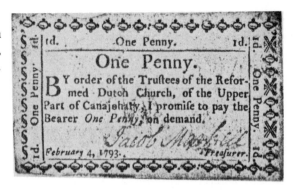

1d
2d
3d
4d

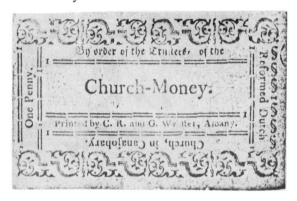

Reformed Dutch Church at Schenectady ★
September 6, 1790 and August 8, 1793

£1,000 in Church Money issued by the Consistory of the Reformed Dutch Church at Schenectady, Albany County, with written signature of Dominie Dirck Romeyn on the 1790 issue and printed signature on the 1793 issue. The 1790 issue has red faces and black backs, and is larger than the 1793 issue. Printed by C. R. & G. Webster of Albany.

| Sept. 6, 1790: | 1d | 2d | 3d | 6d |
| Aug. 8, 1793: | 1d | 2d | 3d | |

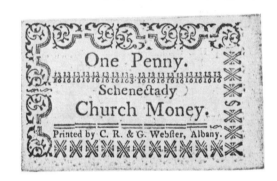

Reformed Dutch Church at Stone Arabia ★ **September 1792**

Church Money of the Consistory of the Reformed Dutch Church at Stone Arabia, Montgomery County, signed by DeWit Peck. Printed by C. R. & G. Webster of Albany. Other denominations probable.

1d
2d

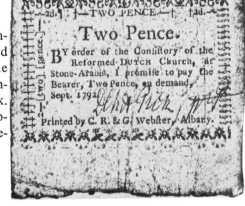

Reformed German Church in Herkemertown ★ June 3, 1793
Church Money issued by the trustees at "Herkemer on the Flatts," Montgomery County. Typeset face hand signed by William Petry. HERKEMER CHURCH MONEY on typeset back. Other denominations probable.

4d
6d

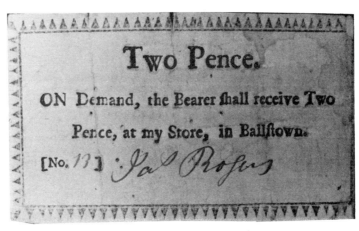

James Rogers ★ Undated
Small change notes issued in Ballstown, Albany County. Blank backs. Other denominations probable.

2d
4d
6d

Isaac Schultz ★ June 1, 1791
Small change notes issued at New Windsor, Ulster County. Other denominations probable.

1d
5d

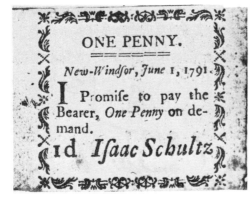

Shepard & Allen ★ February 8, 1793
Small change notes issued in Germanflatts, Montgomery County.

1d

Society of Mechanics at Hudson ★ January 17, 1793
Small change notes issued at Hudson, Columbia County.

1d

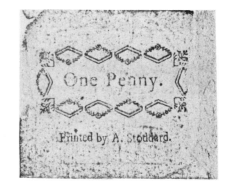

Solomon Tryon ★ Undated
Small change notes issued at Ballstown, Albany County.
Blank backs. Printed by C. R. & G. Webster of Albany.

1d
2d
3d
4d
6d
7d

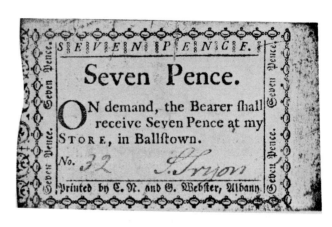

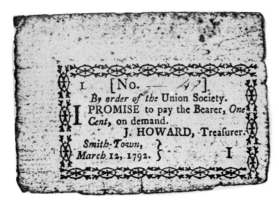

Union Society ★ March 12, 1792
Small change notes issued at Smith-Town, Suffolk County, in cents instead of New York pence. Hand numbered. Blank backs.

1¢

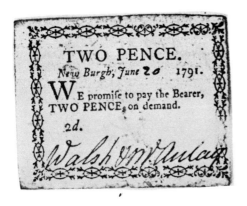

Walsh & Loudon ★ January 1, 1793
Small change notes issued at Newburgh, Ulster County. Blank backs. Other denominations probable.

1d

Walsh & McAuley ★ June 20, 1791
Small change notes issued at Newburgh, Ulster County. Day of issue written in. Blank backs. Other denominations probable.

2d

Insufficiently Identified ★ 1790, etc.

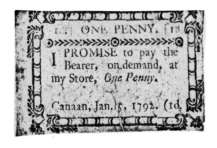

Insufficiently Identified ★ 1790, etc.

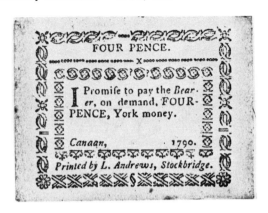
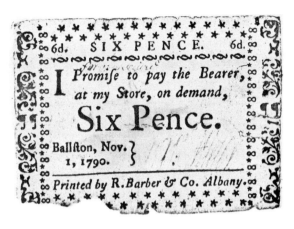
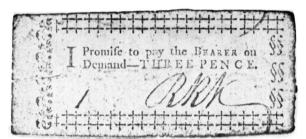

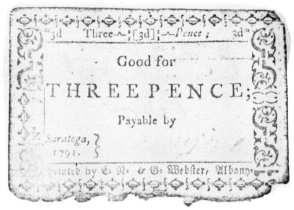

NEW YORK REFERENCES

John M. Connor Estate Collection, Samuel T. Freeman & Co., Auctioneers, Phila., Nov. 7, 1970.

Forrest W. Daniel, "How many varieties?" *Paper Money* (November 1975).

Berthold Fernow, "Coins and Currency of New York," in Vol. IV of James G. Wilson's *Memorial History of the City of New York* (New York, 1893), Chap. X, pp. 297-343.

John H. Hickcox, *History of the Bills of Credit or Paper Money Issued by New York* (Albany, 1866).

Don C. Kelly, "A Colonial New York Counterfeit," *Paper Money* (March 1975).

George M. Korb, "Schenectady Church Money," *The Numismatist,* Vol. 52, No. 11, p. 853 (Nov. 1939).

Howard H. Kurth, "The Albany Church Pennies," *Numismatic Scrapbook Magazine,* April 1944, p. 284.

Eric P. Newman, "The Two Pound New York 1771 Issue," *Paper Money* (January 1976).

New York State Library, *Catalogue of the medals, coins, paper money, etc., in the New York State Library: 1856* (Albany, 1857) pp. 149-212.

Kenneth Scott, *Counterfeiting in Colonial New York* (New York, 1953).

————, "Counterfeiting in New York during the Revolution," *New York Historical Society Quarterly* (July 1958).

————, "A British Counterfeiting Press in New York Harbor," *New York Historical Society Quarterly* (April 1955).

Horace White, "New York's Colonial Currency," *Sound Currency* (New York, 1898).

Laws, archives and other public records.

NORTH CAROLINA

GENERAL EMISSIONS

1712-13
1715
October 19, 1722 Act
November 27, 1729 Act
1734(5)
1735
April 4, 1748 Act
March 9, 1754 Act
1756-7
May 28, 1757 Act
November 21, 1757 Session Act
May 4, 1758 Act
December 22, 1758 Act
July 14, 1760 Act
April 23, 1761 Act
December 1768 Act
December 1771 Act
August 21, 1775 Session Act
April 2, 1776
1778 (August 8, 1778 Act)
May 15, 1779 Act
1780 (April 17, 1780 Session Act)
May 10, 1780 Act
January 18, 1781 Session Act
May 17, 1783 Act
December 29, 1785 Act

SPECIAL ISSUERS

James Murray * 1757 with Written Date
Joseph Ross * January 1800, etc.

1712-13

£4,000 in interest bearing Bills of Credit authorized in 1712 and £8,000 in 1713 issued to pay the expenses of the Tuscarora War. Interest discontinued on Mar. 25, 1715 under Act of 1714. Handwritten in their entirety because no printer was in the Colony.

£3 [500]	£5 [500]	£10 [300]	£20 [250]

1715

£24,000 in indented handwritten Bills of Credit authorized in 1714 and made legal tender at regulated commodity rates. Wax colony seal on bills. Blank backs. Signers are Christopher Gale, Tobias Knight, Edward Moseley, and Daniel Richardson.

2s6d [720]	8s [150]	20s [3,000]	£5 [450]	£15 [300]
5s [3,000]	10s [3,300]	£3 [300]	£10 [480]	£20 [300]

October 19, 1722 Act

£12,000 in indented handwritten Bills of Credit issued pursuant to Oct. 19, 1722 Act. Paper covered wax colony seal attached. Legal tender at regulated commodity rates. Signers are Christopher Gale, John Lovick, and Edward Moseley.

12d	[1,000]
2s	[1,000]
2s6d	[1,000]
5s	[1,000]
7s6d	[1,000] ©
10s	[1,000] ©
20s	[1,000]
40s	[1,000]
£3	[1,000] ©
£5	[920] ©

Ⓐ

November 27, 1729 Act

£40,000 in indented handwritten Bills of Credit issued pursuant to the Nov. 27, 1729 Act. Paper covered wax colony seal or wax seal over thread. Signers are William Downing, John Lovick, Edward Moseley, Cullen Pollock, and Thomas Swann.

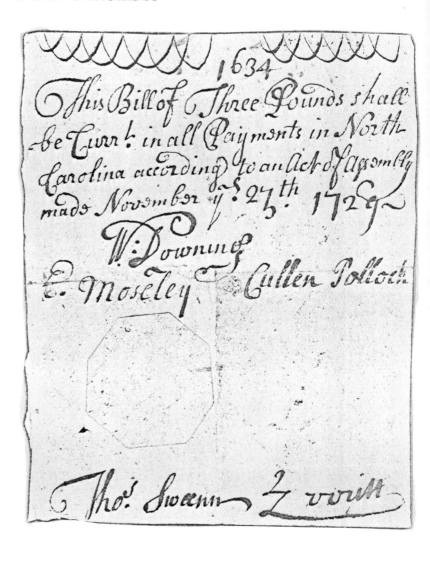

12d	[2,000]	
2s	[2,000]	
2s6d	[2,000]	
5s	[2,000]	
7s6d	[2,000]	
10s	[2,000]	
20s	[4,000]	
40s	[3,000]	©
£3	[4,000]	©
£5	Denomination in red ink [1,840] ©	
£10	[600]	

©

1734(5)

£40,000 in indented Lawful Money Bills without legal tender status and authorized on Mar. 1, 1734(5) to exchange for handwritten bills of the Nov. 27, 1729 issue which were worn and some of which had been counterfeited. Engraved and containing the date in the vignette. Signers are Eleazar Allen, James Castollan, William Downing, and Cullen Pollock.

1s	
2s6d	
5s	
10s	
20s	Crowned Lion
40s	
£3	
£5	
£10	Winged Stirrup ©

©

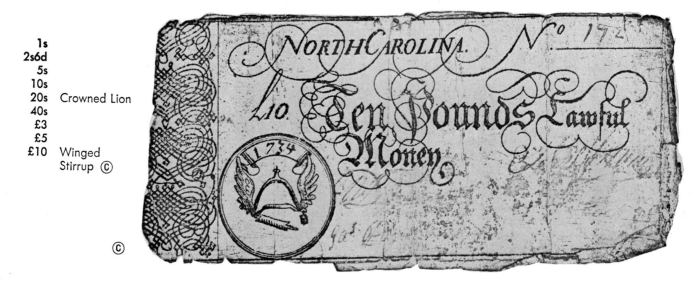

266

1735

£12,500 (£10,000 and £2,500) in indented Lawful Money Bills without legal tender status and authorized on March 1, 1734(5). The same engraved plates as the previous issue with the date modified to 1735. Same signers as previous issue.

1s	
2s6d	
5s	
10s	
20s	Crowned Lion Ⓒ
40s	
£3	
£5	
£10	Winged Stirrup

Ⓒ

April 4, 1748 Act

£21,350 in indented Bills of Credit issued pursuant to the April 4, 1748 Act which provided for redemption of all outstanding bills at 7½ in old bills for 1 in new bills. New bills were made legal tender at Proclamation Money rates, namely 4s in new bills to 3s sterling. The balance were to be expended for fortifications and public debts. Printed from engraved copper plates. Signers are Eleazar Allen, Edward Moseley, John Starkey, and Samuel Swann.

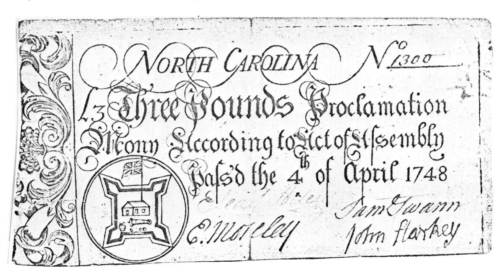

				Fair
4d	Denomination in circle [2,000]			
8d	Denomination in circle [2,000]	7s6d	Harp [2,000]	
1s	Denomination in circle [2,000]	9s	Crowned Lion [2,000]	
1s6d	Denomination in circle [2,000]	10s	Horse [2,000]	
2s	Thistle [2,000]	15s	Rampant Lion [2,000]	
2s6d	Crowned Rose [2,000]	20s	Unicorn [2,000]	125.00
3s	Plumes [2,000]	30s	Winged Stirrup [2,000]	125.00
5s	Crown [2,000]	40s	Drum, cannon & flags [2,000]	125.00
6s	Fleur de Lys [2,000]	£3	Fort Johnson & Union Jack [2,000]	125.00

March 9, 1754 Act

£40,000 in indented Bills of Credit issued pursuant to the March 9, 1754 Act and being legal tender at Proclamation Money rates. The aggregate value of the authorized number of each denomination is only £39,650 instead of £40,000 specified. The unusual denominations of 2s8d and 26s8d are respectively 8 groats and 80 groats, the groat (4d) being the lowest circulating denomination. Printed from engraved copper plates. Signers are Lewis De Rosset, John Starkey, John Swann, and Samuel Swann.

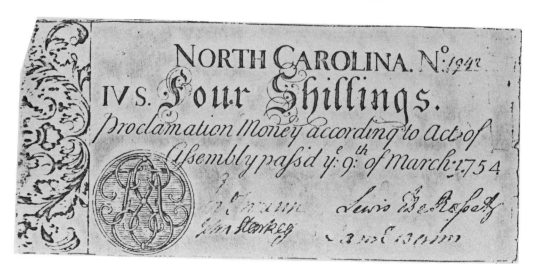

								Fair
4d	Key [10,333]		1s	Bear [10,000]		15s	Armor [6,000]	...... 75.00
4d	Mountain Lion [10,333]		1s	N.C. monogram [10,000]		20s	Crown [6,000]	...... 75.00
4d	Monogram [10,333]		2s8d	Snail [11,000]		26s8d	Bible [4,000]	.... 100.00
8d	Butterfly [20,000]		4s	Monogram [10,000]		30s	House [4,000] ⓒ	... 85.00
8d	Boar [20,000]		5s	Squirrel [8,000]		40s	Church [2,500] ⓒ	.. 100.00
1s	Swan [10,000]		10s	Bird [8,000]				

1756-7

£3,400 (Report of 1764 stated £3,600) in Public Notes of Credit payable in Proclamation Money with 6% interest on Nov. 10, 1757 and authorized at Session ended Sept. 13, 1756. Printed from set type. The denomination and some portions of the date are handwritten. Signer is John Starkey.

£5
£10
£20
£50

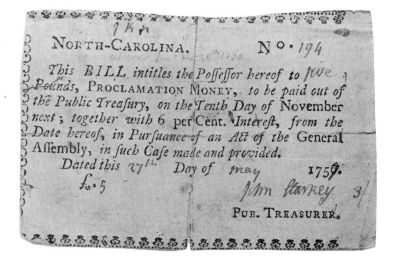

James Murray ★ 1757 with Written Date

£320 in private unauthorized Notes of James Murray payable to bearer and purporting to be receivable for Quit Rents and other amounts due to the Crown in four North Carolina counties. Certified by John Rutherford as Receiver General. Murray was unwilling to accept his own notes except for goods sold at high prices and for delinquent debts. The issue was invalidated by the Governor on Dec. 5, 1757. Both Murray and Rutherford were suspended from their public offices.

20s

May 28, 1757 Act

£5,306 in Public Notes of Credit payable in Proclamation Money with 6% interest on Sept. 29, 1758 pursuant to the May 28, 1757 Act. Typeset with date and denominations written in. Signers are Thomas Barker and John Starkey.

10s	per Cent.
10s	per Centum
20s	per Cent.
20s	per Centum
40s	per Cent.
40s	per Centum
£5	per Cent.
£5	per Centum

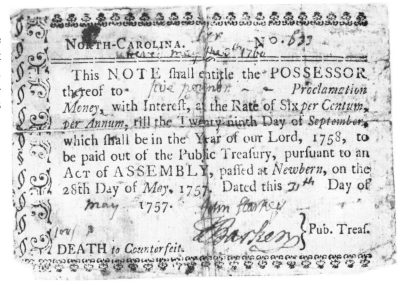

November 21, 1757 Session Act

£7,000 and £2,500 in Public Notes of Credit payable with 6% interest on Dec. 10, 1758 and authorized at Session ended on Nov. 21, 1757. Dated by hand in 1757 and 1758. Receivable for taxes. Typeset. Signers are Thomas Barker and John Starkey.

10s	
20s	
40s	
£5	Payment hyphenated
£5	Payment not hyphenated

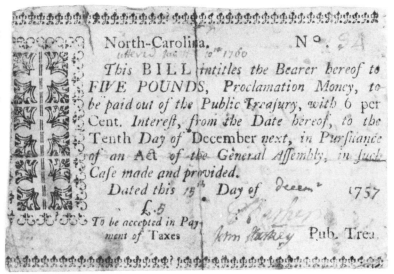

May 4, 1758 Act

£7,000 in legal tender Treasury Notes payable with 6% interest in Proclamation Money on Dec. 12, 1759 and authorized on May 4, 1758. Dated and issued in 1758 and 1759. All prior note issues were also made legal tender. Typeset. Signers are Thomas Barker and John Starkey.

10s	[2,000]
20s	[4,000]
40s	[1,000]

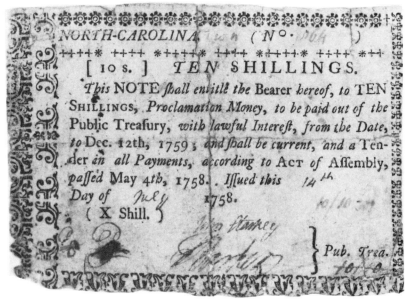

December 22, 1758 Act

£4,000 in legal tender Treasury Notes payable in Proclamation Money with 6% interest on June 10, 1761 and authorized by the Dec. 22, 1758 Act. Hand dated in 1758 and 1759. A reissue of this and prior issues without interest up to a total of £5,500 was approved at the Session ending May 8, 1759. Printed from set type. Signers are Thomas Barker and John Starkey.

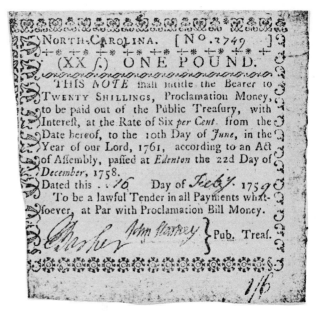

10s
20s (£1)   Two border varieties
           Part of m in "from" over n in "in"
           None of m in "from" over n in "in"
40s (£2)

July 14, 1760 Act

£12,000 in Bills of Credit made legal tender at Proclamation Money rates and authorized by the July 14, 1760 Act. Typeset. Signers are Lewis De Rosset, John Starkey, John Swann, and Samuel Swann.

		Fair	Good	V.G.
4d	[2,000]			
6d	[2,000]			
8d	[4,500]			
1s	[4,000]			
2s	[2,500]			
2s8d	[5,000]			
5s	[4,000]	75.00	100.00	150.00
10s	[2,300]	100.00	150.00	200.00
20s	[2,000]	100.00	150.00	200.00
30s	[1,000]	125.00	175.00	225.00
40s	[1,000]	125.00	175.00	225.00
£3	[1,000]	125.00	175.00	225.00

April 23, 1761 Act

£20,000 in Bills of Credit made legal tender at Proclamation Money rates by the April 23, 1761 Act. Printed from set type. Signers are the same as on the previous issue.

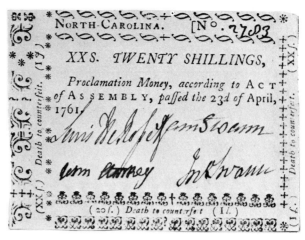

		Fair	Good	V.G.
4d	[5,000]			
6d	[5,000]			
8d	[5,000]			
1s	[5,000]			
2s	[5,000]			
2s6d	[3,000]			
3s	[3,000]	75.00	100.00	150.00
4s	[2,720]	75.00	100.00	150.00
5s	[3,000]	75.00	100.00	150.00
10s	[3,000]	75.00	100.00	150.00
15s	[3,000]	75.00	100.00	150.00
20s	[6,506]	50.00	75.00	100.00
30s	[1,000]	125.00	175.00	225.00
40s	[1,000]	125.00	175.00	225.00
£3	[1,000]	125.00	175.00	225.00

NORTH CAROLINA

December 1768 Act

£20,000 in Debenture Bills payable in Proclamation Money after June 10, 1772 and authorized by the Dec. 5, 1768 Act. Printed from type on thin paper. Signers are Richard Caswell, Lewis De Rosset, James Hasell, and Thomas C. Howe.

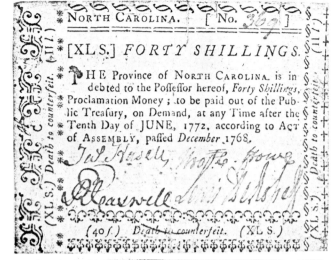

		Fair	Good	V.G.
2s6d	1768 on 6th line .	75.00	100.00	150.00
2s6d	1768 on 7th line .	75.00	100.00	150.00
5s	. . . .	75.00	100.00	150.00
10s	. . . .	75.00	100.00	150.00
20s	. . . .	75.00	100.00	150.00
40s	. . . .	125.00	175.00	225.00
£3	. . . .	125.00	175.00	225.00
£5	. . . .	125.00	175.00	225.00

December 1771 Act

£60,000 in Debenture Bills issued pursuant to a Dec. 1771 Act and payable in Proclamation Money. The three highest denominations are larger than the other denominations. Printed from engraved plates containing a vignette in the lower left corner. Signers are Richard Caswell, Lewis De Rosset, John Harvey, and John Rutherfurd.

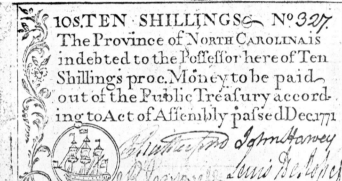

The blank backs of £1 and higher denominations usually contain the stamped name of I. ASHE (John Ashe, Treasurer of the Southern District of North Carolina) or the written name of Montfort (Joseph Montfort, Treasurer of the Northern District of North Carolina). The front sometimes has written initials such as IXθ. These apparently were used as a protective control feature.

		Good	V.G.	Fine	V.F.
1s	Basket of fruit [20,000]	30.00	65.00	100.00	150.00
2s6d	Duck [16,000]	30.00	50.00	90.00	125.00
2s6d	House. Shading on house strengthened in late printing [16,000]	30.00	50.00	90.00	125.00
5s	Quill pens [20,000]	30.00	50.00	90.00	125.00
10s	Ship. Shading on ship strengthened in late printing [10,000]	30.00	50.00	90.00	125.00
£1	Bear representing the constellation Ursa Minor. Shading on bear strengthened in late printing [10,000]	30.00	50.00	90.00	125.00
30s	Hand holding dagger [4,000] ⓒ	40.00	65.00	100.00	150.00
£2	Bird with olive branch. PAX REDDITA (Peace restored) MAY 1771 [5,000] ⓒ	40.00	65.00	100.00	150.00
£3	MAGNA CHARTA [3,000]	50.00	75.00	125.00	175.00
£5	Drum, cannon & flags [2,000]	60.00	90.00	135.00	200.00

August 21, 1775 Session Act

$125,000 in Bills of Credit authorized by the Sept. 7, 1775 Resolution and payable in Spanish milled dollars. Engraved bills with ornamental borders and unusual vignettes in the lower left corner. Signers are Richard Caswell, Richard Cogdell, Samuel Johnston, Thomas Jones, and Andrew Knox. This issue and the April 2, 1776 issue were to be exchanged pursuant to the Aug. 8, 1778 Act for the Aug. 8, 1778 issue or become invalid by May 1, 1779. This was extended to May 1, 1780 at the Jan. 19, 1779 Session, to May 1, 1781 by the Act of April 17, 1780, and to Feb. 4, 1784 by the Act of April 14, 1781.

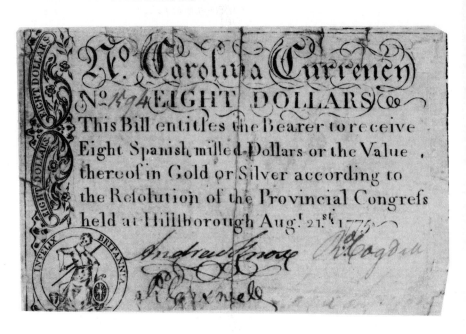

		Fair	Good	V.G.
$1/4	Key [4,000]	300.00	500.00	750.00
$1/2	Drum, cannon and flags [4,000]	300.00	500.00	750.00
$1	Hermes. 12 UNITED COLONIES [4,000]	300.00	500.00	750.00
$2	[4,000]	300.00	500.00	750.00
$3	Masonic emblems [4,000]	300.00	500.00	750.00
$4	Masonic emblems. AERA OF MASONRY 5775 [4,000] ©	300.00	500.00	750.00
$5	State House [4,000]	300.00	500.00	750.00
$8	Britannia stabbing herself. INFELIX BRITANNIA (Unhappy England) [4,000]	300.00	500.00	750.00
$10	Twelve arms supporting liberty cap. HANC TUEMUR HAC NITIMUR (This we guard, for this we strive) [3,000]	300.00	500.00	750.00

April 2, 1776

$1,250,000 (£500,000) in Bills of Credit of which $250,000 were authorized on April 22, 1776 and $1,000,000 on May 9, 1776. Engraved on copper plates by GL (apparently Gabriel Lewyn, a Baltimore goldsmith) whose initials appear on a few varieties. Vignettes on each bill. Some bills contain mottoes. Printed on thin laid paper. Some of the bills show part of a crown as a watermark. Fractional denominations are smaller than the higher denominations. The original plate for the $20 bill exists. Signers are Willis Alston, J. Bradford, William Haywood, G. Hill, Benjamin McCulloch, David Sumner, J. Webb, and William Williams. See the prior issue for the redemption history.

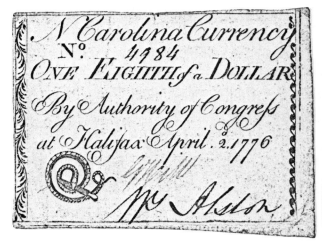

		Good	V.G.	Fine
$1/16	Beetle [13,333]	150.00	200.00	300.00
$1/16	Butterfly [13,333]	150.00	200.00	300.00
$1/16	Cornucopia [13,333]	150.00	200.00	300.00
$1/16	Griffin [13,333]	150.00	200.00	300.00
$1/16	Nautilus [13,333]	150.00	200.00	300.00
$1/16	Vase of Flowers [13,333]	150.00	200.00	300.00
$1/8	Dog [12,500]	150.00	200.00	300.00
$1/8	Heron [12,500]	150.00	200.00	300.00
$1/8	Lion [12,500]	150.00	200.00	300.00
$1/8	Monogram with mirrored H [12,500]	150.00	200.00	300.00
$1/8	Monogram JM [12,500]	150.00	200.00	300.00
$1/8	Sculpin [12,500]	150.00	200.00	300.00
$1/8	Snake biting sword in scabbard [12,500]	150.00	200.00	300.00
$1/8	Steer [12,500]	150.00	200.00	300.00
$1/4	Bird flying [12,500]	125.00	175.00	275.00
$1/4	Three fish [12,500]	125.00	175.00	275.00
$1/4	Hare [12,500]	125.00	175.00	275.00
$1/4	Monogram FB in black script [12,500]	125.00	175.00	275.00
$1/4	Monogram NCSN (State of North Carolina) in white script [12,500]	125.00	175.00	275.00
$1/4	Sea urchin [12,500]	125.00	175.00	275.00
$1/4	Shark [12,500]	125.00	175.00	275.00
$1/4	Tuna [12,500]	125.00	175.00	275.00
$1/2	N. AMERICAN BEAR [12,500]	125.00	175.00	275.00
$1/2	Cock Fight [12,500]	125.00	175.00	275.00
$1/2	Crow and pitcher [12,500] ©	125.00	175.00	275.00
$1/2	Hunter, dog, and target. HIT OR MISS. No day in date [12,500] ©	125.00	175.00	275.00
$1/2	Monogram with toothed border of triangles [12,500]	125.00	175.00	275.00
$1/2	Monogram with toothed border of radial lines. Engraver's initials G L in left border [12,500]	125.00	175.00	275.00
$1/2	Owl [12,500]	125.00	175.00	275.00
$1/2	Ship [12,500]	125.00	175.00	275.00
$1	Duck [10,000]	100.00	150.00	250.00
$1	Raccoon [10,000]	100.00	150.00	250.00
$1	Justice [10,000]	100.00	150.00	250.00
$1	Scroll with denomination in black [10,000]	100.00	150.00	250.00
$1	Scroll with denomination in white [10,000]	100.00	150.00	250.00
$1	Snake strangling bird [10,000]	100.00	150.00	250.00
$2	Deer [10,000]	100.00	150.00	250.00
$2	Fox. Engraver's initials G L [10,000]	100.00	150.00	250.00
$2 1/2	Hand clasping thirteen arrows. VIS UNITATIS (The power of unity) [10,000]	125.00	175.00	225.00
$2 1/2	Liberty cap over altar. LIBERTAS & NATALE SOLUM (Liberty and our native land) [10,000]	125.00	175.00	225.00
$3	Alligator at top. Beaver on left [10,000]	75.00	125.00	225.00
$3	Beehive [10,000]	75.00	125.00	225.00
$4	Bee [10,000]	75.00	125.00	225.00
$4	Sheaf of wheat [10,000]	75.00	125.00	225.00
$5	Raven [10,000]	75.00	125.00	225.00
$5	Triton. Engraver's initials G L. Error of **d2** instead of **2d.** A face is in the O in the top border [10,000] ©	75.00	125.00	225.00
$6	Goat [10,000]	75.00	125.00	225.00
$6	Squirrel eating nut [10,000]	75.00	125.00	225.00
$7 1/2	U. S. Flag with 13 Stripes and Union Jack. Engraver's initials G L [10,000]	125.00	175.00	275.00

		V.G.	Fine	V.F.
$8	Leopard [10,000]	125.00	225.00	350.00
$8	Rooster [10,000]	125.00	225.00	350.00
$10	Cupid [10,000]	125.00	225.00	350.00
$10	Peacock [10,000]	125.00	225.00	350.00
$12 1/2	Eagle carrying broken arrows. DEUS NOBISCUM (God be with us) [3,000]	225.00	350.00	500.00
$15	Boar [5,000] ©	150.00	250.00	375.00
$20	Rattlesnake. DON'T TREAD ON ME. Engraver's initials G L [5,000]	150.00	250.00	375.00

1778 (August 8, 1778 Act)

£850,000 ($2,125,000) in legal tender Bills of Credit payable in Spanish milled dollars pursuant to Aug. 8, 1778 Act. A total of 200,000 bills of $1/16 denomination was originally authorized but reduced to 12,500 at the Session ended Jan. 19, 1779. A total of £24,876 5s of various denominations (including all $1/16) was not printed because of a smallpox epidemic affecting the printer and subsequently $50 bills with 1780 on the back were authorized at the Session begun on April 17, 1780 to replace the unprinted quantity. Printed from type by James Davis both on dark coarse mica flaked paper and on thin unsized paper. Printed backs. Denominations of $4 and higher have two signers while others have only one. Signers are Joseph Armitage, M. Caswell, R. Caswell, S. Caswell, Jesse Cobb, Richard Cogdell, James Coore, David Cox, Jr., Oroondates Davis, Benjamin Exum, James Green, Thomas Harvey, Benjamin Hawkins, Joseph Jones, James Kenan, James Kerr, John Lillington, C. Markland, H. Machilwien, Thomas Satterwhite, William Sharpe, R. White, and James Williams.

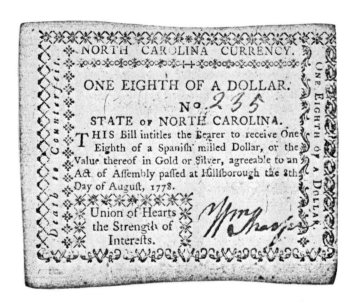

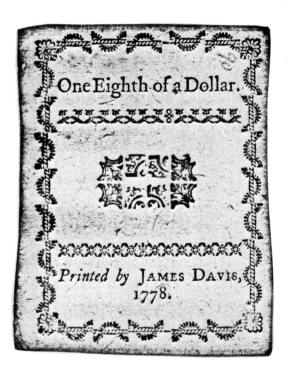

		V.G.	Fine	V.F.
$1/8	UNION OF HEARTS THE STRENGTH OF INTERESTS [100,000]	50.00	75.00	100.00
$1/4	INDEPENDENCE [100,000]	45.00	70.00	90.00
$1/2	BEHOLD! A NEW WORLD [100,000]	40.00	65.00	85.00
$1	LIBERTY AND PEACE, THE REWARD OF VIRTUOUS RESISTANCE [31,250]	40.00	65.00	85.00
$1	VIRTUOUS COUNCILS THE CEMENT OF STATES [31,250]	40.00	65.00	85.00
$2	VIRTUOUS COUNCILS THE CEMENT OF STATES [25,000]	45.00	70.00	90.00
$4	A LESSON TO ARBITRARY KINGS, AND WICKED MINISTERS [12,500]	50.00	75.00	100.00
$5	BEHOLD! A NEW WORLD [12,500]	35.00	60.00	80.00
$5	INDEPENDENCE [12,500]	65.00	100.00	150.00
$5	A LESSON TO ARBITRARY KINGS AND WICKED MINISTERS [12,500]	35.00	60.00	80.00
$5	THE RISING STATES [12,500]	35.00	60.00	80.00
$10	INDEPENDENCE [16,666]	35.00	60.00	80.00
$10	PERSECUTION THE RUIN OF EMPIRES [16,666] ©	35.00	60.00	80.00
$10	UNION OF HEARTS THE STRENGTH OF INTERESTS [16,666]	35.00	60.00	80.00
$20	AMERICAN VIRTUE TRIUMPHANT [12,500]	45.00	70.00	90.00
$25	SIC TRANSIT GLORIA MUNDI (Thus passes the glory of the world) [10,000] ©	45.00	70.00	90.00
$40	FREEDOM OF SPEECH AND THE LIBERTY OF THE PRESS [3,125]	50.00	75.00	100.00
$50	THE RISING STATES [5,000]	50.00	75.00	100.00
	(See issue of April 17, 1780 for other mottoes)			
$100	FREEDOM OR AN HONORABLE DEATH [2,500]	60.00	90.00	125.00

NORTH CAROLINA

May 15, 1779 Act

£500,000 ($1,250,000) in legal tender Bills of Credit payable in Spanish milled dollars and authorized by May 15, 1779 Act. Engraved top border cut on both face and back, otherwise typeset. Printed on light coarse paper by Hugh Walker in Wilmington. Signers are John Hunt, Thomas Person, and John Taylor.

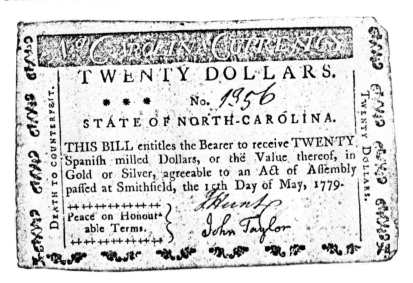

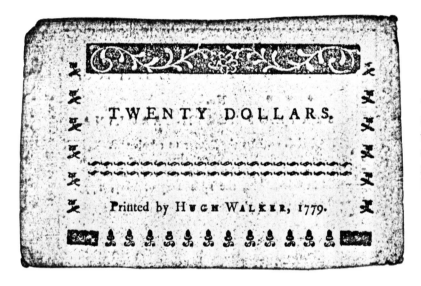

"Secret" typographical marks intended to appear as ink smears were inserted in order to detect counterfeits, but the counterfeiters faithfully copied the secret marks. These marks on each denomination are described below.

		V.G.	Fine	V.F.
$5	BE FREEDOM AND INDEPENDENCE STEADILY PURSUED.			
	Small u over y of May [10,000]	50.00	75.00	100.00
$5	GOOD GOVERNMENT ALWAYS REVERE. Umlaut over e in Silver [10,000]	50.00	75.00	100.00
$10	AMERICAN UNION FOR EVER. DRATH instead of DEATH.			
	Small u over y of May [10,000]	50.00	75.00	100.00
$10	VIRTUE EXCELS RICHES. Dash over y of Assembly [10,000]	50.00	75.00	100.00
$20	PEACE ON HONOURABLE TERMS. Umlaut over e of second the [10,000]	55.00	85.00	125.00
$25	A FREE COMMERCE. Q instead of O in right border [6,000]	55.00	85.00	125.00
$25	AMERICAN FORTITUDE DISPLAYED. Top border lettering is a			
	mirrored image. The period after No is missing [6,000]	55.00	85.00	125.00
$50	A RIGHTEOUS CAUSE THE PROTECTION OF PROVIDENCE.			
	Circumflex over e in Silver [2,000]	100.00	150.00	200.00
$100	A FREE COMMERCE. Q instead of O in right border [1,000] ©	100.00	150.00	200.00
$250	A RIGHTEOUS CAUSE THE PROTECTION OF PROVIDENCE.			
	Circumflex over e in Silver and dash over first i in Smithfield [1,000] ©	100.00	150.00	200.00

1780 (April 17, 1780 Session Act)

£29,876 5s ($74,700) being the balance of the total of the Aug. 8, 1778 issue which was not printed because of the smallpox epidemic, was reauthorized at the April 17, 1780 Session for $50 denominations only. Identical in style to the 1778 issue with mottoes from lower denominations of that issue, but with the date on the back changed to 1780. The Aug. 8, 1778 Act remains in the text on the face. Same signers as the 1778 issue. By another Act passed at the April 17, 1780 Session three inspectors were to be appointed in each county to examine bills and to write COUNTERFEIT in large letters on such counterfeit bills as they found.

$50 INDEPENDENCE [498]
$50 LIBERTY AND PEACE, THE REWARD OF VIRTUOUS RESISTANCE [498]
$50 PERSECUTION THE RUIN OF EMPIRES [498]

May 10, 1780 Act

£1,240,000 ($3,100,000) in legal tender Bills of Credit authorized by the May 10, 1780 Act giving the Governor the right to issue more bills. The Governor apparently added to the issue of $25, $100 and $500 bills and created the new denominations of $200, $300, $400, and $600. Printed from type on both thick and thin paper by James Davis. Printed backs. Signers are John Ashe, Waightsill Avery, Jonathan Cooke, J. W. Caron, James Coore, David Cox, Jr., M. Frank, James Green, Jr., Is. Guion, Joseph Leech, and H. Vipon. This issue and many prior issues depreciated to 800 for 1 and some remained in circulation so depreciated into the nineteenth century.

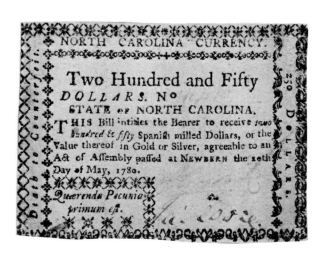

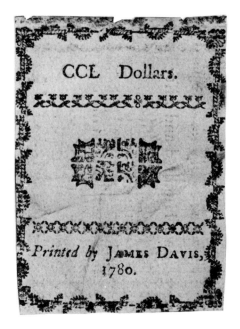

NORTH CAROLINA

		V.G.	Fine	V.F.
$25	DULCE PRO PATRIA MORI (It is pleasing to die for one's country) [8,000 plus] ...	50.00	75.00	100.00
$25	HORA PACIS & LIBERTATIS APPROPINQUAT (The time for peace and freedom is approaching). In the text the S is omitted from DOLLARS [8,000]	50.00	75.00	100.00
$25	JUSTITIA ADDIT FIDUCIAM (Justice adds trust) [8,000]	50.00	75.00	100.00
$25	QUID NON VIRTUTE EFFICIENDUM (What is not to be accomplished by virtue) [8,000 plus]	50.00	75.00	100.00
$25	TERRA LIBERA NOTAM PRAETII IN ME POSUIT (A free land placed a mark of value on me). Center bar of F in FIVE missing [8,000]	50.00	75.00	100.00
$25	VIM VI REPELLAMUS (By force let us repel force) [8,000]	50.00	75.00	100.00
$50	FUNDAMENTUM MIHI AERE PERENNIUS (A foundation for me more enduring than bronze) [8,000]	60.00	90.00	125.00
$100	FORTIS CADERE CEDERE NON POTEST (A brave man cannot fall) [5,000 plus] ..	65.00	100.00	150.00
$200	UT QUOCUNQUE PARATUS (As prepared in every way)	100.00	150.00	250.00
$250	QUAERENDA PECUNIA PRIMUM EST (Money has to be sought first). "T" in "This" in ornamented box [1,000]	75.00	110.00	175.00
$250	QUAERENDA PECUNIA PRIMUM EST. "T" in "This" not boxed [1,000]	75.00	110.00	175.00
$300	AUT NUMQUAM TENTES AUT PERFICE (Either finish or never begin)	100.00	150.00	250.00
$400	MUTARE VEL TIMERE SPERNO (I refuse to change or to fear)	100.00	150.00	250.00
$500	DIVITIAE REIPUBLICAE DANT MIHI PRETIUM (The wealth of the republic gives me value). "T" in "This" in ornamented box [500]	85.00	125.00	200.00
$500	DIVITIAE REIPUBLICAE DANT MIHI PRETIUM. "T" in "This" not boxed [500 plus]..	85.00	125.00	200.00
$600	CRESCIT SUB PONDERE VIRTUS (Virtue grows under pressure)	100.00	150.00	250.00

January 18, 1781 Session Act

$26,250,000 in bearer Certificates payable with 6% interest after March 1, 1782 and issued for enlistment in the State militia. Handwritten dates in the spring of 1781 at which time depreciation was $250 in paper money for $1 in specie. The issuing committee consisted of James Coore and William Pasteur. The issue was protected by a separate counterfeiting provision. Signed by Robert Lanier as State treasurer.

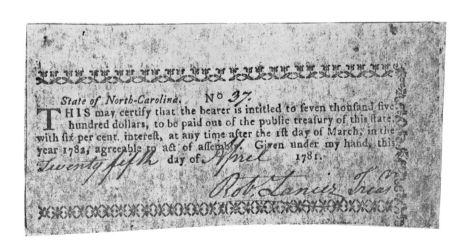

$7,500 [3,500]

NORTH CAROLINA

May 17, 1783 Act

£100,000 ($250,000) in legal tender Bills payable in Spanish Dollars and authorized by May 17, 1783 Act. Printed from border and vignette cuts and set type by Thomas Davis at Halifax. Typeset backs. Signers are John Hunt and Benjamin McCulloch. See redemption history under December 29, 1785 issue.

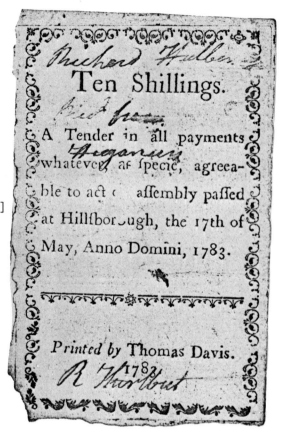

6d	Bird [20,000]	
1s	[10,000]	
2s	Corinthian column. IN RECTO DECUS (Honor in the right) [40,000]	
5s	[20,000]	
10s	Ships. COMMERCIO (Commerce) [20,000] Ⓒ	
20s	Justice. DO AS YOU WOULD BE DONE BY [20,000] Ⓒ	
20s	Crown and book [20,000] Ⓒ	
40s	Angel Gabriel and church [20,000] Ⓒ	

Ⓒ

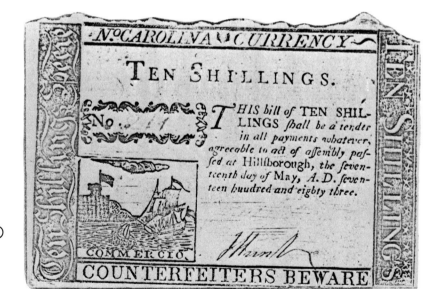

The history of the circulation and redemption of this issue follows the listing of the December 9, 1785 issue.

278

NORTH CAROLINA

December 29, 1785 Act

£100,000 ($250,000) in legal tender Bills of Credit authorized by Dec. 29, 1785 Act. Decorative border and vignettes on the face. The balance of the face and all of the back is typeset. Printed by Thomas Davis on thick paper watermarked NORTH CAROLINA. Test specimens on blue paper. Signers are John Hunt and Absalom Tatom.

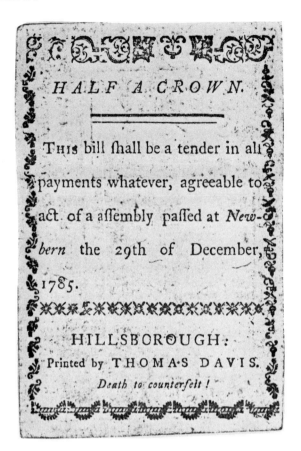

6d	Thirteen stars [25,000]	
1s	Wreath [25,000]	
2s	Plough [25,000]	
2s6d	Phoenix. MELIOR RESURGO (I return improved) [25,000]	
5s	Ship near fort. COMMERCE [25,000]	
10s	Crown and Book [25,000] Ⓤ	
20s	Angel Gabriel and church [25,000] Ⓒ	
40s	Justice [24,375] Ⓤ Ⓒ	

North Carolina's specie notes issued under the May 17, 1783 and December 29, 1785 Acts remained in circulation until 1816, a period of twenty-nine years after the U.S. Constitution prohibited issuance of Bills of Credit by States. Property taxes were first intended to create a sinking fund for specie note redemption along with the proceeds of confiscated Tory property. The State remained in such poor financial condition that redemption of its specie notes was of low priority. At the Nov. 2, 1789 Session of the State Legislature, specie notes were ordered to be redeemed in specie by January 1, 1791, but this Act was repealed at the Nov. 1, 1790 Session because the State had no available specie. Thereafter the State's annual sinking fund was eliminated year by year from 1792 through 1810 and no specie notes were redeemed. These notes had depreciated 20% below specie value and so remained. By 1800 about $300,000 (equal to a face value of £166,667) were in circulation. In 1804 when the legislature incorporated the Bank of Cape Fear and the Bank of Newbern with the right to issue circulating notes the State of North Carolina realized that profits from banking might pay the State's debts (including the specie notes). Whereupon in 1805 the State Bank of North Carolina was incorporated with a capitalization of 8,000 shares at $50 each, the first $10 payable in specie, the next $10 "in the paper currency of this State at the rate of ten shillings for a dollar," and other installments as the directors would determine. The State could subscribe to 2,000 shares but was to be loaned part of its subscription payment by the bank. Half of the State's dividends were to be used to redeem its paper money. This scheme was so impractical that it was repealed at the November 1806 Session. During the same session the State granted itself the right to buy an aggregate of 250 shares in the Bank of Cape Fear and the Bank of Newbern if those banks agreed to accept in payment for the shares the currency which the State had in its treasury. This was equivalent to putting more State paper money in circulation and the plan was rejected. At the November 1810 Session the State Bank of North Carolina was again incorporated with the right of the State to buy 2,500 shares out of 16,000 at $100 each, payable in U. S. Bonds then owned by the State and any balance to be paid in specie at the convenience of the State. The 1783 and 1785 specie notes were to lose their legal tender status when the bank opened. Other subscribers could pay for their shares to the extent of one-fourth in State currency. All dividends due the State were to be used to pay off the State currency. This plan failed to materialize and at the November 1811 session the Bank was required to redeem all State currency by Dec. 18, 1816 and not to recirculate any which was received. When the War of 1812 caused a small change shortage the State approved $82,000 in fractional Treasury Notes at the November 1814 Session in violation of the United States Constitution and used the notes to buy 410 newly issued shares in the Bank of Cape Fear and 410 in the Bank of Newbern. After Jan. 1, 1816 the 1783 and 1785 specie notes were to lose their legal tender status at these two banks but not at the State Bank of North Carolina. The Bank of Cape Fear and the Bank of Newbern had their charters extended and their capitalization increased on condition they would redeem the 1783 and 1785 specie notes if the State Bank of North Carolina dissolved before Dec. 18, 1816. The Governor was ordered to remove all legal tender status of the 1783 and 1785 issues when the redemption was accomplished. At the November 1816 Session $80,000 more fractional Treasury bills were authorized to be issued by the State and to be used to pay the State's obligations at the State Bank of North Carolina. Thus the 1783 and 1785 specie notes were finally discharged by the substitution of new illegal issues of North Carolina paper money, but necessity had dictated this action.

Joseph Ross ★ January 1800, etc.
Private bearer scrip issued at Raleigh. Blank back. Dark brown paper.

3d
6d

NORTH CAROLINA REFERENCES

Douglas B. Ball, "North Carolina's Illegal Bills of Credit 1814-1823," *The Numismatist,* Vol. 60, No. 5, p. 571 (May 1967).

Charles J. Bullock, "The Paper Currency of North Carolina," *Essays on the Monetary History of the United States* (New York, 1900).

(Thomas Fitzgerald), "1759 North Carolina Colonial Note," *Paper Money,* Vol. XIII, No. 4, p. 160 (1974).

Lyman H. Low, "Masonic Emblems on Continental Money," *American Journal of Numismatics* (January 1892).

Mattie E. Parker, *Money Problems of Early Tar Heels* (Raleigh, 1945, etc.).

Kenneth Scott, "Counterfeiting in Colonial North Carolina," *The North Carolina Historical Review,* Vol. 34, p. 467 (1957).

Laws, archives, newspapers and other public records.

See general references, catalogs, and listings following the Introduction.

NORTHWEST
TERRITORY

Compagnie de Scioto ⋆ 1790

Small change notes written in French and issued by the Scioto Company which was formed about 1789 by William Duer, Assistant Secretary of the Treasury of the United States under Alexander Hamilton, as part of a scheme to sell to French immigrants land obtained by Duer as a veteran of the Revolutionary War under a Northwest Territory bounty program. When 500 French land purchasers arrived in 1790 the land they had bought had been forfeited to the United States for non-payment and the group was sent nearby (now Gallipolis, Ohio) to homestead on land of the Ohio Company. The notes are signed by William Duer as Sur-Intendant (Superintendent). Duer (also while a government official) had been a silent partner in the copper coinage contract granted to James Jarvis in 1787 by the United States.

3¢   6¢   9¢   12¢

REFERENCE

S. Fred Rosenthal, "An Ohio Numismatic Rarity," *Western Reserve Historical Society News,* September 1962.

PENNSYLVANIA

GENERAL EMISSIONS

April 2, 1723
January 17, 1723(4)
March 25, 1726
September 15, 1729
April 10, 1731
August 10, 1739
August 1, 1744
August 1, 1746
May 16, 1749
October 1, 1755
January 1, 1756
October 1, 1756
March 10, 1757
July 1, 1757
May 20, 1758
April 25, 1759
June 21, 1759
May 1, 1760
June 18, 1764
June 15, 1767

March 1, 1769
March 10, 1769
March 20, 1771
April 3, 1772
March 20, 1773
October 1, 1773
March 25, 1775
April 10, 1775
July 20, 1775
October 25, 1775
December 8, 1775
April 25, 1776
April 10, 1777 in Black
April 10, 1777 in Red and Black
April 29, 1780
June 1, 1780
April 20, 1781
March 21, 1783 Act
March 16, 1785 Act

SPECIAL ISSUERS

Evan Morgan ★ June 1729
Joseph Gray ★ May 1746
Philadelphia Merchants ★ December 1766
Ignace Labate ★ October 25, 1775
Joseph Ogden ★ January 18, 1777
William Milnor ★ January 20, 1777
Joseph Sommerville ★ February 1, 1777
Bank of North America ★ 1782, etc.
Bank of North America ★ August 6, 1789
John Wray and James Lamberton ★ September 5, 1789
William Peterson ★ October 1, 1789
Fred Hubley ★ December 13, 1789
Bank of the United States ★ 1791, etc.
Delaware and Schuylkill Canal Navigation
    Company ★ March 1793, etc.
Bank of Pennsylvania ★ March 1793, etc.

April 2, 1723

£15,000 in indented legal tender Loan Office Bills approved by the Act of Mar. 23, 1723 and dated April 2, 1723. They were redeemable by April 2, 1731 and were to be invalid after Aug. 2, 1731. Of this total £11,000 was to be loaned on security of land, houses, or silver plate at 5% interest with principal repayable in eight equal annual installments. Cast cuts including Arms of the Penn family, otherwise typeset. Blank backs. Signers are Anthony Morris, Francis Rawle, Charles Read, and Benjamin Vining.

```
 1s  [8,000]  ©
 2s  [6,000]
2s6d [4,000]
 5s  [6,000]  ©
10s  [6,000]
15s  [4,000]
20s  [6,000]
```

January 17, 1723(4)

£30,000 in indented legal tender Loan Office Bills approved by the Act of Dec. 12, 1723. Originally due July 17, 1736 but accelerated to Mar. 1, 1731(2) by the Act of Jan. 4, 1730(1). Of this amount £26,500 was to be loaned on security with principal repayable over 12½ years. On bills of 5s and over the number of crowns equivalent to the denomination was included in the text to prevent raising the bills by alteration. Elaborate cut for indenture. Blank backs. Signers are Samuel Hudson, Anthony Morris, Frank Rawle, and Charles Read.

1s	[7,000]	©
1s6d	[4,000]	
2s	[6,000]	
2s6d	[6,000]	
5s	[6,000]	©
10s	[5,000]	
15s	[8,000]	
20s	[18,000]	

March 25, 1726

£10,000 in indented legal tender Bills issued to replace worn bills of prior issues pursuant to the Mar. 5, 1726 Act. Reemission of prior issues was authorized by the same Act so that the Province could borrow bills from the General Loan Office, expend them and repay by Jan. 16, 1730(1). Signers are Evan Owen, Thomas Tresse, and John Wright.

1s [9,000]   1s6d [10,000]   2s [3,000]   2s6d [8,000]   5s [20,000]   10s [5,000]

Evan Morgan ★ June, 1729

Small change bills printed by Benjamin Franklin for a Philadelphia shopkeeper, Evan Morgan. These bills are mentioned in Franklin's account book and he accepted some in payment for his work. Other denominations are probable.

5d   8d [1,000]

284

PENNSYLVANIA

September 15, 1729

£30,000 in indented legal tender Loan Office Bills approved by the Act of May 10, 1729 and due on Sept. 15, 1745, by which date the 16 year secured loans for which the bills were issued were to be repaid. Printed by Andrew Bradford, although Benjamin Franklin erroneously claimed that he printed the bills. Blank backs. Signers are Abraham Chapman, Edward Horne, John Parry, and Thomas Tresse.

1s	[10,500]	5s	[16,000] ©
1s6d	[17,000]	10s	[12,000]
2s	[12,000]	15s	[2,000]
2s6d	[4,000]	20s	[15,000]

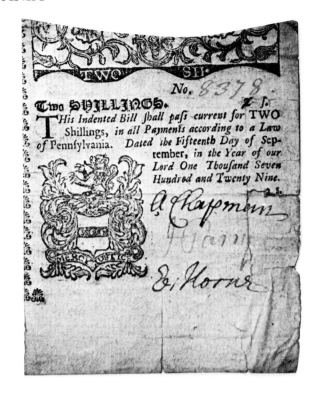

April 10, 1731

£40,000 in legal tender Bills approved Feb. 6, 1730(1) along with authority to reemit £45,000 in prior issues. Printed by Benjamin Franklin. Signers are Job Goodson, Thomas Griffiths, Joseph Kirkbride, and John Parry.

1s	[4,000]	5s	[12,000]
1s6d	[4,000]	10s	[10,000]
2s	[5,000]	15s	[8,000] ©
2s6d	[8,000]	20s	[24,000] ©

August 10, 1739

£80,000 in legal tender Bills issued pursuant to the May 1, 1739 Act primarily to replace prior issues which had been extensively counterfeited. All prior emissions were made uncurrent after Aug. 10, 1740. Only £11,110 5s of the issue were to be used for 16 year loans. Approved by the Crown on May 12, 1740. This style of bill generally continued in use through 1776. The number of crowns is keyed to each of the four highest denominations which have Pensilvania deliberately misspelled to act as a secret check to detect alterations from the lower denominations. The backs of the four highest denominations contained an identical nature print in various positions. Benjamin Franklin in printing this issue introduced nature printing on Pennsylvania paper money as a major deterrent to counterfeiters. Signers are Abraham Chapman, Joseph Harvey, Thomas Leech, William Monington, and Samuel Smith.

1s	[10,000]
18d	[10,000]
2s	[10,000]
2s6d	[10,000]
5s	A & B Plate letters [30,000]
10s	A, B, C, & D Plate letters [40,000] ©
15s	A & B Plate letters [20,000]
20s	A & B Plate letters [34,000] ©

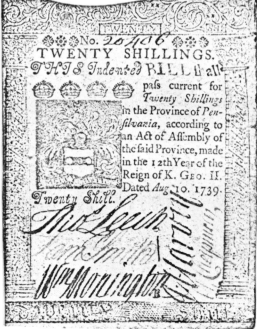

PENNSYLVANIA

August 1, 1744

£10,000 in legal tender Bills of Credit authorized by the May 26, 1744 Act to replace tattered bills of prior issues. Printed by Benjamin Franklin from type and cast cuts. Blank back. Signers are Abraham Chapman, Peter Lloyd, and James Morris.

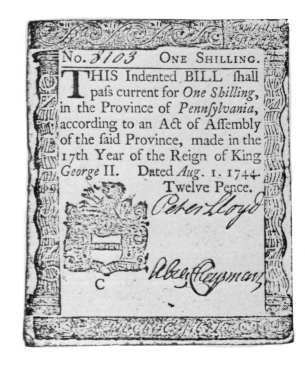

1s	Plate letters A, B, & C [20,000]
18d	Plate letters A, B, & C [20,000]
2s	Plate letters A, B, & C [20,000]
2s6d	Plate letters A, B, & C [20,000] ©
5s	[12,000]

Joseph Gray ★ May, 1746

£27 10s in "running change" issued by Joseph Gray as a private individual to provide a supplement to the small amount of copper coin in circulation. Printed by Benjamin Franklin.

2d [600]   **3d** [600]   **6d** [600]

August 1, 1746

£5,000 in legal tender Bills authorized by the June 24, 1746 Act to replace worn bills of prior issues and to be current until Oct. 15, 1762. Pence denominations are small in size and contain type set in curved lines. Bills of 20s are similar to the Aug. 10, 1739 issue, and have the same nature print on the back. Printed by Benjamin Franklin. Signers are John Hall, Joseph Harvey, James Mitchell, James Morris, and Joseph Trotter. Three signers are on the 20s and two signers on the others.

4d	[30,000]
6d	[30,000]
9d	[30,000]
20s	Plate letters A, B, C, & D [2,625]

286

PENNSYLVANIA

May 16, 1749

£5,000 in legal tender Bills authorized by the Feb. 4, 1749 Act to replace worn bills of prior issues. Printed by Benjamin Franklin and David
Hall with a cut of Penn Arms, border cuts as well as ornamental and
regular type. Blank backs. Signers are John Davis, Joseph Hamton,
John Jervis, William Trotter, and James Webb.

3d	Plate letters A, B, & C [60,000]	©
4d	Plate letters A, B, & C [60,000]	
6d	Plate letters A, B, & C [60,001]	
9d	Plate letters A, B, & C [46,666]	©

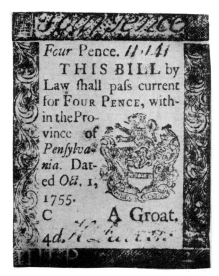

October 1, 1755

£10,000 in legal tender Bills authorized June 28, 1755 to exchange for
torn bills of prior issues. The four lowest denominations are small in
size. Only the 5s and 10s have printed backs which are complex nature
prints later used on Continental Currency. Variations in the spelling of
the provincial name (Pensylvania, Pensilvania, Pennsylvania and Pennsilvania) continue to be used to detect alteration of denominations. The
number of crowns is keyed to each of the two highest denominations.
Printed by Benjamin Franklin and David Hall. Signers are included
under the May 1, 1760 issue. One signer for the four lowest denominations and three signers for the others.

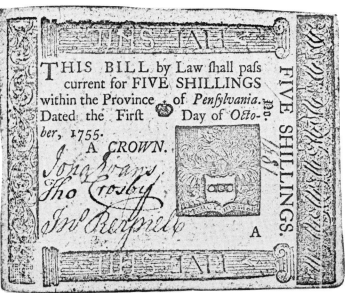

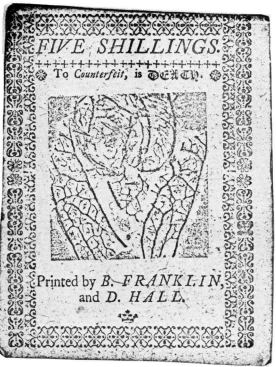

		Fair	Good
3d	Plate letters A, B, & C [15,000]		
4d	Plate letters A, B, & C. Pensylvania [11,250]		
6d	Plate letters A, B, & C [10,000]		
9d	Plate letters A, B, & C [10,000]		
1s	Plate letters A & B. Pennsylvania [10,000]		
18d	Plate letters A & B. Pensilvania [10,000]		
2s	Plate letters A & B [10,000]		
2s6d	Plate letters A & B [10,000]		
5s	Plate letters A & B. Pensylvania [10,000] ...	100	200
10s	Plate letters A & B. Pensylvania. Reversed S on columns [6,000]	100	200

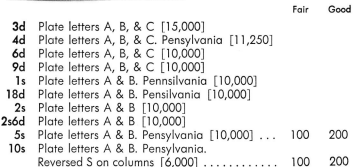

PENNSYLVANIA

January 1, 1756

£55,000 in legal tender Bills authorized during the Session ended Nov. 3, 1755 and good until Jan. 1, 1760. This emission and those in the four subsequent years were primarily to support military expeditions during the French and Indian War. These emissions were to be redeemed by tax levies, as distinguished from Loan Office operations. Penn Arms are on the face and a nature print on the back. The number of crowns is keyed to each of the four highest denominations. Printed by Benjamin Franklin and David Hall on "good strong paper." Signers are included under the May 1, 1760 issue.

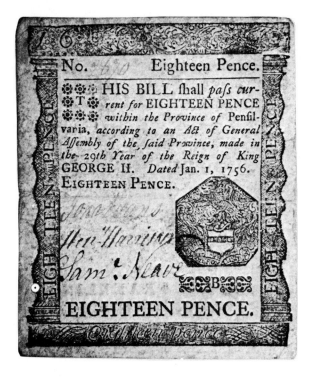
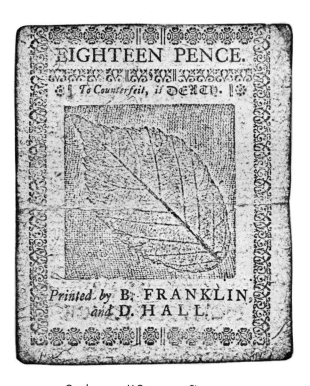

				Good	V.G.	Fine
1s	Plate letters A & B. Pensilvania	[20,000]	....	100.00	150.00	200.00
18d	Plate letters A & B. Pensilvania	[30,000]	....	100.00	150.00	200.00
2s	Plate letters A & B. Pensilvania	[30,000]	....	100.00	150.00	200.00
2s6d	Plate letters A & B. Pennsylvania	[30,000]	....	100.00	150.00	200.00
5s	Plate letters A & B. Pensilvania	[20,000]	....	100.00	150.00	200.00
10s	Plate letters A & B. Pennsilvania. Reversed S on columns	[20,000]	....	75.00	100.00	150.00
15s	Plate letters A & B. Pennsylvania	[20,000]	....	75.00	100.00	150.00
20s	Plate letters A & B. Pensylvania	[15,000]	....	75.00	100.00	150.00

October 1, 1756

£30,000 in legal tender Bills authorized by the Sept. 21, 1756 Act and good until Oct. 1, 1766. Similar in form to the Jan. 1, 1756 issue and having the same variations in the spelling of the name of the Province and the same assignment of nature prints to the back of each denomination. The number of crowns is keyed to each denomination. Printed by Benjamin Franklin and David Hall. Signers are included under the May 1, 1760 issue.

				Good	V.G.	Fine
5s	Plate letters A & B. Pensilvania	[12,000]	....	100.00	150.00	200.00
10s	Plate letters A & B. Pennsilvania. Reversed S on columns	[12,000]	....	100.00	150.00	200.00
15s	Plate letters A & B. Pennsylvania	[12,000]	....	100.00	150.00	200.00
20s	Plate letters A & B. Pensylvania	[12,000]	....	100.00	150.00	200.00

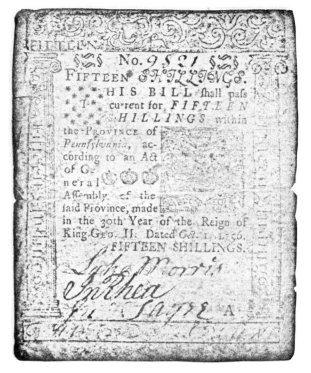

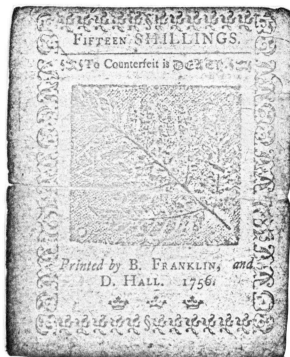

March 10, 1757

£45,000 in legal tender Bills authorized at the Session begun Oct. 14, 1756 and good until Mar. 10, 1761. Similar in form to the Jan. 1, 1756 issue and having the same variations in the spelling of the name of the Province and the same assignment of nature prints to the back of each denomination. The number of crowns is keyed to each denomination. Printed by Benjamin Franklin and David Hall. Signers are included under the May 1, 1760 issue.

			Good	V.G.	Fine
5s	Plate letters A & B. Pensilvania	[18,000]	75.00	100.00	150.00
10s	Plate letters A & B. Pennsilvania. Reversed S on columns	[18,000]	75.00	100.00	150.00
15s	Plate letters A & B. Pennsylvania	[18,000]	75.00	100.00	150.00
20s	Plate letters A & B. Pensilvania	[18,000]	75.00	100.00	150.00

July 1, 1757

£55,000 in legal tender Bills authorized by the June 17, 1757 Act and good until Mar. 1, 1761. Similar in form to the Jan. 1, 1756 issue and having the same variations in the spelling of the name of the Province and the same assignment of nature prints to the back of each denomination. The number of crowns is keyed to each denomination. Printed by Benjamin Franklin and David Hall. Signers are included under the May 1, 1760 issue.

				Good	V.G.	Fine
5s	Plate letters A & B. Pensilvania	[22,000]	. . . .	65.00	85.00	125.00
10s	Plate letters A & B. Pennsilvania. Reversed S on columns.	[22,000]	. . . .	65.00	85.00	125.00
15s	Plate letters A & B. Pennsylvania	[22,000]	. . . .	65.00	85.00	125.00
20s	Plate letters A & B. Pensylvania	[22,000]	. . . .	65.00	85.00	125.00

May 20, 1758

£100,000 in legal tender Bills authorized by the April 22, 1758 Act and good until Mar. 1, 1764. Similar in form to the Jan. 1, 1756 issue. The four lowest denominations have blank backs. The four highest denominations have the same assignment of nature prints as the Jan. 1, 1756 and intervening issues. The number of crowns is keyed to each of the highest denominations. Printed by Benjamin Franklin and David Hall. Signers are included under the May 1, 1760 issue.

				Good	V.G.	Fine
1s	[14,290]					
18d	[14,285]					
2s	[14,285]					
2s6d	[14,285]					
5s	Plate letters A & B. Pensilvania	[38,000]	. . . .	75.00	100.00	150.00
10s	Plate letters A & B. Pennsilvania. Reversed S on columns	[38,000]	. . . .	75.00	100.00	150.00
15s	Plate letters A & B. Pennsylvania	[38,000]	. . . .	75.00	100.00	150.00
20s	Plate letters A & B. Pensylvania	[38,000]	. . . .	75.00	100.00	150.00

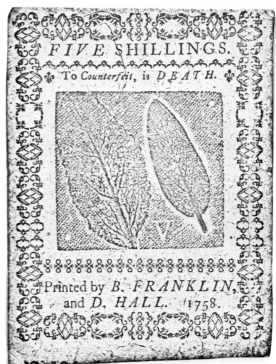

April 25, 1759

£100,000 in legal tender Bills issued pursuant to the April 17, 1759 Act and good until Mar. 1, 1767. This and all prior issues were extended until Oct. 15, 1769. Similar in form to the Jan. 1, 1756 issue. The two highest denominations are printed on both face and back in red and black by Benjamin Franklin and David Hall. The number of crowns is keyed to each of the four lowest denominations. Signers are included under the May 1, 1760 issue.

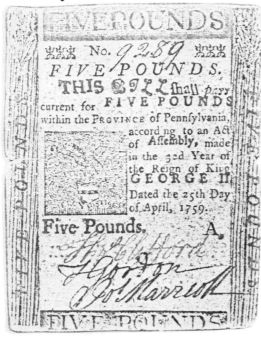

				Good	V.G.	Fine
5s	Plate letters A & B. Pensilvania	[10,000]	.....	100.00	150.00	200.00
10s	Plate letters A & B. Pennsilvania. Reversed S on columns	[10,000]	.....	100.00	150.00	200.00
15s	Plate letters A & B. Pennsylvania	[10,000]	.....	75.00	100.00	150.00
20s	Plate letters A & B. Pensylvania	[10,000]	.....	75.00	100.00	150.00
50s	Plate letters C & D. Pensylvania	[10,000]	.....	75.00	100.00	150.00
£5	Plate letters A & B. Pennsylvania	[10,000]	.....	75.00	100.00	150.00

PENNSYLVANIA

June 21, 1759

£36,650 in Bills approved by the Act passed at the Session ending May 21, 1759, but repealed by the Crown in June 1760. The bills were issued before the repeal occurred and were withdrawn when the repeal was known. Similar in style to the high denominations of the April 25, 1759 issue and with the corresponding nature prints. Printed on both face and back in red and black by Benjamin Franklin and David Hall. Signers are included under the May 1, 1760 issue.

50s   Plate letters C & D. Pensylvania [4,888]

£5   Plate letters A & B. Pennsylvania [4,886]

May 1, 1760

£100,000 in Bills authorized by the April 12, 1760 Act. The two highest denominations are printed in red and black on both face and back by Benjamin Franklin and David Hall. The pence denominations are small in size and have typeset backs. The number of crowns is keyed to the denominations from 5s through 20s. Detector specimens on blue paper. An Act of April 17, 1761 for an additional £30,000 in 50s and £5 bills was disapproved by the Governor. Signers of issues from Oct. 1, 1755 through May 1, 1760 are John Baynton, Daniel Benezet, James Benezet, Thomas Bourne, George Bryan, Robert Bully, Samuel Burge, Stephen Carmick, Thomas Carpenter, Peter Chevalier, James Child, Matthew Clarkson, Thomas Clifford, Redmond Conyngham, Thomas Coombe, Jacob Cooper, Thomas Crosby, Thomas Davis, Matthew Drason, Jacob Duche, Edward Duffield, James Eddy, George Emlen, Jonathan Evans, William Fisher, Plunket Fleeson, Enoch Flower, Joseph Fox, Joseph Galloway, Thomas Gordon, William Grant, Isaac Greenleafe, William Griffiths, Henry Harrison, Samuel Hazard, Joseph Hillborn, William Hopkins, Joshua Howell, Samuel Howell, John Hughes, Charles Humphreys, James Humphreys, Abel James, John Jervis, Charles Jones, Isaac Jones, Owen Jones, Edmund Kearney, Joseph King, Jacob Lewis, William Logan, John Lynn, Joseph Marriott, Charles Meredith, Thomas Moore, Evan Morgan, Joseph Morris, Luke Morris, Samuel Morris, William Morris, Jr., George Morrison, Samuel Neave, George Okill, John Ord, Joseph Parker, Isaac Paschall, Richard Pearne, James Pemberton, Edward Penington, Francis Rawle, Joseph Redman, Peter Reeve, John Reynell, John Rhea, Samuel Rhoads, Jr., Joseph Richardson, Daniel Roberdeau, Hugh Roberts, Daniel Rundle, Samuel Sansom, Joseph Saunders, Thomas Say, John Sayre, William Shippen, Atwood Shute, Buckridge Sims, John Smith, Samuel Smith, Thomas Smith, Charles Steadman, Joseph Stretch, Amos Strettell, John Swift, John Taylor, Charles Thomson, Thomas Tilbury, William Vanderspiegel, James Wharton, Joseph Wharton, Jr., Samuel Wharton, Thomas Wharton, Daniel Williams, Richard Wister, Stephen Woolley, and Thomas Yorke.

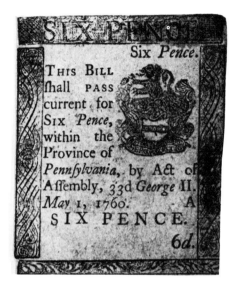

			Good	V.G.	Fine
3d	Plate letters A, B, & C [10,909] Ⓤ				
4d	Plate letters A, B, & C [10,909] Ⓤ				
6d	Plate letters A, B, & C [10,909] Ⓤ				
9d	Plate letters A, B, & C [10,909] Ⓤ				
5s	Plate letters A & B. Pensilvania [9,900]		100.00	150.00	200.00
10s	Plate Letters A & B. Pennsylvania. Reversed S on columns [9,900]		100.00	150.00	200.00
15s	Plate letters A & B. Pennsylvania [9,900]		100.00	150.00	200.00
20s	Plate letters A & B. Pensilvania [9,900] Ⓒ . . .		75.00	100.00	150.00
50s	Plate letters C & D. Pensylvania [9,900]		75.00	100.00	150.00
£5	Plate letters A & B. Pennsylvania [9,900] Ⓒ . . .		75.00	100.00	150.00

June 18, 1764

£55,000 in legal tender Bills authorized by the May 30, 1764 Act and good until Oct. 1, 1772. Later in 1764 Parliament prohibited a legal tender status for any colonial paper money. The four lowest denominations are small in size and have typeset backs. Other denominations have nature prints on the back. Printed by Benjamin Franklin and David Hall using British Arms instead of Penn Arms. Signers are William Bingham, Jonathan Bringhurst, Thomas Clifford, George Clymer*, George Dillwyn, Henry Drinker, Jonathan Evans, John Gibson, Jr., Henry Harrison, A. Hillborn, Samuel Hudson, Jonathan Hughes, Jr., Joseph Jacobs, Abel James, William Lloyd, T. Mayburry, J. Mease, Jr., Jonathan Mifflin, Benjamin Morgan, S. P. Moore, Cadwalader Morris, Samuel Morris, Jr., Samuel Neave, Charles Pettit, Peter Reeve, Samuel Rhoads, Jr., G. Roberts, Joseph Saunders, Jacob Shoemaker, Jr., Joseph Sims, Jr., Joseph Stamper, Isaac Stretch, Joseph Stretch, E. Story, and Thomas Wharton.

*Bills bearing the signature of George Clymer, signer of the Declaration of Independence, are very rare.

			Good	V.G.	Fine
3d	Plate letters A, B, & C. Pennsilvania [80,000] ...		65	85	125
4d	Plate letters A, B, & C. Pensylvania [60,000] ...		65	85	125
6d	Plate letters A, B, & C. Pennsylvania [60,000] ...		65	85	125
9d	Plate letters A, B, & C. Pennsylvania [60,000] ...		65	85	125
1s	Plate letters A & B. Pennsilvania [37,000]		65	85	125
1s6d	Plate letters A & B [22,000]		65	85	125
2s	Plate letters A & B [20,000]		65	85	125
2s6d	Plate letters A & B [20,000]		65	85	125
5s	Plate letters A, B, C, & D. Pensylvania [40,000] ..		65	85	125
10s	Plate letters A & B. Pennsilvania. Reversed S on columns [20,500]		65	85	125
20s	Plate letters A & B. Pennsylvania [21,000]		65	85	125

PENNSYLVANIA

Philadelphia Merchants ★ December 1766

£20,000 in Promissory Notes issued by a group of Philadelphia merchants in Dec. 1766 to alleviate a shortage of circulating public money. Payable to bearer in Aug. 1767 with 5% interest. The thought of anyone having the uncontrolled right to issue "valueless" currency caused 200 tradesmen to present a remonstrance to the Assembly in Jan. 1767 for prohibition of such practices.

£5 [4,000]

June 15, 1767

£20,000 in Bills approved by the May 20, 1767 Act after consideration of a further proposal by the merchants to issue privately £20,000 in £5 notes bearing 5% interest. Two separate nature prints from prior issues were printed on the back of each denomination. The denomination is cut into the nature prints after casting. The face has a cut of Penn Arms and states that the bills are indented but they are not. Printed by David Hall and William Sellers, successors to Franklin and Hall. Test bills are on blue paper. Signers are John Gibson, Isaac Greenleafe, Isaac Jones, J. Mease, John Nixon, Israel Pemberton, John Reynell, Samuel Rhoads, Jr., Joseph Richardson, Daniel Roberdeau, and Thomas Wharton.

40s	Plate letters A, B, C, & D [2,000] Ⓓ
£4	Plate letters A & B [1,000] Ⓓ
£6	Plate letters A, B, C, & D [2,000] Ⓓ

March 1, 1769

£16,000 in Bills of Credit issued pursuant to the Feb. 18, 1769 Act. Penn Arms are on the face and nature prints are on the back. Called for redemption because of the extensive circulation of excellent counterfeits. Printed by David Hall and William Sellers. Face states bills are indented, but they are not. Signers are John Gibson, Jr., Isaac Greenleafe, Isaac Jones, John Nixon, Israel Pemberton, John Reynell, Joseph Richardson, Daniel Roberdeau, and Thomas Wharton.

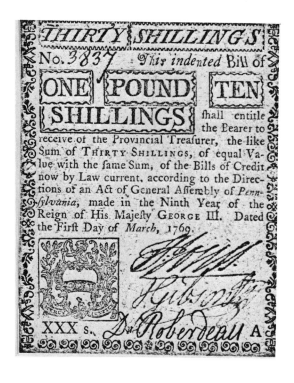

		Good	V.G.	Fine
8s	Pensilvania [1,000]	125.00	200.00	300.00
12s	Pensylvania [1,000]	125.00	200.00	300.00
£1 10s (30s)	Plate letters A, B, & C. Pennsylvania [4,000] ©	100.00	150.00	250.00
£3	Plate letters A & B. Pennsilvania [3,000] ©	100.00	150.00	250.00

March 10, 1769

£14,000 in Bills known as "Bettering House Money" and authorized by the Feb. 18, 1769 Act for the relief and employment of the Poor in Philadelphia. The four lowest denominations are small in size. The eight lowest denominations have blank backs. The four highest denominations have nature prints on the back. The bills state that they are indented but they are not. Printed by Hall & Sellers. Signers are Samuel Burge, Stephen Collins, Joseph Fox, Abel James, Jacob Lewis, Luke Morris, John Parrock, James Penrose, Samuel Rhoads, Jr., Thomas Say, Charles Thomson, and Joseph Wharton, Jr. One signer is on the four lowest denominations and three are on the others.

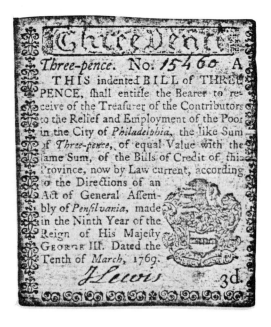

		Good	V.G.	Fine
3d	Plate letters A, B, & C. Pensilvania [30,000] ©	100.00	125.00	175.00
4d	(Groat) Plate letters A, B, & C. Pennsylvania [30,000]	100.00	125.00	175.00
6d	Plate letters A, B, & C. Pensilvania [30,000]	100.00	125.00	175.00
9d	Plate letters A, B, & C. Pennsylvania [30,000]	100.00	125.00	175.00
1s	Plate letters A, B, C, & D. Pennsylvania [30,000] ©	75.00	100.00	150.00
18d	Plate letters A, B, C, & D. Pennsylvania [30,000] ©	75.00	100.00	150.00
2s	Plate letters A, B, C, & D. Pensilvania [20,000]	75.00	100.00	150.00
2s6d	(Half Crown) Plate letters A & B. Pensilvania [12,000]	75.00	100.00	150.00
5s	(Crown) Plate letters A, B, C, & D. Pennsylvania [5,000]	75.00	100.00	150.00
10s	Asterisk follows date on face. On lower border 12 identical ornaments to right of colon. Pensilvania [1,000]	75.00	100.00	150.00
10s	No asterisk follows date on face. On lower border 11 identical ornaments to right of colon. Pensilvania [1,000]	75.00	100.00	150.00
15s	Pennsylvania [1,000]	75.00	100.00	150.00
20s	Pennsylvania [1,000]	75.00	100.00	150.00

March 20, 1771

£15,000 in Bills authorized by the Mar. 9, 1771 Act for the defense of Philadelphia, but used for paving streets. Penn Arms are on the face with cast border cuts. Nature prints on the back. Printed in red and black on the face with the number of crowns keyed to each denomination. Printed by David Hall and William Sellers on paper containing mica flakes. Signers are Stephen Collins, Isaac Cox, Joel Evans, William Fisher, Francis Hopkinson*, Joshua Howell, Robert Strettell Jones, Thomas Mifflin, Joseph Morris, Luke Morris, Daniel Roberdeau, and Jacob Shoemaker.

		V.G.	Fine	V.F.
5s	Plate letters A & B. Pensilvania [6,000]	35.00	75.00	100.00
10s	Plate letters A & B. Pensylvania. Reversed S on columns [6,000] ...	35.00	75.00	100.00
15s	Plate letters A & B. Pennsilvania [6,000]	35.00	75.00	100.00
20s	Plate letters A & B. Pennsylvania [6,000] ©	35.00	75.00	100.00

*Signature of Francis Hopkinson, signer of the Declaration of Independence, triples the value shown.

April 3, 1772

£25,000 in Bills issued pursuant to the Mar. 21, 1772 Act. The pence denominations are small in size and their backs are typeset. The back of the 2s6d has a chevron design cut. The other backs have nature prints. First appearance of the name of James Smither as engraver of border cuts. Printed by Hall & Sellers on paper containing mica flakes. The face of the 40s is printed in red and black. Signers are Clement Biddle, Thomas Clifford, Samuel Coates, Thomas Coombe, Isaac Cox, Joseph Dean, Joel Evans, Thomas Fisher, Samuel Howell, Jr., Adam Hubley, Samuel Hudson, Charles Humphreys, John Mifflin, Anthony Morris, Jr., Cadwalader Morris, John Morton*, Samuel Pleasants, Joseph Pemberton, John Sellers, Joseph Sims, Jr., Joseph Swift, Jeremiah Warder, Jr., James Wharton, and Benjamin Wynkoop. One signer for the four lowest denominations and three for the others.

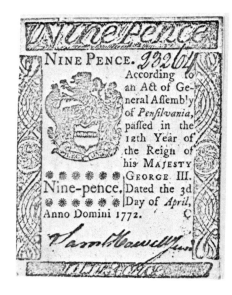

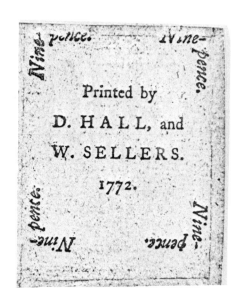

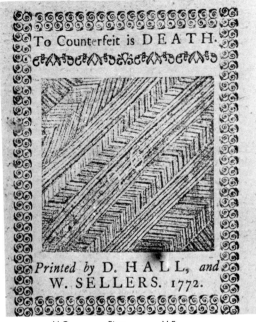

		V.G.	Fine	V.F.
3d	Plate letters A, B, & C. Pennsilvania [33,962]	25.00	35.00	50.00
4d	Plate letters A, B, & C. Pennsilvania [33,963]	25.00	35.00	50.00
6d	Plate letters A, B, & C. Pennsilvania [33,962]	25.00	35.00	50.00
9d	Plate letters A, B, & C. Pensilvania [33,962]	25.00	35.00	50.00
1s	Plate letters A & B. Pennsylvania [33,962]	20.00	30.00	40.00
18d	Plate letters A & B. Pennsilvania [33,962]	20.00	30.00	40.00
2s	Plate letters A & B. Pennsylvania [33,962]	20.00	30.00	40.00
2s6d	Plate letters A & B. Pensilvania [33,962]	20.00	30.00	40.00
40s	Plate letters A, B, C, & D. Pennsylvania.			
	J. SMITHER SCULP in top border cut [5,000]	50.00	100.00	150.00

*Signature of John Morton, signer of the Declaration of Independence, doubles the value shown.

March 20, 1773

£12,000 in Bills for the construction of the Cape Henlopen Lighthouse, and piers and buoys, pursuant to the Feb. 20, 1773 Act. A
cast cut of a lighthouse is on the back with the denomination
incised. Printed by Hall & Sellers on paper containing mica flakes.
Detector bills are on blue paper. Signers are Charles Jervis, Henry
Keppele, Jr., Frederick Kuhl, Benjamin Shoemaker, John Stein-
metz, and Jacob Winey.

			V.G.	Fine	V.F.
4s	Plate letters A & B. Pensilvania [6,000] Ⓓ		30.00	40.00	55.00
6s	Plate A. Penn Arms upside down. Pennsilvania [3,000] Ⓓ		45.00	55.00	75.00
6s	Plate B. Penn Arms in proper position. Pennsilvania [3,000] Ⓓ ...		30.00	40.00	55.00
14s	Plate letters A & B. Pensilvania [6,000] Ⓓ		30.00	40.00	55.00
16s	Plate letters A & B. Pennsilvania [6,000] Ⓓ		30.00	40.00	55.00

October 1, 1773

£150,000 in Bills authorized by the Feb. 1, 1773 Act to revive the Loan Office system. A cast cut of a farming scene is on the back. The number of crowns is keyed to each of the five highest denominations. The face is printed in red and black with one border being in both colors and with denomination worked into the set type in red on the four highest denominations. Printed by Hall & Sellers on paper containing mica flakes and blue fibres. Signers are Joseph Allen, Barnaby Barnes, Stephen Carmick, William Crispin, Benedict Dorsey, George Emlen, Jr., John Field, Samuel Fisher, William Fisher, Jr., Jacob Harman, James Hartley, Owen Jones, Jr., Reynold Keen, Thomas Leech, Mordecai Lewis, John Lownes, Benjamin Marshall, Charles Meredith, Joseph Mifflin, Samuel Miles, Benjamin Morgan, Joseph Pemberton, James Stephens, Alexander Tod, Robert Tuckniss, Abraham Usher, Isaac Wharton, Richard Willing, William Wishart, and William Wister.

		Fine	V.F.	E.F.
18d	Pensilvania [28,318]	20.00	25.00	35.00
2s	Pensilvania [28,319]	20.00	25.00	35.00
2s6d	Pensilvania [28,318]	20.00	25.00	35.00
5s	Pensilvania [28,318]	20.00	25.00	35.00
10s	Pensilvania. Red X [28,300]	20.00	25.00	35.00
15s	Pensilvania. Red XV [28,300]	20.00	25.00	35.00
20s	Pennsilvania. Red I meaning £1 [28,300]	20.00	25.00	35.00
50s	Pennsilvania. Red L [28,300] Ⓒ	20.00	25.00	35.00

March 25, 1775

£6,000 in Bills for the Cape Henlopen Lighthouse, and buoys and piers, pursuant to the Mar. 18, 1775 Act. In the same style as the Mar. 20, 1773 issue. Printed by Hall & Sellers on paper containing mica flakes. Signers are Samuel Coates, Ezekiel Edwards, Richard Vaux, Charles Wharton, James Wharton, and William Wishart.

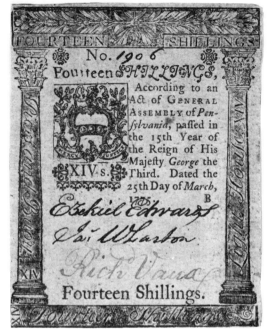
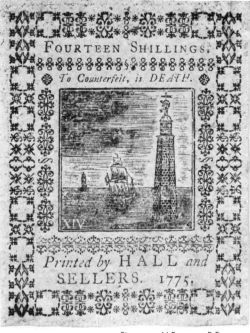

			Fine	V.F.	E.F.
4s	Plate letters A & B. Pensilvania	[3,000]	45.00	65.00	100.00
6s	Plate letters A & B. Pennsylvania	[3,000]	45.00	65.00	100.00
14s	Plate letters A & B. Pensylvania. Inverted back	[3,000]	45.00	65.00	100.00
16s	Plate letters A & B. Pennsylvania. Inverted back	[3,000]	45.00	65.00	100.00

April 10, 1775

£25,000 in Bills for the construction of jails and correctional institutions pursuant to the Mar. 18, 1775 Act. The face is similar to the same denominations of the April 25, 1759 issue. A view of the Walnut Street Workhouse (the city jail of Philadelphia) is on the back and the text above and below it is upside down. Printed by Hall & Sellers in red and black on both the face and back. The paper contains mica flakes. Signers are Job Bacon, Lindsay Coats, and Edward Roberts.

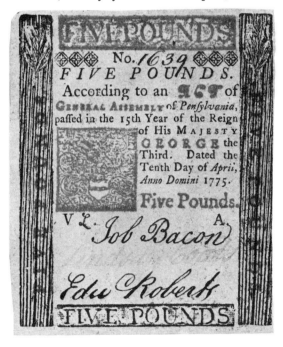

				Fine	V.F.	E.F.
50s	Plate C. Pennsilvania	[1,667]	.....	50.00	80.00	125.00
50s	Plate D. Pennsylvania	[1,667]	.....	50.00	80.00	125.00
£5	Plate A. Pensylvania	[1,667]	.....	50.00	80.00	125.00
£5	Plate B. Pensilvania	[1,666]	.....	50.00	80.00	125.00

July 20, 1775

£35,000 in Bills issued pursuant to the June 30, 1775 Resolve. This and subsequent issues were known as Resolve Money because the approval of the Royal Governor was not given. English Arms are revived on the face. The number of crowns is keyed to each denomination. Printed by Hall & Sellers on paper containing mica flakes and blue silk thread. Reuse of separate nature prints for each denomination. Signers are William Allen, Jr., John Benezet, Lambert Cadwalader, Sharp Delany, Isaac Howell, Adam Hubley, James Mease, John Mease, Samuel C. Morris, Thomas Pryor, John Purviance, and Godfrey Twells.

			Fine	V.F.	E.F.
10s	Plate A. Reversed S on left column. Pennsylvania [3,500]		30.00	40.00	50.00
10s	Plate B. Reversed S on right column. Pennsylvania [3,500]		30.00	40.00	50.00
20s	Plate A. Capital letters on right column. Pennsylvania [3,500]		30.00	40.00	50.00
20s	Plate B. Capital letters on left column. Pennsylvania [3,500]		30.00	40.00	50.00
30s	Plate A. Pensylvania [3,500]		30.00	40.00	50.00
30s	Plate B. Pensilvania [3,500]		30.00	40.00	50.00
40s	Plate A. Pensilvania. J. SMITHER SCULP. [3,500]		30.00	40.00	50.00
40s	Plate B. Pensilvania. J. SMITHER SCULP. [3,500]		30.00	40.00	50.00

PENNSYLVANIA

October 25, 1775

£22,000 in Bills issued pursuant to the Sept. 30, 1775 Resolve. The Penn Arms are on all denominations. The four lowest denominations are small in size and have typeset backs. The 2s6d has a chevron design on the back. All others have nature prints on the back. The number of crowns is keyed to each of the four highest denominations. Printed on paper containing mica flakes and blue silk threads. Signers are Abel Evans, Henry Hale Graham, Adam Grubb, Isaac Howell, Richard Humphreys, Charles Jervis, Francis Johnston, Philip Kinsey, John Knowles, Thomas Shoemaker, Thomas Tilbury, and Jonathan Warder. One signer is on the four lowest denominations and three signers are on the others.

			Fine	V.F.	E.F.
3d	Plate letters A, B, & C. Pennsylvania [15,849]		15.00	25.00	35.00
4d	Plate letters A, B, & C. Pennsilvania [15,849]		15.00	25.00	35.00
6d	Plate letters A, B, & C. Pensylvania [15,850]		15.00	25.00	35.00
9d	Plate letters A, B, & C. Pensilvania [15,849]		15.00	25.00	35.00
1s	S for Smither in top border. Pensylvania [15,849] ..		15.00	25.00	35.00
18d	Pennsilvania [15,849]		15.00	25.00	35.00
2s	Pensylvania [15,849]		15.00	25.00	35.00
2s6d	(Half Crown) Plate A. Pennsylvania [15,849]		15.00	25.00	35.00
5s	(Crown) Pennsylvania [6,000]		20.00	30.00	40.00
10s	Pennsylvania [6,000]		20.00	30.00	40.00
15s	Pensilvania [6,000]		20.00	30.00	40.00
20s	Pensylvania [6,000]		20.00	30.00	40.00

Ignace Labate, etc. ★ October 25, 1775

Typeset bills payable in Pennsylvania currency and issued at Pittsburgh with various signatures. Apparently a standard form for general use by merchants. Blank backs.

6d
1s
2s

December 8, 1775

£80,000 in Bills issued pursuant to the Nov. 18, 1775 Resolve. Similar in style to the July 20, 1775 issue and with British Arms. The number of crowns is keyed to each denomination. Printed on paper containing blue silk thread. Signers are Cornelius Barnes, Matthew Clarkson, William Crispin, George Douglass, Abel Evans, Nicholas Fairlamb, Josiah Hewes, William Kenly, Thomas Leech, Charles Moore, Thomas Moore, Samuel C. Morris. Sketchly Morton, Elisha Price, Joseph Redman, William Smith, Peter Thomson, Godfrey Twells, and Andrew Tybout.

		Fine	V.F.	E.F.
10s	Plate A. Reversed S on left column [8,000]	15.00	25.00	35.00
10s	Plate B. Reversed S on right column [8,000]	15.00	25.00	35.00
20s	Plate A. Capital letters on right column [8,000]	15.00	25.00	35.00
20s	Plate B. Capital letters on left column [8,000]	15.00	25.00	35.00
30s	Plate letters A & B. Pensilvania [16,000]	15.00	25.00	35.00
40s	Plate letters A & B. Pensilvania. J. SMITHER SCULP. [16,000]	15.00	25.00	35.00

PENNSYLVANIA

April 25, 1776

£85,000 in Bills issued pursuant to the April 6, 1776 Resolve. Similar in size and style to the Oct. 25, 1775 issue, except that British Arms are on denominations of 1s and over. The number of crowns is keyed to each of the three highest denominations (not on 10s). Printed on paper containing mica flakes and blue silk threads. Signers are Cornelius Barnes, Benjamin Betterton, William Clifton, William Crispin, George Douglass, Abel Evans, Josiah Hewes, William Kenly, Hugh Lloyd, Charles Moore, Thomas Moore, Samuel C. Morris, Sketchly Morton, Elisha Price, Joseph Redman, William Smith, Peter Thomson, and Andrew Tybout. One signer is on the four lowest denominations, two signers are on the four middle denominations and three signers are on the highest four.

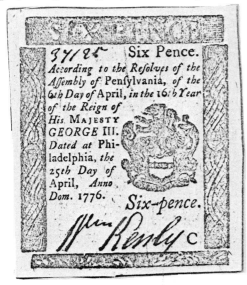
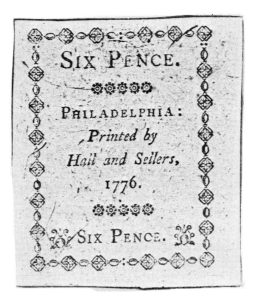
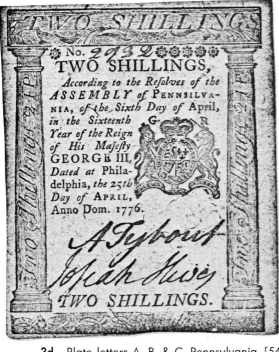
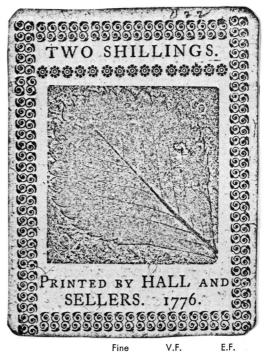

			Fine	V.F.	E.F.
3d	Plate letters A, B, & C. Pennsylvania [54,545]		10.00	20.00	35.00
4d	Plate letters A, B, & C. Pensilvania [54,546]		10.00	20.00	35.00
6d	Plate letters A, B, & C. Pensilvania [54,546]		10.00	20.00	35.00
9d	Plate letters A, B, & C. Pensilvania [54,545]		10.00	20.00	35.00
1s	Pennsylvania. S for Smither in top border [28,572]		15.00	25.00	40.00
18d	Pennsylvania [28,571]		15.00	25.00	40.00
2s	Pennsilvania [28,572]		15.00	25.00	40.00
2s6d	Pennsylvania [28,571]		15.00	25.00	40.00

		Fine	V.F.	E.F.
10s	Plate A. Pennsylvania. Reversed S on right column [7,000]	20.00	35.00	45.00
10s	Plate B. Pennsilvania. Reversed S on left column [7,000]	20.00	35.00	45.00
20s	Plate A. Pennsilvania. Capital letters on right column [7,000] ...	20.00	35.00	45.00
20s	Plate B. Pennsilvania. Capital letters on left column [7,000]	20.00	35.00	45.00
30s	Plate A. Pensylvania [7,000]	20.00	35.00	45.00
30s	Plate B. Pensilvania [7,000]	20.00	35.00	45.00
40s	Plate A. Pensylvania. J. SMITHER SCULP. [7,000]	20.00	35.00	45.00
40s	Plate B. Pensilvania. J. SMITHER SCULP. [7,000]	20.00	35.00	45.00

Joseph Ogden ★ January 18, 1777

Private issue of Joseph Ogden, operator of the Middle Ferry across the Schuylkill River at Philadelphia, to make change in collecting fares. Typeset with ornamental type as borders. Blank backs. Watermarks in the paper are PPD and the motto WORK & BE RICH. Signed by Joseph Ogden.

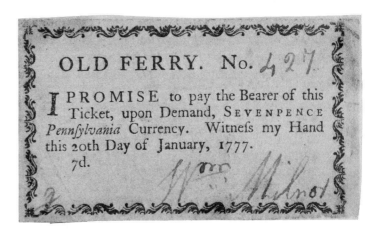

		Unc.
3d	Ⓤ	100.00
4d	Ⓤ	100.00
5d	Ⓤ	100.00
6d	Ⓤ	100.00
9d	Ⓤ	100.00

Ⓤ

William Milnor ★ January 20, 1777

Private small change issue by the operator of "Old Ferry" across the Delaware River from the foot of Market Street in Philadelphia. Other denominations are probable.

3d
7d

Joseph Sommerville ★ February 1, 1777

Private issue of Joseph Sommerville at Hanna's Town near Pittsburgh. Archaeological excavation at this site has yielded many types of coins circulating in Colonial America. Signer's initials printed. Blank back.

1s

306

PENNSYLVANIA

April 10, 1777 in Black

£200,000 in Bills issued pursuant to the Mar. 20, 1777 Act for army support. Arms of the Commonwealth of Pennsylvania were introduced on money. Pence denominations are small in size, each plate letter variety having a different face border. All higher denominations have a new oblong shape and a cast cut of the same farming scene on the back. Printed by John Dunlap in black on paper watermarked PENSYL on one line and VANIA below. By the Mar. 3, 1778 Act all prior issues were to be exchanged for this issue by June 1, 1778. By the Acts of Dec. 23, 1780, April 7, 1781, and Dec. 4, 1789 this and prior issues were exchangeable at 75 for 1 and were to become invalid after Jan. 1, 1791. Bills numbered in red ink. Signers are Philip Alberti, Frederick Antes, Benjamin Betterton, John Browne, Levi Budd, James Cannon, James Davidson (Davison), Caleb Davis, William Evans, Joseph Gardner, Andrew Hodge, Isaac Howell, Whitehead Humphreys, Benjamin Jacobs, William Kenly, Henry Leuthauser, Robert Loller, Joseph Parker, Michael Shubart, Samuel Smith, Isaac Snowden, William Thorne, William Will, and I. Young, Jr. One signer is on the eight lowest denominations and two signers are on the others.

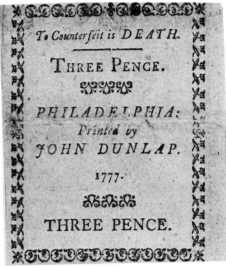

			Fine	V.F.	E.F.
3d	Plate A	[50,000]	10.00	15.00	25.00
3d	Plate B	[50,000]	10.00	15.00	25.00
3d	Plate C	[50,000]	10.00	15.00	25.00
4d	Plate A	[50,000]	10.00	15.00	25.00
4d	Plate B	[50,000]	10.00	15.00	25.00
4d	Plate C	[50,000]	10.00	15.00	25.00
6d	Plate A	[50,000]	10.00	15.00	25.00
6d	Plate B	[50,000]	10.00	15.00	25.00
6d	Plate C	[50,000]	10.00	15.00	25.00
9d	Plate A	[50,000]	10.00	15.00	25.00
9d	Plate B	[50,000]	10.00	15.00	25.00
9d	Plate C	[50,000]	10.00	15.00	25.00
1s	[30,000]		15.00	20.00	30.00
1s6d	[30,000]		15.00	20.00	30.00
2s	[30,000]		15.00	20.00	30.00
3s	[30,000]		15.00	20.00	30.00
4s	[30,000]		15.00	20.00	30.00
6s	[30,000]		15.00	20.00	30.00
8s	[30,000]		15.00	20.00	30.00
12s	[30,000]		15.00	20.00	30.00
16s	[30,000]		15.00	20.00	30.00
20s	[30,000]		15.00	20.00	30.00
40s	[12,670]		20.00	25.00	35.00
40s	Back of £4				
£4	[12,665]		20.00	25.00	35.00
£4	Back of 40s				

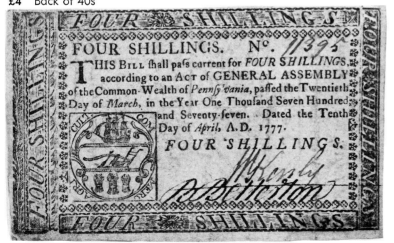

April 10, 1777 in Red and Black

The balance of the £200,000 issue of same date was printed in red and black on both the face and back, except 40s and £4 which are printed in black on the back. Additional typeset black border added on face of 40s and £4. The number authorized was included in the black issue. The numbering overlaps that of the black issue. The same paper and signers as the black issue.

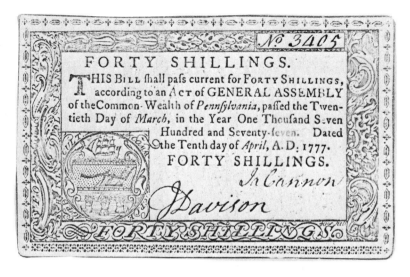

	Fine	V.F.	E.F.
1s	20.00	30.00	50.00
1s6d	20.00	30.00	50.00
2s	20.00	30.00	50.00
3s	20.00	30.00	50.00
4s	20.00	30.00	50.00
6s	20.00	30.00	50.00
8s	20.00	30.00	50.00
12s	20.00	30.00	50.00
16s	20.00	30.00	50.00
20s	20.00	30.00	50.00
40s	25.00	40.00	60.00
£4	25.00	40.00	60.00

April 29, 1780

£100,000 in "Island Money" was issued to purchase provisions for the Army pursuant to the Mar. 25, 1780 Act. Secured by land including Province Island in Kingsessing and payable with 5% interest on June 1, 1784. Made legal tender by the Dec. 23, 1780 Act but the value sank to 3 for 1 in specie in 1781. The date of invalidity was finally extended to Jan. 1, 1793 by the April 7, 1791 Act and the issue redeemed with specie. Printed by John Dunlap on paper watermarked PENSYL on one line and VANIA below. A new set of nature prints on the backs. Signers are William L. Blair, Philip Boehm, Levi Budd, Robert Cather, Nathan Jones, John Knox, John Miller, Jedediah Snowden, William Thorne, Charles L. Treichel, Joseph Watkins, and Daniel Wister.

5s [8,696]		30s [8,696]	
10s [8,696]		40s [8,694]	
15s [8,696]		50s [8,696]	
20s [8,696]		60s [8,696]	

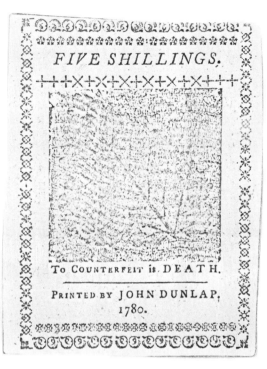

June 1, 1780

$1,250,000 in "Dollar Money" payable in Spanish milled dollars by Dec. 31, 1786 with 5% interest was authorized by the June 1, 1780 Act pursuant to the Continental Congress Resolution of Mar. 18, 1780, guaranteeing the payment of the bills and making the amount issued dependent upon the amount of Continental Currency exchanged at $40 (old) for $1 (new). Redemption, extension and destruction of the issue was provided for in the Acts of Dec. 19, 1780, Mar. 17, 1786, Mar. 22, 1788, Nov. 22, 1788 and April 10, 1792 with final invalidity on July 1, 1792. Face is in black. Back is in red and black.

Printed by Hall & Sellers on paper watermarked CONFEDE on one line and RATION below. Face border cuts and back cut surrounding emblem were engraved by Henry Dawkins. Border cuts and emblem on the back are from the Jan. 14, 1779 issue of Continental Currency. Sometimes surcharged INT. PD. 1 YEAR. Signers are William L. Blair, Philip Boehm, Levi Budd, Robert Cather, Nathan Jones, John Knox, John Miller, Jedediah Snowden, Michael Shubart, and Daniel Wister. Guaranty is signed by Richard Bache and Thomas Smith.

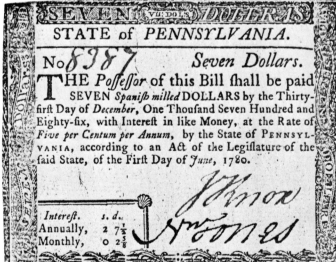

		V.G.	Fine	E.F.
$1	[25,000]	250.00	325.00	450.00
$2	[25,000]	250.00	325.00	450.00
$3	[25,000]	250.00	325.00	450.00
$4	[25,000]	250.00	325.00	450.00
$5	[25,000]	250.00	325.00	450.00
$7	DOLLRAS misspelled [25,000] .	250.00	325.00	450.00
$8	[25,000]	250.00	325.00	450.00
$20	[25,000]	250.00	325.00	450.00

PENNSYLVANIA

April 20, 1781

£486,500 (£500,000 less £13,500) in NEW BILLS issued pursuant to the April 7, 1781 and Jan. 31, 1783 Acts to support the Army and to exchange for the April 10, 1777 and prior issues at depreciated rates. Printed by John Dunlap on paper watermarked PENSYLVANIA in two lines. Pellets in the Arms are keyed to the denominations. The four lowest denominations are small in size and have typeset backs. Chevron pattern is on the 2s6d and a farming scene from the April 10, 1777 issue is on the £5. The backs of others have previously used

nature prints. Trial specimens of some backs exist. Signers are Richard Bache, John Baynton, Philip Boehm, Jacob Barge, James Budden, Joseph Bullock, Samuel Caldwell, David H. Cunningham, Joseph Dean, Tench Francis, Isaac Howell, Jacob S. Howell, Robert Knox, John Mease, Samuel Meredith, Jonathan Mifflin, John Miller, Cadwalader Morris, John Patten, Thomas Pryor, John Purviance, David Schaffer, Jr., Michael Shubart, and Joseph Wharton. The seven lowest denominations have one signer and the others have two signers.

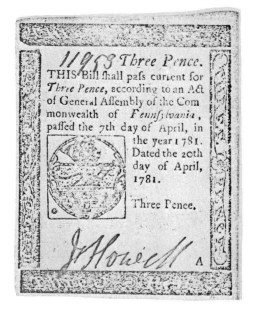

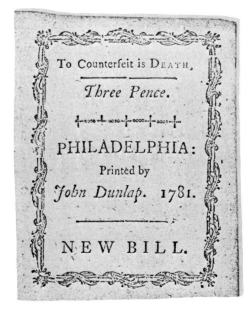

		Good	V.G.	Fine
3d	Plate A. Pence misspelled PENEE at end of text [20,000]	75.00	100.00	150.00
3d	Plate B [20,000]	50.00	60.00	90.00
6d	Plate A. Lower border words separate [20,000]	50.00	60.00	90.00
6d	Plate B. Lower border words too close [20,000]	50.00	60.00	90.00
9d	Plate A. Lower border letters are black [20,000]	50.00	60.00	90.00
9d	Plate B. Lower border letters are white [20,000]	50.00	60.00	90.00
1s6d	[20,000]	60.00	75.00	100.00
2s	Plate A [20,000]	60.00	75.00	100.00
2s6d	Plate A [20,000]	60.00	75.00	100.00
5s	Plate A [20,000]	60.00	75.00	100.00
10s	[29,076]	75.00	100.00	150.00
15s	[29,076]	75.00	100.00	150.00
20s	[29,077]	75.00	100.00	150.00
30s	DNNLAP misspelled [29,077]	75.00	100.00	150.00
40s	[29,077]	75.00	100.00	150.00
50s	[29,077]	75.00	100.00	150.00
60s	[29,077]	75.00	100.00	150.00
£5	[29,077]	75.00	100.00	150.00

Bank of North America ★ 1782, etc.

The Bank of North America, sponsored primarily by Robert Morris, was perpetually incorporated by the Continental Congress on Dec. 31, 1781 with a capital of $400,000 divided into 1,000 shares of $400 each. The Ordinance of incorporation provided that the bank had no authority to exercise any power in any State contrary to the laws of such State. It was permitted to issue bank notes in accordance with a Plan previously submitted to Congress on May 17, 1781 and approved by Congress on May 26, 1781. These bank notes were to be accepted in all payments due to the United States and the States themselves. The United States purchased and paid for 633 shares and promptly borrowed the money back for governmental purposes. The bank opened for business in Philadelphia on Jan. 7, 1782.

In Pennsylvania the bank was separately incorporated on April 1, 1782, followed by an annulment of the charter on Sept. 13, 1785 and a reincorporation for 20 years on Mar. 17, 1787. It was incorporated in New York on April 11, 1782 and granted the exclusive right to conduct the banking business in that State during the remainder of the War. Massachusetts gave it corporate status on Mar. 8, 1782 and Delaware also did on Feb. 2, 1786. Delaware had previously protected the Bank's circulating notes with a special counterfeiting law on Feb. 8, 1783 as did Rhode Island in Jan. 1782. On Jan. 7, 1782, Connecticut made bank notes of the Bank of North America receivable there for taxes.

Although the bank notes originally issued by the Bank of North America were discounted as much as 15% in exchange for specie, they circulated at par before the year 1782 ended. These bank notes were engraved and had partially written dates. The earlier emissions were signed by Thomas Willing as president (1781-92) and by Tench Francis as cashier (1781-92), followed by John Nixon as president (1792-1808) and Richard Wells as cashier (1792-1800). No normal genuine notes of the 18th century other than small change notes issued in 1789 have been located and the source of information about dollar denomination notes has been obtained from proof, counterfeit and altered notes.

The Pennsylvania Bank (1780-84), acting originally as an unincorporated predecessor in Philadelphia, did not issue circulating bank notes and supported the circulation of Commonwealth of Pennsylvania specie issues of April 29, 1780 and April 20, 1781. Its request for a charter was denied in 1784 when sponsored by interests competing with the Bank of North America.

The Bank of North America, although it lost its name through merger, is still in operation as the First Pennsylvania Banking and Trust Company which is the oldest banking institution in the United States.

Original Issue:

The original issue of bank notes has an oval of 13 stars at the top for initialing; the word BANK in script on the left end; no engraved plate letters or officers' titles; and only 17 of the date on the plate. Blank backs. Other denominations are probable.

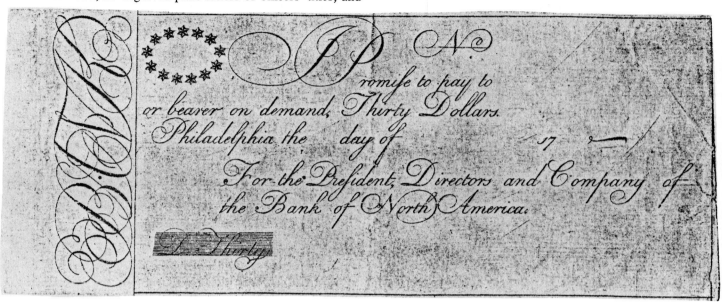

$10 ⓒ $30 Ⓤ

Second Issue:

The second issue of bank notes has the denomination in an oval of 13 stars at the top; the denomination in block letters on the left end with the word BANK superimposed on it in script; engraved plate letters and officers' titles; and 179 of the date on the plate. The back contains a large multiple mirror-image denomination printed in script and visible through the face of the note. Other denominations are probable.

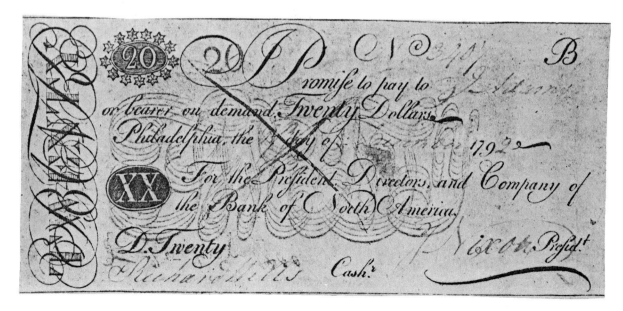

$5 $20 Ⓤ Ⓒ $50

March 21, 1783 Act

$300,000 in Treasury Notes payable in specie after July 1, 1784 pursuant to the Mar. 21, 1783 Act. Typeset with indented left border. Signers are David Rittenhouse and Thomas Smith.

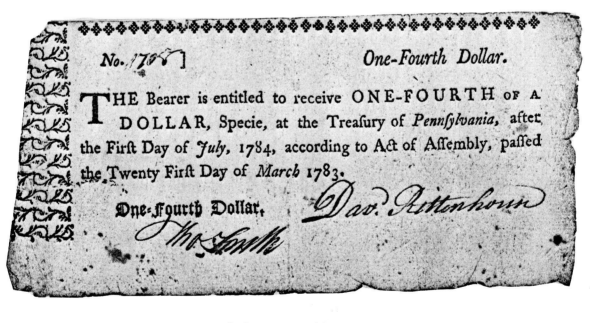

$1/4	$6
$1	$12
$2	$15
$3	$20

PENNSYLVANIA

March 16, 1785 Act

£150,000 in Bills printed by Francis Bailey on paper watermarked PENSYLVANIA in two lines. The Commonwealth Seal in various shapes is on the face. The backs have a new set of nature and cloth prints. Signers are John Baker, James Bayard, Peter Baynton, Robert Bridges, Levi Budd, Samuel Caldwell, John Chaloner, James Collins, John Duffield, Edward Fox, James Glentworth, George Goodwin, William Grey, Stacy Hepburn, Thomas Irwin, H. Kammerer, Reynold Keen, Joseph Ker, George Latimer, George Leib, J. Loughead, Joseph Marsh, James McCrea, Francis Mentges, John Miller, Samuel Murdoch, Andrew Pettit, Joseph Redman, John Rhea, Charles Risk, J. Shortworth, Michael Shubart, Robert Smith, William Smith, John Steele, John Taylor, William Tilton, William Turnbull, Andrew Tybout, Francis Wade, and William Wirtz. The two lowest denominations have one signer, the next three have two signers and the others have three signers.

			V.G.	Fine
3d ($3/90)	[54,546]	....	65.00	85.00
9d ($9/90)	[54,546]	....	65.00	85.00
1s6d ($18/90)	[54,546]	....	65.00	85.00
2s6d	BAILLY misspelled	[54,546] ...	65.00	85.00
5s ($2/3)	[54,546]	....	65.00	85.00
10s ($1 1/3)	[54,545]	....	65.00	85.00
15s ($2)	[54,546]	....	65.00	85.00
20s ($2 2/3)	[54,545]	....	65.00	85.00

Bank of North America ★ August 6, 1789

Bank of North America small change bills payable in specie were issued because of the "copper panic" of July 1789 when circulating copper coin was refused. Printed by Benjamin F. Bache on paper furnished by Benjamin Franklin which had a polychromed or marbled border on one edge. The signature of Tench Francis is printed.

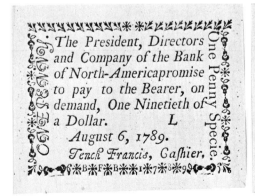

	V.F.
$1/90 (1d) Plate letters A, B, C, D, E, F, G, H, I, K, L, & M [12,000] ...	350.00
$3/90 (3d) Plate letters A, B, C, & D. Polychromed [4,000]	700.00

John Wray and James Lamberton ⋆
September 5, 1789
Small change notes issued at Carlisle. Engraved allegorical backs with trees, field, sun, church, man, mortar and liberty cap on pole. Printed by Kline & Reynolds of Carlisle. Numbered.

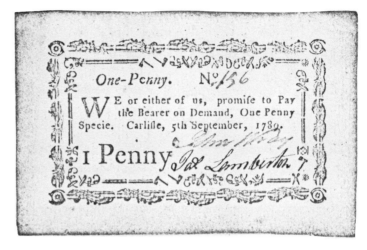

1d Ⓤ
3d Ⓤ

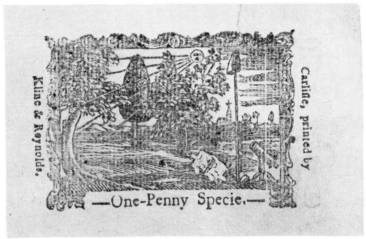

William Peterson ⋆ **October 1, 1789**
Private small change notes issued at Philadelphia and payable in Pennsylvania currency. Blank backs. Other denominations probable.

3d

Fred Hubley ⋆ **December 13, 1789**
Private small change notes issued at Schuylkill, Middle Ferry. Blank backs. Other denominations probable.

2d

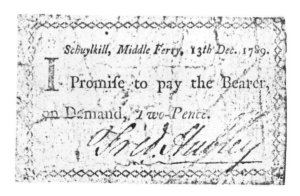

PENNSYLVANIA

Bank of the United States ★ 1791, etc.

Alexander Hamilton in 1779 urged Robert Morris to sponsor the organization of a national bank of issue, using land as security for its notes. Further promulgation of the plan in 1780, 1781, and 1790 culminated in the passage on February 25, 1791 of an Act of Congress incorporating the Bank of the United States with a capital of $10,000,000 divided into 25,000 shares of $400 each. The bank is referred to as the "first bank" to distinguish it from the federally chartered "second bank" of the same name (1816-36, and thereafter as a Pennsylvania corporation). Although the first bank was a private corporation with a 20 year life, the Federal government bought 5,000 shares and became a major depositor and borrower. The United States had not been granted the right to issue its own paper money under the U.S. Constitution which had become effective in 1789. Circulating notes of the Bank of the United States were given legal tender status for all debts due to the United States, including import duties. The principal office was established in Philadelphia in 1791. The Bank of the United States and its branch offices operated successfully and without a legal test of its constitutionality, liquidating on the expiration of its charter in 1811. Between 1796 and 1802 the Federal government sold its

shares in the Bank at a substantial profit. Most bank records were apparently destroyed and the principal sources of information are the reports to Congress made in 1809 and 1811.

The total amount of bank notes issued by the Bank of the United States up to 1811 was $6,152,553 of which $5,037,125 was then outstanding. Of this total the Philadelphia office or parent bank emitted $1,687,893 of which $1,561,833 was then outstanding. The parent bank issued engraved bank notes with the denomination spelled out in a panel on the left end. The counterfeiting of notes of the Bank of the United States was made a Federal crime by Act of June 27, 1798.

Virtually all of the circulating notes of the bank were fully redeemed in specie on liquidation in 1811 and normal examples of genuinely issued bank notes have not been located. A few proof notes and some genuine notes with raised denominations have survived. The principal source of bank note information, however, is from counterfeits made for circulation and a secret circular of the Bank dated Dec. 31, 1791. Most counterfeits have one or more inked x marks on their faces indicating that they were presented to some bank and rejected.

First type (1791, etc.) for parent bank and referred to as "old plates":

Thirteen stars above a heraldic eagle which is near the upper left corner of the notes. A script denomination in the panel on the left end. The numeral at the top is in a beaded oval. For protection against alteration the oval is vertical for the $3 and $5 and horizontal for the $10 and higher denominations. The numeral on the $5 is in red. The date is written in by completing the 179 engraved in the plate, but after 1800 the plate appears to have been modified by removing the engraved numerals of the year. White linen paper with red silk

threads. Each note was watermarked UNITED STATES in script capitals and contained a portion of the watermarked word BANK in large script capitals. Probably engraved by John Draper. Signed by Thomas Willing as president and John Kean as cashier (later by George Simpson as cashier). The original plate letters were A and B on the $5, $20 and $100; A, B, C, and D on the $10; and none on the others. Some subsequent bank note plates for the same denominations contained plate letters continuing in alphabetical order.

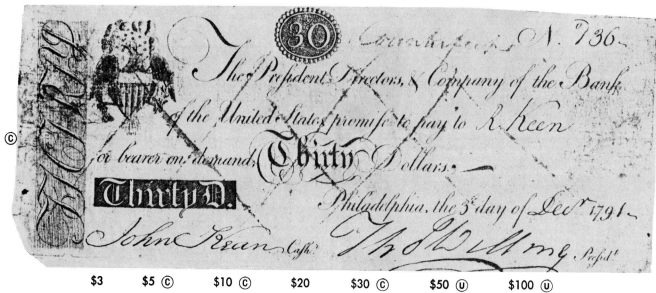

$3 $5 © $10 © $20 $30 © $50 Ⓤ $100 Ⓤ

PENNSYLVANIA

Second type (1794, etc.) for parent bank and also referred to as "old plates":

Similar to first type except that the eagle with 13 stars above it is in the center of the notes and the denomination is shown in two counters instead of one at the top of the notes. The script capitals in the left end panel do not intertwine. Signed by Thomas Willing as president and George Simpson as cashier. Various plate letters. Other denominations probable.

(U)

$5 (U) $10 $20 (U)

Third type (1795, etc.) for parent bank and referred to as "new plates":

A heraldic eagle is within a vertical oval frame of 15 stars in the lower portion of the note and is equidistant from the sides of the note. Capital letter denomination in the left end panel. Engraved by William Harrison, Sr. Signed by Thomas Willing as president and George Simpson as cashier. Various plate letters. Similar 19th century issues were also issued.

(U)

$5 (C) (U) $10 (C) $20 (C) $50 (C) $100 (C)

PENNSYLVANIA

Post Notes for parent bank (1791, etc.):

Notes payable at a future date rather than on demand and requiring endorsement. The eagle with the Arms of the United States has its wings fully extended in a flying position instead of being in an erect position with wings partially open. On bills with engraved denominations these denominations are engraved in six places on the plate. On bills where the amount is written in by hand it is inserted in four places. Red silk threads in white linen watermarked paper. Each note contains the watermark UNITED STATES in script capitals and a portion of the word BANK in large script capitals. No examples have been located.

$5 $10 $20 $30 $50 $100 $500 $1000   Various

New $50 engraved in 1798 by William Harrison, Sr.

Branch Offices of Discount and Deposit:

Offices of Discount and Deposit of the Bank of the United States were established in New York, Boston, Baltimore and Charleston in 1792, in Savannah in 1793, in Norfolk in 1795, in Washington in 1800, and in New Orleans in 1804. Each branch office had its own president and cashier. Nevertheless the notes issued by the branch offices were signed by the president and cashier of the parent bank, and contained the handwritten name of the issuing office in a blank space in the engraved text. The notes of the branch offices had the word DEPARTMENT in a panel engraved on the left end and the engraved note form for each denomination was interchangeable for use by all branch offices. Some branch office notes for protection prior to original emission were payable to the order of the president of the branch office and required his endorsement on the back before issuance, but others were payable to him or the bearer and did not require endorsement. To make branch offices more self reliant the note issues of any branch were to be redeemed in specie only at the branch office of issue and not at the parent bank or other branches. The basic varieties of branch office issues are as follows:

I. An eagle in flying position bearing the Arms of the United States as used on the post notes of the parent and with the word DEPARTMENT in capital letters on the panel at the left end. The plate was engraved by John Draper whose name, J. Draper, is on the left end.

$50 Ⓤ

II. A heraldic eagle with 13 stars above it as used on the first type of parent bank note issues and with the word DEPARTMENT in script on the panel at the left end.

III. A heraldic eagle in an oval frame of 15 stars as used on the third type of parent bank note issues and with the word DEPARTMENT in capital letters on the panel at the left end. This emission continued into the nineteenth century.

Illustrations of and further data on branch office note issues are given under the State in which the branch office was located.

Delaware and Schuylkill Canal Navigation Co. ★
March 1793, etc.

Promissory notes issued in Philadelphia by the President, Managers and Company of the Delaware and Schuylkill Canal Navigation and payable to William Gonett whose endorsement is on the back. Various written dates in 1793. Signed by Tench Francis, former cashier of the Bank of North America whose name appears on its notes. Printed by R. Aitken & Son. Impressed with company seal. Dollar denominations on thick laid paper watermarked PENSYL on one line and VANIA below, being the same paper as used on 1781 and 1785 Pennsylvania State issues. Blank backs. Other denominations probable.

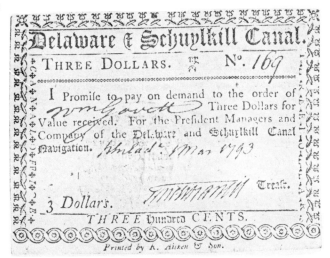

10c (9d)
20¢ (1s6d)
40¢ (3s)
$3 (300¢)
$4 (400¢)

Bank of Pennsylvania ★ March 1793, etc.

Incorporated on Mar. 30, 1793 until Mar. 3, 1813 with a capital limited to $3,000,000 the Bank of Pennsylvania was established at Philadelphia and given the right to establish branches. The Commonwealth was entitled to subscribe up to $1,000,000 in capital and the bank notes were to be receivable in all payments due to the Commonwealth. The Bank of North America, if it surrendered its charter, was given the right to subscribe to 2000 shares at $400 each within three months but that was not done. The president and either the treasurer or the cashier were to sign all bank notes. Blank backs. Other denominations probable.

$5 $10 © $20 © $50

PENNSYLVANIA

PENNSYLVANIA REFERENCES

George H. Blake, "A Rare Colonial Note," *The Numismatist* (July 1912).

"The First Bank of the United States," *Numismatic Scrapbook Magazine* (November 1940).

Harrold E. Gillingham, *Counterfeiting in Colonial Pennsylvania* (New York, 1939).

———, "Philadelphia Ferry Paper Money of 1777," *The Numismatist* (October 1936).

———, "Counterfeiting in Colonial Days," *The Numismatist* (June 1929).

———, "One Penny Bank Note of 1789," *The Numismatist* (April 1934).

William J. Harrison, "The Search for Some Facts about the Bank of the United States Notes," *Paper Money* (July 1975).

John T. Holdsworth and Davis R. Dewey, *The First and Second Banks of the United States* (Washington, 1910).

Richard T. Hoober, "Franklin, the Money Printer," *Numismatic Scrapbook Magazine* (February 1966).

———, "Colonial Paper Currencies of Pennsylvania and New Jersey," *The Numismatist* (December 1944). Reprinted.

———, "The Financial History of Colonial Pennsylvania," *Paper Money* (May 1975 et seq.).

Richard A. Lester, "Currency Issues to Overcome Depressions in Pennsylvania, 1723 and 1729," *Journal of Political Economy* (Chicago, 1938), pp. 324-375.

Lawrence Lewis, *A History of the Bank of North America* (Philadelphia, 1882).

C. W. McFarlane, "Pennsylvania Paper Currency," *Annals of the American Academy of Political and Social Science* (July—December 1896).

C. William Miller, *Benjamin Franklin's Philadelphia Printing* (Philadelphia, 1974).

Eric P. Newman, "Nature Printing on Colonial and Continental Currency," *The Numismatist* (February 1964, etc.), reprinted.

———, "Franklin and the Bank of North America," *The Numismatist* (December 1956).

———, "Franklin Making Money More Plentiful," *Proceedings of the American Philosophical Society* (Philadelphia, October 1971).

Henry Phillips, Jr., *An Historical Sketch of the Paper Money Issued by Pennsylvania* (Philadelphia, 1862), reprinted in *Historical Sketches of the Paper Currencies of the American Colonies* (Roxbury, 1865). Also reprinted in 1969.

John M. Richardson, "A Few of the Very Many Signers of Colonial Notes of Pennsylvania," *Coin Collector's Journal* (July 1936).

Kenneth Scott, *Counterfeiting in Colonial Pennsylvania* New York, 1955).

Laws, archives and other public records.

See general references, catalogs, and listings following the Introduction.

RHODE ISLAND

GENERAL EMISSIONS

August 16, 1710
July 5, 1715
July 5, 1715 redated 1721
July 5, 1715 redated 1724
July 5, 1715 redated 1726
June 14, 1726
July 5, 1715 redated 1728
June 14, 1726 redated 1728
July 5, 1715 redated 1731
June 14, 1726 redated 1731
July 5, 1715 redated 1733
June 14, 1726 redated 1733
July 5, 1715 redated 1737
August 15, 1737
August 15, 1737 redated 1738
August 22, 1738
December 2, 1740
February 2, 1741(2)
February 14, 1743(4)
February 14, 1743(4) redated 1744(5)
February 14, 1743(4) redated 1745
February 14, 1743(4) redated 1746
February 14, 1743(4) redated 1746(7)
February 14, 1743(4) redated 1747(8)
March 18, 1750(1)
March 18, 1750(1) redated 1755
February 27, 1756

August 1756
May 8, 1758
December 23, 1758
March 15, 1759
April 4, 1759
June 23, 1759
March 10, 1760
May 12, 1760
March 20, 1762
April 10, 1762
May 8, 1762
November 1, 1762
March 1, 1766
February 28, 1767
May 3, 1775
June 16, 1775
June 29, 1775
November 6, 1775
January 15, 1776
March 18, 1776
September 5, 1776
1777 Written Dates
May 12, 1777
1778-9 Written Dates
June 1780 Act
July 2, 1780 Act
May 1786 Session

SPECIAL ISSUERS

Providence Bank ★ 1791, etc.
Bank of Rhode Island ★ 1795, etc.
Washington Bank ★ 1800, etc.
Washington Bank ★ August 22, 1800
Bank of Bristol ★ 1800, etc.

August 16, 1710

£13,300 (£5,000, £1,000, £1,000, £6,000 and £300) in legal tender indented Bills of Credit authorized respectively by the Acts of May 3, 1710, Oct. 25, 1710, Nov. 27, 1710, June 28, 1711 and Nov. 14, 1711 for the Annapolis Royal Expedition expense. Receivable for taxes and redeemable by the Colony after 5 years.

Engraved on two face plates. Because of counterfeit £3 bills the issue was declared invalid after May 1, 1719 by an Act passed at the June 17, 1718 Session. Signers are John Coggeshall, Job Greene, Joseph Jenckes, John Odlin, Nathaniel Sheffield, and John Wanton.

```
2s
2s6d
5s
10s
20s
40s
£3 ©
£5
```

July 5, 1715

£40,000 (£30,000 and £10,000) in indented Bills of Credit authorized by the July 5, 1715 and Oct. 26, 1715 Acts for 5% 10 year mortgage loans and known as the First Bank. The loans were extended to 1728 and then amortized over 10 more years. Interest on the loans was to be used for repairing Fort Ann. The four lowest denominations were on one plate and the other six denominations apparently on another plate. Engraved and printed by Samuel Vernon. The backs were not to be covered because they had distinctive engraved designs. Because of counterfeits of this and the following issue all 40s and £5 bills were recalled by May 1, 1727 pursuant to the June 1726 Act. Signers are Job Almy, James Brown, Nathaniel Coddington, Benjamin Ellery, Robert Gardner, and John Wanton.

The Arms contain the motto IN TE DOMINE SPERAMUS (In you, Lord, we have hope).

12d	[4,000]	
2s6d	[4,000]	
3s	[4,000]	
4s6d	[4,000]	
5s	[3,341]	
10s	[3,341]	
20s	[3,209]	
40s	[3,209]	©
£3	[3,209]	
£5	[3,209]	©

July 5, 1715 redated 1721

£40,000 in Bills of Credit loaned pursuant to the May 1721 Act for five years with interest payable in flax and hemp. Known as the Second Bank. These loans were first extended by the Dec. 29, 1724 Act to 10 years; then by the June 1728 Act to a 23 year duration which latter Act was repealed on Dec. 24, 1729. Printed from the same plates as the previous issue with "1721" added on the face without disturbing the prior date. Because of counterfeits of this and the prior issue all 40s and £5 bills were called by May 1, 1727 pursuant to the June 1726 Act. Signers are Nathaniel Coddington, William Coddington, Robert Gardner, Jonathan Nichols, Edward Thurston, and John Wanton.

12d
2s6d
3s
4s6d
5s
10s
20s
40s ©
£3
£5

July 5, 1715 redated 1724

£2,000 in Bills of Credit issued pursuant to the Feb. 1723(4) Act. Printed from the same plates as the July 15, 1715 issue with "1724" added on the face without disturbing prior dates. By the Oct. 1724 Act the custom of tearing bills into half and quarter sections was pro-hibited after Jan. 1, 1724(5), but the practice started anew and was prohibited again by the Oct. 1734 and June 1735 Acts which were repealed in favor of a June 1737 Act providing for redemption of sections and in-validity after Jan. 1, 1738. Same signers as prior issue.

12d	3s	5s	20s	£3
2s6d	4s6d	10s	40s	£5

July 5, 1715 redated 1726

Part of £46,634 5s issued pursuant to the June 14, 1726 Act. Printed from the "small" plate of the previous issue with "1726" added on the face without disturbing prior dates. Generally the same signers as the previous issue.

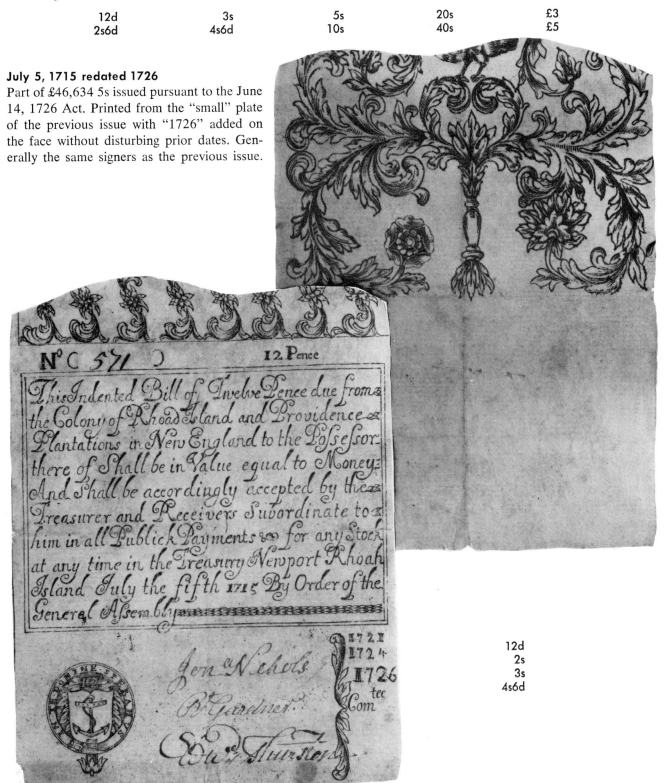

12d
2s
3s
4s6d

June 14, 1726

Part of £46,634 5s in indented Bills of Credit issued pursuant to the June 14, 1726 Act to replace outstanding bills of the prior issues, particularly the 40s and £5 which had been counterfeited. This necessitated engraving a new face and back plate. The new back plate has an elaborately detailed leaf and bird design. Generally the same signers as the prior issues.

5s	10s	20s	40s	£3	£5

July 5, 1715 and June 14, 1726 both redated 1728

£49,000 (£40,000, £3,000, £2,000, £3,000 and £1,000) in indented Bills of Credit issued pursuant to Feb. 1727(8), May 1728, June 1728 and Feb. 1730(1) Acts for replacement of all prior issues, for reloaning as the Third Bank, and for repair of Fort Ann. Silver was then valued at 18s per ounce. The four lowest denominations are from the same small plate used for the 1726 redating and the others from the plates prepared for the June 14, 1726 issue. The date "1728" was added to the face plates without disturbing prior dates. Printed by Samuel Vernon. Signers are Jahleel Brenton, William Coddington, John Gardner, George Goulding, Daniel Updike, and John Wanton.

12d	5s	£3
2s6d	10s	£5
3s	20s	
4s6d	40s	

RHODE ISLAND

July 5, 1715 and June 14, 1726
both redated 1731

£60,000 in indented Bills of Credit issued pursuant to the June 1731 and Oct. 1731 Acts for 5% 10 year delayed amortization mortgage loans and known as the Fourth Bank. Silver was then valued at 22s per ounce. The date "1731" was added to the same face plates as were used for the 1728 redating without disturbing the prior dates. The bills were printed by Samuel Vernon. There were £2,500 in 10s and lower denominations. Signers are Jahleel Brenton, William Coddington, George Goulding, Daniel Updike, Gideon Wanton, and John Wanton.

12d
2s6d
3s
4s6d
5s
10s
20s
40s
£3
£5 ©

**July 5, 1715 and June 14, 1726
both redated 1733**

£104,000 (£100,000 and £4,000) in indented Bills of Credit issued pursuant to the July 1733 Acts for mortgage loans (constituting the Fifth Bank) and for cannon for Fort George. Silver was then valued at 25s per ounce. The bills were printed from the same plates used for 1731 redating with the date "1733" added without disturbing prior dates. Signers are Jahleel Brenton, William Coddington, George Goulding, Daniel Updike, and John Wanton.

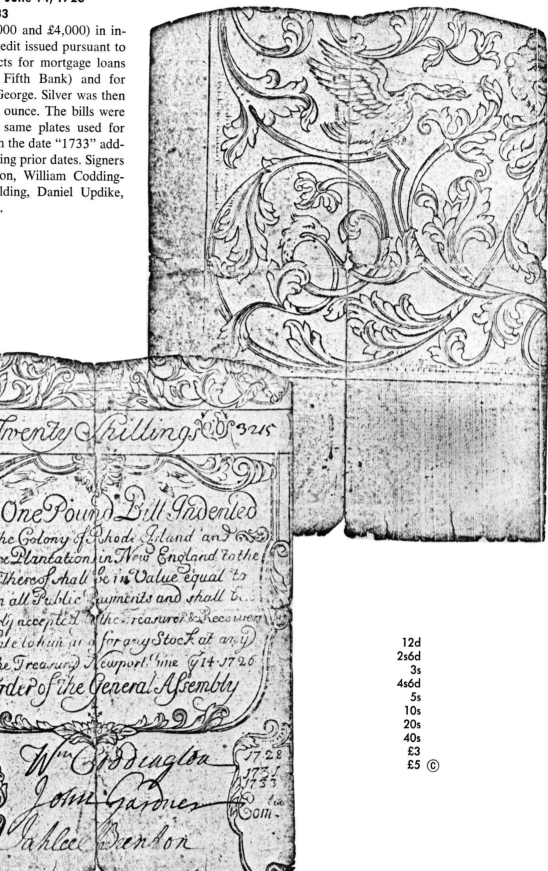

12d
2s6d
3s
4s6d
5s
10s
20s
40s
£3
£5 ©

July 5, 1715 redated 1737

£10,000 in engraved Bills of Credit authorized to be printed from the "small plate" by the June 1737 Act as part of £30,000 to be used to exchange for half and quarter sections of bills of prior issues. Such half and quarter sections were to become invalid by Jan. 1, 1738. Printed from the same small plate as the 1733 redating with "1737" added without disturbing prior dates. The original copper face plate exists. Printed by Samuel Vernon. Signers are Jahleel Brenton, William Coddington, John Gardner, George Goulding, John Potter, and James Sheffield.

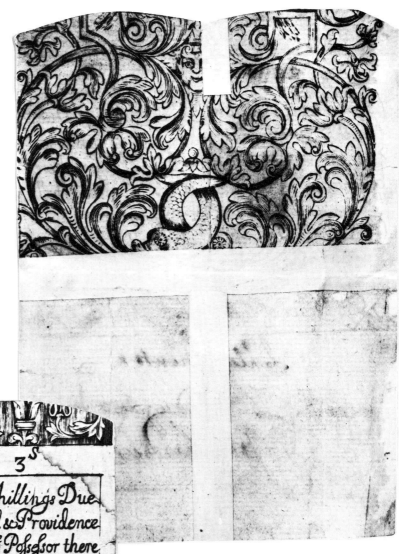

12d Ⓡ
2s6d Ⓡ
3s Ⓡ
4s6d Ⓡ

August 15, 1737

£20,000 out of £30,000 in engraved Bills of Credit authorized by the June 1737 Act to exchange for half and quarter sections of bills of the prior issues. Because the redated "large plate" of the June 14, 1726 issue was in poor condition, as evidenced by instructions to have it "cleaned or new cut," new plates for face and back were engraved for the high denominations. Delays and illness occurred and Samuel Vernon, Jr., had to be substituted for his father as printer. The motto on the Arms was changed to IN TE DOMINE SPERAVI (In you, Lord, I have hoped). Same signers as the issue of July 5, 1715 redated 1737.

£1
£2
£3 ©
£5 ©

August 15, 1737 redated 1738

£10,000 approved by the May 1738 Act and £90,000 out of £100,000 authorized by the Aug. 22, 1738 Act to loan on 20 year delayed amortization mortgages bearing 5% interest and known as the Sixth Bank. Silver was then valued at 27s per ounce. Face of Aug. 15, 1737 plate redated by cutting "1738" above the word "committee." Printed by William Claggett. Deliberately cut up fractional parts of this issue were not to be accepted by the Colony Treasurer. Signers are Jahleel Brenton, John Gardner, George Goulding, John Potter, James Sheffield, Daniel Updike, and John Wanton.

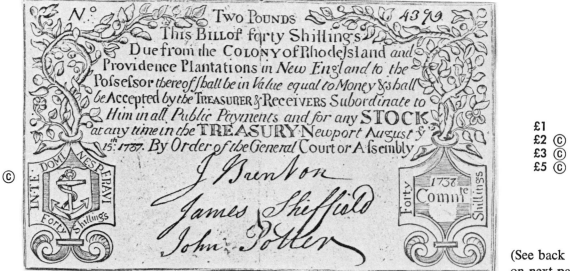

£1
£2 ©
£3 ©
£5 ©

(See back
on next page)

©

August 22, 1738

£10,000 in Bills of Credit as small denominations under the Aug. 22, 1738 Act for loaning £100,000 as the Sixth Bank. Another £10,000 may have been emitted for the Cuba expedition pursuant to the Sept. 16, 1740 Act.

Engraved and printed by William Claggett on one face plate and one back plate, both of which still exist. Same signers as the previous issue.

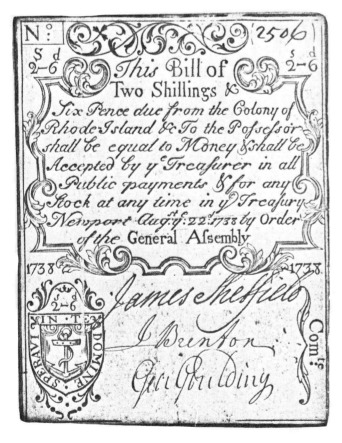

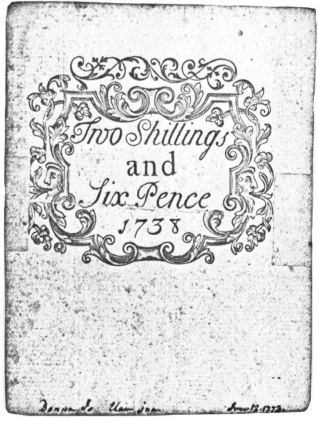

1s ®   2s6d ®   3s ®   5s ®   7s6d   Seaven ®   10s ®

December 2, 1740

£24,000 (£20,000, £2,000 and £2,000) in legal tender New Tenor Bills of Credit issued pursuant to the Acts of Sept. 16, 1740, Dec. 2, 1740, May 6, 1741 and Oct. 6, 1741. Because silver had reached an exchange value of 27s Old Tenor per ounce the Sept. 16, 1740 Act set the New Tenor equivalent at 9s per ounce. It provided for £20,000 in New Tenor bills (5s, 10s, 20s and £2) to be loaned on 20 year amortizing mortgages bearing 4% interest and known as the Seventh Bank. Because of objections by the Crown and others the New Tenor was reset at 6s9d per ounce of silver of sterling alloy equal

to 27s Old Tenor. Interest and two extra appropriations of £2,000 each were to be used for the Cuba expedition. Printed by John Coddington from engraved face and back plates, with some denominations showing Old Tenor and New Tenor equivalents. £4,000 was printed from lower denomination plate. By the June 1742 Act the entire issue was to be exchanged by Oct. 25, 1742 because of counterfeits. Signers are Jahleel Brenton, John Dexter, John Gardner, John Potter, Daniel Updike, and Joseph Whipple.

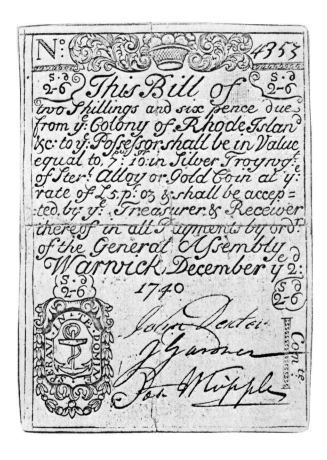

6d	(1 dwt., 12 gr.)	[14,545]
1s	(2 dwt., 23 gr.)	[14,545]
1s6d	(4 dwt., 11 gr.)	[14,545]
2s6d	(7 dwt., 10 gr.)	[14,546]
5s	(14 dwt., 19 gr.)	[5,333] ®
10s	(1 oz., 9 dwt., 15 gr.)	[5,333] ®
20s	(2 oz., 19 dwt., 6 gr.)	[5,333] ® ©
40s	(5 oz., 18 dwt., 12 gr.)	[5,333] ®

February 2, 1741(2)

£24,000 in legal tender New Tenor Bills of Credit issued pursuant to the Feb. 2, 1741(2) Act to replace the entire Dec. 2, 1740 issue because of counterfeits. Same silver equivalent as Dec. 2, 1740 issue. Engraved and printed by William Claggett, £2,000 from the low denomination plate and £22,000 from the high denomination plate. Old Tenor and New Tenor equivalents engraved on the backs. Signers are Jahleel Brenton, John Dexter, John Gardner, Edward Scott, Daniel Updike, and Joseph Whipple.

6d	(1 dwt., 12 gr.) [7,272]
1s	(2 dwt., 23 gr.) [7,272]
1s6d	(4 dwt., 11 gr.) [7,272]
2s6d	(7 dwt., 10 gr.) [7,273]
5s	(14 dwt., 19 gr.) [5,867]
10s	(1 oz., 9 dwt., 15 gr.) [5,867] Ⓒ
20s	Two angels (2 oz., 19 dwt., 6 gr.) [5,866] Ⓒ
40s	(5 oz., 18 dwt., 12 gr.) [5,866] Ⓒ

The motto on the Arms has been changed back to IN TE DOMINE SPERAMVS.

February 14, 1743(4)

£40,000 in New Tenor Bills of Credit issued pursuant to the Feb. 14, 1743(4) Act for 20 year amortizing mortgage loans bearing 4% interest. Known as the Eighth Bank. Same silver equivalent as Dec. 2, 1740 issue. Elaborately engraved face with word SPERAVI in the motto on prior issues changed to SPERAMVS. Back printed from type and ornaments showing New Tenor and Old Tenor equivalents. Signers are James Arnold, Jahleel Brenton, George Brown, John Dexter, Benjamin Nichols, Thomas Richardson, Edward Scott, Daniel Updike, and Gideon Wanton.

The English Arms on this issue are included on Rhode Island bills for the first time.

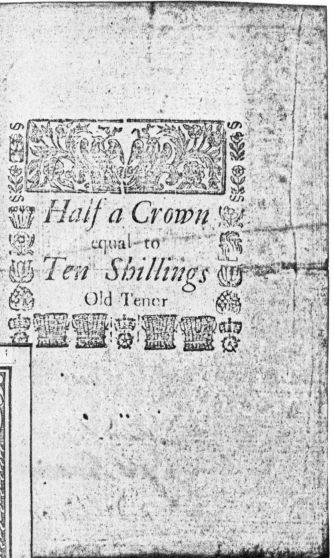

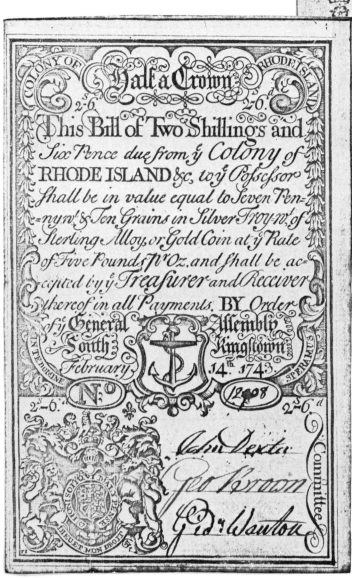

4d (1s4d O.T.)	[30,000]	
6d (2s O.T.)	[20,000]	
1s (4s O.T.)	[20,000]	
2s6d (10s O.T.)	[20,000]	©️
5s (£1 O.T.)	[20,000]	
10s (£2 O.T.)	[10,000]	
20s (£4 O.T.)	[13,500]	
40s (£8 O.T.)	[6,000]	

SPEARMVS in the motto on the Arms of the 6d is misspelled.

February 14, 1743(4) redated 1744(5)

£8,750 (£2,500 and £6,250) in New Tenor Bills of Credit issued pursuant to the Feb. 5, 1744(5) and Mar. 4, 1744(5) Acts for Cape Breton expedition. Same as the four highest denominations of the Feb. 14, 1743(4) issue but with "1744" cut into signature area on the face. Same silver equivalent as Dec. 2, 1740 issue. Old and New Tenor value printed on the back with the date of authorization. Same signers as the Feb. 14, 1743(4) issue plus Gideon Cornell.

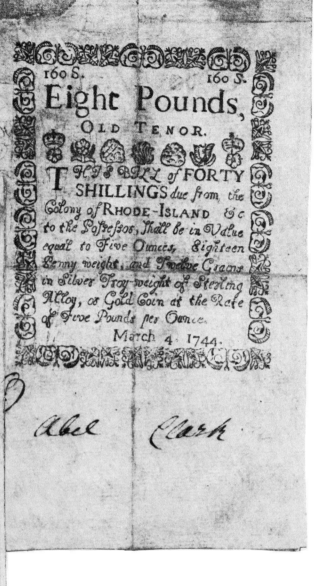

©

5s (£1 O.T.)	[2,334]
10s (£2 O.T.)	[2,333]
20s (£4 O.T.)	[2,333]
40s (£8 O.T.)	[2,333] ©

February 14, 1743(4) redated 1745

£8,750 (£3,750 and £5,000) in New Tenor Bills of Credit issued pursuant to the May 27, 1745 and Sept. 1745 Acts for the Cape Breton expedition. Printed from same face plate as the four highest denominations of the Feb. 14, 1743(4) issue, but with "1745" cut into signature area without changing prior dates. Same silver equivalent as the Dec. 2, 1740 issue. Same signers as Feb. 14, 1743(4) issue.

| 5s (£1 O.T.) | [2,334] | 20s (£4 O.T.) | [2,333] |
| 10s (£2 O.T.) | [2,333] | 40s (£8 O.T.) | [2,333] |

February 14, 1743(4) redated 1746

£11,250 in New Tenor Bills of Credit issued pursuant to the June 2, 1746 Act for Canadian expedition purposes. Printed from the same face plates as previous issues but with "1746" cut into signature area without disturbing other dates. £11,000 from the large denomination plate and £250 from the small denomination plate. Same silver equivalent as the Dec. 2, 1740 issue. The lowest four denominations have blank backs. The misspelling of SPEARMVS in the motto on the 6d has been corrected to SPERAMVS. Same signers as the Feb. 14, 1743(4) issue.

4d (1s4d O.T.) [1,154]	1s (4s O.T.) [1,153]	5s (£1 O.T.) [2,934]	20s (£4 O.T.) [2,933]
6d (2s O.T.) [1,154]	2s6d (10s O.T.) [1,153]	10s (£2 O.T.) [2,933]	40s (£8 O.T.) [2,933]

February 14, 1743(4) redated 1746(7)

£15,000 in New Tenor Bills of Credit issued pursuant to the Feb. 17, 1746(7) Act. From the same face plates as the Feb. 14, 1743(4) redated 1746 issue, but the printed backs contain "Feb. 17, 1746-7." £14,000 printed from the large denomination plate and £1,000 from the small denomination plate. Same silver equivalent as the Dec. 2, 1740 issue. Same signers as the Feb. 14, 1743(4) issue.

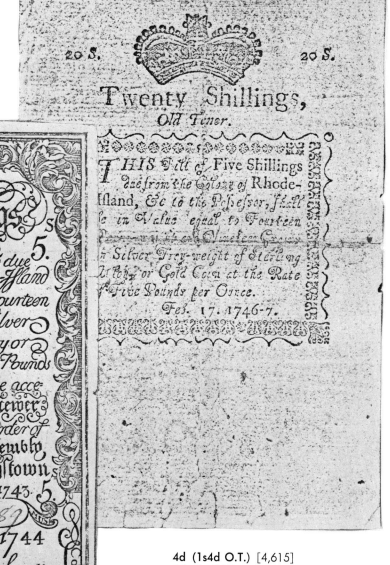

4d (1s4d O.T.)	[4,615]
6d (2s O.T.)	[4,616]
1s (4s O.T.)	[4,616]
2s6d (10s O.T.)	[4,615]
5s (£1 O.T.)	[3,734]
10s (£2 O.T.)	[3,733]
20s (£4 O.T.)	[3,734]
40s (£8 O.T.)	[3,733]

RHODE ISLAND

February 14, 1743(4) redated 1747(8)

£7,500 in New Tenor Bills of Credit issued pursuant to the Feb. 1747(8) Act for a Canadian expedition. The faces of the four highest denominations are the same as the previous issue with "1747" added without disturbing prior dates. The faces of the four lowest denominations are the same as those of the previous issue. On the typeset back of all denominations the date 1747 is used. Same silver equivalent as the Dec. 2, 1740 issue. Same signers as Feb. 14, 1743(4) issue.

The initials T.I. below the anchor on the 6d bill are those of the engraver, Thomas Johnston, and were apparently added when "1746" was engraved onto the low denomination face plate for the issue of Feb. 14, 1743(4) redated 1746.

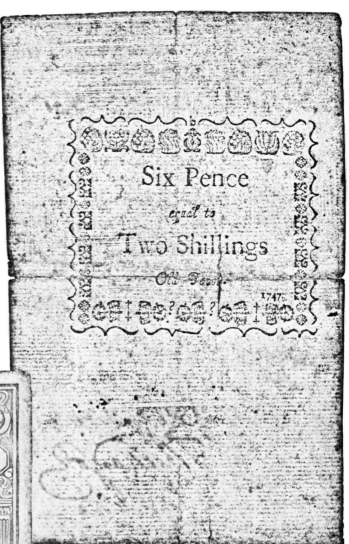

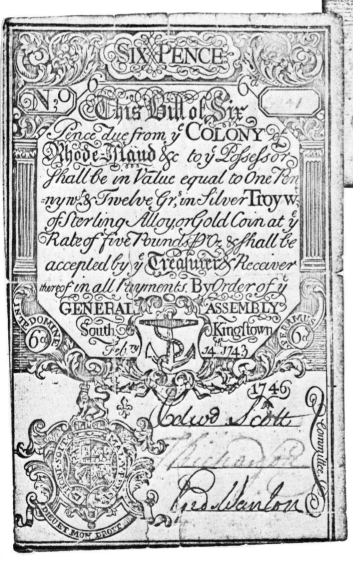

4d (1s4d O.T.)
6d (2s O.T.)
1s (4s O.T.)
2s6d (10s O.T.)
5s (£1 O.T.)
10s (£2 O.T.)
20s (£4 O.T.)
40s (£8 O.T.)

337

March 18, 1750(1)

62,500 ounces of silver of sterling alloy in Bills of Credit without any denomination but equal to £50,000 New Tenor or £200,000 Old Tenor. Under the Act of Mar. 18, 1750(1) the Ninth Bank was created to issue £25,000 in bills with specific denominations. These bills were to be loaned for 6% 5 year mortgages. Sterling alloy was valued at 6s9d sterling per ounce for this emission equal to 13s6d New Tenor or 54s Old Tenor. To pay a higher price for specie than the specified rate was made illegal. The proceeds were to be used for flax, wool, whale oil and codfish subsidies. By the June 1751 Act the subsidies were eliminated, interest was reduced to 5%, loans were extended to 10 years, denominations were to be eliminated from the bills, and one ounce of sterling alloy was made equal to 16s New Tenor or 64s Old Tenor. Old Tenor denominational equivalents were nevertheless for convenience placed on the engraved

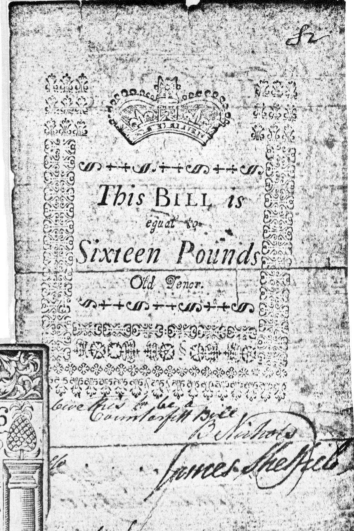

faces and the typeset backs. Signers are James Arnold, Joshua Babcock, George Brown, Obadiah Brown, Samuel Chace, Nicholas Easton, B. Haszard, Jeremiah Lippitt, Benjamin Nichols, James Sheffield, and Gideon Wanton.

15 gr.	(2s O.T.)
1 dwt., 13½ gr.	(5s O.T.)
2 dwt., 12 gr.	(8s O.T.)
6 dwt., 6 gr.	(£1 O.T.)
12 dwt., 12 gr.	(£2 O.T.)
1 oz., 5 dwt.	(£4 O.T.) Ⓡ Ⓒ
2 oz., 10 dwt.	(£8 O.T.) Ⓒ
5 oz.	(£16 O.T.) Ⓒ

Ⓒ

March 18, 1750(1) redated 1755

75,000 ounces of silver of sterling alloy (£240,000 Old Tenor) in Bills of Credit issued pursuant to the Mar., June, Aug., Sept., and Dec. 1755 Acts for the expedition to Crown Point. Printed from the same face plates as the Mar. 18, 1750(1) issue with "1755" added without disturbing the prior date, and "Crown-Point" added to the text of the typeset back. By 1755 depreciation had resulted in 85s Old Tenor being

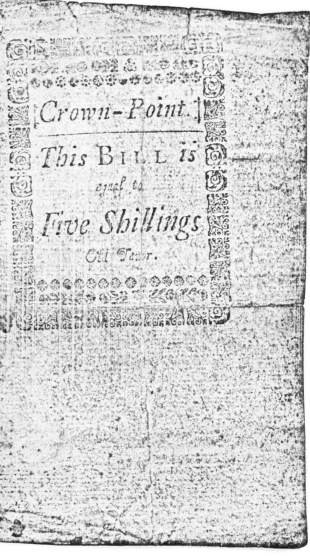

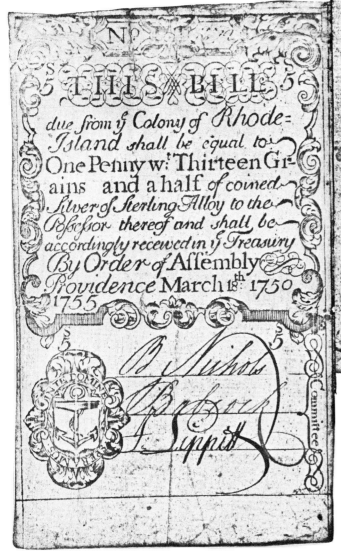

equal to one ounce of silver. Signers are the same as the Mar. 18, 1750(1) issue plus Daniel Updike.

15 gr.	(2s O.T.)	
1 dwt., 13½ gr.	(5s O.T.)	
2 dwt., 12 gr.	(8s O.T.)	
6 dwt., 6 gr.	(£1 O.T.)	
12 dwt., 12 gr.	(£2 O.T.)	
1 oz., 5 dwt.	(£4 O.T.)	1755 redating omitted Ⓡ
2 oz., 10 dwt.	(£8 O.T.)	
5 oz.	(£16 O.T.) Ⓒ	

February 27, 1756

£8,000 in Lawful Money equal to same amount of Massachusetts Bay and Connecticut currency at 6s9d per ounce of silver. Cast cuts on the top and side borders. The body of the bill is in set type with a cast cut of the Colony seal. Small bills of similar size to the Connecticut bills of the same period. Due without interest on Feb. 27, 1758 pursuant to the Feb. 1756 Act and conforming with the Mar. 12, 1750(1) Act of Parliament. Same signers as the Mar. 18, 1750(1) issue.

6d	9d	1s	2s	3s	5s	10s	20s	25s

RHODE ISLAND

August 1756

£6,000 (£4,000 and £2,000) in Lawful Money pursuant to the Aug. 1756 and Sept. 1756 Acts and due without interest in Aug. 1758. Circulation of New Hampshire bills in Rhode Island was prohibited. The same style and signers as the Feb. 27, 1756 issue.

6d	9d	1s	2s	3s	5s	10s	20s	25s

May 8, 1758

£10,000 in Lawful Money with legal tender status issued pursuant to the May 1758 Act and redeemable with 5% interest on May 8, 1763. Protests that rate of interest should be 3% were made. Same style as the Feb. 27, 1756 issue. Printed backs. An issue of bills authorized by the Mar. 17, 1758 Act was not emitted. Signers are Joshua Babcock, Jabez Bowen, Joseph Clarke, Jeremiah Lippitt and Benjamin Nichols.

6d [2,920]	2s [2,920]	10s [2,920]	30s [2,920]
1s [2,920]	5s [2,920]	20s [2,920]	

December 23, 1758

£10,909 1s9d in Lawful Money (£200,000 Old Tenor or 36,363½ Spanish Dollars) issued pursuant to the Oct. 1758 Act and due with 6% interest on Dec. 23, 1763. Same style as the Feb. 27, 1756 issue. Probably the same signers and denominations as the May 8, 1758 issue.

March 15, 1759

£12,000 in Lawful Money issued pursuant to the Feb. 1759 Act and due with 5% interest on Mar. 15, 1764. Same style as the Feb. 27, 1756 issue. Probably the same signers and denominations as the May 8, 1758 issue.

April 4, 1759

£4,000 in Lawful Money issued because it could not be borrowed pursuant to the Feb. 1759 Act and due with 5% interest on April 4, 1764. Same style as the Feb. 27, 1756 issue. Probably the same signers and denominations as the May 8, 1758 issue.

June 23, 1759

£4,000 in Lawful Money issued pursuant to the June 1759 Act and due with 5% interest on June 23, 1762. Same style as the Feb. 27, 1756 issue. Probably the same signers and denominations as the May 8, 1758 issue.

March 10, 1760

£16,000 in Lawful Money for military bounties and wages issued pursuant to the Feb. 1760 Act and due with 5% interest on Mar. 10, 1765. Same style as the Feb. 27, 1756 issue. Called in by the Feb. 1765 Act. Probably the same signers as the May 8, 1758 issue.

6d	9d	1s	2s	5s	10s	20s	30s

May 12, 1760

£11,000 (£10,000 and £1,000) in Lawful Money issued under the May 1760 Act for military expense and for a court house. Due with 5% interest on May 12, 1765. Same style as the Feb. 27, 1756 issue. Called for re- demption by the Feb. 1765 Act. Signers are Joseph Clarke, John Dexter, Jonathan Easton, Augustus John- son, Jeremiah Lippitt, Benjamin Nichols, and James Sheffield.

5s	10s	20s	30s

March 20, 1762

£5,000 in Lawful Money issued under the Feb. 1762 Act for military bounties and wages. Due with 5% in- terest on Mar. 20, 1767. Same style as the Feb. 27, 1756 issue. Called for redemption by the Feb. 1767 Act. Signers are Job Bennett, Jr., Walter Cranston, Jonathan Easton, John Jepson, Nathaniel Mumford, Elias Thomp- son, and John Wanton. Bills authorized under the Mar. 1761 Act were not issued.

3d [2,463]	9d [2,463]	2s [2,463]	10s [1,368]	30s [1,368]
6d [2,463]	1s [2,463]	5s [1,368]	20s [1,368]	

April 10, 1762

£2,000 in Lawful Money issued for military bounties under the Mar. 1762 Act and due with 5% interest on April 10, 1767. Same style as the Feb. 27, 1756 issue. Called for redemption by the Feb. 1767 Act. Same signers as the Mar. 20, 1762 issue plus Edward Thurston.

5s	10s	20s	30s

May 8, 1762

£2,000 in Lawful Money issued for military bounties and wages under the May 1762 Act and due with 5% inter- est on May 8, 1767. Same style as the Feb. 27, 1756 issue. Called for redemption by the Feb. 1767 Act. Same signers as the April 10, 1762 issue except that John Davis was substituted for John Wanton.

5s [615]	10s [615]	20s [615]	30s [615]

November 1, 1762

£4,000 in Lawful Money issued for military services under the Sept. 1762 Act and due with 5% interest on Nov. 1, 1767. In 1763 the State set a scale of de- preciation for paper money beginning at 56s per ounce in 1751 and ending at 140s per ounce in 1763. Same style as the Feb. 27, 1756 issue. Same signers as the May 8, 1762 issue.

3d [2,000]	9d [2,000]	2s [2,000]	4s [2,000]	10s [2,000]
6d [2,000]	1s [2,000]	3s [2,000]	5s [2,000]	20s [1,350]

March 1, 1766

£1,000 in Lawful Money pursuant to the Feb. 1766 Act to be issued if the amount could not be borrowed. Only £659 6s8¾d was emitted and made due without interest on Mar. 1, 1768. Same style as the Feb. 27, 1756 issue. Signers are Metcalfe Bowler, Thomas Free- body, and John Jepson.

3d [8,000]	9d [4,000]	2s [1,000]	5s [1,000]
6d [4,000]	1s [3,000]	3s [1,000]	

RHODE ISLAND

February 28, 1767

£2,000 in Lawful Money pursuant to the Feb. 1767 Act due without interest on Feb. 28, 1769. Same form as the Feb. 27, 1756 issue. Signers are Metcalfe Bowler, Thomas Freebody, John Jepson, and Gideon Wanton.

4d [3,000]
8d [3,000]
1s [1,000]
2s [1,000]
3s [1,000]
4s [1,000]
6s [1,000]
10s [1,000]
20s [550]

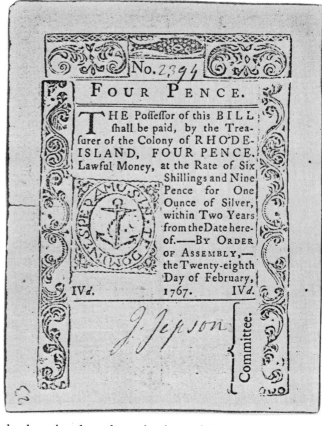

May 3, 1775

£20,000 Lawful Money in legal tender Bills of Credit due on May 3, 1777 or May 3, 1780 with 2½% interest pursuant to the May 3, 1775 Act. Set type within border cuts. Printed by John Carter on thin laid paper. Typeset backs printed on denominations of 5s and over. Entire issue replaced with non-interest bearing bills of the Jan. 15, 1776 issue. Signers are Metcalfe Bowler, Joseph Clarke, John Cole, Thomas Greene, and Henry Ward.

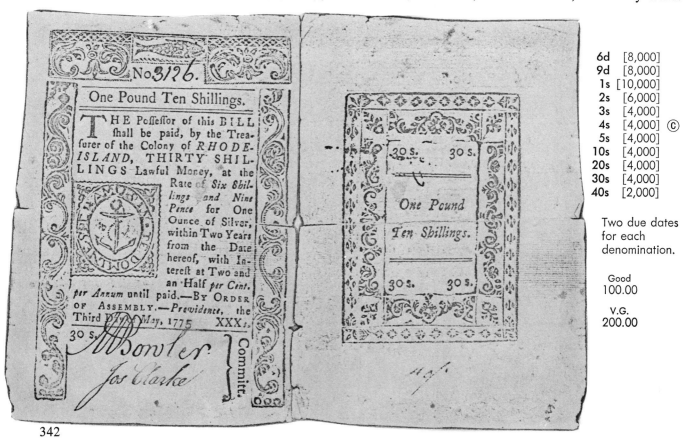

6d [8,000]
9d [8,000]
1s [10,000]
2s [6,000]
3s [4,000]
4s [4,000] ©
5s [4,000]
10s [4,000]
20s [4,000]
30s [4,000]
40s [2,000]

Two due dates for each denomination.

Good 100.00

V.G. 200.00

342

June 16, 1775

£10,000 Lawful Money in legal tender Bills of Credit due on June 16, 1777 or June 16, 1780 with 2½% interest pursuant to the June 16, 1775 Act. Same form as the May 3, 1775 issue except issued at East Greenwich.

Two due dates for each denomination. Entire issue replaced with non-interest bearing bills of the Jan. 15, 1776 issue. Same signers as the May 3, 1775 issue.

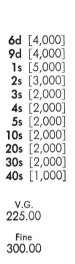

6d	[4,000]
9d	[4,000]
1s	[5,000]
2s	[3,000]
3s	[2,000]
4s	[2,000]
5s	[2,000]
10s	[2,000]
20s	[2,000]
30s	[2,000]
40s	[1,000]

V.G.
225.00

Fine
300.00

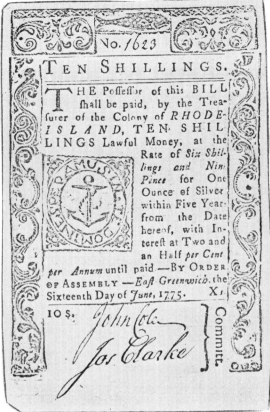

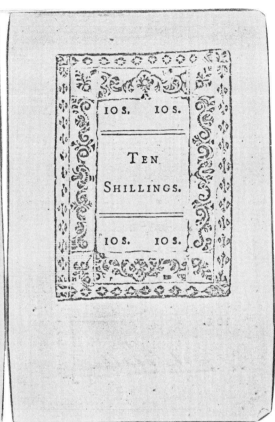

June 29, 1775

£10,000 Lawful Money in legal tender Bills of Credit due June 29, 1777 or June 29, 1780 with 2½% interest pursuant to the June 29, 1775 Act. Same form of face and back as the May 3, 1775 issue. Two due dates for each denomination. The longer maturity bills have odd numbering and the shorter maturity bills have even numbering. Entire issue replaced with non-interest bearing bills of the Jan. 15, 1776 issue. Same signers as the May 3, 1775 issue.

		Good	V.G.
6d	[4,000]	200.00	275.00
9d	[4,000]	200.00	275.00
1s	[5,000]	200.00	275.00
2s	[3,000]	200.00	275.00
3s	[2,000]	225.00	300.00
4s	[2,000]	225.00	300.00
5s	[2,000]	225.00	300.00
10s	[2,000]	225.00	300.00
20s	[2,000]	225.00	300.00
30s	[2,000]	225.00	300.00
40s	[1,000]	250.00	325.00

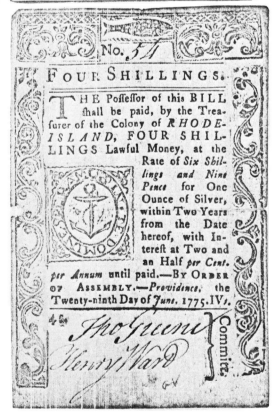

RHODE ISLAND

November 6, 1775

£20,000 Lawful Money in legal tender Bills of Credit due Nov. 6, 1780 without interest pursuant to the Nov. 6, 1775 Act. Same form as the May 3, 1775 issue. Bills of 10s and over were called for redemption by Nov. 1, 1778 pursuant to the Oct. 1777 Act. Signers are Metcalfe Bowler, Joseph Clarke, John Cole, John Dexter, John G. Wanton, and Henry Ward. Lowest five denominations had two signers and the others had three signers.

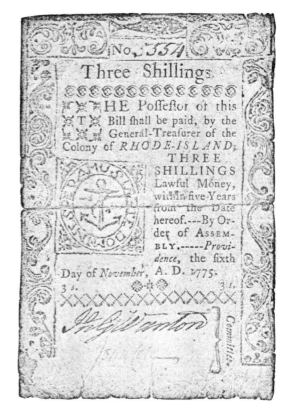

		Good	V.G.
6d	[20,000]	75.00	100.00
9d	[16,000]	75.00	100.00
1s	[20,000]	75.00	100.00
2s	[12,000]	80.00	110.00
3s	[8,000]	85.00	125.00
5s	[6,000]	85.00	125.00
10s	[5,000]	85.00	125.00
20s	[4,000]	90.00	135.00
30s	[3,000]	90.00	135.00
40s	[1,500]	100.00	150.00

January 15, 1776

£40,000 Lawful Money in legal tender Bills of Credit due Jan. 15, 1781 without interest. Issued pursuant to the Jan. 15, 1776 Act to replace interest bearing issues of May 3, 1775, June 16, 1775 and June 29, 1775. Same form as the May 3, 1775 issue. Bills of 10s and over were called for redemption by Nov. 1, 1778 pur-

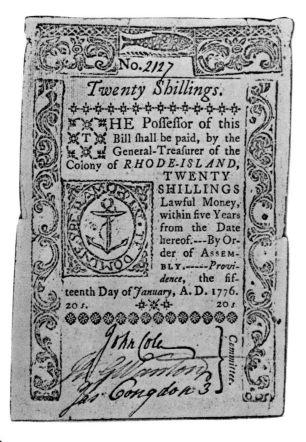

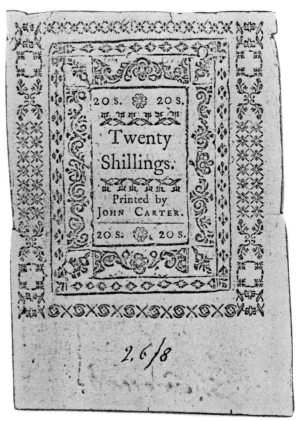

suant to the Oct. 1777 Act. Signers are Welcome Arnold, Joseph Clarke, John Cole, James Congdon, 3rd,

John Dexter, Thomas Greene, and John G. Wanton. Three signers on 5s and over. Two signers on others.

		Good	V.G.
6d	[6,000]	60.00	100.00
9d	[6,000]	60.00	100.00
1s	[6,000]	60.00	100.00
2s	[5,000]	60.00	100.00
3s	[7,500]	60.00	100.00
4s	[6,000]	60.00	100.00

		Good	V.G.
5s	[6,000]	60.00	100.00
10s	[6,000]	60.00	100.00
20s	[6,000]	60.00	100.00
30s	[6,000]	60.00	100.00
40s	[4,000]	60.00	100.00
60s	[3,000]	80.00	125.00

March 18, 1776

£20,000 Lawful Money in legal tender Bills of Credit due Mar. 18, 1782 without interest and issued pursuant to the Mar. 1776 Act. Same form as the May 3, 1775 issue but issued at East Greenwich. Bills of 10s and over

were called for redemption by Nov. 1, 1778 pursuant to the Oct. 1777 Act. Signers are Welcome Arnold, Joseph Clarke, John Cole, James Congdon, John Dexter, William Ellery*, Thomas Greene, and John G. Wanton.

*Signer of the Declaration of Independence

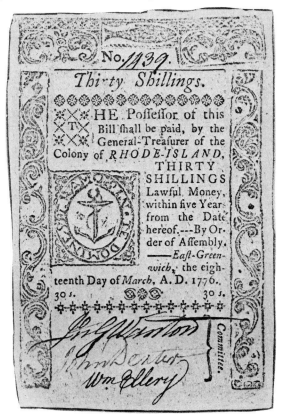 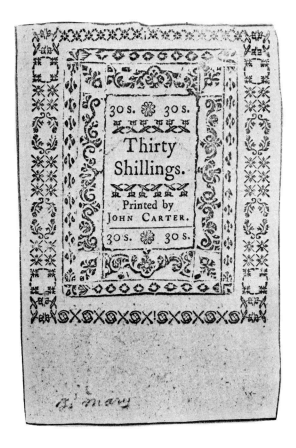

9d [2,400]	3s [3,000]	10s [3,000]	40s [2,000]
1s [2,000]	4s [3,000]	20s [3,000]	60s [1,600]
2s [2,100]	5s [3,000]	30s [3,000]	

RHODE ISLAND

September 5, 1776

$66,670 (£20,001 Lawful Money) in legal tender Bills of Credit due on Sept. 5, 1782 pursuant to a Sept. 1776 Act. New border cuts and Arms on face. New borders on backs of $1 and over. Blank backs on $½ and below. Printed on thick paper by John Carter. Bills of $2 and over were called for redemption by Nov. 1, 1778 pursuant to an Oct. 1777 Act. Signers are Welcome Arnold, Joseph Clarke, John Cole, James Congdon, John Dexter, Thomas Greene, Jonathan Hazard and John G. Wanton. A £10,000 issue authorized at the July 18, 1776 Session was not emitted.

		Good	V.G.
$1/16	[8,000]	100.00	150.00
$1/8	[4,000]	100.00	150.00
$1/4	[4,000]	100.00	150.00
$1/2	[4,000]	100.00	150.00
$1	[2,000]	100.00	150.00

$2	[600]	$7	[600]
$3	[600]	$8	[600]
$4	[600]	$10	[667]
$5	[600]	$20	[600]
$6	[600]	$30	[700]

1777 Written Dates

£50,000 ($166,667) in legal tender Treasury Notes payable 5 years after date with 4% interest and issued for circulation pursuant to the Feb. 1777 Act for money borrowed. Payable to the order of named persons and endorsed in blank. The sum of $86,000 was to be issued in specified denominations from $5 to $30 and the remainder was to be issued in denominations requested by the lender. Denominations over $30 were handwritten. Borders and Arms are same as in the Sept. 5, 1776 issue. Backs are blank. Signed by Joseph Clarke. These notes were refinanced pursuant to an Oct. 1782 Act by the issuance of 5 year 6% notes payable in Lawful Silver Money to the individuals making the exchange.

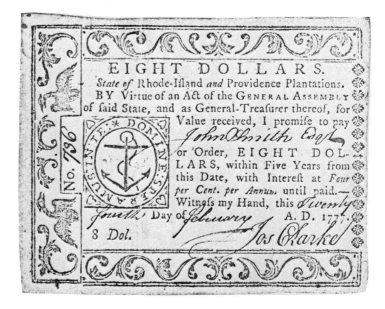

$5	$7	$10	$30
$6	$8	$20	Various

RHODE ISLAND

May 22, 1777

$15,000 (£4,500 Lawful Money) in legal tender Bills of Credit issued pursuant to the May 1777 Act to relieve the shortage of small change. Due May 22, 1785. Typeset and with blank backs. Signers are Paul Allen, James Arnold, Welcome Arnold, William Bowen, John I. Clark, Theodore Foster, George Olney, Joseph DeH. Russell, Ebenezer Thompson, and Olney Winsor.

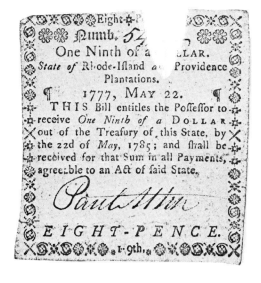

				Good	V.G.
$1/36	(2d)	[15,080]	....	75.00	100.00
$1/24	(3d)	[15,000]	....	75.00	100.00
$1/18	(4d)	[15,000]	....	75.00	100.00
$1/12	(6d)	[15,000]	....	75.00	100.00
$1/9	(8d)	[15,000]	....	75.00	100.00

				Good	V.G.
$1/8	(9d)	[15,000]	....	75.00	100.00
$1/6	(1s)	[15,000]	....	75.00	100.00
$1/4	(1s6d)	[12,000]	....	80.00	110.00
$1/3	(2s)	[8,490]	....	90.00	125.00

1778-9 Written Dates

£40,000 in Treasurer's 6% 3 year Notes issued to exchange for all prior Rhode Island bills of $1 and over pursuant to the May 28, 1778 Act. Payable to the order of individuals making the exchange and endorsed by them. The £10 denomination and portions of the date are also handwritten. All prior bills of $1 and over were made invalid after July 1, 1779. Signer is Joseph Clarke.

£10 [4,000]

Non-circulating Treasurer's Notes were issued both before and after this emission, but did not relate to paper money except for those issued under the October 1782 Act as heretofore mentioned.

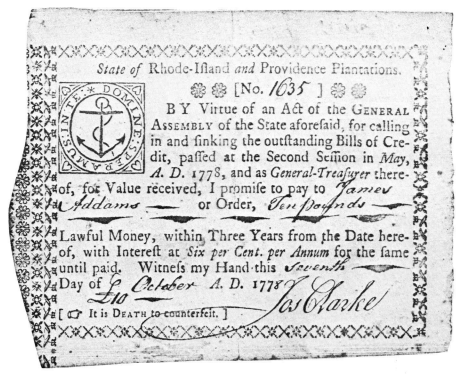

June 1780 Act

£20,000 in legal tender Lawful Money payable in specie with 5% interest on Jan. 1, 1781 out of confiscated real estate. Printed by B. Wheeler. Legal tender prompt-ly suspended. Signers are Metcalfe Bowler, Adam Comstock, Caleb Harris, Benoni Pearce, and Thomas Rumreill.

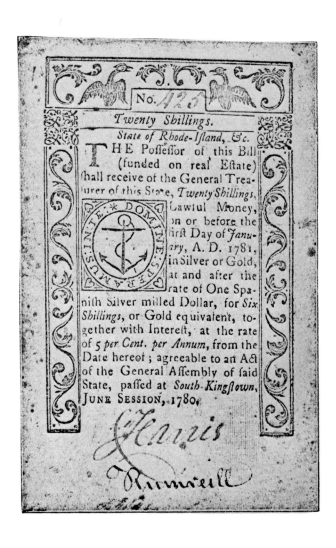

6d	[8,000]
9d	[8,000]
1s	[10,000]
2s	[6,100]
3s	[4,600]
4s	[4,000]
6s	[3,000]
9s	[Issued but not authorized]
10s	[4,000]
20s	[4,000]
30s	[4,000]
40s	[2,000]

RHODE ISLAND

July 2, 1780 Act

£39,000 ($130,000) in legal tender Bills of Credit payable in Spanish milled Dollars by Dec. 31, 1786 with 5% interest was authorized by the July 24, 1780 (not July 2, 1780 as appears on bills) and Mar. 1781 Acts pursuant to a Continental Congress Resolution of Mar. 18, 1780 guaranteeing the payment and making the amount issued dependent upon the amount of Continental Currency exchanged at $40 (old) for $1 (new). Face in black and back in red and black. Printed by Hall & Sellers in Philadelphia on paper watermarked CONFEDERATION in two lines. The face border cuts and back cut surrounding the emblem were engraved by

Henry Dawkins. The border cuts and emblems on the backs are from Jan. 14, 1779 issue of Continental Currency. Sometimes endorsed on the face "Int. Pd. one Yr." Interest was required to be calculated from April 1, 1781 because the bills were not issued until Jan. 1, 1781. The guaranty on the back is sometimes unsigned because many bills were liberated from the unissued supply. The Resolve of June 1788 required their exchange for the May 1786 issue. Signers are Metcalfe Bowler, Adam Comstock, Caleb Harris, and Thomas Rumreill. Guaranty is signed by Jonathan Arnold and Joseph Clarke.

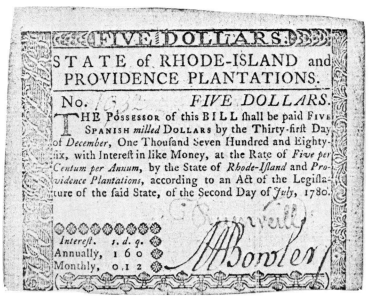
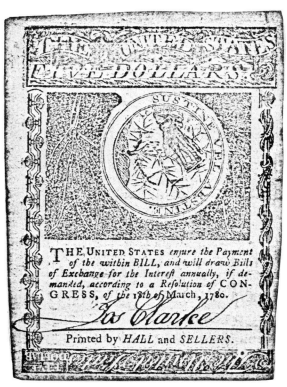

	Fine	V.F.	Unc.			Fine	V.F.	Unc.
$1 [2,600] Ⓤ	15.00	25.00	40.00	$5 [2,600] Ⓤ		15.00	25.00	40.00
$2 [2,600] Ⓤ	15.00	25.00	40.00	$7 [2,600] Ⓤ		15.00	25.00	40.00
$3 [2,600] Ⓤ	15.00	25.00	40.00	$8 [2,600] Ⓤ		15.00	25.00	40.00
$4 [2,600] Ⓤ	15.00	25.00	40.00	$20 [2,600] Ⓤ		15.00	25.00	40.00

RHODE ISLAND

May 1786 Session

£100,000 in legal tender Bills of Credit issued pursuant to May, June and Aug. 1786 Acts for amortizing 4% 7 year loans on realty and known as the Tenth Bank. The legal tender provision was to be enforced by courts summarily without jury trial. In the celebrated proceeding of Trevett vs. Weeden the law was declared invalid for denying trial by jury and there was established the common law principle of trial by jury as a fundamental right of United States citizenry. By the Dec. 1786 Act the illegal features were repealed but the legal tender status was retained. Legal tender was finally repealed by the Sept. 1789 Act by which time the issue had depreciated down to 10% of its original value. Over 96%

of the issue was burned by the State between 1793 and 1803. "Death to Counterfeit" was required to be placed on all bills, but was omitted on the four lowest denominations which had blank backs. By the Dec. 1786 Act the four lowest denominations were approved in their original form. The bills are similar to the Sept. 5, 1776 issue but farm equipment in the State Arms was included on some denominations. Printed by Southwick and Barber on bluish and cream paper. Signers are Samuel Allen, Elijah Cobb, Job Comstock, Jonathan Hazard, and N. Knight. Three signers were required on the three highest denominations and two signers on the others.

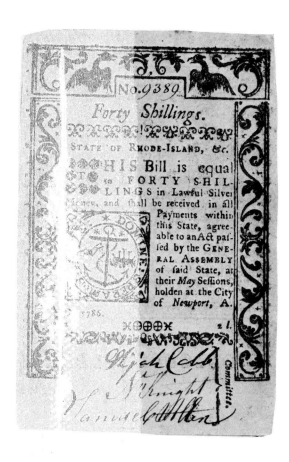

	Fine	V.F.	Unc.
6d [16,000]	20.00	35.00	50.00
9d [16,000]	20.00	35.00	50.00
1s [16,000]	20.00	35.00	50.00
2s6d [16,000]	20.00	35.00	50.00
3s [16,000]	20.00	35.00	50.00
5s [16,000]	20.00	35.00	50.00

	Fine	V.F.	Unc.
6s [16,000]	20.00	35.00	50.00
10s [16,000]	20.00	35.00	50.00
20s [12,000]	20.00	35.00	50.00
30s [10,000]	20.00	35.00	50.00
40s [10,000]	20.00	35.00	50.00
£3 [10,000]	20.00	35.00	50.00

Providence Bank ★ 1791, etc.

The Providence Bank was incorporated on Nov. 5, 1791, having begun to operate in Providence in October, 1791. Its capital was $250,000 divided into 6,250 shares of $400 each, 125 shares being reserved for the United States or the Bank of the United States and 50 shares being reserved for the State. The capital could be doubled. Its bank notes were protected by a counterfeiting provision in the charter.

$1	$2	$3	$5	$10	$20	$30	$50	$100

Bank of Rhode Island ★ 1795, etc.

The Bank of Rhode Island was incorporated on Oct. 28, 1795 to operate at Newport. Its capital was $100,000 divided into 500 shares of $200 each with the right to increase to $500,000. Its bank notes were protected by a counterfeiting provision in the charter. Bank notes dated in the 18th century have not been located.

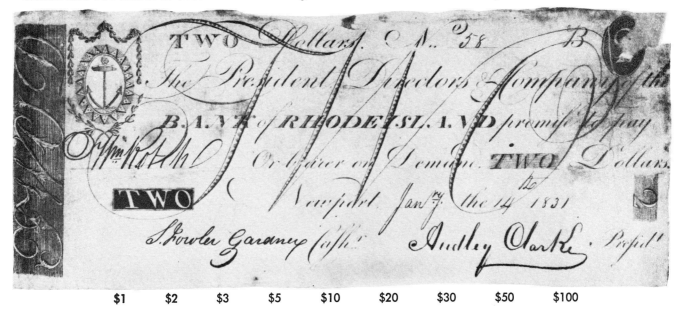

$1	$2	$3	$5	$10	$20	$30	$50	$100

Washington Bank ★ 1800, etc.

The Washington Bank was incorporated during the June 1800 Session with a capital of $50,000 divided into 1,000 shares of $50 each with the right to increase its capital to $150,000. The bank notes were engraved by Amos Doolittle of New Haven. The $1 notes are the first paper money to contain a vignette of George Washington.

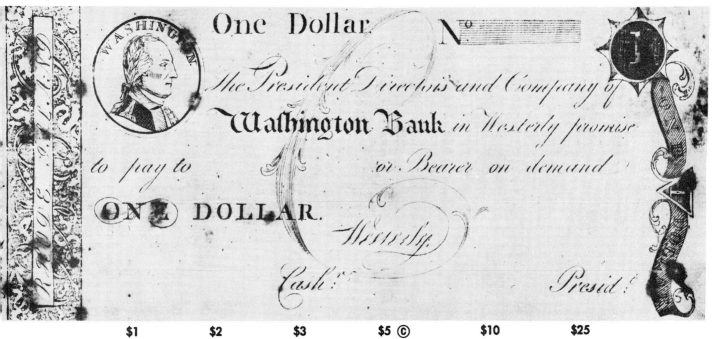

$1	$2	$3	$5 ©	$10	$25

Washington Bank ★ August 22, 1800

Small change notes issued by the Washington Bank at Westerly. Signed by R. Babcock and A. Clarke. Blank backs. Other denominations were issued.

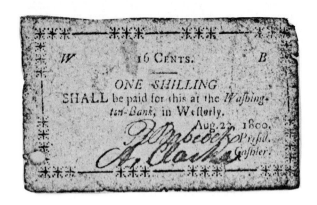

8d (11¢)
1s (16¢)

Bank of Bristol ★ 1800, etc.

The Bank of Bristol was incorporated at the June 1800 Session to operate at Bristol. Its capital was $80,000 divided into 800 shares of $100 each with the right to increase to $300,000. Its bank notes were protected by a counterfeiting provision in the charter.

$1 $2 $3 $5 $10 $20 $50

RHODE ISLAND REFERENCES

Richard LeBaron Bowen, *Rhode Island Colonial Money and its Counterfeiting 1647-1726* (Providence, 1942).

Elston Bradfield, "The Man Who Would Not Accept Paper Money," *The Numismatist* (January 1950).

"Colonial Notes of Rhode Island," *The Numismatist* (January 1912).

Andrew McFarland Davis, "The Emissions of Neighboring Governments—Rhode Island," *Currency and Banking in the Province of Massachusetts Bay* (New York, 1901).

Elisha R. Potter, *A Brief Account of Emissions of Paper Money Made by the Colony of Rhode Island* (Providence, 1837), reprinted (Roxbury, 1865).

—— and Sidney S. Rider, *Some Account of the Bills of Credit or Paper Money of Rhode Island* (Providence, 1880).

Kenneth Scott, *Counterfeiting in Colonial Rhode Island* (Providence, 1960).

James M. Varnum, *The Case of Trevett Against Weeden* (Providence, 1787).

Laws, archives and other public records.

See general references, catalogs, and listings following the Introduction.

SOUTH CAROLINA

GENERAL EMISSIONS

May 8, 1703 Act
July 5, 1707 Act
February 14, 1707(8) Act
April 24, 1708 Act
March 1, 1710(1) Act
November 10, 1711 Act
June 7, 1712 Act
August 27, 1715 Act
March 24, 1715(6) Act
June 30, 1716 Act
August 4, 1716 Act
February 20, 1718(9) Act
June 18, 1720 Act
December 10, 1720 Act
1723
1731
August 20, 1731 Act
March 5, 1736(7) Act
April 5, 1740 Act
September 19, 1740 Act
June 30, 1748
1750-1769 Written Dates
May 16, 1752 Act

July 6, 1757 Act
1760 First Issue
1760 Second Issue
July 25, 1761
May 29, 1762 Act
1767 Written Dates
January 1, 1770
April 7, 1770
April 10, 1774
June 1, 1775
June 10, 1775
November 15, 1775 Order
March 6, 1776 Resolve
October 19, 1776 Ordinance
1777 (December 23, 1776 Act)
February 14, 1777 Ordinance
April 10, 1778
February 8, 1779 Ordinance
1786
May 1, 1786
1787
1788

SPECIAL ISSUERS

Traders and Planters Bank ★ 1730
Promissory Notes of Citizens ★ April-May 1775
City of Charleston ★ (1786)
City of Charleston ★ July 6, 1789
Bank of South Carolina ★ 1792, etc.
Bank of the United States (Charleston Office) ★ 1792, etc.

May 8, 1703 Act

£6,000 (£4,000 sterling at 50% advance) in indented interest bearing legal tender Bills of Credit, known as "Country Bills," were issued to pay for the St. Augustine expedition. Engraved by Joseph Massey and containing the Colony seal. The Dec. 20, 1703 Act called £3,000 for redemption by Mar. 9, 1703(4) and the Nov. 4, 1704 Act called the balance for redemption by Mar. 9, 1705(6). Apparently this was not accomplished because the April 9, 1706 Act continued the remainder in circulation until they were exchanged pursuant to the July 5, 1707 Act. Signers are James Moore, Alexander Parris, and James LeSerurier (Smith). Additional denominations are probable.

50s   £20

July 5, 1707 Act

£8,000 (£5,333 6s8d sterling at 50% advance) in indented Proclamation Money Bills issued to exchange for the prior issue and to finish Charleston fortifications, etc. Legal tender up to 40s and receivable for taxes. Originally to be redeemed in two years, but extended by the Acts of July 12, 1707, July 24, 1708 and Mar. 1, 1710(1) until July 12, 1716. Signers are Richard Beresford, Thomas Broughton, Thomas Nairne, Thomas Smith, and William Smith.

20s [400]   40s [300]   £4 [400]   £6 [300]   £10 [180]   £20 [90]

February 14, 1707(8) Act

£3,000 in indented Bills of Credit issued pursuant to the Feb. 14, 1707(8) Act to exchange for prior issues and to raise armed forces. After issuance the law was repealed by the April 24, 1708 Act.

20s [3,000]

April 24, 1708 Act

£5,000 (£3,333 6s8d sterling at 50% advance) in indented Bills of Credit authorized by the April 24, 1708 Act. Signers are Richard Beresford, Thomas Broughton, George Logan, John Abraham Motte, and William Smith.

20s   40s

March 1, 1710(1) Act

£3,000 (£2,000 sterling at 50% advance) in indented legal tender Bills of Credit were issued pursuant to the Mar. 1, 1710(1) Act to create change. £1,000 were to be exchanged for worn bills. Signers are Richard Beresford, Thomas Broughton, Robert Daniell, Samuel Eveleigh, William Gibbon, Henry LeNoble, George Logan, and Alexander Parris.

5s [8,000]   10s [2,000]

November 10, 1711 Act

£4,000 (£2,666 13s4d sterling at 50% advance) issued to aid North Carolina in defending itself against attacks of the Tusquerora Indians, and thus referred to as Tusquerora Bills. Denominations are not known.

June 7, 1712 Act

£52,000 (£34,666 13s4d sterling at 50% advance) in indented Bills of Credit made legal tender up to 40s by the June 7, 1712 Act. Of this total £32,000 was to be loaned for 12 years on real estate mortgage security, £16,000 was to be exchanged for all outstanding bills except the Tusquerora Bills, and £4,000 was for general expenses. Known as "Bank Bills" and being the first use of paper money in America to stimulate economic progress. Signers are Richard Beresford, Thomas Broughton, Benjamin Godin, George Logan, Arthur Middleton, Joseph Morton, William Rhett, Peter Slann, and Christopher Wilkinson. Other denominations are probable.

5s   £20

August 27, 1715 Act

£30,000 (£15,000 sterling at 100% advance) in indented engraved Bills of Credit were issued for fighting Indians and were receivable for taxes. Made legal tender by the June 30, 1716 Act. Signers are C. Hathaway, Thomas Hepworth, Anthony Mathews, and Robert Tradd. Other denominations are probable.

£4

March 24, 1715(6) Act

£5,000 authorized for military expenses and made legal tender by the June 30, 1716 Act. Denominations are not known.

June 30, 1716 Act

£15,000 (£5,000 sterling at 200% advance) for military expenses. Signers are Andrew Allen, William Bull, Jonathan Drake, Anthony Mathews, and Robert Tradd. Other denominations are probable.

£5   £20

August 4, 1716 Act

£15,000 (£5,000 sterling at 200% advance) in Bills of Credit to buy the services of 32 white mercenary soldiers. Denominations are not known.

February 20, 1718(9) Act

£15,000 (£3,000 sterling at 400% advance) in interest bearing "Rice Bills" issued in anticipation of collection of taxes in rice at 30s per hundredweight (112 pounds). Those redeemed from this and the following issue were reissued pursuant to the Sept. 21, 1721 Act by endorsing "Interest already paid" in red ink across the face. By the 1721 Act taxes were made payable in paper medium instead of rice because of a rise in the price of rice due to inflation. Denominations are not known.

June 18, 1720 Act

£19,000 (£3,800 sterling at 400% advance) in "Rice Bills" issued in anticipation of collection of taxes in rice at 25s per hundredweight (112 pounds). £15,000 from this and the previous issue were reissued as legal tender bills pursuant to the Sept. 21, 1721 Act which was repealed by the Crown on Aug. 27, 1723 leaving the financial affairs of South Carolina in chaos. Denominations are not known.

SOUTH CAROLINA

December 10, 1720 Act

"Rice Orders" payable to bearer in well cleaned merchantable rice in March 1723(4) out of 1,200,000 pounds of rice to be collected in taxes. Legal tender at 30s per hundredweight (112 pounds). Signers are Samuel Eveleigh, William Gibbon, and Robert Tradd. Other denominations are probable.

One hundredweight

1723

£120,000 (£20,000 sterling at 500% advance) in indented legal tender Bills of Credit authorized by the Feb. 23, 1722(3) Act. £80,000 was to be exchanged for all outstanding issues which were to be invalid after Dec. 1, 1723. £40,000 was for public expenses. The Feb. 23, 1722(3) Act was repealed by the Crown on Aug. 27, 1723 after the bills had been issued. The Act of Feb. 15, 1723(4) revived the bills but provided for removal of the four highest denominations from circulation by requiring their use for tax payments. Invalidity of prior outstanding issues was originally deferred to Oct. 15, 1724 and subsequently to Aug. 20, 1738. Printed from copper plates by Joseph Massey. Signers are William Dry, Thomas Hepworth, and Henry Howser.

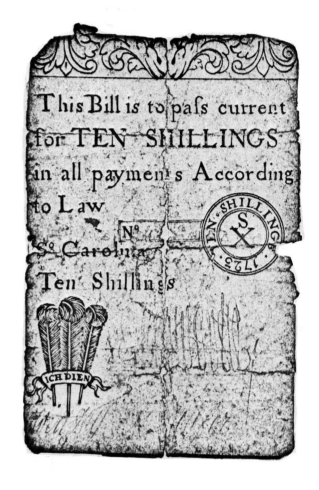

5s	Crown above rose [27,130]	£4	[2,000]
6s3d	Crown above plume [27,130]	£6	[2,000]
7s6d	[27,130]	£8	[1,000]
10s	Plume. ICH DIEN (I serve) [27,130]	£12	[1,000]
£1	[2,000]	£15	[1,000]
£2	[2,000]	£20	[1,000]

Traders and Planters Bank ★ 1730

£50,000 in circulating Promissory Notes bearing 10% interest were issued by a private bank formed by 17 merchants and about 7 planters without authority and using £10,000 in Bills of Credit of the Colony as paid in capital. The Notes contained a vignette of a "drowning Man imploring Assistance." Denominations are unknown.

1731

£106,500 (£15,214 5s8½d sterling at 600% advance) in indented engraved legal tender Bills of Credit authorized by an Aug. 20, 1731 Act to exchange for all outstanding bills. Bills of 4s6d denominations were issued without authority but ratified by the May 4, 1733 Act. All prior issues were originally made invalid after June 1, 1732, but were extended to Mar. 25, 1733(4) by the May 4, 1733 Act. Because of counterfeits, genuine £3, £4, and £15 bills were called in by the June 7, 1735 Act and were reissued after overprinting. An additional emission of £10,000 was authorized by the June 7, 1735 Act to replace worn bills. Signers are Othniel Beale, John Champneys, John Hammerton, Gabriel Manigault, Charles Pinckney, Roger Saunders, and Francis Yonge.

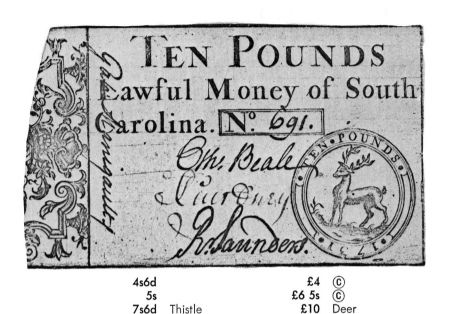

4s6d		£4	©
5s		£6 5s	©
7s6d	Thistle	£10	Deer
20s	©	£12 10s	©
£2		£15	©
£3	©	£20	

August 20, 1731 Act

£104,775 1s3¼d (£14,967 17s4d sterling at 600% advance) in Public Orders payable to bearer and carrying 5% interest were also authorized by an August 20, 1731 Act and were receivable for taxes until March 25, 1738. Signed by Eleazar Allen, Paul Jennys, and Alexander Parris.

£5	£6 5s	£12 10s	£25	£50

March 5, 1736(7) Act

£35,010 in non-interest bearing Public Orders receivable for taxes within 5 years. Signers are John Champneys, John Dart, James Kenlock, Anthony Mathews, and Isaac Mazyck.

£6 [1,945]	£12 [1,945]

April 5, 1740 Act

£25,000 (£3,333 sterling at 700% advance) in non-interest bearing Public Orders receivable for taxes within 4 years. Signers are Edmund Atkin, Robert Austin, William Bull, Jr., John Dart, Thomas Drayton, and Jordan Roche.

£4 [3,124]	£8 [1,563]

357

September 19, 1740 Act

£11,508 (£1,438 10s sterling at 700% advance) in non-interest bearing Public Orders receivable for taxes within 4 years. Signers are Robert Austin, William Bull, Jr., John Colleton, Thomas Drayton, and Jordan Roche.

£4 [959]   £8 [959]

June 30, 1748

£106,500 in engraved indented legal tender Bills of Credit authorized by the May 20, 1748 Act and issued to exchange for all outstanding bills of prior issues. Denominations of £1 and below are smaller than the higher denominations. Signers are William Bull, Jr., William Cattell, Jr., John Dart, Branfill Evance, David Hext, Isaac Mazyck, and William Pinckney. The engraved copper plate for the £1 exists and the plate for the £10 may exist.

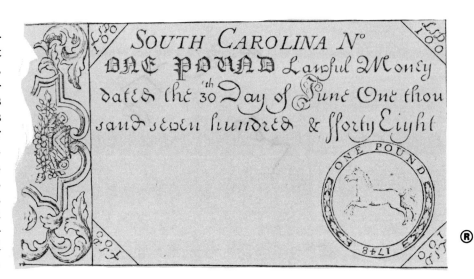

2s6d	[30,000]	£1	Horse [12,508] ®
5s	[30,000]	£2	[3,000]
6s3d	[15,000]	£5	Sheaf [2,350]
7s6d	[15,000]	£10	Deer [2,700] ®
10s	[12,509]	£20	Lion on Crown [1,070]

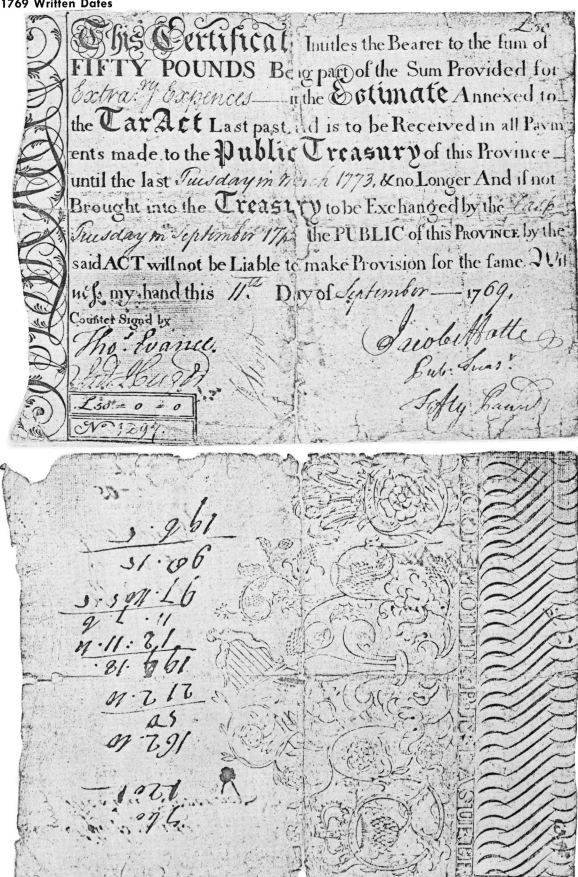

This Certificat Intitles the Bearer to the sum of FIFTY POUNDS Being part of the Sum Provided for Extrary Expences in the Estimate Annexed to the Tax Act Last past, and is to be Received in all Payments made to the Public Treasury of this Province until the last Tuesday in March 1773, & no Longer And if not Brought into the Treasury to be Exchanged by the said Tuesday in September 177 the PUBLIC of this Province by the said ACT will not be Liable to make Provision for the same. Witness my hand this 11th Day of September 1769,

Counter Signd by

Tho. Evance.

Jacob Motte
Pub: Treas:

Fifty Pounds

L 50 . 0 . 0

No 1297

1750-69 Written Dates (Continued)

Indented engraved Public Orders or Tax Certificates of the Public Treasurer payable to bearer and issued for circulation to meet annual Colony expense. Receivable for taxes in succeeding periods and with specific invalidity dates. Elaborately engraved backs with JACOB MOTTE P. TREASURER during his incumbency. Authorized under the taxing acts of May 31, 1750; May 17, 1751; May 1753; May 11, 1754; May 20, 1755; July 6, 1756; May 1757; May 19, 1758; April 7, 1759; July 31, 1760; July 30, 1761; May 29, 1762; Oct. 6, 1764; April 6, 1765; July 2, 1766; May 28, 1767; April 12, 1768; and Aug.

23, 1769. No detail has been found covering Tax Certificates which were issued from 1733 to 1750. Signers are Thomas Bee, Thomas Blake, William Blake, Samuel Brailsford, Miles Brewton, Daniel Doyley, William Drayton, Alexander Fraser, Thomas Gadsden, Daniel Huger, Benjamin Guerard, Rawlins Lowndes, John Mathews, John McQueen, Arthur Middleton*, Jacob Motte, David Oliphant, John Parker, Peter Porcher, Jeremiah Savage, Benjamin Simons, Peter Taylor, Benjamin Waring, and William Wragg.

*Signer of the Declaration of Independence

£5	£10	£20	£30	£50

May 16, 1752 Act

£20,000 in legal tender Bills of Credit issued to replace worn bills and June 30, 1748 bills which were on "bad paper." Signers are Alexander Vander Dussen, Edward Fenwicke, Rawlins Lowndes, Robert Pringle, Jordan Roche, George Saxby, and Thomas Smith.

5s	6s3d	£1	£2	£5	£10

July 6, 1757 Act

£229,300 in Public Orders. Of these £160,000 were for Howarth's regiment and were to be current until November 30, 1762; and £69,300 were for fortifications at Charleston and Fort Johnson and were to be current until June 14, 1766. Signers are Egerton Leigh, Peter Manigault, James Michie, Charles Pinckney, George Ronpell, and George Saxby.

£10 [8,000]	£20 [7,465]

1760 First Issue

£316,693 2s5d in Public Orders authorized by the July 31, 1760 Act. Indented engraved Orders payable to bearer and good for taxes until Nov. 30, 1765. The day and month were written in ink. Issued primarily for expenses of Lyttelton's Expedition. Signers are Samuel Carne, Rawlins Lowndes, Peter Manigault, Isaac Mazyck, William Moultrie, William Roper, and Benjamin Smith.

£25 DEBELLARE BARBAROS RENOVA ANIMUM (Renew the spirit to fight the Barbarians) [6,334]

£50 [3,167]

SOUTH CAROLINA

1760 Second Issue

£125,000 in Public Orders authorized by the Aug. 20, 1760 Act. Indented engraved Orders payable to bearer and good for taxes until Nov. 30, 1766. Issued primarily for the expense of Middleton's Regiment. The day and month were written in ink. Signers are Richard Beresford, William Drayton, Christopher Gadsden, David Grame, Henry Laurens, and John McQueen.

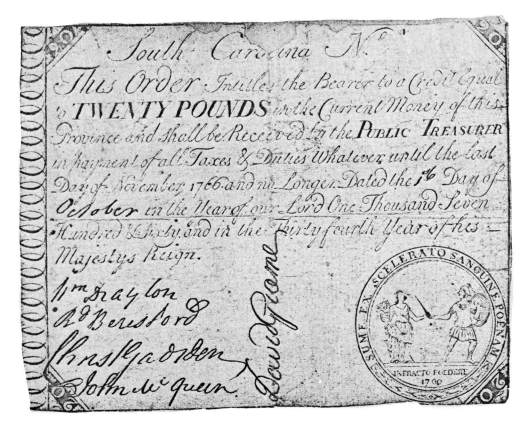

£20 SUME EX SCELERATO SANGUINE POENAM (Exact punishment from guilty blood). INFRACTO FOEDERE (By treaty unbroken) [6,250]

July 25, 1761

£20,000 in indented engraved Bills of Credit authorized by the July 25, 1761 Act to replace worn bills. Signers are Jacob Motte, Jr., John Rutledge, John Savage, Ebenezer Simmons, Jr., Thomas Smith, William Williamson, and John Wragg.

2s6d
5s
7s6d
10s
£1 ©

©

May 29, 1762 Act

£6,000 in Proclamation Money Certificates issued by Directors appointed to regulate the trade on behalf of the Colony with the Cherokee Indians. Signers are Thomas Lambole, Thomas Shubrick, Gabriel Manigault, John Savage, and Thomas Smith.

£2

1767 Written Dates

£60,000 in indented engraved Public Orders payable to bearer and authorized by the April 18, 1767 Act. Receivable for taxes until Sept. 29, 1772. The date is written in ink. Issued to build the Exchange and Customs House and the New Watch House in Charleston.

A handwritten "a" is in each quadrant of all specimens examined. Signers are Miles Brewton, Benjamin Dart, Henry Laurens, Thomas Lynch, Peter Manigault, J. Parsons, Charles Pinckney, Sr., John Rutledge, and Benjamin Smith.

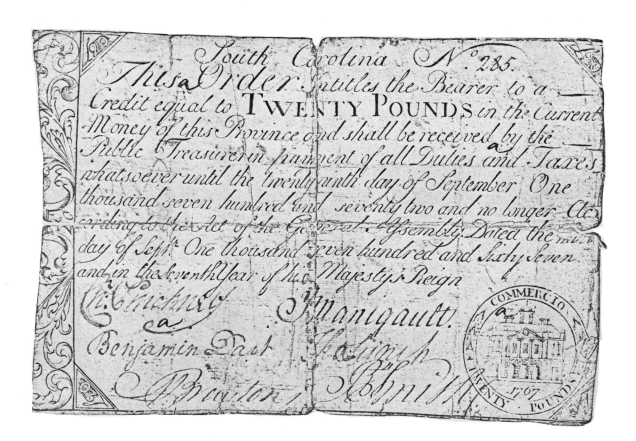

£20 Public building. COMMERCIO (Trade) [3,000]

January 1, 1770

£106,500 in legal tender indented engraved Bills of Credit authorized by the Aug. 23, 1769 Act to exchange for all prior issues. Bills of £2 and over are larger than bills of £1 and under. Prior bills were to be invalid after Aug. 23, 1771. Signers are Thomas Bee, Benjamin Dart, Thomas Evance, Daniel Horry, John Lloyd, John Parker, and Benjamin Waring.

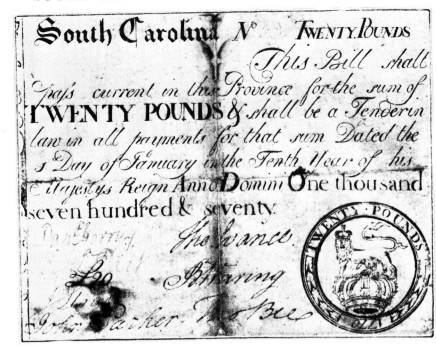

2s6d	[30,000]
5s	[30,000]
6s3d	[15,000]
7s6d	[15,000]
10s	[12,509]
£1	[12,508]
£2	[3,000]
£5	[2,355]
£10	Stag [2,700]
£20	Lion on Crown [1,070]

April 7, 1770

£70,000 in engraved indented Public Orders payable to bearer and authorized by the April 7, 1770 Act. Receivable for taxes until Mar. 25, 1775. Proceeds to be used for building Court Houses, gaols, etc. Signers are Benjamin Elliot, Isaac Hayne, James Parsons, Charles Cotesworth Pinckney, John Poaug, Philip Porcher, and Thomas Smith.

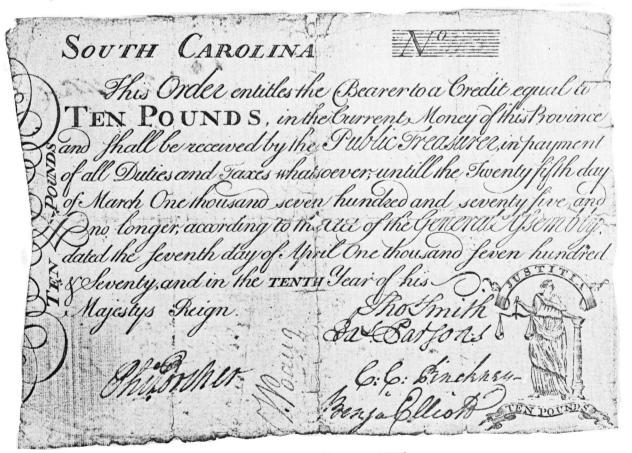

£10   JUSTITIA (Justice) [7,000]

April 10, 1774

Indented engraved Certificates of Audited Accounts approved in the Commons House of Assembly by the Mar. 24, 1774 Resolution. Backs are elaborately engraved. Payable out of next taxes to be levied. The date and denomination are written in ink. Signers are Thomas Bee, Miles Brewton, Gideon Dupont, Jr., Thomas Farr, Jr., Christopher Gadsden, Rawlins Lowndes, and Charles Pinckney, Sr. Miscellaneous odd sums less than £100 were not intended for use as currency.

£100

SOUTH CAROLINA

Promissory Notes of Citizens ★ April-May 1775

Indented private promissory notes jointly signed by Miles Brewton, Benjamin Huger, Thomas Lynch, Henry Middleton, and Roger Smith to finance war expenditures prior to the organization of the Provincial Congress. This issue was apparently to be the ultimate responsibility of the Colony. Engraved faces and backs. Printed on thin paper. Handwritten dates from April 18 to May 23, 1775.

£20
£50

June 1, 1775

£1,000,000 in engraved Certificates authorized by the Provincial Congress on June 14, 1775 following a Resolution passed June 1, 1775 by the Commons House of Assembly. On Feb. 6, 1776 the Provincial Congress increased the number of £50 certificates from £3,000 to £6,000 and correspondingly reduced the number of £5 certificates from £50,000 to £20,000. Only the £20 and £50 have decorative backs as specified by the Council of Safety on June 26, 1775, which backs were engraved by James Oliphant. Printed on thin weak paper. Signers are Peter Bacot, John Berwick, Edward Blake, William Bull, Jr., John Canard, John Colcock, Thomas Corbett, Gideon DuPont, Jr., John Edwards, John L. Gervais, William Gibbes, Robert Ladson, Aaron Loocock, John Loyas, Thomas Middleton, Jacob Motte, Alexander Moultrie, John Neufville, William Parker, Robert Parsons, R. A. Rapley, Thomas Savage, and Benjamin Waring.

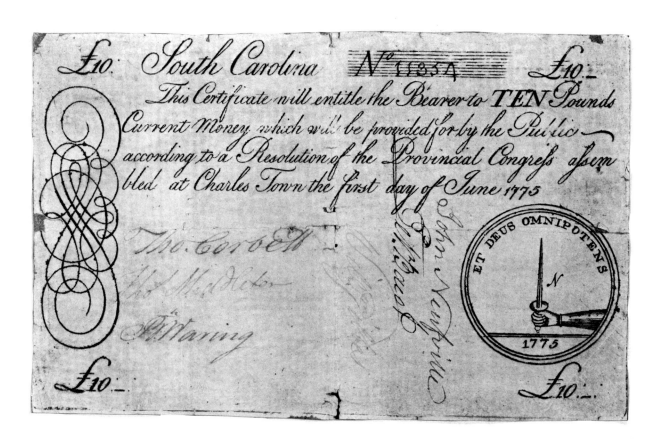

		Good	V.G.	Fine
£5	AUSPICIUM SALUTIS (An auspice of well-being). Splay of 12 arrows representing the United Colonies [20,000]	95.00	125.00	175.00
£10	ET DEUS OMNIPOTENS (And Almighty God). Hand holding sword [40,000]	85.00	115.00	165.00
£20	FIDES PUBLICA (Public trust). Clasped hands [10,000]	95.00	125.00	175.00
£50	POST TENEBRAS LUX (After the darkness light). Woman frightened by a storm and standing next to a tree [6,000]	125.00	165.00	225.00

June 10, 1775

Commons House of Assembly Certificates of Audited Accounts approved by the June 1, 1775 Resolution. Indented engraved certificates with the denomination written in. Similar to the April 10, 1774 certificates. The engraved back is from the same plate as high denominations of the June 1, 1775 issue and containing the motto FOR THE PUBLIC GOOD. Signers are David Deas, Gideon Dupont, Jr., Thomas Farr, Jr., Elias Horry, Jr., Thomas Horry, Theodore Gaillard, Jr., William Gibbes, Isaac Motte, and Charles Pinckney.

£50

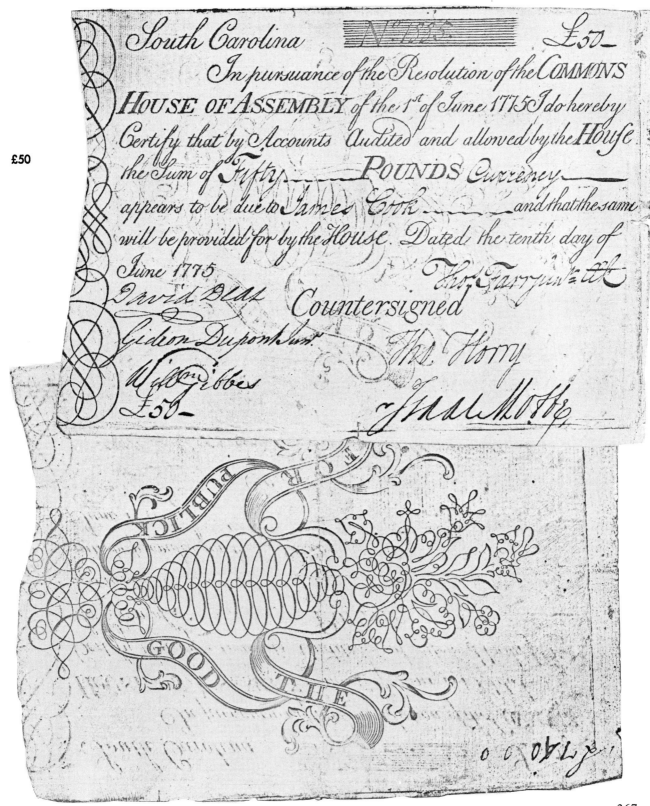

November 15, 1775 Order

£120,000 in Bills of Credit authorized by the Provincial Congress. Engraved and printed by James Oliphant. The four lowest denominations are 2½" x 3", the next three are 2⅜" x 3⅝" and the three highest are 2½" x 4⅜". Signers are John Berwick, P. Bocquet, Jr., Daniel Cannon, Philotheos Chisselle, Paul Douxsaint, Alexander Gillon, G. A. Hall, William Heirving, Ralph Izard, Peter Leger, John W. McQueen, T. Middleton, Jr., R. W. Powell, F. Salvador, Berwick Simon, M. Simons, Anthony Simmons, Roger Smith, A. Toomer, Paul Townsend, Joseph Vivree, Benjamin Waring, and Edward Weyman.

		Good	V.G.	Fine
2s6d	[10,000]	150.00	250.00	350.00
5s	[10,000]	150.00	250.00	350.00
7s6d	[10,000]	150.00	250.00	350.00
10s	[10,000]	150.00	250.00	350.00
15s	[10,000]	150.00	250.00	350.00
20s	[10,000]	150.00	250.00	350.00
30s	[10,000]	150.00	250.00	350.00
£2	UTRUM HORUM MAVIS ACCIPE (Accept whichever of these you prefer [10,000]	150.00	250.00	350.00
£2 10s	PRO LIBERTATE (For freedom) [10,000]	150.00	250.00	350.00
£3	ULTIMA RATIO (The final reckoning) [10,000]	150.00	250.00	350.00

SOUTH CAROLINA

March 6, 1776 Resolve

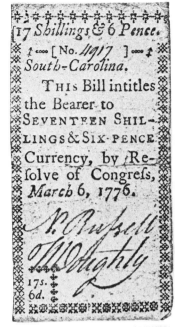

[17 Shillings & 6 Pence.
⁂ [No. 1917] ⁂
South-Carolina.
THIS Bill intitles
the Bearer to
SEVENTEEN SHIL-
LINGS & SIX-PENCE
Currency, by Re-
solve of Congress,
March 6, 1776.

17s.
6d.

£15
South Carolina Nᵒ 3281
THIS BILL intitles the Bearer to
FIFTEEN POUNDS Currency by
a resolution of CONGRESS. March 6, 1776
Jacob Motte
£15
£15

South Carolina Nᵒ 3191 £50.
This Bill entitles the Bearer to Fifty
Pounds Currency by order of the Congress March 6ᵗ
1776
FIFTY POUNDS

One Pound Fifteen Shillings.
[No.]
SOUTH-CAROLINA.
THE Bearer is intitled to ONE
POUND FIFTEEN SHILLINGS
Currency, by Resolve of Congress,
March 6, 1776

1l.
15s

March 6, 1776 Resolve (Continued)

£750,000 in Bills of Credit authorized by the Second Provincial Congress of South Carolina. Denominations of £3 and below were printed by Peter Timothy in red and black from typeset forms with various ornaments including Hebrew and Greek letters. Denominations of 17s6d and below are 3¼″ x 1¾″ and those from £1 10s through £3 are 2⅜″ x 3¼″. The £15 and £25 are engraved and are 3¼″ x 4¾″. The £50 and £100 are engraved and are 3½″ x 5⅜″. The denominations from £15 through £100 are printed on both white and bluish paper. Only the £50 and £100 have printed backs and these contain the motto DEUS PUGNAVIT ET DISSIPANTUR. Signers are Edward Blake, John Deas, William Doughty, Peter Fayssoux, James Fisher, William Gibbes, William Greenwood, Elias Horry, Jr., John Huger, Alexander Inglis, Thomas Jones, Samuel Legare, Peter Leger, John Mathews, John McCall, Jacob Motte, Alexander Moultrie, John Parker, Samuel Prioleau, Jr., N. Russell, Thomas Savage, John Scott, Roger Smith, J. Ward, Thomas Waring, and John Webb.

		Good	V.G.	Fine
1s3d	[10,000]	175.00	250.00	300.00
2s6d	[10,000]	175.00	250.00	300.00
3s9d	[10,000]	175.00	250.00	300.00
5s	[10,000]	175.00	250.00	300.00
6s3d	[12,000]	175.00	250.00	300.00
12s6d	[10,000]	175.00	250.00	300.00
17s6d	[10,000]	175.00	250.00	300.00
£1 10s	[6,000]	175.00	250.00	300.00
£1 15s	[10,000]	175.00	250.00	300.00
£2	[5,500]	175.00	250.00	300.00
£2 5s	[10,000]	175.00	250.00	300.00
£3	[5,000]	175.00	250.00	300.00
£15	Rattlesnake attacking British Lion. MAGNIS INTERDUM PARVA NOCENT (Sometimes small things do harm to big ones) [9,000]	100.00	125.00	200.00
£25	Flourishing tree and fallen tree. MELIOREM LAPSA LOCAVIT (Having fallen it found a better place) [5,200]	125.00	150.00	225.00
£50	Trophies. ANIMIS OPIBUSQUE PARATI (Prepared in spirit and in resources) [3,700]	150.00	185.00	300.00
£100	Thirteen hearts. QUIS SEPARABIT (Who will separate) [2,000]	150.00	185.00	300.00

October 19, 1776 Ordinance

£130,000 ($80,000) in Bills of Credit authorized by the General Assembly on Oct. 19, 1776 to be legal tender at 32s6d in South Carolina currency for one Spanish milled Dollar. Engraved plates with emblems were used to print the faces. Backs are typeset. Thick brownish paper. Signers are John Berwick, Edward Blake, **Peter** Bocquet, Jr., John S. Dart, Benjamin Elliot, Richard Mercer, Philip Neyler, William Parker, William Scott, Jr., Keating Simons, Maurice Simons, and Anthony Toomer.

			Good	V.G.	Fine
$1	(£1 12s6d)	Palm tree. NUSQUAM SUB MOLE FATISCIT (Nowhere does it weaken under weight) [5,000]	80.00	125.00	200.00
$2	(£3 5s)	Tree. SE SUSTULIT IPSA (It raises itself up) [2,500]	80.00	125.00	200.00
$4	(£6 10s)	Elephant. INFESTUS TANTUM INFESTIS (Hostile only to the hostile) [2,500]	80.00	125.00	200.00
$6	(£9 15s)	Wind and waves. TURBAT SED EXTOLLIT (It disturbs but it elevates) [2,500]	80.00	125.00	200.00
$8	(£13)	Wind on rock. IMPAVIDE (Fearlessly) [2,500]	80.00	125.00	200.00
$10	(£16 5s)	Drum and flags. TUTA PEDAMINE VIRTUS (Honor safe in its support) [2,500]	80.00	125.00	200.00

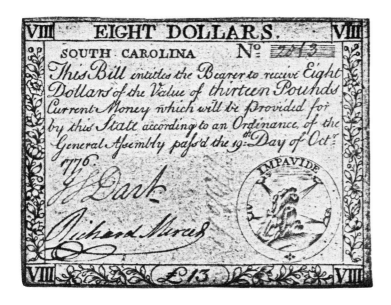

1777 (December 23, 1776 Act)

$308,000 (£500,500) in Bills of Credit authorized by the Act of Dec. 23, 1776. An additional $307,384 was approved if the equivalent sum could not be borrowed. It was not issued. (See issue under Feb. 14, 1777 Ordinance.) Printed with wood cut borders and emblems. Books by J. C. Weigels, Nicholas Verien, and Joachim Camerarius were the source of the emblems and mottoes. The backs were ornamented with Hebrew and Greek letters and other typeset insignia. Printed by Peter Timothy on thick brownish paper. The first $2 and $4 denominations contain a typesetter's error, whereby the date of the Act was printed as Dec. 23, 1777 instead of Dec. 23, 1776, but this error was corrected in brown ink on bills not yet put into circulation. The balance of $2 and $4 bills were printed correctly. Signers are William Ancrum, Edward Blake, George Cooke, John Dart, James Fisher, William Gibbes, William Greenwood, Thomas Jones, Edward Lightwood, John McCall, William Parker, William Price, Nathaniel Russell, Peter Timothy, James Wakefield, Joshua Ward, John Webb, and Plowden Weston. Five signers are on all issued bills, but partially signed unissued remainders appear more often.

			Good	V.G.	Fine
$1	(£1 12s6d)	Tree. PER ARDUA SURGO (I rise through adversity). The m in Timothy is inverted [13,000] Ⓤ	75.00	175.00	275.00
$2	(£3 5s)	Rooster. ET SOLI ET MARTI (For the Sun and for Mars) [10,000] Ⓤ	75.00	175.00	275.00
$2	(£3 5s)	Text on face is misdated December 23, 1777 Ⓤ	100.00	225.00	350.00
$3	(£4 17s6d)	Oracle. FATA VIAM INVENIENT (The fates will find a way) [10,000] Ⓤ	75.00	175.00	275.00
$4	(£6 10s)	Ship. THE ACTAEON. IRAM PRUDENTIA VINCIT (The Actaeon. Wisdom overcomes anger) [10,000] Ⓤ ..	75.00	175.00	275.00
$4	(£6 10s)	Text on face is misdated December 23, 1777 Ⓤ	100.00	225.00	350.00
$5	(£8 2s6d)	Horse. DOMINUM GENEROSA RECUSAT (The well born refuses a master) [5,000] Ⓤ	75.00	175.00	275.00
$6	(£9 15s)	Camel. NEC ONUS NEC META GRAVABIT (Neither burden nor danger will force me down) [10,000] Ⓤ	75.00	175.00	275.00
$8	(£13)	Sailing ship. MULTORUM SPES (The hope of many) [10,000] Ⓤ	75.00	175.00	275.00
$20	(£32 10s)	Bull. AUT MORS AUT VICTORIA (Either death or victory) [2,000] Ⓤ	75.00	175.00	275.00

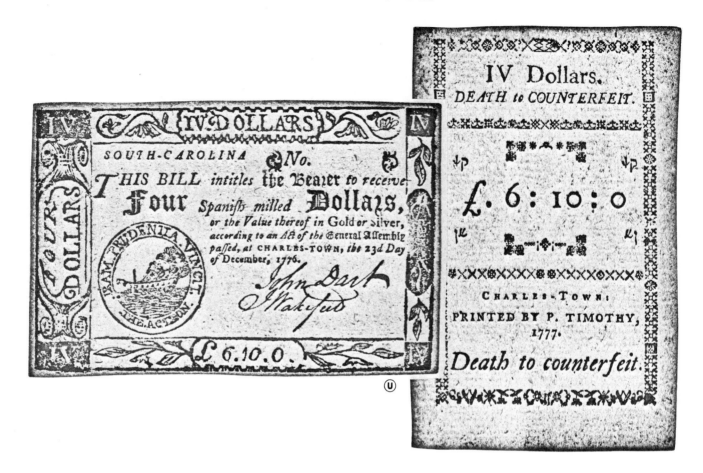

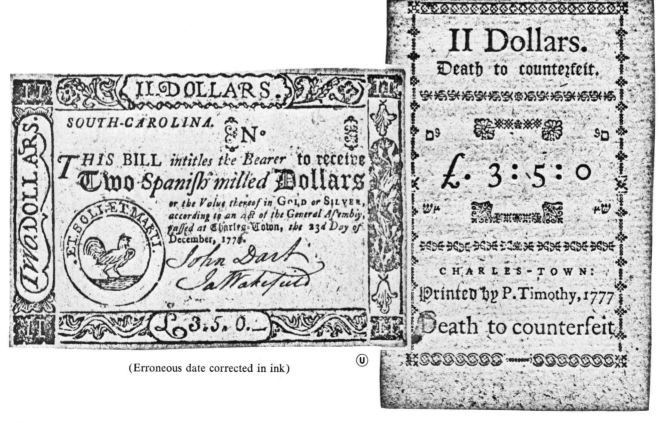

(Erroneous date corrected in ink)

SOUTH CAROLINA

February 14, 1777 Ordinance

$308,000 (£500,500) in Bills of Credit authorized by the Feb. 14, 1777 Ordinance because the amount to be borrowed under the Dec. 23, 1776 Act was not obtainable. Engraved face plates containing emblems and mottoes. Backs are typeset. Printed on dark brown paper. Signers are William Banbury, Edward Blake, Samuel Legare, William Logan, William Parker, and R. W. Powell.

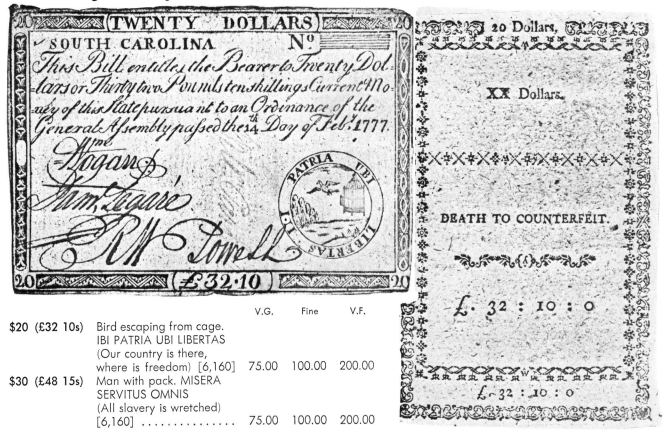

		V.G.	Fine	V.F.
$20 (£32 10s)	Bird escaping from cage. IBI PATRIA UBI LIBERTAS (Our country is there, where is freedom) [6,160]	75.00	100.00	200.00
$30 (£48 15s)	Man with pack. MISERA SERVITUS OMNIS (All slavery is wretched) [6,160]	75.00	100.00	200.00

December 23, 1777 Act

See 1777 (December 23, 1776 Act)

April 10, 1778

£100,000 in legal tender Lawful Money was authorized by General Assembly on Mar. 28, 1778 with the right of the president and Council to issue an additional $1,000,000. Printed on thin paper from engraved plates, the plate for the 20s still being in existence. Signers are John Beale, William Burrows, Jr., Macartan Cambell, Henry Crouch, William H. Gibbes, Thomas Inglis, Nicholas Langford. William Mathews, John Neufville, Jr., John Peronneau, Charles Pinckney, Jr., Thomas Radcliffe, Jr., Jacob Read, William Roper, and Jonathan Sarrazin.

		V.G.	Fine	V.F.
2s6d	Cornucopiae [30,000] .	40.00	60.00	100.00
3s9d	Beaver [30,000]	40.00	60.00	100.00
5s	Phoenix [30,000]	40.00	60.00	100.00
7s6d	Beehive [30,200]	40.00	60.00	100.00

		V.G.	Fine	V.F.
10s	Palmetto [30,001]	40.00	60.00	100.00
15s	Sun [20,000]	40.00	60.00	100.00
20s	Horse [20,000] ®	40.00	60.00	100.00
30s	Hope & anchor [14,533].	40.00	60.00	100.00

February 8, 1779 Ordinance
$1,000,000 in Bills of Credit authorized by the Feb. 8, 1779 Ordinance with the right to issue $3,000,000 more if that sum could not be borrowed. The original $1,000,000 was to be in $40, $60, $80 and $100 denominations only. The denominations of the balance were not specified, but included the $50, $70, and $90 in that group. Faces and backs elaborately engraved by Thomas Coram of Charleston who signed only the new denominations of the later group. Originally legal tender but legal tender status on this and all prior issues was revoked by the Act of Feb. 6, 1782. Printed on both white and bluish paper. Signers are Charles Atkins, Joseph Atkinson, James Bentham, John Blake, George Cooke, Arthur Downes, Theodore Gaillard, Jr., John Hopton, Alexander Inglis, William Morgan, Philip Prioleau, John Scott, John Smyth, Edward Trescot, Plowden Weston, Sims White, and Robert Williams.

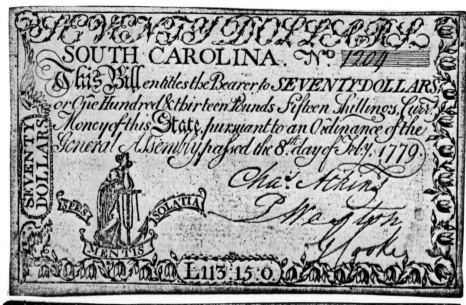

			V.G.	Fine	V.F.
$40	(£65)	Ceres. MINIME VIOLANDA FIDES (Trust by no means is to be violated). Angel blowing trumpet and holding book entitled ANNALS OF AMERICA [2,000]	150.00	200.00	325.00
$50	(£81 5s)	Providence and globe. PROVIDENTIA NOSTRIS PRAESIDEAT (Let foresight guide our people). Atlas holding a boulder (Signed by Coram)	100.00	150.00	250.00
$60	(£97 10s)	Figure and cornucopia. MUTUA DEFENSIO TUTISSIMA (Mutual defense is safest). Lyre, horns and flags [5,000]	100.00	150.00	250.00
$70	(£113 15s)	Hope with anchor. SPES MENTIS SOLATIO (Hope is the consolation of the mind). Prometheus bound and attacked by vulture (Signed by Coram)	100.00	150.00	250.00
$80	(£130)	Man with sword. CONSTANTIA DURISSIMA VINCIT (The firmest constancy will conquer). Shield, liberty cap, etc. [4,000]	100.00	150.00	250.00
$90	(£146 5s)	Warrior. ARMIS CONCURRITE CAMPO (Run together on the field with arms). Hercules strangling a lion. Reverse has a curious No near D of DOLLARS (Signed by Coram)	120.00	175.00	275.00
$100	(£162 10s)	Athena. GLORIAE FUNDAMENTUM FORTITUDO (Bravery is the foundation of glory). Palmetto, drum, flags, etc. [3,000]	150.00	200.00	325.00

1786

£83,184 in Special Indents to raise money for the year 1786 authorized by the Mar. 22, 1786 Act. Typeset and receivable for taxes for the years 1784, 1785, and 1786.

Signers are Peter Bocquet, Jr., T. Bourke, J. Drayton, Alexander Frazier, Jr., Thomas Ogier, and William Price.

2s6d	FIDES PUBLICA (Public trust) [2,000]
5s	[3,736]
10s	[2,000]
£1	[2,000]
£1 10s	[2,000]
£3	[2,000]
£5	[2,000]
£10	[2,000]
£20	[2,000]

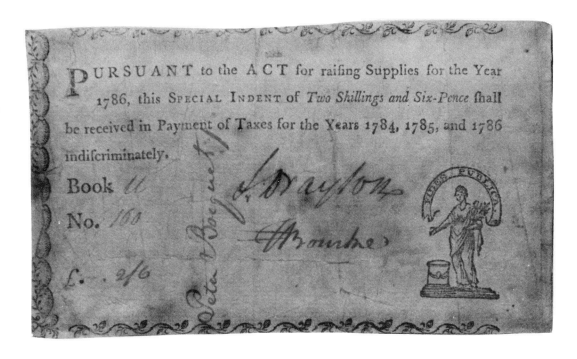

May 1, 1786

May 1, 1786 (Continued)

£100,000 in Loan Office Bills of Credit authorized by the Acts of Oct. 12, 1785 and Mar. 22, 1786 and receivable for taxes until May 1, 1791 on a par with specie. Secured by land mortgages or specie. The use for taxes was extended by the Act of Feb. 19, 1791. Engraved by Abernethie of Charleston. Denominations of 2s6d and 5s were originally authorized but subsequently revoked before issuance. Signers are John Huger, T. Jones and John Postell. Previous attempts by the Acts of May 29, 1736 and June 17, 1746 to reestablish a General Loan Office currency had been disapproved by the Crown.

£1   HONOR ET JUSTITIA (Honor and justice) [6,250]
£2   PRAEMIUM INDUSTRIAE (The reward of industry) [6,250]

£3   HINC OPES (Hence our wealth) [6,250]
£10   VOX POPULI (The voice of the people) [6,250]

City of Charleston ★ (1786)

£8,650 in Bills of the City of Charleston authorized by the July 12, 1786 and Oct. 20, 1786 City Ordinances to provide small denominations which were lacking in the May 1, 1786 State Loan Office issue. The City deposited £8,650 in Loan Office Bills with the Loan Office to secure the City issue. The city ordinances were repealed in July 1788. Printed by Abernethie. Signers are John Huger, T. Jones, Thomas Ropers, and John Webb. Other denominations are probable.

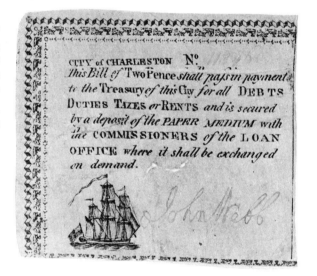

2d
5s3d   ABERNETIHE misspelled
10s

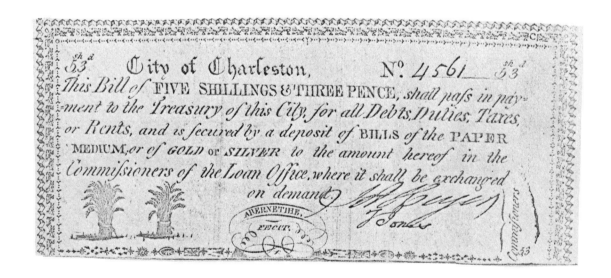

1787

£64,000 in Special Indents to raise money for the year 1787 and authorized by the Mar. 28, 1787 Act. Typeset and receivable for taxes for the years 1784, 1785, 1786 and 1787. Signers are Peter Bacot, James Ballantine, James Kennedy, William Roper, and Edward Trescot.

Ⓤ

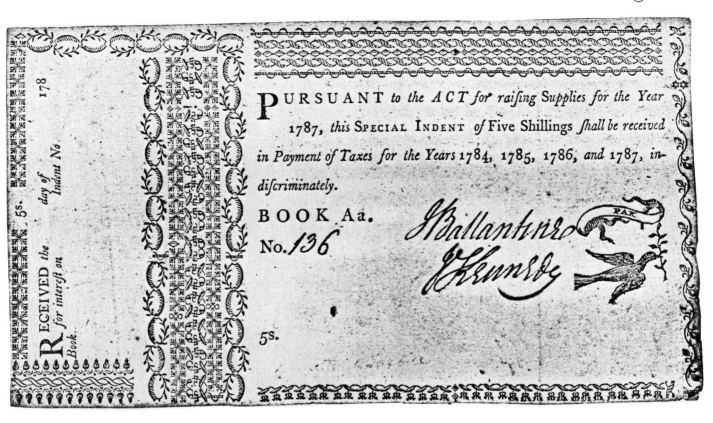

2s6d [1,000]	£1 [2,000]	£6 [2,000]
5s PAX [3,500] Ⓤ	£3 [1,000]	£10 [2,000]
10s [2,000]	£5 [1,000]	£20 [1,000]

1788

£125,000 in Special Indents to raise money for the year 1788 and authorized by the Feb. 27, 1788 Act. Receivable for taxes for the years 1784 through 1788 inclusive. Typeset. Signers are James Ballantine, Jacob Deveaux, and James Kennedy.

1s [1,000]	10s [2,400]	£3 [1,200]	£10 [3,622]
1s6d [1,000]	£1 [2,000]	£5 [4,000]	£20 [2,000]
5s [3,500]	£2 [1,489]	£6 [3,000]	

SOUTH CAROLINA

City of Charleston ★ July 6, 1789

City of Charleston Treasury Notes engraved by Abernethie and receivable in all payments due the city. Signers are S. Beach, L. Foster, James O'Hear, and C. Warham.

6d	Beehive
9d	Alligator
1s3d	Tobacco and hemp rope. TREASUSY misspelled (U)
2s	Lighthouse
2s6d	Cotton plant

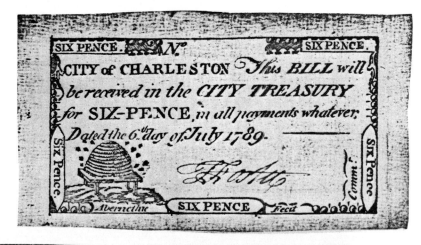

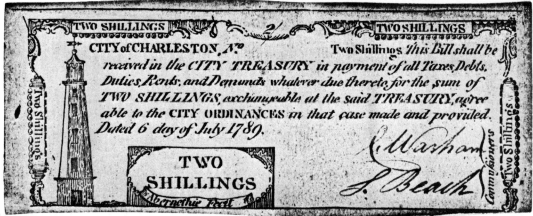

Bank of South Carolina ★ 1792, etc.

The Bank of South Carolina as a private unincorporated bank commenced business in Charleston by April 1792 and its bank notes were made acceptable at the Charleston Office of Discount and Deposit of the Bank of the United States (first bank) on Aug. 28, 1792. These bank notes were engraved by Creed whose name appears on them. Double numbering was provided for on some denominations. The higher denominations were larger in size than the lower denominations to prevent alteration. Thomas Jones signed the early bills as president. The bank was incorporated on Dec. 19, 1801 for 21 years with a capital of $640,000 and a debt limitation (including bank notes) of its specie deposits plus three times its capital. (U)

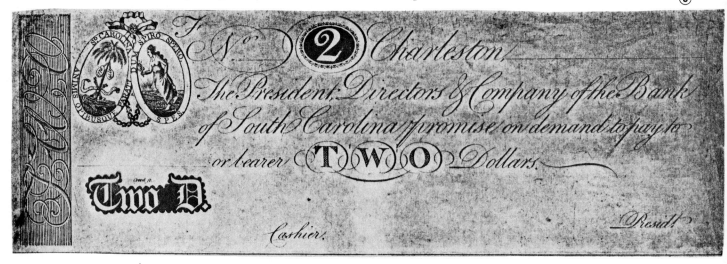

$1	Plate letters A, B, C, D, & E (U)
$2	Plate letters F, G, H, J, & K (U)
$5	Plate letters A, B, C, & D

$10	Plate letters A & B
$20	Plate letters M, N, O, P, & Q
$100	Plate letters R, S, T, U & V

Bank of the United States * 1792, etc.

The Charleston Office of Discount and Deposit of the Bank of the United States (first bank) operated from 1792 to 1811 and issued $802,735 in circulating bank notes. A fuller description of these branch bank notes and other branch bank data is included under the Pennsylvania listings.

A flying eagle bearing the Arms of the United States:

| $5 | $10 | $20 | $50 | $100 |

A heraldic eagle with 13 stars around its head: Ⓒ

| $5 | $10 | $20 Ⓒ | $50 | $100 |

A heraldic eagle in an oval frame containing 15 stars: Ⓒ

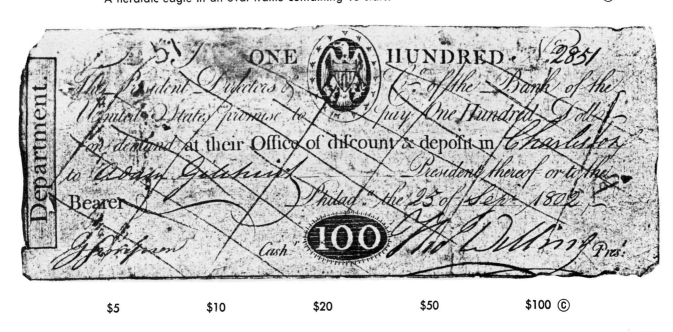

| $5 | $10 | $20 | $50 | $100 Ⓒ |

SOUTH CAROLINA

SOUTH CAROLINA REFERENCES

An Account of the Rise and Progress of the Paper Bills of Credit in South Carolina (1739), reprinted in Vol. IX of *Statutes at Large of South Carolina* (Columbia, 1841), etc.

An Essay on Currency (Charleston, 1734), reprinted.

W. A. Clark, *The History of the Banking Institutions Organized in South Carolina Prior to 1860* (Columbia, 1922).

Condy Raguet, *A Treatise on Currency and Banking* (1840).

David Ramsay, "Fiscal History of South Carolina," *The History of South Carolina* (Charleston, 1809).

Kenneth Scott, "Some Counterfeiters of Provincial Currency," *The South Carolina Historical Magazine,* Vol. 57, p. 14 (1956).

"South Carolina Colonial Notes," *The Coin Collector's Journal* (March 1880).

Laws, archives and other public records.

See general references, catalogs, and listings following the Introduction.

VERMONT

February 1781

£25,155 in legal tender Bills of Credit authorized by the Act of April 14, 1781 for carrying on the War and increasing the amount of paper money in circulation. Redeemable by June 1, 1782 on the basis of 1 Spanish milled Dollar or its gold equivalent for 6s in bills. By an earlier Act of February 22, 1781 a total issue of only £5,590 was approved with similar provisions but was not acted upon. When the £25,155 issue was printed the date of the earlier Act was included by error. This error was subsequently ratified by the Act of June 27, 1781. Legal tender was revoked as of June 1, 1782 by the Act of February 28, 1782, but the bills retained their validity for tax payments. By the Act of October 27, 1781 the Treasury was denied the right to recirculate the bills and

a committee to burn them was appointed. The engraved seal shows 13 joined links and one loose link exemplifying Vermont's objection to being excluded from being one of the original colonies asserting statehood. The motto VERMONT CALLS FOR JUSTICE emphasizes this desire for recognition. The border cuts on the face and back have set type within them. On the lowest five denominations the redemption basis was stated as 6s8d per ounce in silver and the highest three denominations used the equivalent statutory language of Spanish milled Dollars at 6s per dollar. Printed by Spooner and Green on thin weak paper. Signers are John Fasset, Peter Olcott, J. Porter, and E. Walbridge.

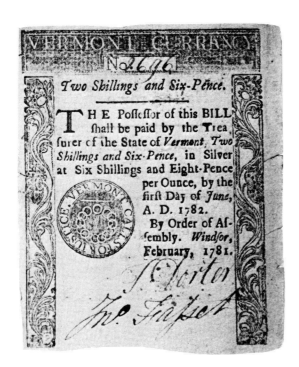

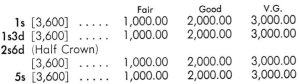

		Fair	Good	V.G.
1s	[3,600]	1,000.00	2,000.00	3,000.00
1s3d	[3,600]	1,000.00	2,000.00	3,000.00
2s6d	(Half Crown)			
	[3,600]	1,000.00	2,000.00	3,000.00
5s	[3,600]	1,000.00	2,000.00	3,000.00

		Fair	Good	V.G.
10s	[3,600]	1,000.00	2,000.00	3,000.00
20s	(One Pound)			
	[3,600]	1,000.00	2,000.00	3,000.00
40s	[3,600]	1,000.00	2,000.00	3,000.00
£3	[3,600]	1,000.00	2,000.00	3,000.00

VERMONT REFERENCES

"Bills of Credit—1781," *Records of the Governor and Council of the State of Vermont* (Montpelier, 1875).

Terrence G. Harper, "Vermont Paper Money," *Numismatic Scrapbook Magazine* (March 1964).

Richard T. Hoober, "Colonial Finances in Vermont," *The Numismatist* (January 1951).

Sanborn Partridge, "Some Comments on the Vermont Notes of 1781," *Colonial Newsletter* (April 1975).

Henry Phillips, Jr., "Vermont Paper Money," *Historical Sketches of the Paper Currency of the American Colonies* (Roxbury, 1865).

Charles N. Schmall, "Historical Note on the Colonial Coinage and Paper Money of Vermont," *Numismatic Scrapbook Magazine* (August 1946).

"Vermont Paper Money," *Historical Magazine* (May 1863).

Ted N. Weissbuch, "A Chapter in Vermont's Revolutionary War Finance," *Vermont History* (January 1961), reprinted.

Laws, archives and other public records.

See general references, catalogs, and listings following the Introduction.

VIRGINIA

GENERAL EMISSIONS

June 1755
December 11, 1755
March 1756
June 8, 1757 Act
October 12, 1758 Act
April 5, 1759 Act
November 21, 1759 Act
March 11, 1760 Act
May 24, 1760 Act
April 7, 1762 Act
1770 (November 7, 1769 Act)
July 11, 1771 Act
April 1, 1773 James River Bank Forms
March 4, 1773 Act (September 1773)
July 17, 1775 Ordinance Small Size Notes
July 17, 1775 Ordinance Large Size Notes

September 1, 1775 James River Bank Forms
May 6, 1776 Ordinance
October 7, 1776 Act
May 5, 1777 Act
October 20, 1777 Act
May 4, 1778 Act with Handwritten Date
May 4, 1778 Act with Printed Date
October 5, 1778 Act
May 3, 1779 Act
May 1, 1780 Act with Handwritten Date
July 14, 1780 Act
July 25, 1780
October 16, 1780 Act with Printed Back
October 16, 1780 Act for Clothing the Army
March 1, 1781 Act
May 7, 1781 Act

SPECIAL ISSUERS

F. James Doudas ★ May 5, 1777
John Hough, Jr. ★ (Undated)
Bank of Alexandria ★ 1793, etc.
Bank of the United States (Norfolk Office) ★ 1795, etc.

June 1755

£20,000 in legal tender Treasury Notes issued for French and Indian War needs pursuant to the Act passed at the May 1755 Session and redeemable with 5% interest by June 30, 1756. The signer is John Robinson. Denominations are unknown.

December 11, 1755

£40,000 in legal tender Treasury Notes authorized on Aug. 5, 1755 and redeemable with 5% interest by June 30, 1760. Issued up to Aug. 1, 1756 and some probably bear intervening dates. By the Act of April 14, 1757 interest was terminated on Dec. 1, 1757 and all notes called for exchange by Dec. 1, 1759 because of counterfeits. Signers are John Chiswell, Peyton Randolph, and John Robinson. Several additional denominations apparently existed.

10s ©
£5 ©

March 1756

£65,000 (£25,000, £30,000, and £10,000) in legal tender Treasury Notes issued pursuant to the Mar. 25, 1756 Act and redeemable with 5% interest on Dec. 15, 1757 as to £10,000 and on June 30, 1760 as to £55,000. By the Act of April 14, 1757 interest was terminated on Dec. 1, 1757 and the notes called for exchange by Dec. 1, 1759. Signers are Robert Carter Nicholas, Peyton Randolph, and John Robinson. Denominations are unknown.

June 8, 1757 Act

£179,962 10s (£80,000 for expenses and £99,962 10s to exchange for the two prior emissions) in legal tender Treasury Notes without interest redeemable by Mar. 1, 1765. An additional issue of £32,000 was approved at the May 1758 Session. The redemption was extended to Oct. 20, 1769 at the Nov. 1761 Session. Ornamented cast borders surrounding typeset text and a small cast cut of the Colony seal in the upper left or upper right.

The motto on the seal is EN DAT VIRGINIA QUARTAM (Behold Virginia contributes one quarter of the Arms). Printed on thin laid paper by William Hunter. Signers are Philip Johnson, Robert Carter Nicholas, Edmund Pendleton, John Randolph, Peyton Randolph, and Benjamin Waller. One signer for the four lowest denominations and two for the others.

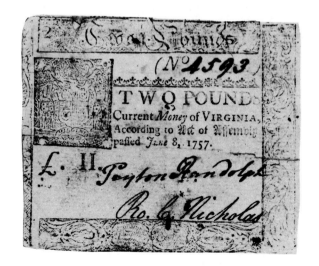

1s [33,000+] ©
1s3d [33,000+]
2s6d [30,000+]
5s [30,000+]
10s [30,000+]
20s [30,000+] ©
£2 [6,000+]
£3 [6,000+] ©
£5 [6,000+]
£10 [6,000+]

VIRGINIA

October 12, 1758 Act

£57,000 in legal tender Treasury Notes redeemable without interest by Sept. 14, 1766. The redemption date was extended to Oct. 20, 1769 at the Nov. 1761 Session. The Colony seal is larger than in the previous issue. New cast border cuts. In excavations at Colonial Williamsburg cast lead cuts for one border and one seal have been found next to the printing shop. Printed by William Hunter on thin laid paper. Signers are Philip Johnson, Robert Carter Nicholas, Edmund Pendleton, John Randolph, Peyton Randolph, and Benjamin Waller. One signer for the four lowest denominations and two for the others.

1s (12d) [20,000]
1s3d [20,000]
2s6d [25,000]
5s (Crown) [25,000]
10s (2 Crowns) [25,000]
20s (4 Crowns) [25,000]
£2 (40s) [25,000]
£3 (12 Crowns) [25,000] ©
£5 (20 Crowns) [25,000]

April 5, 1759 Act

£52,000 in legal tender Treasury Notes redeemable without interest by April 20, 1768. The redemption date was extended to Oct. 20, 1769 at the Nov. 1761 Session. Similar to the previous issue. Signers are George Braxton, Philip Johnson, Robert Carter Nicholas, John Randolph, Peyton Randolph, and Benjamin Waller. One signer for the four lowest denominations and two signers for the others.

1s [17,778]
1s3d [17,778]
2s6d (30d) [20,000]
5s (Crown) [20,000]
10s (2 Crowns) [15,000] ©
20s (4 Crowns) [15,000] ©
£2 (40s) [2,000]
£3 (12 Crowns) [2,000]
£5 (20 Crowns) [2,000]

November 21, 1759 Act

£10,000 (£5,000 and £5,000) in legal tender Treasury Notes redeemable without interest by Oct. 20, 1769. Similar to the Oct. 12, 1758 issue. Signers are Robert Carter Nicholas, Peyton Randolph, and perhaps others. Additional denominations may have been issued.

£3 (12 Crowns)
£5 (20 Crowns)

March 11, 1760 Act

£20,000 in legal tender Treasury Notes redeemable by Oct. 10, 1768. Redemption date extended to Oct. 20, 1769 at the Nov. 1761 Session. Similar to the Oct. 12, 1758 issue. Signers are Robert Carter Nicholas, John Randolph, and Peyton Randolph. One signer for the two lowest denominations and two signers for the others.

2s6d (30d) [5,334]
  5s (Crown) [5,333]
  £2 (40s) [1,800] ©
  £3 (12 Crowns) [1,800]
  £5 (20 Crowns) [1,800] ©

May 24, 1760 Act

£32,000 in legal tender Treasury Notes redeemable by Oct. 20, 1769. Similar to the Oct. 12, 1758 issue. Signers are George Braxton, James Cooke, Philip Johnson, Robert Carter Nicholas, John Randolph, Peyton Randolph, and Benjamin Waller. One signer for the four lowest denominations and two signers for the others.

  1s [16,670]
1s3d [16,664]
2s6d (30d) [7,000]
  5s (Crown) [7,000] ©
 10s (2 Crowns) [7,000] ©
 20s (4 Crowns) [7,000]
  £2 (40s) [1,700]
  £3 (12 Crowns) [1,700]
  £5 (20 Crowns) [1,700]

April 7, 1762 Act

£30,000 in legal tender Treasury Notes redeemable by Oct. 20, 1769 and issued pursuant to the April 7, 1762 Act. Similar to the Oct. 12, 1758 issue. Signers are John Blair, Jr., Philip Johnson, Robert Carter Nicholas, John Randolph, Peyton Randolph, and Benjamin Waller. One signer for the two lowest denominations and two signers for the others.

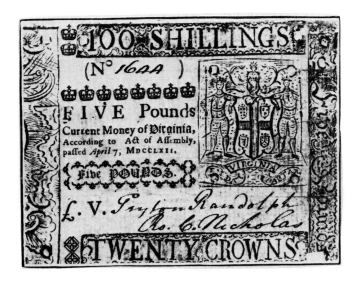

2s6d [6,600]
5s [6,700]
10s [5,000]
20s (4 Crowns) [5,000]
£2 (40s) [2,000] ©
£3 (12 Crowns) [2,000]
£5 (20 Crowns) [2,000] ©

1770 (November 7, 1769 Act)

£10,000 in Treasury Notes without legal tender status redeemable by Nov. 20, 1771 and authorized on Nov. 7, 1769. Ornamented borders and a large artistic Colony seal cut by William Waddill. Printed from cast cuts and type by William Rind. Signers are John Blair, Jr., and Peyton Randolph.

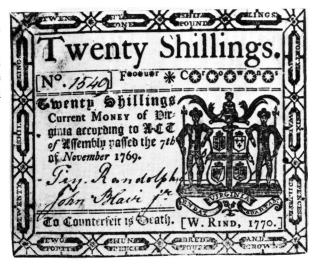

20s (4 Crowns) ©
£2 (8 Crowns)
£5 (20 Crowns) ©

July 11, 1771 Act

£30,000 in Treasury Notes without legal tender status and redeemable by Dec. 10, 1775. Similar to 1770 issue. Printed by William Rind with cuts made by William Waddill. "W.N.Pr." or "Wm.Nn.Pr." refers to William Nelson, President of the Council. The word TOBACCO refers to the fact that the issue was to pay for tobacco lost by floods. Virginia in 1730 had begun the use of public warehouse receipts for tobacco and these "Hogshead" notes or transfer notes were freely used in lieu of money. It was the loss of such stored tobacco that forced the Colony to make good its tobacco warehouse receipts by this issue of money. Signers are John Blair, Jr. and Peyton Randolph.

£2 (8 Crowns) ©
£3 (12 Crowns)
£5 (20 Crowns) ©

VIRGINIA

April 1, 1773 James River Bank Forms

In an emergency arising out of the discovery in Jan. 1773 of an extensive circulation of deceptive counterfeits of the Treasury Notes authorized Nov. 1769 and July 1771 those issues were recalled for immediate exchange by Act of Mar. 4, 1773. Treasurer's Promissory Notes in the sum of £36,384 without legal tender status were approved for the exchange and were payable by Dec. 10, 1775. The best available currency paper was the engraved forms previously brought to Virginia from England by Col. Thomas Tabb for circulating notes to be issued by a proposed private bank to be named the James River Bank. The Crown refused to approve the bank. The forms were accepted by the Virginia Assembly for use as indented Promissory Notes of the Virginia Treasury on condition that the backs were printed and on condition that other notes on English paper would be substituted by June 1, 1774 for the forms to be initially issued. The faces of the James River Bank forms were filled in by hand using parentheses to eliminate inapplicable text. The backs were printed with the denomination and a typeset border. The notes were indented. Signers are John Blair, B. Dandridge, Robert Carter Nicholas, and Peyton Randolph.

	Good	V.G.	Fine			Good	V.G.	Fine
20s	150.00	225.00	350.00		£8	250.00	400.00	700.00
£3	150.00	225.00	350.00		£12	250.00	400.00	700.00
£5	150.00	225.00	350.00					

VIRGINIA

March 4, 1773 Act (September 1773 Issue)

£36,384 to be substituted by June 1, 1774 for Treasurer's Promissory Notes issued on James River Bank forms was authorized by the Mar. 4, 1773 Act. Elaborately engraved by Harry Ashby of London and printed in England on fine laid paper. The notes did not reach Virginia until Sept. 1773 and were then completed, indented and emitted. Signers are John Blair, B. Dandridge, Philip Johnson, William Norvell, and Peyton Randolph. Countersigned by Robert Carter Nicholas on the back. The original copper plate used for printing the £3 notes exists.

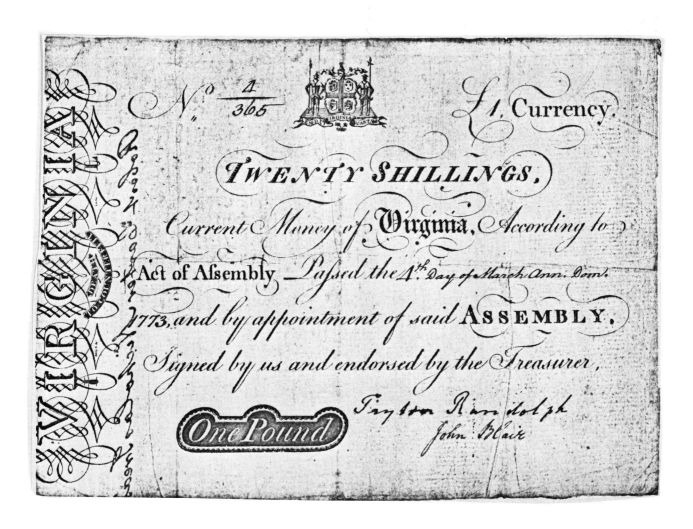

	Good	V.G.	Fine		Good	V.G.	Fine
20s (£1)	100.00	250.00	400.00	£3	100.00	250.00	400.00
£2	100.00	250.00	400.00	£5	100.00	250.00	400.00

VIRGINIA

July 17, 1775 Ordinance Small Size Notes

£350,000 in Treasury Notes redeemable by Jan. 1, 1784 were authorized at the July 17, 1775 Richmond Convention. New designs and different paper were required. Heavy rag paper containing blue fibres was obtained and used. Borders, Arms, and text were separately engraved and combined for printing. Test proofs of the borders and Arms for the 1s3d and 2s6d have the Arms on the left instead of the right side and have the side borders positioned in the same manner as the May 6, 1776 issue rather than that of this July 17, 1775 issue. There was insufficient paper available to complete the emission and two additional issues followed, one on the 1773 Ashby forms and one on the James River Bank forms. Signers are John Burnell, John Dixon, Philip Johnson, Henry King, George Lyne, John H. Norton, William Norvell, John Pendleton, Josiah Parker, Edmund Randolph, and John Tazewell. One signer for the two lowest denominations and two signers for the others.

		Good	V.G.	Fine
1s3d	(Pistareen). "and" in denomination in text [25,000] .	25.00	50.00	75.00
1s3d	(Pistareen). "&" in denomination in text [25,000] ..	25.00	50.00	75.00
1s3d	Proof of border cuts and Arms only			
2s6d	"SIXPENCE" in one word [25,000]	25.00	50.00	75.00
2s6d	"Six Pence" in two words [25,000] ©	25.00	50.00	75.00
2s6d	Proof of border cuts and Arms only			
5s	(Crown)	25.00	50.00	75.00
7s6d	....	25.00	50.00	75.00
10s	(2 Crowns)	25.00	50.00	75.00
12s6d	....	40.00	75.00	100.00
20s	FOWR CROWNS misspelled in right border	40.00	75.00	100.00
£2	(8 Crowns)	40.00	75.00	100.00
£3	(12 Crowns)	40.00	75.00	100.00

VIRGINIA

July 17, 1775 Ordinance Large Size Notes

After the supply of new rag paper for the small notes prepared under the July 17, 1775 Ordinance was exhausted, the use "of other proper paper to make up the deficiency" was approved at the Dec. 1775 Session. Since some note forms engraved by Harry Ashby were left over from the Sept. 1773 emission, such forms were used by filling in appropriate text in ink and by eliminating inapplicable portions by the use of parentheses. Signers are Philip Johnson, William Norvell, and John Tazewell. Countersigned on the back by Robert Carter Nicholas.

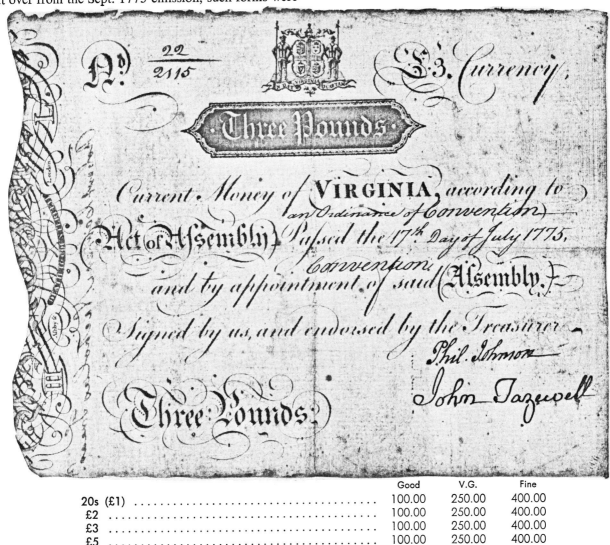

	Good	V.G.	Fine
20s (£1)	100.00	250.00	400.00
£2	100.00	250.00	400.00
£3	100.00	250.00	400.00
£5	100.00	250.00	400.00

September 1, 1775 James River Bank Forms

After the supply of paper for both the small notes and the large Ashby notes was exhausted, the supply of James River Bank forms which had not been used for the April 1, 1773 issue were filled in to complete the emission authorized under the July 17, 1775 Ordinance. Inapplicable words were not eliminated by being enclosed within parentheses, as had taken place in the April 1, 1773 issue. The backs were left blank, but some note forms had printed backs left over from the printing of backs for the April 1, 1773 issue and were used. Signers are B. Dandridge, Philip Johnson, Robert Carter Nicholas, William Norvell, and Josiah Parker.

		Good	V.G.	Fine
10s				
20s	With and without engraved lines for fill in	90.00	125.00	300.00
20s	Printed back	90.00	125.00	300.00
£4	....	90.00	125.00	300.00
£5	With and without engraved lines for fill in	90.00	125.00	300.00
£8	....	90.00	125.00	300.00
£10	....	90.00	125.00	300.00
£12	With and without engraved lines for fill in	90.00	125.00	300.00

May 6, 1776 Ordinance

£100,000 ($333,333) in legal tender Treasury Bills authorized on May 6, 1776 and redeemable by Jan. 1, 1784. Cast cuts from the July 17, 1775 small size issue were shifted and modified for corresponding shilling denominations and new border cuts and new State Arms were prepared for the dollar denominations. The principal insignia on the reverse of a Spanish milled Dollar is used on one denomination of this and the next three State issues. Printed on heavy rag paper containing blue fibres. The original engraved sections for the 20s denomination exist. Signers are Thomas Davis, John Dixon, John Carter Littlepage, Richard Morris, John H. Norton, Blonet Pasteur, and George Seaton. One signer for the four lowest denominations and two signers for the others.

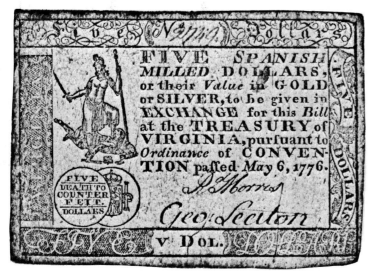

		Good	V.G.	Fine
$1/6	(1s) [24,561]	30	50	75
1s3d	"and" [6,667]	50	75	100
1s3d	"&" [6,667]	50	75	100
$1/3	(2s) [24,561]	30	50	75
2s6d	SIXPENCE [6,667] ..	50	75	100
2s6d	Six Pence [6,666] ...	50	75	100
5s	[10,000]	50	75	100
7s6d	[10,000]	50	75	100
10s	[10,000]	50	75	100
12s6d	[10,000]	50	75	100
20s	FOWR CROWNS misspelled [1,000] ..	75	100	200
$4	(24s) [24,561] © ...	30	50	75
$5	(30s) Spanish Dollar insignia [24,561] ...	30	50	75
£2	[1,000]	75	100	200
£3	[1,000]	75	100	200
£4	[1,000]	75	100	200

VIRGINIA

October 7, 1776 Act

£400,000 ($1,333,333) in legal tender Treasury Bills under the Oct. 7, 1776 Act redeemable by Jan. 1, 1790. Borders for integral dollar denominations of the previous issue were reused and new cuts for text and designs prepared for the fractions. SIC SEMPER TYRANNUS (Ever thus to tyrants) is misspelled and added to $4 and higher denominations. Heavy rag paper containing blue fibres. Signers are B. Dickson, Blonet Pasteur, and James Wray.

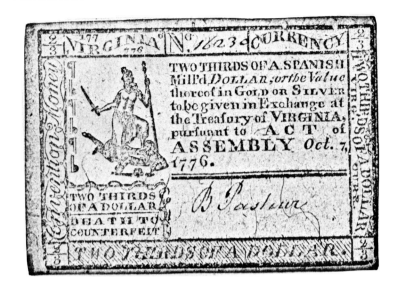

	V.G.	Fine	V.F.
$1/6	30.00	50.00	80.00
$1/3	30.00	50.00	80.00
$2/3	30.00	50.00	80.00
$1 Spanish Dollar			
insignia Ⓒ	30.00	50.00	80.00
$4	30.00	50.00	80.00

	V.G.	Fine	V.F.
$5	30.00	50.00	80.00
$6	30.00	50.00	80.00
$8	30.00	50.00	80.00
$10	30.00	50.00	80.00
$15	30.00	50.00	80.00

May 5, 1777 Act

$1,000,000 in legal tender Treasury Bills authorized by the May 5, 1777 Act and redeemable on Dec. 1, 1784. Similar to the Oct. 7, 1776 issue except that the printed date is partly removed from the cuts and replaced with writing. Heavy rag paper containing blue fibres and mica. Signers are B. Dickson, Blonet Pasteur, L. Wood, and James Wray. Reprints were made privately from complete and broken forms seized at Richmond during the Civil War.

	Good	V.G.	Fine
$1/6	30.00	50.00	80.00
$1/3	30.00	50.00	80.00
$2/3	30.00	50.00	80.00
$1 Spanish Dollar			
insignia Ⓡ ...	30.00	50.00	80.00
$4	30.00	50.00	80.00
$5	30.00	50.00	80.00
$6	30.00	50.00	80.00
$8	30.00	50.00	80.00
$10 Ⓡ	30.00	50.00	80.00
$15	30.00	50.00	80.00

F. James Doudas ★ May 5, 1777

Private small change circulating note issue of F. James Doudas of Winchester. Even though State currency was issued in dollar denominations small transactions were routinely conducted in Virginia pence. Other denominations probable.

3d

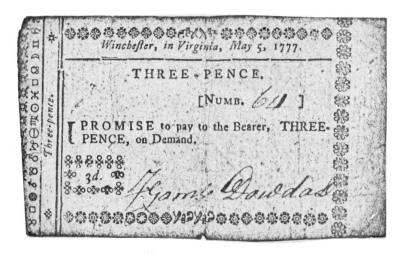

John Hough, Jr. ★ Undated

Private small change note without date or city of emission, but issued by John Hough, Jr. of Loudoun County during the American Revolution. Crudely engraved plate with the initials G W apparently referring to George Washington. Other denominations probable.

9d ($1/8, 3/4s)

October 20, 1777 Act

$1,700,000 in legal tender Treasury Bills authorized by Oct. 20, 1777 Act and redeemable by Dec. 1, 1784. Printed from the same forms used for the May 5, 1777 issue and with the date partly written in by hand. Heavy rag paper containing blue fibres. Signers are B. Dickson, L. Wood, and James Wray.

	Good	V.G.	Fine
$1/6	20.00	40.00	60.00
$1/3	20.00	40.00	60.00
$2/3	20.00	40.00	60.00
$1 Spanish Dollar insignia	20.00	40.00	60.00
$4	20.00	40.00	60.00
$5	20.00	40.00	60.00
$6	20.00	40.00	60.00
$8	20.00	40.00	60.00
$10	20.00	40.00	60.00
$15	20.00	40.00	60.00

May 4, 1778 Act with Handwritten Date

$600,000 in Treasury Bills without legal tender status were authorized by the May 4, 1778 Act and were redeemable by Dec. 1, 1785. Printed from the same forms used for the two previous State issues and with the date written in by hand. The total authorized was only partially issued when a printed date was adopted (see next issue). Signers are L. Wood and James Wray.

		Good	V.G.	Fine
$1/6	....	75.00	100.00	150.00
$1/3	....	75.00	100.00	150.00
$2/3	....	75.00	100.00	150.00
$1	Reverse of a Spanish Dollar ..	75.00	100.00	150.00
$4	....	75.00	100.00	150.00
$5	....	75.00	100.00	150.00
$6	....	75.00	100.00	150.00
$8	....	75.00	100.00	150.00

May 4, 1778 Act with Printed Date

The balance of $600,000 in Treasury Bills not emitted under the previous issue. Newly engraved cuts for borders as well as State insignia. A two letter control system in the upper left hand corner was introduced and constitutes the first use in America of series designation in combination with numbering of paper money. The date is typeset and is inserted into the cast cuts of the engraved text. The spelling of TYRANNUS on the Arms in prior issues was corrected to TYRANNIS in the new cuts. Printed both on thick rag paper containing blue fibres and on thin laid paper. Signers are L. Wood and James Wray.

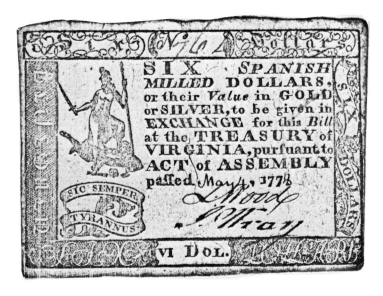

		Good	V.G.	Fine
$1/6	Thick paper ...	65.00	85.00	125.00
$1/6	Thin paper	55.00	75.00	115.00
$1/4	Thick paper ...	65.00	85.00	125.00
$1/4	Thin paper	55.00	75.00	115.00
$1/3	Thick paper ...	65.00	85.00	125.00
$1/3	Thin paper	55.00	75.00	115.00
$2/3	Thick paper ...	65.00	85.00	125.00
$2/3	Thin paper	55.00	75.00	115.00
$1	Thick paper ...	65.00	85.00	125.00
$1	Thin paper	55.00	75.00	115.00
$3	Thick paper ...	65.00	85.00	125.00
$3	Thin paper	55.00	75.00	115.00
$4	Thick paper ...	65.00	85.00	125.00
$4	Thin paper	55.00	75.00	115.00
$5	Thick paper ...	65.00	85.00	125.00
$5	Thin paper	55.00	75.00	115.00
$6	Thick paper ...	65.00	85.00	125.00
$6	Thin paper	55.00	75.00	115.00
$7	Thick paper ...	65.00	85.00	125.00
$7	Thin paper	55.00	75.00	115.00
$10	Thick paper ...	65.00	85.00	125.00
$10	Thin paper	55.00	75.00	115.00
$15	Thick paper ...	65.00	85.00	125.00
$15	Thin paper	55.00	75.00	115.00

October 5, 1778 Act

$1,700,000 (£510,000) in Treasury Bills without legal tender status and redeemable by Dec. 1, 1785 were approved by the Oct. 5, 1778 Act. By an Act passed at the Mar. 1781 Session this issue was given legal tender status. Printed on thin laid paper. The denominations of $15 and below are similar to the May 4, 1778 printed date issue and have the same cuts. The two letter control system was reused on those denominations, the control letters being typeset as well as the date. The two highest denominations are very large indented typeset bills. Signers are Edward Archer, Jonathan Boush, Bolling Stark, L. Wood, and James Wray. Reprints are from a form seized at Richmond during the Civil War.

	V.G.	Fine	V.F.
$1/6	80.00	110.00	150.00
$1/4	80.00	110.00	150.00
$1/3 ⓡ	80.00	110.00	150.00
$2/3	80.00	110.00	150.00
$1	80.00	110.00	150.00
$3	80.00	110.00	150.00
$5	80.00	110.00	150.00
$7	80.00	110.00	150.00
$10	80.00	110.00	150.00
$15	80.00	110.00	150.00
$50 (£15)	100.00	140.00	200.00
$100 (£30)	100.00	140.00	200.00

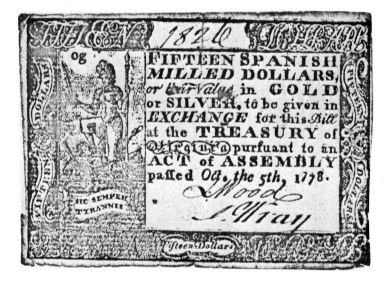

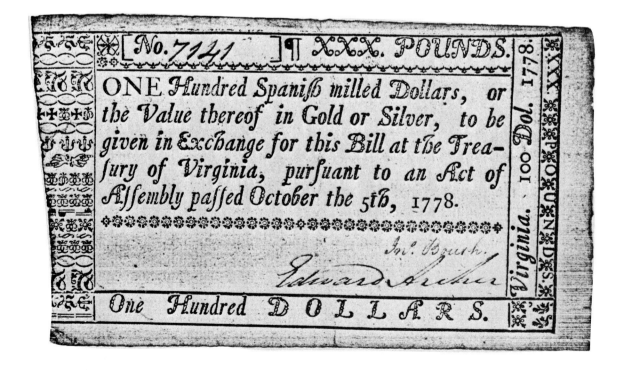

May 3, 1779 Act

£1,000,000 ($3,333,333) in Treasury Bills without legal tender status and redeemable by Dec. 1, 1786 were approved by the May 3, 1779 Act. By an Act passed at the Mar. 1781 Session this issue was given legal tender status. Printed on thin laid paper. Denominations of $15 and below are similar to May 4, 1778 printed date issue and similar denominations of the Oct. 5, 1778 issue. The typeset two letter control system was reused on those denominations as well as the same cuts. The date is typeset. The two highest denominations are very large indented typeset bills similar to the same denominations in the Oct. 5, 1778 issue, but with a ship in the left border. Signers are Edward Archer, Jonathan Boush, H. Cocke, James Cocke, A. Craig, Thomas Everard, J. Hopkins, J. Menitree, H. Randolph, J. Rose, G. Smith, and James Wray.

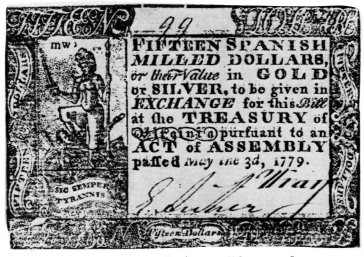

	Good	V.G.	Fine
$3 ⓇR	100.00	140.00	200.00
$5	100.00	140.00	200.00
$7	100.00	140.00	200.00
$10	100.00	140.00	200.00
$15	100.00	140.00	200.00
$50 (£15)	125.00	175.00	250.00
$100 (£30) Ⓒ ..	125.00	175.00	250.00

May 1, 1780 Act with Handwritten Date

$1,666,666 (£500,000) in Treasury Bills were authorized by the May 1, 1780 Act and redeemable in Spanish milled Dollars on Dec. 31, 1786 with 5% interest. The issue was limited to 1/20th of amount of Continental Currency exchanged at $40 (old) for $1 (new) pursuant to the Resolution of the Continental Congress passed Mar. 18, 1780 guaranteeing payment. Without legal tender status until the Act of Oct. 1780, but restricted by the Act of May 1781. Printed by Hall and Sellers in Philadelphia on paper watermarked CONFEDERATION in two lines. Backs are red and black. Face border cuts and back cut surrounding the emblem were engraved by Henry Dawkins. Border cuts and the emblem on the back are from the Jan. 14, 1779 issue of Continental Currency. Handwritten dates of issue as late as Oct. 9, 1781 were added above the interest box in the lower left corner of the face. Signers are Jonathan Boush, A. Craig, John Lyne, H. Randolph, J. M. Simmons, Bolling Stark, James Turner, B. Webb, and L. Wood. Guaranty signed by Charles Fleming and Forster Webb.

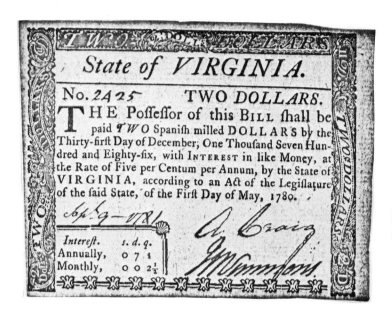
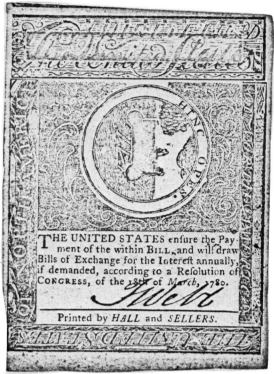

		V.G.	Fine	V.F.
$1	[33,333]	150.00	200.00	275.00
$2	[33,333]	150.00	200.00	275.00
$3	[33,333] ⓤ	150.00	200.00	275.00
$4	[33,333]	150.00	200.00	275.00

		V.G.	Fine	V.F.
$5	[33,333]	150.00	200.00	275.00
$7	[33,333]	150.00	200.00	275.00
$8	[33,333]	150.00	200.00	275.00
$20	[33,333]	150.00	200.00	275.00

July 14, 1780 Act

£2,000,000 ($6,666,666) in Treasury Bills were redeemable at $1 in specie for $40 in bills by Dec. 31, 1784 and were authorized by the July 14, 1780 Act. Without legal tender status until the Act of Oct. 1780 which was revoked in Nov. 1781. Typeset and printed on very thin paper. Denominations were printed on the back. Two control letters are on denominations of $35 and over.

There apparently was an insufficiency in the quantity of Old English type available so that errors in spelling of words set with that type are found in this and subsequent issues. Signers are Edward Archer, J. Hopkins, John Lyne, H. Randolph, J. M. Simmons, Bolling Stark, James Turner, and L. Wood.

			Good	V.G.	Fine
$3 1/3	(20s)	....	40.00	60.00	100.00
$6 2/3	(£2)	....	40.00	60.00	100.00
$10	(£3)	QILL	40.00	60.00	100.00
$13 1/3	(£4)	....	40.00	60.00	100.00
$15	(£4 10s)	....	40.00	60.00	100.00
$20	(£6)	....	40.00	60.00	100.00
$35	(£10 10s)	....	40.00	60.00	100.00
$45	(£13 10s)	....	40.00	60.00	100.00
$55	(£16 10s)	DOLLANS	40.00	60.00	100.00
$60	(£18)	DILL instead of BILL ..	45.00	70.00	115.00
$80	(£24)	Lower border text upside down	40.00	60.00	100.00
$100	(£30)	....	40.00	60.00	100.00

July 25, 1780

Treasurer's Notes payable in "nett inspected tobacco" as bounties for enlistment in the Continental Army. Signed by George Brooke. These notes probably did not circulate as money, but tobacco and tobacco receipts remained in use as a substitute for money into the nineteenth century.

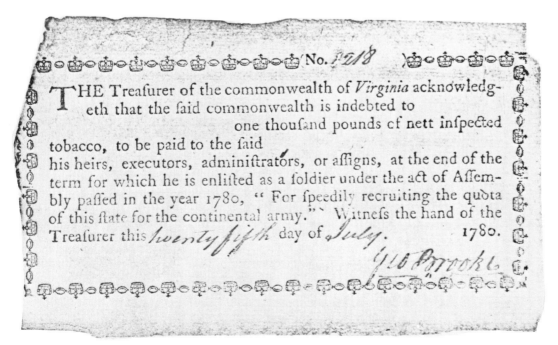

1,000 pounds of tobacco.

October 16, 1780 Act with Printed Back

£6,000,000 with the right of the officials to increase to £10,000,000 the amount of legal tender Treasury Bills redeemable by Dec. 30, 1790 at $1 specie for $40 in bills pursuant to two Oct. 16, 1780 Acts. Legal tender status was terminated at the May 1781 Session. Printed on very thin paper with denominations on the back. Two control letters above text. Signers are J. Hopkins, John Lyne, J. M. Simmons, Bolling Stark, and James Turner.

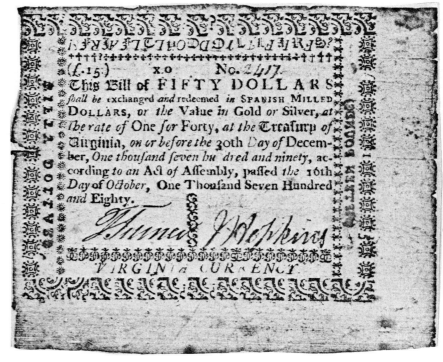

			V.G.	Fine	V.F.				V.G.	Fine	V.F.
$50	(£15)	....	40.00	75.00	125.00	$300	(£90)	....	40.00	75.00	125.00
$100	(£30)	Tnis instead				$400	(£120)	HUNDNED ..	40.00	75.00	125.00
		of This	40.00	75.00	125.00	$500	(£150)	QILL	40.00	75.00	125.00
$200	(£60)	....	40.00	75.00	125.00						

October 16, 1780 Act for Clothing the Army

The amount of Bills to be issued pursuant to an additional Oct. 16, 1780 Act was to be sufficient to buy 1,500 hogsheads of tobacco to create a fund "for the more effectual and speedy clothing the Army." Printed on very thin laid paper with no control letters. Blank backs. Signers are J. Hopkins, J. M. Simmons, Bolling Stark, James Turner, and B. Webb.

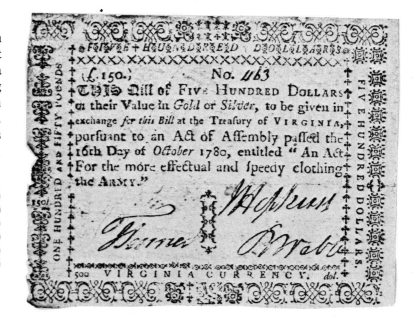

			V.G.	Fine	V.F.
$100	(£30)	....	300	500	750
$200	(£60)	....	300	500	750
$300	(£90)	....	300	500	750
$400	(£120)	HUNDNED .	300	500	750
$500	(£150)	QILL	300	500	750
$1,000	(£300)	....	400	600	1,000

March 1, 1781 Act

£10,000,000 with the right to be increased to £15,000,000 in legal tender Treasury Bills redeemable by Dec. 30, 1792 at $1 specie for $40 in bills. Legal tender was terminated at the Nov. 1781 Session. Printed both on very thin laid paper and on thick laid paper. Signers are A. Craig, J. Hopkins, John Lyne, W. Martin, L. Patterson, H. Randolph, J. Rose, J. M. Simmons, Bolling Stark, James Turner, B. Webb, and Forster Webb.

			V.G.	Fine	V.F.
$20	(£6)	....	40	75	125
$50	(£15)	....	40	75	125
$80	(£24)	....	40	75	125
$150	(£45)	DOLLARAE ..	40	75	125
$250	(£75)	DOLLAR8 ...	40	75	125
$500	(£150)	OIVE	40	75	125
$750	(£225)	D omitted in			
		POUNS. QILL	50	100	150
$1,000	(£300)	©	50	100	150

May 7, 1781 Act

£20,000,000 in legal tender Treasury Bills redeemable by Dec. 30, 1794 at $1 specie for $40 in bills. By an Act at the Nov. 1781 Session legal tender status was terminated, all Virginia issues called for redemption at $1 specie for $1,000 in bills, and all bills to become worthless by Oct. 1, 1782. Printed by John Dunlap of Philadelphia. Bills of $100 and over are larger and have cast border cuts. Signers are John Boush, A. Craig, J. Hopkins, John Lyne, H. Randolph, J. Rose, J. M. Simmons, and Bolling Stark.

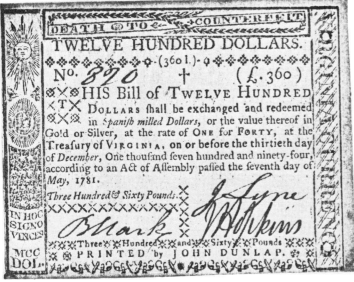

			Good	V.G.	Fine
$10	(£3)	.....	50.00	100.00	150.00
$15	(£4 10s)	.....	50.00	100.00	150.00
$25	(£7 10s)	.....	50.00	100.00	150.00
$30	(£9)	.....	50.00	100.00	150.00
$35	(£10 10s)	.....	50.00	100.00	150.00
$40	(£12)	.....	50.00	100.00	150.00
$50	(£15)	.....	50.00	100.00	150.00
$70	(£21)	.....	50.00	100.00	150.00
$75	(£22 15s)	.....	50.00	100.00	150.00
$100	(£30)	.....	50.00	100.00	150.00
$200	(£60)	WF in lower border	50.00	100.00	150.00
$500	(£150)	.....	50.00	100.00	150.00
$1,000	(£300)	.....	55.00	110.00	165.00
$1,200	(£360)	.....	60.00	120.00	180.00
$1,500	(£450)	.....	65.00	130.00	200.00
$2,000	(£600)	.....	75.00	140.00	250.00

VIRGINIA

Bank of Alexandria ⋆ 1793, etc.

The Bank of Alexandria was incorporated in 1792 for a period originally expiring January 1, 1803 with a capital of $150,000 divided into shares of $200 each. Its circulating notes and other debts could not exceed four times its paid in capital. Bank notes less than $5 were prohibited. Death without benefit of clergy was provided for printing or passing a counterfeit of its bank notes. Early denominations are unknown.

Bank of the United States ⋆ 1795, etc.

The Norfolk Office of Discount and Deposit of the Bank of the United States (first bank) operated from 1795 to 1811 and issued $283,900 in circulating bank notes. A fuller description of branch bank notes and other branch bank data is included under Pennsylvania listings.

A flying eagle bearing the Arms of the United States:

$5	$10	$20	$50	$100

A heraldic eagle with 13 stars around its head:

$5	$10	$20	$50	$100

A heraldic eagle in an oval frame containing 15 stars:

$5	$10	$20	$50	$100

VIRGINIA REFERENCES

Robert A. Brock, "Virginia Colonial Money 1700-1800," *American Journal of Numismatics* (January 1878).

R. W. Church, "Paper Money Issued for Virginia under the Ordinance of the Convention of July 17, 1775," *Numismatic Scrapbook Magazine* (September 1942).

Percy S. Flippen, *The Financial Administration of the Colony of Virginia* (Baltimore, 1915).

Richard T. Hoober, "Financial History of Colonial Virginia," *The Numismatist* (November 1953, etc.).

Frances N. Mason, *John Norton & Sons, Merchants of London and Virginia* (Richmond, 1937).

Eric P. Newman, *Coinage for Colonial Virginia* (New York, 1957).

"Paper Money in Colonial Virginia," *William & Mary Quarterly* (Richmond, 1912).

Henry Phillips, Jr., "Historical Sketch of the Bills of Credit Issued by Virginia," *Historical Sketches of the Paper Currency of the American Colonies* (Roxbury, 1865).

Preface to the *Journal of the House of Burgesses of Virginia 1761-65* (Richmond, 1905).

William Z. Ripley, *The Financial History of Virginia, 1609-1776* (New York, 1893).

William M. Royall, "Virginia Colonial Money and Tobacco's Part Therein," *Virginia Law Journal* (Richmond, 1877).

Kenneth Scott, "Counterfeiting in Colonial Virginia," *Virginia Magazine of History and Biography* (January 1953).

Farran Zerbe, "Virginia Colony Notes on James River Bank Blanks," *The Numismatist* (August 1918).

Laws, archives, newspapers and other public records.

See general references, catalogs, and listings following the Introduction.

APPENDIX A

Sheet Structure

The position and number of bills on uncut sheets are often of numismatic importance and a compilation of data from existing sheets, partial sheets, reprinted sheets, documents, and plates is set forth below.

The placement of the denominations in the list relates only to the face of the bills. Sometimes the backs are printed adjacent to and on the same surface as the face, producing a double sheet when the other side is similarly printed. When this occurs the designation (B) is used to indicate that structure and the double sheet will have double the number of bills listed.

The listing of the face denominations begins at the upper left and proceeds down vertically. The symbol # is used to separate that column from the next column of bills to the right, etc. In positioning the sheet for listing the faces of some bills are not always right side up.

Where a multiple printing of the same impression occurs in an adjacent area on either side of the same sheet the letter (M) is used to indicate that structure and the sheet will have double the number of bills listed.

In some instances each surface of a sheet has both adjacent backs and multiple impressions. Such sheets will be followed by (B) (M) and will contain quadruple the number of bills listed.

The unit of money is not given unless more than one type of money unit appears on a sheet. The plate letters, wherever they occur, are included next to the denominations.

Continental Currency
CC/05/10/75: 1, 2, 3, 4 # 8, 7, 6, 5. (B). Variations occur with $30 substituted for one of the listed denominations.
CC/11/29/75: 1, 2, 3, 4 # 8, 7, 6, 5. (B)
CC/02/17/76: 1/6 A, 1/3 A, 1/2 A, 2/3 A # 1/6 B, 1/3 B, 1/2 B, 2/3 B # 1/6 C, 1/3 C, 1/2 C, 2/3 C. (B)
CC/02/17/76: 1, 2, 3, 4 # 8, 7, 6, 5. (B)
CC/05/09/76: 1, 2, 3, 4 # 8, 7, 6, 5. (B)
CC/07/22/76: 30, 2, 3, 4 # 8, 7, 6, 5. (B)
CC/11/02/76: 30, 2, 3, 4 # 8, 7, 6, 5. (B)
CC/02/26/77: 30, 2, 3, 4 # 8, 7, 6, 5. (B)
CC/05/20/77: 30, 2, 3, 4 # 8, 7, 6, 5. (B)
CC/04/11/78: 40, 30, 20, 4 # 8, 7, 6, 5. (B)
CC/09/26/78: 60, 50, 40, 30 # 20, 8, 7, 5. (B)
CC/01/14/79: 20, 80, 70, 5 # 4, 3, 2, 1. (B)
CC/01/14/79: 65, 60, 55, 50 # 45, 40, 35, 30. (B)

Connecticut
CN/10/11/77: 2, 3, 4, 5, 7. (M)

Delaware
DE/01/01/53: 1, 1 # 1/6, 1/6 # 2, 2 # 2/6, 2/6
DE/01/01/53: 1, 1 # 5, 5 # 10, 10 # 2/6, 2/6
DE/01/01/53: 1, 1 # 5, 5 # 1/6, 1/6 # 2/6, 2/6
DE/01/01/53: 5, 5 # 1/6, 2/6
DE/01/01/76: 5, 6 # 4, 10. (B) (M)
DE/05/01/77: 4d, 3d # 9d, 6d. (B) (M)
DE/05/01/77: 18d, 20s # 2s6d, 10s # 15s, 5s # 4s, 6s. (B)

Georgia
GA/00/00/76 Blue Seal Dollar Issue: 1, 4 # 4, 10. Variations occur.
GA/00/00/76 Maroon Seal: 2, 4 # 20, 10
GA/00/00/76 Fractional Issue: 1/2, 1/2, 1/2, 1/2 # 1/4, 1/4, 1/4, 1/4. Variations occur.
GA/00/00/76 Undated: 3, 4, 5, 8 # 10, 4, 5, 8
GA/00/00/77 Without Resolution date: 3, 3, 3, 3 # 3, 3, 3, 3
GA/06/08/77: 1/10, 1/5, 1/4, 1/3 # 2/5, 1/2, 2/3, 3/4. Variations occur.
GA/06/08/77: 1, 2, 3, 4 # 5, 6, 7, 8
GA/09/10/77: 4/5, 4/5, 4/5, 4/5, 4/5 # 1/2, 1/2, 1/2, 4/5, 4/5. Variations occur.
GA/09/10/77: 1, 2, 3, 4 # 5, 6, 7, 8
GA/05/04/78: 20, 20 # 20, 20. (B)
GA/05/04/78: 40, 40 # 30, 30. (B)

Maryland
MD/00/00/33: 1, 1, 1, 1, 1
MD/00/00/33: 1s6d, 1s6d, 1s6d, 1s6d, 1s6d
MD/00/00/33: 2s6d, 2s6d, 2s6d, 2s6d, 2s6d
MD/00/00/33: 5, 5, 5, 5, 5
MD/00/00/33: 10, 10, 10, 10, 10
MD/00/00/33: 15, 15, 15, 15, 15
MD/00/00/33: 20, 20, 20, 20, 20
MD/04/10/74: 2, 1, 2/3, 1/3. Probably additional denominations on sheet.
MD/06/08/80: 8, 4, 1, 1/2 # 6, 2, 2/3, 1/3

Massachusetts
MS/11/21/02: 5, 20 # 10, 40
MS/07/08/75: 20, 14, 6
MS/07/08/75: 16, 15, 9
MS/07/08/75: 10, 18, 12
MS/12/07/75: 4s6d, 7s # 1s6d, 3s # 2s8d, 3s4d # 1s4d, 8d
MS/11/17/76: 22, 48 # 16, 42 # 14, 36 # 10, 28
MS/10/16/78: 4s6d, 8d, 2d # 4s, 9d, 3d # 3s, 12d, 4d # 2s, 1s6d, 6d

Double Sheet of the February 17, 1776 Continental Currency Fractional Issue
(About one-third actual size)

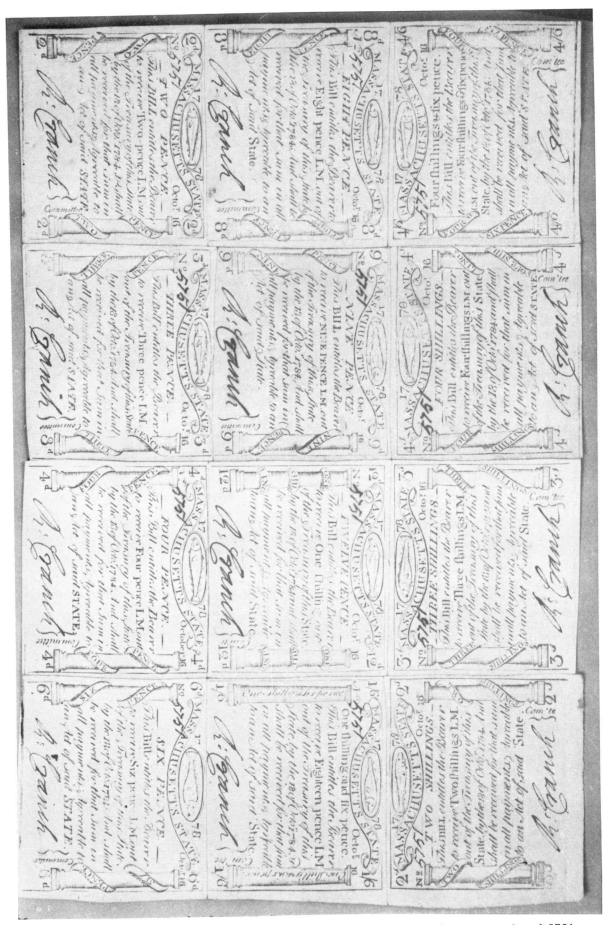

Reconstructed sheet of the October 16, 1778 Massachusetts issue with all bills numbered 5751.

Massachusetts (Continued)
MS/00/00/79: 5s6d, 4s8d, 3s6d, 2s # 5s4d, 4s6d, 3s, 1s6d # 5s, 4s, 2s6d, 1s

New Hampshire
NH/05/20/17 redated 00/00/29: 15s, £3 10s # 30s, £4
NH/04/05/37: 3, 2 # 5, 10
NH/08/07/40: 100, 40 # 60, 20
NH/04/03/42: 7s6d, 40s # 20s, 10s. Backs only.
NH/06/01/56: 6d, 5s, 3s # 1s, 3s9d, 7s6d
NH/06/01/56: 15s, 10s # £3, 30s
NH/06/20/75: 40, 20, 6, 1

New Jersey
NJ/03/25/76: 3s B, 6s B, 18d B, 15s, 1s A, 6s A # 3s A, 12s B, 18d C, 12s A, 1s B, 1s C
NJ/03/25/76: 3s B, 6s B, 18d B, 15s, 1s A, 30s # 3s A, 12s B, 18d C, 18d A, 1s B, 1s C
NJ/03/25/76: £3. (B) (M)
NJ/06/09/80: 5, 7, 8, 20 # 1, 2, 3, 4. (B)

New York
NY/05/31/09: 10 # 10 # 5 # 5
NY/11/01/09: 4 # 4. (M)
NY/11/01/09: 16 # 20. (M)
NY/03/05/76: 4, 4 # 4, 4. (M)
NY/03/05/76: 8, 8 # 8, 8. (M)

North Carolina
NC/04/23/61: 20, 5 # 15, 10. (M)
NC/12/00/71: 2s6d House, £1, 10s # 2s6d Swan, 5s, 1s

Pennsylvania
PA/06/15/67: 40s, £4, £6. (B)
PA/07/20/75: 20, 20 # 30, 30 # 10, 10 # 40, 40. (B)
PA/10/25/75: 3 A, 4 A, 6 A, 9 A # 3 B, 4 B, 6 B, 9 B # 3 C, 4 C, 6 C, 9 C. (B)
PA/10/25/75: 1s, 2s6d # 18d, 2s. (B) (M)
PA/04/25/76: 3 A, 4 A, 6 A, 9 A # 3 B, 4 B, 6 B, 9 B # 3 C, 4 C, 6 C, 9 C. (B)

PA/04/25/76: 18d, 1s # 2s, 2s6d. (B) (M)
PA/01/18/77: 3, 6 # 4, 9 # 5. (M)
PA/04/10/77: 3 A, 4 A, 6 A, 9 A # 3 B, 4 B, 6 B, 9 B # 3 C, 4 C, 6 C, 9 C. (B)
PA/04/10/77: 1s, 18d, 2s, 3s, 4s # 6s, 8s, 12s, 16s, 20s. (B)
PA/03/16/85: 20s, 10s, 2s6d, 9d # 15s, 5s, 18d, 3d
PA/08/06/89: 3 D, 1 D, 1 H, 1 M # 3 C, 1 C, 1 G, 1 L # 3 B, 1 B, 1 F, 1 K # 3 A, 1 A, 1 E, 1 I

Rhode Island
RI/08/22/38: 1s, 2s6d, 3s # 5s, 7s6d, 10s
RI/05/22/77: 1/12, 1/4 # 1/18, 1/6 # 1/24, 1/8 # 1/36, 1/9. (M)
RI/07/02/80: 5, 7, 8, 20 # 1, 2, 3, 4. (B)
RI/05/00/86: 1s, 2s6d # 6d, 9d. (M)
RI/05/00/86: 10, 3 # 6, 5. (B)
RI/05/00/86: 60, 20 # 40, 30. (B)
RI/00/00/1800, Washington Bank: 1, 1, 1, 1

South Carolina
SC/12/23/76: 1, 2, 3, 4. (B). (Includes both dating errors.)
SC/12/23/76: 2, 3, 4, 20. (B)
SC/12/23/76: 5, 6, 8, 1. (B)
SC/04/10/78: 2s6d, 5 # 3s9d, 10s
SC/04/10/78: 7s6d, 20s # 15s, 30s
SC/02/08/79: 50. (B)
SC/02/08/79: 70. (B)
SC/02/08/79: 90. (B)
SC/02/08/79: 100. (B)

Virginia
VA/10/20/77: 6, 4, 8, 5. (B)
VA/05/01/80: 5, 7, 8, 20 # 1, 2, 3, 4. (B)
VA/03/01/81: 1,000, 750, 500 # 250, 150, 50. (M)
VA/05/07/81: 50, 100, 200, 500 # 1,000, 1,200, 1,500, 2,000. (M)

APPENDIX B

Description of Counterfeits

Circulating counterfeits of early American paper money, as stated in the Introduction, are significantly important because of the information they reveal. They are as much a part of monetary history as genuine bills. The description of many of such counterfeits is not possible for several reasons. Many of the counterfeits, particularly those made in the first half of the eighteenth century, have not been located. In other cases counterfeits have been located (some being marked COUNTERFEIT), but the genuine bills to compare them with have not been found. Some counterfeits are known only through their being evidence at the trials of counterfeiters and some of those have been "liberated" from the public records. Other counterfeits are mentioned in Acts of Assembly, newspapers, or other records. Some are identified, not by comparison with genuine issues, but only because their workmanship is not up to the standard of the engravers' or printers' art then being practiced in the place of issue. Others are identified because they are engraved when they should be printed or vice versa. Some are detected by forged signatures. Some altered bills are inaccurately referred to as counterfeits and such records may result in the listing of some counterfeits when no such counterfeits exist.

The British and Tory sponsorship of counterfeiting of Continental Currency and American State issues during the American Revolution introduced a new technique in economic warfare. These counterfeits have a special significance. This was described at the time as "a fair advantage over an enemy." Those counterfeits were prepared in both Europe and America and were freely given to those who were willing to pass them. Some of the counterfeits of Continental Currency are poorly described in a large official broadside which is illustrated herein.

There is no prohibition against the retention of counterfeits of early American paper money and they may be sold and exchanged on the basis of what they are.

Continental Currency

CC/05/10/75—$30: Engraved. Ink is usually pale. Top of second L in BILL is slightly lower than the top of the first L. Period after 1775 is at the same level as the center of the lower part of 5 instead of at top of the lower part. In the motto CIES of FACIES is closer to the outside circle than to the inside circle. Plates cut by Henry Dawkins.

CC/11/22/75—$5: Fictitious date of issue. The little finger of the hand in the vignette extends far to the right of the center branch instead of ending just left of it. V is omitted inside the nature printed back.

CC/02/17/76—$2/3: Plate B. Base of G in CONGRESS very low. Second PH in PHILADELPHIA is much larger than other letters on same line. Baseline of February is very wavy.

CC/02/17/76—$2/3: Engraved. No plate letter. (Only information is from the Pennsylvania Archives, First Series, Vol. V, p. 258 and Vol. XI, p. 234.) This may have been modified to plate letter B described above.

CC/02/17/76—$4: Crude. Engraved. No description. (Only information is from the Pennsylvania Archives, First Series, Vol. V, p. 258, Vol. XI, p. 234 and the Pennsylvania Gazette of July 16, 1777.)

CC/05/09/76—$8: Engraved. On whitish paper containing mica. In the second to there is an old style s instead of a t. G instead of C in GONGRESS. Top of 1 in date is higher than the tops of 77.

CC/05/09/76—$8: Engraved. Top of T in EIGHT beneath top border is straight instead of curved. B in Bearer is partly under left upright of H in THIS instead of to the right of the upright.

CC/05/09/76—$8: Crudely engraved. B in Bearer entirely under right arm of T. J in MAJORA is reversed.

CC/07/22/76—$7: Base of V in the first SEVEN is very high. Second s in SPANISH tilts right. Second 7 in date lower than the first 7. On the back the stem on the leaf may point to the left or to the right depending upon the juxtaposition of the face and the back.

CC/07/22/76—$30: Top loop of G in Gold is open. Bottom loop of C in Congress is open. Left loop of P in Philadelphia is closed. Base of LL is high in BILL. In the text the I in THIRTY is high. Tops of the middle letters in Congress form a convex curve. J in July is under the second s in passed and the last three letters of July are not capitals.

CC/07/22/76—$30: The above described counterfeit substantially corrected. Three capital letters are substituted for lower case letters in JULY. The J in JULY has been moved under the e of passed. The LL in BILL and I in THIRTY have been aligned with adjacent letters.

CC/07/22/76—$30: Engraved. In the text the base of Y in THIRTY is high; the base of r in receive is low; the O in DOLLARS is too short; and the tops of the middle letters of Congress form a concave curve.

CC/11/02/76—$30: Engraved. "this Bill entitles" is engraved over the same words set farther to the left. Copper face plate exists.

CC/02/26/77—$5: Poorly engraved. N is higher than the adjacent o in NO and the following period is lacking. Comma after second DOLLARS is lacking. The e in Baltimore is much smaller than the e in February. In some specimens the back is in the wrong juxtaposition relative to the face.

CC/02/26/77—$30: Engraved. In the date the base of 6 is level instead of higher than the 2. In SI of the motto the tail of the S is flat and extended.

CC/02/26/77—$30: Engraved. Base of B in Baltimore is very low. On the back the base of Hall is much lower than the base of by.

CC/02/26/77—$30: Engraved. Spanish Dollars is very irregular. BALTIMORE is too large. On the back Sellors is misspelled. (Described in Connecticut Courant of November 10, 1778 and in Mason's Monthly Coin & Stamp Magazine, June 1871.)

CC/05/20/77—$6: Engraved. Many words in text are uneven and too small. Base of V in Value is high above the base line instead of being level with it. Under the vignette the period following DOLLARS is sometimes missing. In some specimens the back is in the wrong juxtaposition relative to the face. (Described in Official Broadside.)

CC/05/20/77—$8: Engraved. Base of second I in MINORIBUS is high. Base line of harp rises to the right instead of being horizontal. Words in text are too short. O and E in CONGRESS are low. (Described in the Official Broadside.)

CC/05/20/77—$8: Crudely engraved note. The 2 in 20 in the date tilts to the left. In some specimens the back is in the wrong juxtaposition relative to the face.

CC/05/20/77—$30: Deceptive counterfeit with broken M in May as in genuine. Bottom of s in FACIES touches circle instead of being clear of the line. Y in second THIRTY is slightly higher rather than slightly lower than T. Top of f in thereof is the same distance from the border as the comma above while on genuine f is much closer. Dot over second i in Philadelphia is under the center of the lower curve of s above rather than just left of it.

CC/07/02/77—$30: Fictitious date of issue. Period instead of comma after July 2. Philadelphia.

CC/03/12/78—$40: Fictitious date of Yorktown type. Engraved crudely. In the first Dollars the bases of ars are too high. In Resolution the bases of ion are higher than the bases of other letters in that line. The comma after Congress is omitted.

CC/04/11/78—$4: Crudely engraved. R touches s in MORS. Top of oversized h in the second the is higher than the bottom of p in Spanish.

CC/04/11/78—$5: Engraved. In SPANISH the A is too short and too near N. First s in CONGRESS smaller than second s. No comma after April. (Described in the Official Broadside.)

CC/04/11/78—$7: Crudely engraved. The tail of the s in Resolution sweeps under the R. The second s in CONGRESS tilts to the right.

CC/04/11/78—$8: Engraved. The G in Gold is too large and too low. In the top border the 8 is black instead of white. (Described in the Official Broadside.)

CC/04/11/78—$20: Engraved. Base of second L in DOLLARS in the text is lower than the base of the first L. The A in DOLLARS in the text is much smaller than the adjacent R. The lower case letters of Continental Currency on the right side border are black instead of white. (Described in the Official Broadside and shown on the accompanying illustration.)

CC/04/11/78—$40: Engraved. In the first Forty the base of r is higher than the base of the adjacent o, but the top of r is on the same level as the top of the adjacent o. In the second Dollars the bases of the letters ol are too high. In the second or the base of the r is far below the base of o. In 11th the top of the first numeral is lower than the top of the second numeral. (Poorly described in the Official Broadside.)

CC/04/11/78—$40: Engraved. In the top border the right arm of U does not have a vertical portion and the left leg of A is thicker than the right leg. In Bearer the bases of earer are far above the base of B. The base of re in receive is far below the adjacent to. In thereof the bases of th are much lower than the bases of subsequent letters. The top of the second s in passed is higher than the top of the first s. (Described in the Official Broadside.)

CC/04/11/78—$40: Engraved. In the first Forty the end of the tail of y turns vertically upward. The base of a in according is lower than the base of the adjacent c. The base and top of r in receive slant upward to the right. The bases of the letters in thereof are all well below those in Value. On the back there are only 4 pairs of leaves instead of 5 pairs. (Described in the Official Broadside.)

CC/09/26/78—$40: In Spanish the h is mostly over the o in or rather than the r. The comma after the second Dollars is opposite the top of s. S in Sept. is mostly under g instead of r in Congress.

CC/09/26/78—$40: Base of m in milled slopes down to the right. Base of o in second Dollars higher than the base of D. (Engraved copper face plate in the Smithsonian Institution.)

CC/09/26/78—$40: B in BILL under the left side instead of under the center of D in Dollars. Left side of b in by just left of R in Resolution instead of under right tip of a.

CC/09/26/78—$40: End of loop of second l in first Dollars almost horizontal instead of sloping down to the left. Base of r in first Dollars slightly higher than the base of adjacent letters. Base of second to higher than the bases of adjacent words. Hyphen after Con

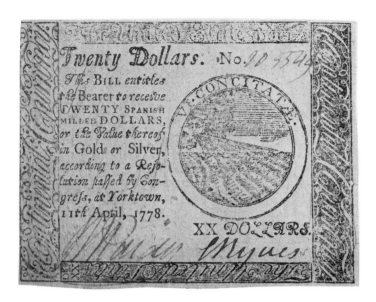

Genuine Bill

Typeset text on face. Nature print of leaf on back.

Counterfeit Bill

Engraved text on face. Engraved leaf print on back.

slopes down to the right. The A in CONFEDERATION is small.

CC/09/26/78—$50: Comma after Philadelphia omitted. Bases of the last three letters in Philadelphia rise to the right. Base of bearer much higher than the base of the adjacent to. Center letters of value slope down to the right.

CC/09/26/78—$50: Previous counterfeit corrected by inserting a comma after Philadelphia and moving the

letters in that line to make a place for it. Other defects remain unchanged.

CC/09/26/78—$50: The top of the left border should have an inverted FIFTY D, but erroneously has an E as its first letter. Base of the r in Dollars in the text is too high. The left base of R in Resolution is too high. Last two letters of passed have their bases too high.

CC/09/26/78—$60: Deceptive. The dot over the i in

DESCRIPTION
OF
COUNTERFEIT BILLS,

Which were done in Imitation of the True Ones ordered by the Honorable the CONTINENTAL CONGRESS, Bearing Date 20th May, 1777, and 11th April, 1778.

EIGHT Dollar Bill, dated May 20, 1777, signed Jn. Taylor and Aq. Norris, is done from a Copperplate, the Letters of which are not only irregular, but by having been engraved, appear more delicate than in the true Bills, which are done with Type, have a smaller aspect, especially in the Words "*Spanish milled, Silver, Philadelphia,*" &c.—The Figures 1777, as well on the back as the front, appear less than in the true Bills.—In the Border at the Top of the Bill over the Words "United States," the two L's in the Word "Dollars" are more irregular and more from a straight Line than in the true Bills.

Six Dollar Bills, dated May 20, 1777, signed Jn. Taylor and Aq. Norris, or R. Smith and A. M'Callister, or G. Young and C. Lewis, are also done from a Copperplate, the Letters of which appear for the same Reason more delicate than in the true Bills, and are also more irregular, particularly the Word "entitles," which stands higher than the rest of the line, and the V in the Word "Value" is placed too high and not on a line with the rest of the Word.— After the Words "Six Dollars" under the Device in the true Bills there is a full stop, in the Counterfeits there is none.—On the Back of the Bill the Leaf is much plainer in the Counterfeits than in the true Bills, the Letters there being also more delicate, and the Figures "1777" have a smaller Appearance than in the genuine Bills.

Forty Dollar Bill, dated April 11, 1778, signed D. Reintzel and S. Bryson, or D. Reintzel and J. Snowden, done from a Copperplate, of which the same Remark may be made as to the Delicacy or Neatness of the Letters as in the preceeding Descriptions.—Yet the whole of the Letters in the Words "THE UNITED STATES," in the top Border of the Bill, appear stronger, tho' not so uniform or so well shaped as those in the true Bills.—In the Border at the right hand (or end) of the Counterfeit Bill the Words "*FORTY* DOLLARS" (which are in white Letters) are ill done, besides having an *E* instead of an *F* in the same.—The larger Leaf on the Back of the true Bills having beside the Branch at the upper end, five Branches on each Side of the Stem, the lowermost of which are not very plain and smaller than the rest; the two last mentioned are entirely omitted in these Counterfeits.

Another species of the Forty Dollar Bills of the same date, signed D. Reintzel and J. Snowden, also done from a Copperplate, of which the same Remark may be made as to the Delicacy or Neatness of the Letters as in the former Descriptions. The Letters however in the whole of the Bill are very irregular, several being larger than the adjoining ones, and almost all the lines crooked, some being placed too high and others too low. In the Border at the right Hand of the Counterfeit Bill the white Letters *FORTY* DOLLARS are ill done and irregular; the O and particularly the first L in the word "DOL-LAS" being smaller than the rest.—The Remark in the Description of the first Forty Dollar Bill as to the white Letters in the top Border of the Bill, may also with Justice be made here, viz. That they appear stronger tho' not so uniform or so well shaped as those in the true Bills, particularly the A having the first Stroke broader than the last.—As to the large Leaf on the Back of the Bill, the Reverse of what was observed in the Description of the first Forty Dollar Bill may be noticed here, as the whole of the Leaf, as well as the two bottom Branches thereof, are all considerably more plain and distinct than in the true Bills; and the ground Work (Back of the Leaf) more plain and coarser, tho' not so regular.—The Letters in the Words "Printed by HALL & SELLERS" are more delicate and are differently shaped than in the true Bills.

Of the Twenty Dollar Bills, dated the 11th April, 1778, signed D. Reintzel and J. Snowden, or D. Reintzel and S. Bryson, done from a Copperplate, the same Remark may be made as to the Delicacy of the Letters as in the preceeding Descriptions, and may be easily discovered from the true Bills, as the Ornaments as well as the Words "Continental Currency," in the Borders to the left and thofe on the right Hand of the Bill are both black, whereas in the true Bills thofe to the left Hand are black and thofe to the right Hand are white; the Counterfeits indeed left the broad Strokes in the two C's in the Border at the right Hand of the Bill, as well as a few of the Ornaments in the fame, open, as if they had intended them for white.—Some of thofe Bills have Particles of gold Leaf thrown here and there upon them, in Imitation of the Ifinglafs on the genuine Bills.

The Eight Dollar Bill, dated 11th April, 1778, figned D. Reintzel and J. Snowden, is alfo done from a Copperplate, and therefore the like Remark may be made as to the Delicacy of the Letters, as is already mentioned.—The Letter G in the Word "*Gold*" is not only too large in Proportion to the reft of the Word, but is placed too low, it not being in a Line with the reft.—In the Border at the Top of the Bill, under and between the Words "THE" and "UNITED," is placed a black 8 inftead of a white 8.

Of the Five Dollar Bill, dated 11th April, 1778, figned D. Reintzel and J. Snowden, done from a Copperplate, the fame may be obferved as in the preceeding Defcriptions, refpecting the Delicacy of the Letters, with this that they differ very much in Shape or Countenance from the Type, befide being evidently irregular; the A in the Word "SPANISH" and the R and the *e* in the Word "*Refolution*" being too low and not on a Line with the reft of the Word.—The Cuts of the Leaves on the Back of the genuine Bill are done from real Leaves, as the Fibres readily fhew; whereas thofe in the Counterfeits appear not like Nature but like Imitations, the Strokes for the Fibres being too regular.

Another Counterfeit Forty Dollar Bill, dated 11th April, 1778, is figned J. Duncan and R. Davis, (who by the bye were never figners of Continental Money) the Back of which appears as if done from a Copperplate, and the Words in the front as if done with Types; the Borders and Devices as if cut in Metal. I am forry to fay that this Bill is rather fo good an Imitation that it is really dangerous to moft People. I will however point out a few other Marks, viz. The firft N in the Word *Confederation* (in the Device) is not placed fo fquare as in the true Bills, the laft Stroke of the faid Letter leaning more than it fhould do; indeed the whole of the Letters of the Word Confederation are not quite fo bold as thofe in the genuine Bills. The Stars in the Device appear more open in the Center of each of them than thofe in the true Bills, which appear moftly clofed. In the Word Forty at the Top of the Bill the Tail of the y in the Counterfeits comes nearer to the Bottom of the t than in the true Bills; the o in the fame Word appears on a Level with the reft of the Word, whilft in the true Bills it is placed rather lower than the r which follows it. In this Counterfeit (like one of the others) the larger Leaf on the Back (exclufive of the top Branch) has but four Branches on each Side thereof, while the true Bills have five Branches on each Side, of which the two lowermoft are the moft faint, as is already mentioned.

Note: In fome of the Bills of different Denominations D. Remzell is figned for D. Reintzell. It may be further neceffary to obferve that it is very probable there may be other Names affixed as Signers to fome or all of the different Denominations than are noticed in the preceeding Defcriptions, having mentioned in the foregoing only fuch as I have feen.

Some Perfons in the United States having been much alarmed on comparing of Bills of Credit, by finding Bills of the fame Denomination and Date to differ from each other in refpect to the Letters, fome having broken Letters and others not, and frequent Conclufions having been drawn that the former were true Bills, and the broken Letters were originally made as private or fecret Marks: It is therefore become neceffary to inform, That thofe were not intended as Marks, but that at the firft Beginning of printing an Emiffion the Letters were whole, and that during printing the Emiffion, from hard Lumps or Gravel or Sand in the Paper, with the Force of the Prefs, thofe Letters at different Times were accidentally and unobfervedly broken.

Permit no copy of thefe defcriptions to be taken unlefs at the requeft of the Executive Authority of the State to be placed in confidential hands

Official Broadside

receive is on the left instead of slightly to the right of the dot over the i of milled below. In the text the base of x in Sixty is in line with instead of lower than the base of the adjacent t. The upper end of the first s in Congress aims diagonally upward instead of curling downward.

CC/09/26/78—$60: The base of r in or in each use is lower than the adjacent o. The first c in according is low and the second c is small. The top of the comma after Philadelphia is above the center of the previous a. The left end of the v in receive curls down. In the top border there are no curved brackets around the n in Currency.

CC/01/14/79—$65: Crudely engraved. First c smaller than second c in according.

CC/01/14/79—$80: Crude. In the first Eighty ht tilts

to the right. No space between inGOLD.

CC/01/14/79—$80: Upright of t in the first Eighty slightly left instead of right of upright of E below. Tail of R in Resolution ends over the center of f below instead of to the right of the f. The space between EC of SECULORUM is abnormally wide.

CC/10/09/80—$500: Fictitious Resolution date and fictitious denomination. No genuine $500 denomination in any Continental Currency issue. Borders of face crudely cut. Long bright red stripe over large FIVE HUNDRED DOLLARS in which F is too large and i is not a capital. The word, Resolution, is improperly hyphenated. Period after Confede in Confederation which is also improperly divided. On the right side of the face the H in HUNDRED is too small.

Counterfeit with fictitious date of issue
and fictitious denomination.

Connecticut

CN/05/10/75—40s: Second s in ASSEMBLY tilts to right. Plates cut by Henry Dawkins.

CN/03/01/80—40s: r in Hartford and in March are normal in size instead of being too large as in originals.

CN/06/01/80—20s: Four ornaments in a vertical row directly under the space between GS of SHILLINGS instead of under the left side of s.

CN/06/01/80—40s: The base of S in Shil in the fifth line of the face text is on the base line and not well below it as in the genuine.

Maryland

MD/10/01/48—20s: Crudely engraved. The upright of D in Day tilts left.

MD/03/01/70—$6: Crudely engraved. The top of x in the first SIX is larger than the bottom. s in BILLS is high.

Massachusetts

MS/12/07/75—36s: Engraved. Masts on ships are vertical instead of sloping up to the right.

MS/12/07/75—42s: The 5 in the date has a short top bar. The s in the second use of payments is small. The baseline of the first two letters in Committee is high and the base of the first t is higher than the base of the second t. Plates cut by Henry Dawkins. Face plate at the American Antiquarian Society.

MS/06/18/76—2s6d: Modern instead of eighteenth century s in 2s6 in the upper right corner inside the border.

MS/06/18/76—5s: Fourth line of the text very wavy.

MS/06/18/76—24s or $4: T in Treasury directly over 1 of 18 and not to its right.

MS/11/17/76—48s: In each 48 at the bottom the 4 is smaller than the 8. The lanyards on the sailing ships are omitted.

MS/05/05/80—$7: Large S of Seven is below space between CH of MASSACHUSETTS instead of under second A.

MS/05/05/80—$20: N in No. has slanting uprights instead of vertical uprights. The diagonal of N in the watermark is reversed.

New Hampshire

NH/11/03/75—30s: 1780 due date. Base of second t in Thirty lower than base of adjacent r. Very deceptive.

NH/11/03/75—40s: 1779 due date. Seventh ornament after 1779 is directly over the second sunburst in the line below instead of being over the first sunburst. The period after No is missing.

NH/11/03/75—40s: 1782 due date. Period after hereof below e instead of n in Payments.

New Jersey

NJ/12/31/63—12s: Plate A. The 1 in 1763 is over the right side instead of the left side of the L below.

NJ/12/31/63—15s: Plate B. Crude engraving. The base of the E in Eighteen is low.

NJ/12/31/63—£3: Plate B. The base of D in December is high.

NJ/04/16/64—30s: Plate B. Rays of sun reach circumference. Shilligns misspelled on back.

NJ/04/16/64—30s: Plate B. Above counterfeit with corrected spelling of Shillings on back.

NJ/09/06/80—$5: In the horizontal line of ornaments there are 14 X's on each side of the circular ornament instead of 15 on the left side and 13 on the right. The N in ABSTINE is deformed.

New York

NY/02/16/71—10s: Single horizontal hyphen in first New-York in text instead of double hyphen rising to the right.

NY/02/16/71—10s: s in x.s. much smaller than x and tilted to the left.

NY/02/16/71—£1: In the text the diagonal of the N in POUND does not reach the top of the left upright.

NY/02/16/71—£3: Each 1 in 1771 tilts to the right instead of being upright.

NY/02/16/71—£5: Second T in CIVITAT is over the space to the right of to instead of being over the t of to. Comma over e in Payments instead of over m.

NY/02/16/71—£5: The base line on which the settler and the Indian are standing slants down from left to right instead of being level.

NY/02/16/71—£10: Period within Arms directly over upright of second T in CIVITAT instead of being over right edge of T.

NY/06/15/80—$20: In lower left corner the base of I in Interest is low.

NY/02/20/90—City of New York—2d: On the back

the middle letter in TWO is upside down.

NY/06/22/90—N. Y. Mfg. Soc.—1d: Demand is misspelled Demanb.

NY/06/22/90—N. Y. Mfg. Soc.—3d: Insufficient space between THREE and PENCE at the top.

North Carolina

NC/12/00/71—30s: The lower part of the upright of the obsolete s in Treasury tilts slightly to the right.

NC/04/02/76—$1/2 Crow: Crossbar of H in HALF rises slightly to the left.

NC/04/02/76—$1/2 Hunter: Crude. Second L in DOLLAR narrower than first L.

NC/08/08/78—$10 Persecution: In the top border R in NORTH is too large and O in CAROLINA is too high.

NC/08/08/78—$25: Crude. On the top border N in CAROLINA is reversed.

NC/05/15/79—$100: Crude. In the right border DR in HUNDRED is too large.

NC/05/15/79—$250: Third line of body text slopes down to right.

NC/05/17/83—20s Crown: Top of large Y in first TWENTY higher than crossbar of adjacent T.

NC/05/17/83—20s Justice: Each s in SHILLINGS differs in shape.

NC/05/17/83—20s Justice: Base of each s in SHILLINGS is high.

NC/05/17/83—40s: Engraved text. Second s in second SHILLINGS has much larger top than bottom.

NC/12/29/85—20s: Final period under v instead of under se of seven.

NC/12/29/85—40s: The forearm holding the sword slants downward from the horizontal.

Pennsylvania

PA/03/01/69—£1 10s: Plate C. Base of B in Bills is low.

PA/03/20/71—20s: Plate A. Engraved. The upright of T in This is above the right side of h in Shillings below instead of the left side.

PA/00/00/92—$20 Bank of North America: Right top of c in America touches the adjacent a. Tail of y in twenty in lower left touches base of n.

Virginia

VA/07/15/75—2s6d: SIX in text is all capitals instead of ix being in lower case letters.

VA/05/06/76—$4: Crude. The word to is in the eighth line of the text instead of the seventh line. No period after date.

VA/10/07/76—$1: Upright of P in SPANISH tilts to right.

VA/05/03/79—$100: In the lower border the uprights of u in Hundred are not parallel to the uprights of n.

VA/03/01/81—$1,000: On left border s in THOUSAND is reversed.

APPENDIX C

Exchange Value of a Spanish Dollar in
Colonial and State Shillings and Pence
During Critical Years

(See Appendix D for the American Revolutionary War period depreciation table)

	1740	1748	1761	1774	1783**
NH	23/1	49/6	6*	6	6
VT	—	—	—	—	6
MS	23/1	49/6	6*	6	6
RI	23/1	49/6	6*	6	6
CN	23/1	49/6	6*	6	6
NY	7/3	8/6	8	8	8
PA	7/10	8/1	7/6	7/6	7/6
NJ	7/10	8/1	7/6	7/6	7/6
DE	7/10	8/1	7/6	7/6	7/6
MD	11/6	9	6/6	7/6	7/6
VA	5/5	5/7½	5/7½	6	6
NC	63	45	6/6*	8	8
SC	36	32/6	32/6	32/6	4/8
GA	4/6	4/6	4/6	4/8	4/8

*New Tenor based upon the revaluation of 45 shillings in Old Tenor for a Spanish Dollar.
**Reestablished tenor for paper money issues payable in specie and emitted after the collapse in value of the regular Revolutionary War paper money issues.

APPENDIX D

Revolutionary War Depreciation Tables

The Federal government and many of the States subsequently adopted tables showing the depreciation of their paper money during the Revolutionary War in order to help adjust transactions entered into or payments made during the War. Such tables were reassembled for the United States House of Representatives on January 30, 1828, and are published in detail in American State Papers—Financial, Vol. 5, p. 763 and elsewhere. A simplified consolidated and abbreviated digest of the ratio of paper money to the original value of the Continental Currency and the State issues is as follows as of the first day of each month:

Date	CC	MS NH RI	NY CN	PA DE	NJ	MD	VA	NC	SC
Jan. 1777	1	1.05	1	1.5	1.2	1.5	1.5	1	1
Feb. 1777	1	1.07	1	1.5	1.1	1.5	1.5	1	1
Mar. 1777	1	1.09	1	2	2.1	2	2	1.25	1
April 1777	1	1.12	1	2.5	3.1	2.5	2.5	1.5	1.08
May 1777	1	1.15	1	2.5	4.1	2.5	2.5	1.5	1.17
June 1777	1	1.20	1	2.5	2.0	2.5	2.5	1.75	1.25
July 1777	1	1.25	1	3	2.25	3	3	2	1.39
Aug. 1777	1	1.50	1	3	2.5	3	3	2.13	1.52
Sept. 1777	1	1.75	1	3	2.75	3	3	2.25	1.66
Oct. 1777	1.10	2.75	1.09	3	3	3	3	2.5	1.86
Nov. 1777	1.21	3.00	1.21	3	3	3	3	2.5	2.06
Dec. 1777	1.33	3.10	1.33	4	3	4	4	3	2.26
Jan. 1778	1.46	3.25	1.46	4	4	4	4	3.5	2.21
Feb. 1778	1.60	3.50	1.60	5	4	5	5	3.5	2.11
Mar. 1778	1.75	3.75	1.75	5	4	5	5	3.75	2.67
April 1778	2.01	4.00	2.03	6	5	6	5	4	3.17
May 1778	2.30	4.00	2.30	5	5	5	5	4	3.28
June 1778	2.65	4.00	2.65	4	5	4	5	4	3.47
July 1778	3.01	4.25	3.03	4	5	4	5	4	3.54
Aug. 1778	3.48	4.50	3.48	5	5	5	5	4.25	3.61
Sept. 1778	4.00	4.75	4.00	5	5	5	5	4.5	3.80
Oct. 1778	4.66	5.00	4.64	5	5	5	5	4.75	4.05
Nov. 1778	5.45	5.45	5.45	6	6	6	6	5	5.20
Dec. 1778	6.35	6.34	6.34	6	7	6	6	5.5	6.29
Jan. 1779	7.42	7.42	7.42	8	8	8	8	6	7.61
Feb. 1779	8.68	8.68	8.68	10	10	10	10	6.5	8.32
Mar. 1779	10.0	10.0	10.0	10.5	12	10	10	7.5	8.93
April 1779	10.5	11.0	11.0	17	16	17	16	10	9.66
May 1779	12.2	12.2	12.2	24	20	24	20	10	8.32
June 1779	13.4	13.4	13.4	20	20	20	20	12.3	11.8
July 1779	14.8	14.8	14.9	19	20	20	21	15	14.6
Aug. 1779	16.3	16.3	16.3	20	24	20	22	18	16.4
Sept. 1779	18.0	18.0	18.0	24	24	24	24	21	16.2
Oct. 1779	20.4	20.3	20.3	30	30	30	28	25	20.4
Nov. 1779	23.0	23.1	23.4	38.5	36	38.5	36	27	26.0
Dec. 1779	26.0	25.9	26.0	41.5	40	41.5	40	30	32.3
Jan. 1780	29.4	29.3	29.3	40.5	42	40	42	32	37.8
Feb. 1780	33.2	33.2	33.3	47.5	50	47	45	35	42.2

Date	CC	MS NH RI	NY CN	PA DE	NJ	MD	VA	NC	SC
Mar. 1780	37.5	37.4	37.3	61.5	60	60	50	40	46.6
April 1780	40*	40.0	40.0**	61.5**	60	60	60	50	51.0
May 1780		44.0**		59	60	60	60**	60	52.5
June 1780		62.0		61.5	60**	60**	65	75	
July 1780		69.0		64.5	60	60	65	90	
Aug. 1780		70.0		70	60	65	70	100	
Sept. 1780		71.0		72	60	75	72	125	
Oct. 1780		72.0		72	75	85	73	150	
Nov. 1780		73.0		74	75	90	74	175	
Dec. 1780		74.0		75	75	100	75	200	
Jan. 1781		75.0		75	75	110	75	210	
Feb. 1781		75.0		75	90	120	80	225	
Mar. 1781		75.0		125	100	140	90	250	
April 1781		82.0		160	120	160	100	260	
May 1781		90.0		225	150	280	150	300	
June 1781		100				280	250	350	
July 1781							400	400	
Aug. 1781							500	500	
Sept. 1781							600	550	
Oct. 1781							700	600	
Nov. 1781							800	675	
Dec. 1781							1,000	725	
Jan. 1782								800	
Dec. 1782								800**	

*To be exchanged at the rate of $40 for $1 by the States pursuant to Mar. 18, 1780 Resolution of the Continental Congress.

**Depreciation after the date designated is not related to new currency issues payable in specie or issues guaranteed by the United States. It is based upon the prior regular issues in circulation.

There are only occasional references to the value of Georgia bills. By May 4, 1778 a depreciation of 5.31 to 1 had taken place. The bills were made acceptable for taxes by the Ordinance of February 22, 1785 at the rate of $1,000 in bills for $1 in specie.